The New British Politics

Visit the Politics Chamber at **www.pearsoned.co.uk/politicschamber** to access a wealth of valuable politics resources, including:

- Guides to studying politics
- Short essays on the political process, from speech-writing to committee work
- Information on careers in politics
- An archive of updates and essays on various aspects of the contemporary political scene

From the Politics Chamber, click through to the companion web site for *The New British Politics, fourth edition* or visit the web site directly at **www.pearsoned.co.uk/budge**. Here you will find:

- Multiple choice questions to help test your learning
- A guide to essay writing for students of politics
- Statistical data sets
- Links to relevant sites on the web
- Updates on a range of political topics

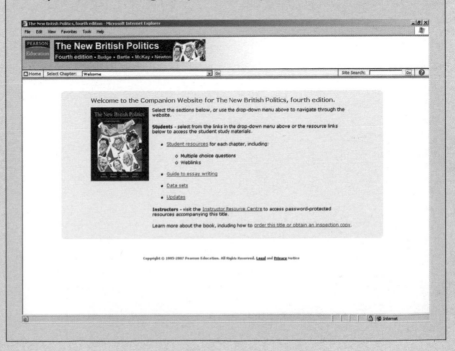

We work with leading authors to develop the
strongest educational materials in politics,
bringing cutting-edge thinking and best learning
practice to a global market.

Under a range of well-known imprints, including
Longman, we craft high quality print and
electronic publications which help readers to
understand and apply their content,
whether studying or at work.

To find out more about the complete range of our
publishing, please visit us on the World Wide Web at:
www.pearsoned.co.uk

The New British Politics

Fourth edition

IAN
BUDGE

DAVID
McKAY

KEN
NEWTON

JOHN
BARTLE

PEARSON

Longman

Harlow, England • London • New York • Boston • San Francisco • Toronto • Sydney • Singapore • Hong Kong
Tokyo • Seoul • Taipei • New Delhi • Cape Town • Madrid • Mexico City • Amsterdam • Munich • Paris • Milan

Pearson Education Limited
Edinburgh Gate
Harlow
Essex CM20 2JE
England

and Associated Companies throughout the world

Visit us on the World Wide Web at:
www.pearsoned.co.uk

First published 1998
Second edition published 2001
Third edition published 2004
Fourth edition published 2007

ISBN-13: 978-1-4058-2421-7

British Library Cataloguing-in-Publication Data
A catalogue record for this book is available from the British Library

Library of Congress Cataloging-in-Publication Data
A catalog record for this book is available from the Library of Congress

10 9 8 7 6 5 4 3 2 1
10 09 08 07

Typeset in 10/12pt Times by 35
Printed and bound by Mateu Cromo Artes Graficas, Spain

The publisher's policy is to use paper manufactured from sustainable forests.

Contents

Part 8   Assessment   **629**

Supporting resources

Visit www.pearsoned.co.uk/politicschamber to find valuable politics resources

Politics Chamber
- Guides to studying politics
- Short essays on the political process, from speech-writing to committee work
- Information on careers in politics
- An archive of updates and essays on various aspects of the contemporary political scene

Companion Web site
Visit www.pearsoned.co.uk/budge for:
- Multiple choice questions to help test your learning
- A guide to essay writing for students of politics
- Statistical data sets
- Links to relevant sites on the web
- Updates on a range of political topics

For more information please contact your local Pearson Education sales representative or visit www.pearsoned.co.uk/politicschamber

Guided tour

The fourth edition of *The New British Politics* has been produced to bring to your fingertips a wealth of materials that will enhance your understanding of British politics past, present and future. As you read through the text you will find a host of embedded features that have been expressly designed to deepen and cement that understanding.

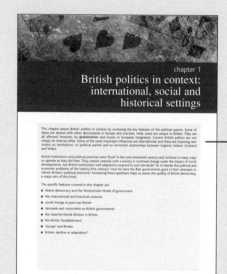

Each chapter opens with an **Introductory** section, which lists the topics covered and outlines what you should understand by the end of the chapter.

Briefings are studded throughout the book and, like an informal chat with a junior minister, will bring you up to speed on key movements and theories in double quick time.

Throughout the text **key terms** are drawn to one side and carefully explained in margin notes.

Controversy boxes crop up from time to time to set the scene around some of the more contentious issues in British politics.

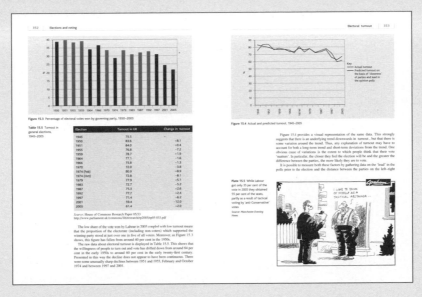

The authors have chosen a plethora of graphs, tables, photos and cartoons to provide visual reinforcement to the sometimes abstract concepts under discussion.

Essays appear at the end of each chapter and are designed to prompt you into marshalling what you have learned and begin the process of formulating your own responses to the issues at hand.

Projects also appear at the end of each chapter. These require you to probe a little deeper than the essay questions (see above) and encourage you to make use of wider resources, a valuable skill for the budding political scientist to develop.

Timelines can be found in most chapters and provide a useful chronological overview of the development of often complex issues.

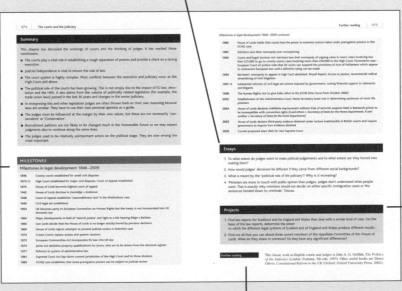

To conclude, each chapter has an annotated **further reading** section. Taken in conjunction with the **useful web sites listing**, this is a valuable pointer for those who wish to study a particular area in greater depth.

Preface

This fourth edition of *The New British Politics* has been updated to focus on the ten years of New Labour government from 1997–2006. To understand contemporary events, of course, you have to put them in context (Chapters 1–4). But most of the book deals with what is going on now in central government (Chapters 5–7), in Europe (Chapters 8–9), and in the regions and localities (Chapters 10–12). Politics is not just about institutions but is also about the pressure groups and parties operating within them (Chapters 13–18). Television and press (Chapter 14), elections and voting (Chapter 15), and Parliament (Chapter 18) are particularly relevant here.

The end result of politics are the policies that affect us all – from the war against crime and terrorism (Chapters 19–22) to the environment, health, welfare, race and gender discrimination and equal opportunities (Chapters 23–26). As students of politics we also need to ask how democracy in Britain has been affected by New Labour (Chapter 27) – particularly in light of growing apathy and, some would say, alienation from the political process.

We present these analyses comprehensively but directly, through text, tables, graphs, photographs and cartoons. Each chapter has a similar structure with an introduction, frequent 'briefings', historical 'milestones', suggestions for essays and projects, a chapter summary, further reading and internet resources. The book has an associated web site and teachers' manual available on request, which should help to promote an interactive relationship with the arguments and information contained here, rather than a purely passive absorption of the points we make. Active debate and argument should additionally be facilitated by the 'controversies' and 'briefings' inserted at key points in the text and also updated for this edition.

The way to use these for your own purposes and to best effect is to plan your route through the book in advance. If you want a comprehensive introduction to British politics, before taking a course or without taking one, the best thing is to read the text right through. The overall order of the chapters is planned for this, so you go in a logical progression from the historical background through governmental processes and political actors to policies and how the system works overall.

Often, however, you will have more specific purposes in mind – for example, the core processes of British government. In that case, read Part 2 on central government and Chapter 18 on Parliament. If relationships with the EU are the focus then Chapters 8 and 9 provide a succinct account. Politics in Ireland, Scotland and

Wales are covered in Chapters 10 and 11. Most topics on which A-level or first-year university students might be asked to write essays appear as separate chapters. If you have a choice of topic or can volunteer one yourself you might score by taking a relatively neglected topic such as politics and law (Chapter 19) or security (Chapter 21), which have quite specialised treatments in the book.

The way you organise your reading of an individual chapter may vary with the time you have. With enough time there is nothing like reading the text right through. For those with less time and a tight focus start with the summary and bullet points at the beginning, read the summary at the end and go over the milestones, then read the bits of the text relevant to you. Chapters are divided into sections to make this easy.

Do not, in any case, try to cope with all the material in the chapter at a first reading. Stick to the text, ignoring the briefings for the time being. The briefings are designed to be free standing. Their purpose is to explain details and references in the main text that you might not understand or which you might want to follow up – after reading the chapter text. The same is true of tables and graphs. They are all commented on and summarised in the text, so on a first or quick reading stick to that. The more specialised material inside and around a chapter is useful for writing essays or papers, and pursuing the topic in relevant papers or books and on the internet.

The companion web site includes advice on how and how not to write essays. In general, use this book as a starting point but do not just reproduce its arguments and material – engage with them, question them (with reasonable arguments!) and extend them. We ourselves have found our judgements on many topics have changed between the first edition of the book (1998) and this one (2007). That is inevitable as events unfold, so never be afraid to challenge and debate our conclusions – but always with arguments and evidence of your own.

We have to take final responsibility for the opinions expressed here, also for any factual errors that may have crept in. Julie Snell has gone beyond processing the manuscript to compiling, collating and formatting. Morten Fuglevand at Pearson has been a model book editor. Without them the book would have been much inferior and we thank them for their help.

Ian Budge
Ken Newton
David McKay
John Bartle
Colchester, Essex
March 2006

List of abbreviations

AA	Automobile Association
ABC	Aubrey, Berry, Campbell (Trial, 1977)
ACAS	Advisory, Conciliation and Arbitration Service
ACPO	Association of Chief Police Officers
AEEU	Amalgamated Electrical Engineering Union
All ER	All England Reports
AMS	additional member system
ASBO	anti-social behaviour order
ASH	Action on Smoking and Health
ATL	Association of Teachers and Lecturers
BBC	British Broadcasting Corporation
BCC	Broadcasting Complaints Commission
BCS	British Crime Survey
BMA	British Medical Association
BPBNC	both parents born New Commonwealth
BSB	British Satellite Broadcasting
BSC	Broadcasting Standards Commission
BSP	Basic State Pension
CAP	Common Agricultural Policy
CAT	computerised axial or computer-assisted tomography
CBI	Confederation of British Industry
CCT	compulsory competitive tendering
CEO	chief executive officer
CFC	chlorofluorocarbon
CFER	Campaign for the English Regions
CFOI	Campaign for Freedom of Information
CGT	capital gains tax
CID	Criminal Investigation Department
CLA	Country Landowners' Association
CLP	Constituency Labour Party
Cm	Command
CND	Campaign for Nuclear Disarmament
CNN	Cable News Network
Con.	Conservative
CONVOTE	Conservation voting support in the current month

COPA	Committee of Professional Agricultural Organisations
COREPER	Committee of Permanent Representatives (ambassadors to the EU)
CPAG	Child Poverty Action Group
CPRS	Central Policy Review Staff
CPS	Crown Prosecution Service
CRA	Constitutional Reform Act (2005)
CRE	Commission for Racial Equality
CSA	Child Support Agency
CSC	Civil Service College
CSD	Civil Service Department
CSI	Committee on the Intelligence Services
CSR	Comprehensive Spending Review
CTC	Child Tax Credit
CWS	companion web site
CWU	Communications Workers Union
DCMS	Department for Culture, Media and Sport
DEA	Department of Economic Affairs
DEL	departmental expenditure limits
DES	Department of Education and Science
DETR	Department of the Environment, Transport and the Regions
Defra	Department for Environment, Food and Rural Affairs
DFES	Department for Education and Skills
DFID	Department for International Development
DHA	district health authority
DIS	Defence Intelligence Staff
DM	Deutschmark
DNA	deoxyribonucleic acid
DoE	Department of the Environment
DoH	Department of Health
DoT	Department of Transport
DRC	Disability Rights Commission
DTI	Department of Trade and Industry
DWP	Department of Work and Pensions
EC	European Community
ECHR	European Convention on Human Rights and Fundamental Freedoms
ECJ	European Court of Justice
ECR	European Court Regulation
ECSC	European Coal and Steel Community
EDP	Economic and Domestic Policy
EEC	European Economic Community
EGO	extra-government organisation
EMS	European Monetary System
EMU	European Monetary Union
EOC	Equal Opportunities Commission
EP	European Parliament
ERASMUS	European Community Action Scheme for the Mobility of University Students
ERM	Exchange Rate Mechanism
ETUC	European Trade Union Confederation
EU	European Union
Euratom	European Atomic Energy Authority
EUROPOL	European Police Office

FCO	Foreign and Commonwealth Office
FMI	Financial Management Initiative
FOI	Freedom of Information
FPTP	first past the post
G7	Group of Seven
GATT	General Agreement on Tariffs and Trade
GCHQ	Government Communications Headquarters
GCSE	General Certificate of Secondary Education
GDP	Gross domestic product
GEC	General Electric Company
GLA	Greater London Authority
GLC	Greater London Council
GM	genetically modified
GMB	General and Municipal
GMG	Glasgow Media Group
GNP	gross national product
GP	general practitioner
GPMU	General Public and Municipal Workers Union
HAT	Housing Action Trust
HMCIC	Her Majesty's Chief Inspector of Constabulary
HMIC	Her Majesty's Inspectorate of Constabulary
HMSO	Her Majesty's Stationery Office
HoC	House of Commons
HRA	Human Rights Act
IBA	Independent Broadcasting Authority
ICPSR	Inter-University Consortium for Political and Social Research
ID card	Identity card
IDEA	Institute for Democracy and Electoral Assistance
IEA	Institute of Economic Affairs
ILEA	Inner London Education Authority
ILO	International Labour Organization
IMF	International Monetary Fund
IPCA	Independent Police Complaints Authority
IRA	Irish Republican Army
IS	Intelligence Services
ITC	Independent Television Commission
ITN	International Television Network
ITV	Independent Television
JCC	Joint Consultative Committee (of the Cabinet)
JIC	Joint Intelligence Committee
JP	Justice of the Peace
JPC	Joint Policy Committee (of the Labour Party)
JSA	Job Seeker's Allowance
Lab.	Labour
LCC	London County Council
LEA	Local Education Authority
Lib. Dem.	Liberal Democrat
LTE	London Transport Executive

M3	A measure of money supply
MAFF	Ministry of Agriculture and Fisheries
MEP	Member of the European Parliament
MIG	Minimum Income Guarantee
MINIS	Management Information Systems for Ministers
MoD	Ministry of Defence
MORI	Market and Opinion Research International
MP	Member of Parliament
MPC	Monetary Policy Committee
MPO	Management Personnel Office
MSFU	Managerial, Scientific and Financial Union
MSPs	Members of the Scottish Parliament
NASUWT	National Association of Schoolmasters and Union of Women Teachers
NATO	North Atlantic Treaty Organisation
NCCL	National Council for Civil Liberties
NCIS	National Criminal Intelligence Service
NCS	National Crime Squad
NDPB	non-department public body
NEC	National Executive Committee (of the Labour Party)
NEDC	National Economic Development Council
Neddy	National Economic Development Council
NFU	National Farmers' Union
NHS	National Health Service
NI	Northern Ireland
NPF	National Policy Forum (of the Labour Party)
NRC	National Reporting Centre
NSM	new social movement
NSPCC	National Society for the Prevention of Cruelty to Children
NUM	National Union of Miners
NUS	National Union of Students
NUT	National Union of Teachers
OCPA	Office of the Commissioner for Public Appointments
ODM	Ministry of Overseas Development
OECD	Organisation for Economic Cooperation and Development
OFCOM	Office of Communications
Ofgas	Office of Gas Supply
Oftel	Office of Telecommunications
Ofwat	Office of Water Regulation
OMCS	Office of the Minister for the Civil Service
OPEC	Organization of Petroleum Exporting Countries
OPS	Office of Public Service
OPSS	Office of Public Service and Science
OSCE	Organization for Security and Cooperation in Europe
PA	Press Association
PAC	Public Accounts Committee
PACE	Police and Criminal Evidence Act
PC	Plaid Cymru
PC	police constable
PC	politically correct
PCA	Parliamentary Commissioner for Administration
PCA	Police Complaints Authority

PCB	Police Complaints Board
PCC	Press Complaints Commission
PCS	Public and Commercial Services
PESC	Public Expenditure Survey Committee
PFI	Private Finance Initiative
PLC	public limited company
PLP	Parliamentary Labour Party
PM	Prime Minister
PMQs	Prime Minister's Questions
PPBS	planning, programming and budgeting systems
PPP	public/private partnerships
PPS	parliamentary private secretary
PR	proportional representation
PRT	petroleum revenue tax
PSBR	Public Sector Borrowing Requirement
PSI	Policy Studies Institute
PSIS	Permanent Secretaries' Committee on the Intelligence Services
PSNCR	Public Sector Net Cash Requirement
PUSS	parliamentary under-secretary of state
QBD	Queen's Bench Division
QC	Queen's Counsel
QMV	qualified majority voting
quangos	quasi-autonomous non-governmental organisations
RAC	Royal Automobile Club
R&D	research and development
RAF	Royal Air Force
RFSR	Russian Federal Socialist Republic
RIPA	Regulation of Investigatory Powers Act
RSG	Rate support grant
RSPB	Royal Society for the Protection of Birds
SDLP	Social Democratic and Labour Party
SDP	Social Democratic Party
SEA	Single European Act
SEU	Social Exclusion Unit
SERPS	State Earnings Related Pension Scheme
SIS	Secret Intelligence Service
SMSP	single-member simple plurality system
SNP	Scottish National Party
SOGAT	Society of Graphical and Allied Trades
STV	Scottish Television
STV	single transferable vote
TEC	Training and Education Council
TGWU	Transport and General Workers Union
TIC	taken into consideration
TUC	Trades Union Congress
UCATT	Union of Construction, Allied Trades and Technicians
UDA	Ulster Defence Association
UHT	ultra heat treated
UK	United Kingdom

UKIP	United Kingdom Independence Party
UKREP	United Kingdom Permanent Representation to the EU
UN	United Nations
UNIEU	Union of Industries of the European Union
USDAW	Union of Shop, Distributive and Allied Trades Workers
USSR	Union of Soviet Socialist Republics
UVF	Ulster Volunteer Force
VAT	value added tax
WLR	Weekly Law Reports
WMD	weapons of mass destruction
WFTC	Working Families Tax Credit
WTC	Working Tax Credit
WTO	World Trade Organization

Acknowledgements

We are grateful to the following for permission to reproduce copyright material:

Figures 1.1 and 1.3 from Labour Force Survey, Office for National Statistics. Reproduced under the terms of the Click-Use Licence; Figure 1.2 from *Social Trends 32*, 2002, Chart 4.25, Office for National Statistics. Reproduced under the terms of the Click-Use Licence; Table 1.2 from Office for National Statistics, 2002, Table 3.19, http://statistics.gov.uk. Reproduced under the terms of the Click-Use Licence; Table 1.3 from *Social Trends 32*, 2002, Table 5.4, Office for National Statistics, and HM Revenue and Customs. Reproduced under the terms of the Click-Use Licence; Figure 1.4 from Office for National Statistics. Reproduced under the terms of the Click-Use Licence; Table 2.1 from http://www.tuc.org.uk, Trades Union Congress; Figure 3.1 from *Social Trends 35*, 2005, Chart 6.15, Office for National Statistics. Reproduced under the terms of the Click-Use Licence; Briefing 4.4 courtesty of Guardian Newspapers Ltd; Table 6.1 from http://www. cabinet-office.gov.uk and HM treasury *Public Expenditure Statistical Analysis 2005*, Table 4.1. Reproduced under the terms of the Click-Use Licence; Figure 7.1 from Official Civil Service and National Statistics figures. Reproduced under the terms of the Click-Use Licence; Table 7.1 from Cabinet Office *Public Bodies 2005* (from the Public Bodies On-Line Directory). Reproduced under the terms of the Click-Use Licence; Table 10.1 from Northern Ireland Office Statistics Research Agency. Reproduced under the terms of the Click-Use Licence; Table 10.2 from CAIN Web Service, 5 May 2005, http://cain.ulst.ac.uk/; Table 11.1 from *ONC Regional Trends 36*, 2001 and *ONC Social Trends*, 2001. Reproduced under the terms of the Click-Use Licence; Table 11.4 from GDP, Office for National Statistics regional accounts; Scottish Executive Economic Advice and Statistics Division. Reproduced under the terms of the Click-Use Licence; Table 12.1 from *Local Government in Britain*, Byrne, A., 2000, London, pp. 84–85, Copyright © Anthony Byrne, 2000. Reproduced by permission of Penguin Books Ltd; Table 13.1 from European Social Survey, http://www.europeansocialsurvey.org; Table 13.4 from Social capital and associational life in *Social Capital* edited by S. Baron *et al.*, Oxford University Press (Maloney, W., Smith, G. and Stoker, G. 2000); Map 15.1 from http://news.bbc.co.uk/1/shared/vote2005/flash_map/html/map05.stm. Reproduced with permission of Ordnance Survey. © Crown Copyright; Figure 19.1 from http://www.hmcourts-service.gov.uk/aboutus/structure/index.htm. Reproduced under the terms of the Click-Use Licence; Figures 19.2 and 21.2 from HMSO. Reproduced under the terms of the Click-Use Licence; Figure 20.2 from *Home Office Statistical Bulletin 11/05, July 2005: Crime in England and Wales*

2004/2005, Table 2.01, p. 25 (for 1995–97 and 2001–05); *Home Office Statistical Bulletin 10/04, July 2004: Crime in England and Wales 2003/2004*, Table 2.01, p. 21 (for 1999). Reproduced under the terms of the Click-Use Licence; Table 22.1 from the NATO website, http://www.nato.int; Figure 23.1 from *Social Trends 36*, 2006, Figure 11.2, Office for National Statistics. Reproduced under the terms of the Click-Use Licence; Figures 24.1 and 24.2 from HM Treasury. Reproduced under the terms of the Click-Use Licence; Table 24.1 from *OECD in Figures*, 2005 Edition, Copyright OECD, 2005; Figure 24.3 from House of Commons Library Research Paper 06/12, *Economic Indicators*, March 2006. Reproduced under the terms of the Click-Use Licence; Figure 24.4 from Office for National Statistics, http://www.statistics.gov.uk/cci/nugget.asp?id=206. Reproduced under the terms of the Click-Use Licence; Figure 25.1 from *Social Trends 36*, 2006, Figure 8.1, Office for National Statistics. Reproduced under the terms of the Click-Use Licence; Figure 25.2 from *Social Trends 36*, 2006, Figure 10.3, Office for National Statistics. Reproduced under the terms of the Click-Use Licence; Table 25.2 from *Social Trends 27*, 1997, Table A.2, HMSO. Reproduced under the terms of the Click-Use Licence; Figure 25.3 from *Social Trends 36*, 2006, Figure 10.6, Office for National Statistics. Reproduced under the terms of the Click-Use Licence; Figure 26.1 from *Social Trends 36*, 2006, Figure A.4, Office for National Statistics. Reproduced under the terms of the Click-Use Licence; Figures 26.2 and 26.3 from *Social Trends 36*, 2006, Figure 5.6, Office for National Statistics. Reproduced under the terms of the Click-Use Licence; Table 26.3 from *The Times*, 11 May 2000, News International Syndication; Table 26.5 from *Social Trends 32*, 2002, Figure 4.8, Office for National Statistics. Reproduced under the terms of the Click-Use Licence.

Plate 1.1 Alamy/Pawel Libera; Plate 1.2 Getty Images/Scott Barbour; Plate 1.3 Corbis/Paul Hardy; Plate 1.4 Alamy/Photofusion; Plate 1.4 Alamy/Education Photos; Plate 2.1 Corbis/Hulton Deutsch; Plate 2.2 Topfoto; Plate 2.3 Empics; Plate 2.4 Alamy/David Hoffman Photo Library; Plate 3.1 Getty Images/Hulton Archive; Plate 3.2 Getty images/Hulton Archive; Plate 3.3 Nicholas Garland/Daily Telegraph; Plate 3.4 Empics; Plate 4.1 Alamy/Jayne Fincher, Photo International; Plate 4.2 Chris Riddell/The Observer 18th May 2003, Centre for the Study of Cartoons & Caricature, University of Kent; Plate 5.1 Cartoon Stock; Plate 6.1 Alamy/Andrew Holt; Plate 6.2 Cartoon Stock; Plate 7.1 Chris Riddell/The Observer 24th March 2002, Centre for the Study of Cartoons & Caricature, University of Kent; Plate 8.1 Daily Express; Plate 8.2 Cartoon Stock; Plate 9.1 Alamy/Image State; Plate 10.1 Empics; Plate 10.2 Empics; Plate 10.3 Topfoto; Plate 11.1 Empics; Plate 11.2 Glasgow Herald; Plate 11.3 Alamy/Photolibrary Wales; Plate 11.4 Alamy/Topix; Plate 12.1 Alamy/Simon Stanmore; Plate 12.2 Nicola Jennings/The Guardian; Plate 13.1 Topfoto; Plate 13.2 Topfoto; Plate 13.3 Topfoto; Plate 14.1 Cartoon Stock; Plate 14.2 Popperfoto; Plate 14.3 Chris Riddell/The Observer 27th August 2003, Centre for the Study of Cartoons & Caricature, University of Kent; Plate 15.1 Getty Images; Plate 15.2 Cartoon Stock; Plate 15.3 Cartoon Stock; Plate 15.4 Cartoon Stock; Plate 15.5 Manchester Evening News; Plate 16.1 Empics; Plate 16.2 Daily Telegraph; Plate 16.3 Empics; Plate 16.4 Daily Telegraph; Plate 16.5 Empics; Plate 16.6 Empics; Plate 17.1 Cartoon Stock; Plate 17.2 Cartoon Stock; Plate 17.3 Empics; Plate 17.4 Empics; Plate 17.5 Peter Brooks/The Times 17th September 1996, Centre for the Study of Cartoons & Caricature, University of Kent; Plate 18.1 Empics; Plate 18.2 Empics; Plate 18.3 Empics; Plate 18.4 Empics; Plate 18.5 Bert Hackett/Gemini/Centre for the Study of Cartoons & Caricature, University of Kent; Plate 18.6 Empics; Plate 19.1 Alamy/Peter Horee; Plate 19.2 Empics; Plate 19.3 Empics; Plate 19.4; Empics; Plate 19.5 MAC(Stan McMurty)/Daily Mail; Plate 19.6 Michael Heath/

The Mail on Sunday 18th May 2003, Centre for the Study of Cartoons & Caricature, University of Kent; Plate 20.1 Empics; Plate 20.2 Peter Schrank/The Independent 23rd February 1997; Plate 20.3 Empics; Plate 20.4 Empics; Plate 20.5 New Statesman 26th February 1999; Plate 20.6 Empics; Plate 21.1 Empics; Plate 21.2 Cartoon Stock; Plate 21.3 Alamy/Steve Atkins; Plate 21.4 Empics; Plate 21.5 Empics; Plate 22.1 Cartoon Stock; Plate 22.2 Michael Cummings/The Times 26th July 1997; Plate 22.3 Topfoto; Plate 23.1 Topfoto; Plate 24.1 Alamy/Robert Harding Picture Library; Plate 24.2 Corbis/Stephen Hird; Plate 24.3 Alamy/Elmtree Images; Plate 24.4 Cartoon Stock; Plate 25.1 Getty Images/Graeme Robertson; Plate 26.1 Topfoto; Plate 26.2 Corbis/David Pollack; Plate 27.1 Getty Images/AFP; Plate 27.2 Getty Images.

In some instances we have been unable to trace the owners of copyright material, and we would appreciate any information that would enable us to do so.

Introduction

chapter 1

British politics in context: international, social and historical settings

This chapter places British politics in context by reviewing the key features of the political system. Some of these are shared with other democracies in Europe and overseas, while some are unique to Britain. They are all affected, however, by **globalisation** and moves to European integration. Current British politics are not simply an internal affair. Some of the most important influences are international, and these are imposing new strains on institutions, on political parties and on territorial relationships between England, Ireland, Scotland and Wales.

British institutions and political practices were 'fixed' in the mid-nineteenth century and continue in many ways to operate as they did then. They coexist uneasily with a society in continual change under the impact of world developments. Are British institutions well adapted to respond to such demands? Or to handle the political and economic problems of the twenty-first century? How far have the Blair governments gone in their attempts to reform Britain's political structure? Answering these questions helps us assess the quality of British democracy, a major aim of this book.

The specific features covered in this chapter are:

- liberal democracy and the Westminster Model of government
- the international and historical contexts
- social change in post-war Britain
- demands and constraints on British governments
- the class/territorial division in Britain
- the British 'Establishment'
- 'Europe' and Britain
- Britain: decline or adaptation?

BRIEFINGS

1.1 Liberal democracy

Liberal democracy exists in states that have regular elections for choosing the government, in which all citizens are entitled to vote, and that guarantee rights for individuals and groups which cannot be taken away. There have been liberal states that guaranteed legal rights without being full democracies (for example, Britain during most of the nineteenth century); and there have been democracies that infringed rights, such as the United States before the granting of federal protection to African-Americans in the 1960s.

Elections are important for maximising the probability that the government will act in accordance with majority wishes – a characteristic which is fundamental to democracy. However, most people would agree that minorities also need to be protected, even against the majority if the majority want to discriminate against them. It is important for minorities to be allowed to persuade others of the correctness of their view and perhaps become the majority later on. This possibility has to be left open if democracy is to function properly. So the protection of minorities is as important in its way as majority rule. Liberalism has traditionally stressed individual rights (freedom of speech, assembly, religion, movement). That is why democracies that incorporate guarantees for such rights are called liberal democracies.

Liberal democracy

Britain is a liberal–democratic state. **Liberal democracy** means that institutions such as the Civil Service and the armed forces, which administer and defend the national territory, operate under the supervision of a regularly elected government and Parliament. These arrangements guarantee citizens certain rights and freedoms. Free elections to choose governments define Britain as a democracy, while the liberal element comes in the form of restrictions on state interference with the lives of private individuals and families.

Making comparisons

Globalisation

The growing linkage of all countries of the world with each other through travel, tourism, trade and electronic communication. As anything done in one area now affects all the others, this means that countries such as Britain can act less and less on their own and so creates a need for international political institutions such as the United Nations (UN) and the European Union (EU).

Britain is one of about 30 fully liberal democracies in Europe and about 50 elsewhere in the world. British institutions, such as Parliament and political parties, are broadly similar to those that operate in other democracies. This is particularly so where other countries are 'parliamentary democracies' like Britain and not 'presidential democracies' like the United States or Russia. In a parliamentary democracy the members of the **government** are drawn from the national legislature or Parliament, and the government itself depends on the support of Parliament. This contrasts with the United States, where the head of government is separately elected and independent of the elected legislature.

Britain was the first parliamentary democracy in Europe. Many of the other European countries modelled their political institutions and ways of doing things on Britain when they too introduced responsible governments and elected parliaments. In the 1950s and 1960s, the British system (known as the '**Westminster Model**') was exported to many of the colonies and territories of Britain's old empire when these countries became independent. As a result, many British procedures and practices exist in other liberal democracies too. Good examples are the ways in which the courts function and some of the ways in which political parties operate.

However, some features of British politics were not copied elsewhere. A good example is Britain's unwritten **constitution**: there is no one basic document that

BRIEFINGS

1.2 The Westminster Model of responsible party government

Britain is a 'representative democracy' because popular votes are usually cast for party candidates who advocate a policy programme, rather than for individual policies themselves (a practice termed 'direct democracy'). The party that gets a majority of candidates elected to the House of Commons then forms the government, until the next election.

The 'Westminster Model', so called after the area of London where the Houses of Parliament stand, is the term used to describe this form of representative democracy. Its most important feature is the fusion of legislative and executive power in the hands of the majority party in the Parliament.

The majority party leader becomes Prime Minister and nominates close party colleagues and supporters to form the Cabinet and government. They make national policy that their majority in the House of Commons can be guaranteed to support, owing to the strict discipline the party leadership in the government enforces on the majority party. All members of the government must support its policy (in public anyway). All Members of Parliament (MPs) of the ruling party vote for government policy. The opposition parties can only oppose, as the Westminster Model denies them any direct power.

This system is supported by many commentators on the grounds that it makes for decisive, strong government and fixes responsibility for government actions on the party in power. The fact that one or other of the two main parties will form the next government gives voters a clear-cut choice between their policy programmes.

The Westminster Model has been criticised, however, for making the ruling party too strong. It creates an 'elective dictatorship' of the majority party leadership, which can ignore all opposition and criticism, however justified, of what they propose to do. Moreover, the fact that an election may transfer total power in a matter of days from a party with one set of policies to another that opposes them (as with Conservatives and Labour in the 1997 general election) creates uncertainty and instability for business and for people in general, who have no secure guidelines on what the future will look like after a complete change of government.

Liberal democracy

The form of government practised in the West that tries to combine representative institutions of government, such as regular and free elections, with liberal values in terms of individual rights and responsibilities.

Government

A general term which refers either to the body that forms the political executive (as in 'the Labour government'), or the institutions of the State (as in 'the British system of government').

specifies the relationships between government, Parliament, the courts and the ordinary citizen.

When other countries made the transition to democracy, often after an internal revolution or defeat in war, they had to make a blueprint of the way their new democratic politics should operate. British institutions and practices evolved more gradually, so there was never a definitive turning point that called for the codification or writing down of the main relationships between institutions and between institutions and the citizenry in one document. (Chapter 4 discusses the constitution in more detail.)

The absence of a codified constitution does not necessarily make Britain less democratic than other democracies. Having regular elections and the opportunity to vote governments in or out is what counts. In many respects, however, it does make British politics different. For example, the absence of a written document that specifies precisely what governments can and cannot do makes it more difficult in Britain to claim that a government has acted unconstitutionally. Some claim that Britain needs a written constitution for precisely that reason. Most governments, contrariwise, feel that they exercise their powers in a reasonable way and that a written constitution would be unnecessarily restrictive and cumbersome.

We can make a judgement as to which side is right by looking at those liberal democracies that do have written constitutions and seeing whether these documents are indeed important in safeguarding individuals and minorities. Or they could be unnecessarily restrictive.

Comparisons with the experiences of other democracies help us to answer important questions about British politics on a factual basis, instead of just advancing

Plate 1.1 The Houses of Parliament, Westminster
Source: Alamy/Pawel Libra

our own opinions. Would a change in the method of electing MPs lead to parties rarely or never having a majority in the House of Commons, and thus encourage them to combine to form coalition governments? Would coalition governments be more representative than single-party ones or would they just be weak and helpless? We can look at other countries such as Italy or the Netherlands to see if such consequences necessarily follow when coalition governments emerge.

International context

Westminster Model

The form of liberal democracy that is modelled on the British Parliament and government in Westminster – the part of London where the Houses of Parliament are located.

Constitution

The fundamental rules or laws governing the relationship between the public institutions of a state.

Making comparisons is useful because it highlights the ways in which British politics resemble those of other countries, and the ways in which they are unique. They also help us to put British politics in an international context. This is important because we cannot really understand British politics unless we take account of developments outside the country. It is easy to lose sight of this during political debates that focus on things British governments can do on their own, such as regulating or deregulating industry or raising and lowering taxes. However, even these actions can have important international dimensions such as their effect on competitiveness or their compatibility with European Union law.

One need only think of British involvement in Afghanistan or Iraq to see that politics in Britain cannot be isolated from what goes on elsewhere in the world. Britain's close rapport with the United States or NATO (the North Atlantic Treaty Organisation) makes this even truer, as does its growing integration into the European Union. Whether or not Britain goes on to form a closer union with the other European countries or continues to stand apart on some issues such as monetary union, the EU and its decisions will affect it ever more closely, often more so than decisions taken by British governments alone.

Historical context

Attitudes to Europe, to British institutions and to political processes all emerge from history. This is probably truer of Britain than of other liberal democracies. Britain was the first major country in the world to base itself on an industrial and commercial economy, to see the bulk of the population shift from the countryside into cities, and to design social and political institutions to deal with that situation. As a result the key British institutions – Parliament, political parties, the Cabinet, Civil Service, local government, trade unions, and financial institutions in the City of London – all took on their modern shape during and after the Industrial Revolution.

Some institutions have adapted to modern developments while others remain essentially unchanged. In the course of the twentieth century other European countries were taken over by dictatorships or defeated in war and occupied. Among the major powers only Britain, owing partly to its island position, managed to avoid this. Most continental European countries thus experienced a sharp break with their political past, which pushed them into changing and updating their political practices. Only Britain had no immediate need to do this.

A degree of stability and continuity has thus characterised British political institutions since the mid-nineteenth century. To take one example, two out of the three big political parties – the Conservatives and Liberal Democrats – date back to the 1870s. The third, Labour, is only slightly younger, having been founded about 1900.

Such stability and continuity may be welcomed as evidence of the strength of British democracy. Particularly during and after the Second World War British institutions stood out as islands of stability and beacons of hope in a chaotic world. When post-war Europe was divided and its democracies were threatened by Communist subversion within and Soviet aggression without, Britain seemed admirably free from internal divisions and was perceived as democratic and strong. These characteristics made Britain the chief ally of the United States in the military and political confrontation with the **Soviet Union** known as the Cold War (1948–88).

The flipside of continuity and stability, however, was a reluctance to keep up with developments, internationally and internally. Eventually, the other European democracies found political stability and replanned their institutions. They recovered economically from the devastation of the Second World War, and spearheaded a move to European integration from which Britain initially stood apart. Germany gained a large share of world trade and challenged Britain for the position of leading ally of the United States. As the Cold War declined in intensity, world bases were abandoned. British colonies were given independence in the face of nationalist and independence movements. Britain's influence on the international scene diminished. In such a situation, parliamentary debates over foreign policy, conducted in the grand style of earlier days, seemed more like a charade to bolster pretensions of grandeur than the world-shaking decisions of the old days.

Indeed, British world preoccupations increasingly looked like excuses for not tackling basic problems nearer at hand, such as relative economic decline and relations with Europe. Overseas preoccupations, together with opposition from French governments, prevented Britain from joining the European Community until 1973. At home they diverted attention from the ever-accelerating social changes that started with the creation of the Welfare State in the late 1940s, continued in the

Soviet Union

The Communist state set up in 1922 on the remnants of the old Russian Empire that was principally responsible for defeating Nazi Germany in the Second World War. As a result it dominated central and eastern Europe as a basis for confrontation with the United States and the West during the 'Cold War' (1948–88). But it split up in 1991–2, leaving Russia as its main successor state.

midst of economic change and immigration in the 1950s, and created growing difficulties thereafter. The inability or reluctance of political leaders to deal with such developments forms the stage on which recent British politics has been played out.

Social change in post-war Britain

The post-war Labour governments (1945–51) consolidated all the existing schemes for health care and social protection into a unified body of legislation, along with institutions to implement it. Collectively these went under the name of the Welfare State.

The basic aim was to ensure that everyone got support in all the major crises of life: poverty, sickness, old age and unemployment. State help was to be provided whether or not recipients could pay. In this sense, the Welfare State was based on the notion of universal rather than selective benefits: all citizens, irrespective of their financial position, were to be provided with Welfare State support. This basic support was supplemented by schemes to provide everyone with decent housing and education.

In themselves, these welfare reforms would have produced major social changes. They allowed poorer groups – generally urban manual workers – to improve their basic standards of living and to get better jobs through improved educational opportunities. This contributed to the breaking down of class barriers and produced more geographical and social mobility (see Table 1.1).[1]

Economic expansion and change also encouraged this, however. In the first 20 years of the post-war period (1945–65) the traditional industries expanded and some prospered. New service sectors such as tourism and personal finance developed. Many of the new jobs were non-manual but attracted sons (and increasingly daughters) from the working class.

BRIEFINGS

1.3 The Welfare State

This is a generic term for the provision by the state of collective goods and services to its citizens: health, education, housing, income support and personal social services for children, the old, the sick, the disabled and the unemployed. The state uses public funds to provide a minimum standard of living, or safety net, for its citizens. There are many different forms of welfare intervention: some work primarily through cash benefits, others by providing services directly; some provide universal benefits, others selective benefits; some try to redistribute incomes and resources, others are more concerned with raising sufficient funds for basic services. Some of these services are highly developed, some are more minimal. The proportion of national wealth spent in Britain on the Welfare State rose particularly rapidly from 1950 to 1980 and from 2000 onwards. The term 'welfare state' also refers very often to the array of institutions – hospitals, health trusts, insurance, employment and training agencies – set up to care for those in need.

---

[1] The major 'class' division is between manual occupations, often involving hard physical effort, and non-manual occupations, which usually involve desk or computer work. Table 1.1, based on social surveys conducted in the 1970s, shows that 18.8 per cent of the population had fathers in manual work but were themselves in non-manual jobs (or had husbands in non-manual jobs). That is to say that almost one-fifth of the old manual working class had 'risen' to the non-manual middle class. This is balanced by the 7.8 per cent who had fathers in non-manual work but were themselves now in manual work (or had husbands who were). Even taking this into account, however, the general movement between generations in the middle of the post-war period was 'up', both in terms of the relative magnitude of these percentages and the fact that the working class was much larger than the non-manual groups.

Table 1.1 Increasing social
mobility among males in
Britain in the 1970s

Father's occupational class	Sons or sons-in-law in occupational class		
	Non-manual	Manual	Total
Non-manual	16.8	7.8	24.6
Manual	18.8	56.6	75.4
Total	35.6	64.4	100%

Source: A. H. Halsey, *Trends in British Society since 1900*, London: Macmillan, 1982, p. 146

Unemployment was low, partly because governments made it a major priority to expand employment. The economy grew every year and provided more jobs. This situation made it easy to absorb refugees from eastern Europe after the end of the war. The prospect of a job attracted growing numbers of immigrants during the 1950s and 1960s, at first from Ireland, then from the colonies and ex-colonies in the West Indies, Africa and the Indian subcontinent.

The arrival of these groups gave Britain for the first time a section of the population that obviously differed from the rest in terms of appearance and, in the case of Asians, in religion and many of their social customs too. Although restrictions on immigration were imposed from 1962 onwards, by 2000 around 4 million of Britain's 59 million people were classified as ethnic minorities, mainly of Asian, Caribbean and African origin.

At 7 per cent of the total this is not enormous. But of course the job seekers concentrated in the more prosperous and populous areas, notably Greater London, the Midlands and (when jobs were available in the 1950s and 1960s) the northern textile towns (see Table 1.2). Their growing presence was sometimes followed by tensions with the white population, which from the 1960s erupted in sporadic rioting and sometimes encouraged racist appeals in elections.

It must be said, however, that Britain is not unique in this respect. Compared with some countries, restraint and goodwill on both sides have usually characterised British race relations. This held true even when economic and social conditions deteriorated in the later 1970s and early 1980s. The presence of immigrants stresses the fact that Britain is a multi-ethnic society (see Figure 1.1). Awareness of this was heightened by the claims of territorial minorities inside Britain – the Scots, Welsh and (Catholic) Northern Irish – to recognition. The overwhelming majority (just over 83 per cent) of the British population live in England. However, the Scots (9.8 per cent or over 5 million), the Welsh (nearly 2.5 per cent or

Table 1.2 Percentage
distribution of ethnic
minorities by region of Great
Britain, 2001

Northern England	1
Yorkshire and Humberside	6
North-west England	8
East Midlands	7
West Midlands	14
Eastern	4
Greater London	46
Rest of south-east England	7
South-west England	2
Wales	2
Scotland	3
Total, Great Britain	100

Source: Office for National Statistics, 2002, Table 3.19, http://statistics.gov.uk. Reproduced under the terms of the Click-Use Licence

Figure 1.1 Ethnic composition of the British population, 2000–1

Source: Computed from Labour Force Survey, Office for National Statistics. Reproduced under the terms of the Click-Use Licence

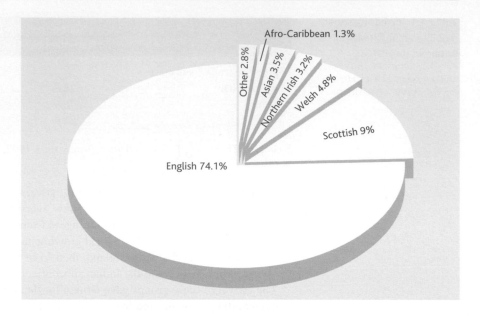

Afro-Caribbean 1.3%

Other 2.8%

Asian 3.5%

Northern Irish 3.2%

Welsh 4.8%

Scottish 9%

English 74.1%

2 million) and Northern Irish (just over 3 per cent) each dominate their own areas of Britain. Each group has generated nationalist parties that seek greater political autonomy and, in some cases, total secession from the British state. Their claims have been fuelled by the fact that the peripheries have been less prosperous than the London and south-east area over the post-war period. Hence, some sections of

Plate 1.2 Britain – a multi-ethnic society

Source: Getty Images/Scott Barbour

Figure 1.2 Unemployment rates by region, spring 2002

Source: Social Trends, **32**, 2002, Chart 4.25, Office for National Statistics. Reproduced under the terms of the Click-Use Licence

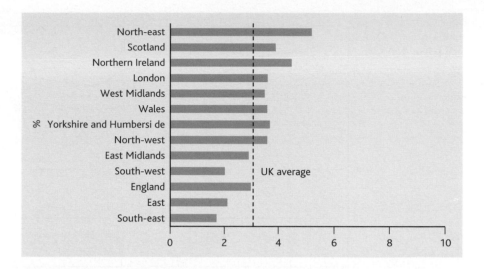

their populations feel they can do better on their own (see Chapters 10 and 11 for a detailed discussion).

The main reason for regional disparities is that traditional industries such as textiles, coalmining, steel and shipbuilding were heavily concentrated in the north, Scotland and Wales and newer light industries such as car manufacture were concentrated in the English Midlands. By the 1980s these industries were facing huge pressure from competitors around the world, particularly East Asia. Thousands of jobs were lost as firms introduced cost-saving measures to improve their efficiency. Meanwhile the governments, committed to '**New Right**' economic policies, refused to intervene to try to save factories and mines from closing, believing that it was up to the management of the industries themselves to respond to the pressures of the market by becoming more efficient.

Economic change was not confined to the unemployed. Many men, for example, dropped out of the labour force altogether, taking early retirement on the basis of their savings or pensions. Many more women took jobs outside the home, until the number of women working approached those of men (see Figure 1.3). Women

New Right

The politicians and theorists of the 1980s who believed in the efficacy of market competition as the best means of guaranteeing political freedom and economic growth.

BRIEFINGS

1.4 Thatcherism and the New Right

'Thatcherism' is a term used to describe the attitudes and policies of the Conservative governments from 1979 to 1990, when Margaret Thatcher was party leader and Prime Minister. These attitudes have been summed up as 'free market, strong state'. On the economic side, the object was to 'get the government out of business' and restore individual initiative. This was achieved by 'privatisation' (selling off) government enterprises such as electricity, water, gas, public housing and railways. Many regulations were abolished and serious attempts made to reduce the number of government employees (from 700,000 to 590,000 in the course of the 1980s).

Strong and authoritative state action was needed, however, to break trade union resistance to these changes or even to initiate them in the first place against internal Conservative Party opposition, parts of the Civil Service, local governments and other groups. Thatcher and her supporters built up state power by strengthening police and security forces (see Chapter 21) and taking powers away from local government (see Chapter 12).

The emphasis of Thatcherism on freeing markets tied in with the thinking of 'neo-liberal' or 'New Right' economists, who saw the market as more efficient than the state (including the Welfare State) at providing everyone with goods and services. Margaret Thatcher is therefore often described as a 'neo-liberal' or 'New Right' politician. (For more on these ideas, see Chapters 2 and 17.)

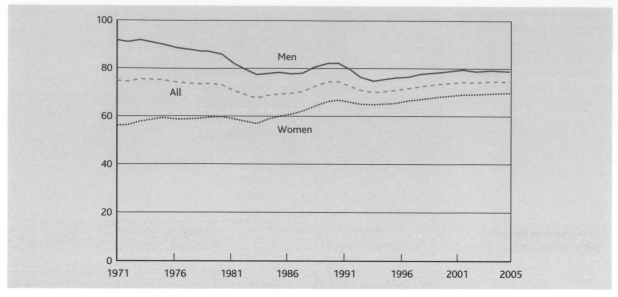

Figure 1.3 Employment rates by gender, United Kingdom 1971–2005

Note: At spring each year. Men aged 16 to 64, women aged 16 to 59. The percentage of the population that is in employment. Data are seasonally adjusted and have been adjusted in line with population estimates published in autumn 2005. See Appendix, Part 4: LFS reweighting, and Historical LFS-consistent time series.

Source: *Social Trends*, **32**, 2002, Chart 4.1, Office for National Statistics. Reproduced under the terms of the Click-Use Licence

tended to be more flexible and to take the service and part-time jobs that now became available.

Unemployment and a changing pattern of family and life cycle employment created new demands on the Welfare State at the same time as the Conservative government wanted to cut social spending and strengthen citizens' self-reliance. As the eligibility criteria for unemployment and social benefits were tightened in order to reduce expenditure and cut taxation, disparities between rich and poor increased (see Table 1.3). Interestingly, these disparities continued to increase throughout the 1990s, so that by 1999 just 1 per cent of the population owned 34 per cent of the wealth (excluding wealth held in housing).

Table 1.3 Distribution of wealth in Britain, 1976–2002

Source: *Social Trends*, **32**, 2002, Table 5.4, Office for National Statistics. Reproduced under the terms of the Click-Use Licence

	1976	1981	1986	1991	1997	2002
Marketable wealth: percentage of wealth owned by:						
Most wealthy 1%	21	18	18	17	22	23
Most wealthy 5%	38	36	36	35	43	43
Most wealthy 10%	50	50	50	47	54	54
Most wealthy 25%	71	73	73	71	75	74
Most wealthy 50%	92	92	90	92	93	94
Marketable wealth less value of dwellings: percentage of wealth owned by:						
Most wealthy 1%	29	26	25	29	30	34
Most wealthy 5%	47	45	46	51	54	58
Most wealthy 10%	57	56	58	64	66	71
Most wealthy 25%	73	74	75	80	83	86
Most wealthy 50%	88	87	89	93	95	97

Note: Data is taken from *Social Trends*, **32**, 2002, Table 5.4 and HM Revenue and Customs. Most people's wealth is the value of their house. When that is taken out of the calculation, in the bottom half of the table, disparities increase markedly.

Post-war Britain therefore remains a remarkably unequal society. In contrast to the immediate post-war period, however, the middle classes are much more numerous. A vote of 40 per cent is enough to give a national party a majority in Parliament and to sustain a government. Thus groups that benefit from the current distribution of income and wealth are numerous enough to vote a government in, regardless of the 20 per cent living in poverty. These social developments partly account for the long tenure of Conservative governments under Mrs Thatcher (1979–90) and John Major (1990–7) who were committed to tax cutting and reducing government spending on the social services. They also help to explain why the New Labour governments have accepted many – although not all – of these policies.

Political demands and institutional constraints

Some critics have argued that this situation is not healthy or stable. If, partly as a result of government policy, groups that are suffering deprivation see no way of changing this through peaceful persuasion and elections, they are liable to react in ways that are undesirable for a democracy. Either they can withdraw altogether from politics (Chapter 15) or back parties with extreme demands or they can threaten to secede from the United Kingdom if they live in a particular area such as Northern Ireland or Scotland.

Of course, the election of an alternative government can bring relief and hopes of reintegrating the marginal groups into society. This is why democracies, which offer such an escape mechanism through elections, are often more strong and stable than they appear.

Not only electoral considerations but international and institutional constraints limit what a British government can do. The two come together in the financial institutions and markets of the City of London. The major British financial institutions, such as banks, trust funds and insurance companies, conduct their worldwide business here. Much of their business consists in buying and selling shares in British and international companies and in lending governments money. The City is a major influence on what foreign lenders and investors think about British economic prospects. It also has a broader influence on British commerce and industry generally.

The major way in which the City's influence is felt is through the price it and other lenders charge the government for loans, or whether it is even prepared to lend money for the day-to-day operations of government in the first place. British governments often spend more than they take in revenue. Any improvement in educational or health standards costs money, which may have to be borrowed. Therefore, all governments are heavily dependent on the goodwill of the financial markets. A loss of goodwill can result in a reduction in the value of the British currency, through the loss of world financial confidence. This could plunge not only the British government but the whole of the economy into crisis.

In the past, City influence pressed particularly on Labour governments because they traditionally needed to tax and spend to fulfil electoral promises. Plans to take more money in taxes rather than leaving it as higher profits reduces the value of shares. Since the mid-1990s, however, the Labour Party has largely abandoned high-tax, high-spending policies in favour of fiscal rectitude (i.e. low taxation and restraints on public spending and inflation). This sea change in policy has had important consequences for British politics and for the British economy. We will return to this in Chapter 3.

Plate 1.3 The City of London. The new building that now houses the London offices of Swiss Re nicknamed 'The Gherkin'. It demonstrates the size, wealth and power of city finance

Source: Corbis/Poul Hardy

BRIEFINGS

1.5 The 'City'

This is a geographical area, referring to the old core of London within the medieval city wall, between the modern centre and the residential East End. Most British financial institutions, including the Stock Exchange and Bank of England, are physically located there. The term is used metaphorically to refer to British financial institutions in general, even though some are located elsewhere.

These institutions dominate the British economy for two reasons. The first is because, collectively, they own most of the large businesses and firms through their shareholdings. Second, manufacturing industry borrows from them to finance production and expansion. Bank decisions about whether to make loans and how much to charge for them thus affect the activity of the whole economy. In addition, the City is the major global centre for insurance and many exchange markets such as currency, precious metals and other commodities.

The City is one of the three leading financial centres of the world (the others being New York and Tokyo). Thus its collective judgements about how well the British economy is performing, and whether to hold on to British currency, influence foreign investors as well. If the City's judgement is negative money markets across the world will sell pounds for ever-decreasing amounts of foreign currency, thus effectively reducing the value of savings in Britain and of sales overseas. This gives financial interests a crucial influence over government economic policy, often to the extent of obliging governments to favour financially prudent policies such as low government debt and low inflation, over expansion of manufacturing industry and of public services.

Class/territorial divisions

The financial markets' desire for expenditure cuts, limited taxation and hence generally limited government tied in very well with Conservative government policies from 1979 to 1997. Financial services directly or indirectly employ millions of the new middle class in south-east England. So the views of the financial markets and the new middle classes form one side of a political division that traditionally separated the Conservative and Labour parties. Labour's core support has usually come from groups that by and large have been disadvantaged by recent social changes and government policies: the unemployed, the shrinking numbers of manual workers represented by trade unions, immigrants and all those dependent on and working in old industries. Only when Labour adopts a more centrist position, which broadens its appeal beyond its core supporters to the mass of middle-class voters, can it win elections. This is precisely what happened in 1997 and later.

Because of the way industry developed in Britain the social divisions separating the parties are also reflected in a territorial division of political opinion. The availability of water power and coal meant that the manufacturing industries of the Industrial Revolution – textiles, coalmining, steel and shipbuilding – were located in the '**Celtic fringe**' – Scotland, Northern Ireland and Wales – and in the Midlands and north of England.

The large new nineteenth-century cities – Glasgow, Newcastle, Manchester, Liverpool, Leeds, Cardiff, Belfast – developed in these regions, along with Birmingham and Nottingham in the Midlands. They housed the new industrial class of manual labourers and factory workers, often in appalling conditions. These cities and their inhabitants depended on manufacturing and extractive industries, unlike London, which remained the seat of government, administration, commerce and finance. Although a large working class grew up in central and east London, the capital and its surrounding area (the 'Home Counties') were the centre of an even larger middle class.

Class contrasts between manual and 'white-collar' workers were thus reinforced in Britain by a territorial division between the geographical areas in which each predominated. From this point of view the Labour (and Liberal) parties have often seemed more like coalitions of Inner London and the British peripheries against the south and south-east England than class-based parties. This is particularly true now, following the Labour victories in the 2001 and 2005 elections. In 2005, 141 out of 197 Conservative MPs came from the south and south-east of England. Also significant is the fact that in 2001 only three Conservative MPs were elected in Wales and one in Scotland.

Divisions between these two territorial/class coalitions go beyond party politics. Financial interests trading worldwide from the City of London need above all a stable currency and low inflation to preserve the value of their cash and investments. This need has often conflicted with the requirement of manufacturing industry for devaluation of the currency to help their exports, and for mildly rising inflation to give people more money to buy their products. In turn, this situation stimulates investment and employment.

Government policy has usually favoured financial prudence because inflation can provoke an immediate financial crisis with both national and international repercussions. Industrial consequences are long term: once older manufacturing industries decline, it is very difficult to revive them. These industrial changes clearly have negative consequences for older mining and manufacturing communities. Contrariwise, the jobs created in other sectors such as finance and retailing are often better paid and less arduous. The problem has been distributing them

Celtic fringe

Coined around 1900 to describe the northern and western peripheries of the British Isles (Scotland, Wales and Ireland) that voted Liberal, Labour or Nationalist rather than Conservative. The term is now used to refer to the Celtic periphery of the UK (Scotland, Ireland and Wales) whatever the voting patterns.

geographically in a way that helps the distressed industrial areas rather than the south-east.

By the mid-1990s the Labour Party had reconciled itself to the fact that, to achieve electoral success, it was obliged to follow a policy of fiscal and monetary restraint. This meant avoiding large tax increases, attempting to balance the national budget and, above all, keeping strict controls on inflation. With the abolition of restrictions on capital movement across national borders during the 1980s and 1990s governments in all countries felt pressure to control inflation and thus prevent a decline in currencies' values. In this sense, the principles represented by the City of London throughout the post-war period (lower taxes, balanced budgets and low inflation) became the economic orthodoxy almost everywhere. As we shall see, this development has had the effect of putting strict limits on what governments of all political complexions can do in terms of public expenditure.

Map 1.1 The regions of the UK

Note: See also Map 11.1 for official UK regions of England.

Plate 1.4 Working-class housing and a middle-class estate

Sources: (left) Alamy/Photofusion; (right) Alamy/Education photos

The British State and the British 'Establishment'

The class/territorial division is at the heart of the left–right cleavage between the British parties, which we discuss in Chapter 17. Labour wants help for disadvantaged groups and regions, the Liberal Democrats desire their greater empowerment, while Conservatives want a strengthening of the existing order and of the disciplines underpinning it. As we have seen, important institutions such as the City of London as well as many business people and business groups have historically sided with the Conservatives. Many commentators have therefore concluded that all the leading British institutions, including **state** institutions such as the Civil Service and the security services, are biased against change and covertly do their best to thwart the left when it achieves power. Some variants of these 'conspiracy' theories saw the whole set of central institutions, including the Crown, judges and even the clergy of the Church of England, as lined up to thwart any left-wing threats to their privileges and position.

Ideas of this kind were quickly discredited when Margaret Thatcher came to power in 1979 and started to change British institutions and practices ruthlessly, without effective resistance from anyone. Speculation about an elite conspiracy was always far fetched – there never was a conspiracy. Bishops figured among the major critics of Conservative policies on the grounds that they were hurting the weak. Civil servants and government departments rarely agreed among themselves: if the Treasury favoured City financiers, the Department of Employment often supported trade unions.

Nevertheless, the Treasury and the Home Office are the most powerful and central of the departments dealing with internal affairs. Spending departments, such as Education and Skills, Health and Transport do not deal with core policies. The Treasury shares its values with the City of London and supports their preferences for tight expenditure controls and tax cutting, putting the maintenance of financial confidence at the top of its list of priorities. A certain structural bias is thus built into British central institutions, which favour the private versus the public, tax cutting against services, London and the Home Counties against the peripheries. However, low inflation and fiscal rectitude have become the orthodoxy for all

State

The set of public bodies and institutions within a given territory that exercise a monopoly of the legitimate use of physical force. In Britain, the state consists mainly of Parliament, the military, the courts, the police, the Civil Service and local government.

political parties. Put another way, they determine the limits of what even the most radical governments can do with taxing and spending. In areas independent of economic policy, and especially constitutional reform, major changes can still be achieved. But the acceptance of economic orthodoxy by all political parties has significantly changed the nature of British politics.

European integration

New international influences are emerging, however, that counteract the newly established orthodoxy. These stem from Britain's increasing integration into the European Union. By creating additional pressures from outside the existing set of British institutions the European Union has tipped the balance towards more 'social' policies. This is because other members of the EU have better social protection than Britain. Having fewer social benefits enables firms to cut prices, particularly if there is no legislation enforcing a minimum wage (as was true in Britain until 1998) or the minimum wage is set at a low level in comparison with other EU states. Other EU governments are therefore afraid that in the single European market, which they are creating, British firms will have a competitive advantage because of lower wage and welfare costs.

Precisely for this reason the Treaty of Maastricht (1993), which envisaged an emerging federal union between EU member states, had a 'Social Chapter' binding all governments to give social rights to workers to ensure a 'level playing field' for competition. The Conservative government of John Major 'opted out' of the Social Chapter, the only one of the member governments to do so (Labour opted in in 1997). The Major government also reserved its position on the question of whether to enter a currency union with the other member states. Such a union would have the advantage of creating a strong, stable European currency that would command international confidence and avoid financial crises better than a purely British pound. However, it would also remove control of financial policy from the British government and Treasury and place it in the hands of a European central bank. For this reason New Labour has been cautious and divided on the issue, with Gordon Brown strongly opposing it as Chancellor of the Exchequer (in charge of financial and economic policy). No Conservative government would agree to join the 'euro' (the new European currency) either, so further integration seems out of the question for Britain at this point.

Britain: adapting to a new international environment

Whether we think European influence is a good or a bad thing, British politics cannot be explained without taking it into account. This would be the case whether Britain were in or out of the EU. So closely are its economy and defence now bound up with Europe that they will be vitally affected by European Union decisions. That is not a choice. The only real question is whether the government chooses to influence European policy from outside or inside.

The inability of Britain to go it alone, evident in the case of Europe and in Britain's extensive cooperation with the world superpower, the United States, seems a far cry from its position in the mid-nineteenth century when it was at the centre of a worldwide Empire and an even more extended trading network. The contrast has prompted many critics to see post-war British politics as a series of unsuccessful attempts to cope with national decline.

'Decline' is an emotive word, with all sorts of implications beyond the specific political area to which it applies. It has undertones of moral and spiritual decay, which did indeed drive analyses of the British situation in the 1980s. A more neutral characterisation of British politics is that they have been adapting to an unstable and shifting world environment, in which the British position has also changed quite radically.

Clearly, the British state is much less powerful militarily and economically at the beginning of the twenty-first century than it was at the beginning of the twentieth century, when it was the leading naval power in the world. This enabled it to trade everywhere and to build up an Empire that at its height covered a quarter of the land area of the world. At the same time Britain was, along with the United States and Germany, a leading world industrial power and the leading provider of investment capital in the new markets of Asia, Africa and South America.

All this was due to the fact that the Industrial Revolution was carried through first in Britain, making British firms the undisputed leaders in a variety of manufactures ranging from textiles to steel. This unique situation could not last. Even to sell their goods abroad British entrepreneurs had to invest in overseas infrastructures such as railways, which then provided the basis for other countries to industrialise too. Their doing so was a precondition for Britain to continue its industrial expansion, as purely agricultural societies could take only a limited supply of British exports.

Clearly, Britain no longer enjoys the commercial and military pre-eminence that it did then. However, it has been on the winning side in two world wars and in the Cold War, and it disengaged from its colonies relatively painlessly. The British were able to recognise the formidable power of local nationalism, and avoided becoming embroiled in the sort of long and corrosive wars fought by France and Portugal in the 1950s and 1960s. Britain has kept its options open in Europe up to the present time. All this looks less like drift and decline than successful adaptation to a changing world situation.

Much of the debate on decline and change, however, focused on the economy rather than directly on foreign affairs. The British share of world trade has fallen consistently over the last 100 years, from one-third in 1899 to one-quarter in 1950, to around one-twentieth today. British economic growth was also sluggish for most of the post-Second World War period. However, since about 1990 the British economy has performed well, consistently outstripping the growth rates of Germany, France, Italy and Japan (see Table 1.4 and Figure 1.4).

The relatively poor performance of the British economy in the 1950–90 period was to have profound effects on British politics. The Labour and Conservative parties competed with one another on how best to redress this situation and allow Britain to 'catch up' with such countries as France, Germany and Japan. As we will see in later chapters, radical alternatives were provided by both the left and the right, which led to a particularly abrasive and confrontational style of politics. Poor

Table 1.4 Annual GDP growth for major industrialised countries, 1962–2001

	1962–72	1977–88	1991–2001
France	4.7	1.6	1.9
Germany	3.6	1.3	1.5
Italy	3.9	2.2	1.6
Britain	2.2	1.8	2.7
United States	3.0	2.3	3.4
Japan	9.2	3.9	1.1

Source: OECD, *OECD in Figures: Statistics of Member Countries*, Paris: OECD, 2002, pp. 14–15

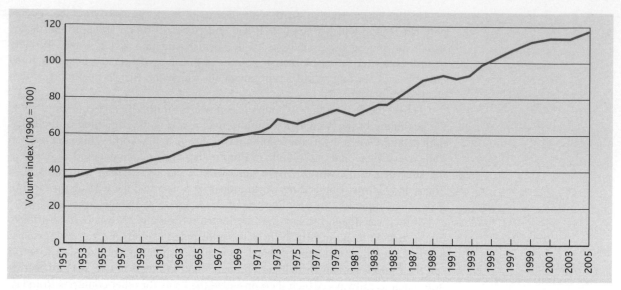

Figure 1.4 Growth of British gross domestic product over the post-war period
Source: Office for National Statistics. Reproduced under the Click-Use Licence

economic performance also led to a sense that British politics was in a state of almost permanent 'crisis' with parties and governments lurching unsteadily in the face of uncontrollable economic events. This sense of economic crisis abated during the 1990s and disappeared after 1997. This helps explain the remarkable renaissance of the Labour Party in British politics, as it has been credited with economic success.

Geographically, Britain is an island group off the north-western shore of Europe. Its proximity to Europe means that it has always been involved in European affairs. Its strategic location on the Atlantic means, however, that it was also in a position to expand westwards. British emigration and trade, therefore, have been predominantly overseas, away from Europe. They ended up creating new English-speaking countries in North America and Australasia, with which Britain has closer cultural links than with France and Germany, despite being much closer to those countries geographically.

Since 1960, British governments have therefore been pulled in two directions, often proving unable to make up their minds between them. The European Union, particularly under the influence of France, has wanted to create a strong European bloc of countries with external trade barriers against the rest of the world. Britain, with strong commercial and, particularly, financial links overseas, has wished the EU to pursue relatively liberal, open trading policies. It has also wanted the EU to cooperate with the United States rather than rival it.

These conflicting pulls are behind British membership of the EU on the one hand and its opposition to an exclusive, federal, largely autonomous and self-sufficient EU on the other. Britain would maximise its influence and prosperity by pressing ahead with integration into the EU, which increasingly seems likely to emerge as a world superpower. Yet this would weaken its overseas links, particularly with the United States, with which it shares a language and – to some extent – a culture. The choice is hard. As an American observer, Dean Acheson, acutely observed in the 1950s, 'Britain has lost an empire but not yet found a role.' It is still hesitating between two roles: that of world free trader and that of good European. Now that New Labour seems as undecided about 'Europe' as previous Conservative governments have been there seems little chance of resolving the conflicting external pulls that Britain has felt for half a century.

Summary

■ Britain is a liberal democracy. As such it shares many political characteristics with other countries that are also liberal democracies, both in Europe and overseas. The most obvious characteristics are regular, free, competitive elections, and parliaments and governments chosen by popular vote.

■ However, Britain also has unique characteristics deriving from its own particular history and geography. Some of the most important of these are associated with the Industrial Revolution. Britain was the first European country to create institutions such as mass parties, a representative Parliament, popular press, trade unions, financial and commodity exchanges and markets.

■ Many of these institutions still exist, largely in their original form. A central question of this book is how well such relatively unchanging institutions serve the needs of a continually changing society, divided between different ethnic groups, classes and regions.

■ A further question is how well they can cope with the international pressures that Britain faces. It has become hard to distinguish between purely national politics and foreign relations, particularly with globalisation and the move to European integration. Britain now has to decide between committing itself fully to Europe or remaining in its present uneasy position between Europe and the United States.

■ British politics can only be explained by a combination of national and international factors, set within a unique historical and geographical context. Historical influences are channelled through the institutions that the country inherited from the late nineteenth century. The origin and development of these institutions are examined in Chapter 2.

Essays

1. What role does the City play in British politics? Has its role been beneficial or detrimental to British interests?

2. Has Britain's military involvement with the Americans in the Middle East permanently isolated it from 'Europe'?

3. What policy differences, if any, now exist between 'New Conservatives' and 'New Labour'?

Projects

1. How would you go about testing whether the class/territorial divide in British politics is increasing or decreasing? Answer with respect to both economic and political influences.

2. What statistics would you use to test the claim that Britain is no longer in 'economic decline'? How reliable are these statistics?

3. Using information available from the annual publication *Social Trends* show that:

   (a) gender inequality in employment in Britain remains high;

   (b) women are, however, generally more important in the workforce.

Further reading

A provocative account of some of the general themes discussed in this chapter is Will Hutton, *The World We're In* (London: Little, Brown, 2002). Andrew Gamble, *The Free Economy and the Strong State* (London: Macmillan, 1988), assessed the 1980s in Britain and also wrote *Britain in Decline* (London: Macmillan, 1989). For the British role in Europe and the world see S. Falla, *New Labour and the European Union* (London: Ashgate, 2002). For lively updates on current developments see the quarterly *Monitor* published by the Constitution Unit at University College London, and the associated web site (see section at end of chapter).

Useful web sites on British politics

Hot links to these sites can be found on the companion web site (CWS) at www.pearsoned.co.uk/budge.

As a general introduction to important web sites concerning British politics, try www.ukpolitics.org.uk, which has many links to other political web sites. There are sites for the main institutions of the British state and government. For example, see the monarchy (www.royal.gov.uk), the Anglican Church (www.cofe.anglican.org), the House of Commons and House of Lords (www.parliament.uk and www.explore.parliament.uk), the new Scottish Parliament (www.scottish.parliament.uk), the Welsh Assembly (www.wales.gov.uk/assembly.dbs) and the Northern Ireland government web site www.nics.gov.uk. Other useful introductory sites related to British politics: www.historylearningsite.co.uk/gbpolitics.htm offers a comprehensive glossary of terms including liberal and representative democracy; for specific information on the Westminster system, as well as data on central and local government in the UK, refer to www.ukpol.co.uk; finally there are accessible complementary resources at www.britpolitics.com.

Political party sites

All the major political parties have web sites, and there are other sites that may be of interest to students of British politics such as www.ucl.ac.uk/constitutionunit/ and www.bubl.ac.uk/uk/parties.htm. See also the following list and subsequent chapters.

Labour www.labour.org.uk

Conservative www.conservative-party.org.uk

Liberal Democrats www.libdems.org.uk

Scottish National Party www.snp.org.uk

Plaid Cymru www.plaid-cymru.wales.com.

(See Chapters 16 and 17 for more links to party sites.)

For further study aids on this subject, please see the self-assessment test for this chapter on *The New British Politics* web site at www.pearsoned.co.uk/budge.

Other sites of interest

The government-sponsored www.ukonline.gov.uk is a recommended source of information for central and local institutions. www.open.gov.uk is a good first point of entry for internet information on the public sector in the UK, as is www.number-10.gov.uk.

www.hmso.gov.uk for Her Majesty's Stationery Office, contains legislation, statutory instruments and other official government publications

www.britannia.com is a private site on all things British, in particular see www.britannia.com/gov

www.bankofengland.co.uk for the Bank of England.

Economic and social statistical data can be found at www.statistics.gov.uk. The Cabinet's site at www.cabinet-office.gov.uk provides valuable information on the ministerial structure, the Civil Service and the public sector. General information about British culture and traditions can be obtained from www.english-heritage.org.uk.

PART 1
History

chapter 2

The first industrial country: ideas and institutions, 1688–1931

From the seventeenth through to the early twentieth centuries Britain experienced two crucial and – in comparison with other countries – unique developments. First, the country made a long and peaceful transition from autocratic monarchy to modern democracy. No other comparable state made this transition entirely through peaceful means. Instead, such countries as Germany, France, Italy and even the United States experienced revolutions, civil war or wars of independence in their evolution to democracy. Second, Britain was the first country to industrialise and make the transition from a predominantly rural society to an overwhelmingly urban one. At the same time, Britain acquired the world's largest colonial empire, which was at once a source of raw materials and cheap agricultural produce and a market for British manufactured goods and financial services. These developments required new political, economic and social institutions, many of which – Parliament, the Civil Service, local government, courts and police, the City of London, the armed forces – are still with us. Externally, Britain got locked into a pattern of relationships with the rest of the world that also persists, although both Britain and the world have changed greatly in the meantime.

How adaptable these institutions have been in the face of dramatic changes to British society and to Britain's role in the world was a question raised in Chapter 1, and will be a theme throughout the book. However, we cannot provide a clear answer until we have looked in detail at how British politics and institutions function in practice. To understand them fully we also need to look at the critical formative period in which they emerged and see what influences shaped them. We do this here, before going on to developments post-1930 in Chapter 3.

This chapter looks at the ways in which industrialisation and urbanisation changed both political institutions and the main ideas that shape politics. Discussion will cover these historical periods and episodes:

- the triumph of parliamentary over royal power, 1688–1830
- urbanisation and the rise of mass democracy, 1830–1928
- the British world system, 1850–90
- institutional change and reform, 1840–1900
- free markets, protection and industry, 1890–1931
- defences against an unstable international environment, 1890–1931
- the rise of socialism and trade union power, 1890–1931.

The triumph of parliamentary over royal power, 1688–1830

A crucial date in English (and hence British) history is 1688, because it marks one of the few occasions when English political institutions made a clean break with the past. Until 1688 royal power was enshrined in the doctrine of the divine right of kings (that monarchs were chosen by God to rule their subjects). In England, James II was openly Catholic and contemptuous of Parliament. The most influential grouping in Parliament, the Whigs, were Protestant and determined to assert parliamentary power over the monarch. James II's insensitivity also offended the other main grouping, the Tories, and in 1688 their leaders invited the Protestant William of Orange and his wife Mary, Protestant daughter of James, to take the English throne. Although James at first resisted, he eventually fled to France and William and Mary acceded to the throne.

A new constitutional settlement, known as the Glorious Revolution, established the necessity of consulting Parliament, especially on matters of taxation. A Bill of Rights was published – not so much a guarantee of citizen rights in the modern sense, as it was a guarantee of the rights of Parliament. These included free elections, free speech in Parliament and the abolition of the monarch's power to dispense and suspend laws. Further refinements were added through the Act of Settlement in 1701 and through the Act of Union with Scotland in 1707 (see Chapter 11).

During the eighteenth century, prime ministers assumed the role of chief executive in the British system. Even so, important residual powers remained with the monarch, including the formal power of dissolving Parliament and appointing a new government. These residual powers continued through the nineteenth century and indeed remain in a much-attenuated form to this day (see Chapter 4).

In spite of free speech in Parliament and free elections, eighteenth-century Britain was hardly democratic. Parliamentary seats could be secured from large landowners or by bribing a few electors. The right to vote was confined to a few men of property. And, of course, the landed aristocracy retained an important role in government through their membership of the upper House of Parliament, the House of Lords. Even so, British elites considered their system free in comparison to the absolutism that characterised most major continental powers. Towards the end of the eighteenth century two foreign events had a profound impact. First, the American War of Independence and the subsequent establishment of democracy in the United States showed up the weaknesses and inadequacies of British politics as practised in the late eighteenth century. Second, the French Revolution showed what could happen to states that denied rights and freedoms to their citizenry – anarchy and rule by the mob. The French Revolution thus provided a salutary lesson on what could happen in states that failed to make a peaceful transition to full democracy.

Urbanisation and the rise of mass democracy, 1830–1928

The ascendancy of parliamentary over royal power was accompanied by dramatic economic developments. First agriculture and then manufacturing experienced rapid technological changes, greatly increasing productivity and speeding the movement of population from the countryside to the towns. The development of factory machinery powered by steam led to the concentration of manufacturing in towns where markets were close by and transport links good. An industrial working class clustered around the new factories and eventually older towns expanded

BRIEFINGS

2.1 The Industrial Revolution

During the eighteenth century technology was increasingly applied to manufacturing processes, from cloth to iron, which had previously been carried out by hand in scattered artisan workshops. The most notable development was the use of mill machinery, which utilised water and steam power to spin and weave cloth and to shape metal. As a result, a large number of unskilled workers could produce more, better quality goods at a lower price. The use of a single power source and of a large, concentrated labour force prompted the invention of the modern factory. When steam was substituted for water power, factories were grouped near to coalfields and close to each other. These groupings of factories and associated workers' housing produced industrial towns and cities, which developed an infrastructure of canals, roads, transport and services. By 1850 more than half the population of Britain lived in such settlements and Britain had become the first urbanised society. The factory owners, professionals and merchants who dominated the new cities formed a new political grouping that wanted a share in political power, and eventually the organised working class also wanted representation to improve their conditions. Thus the economic changes associated with the Industrial Revolution destabilised the old political order in which landed aristocrats and gentry dominated Parliament.

rapidly and new towns were created where previously there had been villages. By 1850 a quarter of the British population lived in cities of over 100,000 and more than a half in conglomerations that could be described as urban. However, most of these areas had no political authority to police, regulate or represent them. The new middle class in the urban areas felt personally threatened by disorder and disease, and wanted in any case to have a healthier and more disciplined workforce in the factories.

Middle-class agitation for local and national change produced the 'Great Reform Act' of 1832 and the repeal of the Corn Laws in 1846. The Great Reform Act was in fact a very limited measure. It extended voting rights to all the wealthy and the upper middle class. Parliamentary reform was followed by municipal reform that set up new councils in urban areas which were able, where they wished, to tackle local health and crime. The **New Poor Law** created uniform, minimal and often harsh facilities for those in desperate need.

The new middle classes followed up these successes by abolishing all protective taxes on imports, notably of food (the repeal of the Corn Laws, 1846). Their reason for wanting this was logical and simple. British industry was incomparably bigger and more efficient than that in other countries and therefore had nothing to fear from competition or imports. What manufacturers did want, however, was cheap food for their workforce, so that wages and prices could be kept down. Protective tariffs on imports of food left food prices high, to the benefit of British farmers and country dwellers in general. The abolition of tariffs on wheat signalled the end of all such protective measures, marking the dominance of urban interests over rural and of the new middle class (the 'bourgeoisie') over the landed gentry.

The abolition of protective tariffs produced the 'great transformation' of British society and of Britain's place in the world. For the first time, a country had taken the gamble of making itself dependent on foreign imports for its basic survival. By the beginning of the twentieth century half of what the British ate was imported, much of it from the Americas and Australasia. This meant in turn that Britain had to export to survive. (It also rendered it particularly vulnerable in the First and Second World Wars to submarine attacks, which sank ships carrying food and munitions.)

New Poor Law

Passed in 1834 to deal with the poor cheaply and efficiently. 'Workhouses' were set up everywhere into which those who needed relief had to go. Conditions inside were harsher than those of the worst-paid employment outside to deter 'welfare dependence'.

BRIEFINGS

2.2 The Reform Acts 1832–1928

The Great (First) Reform Act of 1832 was passed by the unreformed Parliament under pressure from the politically mobilised middle class (industrialists, merchants, and their supporters and dependants). It was a limited measure, abolishing most 'rotten boroughs' (constituencies with very few electors) and 'pocket boroughs' (constituencies controlled by one big landowner), where MPs could buy their seats from electors or obtain it from a landed proprietor. These seats were redistributed to counties or to the large new industrial towns. Inside the redrawn constituencies the vote was given to property holders, resulting in limited numbers of electors in each constituency.

The Great Reform Act was not a very radical measure, but it did show that the electoral system could be changed peacefully in favour of previously excluded groups. Further agitation later in the century brought about:

- the Second Reform Act (1867), which gave the vote to the better-off workmen in towns

- the Third Reform Act (1884), which extended the franchise in towns and gave it to agricultural labourers

- the extension of the vote to the third of adult males who were still excluded, along with women over 30, in 1918

- finally, in 1928, the granting of the vote to women on the same terms as men.

These changes were accompanied by reforms of the constituency system which ensured that constituencies were relatively equal in size, thus weighting votes more equally. It was typical of the cautious and incremental nature of political change in Britain, however, that all reforms left intact the 'first past the post system', in which the individual candidates compete in small constituencies and the one with the most votes wins, whether or not he or she gets a majority of the total votes cast.

Free trade

The idea that trade should not be restricted by protection in the form of tariffs, customs duties or import quotas that are designed to protect the domestic economy from foreign competition.

Liberalism

With a small 'l', liberalism is the political belief that individual rights should be protected by strictly limiting the powers of government.

Liberalism

With a capital 'L' Liberalism refers to the beliefs and policies of the Liberal Party.

Agitators such as John Bright and Richard Cobden who attacked protection did not foresee this military consequence. They were, however, quite prepared to gamble on manufactured exports paying for food imports. Given British industrial supremacy in the world this seemed a safe bet. In support of Corn Law repeal they developed a series of interlocking arguments in favour of **free trade**, that is, the abolition of all protective tariffs on a worldwide basis.

The free trade advocates believed that without 'artificial' tariffs the pressure of competition would force each area of the world to concentrate on what it produced most efficiently. Efficiency might be linked to natural advantages such as the presence of minerals or a beneficent climate. It was marked in practice by the ability to produce and market the good at a lower price than elsewhere in the world, provided political barriers such as tariffs did not distort market judgements. Hence the importance of eliminating them.

In this way universal free markets would stimulate the production of goods, and distribute them at the lowest possible prices, thereby maximising human well-being. They also reduced the possibility of war, whose prime cause was thought to be poverty or covetousness. Now the populations of all countries would enjoy all the benefits that were humanly attainable, or so the argument went.

Free trade ideas fit nicely with the development of parallel ideas relating to the general role of the individual in society. Thinkers such as John Stuart Mill (one of the first proponents of **liberalism**) argued that the state should not interfere with the tastes and choices of individual citizens unless their actions adversely affected others. Mill also argued that the free clash of contrasting political ideas would expose falsehood and lead to the triumph of ideas that were 'true'. Censorship and the restriction of free speech might lead to society being dominated by 'wrong' or

BRIEFINGS

2.3 Free trade, free markets, protectionism, and classical (neo)liberalism

Classical economics (the ideas of Adam Smith, David Ricardo and Jeremy Bentham) concluded that trade and well-being would be maximised in a market of independent producers who could trade freely with each other. Victorian politicians such as Richard Cobden and John Bright adopted this argument enthusiastically on behalf of the new middle class. They believed that once free trade was extended, both nationally and internationally, it would eliminate the causes of war, since everybody would receive the maximum benefits possible from the operation of the market, and this would remove the causes of conflict between nations.

Although this summary of the argument may seem a little naive, belief in free markets and free trade gained new force in the second half of the twentieth century from adherents such as Margaret Thatcher. Many countries accordingly tried to sweep away their own barriers to trade and continue to eliminate them internationally through the General Agreement on Tariffs and Trade (**GATT**) (later renamed the **World Trade Organization (WTO)**).

In the nineteenth century the new free trade ideas seemed to provide an answer to everything and were taken up enthusiastically by reformers and liberals everywhere. Hence their label of 'classical' (or **neo-**) **liberalism**. The antithesis of free trade was protection, where special taxes or tariffs were applied to goods to keep another country's products out. The classic example of this were the Corn Laws in Britain, which excluded cheaper foreign grain in order to raise prices for farmers and were accordingly abolished in 1846.

GATT

General Agreement on Tariffs and Trade – the series of agreements heavily promoted by the United States since the Second World War and designed to promote free trade in all products throughout the world.

World Trade Organization (WTO)

The international organisation set up in 1993 to 'police' the GATT agreements.

Neo-liberalism

The ideas associated with the New Right of the 1980s that market competition is the best means of guaranteeing political freedom and economic growth.

'false' ideas. Moreover, no social group or gender had a monopoly on the truth. By implication, all educated citizens irrespective of background, race, class or gender should participate in the marketplace of ideas. It followed that free speech, universal education and a universal franchise (all should be eligible to vote) were essential to a good society.

Such notions gradually gained currency in Victorian Britain. Clearly they influenced the rise of mass democracy and the idea of 'one man, one vote' (later one person, one vote). It follows that if any individual (although only men until the early twentieth century) wanted to stand for Parliament he or she should be free to do so by making direct appeals to the electorate. During the nineteenth and early twentieth centuries the social make-up of MPs did indeed change, with much larger numbers being drawn from the middle classes and eventually the skilled working classes. Moreover, as the franchise expanded to include the lower middle and working classes so it was necessary for candidates to appeal to the electorate by differentiating themselves from the opposition in a coherent and intelligible manner.

By the second third of the nineteenth century the main vehicle for these appeals were the political parties, which by then had developed effective means of communicating with voters including party manifestos, political advertising and mass meetings or 'hustings' where candidates could speak to voters and exchange views.

Generally, Mill and his adherents were *liberal individualists*. They believed that society should be made up not of strictly stratified social classes, but of individuals exercising their free will both in the marketplace of political ideas and in the economic marketplace. Such beliefs clashed both with older notions of class and privilege and with the new socialist ideas based on equality of condition that were rapidly gaining influence in the second half of the nineteenth century. Political party programmes reflected these contrasting views of society with the Tories (later Conservatives) championing aspects of the old order, the Liberals defending **liberal individualism** and, from 1901, Labour advancing socialism. We will return to this later in the chapter.

The British world system, 1850–90

Liberal individualism

All forms of liberalism imply individualism. But the recent tendency to combine 'liberal' and 'individual' in one phrase suggests neo-liberal views that reject modern liberal ideology – fairly sympathetic to some state intervention – and a return to classical nineteenth-century liberalism, which believes in a minimal state.

A free market in political ideas was thus accompanied by support for an economic free market. Free trade and free competition constitute a set of ideas that British politicians and most parties have been strongly attached to ever since the 1850s. Concrete examples of their influence today are British entry into the European Union (conceived as an extended 'Common Market'), and enthusiasm for opening up world trade in successive GATT (now WTO) negotiations. World trading conditions and British economic competitiveness have changed enormously since the mid-nineteenth century. Regardless of such changes, British policy makers have opened up the country to foreign trade, and done their best to abolish protection internationally, apart from a brief period during the economic recession of the 1930s and the Second World War.

The explanation for this steadfast adherence to free trade and economic liberalism is not simply historical and cultural but also institutional and structural. In the period of its industrial and commercial supremacy Britain created institutions such as the international financial markets in the 'City', and made enormous overseas investments; these depended on world free trade and the unhampered flow of money.

These developments followed naturally from Britain's overwhelming dominance in the world economy from 1850 to 1870. With efficiently produced industrial goods that nobody else could produce as cheaply and which could not all be absorbed by the domestic market, manufacturers depended on overseas outlets. However, something clearly needed to be traded for manufactured goods. Other countries could go into debt, of course, and many did, contributing to a massive growth of British assets overseas. Ultimately, however, they needed to balance their imports with exports.

The abolition of protection in Britain, under the influence of free trade ideas, helped solve the problem. Increasingly, Britain imported food and raw materials for industry (such as raw cotton, timber and mineral ores). The most plentiful supplies of these were in the less developed world, notably North and especially South America, and Australasia.

Consequently, British trade turned increasingly towards these areas. In line with free trade ideas about each country doing what it did best, Britain manufactured, while overseas trading partners raised animals and crops, or dug and quarried, exploiting the extensive natural resources they had and Britain did not.

There was a snag, however. Often the natural resources were inaccessible, or under the control of hostile governments or indigenous peoples who had no desire to trade. To deal with the latter Britain rapidly expanded its direct control of likely territories, converting them into 'colonies'. It used its large and highly trained navy to protect trade routes and the army to destroy indigenous opposition (and often the indigenous peoples). Until around 1880, British naval power was close to being hegemonic – that is it dominated to the extent that no other power could challenge it in size and geographic scope.

In other cases, Britain supported like-minded governments that could subdue internal opposition. In terms of transport, British banks could supply capital for building railways for the transportation of settlers and crops. These were usually built by British-owned companies, which used British iron for the rails, imported locomotives and rolling stock from Britain and employed British personnel, thus creating another British asset overseas.

Britain was able to accept universal free trade in the nineteenth century because its industry and commerce could take on the world. This was an attitude that was natural for the first industrialised country to have but which was obviously much harder for later-developing ones to accept. Primary producers of food and raw materials could accept it for a while. They had products to export that Britain wanted, and by accepting their role as British suppliers they could attract investment and build up their economic infrastructure of roads, railways, houses and supporting facilities.

By the second third of the nineteenth century, however, some European countries (notably Germany) and the United States began to catch up with Britain. Moreover, because they developed their industries later than Britain they could take advantage of the most recent techniques in manufacturing and transport. By 1880, both Germany and the United States were expanding rapidly. Expansion was helped in the continental countries by state subsidies, by tariffs (taxes on imports) and quotas (physical limits on what could be imported) imposed on British goods. These governments, therefore, embarked on a series of measures collectively known as 'protectionism', which went directly counter to all the doctrines of free trade.

Germany was the major exponent of protectionism in the late nineteenth century, but all the developed countries apart from Britain followed suit. Thus the free trade system – an early form of globalisation with London at its centre – that Britain managed to impose on most of the world had its exceptions and dissenters. For a time, however, these were not too important in the British scheme of things – especially as the Empire continued to provide an outlet for British goods. Free trade operated without many impediments until the 1890s, and survived, although with increasing difficulty and interruptions during the First World War, until the great world economic depression of the 1930s. Meanwhile free trade ideas generated internal opposition.

Institutional change and reform, 1840–1900

The reform of Parliament and the municipalities, creation of the New Poor Law to deal with poverty and the abolition of protective tariffs clearly demonstrated the dominance of the industrial, commercial and professional classes over the old landed aristocracy. In the middle years of the nineteenth century this dominance was reinforced through the reform or foundation of a whole series of cultural, economic and political institutions that reflected the values of the Victorian middle classes and catered to their interests. These ranged from the reform of the armed forces and Civil Service, which began to recruit on the basis of open competition and merit rather than the ability to buy a position, to the creation of schools, institutes and later universities in the industrial provinces that trained the children of the new middle classes and 'respectable' skilled working class for positions in trade, business and the professions. The social and geographical extension of the **franchise** led to the election of many more businessmen and professionals to the House of Commons. The reform of the Stock Exchange and commodity exchanges expanded trade and finance, to the benefit of the commercial middle class. Eventually, a national, mass-circulation press and book publishing industry emerged that disseminated middle-class values more widely in a society with rapidly improving literacy rates.

Franchise

In its political sense, the right to vote.

Most of these institutions are familiar because they exist in much the same form today. This is clear in the case of Parliament. As noted earlier, the political struggles of the nineteenth century between reformers and the old landed interest

BRIEFINGS

2.4 Class and its importance in Britain

Britain is a particularly class-conscious society. This is partly because social, and particularly geographical, mobility has been less than in comparable industrialised societies. Britain has not experienced the sweeping social and political changes brought about by revolution and war as experienced in most other European countries or the mass immigration that opened channels of mobility in the United States. Thus the class divisions fixed by the Industrial Revolution remained almost unchanged until the 1940s, although they have been very much modified by economic and industrial changes since then.

The strength of class in Britain lay in the fact that it was reinforced by a whole series of social characteristics and life opportunities. In the industrial cities of the nineteenth century there was a clear demarcation between the areas and type of housing occupied by industrial workers and those of both the lower middle and upper middle class. Each had its own type of school, club, church; each had its own social habits and lifestyle. Manual workers left school at the minimum age, went straight into work, spoke with a local accent and even looked different from the prosperous middle class. They would travel little, marry and die young, earn minimal wages, spend some of their working lives unemployed and live in or near industrial cities.

Of course, there were many exceptions to this pattern and many variations within the working and middle classes. But large blocks of the population were marked out by these cumulative differences. The working class relied on collective action to improve their situation while the middle class were more disposed to adopt individualistic solutions, which their better resources and education made possible. A corollary of this was that the working class increasingly supported Labour, with its message that state intervention could help them, while the 'solid' middle class became increasingly Conservative from the 1880s onwards. Social differences were thus reinforced by political ones.

Plate 2.1 The House of Commons. The Conservative and Labour parliamentary parties face each other on confrontational lines in the debating chamber during Prime Minister's Questions. Liberal Democrats and minor parties have to sit apart on bottom right

Source: Corbis/Hulton Deutsch

led politicians to group themselves in two major parties: Liberals (reformers) and Conservatives (defenders of established interests). By the 1870s both had organised themselves on a countrywide basis and were imposing party discipline on their members.

This meant that the House of Commons, the popularly elected chamber, was regarded as a national forum for the confrontation of two great political parties. All its procedures were arranged so as to focus and enhance this confrontation, from the physical arrangements of the debating chamber that forced MPs of different parties to choose sides, to the procedures for debates and committees that allowed government and opposition to confront each other. The state of the parties from 1868 to 1878, in the first truly reformed parliaments, was thus built into the constitutional arrangements still prevailing in the 2000s. When Labour came to the fore in the 1920s it simply squeezed out the Liberals as a serious competitor for government power.

These consequences of Britain's parliamentary institutions were reinforced by the single-member constituency system that Britain has inherited for electing MPs (Chapter 15). Any one candidate can be elected if he or she receives more votes than any other candidate. This gives an advantage to large parties with strong support across the whole country rather than to a small party with a wide national appeal or small parties such as the Scottish Nationalists with strictly regional support, and explains why today governments are formed by either the Labour or Conservative parties rather than the Liberal Democrats.

Plate 2.2 An Oxbridge college with undergraduates

Source: Topfoto

Another Victorian institution that was to have a strong, if diffuse, influence over national life was the 'public school' (in fact, a particularly exclusive private school open only to the wealthy). Such schools had developed in the eighteenth century to educate aristocrats. From the 1830s onwards they were reformed and opened to the wealthy middle classes. Their aim was redefined as producing Christian gentlemen with a strong moral sense and commitment to public duty. This was to be achieved through the study of Latin and Greek, with literature and history thrown in, and an emphasis on competitive sport.

A by-product of this was the fusion of aristocracy, gentry and upper middle class in a single upper class marked out by accent, background and lifestyle. The contacts made at public school rendered entry to politics and business easier and helped secure advancement. To an extraordinary degree, therefore, most institutions founded in Victorian times were – and to an extent still are – dominated by graduates of public schools and of the exclusive universities, Oxford and Cambridge (known collectively as 'Oxbridge').

This made contacts between the people at the top easier, as they shared a common background. Links were reinforced by the fact that many MPs, particularly in the Conservative Party, came from and continued in business after they were elected. The Victorians approved of MPs having personal wealth, because it made them independent, and of MPs engaging in activities outside Parliament, because it kept them in touch with the broader society. Although MPs were paid from 1911 onwards (a reform that opened the way for those without inherited wealth or high incomes to serve in Parliament) the practice remains of taking directorships, consultancies and other jobs to supplement this. The fact that business links increasingly involve the financial corporations of the City of London reinforces the latter's influence over political decisions.

Free markets, protection and industry, 1890–1931

The Victorians also modernised the Stock Exchange, where the ownership of companies was bought and sold. By extending the idea of a limited liability company – where the maximum individual investors could lose was the value of their holding in the company – they increased the incentives for individuals with money to buy and sell their 'shares' in its ownership as their price fluctuated. Such individuals were usually not actively concerned with the development of the company they bought into. They were simply concerned with the price they could sell the share for. If it fell, they sold rapidly, causing a general collapse of the price. This could bankrupt a company by preventing it raising money through share sales or bank loans (since banks would not lend to a company in trouble). Share prices might fall for many reasons other than bad management – for example a temporary fall in demand that, given time, a firm might overcome. Or companies might wish to invest more of their profits in better machinery to increase profits in later years.

The divorce between investment and management meant, however, that the predominant concern of investors was the current share price, not the underlying performance and prospects of the company. If it failed to pay out high returns each year it would be in trouble, regardless of whether it could promise higher returns in the future.

Such '**short-termism**' on the part of investors has often been criticised. Manufacturing firms are tied to immediate results and cannot make long-term plans to deal effectively with overseas competition. However, one must also realise that it is a structural feature of the economy. British investors simply follow the logic of

Short-termism

A criticism often made by politicians of British managers and investors who are unwilling to pay for research and other developments that do not give an immediate profit.

Plate 2.3 The trading floor of JP Morgan in the City of London
Source: Empics

a free market, in which shares are necessarily a product to be bought and sold. In such a market investors themselves would be in trouble if they let considerations other than immediate profit and loss enter in. This was particularly true for the British financial markets as the world was opened up from 1850 onwards. Banks, insurance companies and individual investors had an increasing choice between various overseas outlets, with high and immediate rates of return. British industrial shares came late into the financial markets in any large quantity. This was because it was easier financing expansion from their high rate of profits than from loans or share sales. The development of more sophisticated and expensive technology ruled this option out. Profits themselves were cut into by a slowdown in the rate of growth during the great depression of 1870–92. Firms amalgamated in order to survive. The new industrial conglomerates turned to banks and the Stock Exchange to finance development by selling their shares.

Britain has thus inherited from the nineteenth century financial markets that are highly efficient, internationally oriented but largely divorced from British industry. A better appreciation of the consequences can be obtained by comparing them with the very different path other countries, particularly Germany, the United States and Japan, took towards industrialisation.

The second, third and fourth industrialising nations could not follow the free trade path marked out by Britain. To open their markets to free competition simply meant that cheaper British products would ruin their home industry. If they wanted to build their own industrial base they had to protect developing industries by imposing taxes on any incoming products that threatened them. This meant that the home consumer had to pay higher prices. By the same token, the industries protected in this way also provided growing opportunities for employment and domestic prosperity.

The economic policies adopted by the continental countries and the United States were thus very different from Britain's internationally focused free trade, where home industry had to compete with foreign imports and other investment opportunities. The concern abroad was rather to nurture home industry and agriculture, consolidate interlocking directorates with banks that facilitated long-term financing and to allow international competition only when industries were strong enough to sustain themselves.

This contrast in attitudes affects present-day relationships, particularly between Britain and its partners in the European Union. For Britain, the attraction of the EU has always been the prospect of abolishing tariffs and extending free markets across Europe, as a preliminary to extending them to the rest of the world. France and Germany, in contrast, have always seen the European Union primarily in terms of building a strong Europe that can protect and develop its industries on a continental rather than a national scale. The British preference for a loose economic association rather than a federal union stems in part from the structure and functioning of its financial markets inherited from the nineteenth century.

The ways in which political ideas developed in Britain paralleled these economic contrasts. In Germany, France and Russia the state played a major role not only in economic development but also in most aspects of social and political life. Citizens came to expect the central 'state' to take a lead in education, law enforcement, transport, and the regulation and finance of industry. In addition, a major rationale for the strong state was military defence. Therefore these countries – and later Japan – maintained large standing armies and eventually developed navies, some of which came to rival the British. Except in France, democracy and democratic institutions remained undeveloped. *Collectivist* rather than *individualist* notions prevailed whereby citizens believed that the interests of central state institutions should take precedence over those of individuals.

Although such ideas were not entirely absent from Britain, they had little influence compared with liberal individualism and older notions of class division and inherited privilege. Liberal individualism was even more influential in the United States where, by mid-century, democracy (for white males at least) was fully developed.

Defences against an unstable international environment, 1890–1931

Eventually, these contrasting ideas of the role of the state were to be tragically played out in two world wars and in the subsequent Cold War. From the late nineteenth century through to 1914, the British were drawn into increasing military competition with the other great powers and in particular Germany. At the same time there was a 'rush for empire' as Britain, France, Germany and other powers established control over almost all of Asia and Africa. Eventually military and economic competition resulted in the First World War, which transformed the role of the United Kingdom in international affairs. Although Britain and its allies (the United States and France) triumphed, the economic, human and military costs were very high. One million British, Empire and Commonwealth soldiers died, Britain incurred massive external debts to finance the war and British industry was obliged to keep producing basic industrial goods (iron and steel, ships, coal, textiles) rather than develop new industries and technologies.

These costs were graphically illustrated in the fortunes of the pound sterling after the war. Historically, the pound was freely convertible into gold and the British currency was effectively the reserve currency for international trade (even foreign governments and firms used pounds to finance international transactions). This system was known as the Gold Standard. After the war, however, international confidence in sterling collapsed and the Bank of England increasingly had to intervene in the foreign exchange markets to maintain full convertibility. Eventually the pressure was too great and Britain abandoned the Gold Standard in the context of deep economic crisis in 1931.

The consequences of maintaining it for so long were little short of disastrous for British industry. Already inefficient by international standards, the strong pound reduced industrial competitiveness further by making imports cheap. Unemployment rose rapidly especially in the older industrial areas. While many other countries such as the United States prospered during the 1920s, Britain remained mired in economic recession – a development that helped precipitate a damaging general strike in 1926. As a result, opinion began to shift towards the idea of protecting British industry from foreign competition through the imposition of tariffs and quotas. We will return to this theme in the next chapter.

On the broader international stage, the First World War shattered the old world order. Imperial Germany was replaced by a smaller republic. The Communist Soviet Union replaced imperial Russia and Japan emerged as a strong regional power. By refusing to sign up to the League of Nations, a new international organisation designed to enforce international order, the United States withdrew into isolationism, although its industrial base went from strength to strength. Above all, the war reduced Britain's international status. The United Kingdom was no longer able to dictate to other countries; its naval hegemony was over and it became just another, albeit important, European power.

Rise of socialism and trade union power, 1890–1931

As British industry suffered increasingly from foreign competition from the 1880s onwards, so insecurity grew. Foreign firms operating from a protected home base took full advantage of free trade to penetrate both the British and colonial markets. Ideological and structural constraints meant that British governments resisted internal pressures to impose protective tariffs until the 1930s, when it became obvious that the First World War had completely disrupted the old world trading arrangements.

For the unskilled working class, these developments aggravated the general precariousness of their position in an unregulated free market. They had no savings to fall back on and no particular skills to make them especially valued. They were employed on a weekly or even a daily basis, and when there was no work they had no money to pay the rent or even to buy the next meal. Prolonged unemployment would force them into a New Poor Law workhouse where their family would be split up and where they would live under conditions deliberately made harder than those of the poorest paid worker outside, to discourage 'dependency' and reduce the tax burden on the working population.

In this situation, workers sought security through organised action. Their first successful attempt was through consumer co-operatives, which reduced prices and shared out profits to their members. Other collective organisations such as funeral and sickness clubs followed. These all operated on the basis that large numbers of tiny contributions could finance a strong collective organisation, which then protected individuals in times of need. Such organisations were often associated with churches, particularly Nonconformist churches and the Catholic Church, the majority of whose adherents were working class.

In spite of this, the middle class resented co-operatives. Small shopkeepers and professionals saw them as offering unfair inducements that undermined the free market in goods and services.

This was even truer when workers banded themselves together to bargain about the price of their labour. Employers saw this as an unfair attempt to raise costs, which in a competitive market would drive them out of business. They much preferred to deal with individuals where they could offer what they felt they could afford on a take it or leave it basis. Workers on their side saw this as an inherently unequal bargain, in which their sole source of support – their wage – could be reduced or cut off according to the vagaries of employers and markets.

The remedy was to join collective organisations – trade unions – that could bargain on a more powerful basis than any individual. If a trade union could persuade the whole workforce of a particular factory or firm to withhold their labour, profits would be severely hit and so it would be worthwhile for an employer to make a better offer, even though this cut into profits to a certain extent. For established interests, trade unions represented a direct attack on the free market, and in the first half of the nineteenth century trade unions were outlawed. In the second half they were severely regulated and restricted by, for example, being made liable for damages caused by anyone who could be regarded as acting as their agent (e.g. a worker on strike).

Employers often brought in non-union labour to break a strike by the existing workforce. 'Pickets' of striking workers confronted these and violence sometimes ensued. Thus the collective responsibility of unions for damage caused by their members was a serious liability for them, rendering them ultra-cautious in their

Plate 2.4 A picket line – a group of strikers

Source: Alamy/David Hoffman Photo Library

BRIEFINGS

2.5 Business cartels versus labour cartels

A **cartel** is an organisation, usually of firms or manufacturers, that aims to establish monopoly control of a particular product so as to regulate its price. In this way market demand by consumers and competition among producers will not drive down the price, which will be decided by what producers think is a reasonable profit over and above their costs of production. The temptation for producers, especially if they face no competition and their product is a necessity of life, is to set the price and their profits very high.

A cartel is a direct attack on the free market, since it undermines or dominates competition. With the growth of big firms and multinational companies many semi-cartels exist today. As they tend to drive prices up and stifle innovation, governments try to regulate them, for example through the Monopolies Commission and regulators such as Ofwat (the Office of Water Regulation) in Britain.

Trade unions can also be seen as cartels, trying to ensure that no worker undercuts another in terms of wages, and thus operating to drive the price of labour up. Late nineteenth-century liberals and business people regarded them as such and opposed them or regulated them closely. Margaret Thatcher and her Conservative governments (1979–90) also looked on unions this way.

Trade unions argue, however, that workers' wages are not just a commodity price to be set by the market. Individual workers competing against each other, and helpless against wealthy companies that can afford to pick and choose, would drive their own wages down. The saving in 'labour costs' would be counterbalanced by increasing human misery in terms of poverty, health, family stability and crime, problems that would affect the rest of society and eventually incur general costs in social security, health care and policing.

Cartel

An arrangement between economic interests to limit competition by controlling their market in some way.

---

actions and weakening their finances. The police normally took the side of the employers, protecting their property and maintaining free access for strike breakers to the factory premises.

Trade unions and their supporters wanted to change the balance of power in the workplace by getting Parliament to absolve them from collective responsibility for individual actions. They also wanted governments to act more neutrally in industrial disputes.

To achieve both objectives they had to gain political power. The Second Reform Act (1867) and the Third Reform Act (1884) gave the vote to substantial numbers of working-class men. In order to attract their votes both the Conservatives and Liberals passed legislation favouring trade unions. Various attempts were also made to organise a specifically 'Labour Party', which eventually emerged in 1900 as an alliance of trade unions, co-operatives and some of the small socialist parties that had already elected a few MPs.

At the same time employers and landowners had been steadily leaving the Liberal Party and joining the Conservatives, whom they saw as more likely to protect their interests at home and abroad. The Liberals became more dependent on working-class votes and Labour Party support in Parliament. This produced a radical shift in the political views of many of their leaders. Retaining individual freedom as a central value, they began to feel that political and social freedom was impossible unless individuals had a reasonable economic basis from which to pursue it. If they did not know where the next meal would come from they would hardly pay any attention to politics.

In line with these ideas, a Liberal government with Labour support passed the National Insurance Act of 1911. This provided for contributions by employees, employers and the state towards the provision of health and unemployment insurance. What this meant was that everyone who had worked and paid contributions

BRIEFINGS

2.6 The rise and fall of union power: trade union legislation 1868–2000

In 1868 the various small trade unions (mainly of craftsmen) that had been locally organised in Britain held a joint meeting resulting in a federation with a governing council, the Trades Union Congress (TUC). The Liberal government's Trades Union Act (1871) gave them legal recognition and protection of funds against embezzlement. The Conservative government's Conspiracy Act (1875) declared that no trade union could be prosecuted for anything that would not be illegal if done by an individual. On this foundation trade unions grew, most importantly by organising unskilled labourers as well as (relatively well-off) craftsmen (the 'new trade unionism' of the 1890s). Trade unions also began to use their funds to send 'Labour' candidates to Parliament. This helped the foundation of a fully fledged Labour Party in 1900.

One stimulus to taking direct political action was the Taff Vale decision by the courts (1901) which decided that a trade union could be held responsible and sued for the actions of members during strikes. The Liberal government's Trades Disputes Act (1906) effectively reversed this decision. Only an individual could be sued for illegal actions. The Trade Union Act (1913) stated that unions could use funds for political purposes if they were separated from general funds, and if members who objected would not be forced to pay into them.

On this legal basis, trade unions grew rapidly from 1906 to 1926, mounting direct actions and strikes with considerable success. Adverse economic conditions after the First World War produced more industrial action, culminating in the general strike of 1926. All trade unionists were called on to strike, basically in support of miners' attempts to avoid wage cuts and dismissals. The Conservative government defeated the strike after a week but took relatively restrained action against the trade unions, stipulating that members had to 'opt in' to paying the political fund rather than 'opt out'.

With the election of the Labour government in 1945 trade unions secured a reversal of this measure. More importantly, they were consulted on all issues relating to labour and industrial relations by the government. The 'closed shop' and factory negotiating committees were recognised as normal practice. Neither Conservative nor Labour governments from 1951 to 1970 challenged the legal powers of trade unions. The Conservative government of Edward Heath (1970–4) tried to regulate trade unions through a special code of industrial law and a special court, the Industrial Relations Tribunal. The miners' strike in 1973–4 precipitated a general strike that brought down the government. The Labour governments of Harold Wilson and James Callaghan (1974–9) tried to conciliate trade unions by reaching formal agreements with them on prices and wages. A failure to agree on wage restraint in 1978 led to a near general strike in 1979 (the 'winter of discontent'). This rendered Labour so unpopular that it lost the general election of 1979.

The 'New Right' Conservative government of Margaret Thatcher regarded trade unions as a major impediment to the free market, echoing the views of free market economists of the late nineteenth century. In a series of legislative measures the 1979–83 and 1983–7 governments:

- required regular trade union ballots on whether they should keep a political fund

- required regular re-election of trade union leaders

- required ballots of members before strike action could be taken

- perhaps most importantly, outlawed secondary picketing, that is, industrial action against any firm not directly involved in an industrial dispute.

Thus strikers could picket a newspaper, for example, if they were in dispute with it. But they could not stop another firm delivering newspapers, even if this was vital to keep the newspaper going. Enterprising employers could thus split their companies into two to avoid union reprisals, since the law would hold that the one not in direct dispute should not be picketed in any way.

Concurrent developments also weakened trade unions. Increased unemployment reduced their membership from 12 million to 7.5 million in the course of the 1980s. In a set-piece confrontation the government defeated a year-long miners' strike in 1984–5, brought about by closures of mines. The media proprietor, Rupert Murdoch, also broke the print and journalists' unions' power in the Wapping dispute (1986–7), with the help of the secondary picketing legislation.

In a curious way, however, the reforms imposed on the unions also helped them, making them internally more democratic, leaner and fitter. In their glory days from 1950 to 1979 they had become very bureaucratised, with policy and leadership chosen by agreement among leaders and little contact with the rank and file. Having to submit themselves to democratic election actually strengthened leaders' claims to represent their members. This was reflected in a cautious return to industrial action in the 1990s, especially as economic conditions gradually became more favourable. Even though the 'New Labour' Party of Tony Blair distanced itself from too close a connection with the trade unions, the unions worked hard for its return to office in 1997 and in 2001. They have been rewarded by British adoption of the European Social Chapter (1997) and the upholding of a minimum statutory wage for all workers. Even so, in 2002 and 2006 the Labour government faced a series of public sector strikes that in character, if not in scale, were similar to those of the 1960s and 1970s.

would get free health care when they were sick, from payments guaranteed by the state. The same applied to unemployment: all who lost their job would be entitled to weekly payments until they found another. When there was a Labour government supported by Liberals (1923–4), a Housing Act was passed to help local councils build subsidised houses to rent to those with little money.

As technological developments encouraged the concentration of production in ever-larger plants, so trade unions became larger as well. It was no longer enough to stop work at one factory in order to get better offers from employers. Firms could always shift work from one factory to another, or even close down factories affected by a strike. What was necessary was to disrupt all the factories controlled by a firm in order to induce it to negotiate.

However, in seeking more members, unions did not grow in accordance with any very rational plan. Although they initially based themselves on one particular group of craftsmen or workers, the desire to reinforce themselves in one factory or inside one company often led to recruitment of very different types.

Moreover two, three, four, or even more unions might operate inside one factory. They might put different demands to management and one might go on strike when others did not, because workers were, and are, a sharply differentiated group. Trade unions representing skilled workers were anxious to maintain 'differentials' between their members' wages and those of unskilled workers. Therefore, when one union obtained its demands another might well strike to obtain more for its members in order to maintain their 'differential'.

The messy nature of British trade unionism, with large unions often overlapping each other, and with multiple unions present in the same factory, is now largely a thing of the past. As Table 2.1 shows, recent mergers and rationalisations have greatly simplified the structure of unions in Britain. The size of the largest unions is quite striking: the 10 largest account for three-quarters of the 6.5 million members in the country as a whole. Note also that by the beginning of the twenty-first century many unions represented service and public sector workers. Just 20 years previously most of the main unions represented workers in manufacturing, mining and transport. Union activity is coordinated by the Trades Union Congress, a committee and annual delegate conference supported by a permanent bureaucracy. But its powers are very limited compared with those of individual unions.

The rise of trade union power and the Labour Party was partly fuelled by the spread of socialist ideas. On the Continent, socialist ideas had taken strong hold in such countries as Germany and France. They came in three varieties. Marxists believed that a transition to a Communist society where the workers own the means of production, control and exchange could only be achieved by the violent overthrow of the existing capitalist order. Social democrats believed that it was possible to make a peaceful transition to socialism through winning representation in

Table 2.1 Major trade unions in Britain, 2005

Union name	Number of members	Industrial or service sector covered
UNISON	1,301,000	Public employees including health workers
AMICUS	1,179,850	All sectors of industry
T & G (Transport and General Workers)	820,118	All sectors of industry including communications
GMB (General and Municipal)	600,106	Distributive sector and local government
USDAW (Shop, Distributive and Allied Trades Workers)	331,703	Shops and stores, transport
PCS (Public and Commercial Services union)	295,063	Government, public sector and private sector IT and service workers
CWU (Communications Workers)	258,696	Electronics, particularly communications
NUT (National Union of Teachers)	239,796	Teachers in state schools, particularly primary schools
NASUWT (National Association of Schoolmasters and Union of Women Teachers)	223,486	Teachers in state schools, particularly secondary schools
UCATT (Union of Construction, Allied Trades and Technicians)	110,886	Building and construction workers
ATL (Association of Teachers and Lecturers)	108,730	Teachers in secondary schools and colleges
PROSPECT	105,044	Engineering, scientific, managerial and professional staff

Source: TUC web site: http://www.tuc.org.uk

national legislatures such as the British Parliament. Perhaps unsurprisingly, social democratic ideas were more influential in countries with democratic institutions such as Britain and Australia than in autocracies such as Germany and Russia where Marxist ideas were dominant. Finally, some on the left believed that it was possible to achieve a good society which combined some common ownership of natural monopolies, such as transport and utilities, welfare state protection for workers, with elements of the capitalist system in naturally competitive sectors of the economy such as retailing and agriculture. Eventually, most social democrats shifted to this last, moderate position, including most members of the Labour Party.

That a moderate form of socialism would develop in Britain is not surprising given the influence of liberal individualist ideas and the absence of revolutionary change. Although many in the Conservative Party feared that a Labour government would bring revolution and the end of capitalism, no Labour government has ever attempted such a project. As later chapters will show, Labour governments instead called for the nationalisation of basic industries, the strengthening of the Welfare State and greater income equality. In addition, the vast majority of Labour MPs and party members were and remain strong supporters of traditional liberal values, including freedom of speech and religion and race and gender equality. In its historical development, British socialism fits well with broader traditions in British society – gradual change through existing institutions and a belief in the intrinsic worth of the individual in society.

Summary

This chapter has concentrated on the most important institutional and ideological features of British politics deriving from Britain's experience as the first urbanised and industrialised nation in the world. To put these developments in their historical setting the milestones section charts the key events, both nationally and internationally, up to 1945.

The political and economic developments of the eighteenth and nineteenth centuries that led to the spread of democracy and Britain's industrial and commercial pre-eminence are:

- a deep attachment to free trade and the ideal of a free competitive market, in Britain, Europe and the world

- the associated rise of liberal individualism and a belief in free speech and the value of the free marketplace of ideas

- the persistence of political and other institutions that continue in an essentially nineteenth-century form (e.g. Parliament, the political parties, the Civil Service, local government)

- a working-class defence against the uncertainties of the free market that relies on collective action and is fuelled by socialist ideas, focused particularly on trade unions and the Labour Party.

MILESTONES

Milestones in British history, 1688–1945

BRITAIN	WORLD
The Glorious Revolution, 1688, established the primacy of parliamentary over royal power	
Late eighteenth century, adversarial party politics in Parliament, but voting limited to the wealthy	American Declaration of Independence, 1776; French Revolution, 1789
1832 Great Reform Act widens the franchise and removes most electoral corrupt practices. Followed by Municipal Reform and New Poor Law	1830 revolutions against absolutist rule break out across Europe
1846 Britain abolishes the Corn Laws and establishes free trade	1848 further often violent revolutions across Europe
Conservative–Liberal alternation in government 1867–86	
Home rule for Canada, 1867	
Second Reform Bill extends franchise, 1867	
Great Economic Depression, 1870–92	Franco-Prussian War, 1870–1 makes newly united Germany dominant on the continent of Europe
Liberal reforms in health, Civil Service, army, universal education, 1868–74	
Trades Union Act, 1871	
Unions protected from liability for individual members' acts, 1875	
Control of Suez Canal and Egypt secures sea route to India; Indian Empire consolidated, 1878	
Expansion in South Africa, 1879–80	
80 Irish Nationalist MPs elected to House of Commons and disrupt parliamentary proceedings, 1874–80	
Irish 'Land War', 1879–83	

Milestones in British history, 1688–1945 continued

BRITAIN	WORLD
Third Reform Act extends franchise further, to almost all adult males, 1884	1884–5: the 'grab for Africa': European powers set out to conquer as much territory as possible; most falls to France and Britain
First Home Rule Bill for Ireland splits Liberal government, which is defeated, 1886	
Conservative predominance in government 1886–1905 (Liberals, 1892–5)	
Local Government Act extends elected councils to counties, 1888	
Second Irish Home Rule Bill defeated, 1893	
Scottish Office centralises Scottish administration in Edinburgh	
Home Rule movements grow in Scotland and Wales during 1890s	Boer War, 1899–1902; Britain conquers independent white republics of South Africa with difficulty
Labour Party founded 1900 with support of trade unions	
Home Rule for Australia and New Zealand, 1901	Anglo-French military cooperation initiated 1904; extended to Russia 1907, creating an informal alliance against Germany
Liberal predominance in government 1905–16	
Trade Union Acts, 1906 and 1913, strengthen unions	Naval arms race between Britain and Germany for dominance of North Sea, 1906–14
Home Rule for South Africa, 1909	
Parliament Act, 1911, strengthens power of House of Commons (elected) against House of Lords (unelected)	
National Health Insurance Act – extensive government intervention to protect and pay sick, unemployed and old, 1911	
Third Irish Home Rule Bill initiated 1912 – Lords' now limited veto can only block it until 1914	
Rising violence by Irish Protestants, paramilitary organisations founded, 1912–14; 'Curragh Mutiny' of army officers in Dublin against having to enforce Home Rule, 1914; Home Rule postponed	First World War begins 1914 – Britain, France and Russia against Germany, Austria–Hungary and Turkey
1915 – submarine attacks almost cut off British food supplies	US enters war against Germany, 1917; German defeat, 1918
	1919–23 Treaties of Versailles and Trianon reduce and disarm Germany, break up Austria–Hungary, create Poland and other new central and eastern European countries and extend French and British control of Arab Middle East
1916–22 Coalition governments between Liberals and Conservatives	
Representation of the People Act (1918) extends franchise to almost all adult males and women over 30	
1919 Britain suspends Gold Standard	
Civil war in Ireland, 1918–22	
Ireland partitioned between Irish Free State and Northern Ireland, 1922	League of Nations set up without United States
	Russian Revolution, 1917–22, Communist government takes over (reduced) Russian empire

Milestones in British history, 1688–1945 continued

BRITAIN	WORLD
Conservative predominance in government 1922–9 (first Labour minority government 1923–4)	
Housing Act provides for subsidised housing, 1924	
General economic depression from 1920 – many strikes by individual unions. Britain re-establishes Gold Standard, 1925	
General strike fails, 1926	
Equal Franchise Act (1928) extends vote to all adult women	
Labour government 1929–31	
Labour splits over cutting social payments, 1931; Britain leaves Gold Standard	Wall Street Crash (collapse of US share values) ushers in Great Depression of 1930s: world trade slumps, millions unemployed in all countries
National coalition governments of rump Labour and Liberals dominated by Conservatives 1931–40	
Cuts in social benefits, abandonment of free trade, protectionist measures create cartels and monopolies to regulate market	1933–9 rise and consolidation of Nazi regime in Germany, rearmament and takeover of adjoining territories; leads to Second World War, 1939
Government of India Act 1936 gives India limited Home Rule as a response to growing nationalist agitation	
Coalition governments of Conservatives, Labour and Liberals 1940–5	
Full wartime planning and control of society and economy	Germans conquer most of European mainland except Russia, 1940
	Germany attacks Russia, 1941
	Japan goes to war against United States and United Kingdom, 1941
	United States enters war on British side, 1941
	Defeat of Germany and Japan, 1945

Essays

1. What were the main electoral reforms of the nineteenth century? Why were they passed and what were their effects on party politics?

2. What were the costs and benefits of the free trade policies pursued by Britain for much of the nineteenth and early twentieth centuries?

3. What are 'liberal individualist ideas'? What influence have they had on British politics?

4. Account for the rise and decline of trade union power in Britain.

Projects

1. Analyse the role of class in the House of Commons over time by researching the educational backgrounds of MPs between 1900 and 2003.

2. Obtain statistical evidence on the patterns of British overseas trade in the twentieth century.

3. Research the changing pattern of trade union membership since 1945. Answer with regard to the level of trade union membership and the type of trade union.

Further reading

Karl Polanyi, *The Great Transformation* (Boston: Beacon Press, 1957) is the classic account of the triumph of free trade in Britain. Eric Hobsbawm's three-volume history traces out the social and economic consequences of the Industrial Revolution. The one most relevant to this chapter is Eric Hobsbawm, *Industry and Empire* (Harmondsworth: Penguin, 1968). Andrew Gamble, *Britain in Decline* (London: Macmillan, 1989) reviews many of the developments discussed in this chapter from a rather pessimistic point of view. P. J. Cain and A. G. Hopkins, *British Imperialism* (Harlow: Longman, 1993) is an influential two-volume account of Britain's imperial and commercial history. Cain, 'British capitalism and the State', *Political Quarterly*, **68** (2), 1997, pp. 95–8, is also relevant.

Useful web sites on institutions and relationships

Hot links to these sites can be found on the CWS at www.pearsoned.co.uk/budge.

There are a variety of excellent sites dealing with the historical evolution of British political, social and economic institutions. A comprehensive introduction to the major developments in different periods can be found at www.spartacus.schoolnet.co.uk/Britain.html. Useful material regarding political and social reforms is also available at www.britishhistory.about.com and this site also contains valuable information on foreign policy relevant to the British Empire.

Additional data can be obtained from www.academicinfo.net/histuk.html. For students willing to dig deeper into British history we suggest you visit the Historical Manuscripts Commission at www.hmc.gov.uk/index.html and the Institute of Contemporary British History at www.history.ac.uk/icbh.

British trade union sites

The Department of Trade and Industry offers constructive information on trade unions and collective rights at www.dti.gov.uk/er/union.htm. History and news about trade unions can be found at the Trades Union Congress site www.tuc.org.uk, the General Federation of Trade Unions www.gftu.org.uk and the public service workers' union www.unison.org.uk. See also the *Guardian*'s special report on trade unions www.guardian.co.uk/unions/archive.

There are a variety of web sites from other trade unions in the UK: for example, the Amalgamated Engineering and Electrical Union, www.aeeu.org.uk; the Communications Workers Union, www.cwu.org; the Transport and General Workers Union, www.tgwu.org.uk; the Public and Commercial Services Union, www.pcs.org.uk; the Broadcasting, Entertainment, Cinematograph and Theatre Union, www.bectu.org.uk; the Association of University Teachers, www.aut.org.uk; the National Union of Students, www.nus.org.uk.

International union sites

For students interested in the international union arena, you can visit the International Labour Organisation at www.ilo.org and also the International Confederation of Free Trade Unions web site at www.icftu.org. Valuable information on this topic is also obtainable from www.global-unions.org as well as www.etuc.org (European Trade Unions Confederation).

chapter 3

From government intervention back to free markets and a 'Third Way': ideas and institutions, 1931–2006

By the early 1930s, the whole system of world free trade had broken down. This was one of the effects of the First World War, where the leading trading nations had fought each other to a standstill. The destructive impact on Germany in particular destabilised international trade and finance – showing that relationships between national economies are not so much competitive as interdependent.

The final breakdown was signalled by the world depression, which began with a general collapse of financial confidence from 1929 to 1931 and continued for most of the 1930s. This chapter discusses major ideological and policy shifts in Britain involving the abandonment of free trade and massive government intervention in economy and society. This was designed both to protect British industry and to guarantee minimum living standards for the population. The reforms initiated by the 'national governments' of the 1930s were carried further by the Labour governments of 1945–51, and supported by both Conservatives and Labour from 1950 to 1979 (the 'social democratic consensus'). Intellectually this was underpinned by **'Keynesian'** economics, which gave a central place to government action to smooth out the economic cycle.

The end of the long post-war boom in the early 1970s demonstrated the limits of government intervention. Free trade and free markets reasserted themselves vigorously under the Conservative governments led by Margaret Thatcher (1979–90), replacing the earlier 'social democratic consensus' with a 'neo-liberal' one. Many of the policies and issues of the new millennium, linked to growing world 'globalisation', thus hark back to the mid-nineteenth century rather than to the 1930s and 1940s. The new element was 'Europe'. The chapter ends with the main ideas underpinning New Labour's 'Third Way' between socialist collectivism and free market capitalism.

The chapter describes:

- the rise of government intervention from 1931 to 1945

- Labour socialism: the creation of the Welfare State and nationalisation of basic industries, 1945–51

- 'social democratic consensus', 1951–79

- the return to free market principles in the 1980s and the emergence of a 'neo-liberal' economic consensus

- New Labour's Third Way, 1997–present.

The rise of intervention, protection and planning, 1931–45

Keynesianism

Economic theories and policies propounded by J. M. Keynes (1883–1946) that advocate government intervention to achieve economic stability, growth and full employment.

Beveridge Report

Produced in 1942 by a government commission chaired by Lord Beveridge (1879–1963), an academic economist, which recommended welfare services and income support for citizens 'from the cradle to the grave'. Its recommendations provided the intellectual basis for both the 'Welfare State' and the 'social democratic consensus' (1945–79).

The collapse of world trade and British industry by 1931 prompted even the Conservative-dominated national governments of the 1930s to intervene in society and the economy. Externally they finally imposed protective tariffs to safeguard what was left of British manufacturing against foreign competition. Internally they forced surviving businesses to merge into cartels and conglomerates to keep prices up and costs down. Their protectionist policies helped the growth of new industries close to the large consumer markets of the Midlands, London and south-east England – cars, washing machines, wireless sets, domestic furnishings and so on. There were almost two manufacturing economies – one based on the old industries in the industrial north and one based on new industries in the Midlands and south.

The problem from the government's point of view was the location of new industry in places that were already reasonably prosperous. Many difficulties could be overcome if some new firms could be persuaded to move out of the congested areas into the depressed ones. A number of commissions and their reports set out planning proposals involving government inducements and controls. The most significant was the **Beveridge Report**, which reported on income maintenance (unemployment benefit, pensions, national assistance, welfare services and health) – thus laying the foundations for the post-war Welfare State. This was not created completely from new – elements of a social support and welfare system had been in place since the early twentieth century – but it was the first time proposals had been made for social support.

Between 1936 and 1945 attitudes towards state intervention were transformed by two events: the acceptance of Keynesian economics and the total modification of the economy during the Second World War. The monetarist orthodoxy accepted by the national governments of the 1930s held that industrial development could only take place if there was general confidence in the currency, maintained by government budgets in which revenues equalled or surpassed expenditures. Keynes showed that such an economy could function well below the level it might attain with full use of available resources. Since the main underused resource was

BRIEFINGS

3.1 Wartime rationing

Very soon after the outbreak of war in September 1939 the government introduced petrol rationing, followed in January 1940 by food rationing. Few British citizens expected rationing to last for long, partly because few expected the war to last for long. In the event almost every commodity, including clothes, fuel and food, was subject to rationing by the end of the war. On most items rationing lasted until the late 1940s and was not completely removed until 1952. Every household was issued with a ration book, containing stamps that had to accompany money purchases.

Ration allowances were meagre – for example, as late as 1951 the meat ration was four ounces per person per week – and designed to provide the very minimum necessary to feed, clothe and heat a family. Rationing was necessary because Britain depended on imports of fuel, food, textiles and other commodities. Shortages in all these developed as production was disrupted by war and enemy action, and as resources were diverted to the armed forces. After the war shortages actually worsened as the demand for food and fuel in war-ravaged Europe soared. In 1947 the fuel quota was reduced during a severe winter and, in 1949, some of the most restrictive rationing was introduced because Britain was running out of the dollars needed to buy goods on the international markets. Most commentators agree that the continuing austerity of the 1940s and early 1950s contributed to the defeat of the Labour government in 1951.

BRIEFINGS

3.2 Orthodox economics and Keynesian economics

Orthodox economics assumes that the most efficient economic organisation is minimal government intervention and free markets. National accounts – the relationship between income (taxes) and expenditure (government spending) – should always be in balance. For a government to spend more than it receives leads to inflation. During the 1930s, however, tax revenues fell as a result of the depression, leading governments to cut expenditure – including unemployment benefits. The Cambridge economist John Maynard Keynes (later Lord Keynes) noted that the effect of this was to reduce the level of total demand in the economy and therefore to depress it even further. He demonstrated that it was possible for the economy to reach equilibrium (that is, when supply matches demand) at a level far below full capacity, with resulting high unemployment. The government therefore needed to stimulate demand by increasing expenditure, the precise opposite of what governments actually did for most of the 1930s. Budget deficits were acceptable, therefore, when the economy was operating below full capacity. Once full capacity had been reached, government accounts should once again be brought into balance. If they were not, inflation would return. The experience of the Second World War seemed to confirm this thesis: massive government spending led to full employment and eventually to labour shortages and inflation. After the war all British governments accepted Keynesian thinking: governments had a duty to maintain full employment via government spending. Not until the 1970s, when rising inflation and rising unemployment occurred at the same time, were the basic principles of Keynesian economics challenged. As a result, orthodox economics became once again a feasible alternative for policy makers.

Orthodox economics

The dominant economic approach before Keynesian theory, which argued for minimal state intervention in the economy.

labour, this implied long-term unemployment for large sections of the workforce. Governments could, however, raise the economy to nearly full capacity by increasing government expenditure and therefore stimulating demand.

The war seemed to confirm the validity of this assumption. Spending on armaments was massively increased in the late 1930s. By June 1943 only 60,000 people were registered as unemployed, and by 1945 few political leaders opposed Keynesian demand management. The war also gave planning an enormous boost, both in theory and practice. Central committees controlled prices, incomes, industrial relations and production. Never before or since has the British economy been so rigidly disciplined.

This policy transformation was accompanied by remarkably little in the way of institutional reform. Although a number of new bureaucracies were created before and during the war, the machinery of central government continued to operate much as it always did. Local government, the Civil Service, Parliament and the 'parties' functioned as before. *Policies* changed but bureaucratic values and practices did not. This contrast continued up to the reassertion of Treasury control under the 'New Labour' governments from 1997 onward.

Founding and administering the Welfare State, 1945–62

Privatisation

The opposite of nationalisation, privatisation is the returning of nationalised industries wholly or partly to the private sector.

Under the government elected in 1945 basic industries were nationalised, the Welfare State created, regional policy strengthened dramatically and land-use planning by local authorities established as mandatory. All these policies remained in place until the 1980s. Only then did Conservative governments challenge them through **privatisation**, the dramatic scaling down of regional policy, and the creation of 'internal markets' in education and health.

Post-war policy was dominated by a driving desire to maintain full employment. Keynesian demand management, **nationalisation** and regional policy were either primarily or partly designed to achieve this and, combined with a generally

Nationalisation

Taking businesses or whole industries into public ownership.

favourable international trading position, did so until 1951. Industry readapted to peacetime conditions quite efficiently and Britain's share of world trade actually increased during these years. Nationalisation and Keynesianism carried with them a marked increase in government intervention. However, there was no support for overall national planning or for new administrative organisations to carry it through. All Labour's political and economic initiatives were channelled through the traditional institutions and ministries. Government structures, although larger, remained much what they had been in the 1930s or for that matter the 1870s. When the Conservatives came to power in 1951 the basic relationships between government, unions, finance and industry were thus almost unchanged. The trade unions played no integrated role in economic or industrial policy. Big business was quite happy to accept a regulative government role, especially in foreign trade, but they too were excluded from central economic policy making. Administrative changes were largely confined to the creation of new bureaucracies to implement the programmes of a burgeoning Welfare State. The public sector had expanded enormously, but the basic tools available to governments to guide and control the public sector changed very little. The divorce between industrial and financial sectors, and between both of these and government, continued to be almost as wide as in the earlier free trade era.

Plate 3.1 The Festival of Britain, 1951. General view of the River Walk showing the sculpture of the Islanders and part of the Skylon. The Festival symbolised post-war hopes for modernisation

Source: Getty Images/Hulton Archive

BRIEFINGS

3.3 Decolonisation and disengagement from empire, 1946–83

The Second World War created not only domestic but also overseas preoccupations for British policy makers. The most important of these was the confrontation between the US-led, and British-supported, North Atlantic Treaty Organisation and the Soviet Union, from 1948–88 (the Cold War). Britain was subsidiary to the United States in this. Successive post-war governments had, however, to deal directly with the vast colonial empire inherited from the nineteenth century, and no longer possible to dominate with military power. The Second World War, fought in the name of freedom and democracy, exacerbated the problem of dealing with the empire since it had stimulated native nationalist movements that demanded independence.

It was clear to the post-war Labour movement that India, with its vast population, would be impossible to control. Independence was accordingly granted in 1948, and internal divisions between Hindus and Muslims met with a deadline for withdrawal, after which they were left to fight it out and separate into India and Pakistan. The same solution was applied to Jews and Arabs in Palestine. In Malaya, the British, allied with Malays, defeated a Chinese Communist insurrection (1948–58).

Withdrawal quickened after a last attempt to assert control in the Middle East failed with an abortive takeover of the Suez Canal in 1956. In the years between 1959 and 1963 Britain granted independence to most of its African colonies. The final stage of the retreat from empire was the strategic defence review of 1967–8, which concluded that Britain could not afford a naval presence east of Suez – a decision that soon also extended to the Mediterranean. These withdrawals left Britain with only vestigial colonial dependencies – one of which, the sparsely inhabited Falkland Islands, involved Britain in war with Argentina in 1982.

On the whole, the disengagement from empire was managed peacefully and skilfully. Friendly governments were left in charge, British interests safeguarded and ties with the West firmly cemented. However, disengagement accentuated Britain's transition from a world to a regional power, and contributed to the crisis of morale in the 1970s and 1980s.

This made it easier for the Conservative governments from 1951 to 1964 to accept most of what Labour had done. They continued to administer the Welfare State, simply relaxing some of the more rigorous measures such as rationing of food and clothes. Such 'decontrol' was possible because of the recovery of world trade and growing prosperity.

In one sense, the Conservatives had little choice. The Welfare State – and especially free universal health care – was immensely popular with the electorate. A sea change had taken place in British politics and society. Following the experience of the 1930s and the Second World War, the British had become convinced that universal welfare provision was essential to the good of society. Recognising this, all political parties became enthusiastic supporters of the Welfare State.

Government intervention, 1962–79

Until about 1960, government intervention in industry was minimal but Keynesian demand management of expenditure and interest rates continued. Aware that Britain's growth rate was falling behind those of France, Italy and Germany, governments after 1960 used Keynesian methods in combination with incomes policy and some embryonic planning devices both to control inflation and to achieve a higher rate of economic growth. Using fiscal and monetary policy to stimulate or depress economic activity in the Keynesian fashion, the government soon found itself in a vicious 'stop–go' cycle characterised by successive rounds of economic stimulation followed by the reining in of demand with expenditure cuts and interest rate hikes.

BRIEFINGS

3.4 'Stop–go' and the British economic cycle

During much of the post-war period British economic management was characterised by periodic rounds of economic growth followed by government-induced deflation to stem the inflationary effects of growth. Typically, the cycle went something like this: in year 1, the government would reduce taxation and interest rates in order to stimulate employment and growth. This in turn led, in year 2, to an upsurge in imports on which the expansion of the British economy depended. With a growing balance of payments deficit the pound would come under pressure on the foreign exchanges, forcing the government, in year 3, to dampen demand by raising interest rates and taxation. This resulted in increased unemployment, and pressure by the trade unions for government action. Given the commitment of all governments to full employment, chancellors of the exchequer would then be obliged, in year four, to stimulate the economy in order to reduce unemployment. The cycle would then begin again. This pattern led to a vicious cycle of under-investment in British industry. It was because British industry was uncompetitive that growth in the economy led to import-led inflation; however, without a period of steady increase in demand with sustained investment, industry could not catch up with its foreign competitors. In other words, as soon as the conditions for sustained investment appeared they were undermined by the government's need to protect the pound.

Not until the 1980s, when the pound was bolstered by North Sea oil revenues, did conditions change in ways which allowed the cycle to be broken, and it was not until the post-1992 period that surviving British industry had become sufficiently competitive to support a period of sustained growth.

Such 'stop–go' tactics became common between 1953 and 1970. A related problem was inflation, which accelerated during 'go' periods and declined during 'stop' periods. Compared with the 1970s and the 1980s inflation was low (Figure 3.1) but, crucially, it was higher than rates in comparable countries. Indeed, as the decade wore on, the fundamental problem with the economy was increasingly defined as failure to achieve a rate of economic growth comparable to other major industrial countries.

The Tories flirted with economic planning during the early 1960s. When elected in 1964 Labour created the Department of Economic Affairs (DEA) in which a full-blown government department was assigned the job of long-term economic planning. The Treasury was confined to its traditional role as short-term controller of expenditure. The DEA's brief was extensive: to devise a longer-term national plan; to revitalise industry and improve efficiency, through planning by industrial sector; to work out a prices and incomes policy; and to reorganise regional policy.

Figure 3.1 UK inflation, 1961–2005

Source: Social Trends, **36**, 2005, Chart 6.15, Office for National Statistics. Reproduced under the terms of the Click-Use Licence

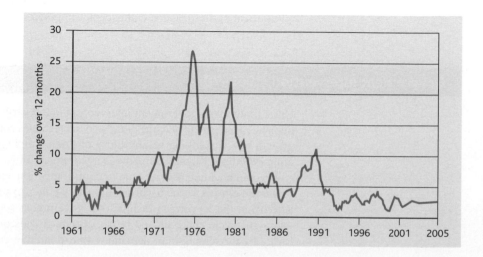

BRIEFINGS

3.5 The changing fortunes of the pound sterling

When the leading industrial countries established fixed exchange rates between currencies at Bretton Woods in 1944, it was agreed that the US dollar would be the main currency of international trade. In addition, however, the pound sterling would also perform this role. In other words, when countries traded with each other they would use either dollars or pounds as a medium of exchange. The pound was accorded this status because a large number of countries used pounds as their main reserve. These included British colonies and dominions but also some Latin American, Middle Eastern and Scandinavian states. Bretton Woods allowed for devaluations but only under emergency circumstances. Britain was, therefore, expected to maintain the value of the pound in relation to the dollar. Any forced devaluation would undermine confidence in the whole sterling area. Under the worst circumstances, a flight from the pound would lead to a collapse in its value. From 1945 until the end of the Bretton Woods system in 1971 successive British governments were under pressure to maintain the value of sterling. The two forced devaluations in 1949 and 1967 were regarded as major government failures, and these pressures intensified the problems of the stop–go cycle (see Briefing 3.4). Most countries gradually moved out of the sterling area during the 1950s and the 1960s. Even after 1971, when currencies floated freely in relation to one another, the problem of currency weakness remained. But this was mainly because the lack of competitiveness of British industry led speculators to believe that the pound was a poor long-term prospect. In 1976 such sentiments led to a run on the currency. Only large loans to the government and intervention from the International Monetary Fund (IMF) prevented economic collapse.

Since then the value of sterling has not been so central to government economic policy, partly because governments have acted more responsibly in fiscal matters and partly because of the existence of a floating exchange rate regime. One major exception was the British involvement with the Exchange Rate Mechanism (ERM) of the European Monetary System (EMS) between 1990 and 1992. (This subject is covered extensively in Chapter 8.)

However, the DEA really operated for less than two years, owing to the accelerating rate of economic crisis from 1965 to 1967. Britain's competitive position had been deteriorating for some years and balance of payments deficits were slowly increasing. Sterling was clearly overvalued, mainly because of the need to maintain the stability of the pound as an **international reserve currency**. The Labour government was committed to economic growth and the expansion of public services and found it impossible to reconcile its policy objectives with economic reality. An already bad situation was aggravated by the government's deference to the official Treasury and City line of giving priority to the value of sterling. In 1966 a serious balance of payments crisis and a crippling seamen's strike coincided, inducing investors to sell pounds. The government opted to abandon national planning and industrial expansion, and instead to safeguard the currency by restricting credit. Under the new chancellor of the exchequer, Roy Jenkins, economic policy reverted almost to a pre-Keynesian strategy: some government expenditure was cut (mainly in defence), foreign loans were repaid and taxes increased. Interestingly, the Jenkins deflation was not so damaging to employment as might have been expected (Figure 3.1), largely because a 1967 devaluation did produce something of an investment boom.

In comparison with the 1945–50 period, Labour had hardly been a radical reforming government. Rather than institute institutional reforms the government simply increased spending on existing programmes, and especially on the Welfare State. Taxation increased dramatically from 32 per cent of **gross domestic product** (GDP) in 1964 to 43 per cent in 1970. The government's failure to carry through a radical programme alienated many supporters within the Labour movement. By 1970 increasingly militant trade unions were demanding more fundamental reforms and were prepared to use their bargaining muscle to extract higher wages from employers.

International reserve currency

A currency that many smaller and third world countries not directly linked with the sponsor country choose to make payments in, because it has a stable value.

Gross domestic product

The total value of all the goods and services bought and sold in the domestic economy.

The new Conservative government of Edward Heath, which unexpectedly won the 1970 election, was intent on reforming industrial relations, by imposing a more rigid framework of law on trade union activity. What transpired was the 1971 Industrial Relations Act, which sought to make unions accept certain legal restrictions on their activities, notably on their right to strike, and to submit themselves to a special court. From its inception, this inspired their fiercest hostility.

Along with other countries, the new government abandoned a fixed exchange rate for its currency, letting international financial markets determine its value. In conjunction with this it negotiated British entry to the European Community (now called the European Union) in 1972. Entry was expected to stimulate British industry by exposing it to new competitive pressures while at the same time opening up new markets.

Strangely, the Conservative government failed to exercise real control either over incomes or over public expenditure and inflation took off, soaring from 6.4 per cent in 1970 to 9.4 per cent in 1971, by far the highest figure since 1950 (Figure 3.1). This situation could not last long. The rapid increases were bound to undermine the balance of payments and Britain's trading position, especially with

Plate 3.2 Minister of Technology, Anthony Wedgwood Benn, opens Oceanology International, the world's first international conference on underwater technology, at Brighton. The Labour government had come to power on a modernising platform in 1964, with Harold Wilson famously speaking of the 'white heat' of technology

Source: Getty Images/Hulton Archive

a floating exchange rate. In a famous 'U-turn' of November 1972, Edward Heath announced a prices and incomes policy. Although at first this was accepted the miners and other unions later resisted controls on wages. Faced with crippling strikes, the government called a general election early in 1974.

The government's U-turn on incomes policy in 1972 was accompanied by another change of heart on industrial policy – now adapted to aid, succour and guide industrial recovery. Bankrupt companies such as Rolls-Royce and Upper Clyde Shipbuilders were bailed out, regional incentives and development grants were strengthened, a Minister for Industrial Development was attached to the new Department of Trade and Industry, and workforce retraining was organised and greatly strengthened. All this did not amount to planning in the sense of economic targets being set over a fixed time period. But it did represent a new institutionalised liaison between government and industry.

When they left office the Conservatives thus presided over a larger public sector than in 1970, in terms of the government share of GDP and the number of enterprises it owned. This demonstrates how much the Heath government was relying on incomes policy to harness inflation. Talk of controlling the money supply, which dominated the policy agenda in the late 1970s, was almost completely absent.

On returning to power in February 1974, the new Labour government continued the Conservatives' interventionist policies while trying to conciliate the trade unions. However, they did so with much greater ideological commitment. Indeed, the party was split between social democratic gradualists and more fundamentalist socialists who were determined to avoid the mistakes of the last Labour government. For about 18 months, the fundamentalists were in the ascendant. The Industrial Relations Act was repealed, a state holding company to encourage investment and improve productivity was created, and a system of planning agreements between industries and state established. A new 'Social Contract' bound both government and trade unions to moderate wage demands. In fact, the Social Contract resulted in anything but moderation. Weekly wage increases jumped from 12.2 per cent in 1973 to 29.4 per cent in 1974. Inflation too bounded ahead, reaching 16.1 per cent in 1974 and a staggering 24.2 per cent in 1975 (Figure 3.1).

BRIEFINGS

3.6 OPEC and the oil crises of the 1970s

Partly as a result of the increased economic activity associated with US intervention in the Vietnam War (1964–72), oil and other commodity prices increased rapidly during the late 1960s and early 1970s. As a result the bargaining power of commodity producers also increased. Most of the world's oil came from Arab states and poorer Third World countries. These formed a cartel called the Organization of Petroleum Exporting Countries to increase the price of oil by bargaining. When war broke out in the Middle East in 1973 OPEC decided to increase the price of oil in order to punish Israel and its Western backers. Within a year oil prices increased fivefold on the world markets, bringing severe inflation to the industrialised countries. Those such as Britain were particularly hard hit, having no indigenous oil supplies. In addition, powerful trade unions were able to insist that wages kept up with or exceeded price increases, thus fuelling further inflation. The disruptive effects of this inflation were considerable and led indirectly to the bailing out of the British economy in 1976 by the International Monetary Fund. Later in the decade a second oil crisis with accompanying price increases was caused by the Iranian revolution. The new regime in Iran was deeply hostile to the West and persuaded OPEC to precipitate another price rise. By 1979–80, however, Britain's North Sea oil began to be extracted. As a result, Britain benefited from the increased oil price and the pound sterling appreciated rapidly on the foreign exchange markets. Since the early 1980s OPEC has often been in disarray as a result of conservation measures in the West, increases in oil production in such areas as Alaska and the North Sea, and internal divisions within the original OPEC countries.

Finally, the Conservatives' quite generous public expenditure targets for 1974 and 1975 were met in full.

The year 1974 was a bad one for all the developed countries. The quadrupling of oil prices by the Organization of Petroleum Exporting Countries (OPEC) in late 1973 precipitated a sharp downturn in world trade and an acceleration of inflation everywhere. A good part of the 1974–5 inflation can be attributed to these international forces.

However, Britain suffered from additional problems. Its industrial competitiveness continued to decline. British trade unions were more successful than those in many other countries in keeping wage rates up to or beyond the rate of inflation. Like the Conservatives before them, Labour announced an incomes policy that, although not statutory, was in effect compulsory. After early compliance by the unions, the government faced growing resentment and industrial unrest, which culminated in a 'winter of discontent' during 1978/9. Most commentators agree that this cost Labour the election in May 1979.

Just as important as incomes policy was the government's conversion to a limited form of **monetarism**. During 1976 the selling of sterling reached panic proportions. Fixed exchange rates (the Bank of England commitment to buy sterling for fixed sums in other currencies) had been abandoned in 1971 and left free to fall. And fall the pound did, to a low of $1.57 at one point (until 1971 the pound was fixed at $2.40). Britain was approaching the point where the government could not meet immediate payments on outstanding debts. In exchange for massive loans from the International Monetary Fund (IMF), Denis Healey, the chancellor, agreed to new controls on the money supply. Interest rates rose to a record 15.5 per cent and public expenditure was cut. After complex negotiations the IMF and the Treasury agreed that the Public Sector Borrowing Requirement (now known as the Public Sector Net Cash Requirement), the amount needed by the government to cover the gap between resources and expenditure, should be trimmed by £3 billion over two years. In fact public spending did not fall quite as rapidly as planned. But the very idea of using public sector spending as the major instrument of economic policy was new, notwithstanding Roy Jenkins' more limited efforts in this direction between 1968 and 1970. These radical adaptations to political and economic reality represented a defeat for 'old Labour' ideas, and although a form of traditional

Monetarism

A revised version of neo-classical economics that, contrary to Keynesianism, argues that government should minimise its involvement in economic matters, except for controlling the money supply as a way of holding down inflation.

Public Sector Net Cash Requirement (PSNCR)

The amount borrowed by government to help finance its annual expenditure.

BRIEFINGS

3.7 The Public Sector Net Cash Requirement (PSNCR)

Put simply, the **PSNCR** (previously known as the Public Sector Borrowing Requirement (PSBR)) is the difference between government revenue and expenditure. After the Second World War, British governments were committed to full employment, and running up the national debt was deemed necessary for this end. With the intervention of the IMF to bail out the economy in 1976, holding down public spending became a priority, and the Conservative government elected in 1979 was determined to make reductions in the PSBR (as it was then called). In 1980 the government launched its medium-term financial strategy, which aimed to reduce the PSBR in stages from 4.8 per cent of GDP in 1979/80 to under 3 per cent by 1983/4. In the event the PSBR increased to 5.7 per cent of GDP in 1980/1 and this induced the government to produce a very deflationary budget in 1981. This, together with a period of sustained economic growth from 1983, reduced the PSBR to 0.9 per cent of GDP in 1986/7 and gave a surplus in the following two years, which was helped by proceeds from selling off nationalised enterprises. By the early 1990s, however, recession took its toll on government revenues and the PSBR once again moved into deficit, reaching over 5 per cent of GDP by 1996. The Labour government elected in 1997 pledged to reduce this figure to well below 3 per cent over a five-year period. Helped by the general recovery of the economy they achieved this by 1999.

BRIEFINGS

3.8 The 'social democratic consensus', 1945–79

This is the name given to the implicit agreement between all political parties, up to 1979, that the fundamental reforms and policies of the post-war Labour government should remain unchanged. The most obvious of these was the Welfare State. Both Conservative and Labour governments of this period increased social benefits and health provisions. Another feature was the acceptance of state ownership of coal, gas, electricity, rail, air transport and telephones. Steel and road transport were partially denationalised and then renationalised throughout the period. The third 'leg' of the consensus was economic management: Keynesian policies of avoiding unemployment by government overspending and relaxation of monetary controls were followed by both Conservatives and Labour. From 1960 both also tried to control prices and incomes directly through various monitoring bodies.

This consensus between the parties broke down under the successive economic crises of the 1960s and 1970s and the confrontations with increasingly aggressive trade unions that income controls provoked. In retrospect we can see it depended on the early post-war prosperity in which Britain shared. When this became more difficult to sustain both state intervention and Keynesian economic policy were discredited and became targets for attack by the Thatcherite Conservative governments of the 1980s and 1990s.

socialism was to return under the leadership of Michael Foot (1979–83), the Labour Party moved steadily to the right.

The combination of incomes policy and public expenditure cuts reduced inflation quite quickly to a low of around 8 per cent between 1978 and 1979 (Figure 3.1). However, unemployment remained stubbornly high. Labour's plans both for industrial reorganisation and social reforms were rendered ineffective by the spending cuts. As with its predecessor, crisis management rather than social reform became the government's overriding preoccupation, and more and more problems focused on the reaction of the trade unions to government intervention.

One further characteristic of this turbulent period was the relative absence of institutional reform. Parliament, the Civil Service, the health service and local government operated in the traditional manner. It is true that controls on public expenditure instilled a sense of crisis in the public sector, but in terms of operating procedures and the relationship between central authority and other public sector actors, very little changed.

The return of the free market, 1979–97

Government intervention, whether of the Labour or the old Conservative variety, seemed increasingly to create more problems than it solved. Perhaps the solution lay in the free trading and free market ideas associated with the golden age of the mid-nineteenth century? These were particularly attractive as they had encouraged hard work, thrift, saving and respect for authority, virtues that many thought the country had lost in the preceding 20 years and which were traditional sources of support for the Conservative Party.

Indeed, the Conservatives under Margaret Thatcher won the general election of May 1979 amid a wave of popular revulsion against the strikes and trade union excesses of the 'winter of discontent'. The new Prime Minister and her closest associates had been converted to the belief that Britain was suffering from political and moral breakdown, traceable to the excessive government intervention fostered by socialism. They believed that the 'nanny state' gave everybody an assurance that they would be bailed out if things went wrong for them. As a result, the public engaged in all sorts of irresponsible behaviour, since they did not have to suffer the consequences of their actions.

According to Thatcherite ideology, those who suffered were the solid moral majority who did behave responsibly, saved for their old age and worked hard. These were denied the fruits of their labour by a swollen state apparatus that took away their savings in taxation and depressed their initiative by over-regulation, while rewarding 'scroungers' and the irresponsible.

A major imperative, therefore, was to cut government down to size and limit its interventions in society. By doing so it could distance itself from those who had usurped its authority, particularly trade unions, and act with force where it had to intervene, notably in support of law and order and free market reform. A strong government could also assert British interests abroad, in collaboration with like-minded US administrations. Bolstered by the enhanced economic growth that these policies would bring it could also push the European Union in a free trade direction.

These ideas inspired government action both under Margaret Thatcher (1979–90) and her successor as Conservative Prime Minister, John Major (1990–7).

Thatcherism, 1979–90

Until 1983, the Thatcher government favoured monetarism: a belief that control of the amount of money circulating in the economy would alone improve general economic efficiency, in spite of the exceptional unemployment it caused (over 11 per cent in 1982). From 1983, however, monetary targets were rarely met and ministers became less and less dependent on the theory. They stuck to their free market philosophy – denationalisation (or 'privatisation'), reducing trade union power, and increasing penalties and incentives in the public sector. The British National Oil Corporation, Jaguar Cars, British Leyland, British Telecom, the Trustee Savings Bank, British Gas, British Airways, Rolls-Royce and many council-owned homes were sold. In the late 1980s water companies, electricity supply and other 'natural monopolies' traditionally within the public sector were also privatised.

Deregulation

The opposite of regulation, it involves the weakening or removal of state regulations in the interests of market competition.

Major legislation in 1980, 1982 and 1984 transformed industrial relations law. 'Closed shops' (i.e. factories where all the workforce have to join a union) had to be approved in a secret ballot by four-fifths of the workers; secondary picketing (i.e. the picketing of firms not themselves party to an industrial dispute) was outlawed; secret ballots were introduced to endorse industrial action, to elect top union officials, and to approve the collection of union political funds. These laws, together with continuing high unemployment, substantially weakened the trade unions. From 1979 to 1995 their membership halved. They were further debilitated by the costly and often violent miners' strike of 1984–5, which ended with a split in the National Union of Mineworkers and an effective victory for the government. Many mines were closed and the remnants of the coal industry were sold off in the mid-1990s.

Unemployment remained the Thatcher government's Achilles' heel. By 1987, the number and scope of youth employment schemes, retraining programmes and other employment creation schemes had increased considerably. However, in 1985, the economy began to expand very rapidly by British standards, culminating in the frenetic 'boom' of 1987–8.

The Thatcher project involved a renewed effort to reduce the size of government and attempts at major institutional reform. High levels of unemployment had become a long-term feature of many inner-city areas, especially in the north, Scotland, Northern Ireland and Wales. Intervention in these areas had traditionally involved high levels of public expenditure on housing, transport and social services, with central government relying on locally elected councils to effect its policies.

Plate 3.3 A Nicholas
Garland cartoon in the *Daily
Telegraph*, 23 September
1981, showing
unemployment about to go
through the 3 million mark
under Thatcher
Source: Nicholas Garland/
Daily Telegraph

The Conservatives, in line with their free market philosophy, sought instead to remove what they saw as the dead hand of Labour-dominated local government. The centrally controlled Youth Training Scheme, channelling the energies of the young unemployed, was extended and made semi-compulsory; enterprise zones with suspension of normal planning regulations were set up under nominated boards; council house sales continued and private renting and buying of houses was encouraged. State schools were given the right to opt entirely out of local authority control and thus gain much greater autonomy. Subsidies for public transport were effectively removed and competition was encouraged. Meanwhile moral and administrative pressure was applied to those receiving Unemployment Benefit to take any form of work available, however low paid and unattractive. Vigorous attempts were made to break away from national pay settlements, so that firms operating in areas of high unemployment could pay less.

In addition, the government embarked on major reforms of the Civil Service, education and health service. Most of these involved introducing market or market-like principles into operating procedures. Until the 1970s there was an implicit assumption that publicly provided services were a good thing. From the 1980s, many politicians, academics and commentators seriously questioned this assumption

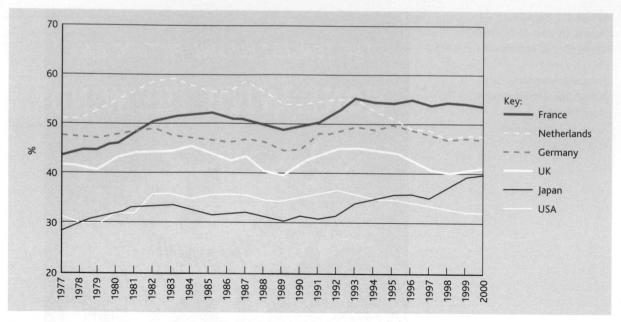

Figure 3.2 Percentage of GDP in the public sector, related countries, 1977–2000

and argued that the private sector (or in some cases private sector practices applied in the public sector) were often superior in terms of quality and value for money.

The attempt to get government out of the economy appeared by the end of the 1980s to have had real but limited success. In areas of traditional strength – finance and services centred on south-east England – free enterprise policies had strengthened Britain's competitive position in an era of growing interdependence and internationalisation of markets. They had accelerated the industrial decline of the outlying areas, however, and events were to show that the recovery was fragile. A further downturn in the global economy from 1990 arrested the move to the market. Spending as a percentage of GDP increased once more after having declined in the early 1980s (Figure 3.2).

The stock market 'crash' of October 1987 convinced the government that they had to lower interest rates to avert a recession. At the same time, the third Thatcher government was less intent on holding down public expenditure. It had a surplus of revenue over expenditure and had eliminated the annual PSBR by 1987. However, the expected downturn in economic activity following the collapse of world stock market prices in October 1987 never transpired. As a result the economy became seriously overheated in 1988, culminating in an inflation rate of close to 10 per cent (Figure 3.1). Remedial action in the form of punitively high interest rates followed rapidly, which in turn depressed the housing and property markets and helped precipitate the 1990–2 recession.

A number of other countries went through a similar boom/slump cycle during the late 1980s and early 1990s. In few others was the initial stimulus to growth and inflation so great or the subsequent deflationary reaction so draconian. Britain experienced a longer, deeper recession than any comparable country except Japan.

Modified Thatcherism, 1992–7

The Conservatives' surprise election victory in 1992, giving them a record fourth term, was not just a confirmation of the Thatcher policies of the 1980s. Some of the Thatcherite agenda was dropped: most importantly, the Major government no longer pursued orthodoxy in the national accounts. Public expenditure was allowed to rise to a point where by 1995 the PSBR was above 6 per cent of GDP. Money was initially pumped into health, education, transport and a range of other areas before further cuts were imposed from 1994 onwards to finance reductions in income tax. But equally much of the Thatcher agenda remained or was even strengthened. This included lower taxes on incomes and profits, further privatisations such as British Rail and increasing competition and self-management within the public sector.

From 1993 the British economy recovered ahead of its European partners and a great deal of the government's energy went into managing the boom to sustain steady growth and avoid a subsequent recession. Much of the Major government's attention had also to be given to relationships with the European Union. Mrs Thatcher had been a strong upholder of British sovereignty – the idea that the British government should always have the last say on what was done on British territory. This had caused tensions with other countries in the EU, particularly France and Germany, which were strong supporters of a closer (and even a federal) European Union.

The single most important move towards European union in the 1980s was the 1986 Single European Act (SEA), which aimed to abolish all restraints to trade within the EU by 1992. To speed up progress it gave the European Commission and European Court greater powers of regulation and intervention, independent of national governments. It also introduced majority voting, on matters related to the development of the market, among member states in the Council of Ministers. (For more detail on the European Union see Chapter 8.)

Moves towards a European free market were wholly in line with Thatcherite thinking. Mrs Thatcher's warm endorsement of the economic aims of the SEA blinded her to its political consequences. Opening up markets demanded strong political intervention, as her own experience in Britain might have warned her. In delegating greater powers to the 'Brussels bureaucracy', even to enforce free trade, she was undermining the autonomy of the British government and Parliament.

This was masked up to 1991 by the fact that British commissioners within the EU, British advisers and many neo-liberal economists were at the forefront in striking down protectionist measures in countries such as France and Germany. Under John Major, however, it became clear that the free market was simply a stage on the road to closer political union. The Treaty of European Union (also known as the Maastricht Treaty) (1992–3) committed countries of the European Union to closer integration of social and economic policies, and to collective decision making in many areas. Britain reserved the right to opt out of the single currency, which it exercised when it abstained from joining the euro in 1999, and refused to accept the Social Chapter on minimal working conditions for European employees (later adopted by the Labour government).

Even so, the Maastricht Treaty seemed to a substantial body of 'Eurosceptics' in the Conservative Party to go too far. Their scepticism was reinforced by the improvement in the British economy after the country was forced out of the European Monetary System, which had obliged members to keep their currencies within narrow limits in relation to each other.

As France and Germany powered ahead with their project of 'ever-closer union', and as the European institutions became more active in Britain, the persistent opposition of the Conservative Eurosceptics spread to other aspects of government activity. They objected to the slackening pace of Thatcherite reform and threatened to vote against a whole series of government measures unrelated to Europe.

With a minuscule majority in Parliament the Major government (itself split internally) took an increasingly negative stance in Europe to retain Eurosceptic support. This in turn alienated the pro-European Conservatives. Supported by much of industry and the City, they wanted to go along with European Monetary Union (EMU), either because they feared the consequences if Britain were left out or because they saw positive benefits for London as the financial centre of a more integrated Union. Divisions both in Cabinet and in Parliament contributed to the impression of an indecisive, do-nothing government, which helped lose them the election of 1997.

There is no doubt that the Conservative governments of the 1979–97 period transformed the political landscape of Britain. Above all, they created a completely new policy agenda. With the collapse of the social democratic consensus in the 1970s Britain had become an ideological battleground between old Labour ideas such as nationalisation and high rates of income tax designed to redistribute wealth, and free market ideas based on individual initiative and self-reliance. To be sure, there were many shades of opinion within the main political parties and between them, but almost all political discourse took on a left versus right character. The Conservative years changed all this. By the mid-1990s almost all politicians accepted that the market was the best mechanism for producing and delivering a wide range of goods and services. This applied not just to traditional industries but also to 'natural' monopolies such as utilities and transport. It might even apply to the ways in which public services such as health, education and law enforcement were delivered. At the same time, few argued for higher taxation. The assumption was that lower rates of income tax provided an incentive to work and to save. Old Labour policies were effectively discredited.

A Third Way? New Labour, 1997–2007

After nearly 18 years in opposition the Labour Party returned to office in May 1997, and accepted most of the Thatcherite agenda, including the need for strict financial discipline and income tax reductions. One of the first things the self-styled 'New Labour' government did was to adhere strictly to the Conservatives' spending plans. Combined with the increased tax revenues that resulted from continuing economic prosperity this resulted in a large budget surplus which allowed some relaxation of spending controls before the next election. Increasingly, Labour steered political debate away from the questions of how industry should be structured and levels of spending and taxation determined, towards an emphasis on the quality of public services, notably health, education and law and order. The hard-line, Eurosceptical Conservative Party under William Hague failed to note this change of emphasis and argued that the future lay in low taxes and reduced public expenditure – a position that helped account for the Conservatives' second defeat in 2001. Hague's successor, Iain Duncan Smith, played down both the European issue and lower taxes and argued that the Conservatives too were interested in improving public services. This line was followed by the new leader, David Cameron, after 2005.

In spite of this emphasis on public services, there is no question that by 1997 the nature of the policy agenda had changed. Old Labour appealed to voters not only on the question of nationalisation but also on issues of wealth and equality. Traditionally, Labour governments had advocated higher taxes for the rich and lower taxes for the poor. At the same time they generally opposed the private provision of such services as education, transport and housing. By 1997 references to redistributive taxation (taxing the better off and redistributing tax revenue to the poor) had almost passed from political discourse. Instead, New Labour wanted to expand the economy, so that everybody would benefit. They no longer opposed

Plate 3.4 The new prime minister, Tony Blair, with his wife, Cherie, at No. 10 Downing Street after winning the 1997 general election

Source: Empics

private education and the private provision of transport, and had become positively enthusiastic about owner-occupied housing.

They also distanced themselves from the trade unions, whose advice was much less important to the government than that of financial interests and in particular proponents of fiscal orthodoxy – a combination of low inflation and a balanced budget. Financial interests dominate the Monetary Policy Committee of the Bank of England, which sets interest rates. Beating inflation and maintaining a stable currency are seen as the prerequisites for a generally healthy economy in the long term, even if there are casualties, especially in manufacturing, in the short term. Central controls on local government spending were maintained and indeed tightened. Tough law and order policies were supported by the first two Labour home secretaries, Jack Straw and David Blunkett, while the prime minister never tired of extolling 'family values'. In general too New Labour shared Mrs Thatcher's suspicions of public employees and the government devised ever tighter means of control of schools and teachers, for example. In many ways therefore Mrs Thatcher's goals of 'free economy, strong state' have been accepted by New Labour.

These policies have been projected to the public as a '**Third Way**' between unfettered capitalism and state socialism. However, it is not easy to pinpoint what exactly the Third Way is. In an influential book published in 1998, the sociologist Anthony Giddens attempted to spell it out. Most of the emphasis is on the 'restructuring of government and civil society', which usually means making government more responsive to a better informed and more politically active public. In policy terms, this translates into making government programmes more *efficient* but not necessarily bigger or more egalitarian. The Third Way also involves copying the

Third Way

The theory that governments should follow policies that are based neither on free market capitalism nor state socialism, but an amalgam of both. In British politics it is closely associated with Blair and New Labour.

BRIEFINGS

3.9 A neo-liberal consensus?

Just as Conservatives and Labour agreed from 1950 onwards on the acceptance of Labour reforms such as the Welfare State, so we can see an implicit agreement between the major parties today on acceptance of the Conservative privatisations of the 1980s, together with their supporting 'free market' philosophy. New Labour and Conservatives agree that the economy is best left to run itself with a minimum of government regulation. What regulation there is will be undertaken on financial grounds, favouring the City of London, and aimed at reducing inflation. Public services are to be run on a 'market model' as far as possible with bigger incentives for efficient providers and penalties for the inefficient. This applies even to the Welfare State, the big holdover from the previous period. Conservatives and Labour differ however over the extent to which social benefits should be raised. Even though they share many of the same policy ideas, therefore, Conservatives and Labour still divide on the extent to which government should intervene in society, by targeting benefits, or reduce its role by taking less in taxes.

best practice of other countries in such areas as welfare and health care. Almost by definition, the Third Way can mean institutional and constitutional reform. While its advocates believe strongly in protecting the weak and vulnerable in society (the disabled, the poor, the sick), they also believe that welfare benefits should go only to the deserving poor or the genuinely needy. As far as income security is concerned, most individuals should be self-reliant rather than depend on the state. Only those who cannot help themselves should be supported by the government. To be fair, in health and education, New Labour supports free provision for all who need it – although it also respects the wishes of those who prefer private provision. However, it no longer believes that income and wealth inequality should be addressed directly through redistributive taxation.

None of this adds up to socialism or even to social democracy as practised in most European countries in the post-Second World War period. But it did mean renewal and reform. New Labour was quite prepared to accept most of the reforms of the Thatcher period because many of them did make government more efficient. Labour also embarked on major constitutional reform, which the Conservatives opposed. This has involved signing the European Convention on Human Rights, and giving devolution to Scotland, Wales and Northern Ireland. In addition the House of Lords has seen hereditary peers ousted and some devolution to a London Assembly and mayor has been implemented.

One final characteristic of Labour's Third Way, which also distinguishes it from earlier Thatcherite ideas, is what has been called *liberal internationalism*. Tony Blair and other Third Way adherents believe that with the proper safeguards, globalisation can produce benefits. These safeguards include international treaties on environmental protection, aid for poorer countries and, most controversially, multilateral military efforts to contain terrorism and the aggression of 'rogue' states such as Iraq. Liberal internationalists also support free trade and such bodies as the EU, the World Trade Organization and the International Monetary Fund. We will return to this theme in later chapters.

By the first years of the twenty-first century, therefore, the ideas that informed British politics had changed. Market values dominated in most areas of economic life, and market-like mechanisms had been introduced to most parts of the public sector. Labour has not dropped its hope of a more egalitarian society, but it assumes that this will come through economic growth and public services that are more efficiently run. In fact, rather than Britain becoming a more equal society it has become more unequal over recent decades. This was not, of course, the

Liberal internationalism

The view of international politics built on individualism which argues that individual rights are superior to nation state rights.

BRIEFINGS

3.10 Inequality in Britain

Among the OECD states (Organisation for Economic Cooperation and Development, which represents the richer industrial countries) it is widely recognised that Britain has a relatively high degree of income and wealth inequality. Along with the United States (and in contrast to such countries as Japan and France) a small number of rich people control a large proportion of wealth. In 2002, for example, the richest 1 per cent of the population owned 23 per cent of the wealth, up from 18 per cent in 1981 (see Table 1.3). More disturbingly, there is evidence that this inequality spreads to other areas of social life, including health and education. People living in Scotland, Wales and the north of England have a considerably lower life expectancy than those living in the south. This difference is largely explicable in terms of income and wealth distribution. More poor people live in Wales and northern Britain than in the south. In education, although standards have been increasing in recent years, so has educational inequality. An OECD report found that a high level of socio-economic segregation in Britain encouraged by private and elite public sector schools has led to a growing gap in educational attainment between rich and poor (*Knowledge and Skills for Life*, OECD, 2000).

Although New Labour is committed to reducing these inequalities some of its policies, such as maintaining grammar and special subject schools, may actually have the opposite effect.

intention of Labour governments, but it has happened nonetheless. Labour has gone further than its predecessors in the area of constitutional change. However, reforms of the 'core' institutions of British political life – Parliament, the Civil Service, local government – have lagged behind. Later chapters will review these developments – or lack of them – in detail.

Summary

This chapter has shown how British governments broke away from free trade doctrines in the 1930s and 1940s to protect industry and society from the consequences of global recession. In particular, governments intervened to:

- nationalise basic industries (coal, steel, transport and public utilities) so as to guarantee price and production levels and a minimum level of service

- use monetary policy to achieve a high level of activity in the economy with top priority being given to full employment

- use planning to direct investment and employment towards reviving older industrial regions and alleviate crowding in the inner cities

- create a comprehensive Welfare State to provide all citizens with basic health care, education and adequate housing.

From the 1950s to the late 1970s few governments challenged these policies. However, it became increasingly difficult to fund them because:

- Britain suffered from chronic balance of payments problems that led to repeated bouts of 'stop–go', i.e. overheating of the economy followed by the need for deflation.

- The international economic environment became more difficult during the 1970s, with the abandonment of fixed exchange rates and the rapid increase in commodity prices.

▶

- Britain's economic performance was poor compared with other countries as strikes and low productivity led to an ever-present sense of economic crisis. The preferred solutions to these problems – incomes policy and economic planning – gradually became discredited.

- By the mid-1970s intellectual and political opinion moved in favour of market solutions to economic problems.

- Since the 1980s a combination of market solutions together with fiscal and monetary discipline have dominated the political agenda. Full employment has been given a lower priority, although the Labour Party remains more concerned about it than the Conservative Party. Similarly, both parties now accept that Welfare State benefits have to be selective rather than universal. The major difference between the parties is on the degree of selectivity, with Labour favouring higher benefit levels.

- By the mid-1990s the performance of the British economy recovered to reach the average of the developed countries.

- New Labour's 'Third Way' involved renewing the relationship between government and citizen through constitutional reform and social justice. From 1999 it also involved an interventionist foreign stance and support for multilateral treaties as well as military intervention to oust dictators.

MILESTONES

Milestones of events, policies and governments, 1931–2006

BRITAIN	WORLD
'National' governments, 1931–40 (MacDonald, Baldwin, Chamberlain), Conservative dominated	
Abandonment of Gold Standard, 1931	World depression, 1928–39
Mass unemployment, 1930–8	Rise of Hitler in Germany
Tariffs on foreign imports, 1931–5	
Formation of industrial cartels, 1931–8	
Marketing boards for Agriculture	
Special Areas Acts, 1935, 1936, 1937	
Rearmament, 1936–40	
Series of reports on land use, town planning, population distribution, 1938–40	Nazi annexations: Austria, 1938, Czechoslovakia, 1939; attack on Poland, 1939, precipitates war
Wartime coalition, 1940–5 (Churchill)	
Unprecedented control of labour, supplies, food, production, 1940–5	Second World War, 1939–45
Beveridge Report on Social Insurance, 1942	
Labour government, 1945–51 (Attlee)	
National Health Service Act, 1946	German surrender, 1945
National Insurance Act, 1946	Japanese surrender, 1945
State ownership of coal industry, gas, electricity, transport and steel	Dislocation of international trade after Second World War
Town and Country Planning Act, 1947	Berlin crisis, 1948–9, marks start of Cold War with Soviet Union and intensification of Western alliance (NATO)
Full employment policy, wage and dividends freeze, control of production in many areas, rationing	Independence of India, Pakistan, Burma and Ceylon, 1948

Milestones of events, policies and governments, 1931–2006 continued

BRITAIN	WORLD
Conservative governments, 1951–9 (Churchill, Eden, Macmillan)	
Deregulation of trade and financial controls	Korean War, 1950–3
Limited denationalisation of iron and steel industry and road transport	World economic growth; invasion of Suez, 1956
	Formation of European Community, 1956
Conservative governments, 1959–64 (Macmillan, Home)	
Wage and price freeze, 1962–3	Independence of most African colonies
Unsuccessful application to join EC, 1962	Détente with Soviet Union, 1960–79
	Relaxation of Cold War and arms race
Labour governments, 1964–70 (Wilson)	
Balance of payments crisis, 1964–6	Britain keeps out of US involvement in Vietnam War, 1964–73
National economic plan effectively abandoned, 1966–7	Increasing liberalisation of world trade under GATT
Increasing credit, wage and dividend restrictions, 1966–9	
Devaluation of pound sterling, 1967	
Unsuccessful application to join EC, 1968	Arab/Israeli War, 1967
Plan to regulate trade union and industrial relations, 1969–70 defeated by trade union and internal Labour opposition	
Intervention of British troops in Northern Ireland, 1969	
Conservative governments, 1970–4 (Heath)	
Floating exchange rate for pound sterling, 1971	Abandonment of Bretton Woods system of fixed exchange rates, 1971–3
Industrial Relations Act, 1971 (legal regulation of trade unions); 'U-turn' from not interfering in industry or wage negotiations to restrictions on wage and salary increases	
Suspension of Northern Ireland Parliament and Direct Rule, 1972	
Reorganisation of local government units into larger ones, 1972–5	
Entry to EEC, 1973	
Easy credit and high inflation, 1973–4	Arab/Israeli War 1973
Successful strikes by National Union of Mineworkers, 1972 and 1974, which disrupt entire country	
Discovery of oil in British North Sea	Rise in world oil prices, 1973–4
Labour governments, 1974–9 (mostly in minority) (Wilson, Callaghan)	
Major election gains by Scottish and Welsh Nationalists, 1974	
High inflation, 1974 onwards	
Social Contract with trade unions, involving limits on prices and incomes and legal concessions, 1975–8	
Referendum for continuing membership of EC, 1975	
Balance of payments crisis, 1976	
Severe credit restrictions and increasing cuts in projected government expenditure, 1976–9	
High and increasing unemployment, 1975 onwards	

▶

Milestones of events, policies and governments, 1931–2006 continued

BRITAIN	WORLD
'Winter of discontent', 1979 (strikes by numerous groups of workers including transport strike)	British oil revenues from North Sea equal payments for foreign oil
Defeat of government proposals for Scottish and Welsh devolution, 1979	
Conservative governments, 1979–97 (Thatcher, Major)	
Policy of restricting stock of money to bring down inflation involves further cuts in government and central restrictions on local government expenditure	Increasing friction between Soviet Union and the West from 1979
	Iranian Revolution and world oil crisis, 1978–81
	World economic depression intensifying up to 1981
Legal restrictions on union's rights to picket during strikes and to extend scope of stoppage	
Falling inflation and greatly increasing unemployment, 1980–2	
Extensive urban riots, 1981	
Foundation of Social Democratic Party and leadership defections from Labour, 1981	Falklands War, 1982
Re-election of Conservatives with large majority, Liberal–Social Democratic Alliance comes close to Labour in terms of votes but not seats, 1983	World economic recovery, 1982–6
Miners' strike, 1984–5: most bitter industrial dispute since war	
Renewed urban riots, 1985	
Unemployment reaches 13 per cent, then begins to fall	Approval of Single European Act 1986 by members of EU including United Kingdom
	Oil and other commodity prices fall, 1986
Renewed balance of payments problems with drop in oil revenues, 1988–97	Relaxation of Soviet–Western relations, 1986–7, serious disarmament negotiations between the Soviet Union and United States
'Privatisation' of many nationalised industries including gas	Single European market planned for mid-1990s
Re-election of Conservatives with large majority, 1987, Labour fails to recover significantly and Alliance fails to break through	
Economic boom, 1987–9, followed by severe recession, 1990–4	Break-up of Soviet Union follows peaceful liberation of east European states, 1989–91
Britain joins Exchange Rate Mechanism, 1990	
Replacement of local rates by Community Charge (poll tax) provokes massive non-payments and riots, 1989–90	
Replacement of Mrs Thatcher as prime minister by John Major, 1990	
Conservatives returned with a majority of 21 with John Major as prime minister, 1992	Gulf War, 1991
Britain forced out of ERM by currency crisis, 1992	Maastricht Treaty on further European union, Britain opts out of Social Charter and reserves decision on monetary union
Increasing internal conflict in Conservative Party between 'Eurosceptics' and pro-Europeans	
Government forced into increasing opposition to 'Europe'	Bosnia crisis 1992–5: British intervention along with other EU members and United States
Slow economic recovery, 1994–6	Intergovernmental conference on closer European Union, 1997
'New Labour' wins election, 1997	

Milestones of events, policies and governments, 1931–2006 continued

BRITAIN	WORLD
Labour governments, 1997– (Blair)	
Bank of England given autonomy to act on interest rates through Monetary Policy Committee	Russia accepts eastward expansion of NATO
Labour endorses strict financial orthodoxy	
British economic performance improves: accelerating boom 1997–2001	
Referendums approve a Scottish Parliament and devolution for Wales, September 1997	
Devolved assemblies start work, September 1999	
	European Monetary Union, 1999, all members join except United Kingdom, Sweden and Denmark (Greece joins later)
'Peace Process' in Northern Ireland succeeds in reaching agreement on a power-sharing Assembly in 1998. Uneasy peace continues although the Assembly is sporadically suspended	Kosovo intervention and bombing of Serbia by United States and United Kingdom, 1999
Labour second landslide victory, 2001	
Slowdown of British economy, 2002–5	Terrorist attacks on United States, September 2001
Unprecedented third Labour election victory, 2005	Allied invasions of Afghanistan 2002 and Iraq 2003
	Stalemates in Middle East and in 'War on Terror'
	EU expands to include ten extra countries, mainly in central and eastern Europe
	Failure of international initiatives to tackle poverty and global warming owing to US opposition
Increasing tensions over efficiency measures for NHS and education within Labour Party under last period of Blair premiership	Defeat of EU proposals for more federal constitution, 2005

Essays

1. Why did government intervene so extensively in society from 1931 to 1951? What remains of this legacy in the early twenty-first century?

2. What was the nature of the post-war 'social democratic consensus'? To what extent has Labour's 'Third Way' broken with this consensus?

3. Why did the question of the 'balance of payments' disappear from British politics after the 1970s?

Projects

1. Write a review of the differences in economic management between the Conservative governments, 1979–1997 and the Labour governments of the subsequent period. Answer with specific reference to the role of taxation in funding public expenditure.

2. Catalogue the main differences between the Conservatives and Labour on the funding and organisation of the Welfare State since 1979.

3. Outline the main privatisations carried out since 1980. Produce a report card on the success and failure of privatisation.

Further reading

A very large literature on British post-war policy exists. A balanced assessment of the question of economic decline is David Coates, *The Question of UK Decline* (London: Harvester Wheatsheaf, 1994).

On the politics of economic change see, for the early period, Samuel H. Beer, *Modern British Politics* (London: Faber, 1965) and, for the 1970s, Keith Middlemas, *Politics in Industrial Society* (London: Deutsch, 1979).

On the Thatcher era see David Marsh (ed.), *Implementing Thatcherite Policies* (Milton Keynes: Open University Press, 1992). On the 1990s see C. Crouch, 'The terms of the neo-liberal consensus', *Political Quarterly*, **68** (4), 1997, pp. 352–60. On New Labour's economic and social policies see Gerald R. Taylor (ed.), *The Impact of New Labour* (London: Macmillan, 1999). On the Third Way, see Anthony Giddens, *The Third Way* (Oxford: Polity, 1998). Giddens replies to his critics in *The Third Way and its Critics* (Oxford: Polity, 2000). David Richards and Martin J. Smith assess New Labour responses to the changing world order in *Governance and Public Policy in the UK* (Oxford: Oxford University Press, 2002).

Useful web sites on the British economy

Hot links to these sites can be found on the CWS at www.pearsoned.co.uk/budge.

For students interested in the historical development of economic theories and practices that shaped modern Britain, there is an excellent set of entries in the Economic History Network at www.eh.net/HE, especially in their 'resources on specific topics' page (www.eh.net/HE/he_resources/topics.php). A comprehensive historical approach to the period surrounding Keynesian economic theory can be found at www.libertyhaven.com/theoreticalorphilosophicalissues/economics/keynesianism/index.html. Contemporary economic models of relevance to today's world are regularly discussed on the web site of the World Economic Forum www.weforum.org.

The main policy goals and achievements of economic and fiscal policy can be found at www.number-10.gov.uk; there are other relevant sites related to economic and fiscal policies. These include the Treasury site www.hm-treasury.gov.uk; the Bank of England, www.bankofengland.co.uk; and the Department of Trade and Industry, www.dti.gov.uk. It might also be worth looking at the British Chambers of Commerce web site at www.chamberonline.co.uk/index.jsp.

A number of societies and research groups provide critical assessments of economic theories such as the Institute of Fiscal Studies, www.ifs.org.uk; the National Institute for Economic and Social Research, www.niesr.ac.uk; the Centre for Economic Policy Research, www.cepr.org; the Adam Smith Society, www.adamsmith.org.uk; the Institute for Economic Affairs, www.iea.org.uk; and DEMOS, www.demos.co.uk. The *Financial Times*, www.ft.com and the *Economist*, www.economist.com offer regular market, financial and economic analysis.

PART 2

Government

chapter 4

A British constitution?

We have seen how historical developments have strongly shaped the present-day institutions of British government and politics. The slowly evolving nature of the British state over hundreds of years, perpetually introducing new processes under old forms, has left its mark, particularly on the constitution. The British 'constitution' is almost unique among the world's democracies for its pre-modern origins, gradual evolution and unwritten status. Until recently most commentators celebrated it for producing strong but flexible and responsive government that has worked well over the centuries. Its major features – parliamentary sovereignty, the rule of law, the unitary state, and responsible and accountable government – were seen as evidence of British pragmatism and political genius. We shall examine these claims in the next set of chapters as we see how government operates in practice under the constitution. In fact many of its original principles were eroded in the 1980s and 1990s by government actions themselves and by membership of the European Union. The constitution also came under criticism for not working as it was supposed to, and for being less democratic than it should be. Some sceptics even questioned whether Britain has a constitution at all, hence the question mark in the chapter title. Demands for reform grew louder in the 1990s, and at the turn of the century New Labour embarked on a major programme of constitutional reform.

This chapter discusses the traditional British constitution, criticisms of it, and the ways in which it has changed in the recent past. It covers:

- the status and sources of constitutional authority
- Parliament, government and the constitution
- the principal doctrines of the traditional 'British constitution'
- the myth and reality of the traditional constitution
- recent constitutional changes
- New Labour's 'constitutional project'.

Britain's 'unwritten' constitution: status and sources

Constitution

A set of fundamental laws that determine what the central institutions and offices of the state are to be, their powers and duties, and how they relate to one another, and to their citizens.

People talk of a country's constitution in two different ways. Sometimes they refer broadly to the general body of laws and rules that define the functions and powers of the state, and its relations with ordinary citizens. In this sense every country, including Britain, has a **constitution**.

At other times they refer to a single document, typically written on vellum and solemnly ratified with a grand seal. Examples are the US Constitution of 1787, and Germany's 'Basic Law' of 1949. In this second sense Britain, along with Israel, is almost unique among democracies: there is no single constitutional document. One

Statute law

The sum total of laws passed by Parliament.

has to visit the British Library (or the cathedrals at Lincoln or Salisbury) to look at Magna Carta of 1215 for anything resembling a written constitution in Britain.

To say that the British constitution is 'unwritten' is misleading. Many laws and rules that regulate Britain's political system are in fact written down. They appear in acts of Parliament (**statute law**), treaties with foreign states, orders in council (government directives made in the name of the Crown), judgments handed down through the ages by the courts (**common law**), European law, and the commentaries of experts (Bagehot and Dicey in the nineteenth century, Jennings and Bogdanor in the twentieth). Table 4.1 defines these sources and gives examples.

Table 4.1 Sources of the British 'constitution'

1 Statutes	Acts of Parliament, which override all other British constitutional sources and account for a growing proportion of the 'constitution'
Examples	■ Representation of the People Acts, 1832–1969 (extended the right to vote) ■ the Peerage Act, 1963 (created life peers) ■ European Communities Act 1972 (UK joined the European Community)
2 Royal prerogative	Functions performed by ministers acting on behalf of the monarch; their authority derives from the Crown, not Parliament. Executed by Orders in Council or through proclamations and writs under the Great Seal. A gradually diminishing sphere of the constitution, but still important for foreign affairs and security matters
Examples	The power to: ■ dissolve Parliament ■ declare war and make treaties ■ dispense honours ■ appoint ministers
3 Common law	This means customary rules, especially 'precedents' established by judicial decisions in particular cases. Important for civil liberties
Examples	■ Freedom of speech and assembly ■ Individual rights in relation to the police and the courts
4 Authoritative commentaries	Books and writings widely recognised as interpretations of constitutional rules
Example	■ T. Erskine May, *Treatise on the Law, Privileges, Proceedings, and Usage of Parliament*, the classic guide to parliamentary procedure
5 Conventions	Established customs and practice that are considered binding but lack the force of law. Applies particularly to the practices of the Crown and the Cabinet
Examples	■ the impartiality of the Speaker of the House ■ Cabinet and ministerial responsibility ■ the prime minister should be a Member of the Commons
6 European Union law	EU law has precedence over UK law, where the two conflict. British courts are required to strike down UK laws that contravene EU law. Important for social and economic legislation, including the rights of workers
Example	■ *Factortame* case: House of Lords judge the UK's Merchant Shipping Act to be unlawful in light of EU agreements

Common law

Law that is overtly made by judges and that has become part of custom and precedent.

However, these writings have never been assembled, codified and ratified into a single document. Moreover, important aspects of Britain's constitutional arrangements are not written down at all, but take the form of widely accepted understandings: constitutional 'conventions'. Britain's constitution is, therefore, more accurately described as partly written and wholly uncodified. It is the unplanned and unsystematic product of slow evolution.

The lack of a single constitutional document in Britain reflects the exceptional continuity of the British state. It has been spared the dictatorships, civil wars, colonisation and foreign invasions that, after liberation, herald a fresh start and a new, written constitution. There has been no historical moment since the 'glorious revolution' of 1688 when an overwhelming need for a new constitution has occurred.

The British 'constitution' also differs from most other countries in another significant respect: it has no special legal status. Written constitutions are normally 'entrenched': they can only be changed by special and often complicated procedures that do not apply to ordinary legislation. For example, an amendment to the US Constitution requires the assent of two-thirds of both Houses of Congress and ratification by the legislatures of three-quarters of the states. In some countries major constitutional changes must be approved by referendum. In Britain, Parliament can repeal or amend a constitutional law exactly as it would any other law. Referendums have increasingly been held, but there is no legal requirement for them.

And last, the British constitution differs from many others where the courts (sometimes a special Constitutional Court) have powers to interpret the constitution and to rule that government legislation or action is unconstitutional. In Britain, the courts have ruled that government and ministerial action are inconsistent with the law, but they cannot rule that the law itself is unconstitutional, although since the Human Rights Act (1998) laws can be declared inconsistent with it.

Parliament, government and the constitution

The British constitution allows for a pronounced concentration of power in the hands of central government to such an extent that the party in government can reshape the constitution to its own advantage. This is because without a written constitution the government of the day can pass a law with considerable constitutional implications, provided only that it can muster a majority vote in the House of Commons. Blatantly partisan constitutional legislation has been rare in Britain since 1918, but there are a few recent examples:

Bill of Rights

A formal statement of the rights and privileges that may be actually or theoretically claimed by citizens. Unlike a modern Bill of Rights, however, the one passed by Parliament in 1689 was more concerned to restrict the royal prerogative and assert the powers of Parliament.

- A 1984 Act required trade unions to ballot their members about political donations, which go mainly to the Labour Party. No matching legislation was introduced requiring companies to ballot their shareholders about political donations, which go mainly to the Conservative Party.

- A 1986 Act abolished the Greater London Council, and the six other metropolitan councils, which were normally under Labour control (see Chapter 12).

- The government's willingness in 1994 to change the ancient **Bill of Rights** (1689) at short notice in order to help one of its MPs sue the *Guardian* shows how easily – and, at times, recklessly – statute law can be used to change the constitution (see Briefing 4.1).

Some of the other sources of constitutional authority listed in Table 4.1 are effectively controlled by the government:

BRIEFINGS

4.1 The Hamilton affair and the amendment of the Bill of Rights of 1689

In 1994 the *Guardian* newspaper published allegations that the MP and trade minister, Neil Hamilton, had accepted payments from the millionaire businessman and owner of Harrods, Mohamed Al Fayed, without recording the payment in the Register of Interests as required by parliamentary rules. Hamilton started libel proceedings against the *Guardian*, which successfully applied to the court to have the action struck out on the ground that in order to defend it properly they would need to rely on evidence of Hamilton's conduct in the House of Commons, which was precluded by the terms of Article Nine of the Bill of Rights of 1689, and by the rules of parliamentary privilege. Many Conservative MPs and peers considered this unfair because it prevented Hamilton from using the courts to clear his name. The government hurriedly passed a new law permitting an MP to waive Article Nine of the Bill of Rights in order to bring a libel action. In the event Hamilton abandoned his libel action, was defeated in the May 1997 general election and soon after was found by the Parliamentary Commissioner for Standards to have acted improperly.

This is a recent example of how government can use its majority in the House of Commons to overturn, at short notice and without careful consultation, a long-established provision of the constitution. This may illustrate either the flexibility of the constitution or the government's ability to alter the constitution for short-term partisan advantage.

(For more detail see Dawn Oliver, 'Regulating the conduct of MPs: the British experience of combating corruption', *Political Studies*, **45**, 1997, pp. 539–58.)

Royal prerogative

Functions performed by ministers on behalf of the monarch. Before a constitutional monarchy was established the Crown had powers that were subject to no check or veto by Parliament, but now the royal prerogative is generally exercised by ministers.

- The **royal prerogative** is exercised by ministers who derive their authority, not from Parliament, but from a wholly compliant Crown.

- Common law and judicial decisions sometimes prove a temporary embarrassment for the government, but can be overturned by an act of Parliament.

- Constitutional conventions only bind the executive to the extent that they are recognised and implemented by the government.

As a result, the British 'constitution' can be little different from 'what the government decides to do'.

The traditional constitution, 1911–72

Despite its untidiness and vagueness on some crucial matters, there was a structure to the British constitution in operation between 1911 (when the Parliament Act reduced the power of the House of Lords) and 1972, when the European Communities Act enabled Britain to join the EU. Its central principles were: a unitary state; parliamentary sovereignty; constitutional monarchy; centralised power; government accountability; and a representative form of democracy. All are important features of the British system of government, and we will discuss them in greater detail in chapters that follow. But a quick review of them here is necessary before looking at the way in which the constitution has started to change in recent times.

Unitary state

A state in which there is a single sovereign body, the central government. Unlike a federal state, the central government of a unitary state does not share power with smaller territorial areas within the state (states, regions or provinces) although it may devolve some powers to them.

The unitary state

The British state is **unitary** rather than federal or confederal. This means that there is only one constitutional centre of power – Parliament – which can create any sort of sub-central system of government it wishes. In federal systems, such as Germany,

Australia, Switzerland and the United States, sub-central levels of government (states, regions and provinces) have their own independent and constitutionally guaranteed status and powers. The federal (i.e. central) government cannot change these, unless it alters the constitution, because power is shared by the different levels of government. There are, of course, regional and local units of government in Britain with powers and duties. But the important point is that they only have these because the Westminster Parliament permits them, not because any constitutional document says so. In fact, central government can create or abolish regional parliaments and councils as it wishes, just as it can change their powers and responsibilities. The Heath government, for example, suspended the 50-year-old Stormont Parliament in Northern Ireland in 1972, replacing it eventually with direct rule from London. The Thatcher government abolished the Greater London Council and the six metropolitan counties in 1986. The Blair government then re-established the Stormont Parliament, London government, and created Welsh and Scottish regional authorities.

It is, of course, true that central government has reformed regional and local government in major ways in other unitary states such as France, Italy and Denmark, yet in these unitary states regional and local government is *relatively* powerful and autonomous compared with Britain. Even among democratic unitary states, political power in Britain is concentrated in central government. Britain is not just a unitary state but a highly centralised one. (For more on the UK's unusual form of unitary state see Chapters 10 and 11.)

Parliamentary sovereignty

A. V. Dicey, the foremost authority on the British constitution in the late nineteenth century, described parliamentary sovereignty as 'the one fundamental law of the British constitution' and 'the ultimate political fact upon which the whole system of legislation hangs'.

Parliamentary sovereignty means that no institution other than Parliament (strictly speaking 'the Queen, Lords and Commons assembled') can make law. An act of Parliament is not subject to, or constrained by, a higher law, such as a written constitution, or another body, such as a regional parliament or a court of law. In this sense, parliamentary sovereignty means that Parliament can do whatever it wants – pass any new law and abolish any old one without *formal* restraint. The British Parliament can make or unmake any law. It cannot be bound by its predecessors, neither can it bind its successors.

Legal power, of course, is not the same as practical power or political power. For example, Parliament has the *legal right* to do all sorts of things that would be unconstitutional in other democracies – to prohibit football, dancing, television and alcohol, even to abolish all elections – but it does not have the *political capacity* to do these things. The constraints on it, however, are practical and political, not legal or constitutional.

Constitutional monarchy

Britain has a 'constitutional monarchy', which means that the Crown plays a largely ceremonial role as head of State and symbol of the national community, having gradually ceded its political powers in the eighteenth and nineteenth centuries. In the nineteenth and early twentieth centuries, the monarch's rights were 'to be informed, to encourage and to warn' in the famous words of Walter Bagehot, the nineteenth-century constitutional expert. In practice, it is not clear that the present-day monarch has even these rights.

Plate 4.1 The Queen at the State opening of Parliament. The Crown plays a largely ceremonial role as head of State and symbol of the national community, having gradually ceded its powers in the eighteenth and nineteenth centuries. The Crown retains the right to dissolve Parliament, on the prime minister's advice, and to choose the prime minister

Source: Alamy/Jayne Fricher, Photo International

Concentrated and centralised power – elective dictatorship?

Just as the political power of the monarchy has dwindled to virtually nothing, so the power of the aristocracy in the House of Lords has dwindled to very little. The 1911 Parliament Act prohibited the House of Lords from blocking financial measures and limited its delaying powers on a non-financial bill. The Lords did not block measures included in the government's election manifesto (the 'Salisbury doctrine'). Occasionally, the Lords defeated a bill sent to it from the Commons, but usually the Commons simply approved the bill again, possibly after minor amendments, and the Lords then accepted it. If the Lords was particularly resistant the government could invoke the Parliament Acts of 1911 and 1949 to bypass the Lords altogether.

The combination of a constitutional monarchy and the diminished powers of the House of Lords means that the House of Commons is supreme. Some constitutional systems provide for two powerful representative assemblies (bicameralism). In Britain's 'asymmetric bicameral' system, the Upper Chamber, the House of Lords, is clearly secondary to the Lower, the House of Commons.

In most other democratic states, the power of the state is restrained by written constitutions and by the courts that interpret them, and it is generally shared between different levels of government (federal, state and local), between different representative assemblies (the upper and lower houses of central government), between different branches of government (the executive and legislative), and between different parties that form coalition governments. In Britain, more than almost any other democracy, power is centralised at the national level, and largely concentrated in the hands of the majority party in the House of Commons – in other words 'elective dictatorship'.

Government accountability

One consequence of the concentration of power, and one of the great merits claimed for the British system, is the accountability of government. Central government cannot easily blame others for its failings – it cannot blame opposition parties or coalition partners, the House of Lords, local government, the courts, the Civil Service, or anybody else for action taken in its name. The electoral system and the party system also create a direct and unbroken chain of accountability that stretches from individual electors right up to the Cabinet and prime minister: electors send a single-party representative for their constituency to Parliament; the majority party in Parliament forms a government; the government creates a Cabinet led by a prime minister; and so the government, Cabinet and prime minister are held directly accountable by the voters for what gets done. Central government has the power and the responsibility, and ultimately it alone can be held accountable.

Representative government

British government is representative government. For much of the nineteenth and twentieth centuries the public elected MPs, who were left to get on with the job of

Plate 4.2 This cartoon captures the idea that the prime minister dominates the Cabinet, referring to the claim that Blair decided to hold a referendum on the euro without discussing the matter with his Cabinet colleagues. The figure dumped in the waste basket is Clare Short, who resigned from the Cabinet in opposition to the Iraq War, but after the war was over

Source: Chris Riddell/The Observer 24th March 2002, Centre for the Study of Cartoons & Caricature, University of Kent

running the country. The principle was enunciated in 1774 by Edmund Burke, who did not mince his words when he told the people who had just elected him as their MP that he was always prepared to listen to them and work hard for them, but that his actions in the House of Commons would always be determined by his own judgement.

Representative government of this type contrasts with participatory or direct democracy, where citizens exercise closer control over their elected representatives by participating more directly in government. Referendums – a direct form of participation – were not used in Britain and are not part of the traditional constitutional order.

Strengths of the traditional constitution

The traditional British constitution was widely thought to have great strengths: it provided a durable and adaptable foundation for democracy; it helped to create stable government; and it produced moderate and effective government. Above all, it was said, it worked.

Durable democracy

The United Kingdom is one of the world's oldest democracies. It has gradually evolved from the Magna Carta in 1215 to its present form, and during this time it has avoided authoritarian and totalitarian governments, military coups and extremist political threats. It has adapted to huge social and economic changes, and survived wars and the rise and decline of the empire. Throughout all this it has protected most of the basic social and political rights of most of its citizens.

Stable government

Most British governments are in office for four or five years, providing a stability and continuity not often found in coalition systems. In post-war Italy and France, for example, there has been much more government instability. There have been unsettled periods in Britain since 1945 (1964–6, 1974, 1976–9) but they have been brief and exceptional.

Moderate government

For the most part, British government has been moderate government. Radical reforming governments have been relatively rare (the 1945–51 Labour government, and the Thatcher governments of 1979–90). Moreover, a broad consensus has usually spanned the two main parties. This was called 'Butskellism' in the 1950s after R. A. B. Butler, on the left wing of the Conservative Party, who had much in common with Hugh Gaitskell, on the Labour right. We have already commented on policy agreement in terms of the Social Democratic Consensus (1951–79) and the New Liberal Consensus (1979–2006).

Effective government

More controversial, and less easily demonstrated, the British constitutional system is said to produce effective government. Because power is centralised in the hands of the majority party in the House of Commons, government is better able to take effective action, so far as any government is able to do this. This does not mean that government policies are good or bad, but that governments can take decisions and implement them. There are not many veto points in the system and governments can take action if they have the will to do so.

The pragmatic virtue – it works

In the last resort, defenders of the traditional British constitution have argued that it works. It provides for stable, moderate, effective and accountable government in normal times, and is flexible enough to respond to crises. For example, although it is a prime example of strong, single-party government, it has moved smoothly into coalition government when the need arose. It did this when the country was threatened by the Great Depression (1931–6) and again during the Second World War (1940–5). The Labour government of 1974–9 was kept in power by an informal parliamentary agreement with the Liberals and Scottish Nationalists.

Similarly, although the United Kingdom is a prime example of a centralised unitary state, there was a degree of devolution to Scotland, Ireland and Wales, even before the creation of the Scottish Parliament and Welsh Assembly in 1999, and the restoration of Home Rule to Stormont. The electoral system is one of the least proportional in the democratic world, but it often produces a government that is close to the opinions of the average elector. The British constitution is a strange and unusual animal, it is true, but its defenders argue (with some merit) that it has worked as well as most democracies, and better than some.

The traditional constitution: myths and reality

Conventions

Constitutional conventions

Unwritten understandings based on custom and practice that are held to be binding and are commonly observed even though they are not enforced by law or sanctions. An example in the British constitution is that of the Crown assenting to bills passed by Parliament.

At the same time, critical voices have grown more insistent in recent times. At the heart of the criticism is the fact that the British constitution is only partly written and wholly uncodified. It depends not on formal, written rules, but on **conventions**, that is, on unwritten understandings based on custom and practice, which are supposed to be observed, but which lack the force of law. 'The British Constitution presumes more boldly than any other the good sense and the good faith of those who work it', said W. E. Gladstone, the nineteenth-century statesman.

Defenders of the traditional constitution emphasise the flexibility of conventions and their ability to fill gaps in the written parts of the constitution. They are what the constitutional expert Lord Norton calls 'the oil in the machinery of the constitution'. Sceptics point out that governments lubricate their own machinery nicely, leaving the opposition's to rust.

Some conventions are so firmly fixed that it is almost impossible to imagine their changing: the Crown assents to bills passed by both Houses of Parliament; the monarch calls on the leader of the largest party in the Commons to form a government; the prime minister always sits in the Commons; the Speaker is impartial; Parliament must meet every year; elections must be held at last every five years.

Other conventions are more fluid. Governments have been known to bend or ignore the conventions if they think they can get away with it. The combination of party discipline, a majority in the Commons and the legal supremacy of Parliament means they often can get away with it. In 1977 the Labour Prime Minister, James Callaghan, decided to allow a free vote on the rules for regulating European elections. Challenged in Parliament to say whether this breached the convention of collective Cabinet responsibility, he nonchalantly replied: 'The convention still applies except in cases I announce that it does not.'

The convention that a government resigns if it loses a vote of confidence is a case in point. In the nineteenth and much of the twentieth century any financial or legislative measure that was central to a government's programme was regarded as a matter of confidence. This understanding was ignored by the Labour government, which was elected with a tiny parliamentary majority of three in October 1974, and became a minority government in March 1977. It was defeated on a number of major measures but insisted that only a defeat on a censure motion required it to resign.

The 1994 Conservative government, beset by a dwindling majority and growing backbench rebellion, took the same line when an important part of its budget was defeated (increased VAT on fuel). Ironically in the same month the Prime Minister, John Major, defined the proposal to increase Britain's contribution to the EU as an issue of confidence in order to pressure reluctant Conservative MPs into supporting it. When is an issue an issue of confidence? When the prime minister says it is?

Ministerial responsibility

'Ministerial responsibility' offers a telling example of how changing political circumstances and government self-interest have together eroded the once firm constitutional convention that ministers are responsible for what they and their officials do (or omit to do). In theory they are answerable to Parliament for their conduct while holding public office and are held accountable – expected to resign – for major personal lapses or departmental errors. Some ministers have resigned for these reasons – David Blunkett and Peter Mandelson both resigned twice. But many have not, even when serious policy errors and departmental mistakes were involved. Recent examples include the following:

- James Prior, the Northern Ireland minister, over the breakout of prisoners at the Maze prison in Belfast in 1983

- Norman Lamont, the Chancellor of the Exchequer, over Britain's forced exit from the Exchange Rate Mechanism in 1992

- Michael Howard, the Home Secretary, over a series of prison escapes in 1994 and 1995

- William Waldegrave, for misleading the Commons, and Sir Nicholas Lyell, the Solicitor General, for wrongly instructing ministers on the arms to Iraq scandal in 1996

- Douglas Hogg, the agriculture minister, over the concealment of 'mad cow' disease in the early 1990s

- Jack Straw, the Home Secretary, for the accidental publication of the addresses of witnesses to the Macpherson inquiry on the police handling of the murder of Steven Lawrence, in 1999

- Jack Straw, the Home Secretary, for the protracted delays in the processing of passport applications in 1999

- Keith Vaz for misconduct in 2001

- Weapons of mass destruction. Some believe that members of the government should have taken responsibility for misinforming the public about Iraq's weapons of mass destruction in 2002–3.

It may no longer be reasonable to hold ministers personally accountable for the actions of thousands of civil servants in their ministry. The huge growth of government, the rapid turnover of ministers, and the delegation of much of the administration to executive agencies at arm's length from the department (see Chapter 7) may well be reasons for weakening the convention in some instances.

This argument might exonerate Prior and Howard, who could not be personally blamed for prison breakouts, but hardly excuses Lamont, Waldegrave, Hogg, Straw and Vaz, who had direct personal responsibility for their errors. They clung to office to avoid damaging their own careers and the government's reputation. The convention, in reality, is to cling on to office for as long as possible to avoid embarrassment, and only resign if forced to. If it is true that the convention of ministerial responsibility often does not work, then one of the mechanisms of government accountability is severely weakened.

Secrecy

The British political system is one of the most secretive among modern democracies (see Chapter 21). Not only are state institutions and officials protected by the sweeping and powerful Official Secrets Act 1989. Freedom of information provisions are, by most democratic standards, weak and ineffective. If a virtue of the British constitution is that it concentrates power in a way that makes government effective, a weakness is that it protects government from close and constant inspection. If we cannot find out what public officials have done, how can we hold them accountable for their actions?

Unaccountable government?

In the 1960s and 1970s Britain was widely admired for its accountable single-party government. In the 1990s it was increasingly criticised for an executive that was too powerful and insufficiently accountable to Parliament and public opinion. The poll tax of the late 1980s was probably the most conspicuous example (see Chapter 12). Hailed as 'one of the worst ideas in the world', it was forced through against the wishes of the great majority, possibly even a majority of Conservative MPs. There is much truth in Gladstone's claim that the British constitution relies heavily on the good sense and good faith of those who work it. What if they lack good sense and good faith?

Inflexibility

It is true that the British constitution has been flexible and adaptable. It is also true that it has difficulty in responding to demands for reform – the reform of the House of Lords has been an unresolved issue for 100 years now. Government secrecy and the electoral system are other examples. The British constitution puts great power in the hands of the government, and they often have no wish to change rules that give them this power.

A democratic deficit?

Critics have pointed to many democratic weaknesses and failings of the traditional constitution – the unelected nature of the House of Lords, the unfairness of the electoral system, the absence of any Bill of Rights, the weakness of freedom of information provisions, secrecy, the over-centralisation of power in the hands of central government and the weakness of regional and local government, the weakness of the House of Commons, the strength of the executive, and an over-reliance on representative rather than participatory forms of government. As the cracks in the traditional constitution began to show more clearly towards the end of the twentieth century, so the movement for constitutional reform grew stronger and the government introduced major constitutional reforms.

Recent constitutional changes

In the Victorian and Edwardian eras (1837–1914) issues of constitutional reform dominated the political agenda, pitched the parties into battle and inflamed the passions of politicians and people alike. The Chartist movement (a popular movement of the 1830s and 1840s that pressed for universal suffrage, a secret ballot, the abolition of the property qualification, equal constituencies, payment of MPs and annual elections), the Home Rule movement in Ireland and the Suffragette movement were associated with mass demonstrations, riots and even violence.

After 1928, when women were given the same voting rights as men, the issue of constitutional reform was pushed into a dark corner by the economic depression of the 1930s and the 1939–45 war, and remained there until the powers and actions of the Conservative governments in 1979–97 raised the issue again. Most citizens do not give it great importance compared with the 'bread and butter' issues of jobs, war, taxes and public services. But opinion polls reveal growing discontent with constitutional arrangements. The reform programme of the Charter 88 movement gave this dissatisfaction a clear focus.

We have referred, so far in this chapter, to the 'traditional' constitution of 1911–72 for the simple reason that the system has changed in the past 25 years. Much of the traditional constitution remains, but starting with Britain's membership of the European Union in 1973 a cumulative series of changes and reforms have had major effects on the British constitution.

Impact of Europe

It is not too much to say that Britain's joining (what was then called) the European Communities caused a constitutional earthquake. Earlier in this chapter we quoted Dicey's comment that parliamentary sovereignty is the one fundamental law of the British constitution. Membership of the EC ended that (see Briefing 4.2) for it was completely unlike any previous international agreement. Signing a foreign treaty or joining an international organisation does not necessarily contravene parliamentary sovereignty. Long before it joined the European Community Britain was a member of the United Nations, the North Atlantic Treaty Organisation and GATT. They imposed obligations on the British government but did not affect the right of Parliament to make or unmake any law.

Joining Europe was altogether different. The act of Parliament that legalised Britain's membership (the 1972 European Communities Act) incorporated the Treaty of Rome, and all the secondary legislation of the EC into British law, as well as the decisions of the European Court of Justice. For all practical purposes the 1972 Act commits Britain to obeying all present and future European laws and, therefore, binds successor Parliaments to accepting European law. Some constitutional commentators argue that parliamentary sovereignty remains intact because Parliament can always repeal the 1972 Act, and rescind any other agreement with the EU. Technically this is so, but it remains a pure technicality so long as the

BRIEFINGS

4.2 European law and parliamentary sovereignty

The sovereignty of Parliament is the dominant characteristic of our political institutions . . . the principle of parliamentary sovereignty means neither more nor less than this, namely, that Parliament thus defined has, under the English Constitution, the right to make or unmake any law whatever; and further, that no person or body is recognised by the law of England as having the right to override or set aside the legislation of Parliament.

A. V. Dicey, *Introduction to the Study of the Law of the Constitution*, London: Macmillan, 1952, p. 29

On the basis of the powers thus conferred on them, the Community institutions can enact legal instruments as a Community legislature legally independent of the Member States. Some of these instruments take effect directly as a Community law in the Member States, and thus do not require any transformation into national law in order to be binding, not only on Member States and their organs, but also on the citizen.

European Commission, *ABC of Community Law*, Luxembourg: European Documentation Series, 1991

chances of leaving the EU are negligible. Meanwhile, British courts must give precedence to European law.

The most striking example of a British court using European law to judge parliamentary legislation is the *Factortame* case, which involved a claim by the owners of a Spanish fishing boat that the Merchant Shipping Act 1988 was contrary to EU law and should not be applied. The House of Lords unanimously held (subject to a European Court of Justice ruling in support of the EC rights claimed by the fishermen) that EU law should prevail over the 1988 Act. The *Factortame* case is significant because it showed, beyond all doubt, that British courts could now do more than declare government actions illegal – they could declare acts of Parliament illegal, which ended the principle of parliamentary sovereignty. There are many similar, although less fundamental, cases of British law being overturned by European law. Briefing 4.3 gives a small but telling example.

In sum, membership of the EU has:

1. brought an end to parliamentary sovereignty; and

2. strengthened the constitutional power of the courts.

Referendums

The United Kingdom has increasingly used national referendums to ratify major constitutional changes, even though referendums do not fit easily with the principles of parliamentary sovereignty and representative democracy, and even though the

BRIEFINGS

4.3 Case 121/85 *Conegate* v. *Commissioners of Customs and Excise* [1986] ECR 1007

Inflatable sex dolls imported into the United Kingdom were seized by Customs and Excise. The importers claimed that seizure was contrary to Article 30 of the EC Treaty, which prohibits obstructions to free trade between member states. The ECJ held that the fact that the goods cause offence was not enough to justify a ban on their import. Imports could not be banned when there was no corresponding prohibition on their internal domestic distribution.

constitution itself does not require referendums for constitutional change. The first, a national referendum on the European Union in 1975, was followed by referendums on Scottish and Welsh devolution in 1979 and 1997 (see Chapter 11). Since then three major referendums have been held, one in 1998 agreeing to the creation of a Greater London Authority, another in 1998 supporting an agreement about the government of Northern Ireland (see Chapter 10), and one in 2004 rejecting an elected assembly for the North East Region of England. Between 2001 and 2004 there were 31 referendums held by local authorities to decide which political structure to adopt (Local Government Act 2000), and a national referendum is promised on whether the United Kingdom should join the euro.

Judicial review

The growth of judicial review started before membership of the EU gave the courts additional power. Some of the most important cases are discussed in Chapter 19, but here it is important to note the following:

■ The courts of Britain have been increasingly willing since the 1960s to take a more proactive role in reviewing the decisions and actions of politicians in both central and local government. A notable example was the Law Lords' rejection by a vote of 8–1 in 2004 of the government's anti-terrorist laws.

■ A small proportion of cases have introduced radically different constitutional principles. For example, in 1993 the House of Lords ruled that the Home Secretary was in contempt of court in his action on an asylum case. The case was important because it deprived ministers of their age-old right to claim Crown immunity for their actions.

■ The number of applications for judicial review has multiplied many times since the early 1980s. Many of them fail, but the growth shows that judicial review, like referendums, are an integral part of the constitutional system.

New Labour's 'constitutional project'

The constitutional implications of membership of the EU, referendums and judicial review are profound in themselves, but the election of New Labour in 1997 resulted in even more far-reaching change.

From the mid-1930s to the mid-1980s the Labour Party was traditionalist about constitutional issues, although a few MPs (e.g. the left-wing MP Tony Benn) supported reform. Most Labour leaders saw little need, given that the system enabled them to win power periodically. Left-wingers such as Michael Foot (Labour leader 1980–3) were as likely to take this view as Labour right-wingers.

Labour's change of heart had several causes:

1. The party had been an impotent opposition for 18 years (1979–97) and the fear that it might not win another election made constitutional reform more attractive, as well as building bridges with the nationalists and Liberal Democrats, who favoured reform and might be required to help Labour form a government.

2. Many were dismayed by what they regarded as the Conservative governments' (1979–97) excessive secrecy, disregard for individual and group rights, and increasing concentration of political power in their own hands.

3. The lack of power of backbench MPs in the two main parties.

4. In theory, the House of Lords acts as a constitutional backstop, but its large Conservative majority on most issues meant that it rarely opposed Conservative government measures.

5. Scottish Labour was converted to the merits of a Scottish Parliament because from 1979 to 1997 Scotland was ruled by a Conservative government, even though an overwhelming proportion of Scots voted against it. Scottish Nationalists effectively exploited this situation to campaign for an independent Scotland, steadily increased their vote, and replaced the Conservatives as the main challengers in Labour areas. For the Labour Party acceptance of a Scottish Parliament – which Labour would anyway expect to dominate – was seen as a small but necessary price to pay for heading off the SNP and 'dishing' the Tories in Scotland.

6. Once the case for a Scottish Parliament was conceded, it followed that the Welsh should have an Assembly of their own (see Chapter 11 on Scotland and Wales), and perhaps also the English regions and the large metropolitan areas as well.

In office the Labour government moved with remarkable speed on some matters, but slowly on others.

Independence for the Bank of England

Within four days of being elected, Gordon Brown, the Labour chancellor of the exchequer, announced to almost everyone's surprise that the Bank of England would follow the pattern of many central banks in Europe, and have the power to set interest rates independently of the government. Although not a major constitutional change in itself, this signalled the willingness of the central government to devolve power.

Human rights

After many calls for a British Bill of Rights, and quite a few failed attempts in Parliament, the Human Rights Act was passed in 1998. This incorporates into British law the European Convention on Human Rights which is implemented by the European Court of Human Rights (ECHR) in Strasbourg (see Chapter 9). British government is now required to ensure that its legislation is consistent with the Convention. One important little corner of the Act, however, tries to protect the old constitutional order. To preserve 'parliamentary sovereignty' (or the myth that it still exists) the courts cannot strike down parliamentary legislation, but can only issue a 'declaration of incompatibility'. It is not clear what would happen if the government or Parliament chose to ignore such a declaration.

In spite of alarm that human rights cases would choke the courts, the Act (implemented in 2000) bedded down successfully. There were, however, a number of important legal decisions flowing from new legislation, including the much publicized case of Diane Pretty who, with the terminal illness of motor-neurone disease, had her case for assisted suicide turned down by the European Court of Human Rights in 2002. In the same year the EHCR overturned the home secretary's decision to keep a serial offender in prison. In 2003 the United Kingdom was criticised by the European Union for its Anti-Terrorism, Crime and Security Act 2001 (the government's response to the 9/11 attacks in the United States) which allowed non-UK nationals to be held in indefinite administrative detention without being charged or having the right of appeal. Detention without charge became an important civil rights issue, and in 2005 the House of Lords defeated a government bill 19 times before emergency legislation was passed giving the home secretary unprecedented powers of control (including curfews, tagging and house arrest) without suspects being charged or convicted.

Scottish and Welsh devolution

After referendums in 1997, the Scottish Parliament and the Welsh Assembly were created (see Chapter 11 for more details of their powers). Some feel these arrangements in Scotland and Wales are inherently unstable. They are not so much final decisions that have been made once and for all. Rather they form a long-term process in which both regions will demand more and more power over their affairs. They also create an anomaly (the 'West Lothian question') whereby Scottish and Welsh MPs can speak and vote on questions of relevance to the English regions that come before the House of Commons, but English MPs in the Commons cannot speak or vote on matters of relevance to Scotland and Wales in areas that come before their elected bodies.

Home Rule in Northern Ireland

Between 1972 and 1997 Northern Ireland was ruled from London, but as a result of the Good Friday Agreement of 1998 (confirmed by a referendum in the same year) the Northern Ireland Assembly at Stormont was re-elected in June 1998. Its powers are similar, but not identical, to those of the Scottish Parliament. The long-term fate of the NI Assembly remains in the balance, however, after devolved government was suspended in October 2002 (see Chapter 10).

London government

The Greater London Authority Act 1999 provides for a directly elected executive mayor of London and a separately elected London Assembly with 25 members. They first took office in July 2000, and have responsibility, in consultation with the 32 London boroughs, for metropolitan-wide policies, including London transport, police, fire, emergency planning, economic development, the environment and culture. Most of the Authority's £3,000 million consolidated budget is met by the central government. The London mayor has little formal political power, but the current holder Ken Livingstone, has high political visibility and is a political influence outside central government. Livingstone's battles with central government over the funding of the London underground have hit the headlines, as has his role in securing the Olympics for London. His controversial congestion charge for vehicles in central London was fiercely criticised when introduced, but is generally regarded as a success.

The House of Lords

As a first stage of reform the House of Lords Act 1999 removed most hereditary peers from the Lords, leaving life peers in control. The second stage of reform is not yet decided, although the opposition parties and many Labour MPs want an almost wholly elected Chamber with greater powers than the present House of Lords.

The Labour government therefore has to decide between a largely appointed or elected Upper House. An appointed House, composed of elder statesmen and eminent figures ('the great and the good') from various fields of life, might lack popular democratic legitimacy. At the same time, a directly elected Upper House (which is strongly favoured by most citizens) would have democratic credentials that could lead it to challenge the House of Commons. This dilemma slowed the second stage of Lords reform after 1999, and stalled it completely in February 2003 when all the government's proposals for reform were rejected by the House of Commons. Since then, the issue has made no progress, but it remains a major issue not least because the Lords have fiercely resisted a good deal of government legislation in recent years. The government's powers to nominate members of the House and make them 'life peers' have frequently caused controversy. In early 2006 a scandal blew up over Labour Party donors being nominated for peerages.

Electoral reform

From the beginning Britain has used the first past the post electoral system in general elections. This simple voting method often produces single-party government in Parliament and stable and accountable single-party government in the House of Commons. It is also associated with electoral unfairness (**disproportionality**), which favours major parties and discriminates against minor ones (see Chapter 15). In the general election of 2005 Labour took 35 per cent of the votes and 55 per cent of the seats, while the Liberal Democrats won 22 per cent of the votes but less than 10 per cent of the seats.

> **Disproportionality**
>
> (the opposite of proportionality) Occurs when the seats in a representative body are not distributed in relationship to votes. Proportionality (proportional representation) occurs, therefore, when there is a close relationship between the distribution of seats and votes.

Labour has contemplated electoral reform for some time, and when it came to power in 1997 it introduced the additional member system for Welsh, Scottish and London Assembly elections (for details of voting systems see Chapter 15). For the London mayoral elections, however, it introduced the supplementary vote, while in elections for the European Parliament it introduced, in accordance with a European directive, a version of the regional list system (the European Parliamentary Elections Act 1999). In Northern Ireland the single transferable vote system is used for the Assembly and the European Parliament. The result is that five different election systems are currently used in the United Kingdom, but the main target of criticism – the use of first past the post voting in general and local elections – remains unreformed.

Labour is deeply ambivalent about reforming the voting system for general elections. Its own commission on electoral reform (the Plant Commission) was divided on the issue. On the one hand, Labour is acutely aware that the Conservatives won four successive elections with a minority of votes between 1979 and 1993, and yet managed to push through unpopular policies such as water and railway privatisation, the poll tax and VAT on fuel. On the other hand, changing to a proportional representation (PR) system would have two major drawbacks for Labour. First, it would lose some seats under PR. Second, since no party has won an absolute majority of votes since 1935, a proportional system would almost certainly mean coalition government in the House of Commons. Electoral reform might well mean the end of single-party Conservative government, it is true, but equally it would mean that Labour would always have to share power with one or more minor parties.

Referendums

New Labour built on the practice of calling referendums on major issues (Welsh and Scottish devolution, London government, Northern Ireland, and a regional authority for the North East of England), and it has promised two more over a new electoral system and Britain joining the euro, when the time comes.

Freedom of information

After delay, backbench revolts and much criticism, the Freedom of Information Act was passed in 2000 and came fully into force in 2005. The Act is supposed to provide a general right of access to all types of recorded information held by public authorities. It places obligations on them to observe these rights within 20 working days of a request, and creates an Information Commissioner to enforce them. However, there are 36 categories of exemption and ministers and local government can use 'harm to public safety' as a reason for refusing to release information. As a result many believe that the Act is no real improvement on the voluntary code of practice it replaced. Nonethless, in the first three months of 2005 a total of 13,400 requests for information were registered and by the end of the year information had been released about a variety of matters, including a police inquiry into a shooting, safety hazards, parking fines, school violence, school funding, plans for nuclear waste disposal sites and food safety. Equally, there have been many delays beyond the 20 working days requirement in the release of information, and by the end of 2005 the Information Commissioner had accumulated more than 1,300 unresolved complaints.

Even if the Freedom of Information Act is a small step forward, two other Acts are a step back. The Regulation of Investigatory Powers Act 2000 gives government access to electronic information previously not available to it, and the Terrorist Act 2000 broadens and strengthens government powers.

Constitutional Reform Act 2005

Constitutional theory argues for a separation of powers to ensure that power is not concentrated in too few hands. This means keeping the political executive (prime minister and Cabinet), the legislative bodies (Lords and Commons) and the judiciary apart. In Britain, however, the Lord Chancellor presides over the House of Lords, is the head of the judicial branch of government, and is a member of the Cabinet. The Constitutional Reform Act of 2005 changed this, providing for an independent Supreme Court of the United Kingdom to take over the powers of the Law Lords, transferring the judicial functions of the Lord Chancellor to a newly created post of President of the Courts of England and Wales, and establishing an independent Judicial Appointments Commission to recommend names for judicial office. It is likely that a new job of Speaker of the House of Lords (a job traditionally performed by the Lord Chancellor) will be created.

Guardians of the constitution

Many of the constitutional reforms are shored up by a set of new public offices created to ensure their proper workings. In addition to the ombudsmen, the National Audit Office and the Civil Service Commissioners, there are also the following:

- the Electoral Commission, for elections, referendums and constituency boundaries

- the Committee on Standards in Public Life to conduct inquiries, reports and research into public attitudes, issues and concerns relating to standards in public life

- the Information Commissioner to promote access to official information and protect personal information

- the Commissioner for Public Appointments to regulate, monitor, report and advise on appointments made by UK ministers and members of the National

BRIEFINGS

4.4 British democracy

I've been thinking a lot since the election about what a lousy system of democracy we've got in this country ... how did we ever get into a position where a government gets a majority of nearly 70 with only 21.5% of the electorate voting for them ... how did we end up in the last parliament with a House of Commons totally unable to hold the executive to account on issues that mattered, and why did we have such a supine cabinet who didn't realise that one of their central roles in our democracy was to hold the prime minister in check? With a couple of honourable exceptions, why didn't they ask to see the Foreign Office papers on Iraq or the attorney general's advice? ... And then I've been asking myself what can we all do about it, because something has to be done.

Greg Dyke, the *Guardian*, 31 May 2005. Greg Dyke resigned as Director General of the BBC in 2004 as a result of heavy criticism of the Corporation over its reporting of Iraq's weapons of mass destruction (see Chapter 14).

Assembly for Wales to the boards of around 1,100 national and regional public bodies, and some bodies in Northern Ireland

■ the Parliamentary Commissioner for Standards to keep the Register of Members' Interests, advise MPs on their conduct and investigate complaints

■ Appointments Commission to recommend people for appointment as non-party-political life peers

■ the Commission for Judicial Appointments to review the judicial and Queen's Counsel appointment procedures and investigate complaints about the operation of those procedures

The incomplete programme

Experts on constitutional matters differ widely on the significance of New Labour's constitutional project. Some claim that British government is pretty much as powerful and unaccountable as it ever was (see Briefing 4.4). Others argue that it has modified but not transformed the cohesive, unitary and flexible nature of the traditional system. A third school claims that the innovations after 1972, and especially 1997, amount to nothing less than a constitutional revolution.

However one views the constitutional reform programme starting in 1997, it is clear that it is unfinished. The Scottish and London authorities are likely to push for greater devolved powers, and a report to the Welsh Assembly has already done so. The fate of the Northern Ireland Assembly still hangs in the balance. Freedom of information is unsatisfactory. Other aspects of reform have run into the sand. Major issues about the House of Lords and the Lord Chancellor's office are unresolved. Regional devolution in England has been shelved after the single, unsuccessful referendum in the north-east. Reform of the voting system in general elections is virtually untouched. Postal voting is easier, although a judge described evidence of electoral fraud in local elections in 2004 as something that would disgrace a banana republic. Electronic voting is being investigated further but that, too, is amenable to fraud. Other fundamental matters have barely been tackled: the relative weakness of the House of Commons, government secrecy, the financing of political parties (an issue revived in 2006 by questions about donations to the Labour Party), the over-centralisation of the political system.

We will return to the issue of democracy and the British constitution at the end of the book (Chapter 27), after looking in greater depth at particular parts of it in the chapters that follow. Meanwhile we can note that the issue remains a hotly contested and topical one which is still far from resolved. Surveys show that nearly two-thirds of the population believe that the way Britain is governed needs 'quite a lot' or 'a great deal of improvement', and over half believe that Britain is becoming less democratic. Once an issue of little interest but great pride, the British constitution is now more of a matter of concern and criticism.

Summary

This chapter has summarised the main sources and features of Britain's 'unwritten constitution', starting from the question of whether it really is a constitution at all. Certainly its informal and diffuse nature leaves it open to manipulation by the powerful central governments it has helped to create, and this has been a source of growing concern. The particular constitutional features highlighted by this chapter are:

■ The partially written and wholly uncodified nature of the British constitution.

■ The extent to which it has to be supplemented by 'conventions', practices or customs that can, however, be radically reinterpreted, or even ignored, if it suits the party in power.

■ The principal doctrines of the traditional constitution: a unitary state; parliamentary sovereignty; constitutional monarchy; power concentrated within central government; government accountability; and representative (rather than direct) democracy.

■ Defenders of the traditional constitution argue that it has produced a durable basis for democracy with stable, effective and moderate government that works pragmatically.

■ Critics argue that the conventions of ministerial and Cabinet accountability do not always work, and that secrecy, inflexibility and too much power in central government's hands create an 'elective dictatorship'.

■ Changes in the traditional constitution were brought about by membership of the EU, and by the willingness of British courts to play a larger role in constitutional matters (judicial review).

■ New Labour's constitutional project resulted in an unprecedented series of reforms between 1997 and 2000. Some argue these have had profound effects on the traditional constitution, some that the effects are modest, but all agree that the reform programme is still incomplete.

MILESTONES

Milestones in British constitutional development

1215	Magna Carta (The Great Charter). English Barons force King John to recognise their personal rights (which later extend to all freemen) and their right to collective consultation about important matters
1296–1306	Edward I begins to summon representatives of towns and counties, regularly, along with the Lords, to agree to taxation for the Scottish wars. In return, the King makes concessions to meet their requests, a process that continues for the next 200 years
1532–59	Parliament is used by the Tudor monarchs to ratify the most important royal actions (settling succession, setting up Protestant Church, etc.)
1640–51	Parliament fights Civil War against Crown and wins. Establishes its supremacy over the Law Courts
1688–9	Bill of Rights. Parliament deposes James II and installs William III as king (the Glorious Revolution). It reaffirms that taxes can only be raised with its consent and affirms specific citizens' rights
1701	Act of Settlement. Parliament establishes (Protestant) succession

Milestones in British constitutional development continued

1707	Act of Union with Scotland. The English Parliament absorbs the Scottish one, but accepts the separate Scottish legal system and Church
1715–1832	The 'Eighteenth-Century Constitution'. The government has to be acceptable to the king but must also maintain a majority in the House of Commons. Party organisations ('Whigs' and 'Tories') develop from time to time to secure and organise this majority
1832	Great Reform Act substitutes election for ownership of seats as the basis for representation in the House of Commons. Election is within small constituencies by plurality vote on the first past the post system
1838	Accession of the 18-year-old Victoria marks end of active involvement of monarch with the government, which is now effectively nominated by the largest party in the House of Commons
1867	Second Reform Act (Representation of the People Act) extends franchise to most male town dwellers
1868–86	Conservative and Liberal parties create mass organisations throughout Britain and alternate in government with support of a Commons majority
1884	Third Reform Act (Representation of the People Act) extends franchise to most male country dwellers
1911	Parliament Act. Reforming Liberal government with support of Commons majority restricts powers of (hereditary) House of Lords: (a) over financial bills, (b) to delaying any legislation for only three years
1918	Representation of the People Act enfranchises all remaining males over 21 and women over 30
1922	Government of Ireland Act sets up regional Parliament and government in Northern Ireland
1928	Representation of the People Act gives women the vote on the same terms as men
1949	Parliament Act. Reforming Labour government restricts delaying powers of House of Lords to one year
1963	Peerage Act. Creation of 'life peers' to serve in House of Lords but not to pass on title to children
1969	Representation of the People Act reduces voting age to 18
1972	European Communities Act. Britain accedes to the EU and accepts that all previous European legislation and judicial decisions are binding and European legislation superior to British legislation
1973–4	UK Parliament abolishes Northern Irish government and Parliament
1986	Single European Act extends competence of EU. Qualified majority voting in the Council of Ministers means that UK government cannot veto European provisions it disagrees with, in the areas where they apply
1993	Treaty of Maastricht further extends European Union's area of jurisdiction and use of qualified majority voting
1997	New Labour government accepts the Social Chapter of the Treaty of Maastricht. Bank of England given powers to set the interest rate. Referendums on Welsh and Scottish devolution
1998	Human Rights Act. Scotland Act. Government of Wales Act. Referendum on the Good Friday Agreement followed by Northern Ireland Act and reintroduction of Home Rule for Northern Ireland. London referendum
1999	First election to Scottish Parliament and Welsh Assembly, under system of proportional representation. Greater London Authority Act. House of Lords Act. European Parliamentary Elections Act to introduce the regional list voting system
2000	Freedom of Information Act. Representation of the People Act (introduces various measures to encourage turnout)
2002	Official proposals for regional government in England
2003	House of Lords reform stalls
2004	Proposals for an elected assembly for the north-east of England rejected in a referendum
2005	Constitutional Reform Act provides for an independent judiciary and reform of the office of Lord Chancellor. Freedom of Information Act comes fully into force.

Essays

1. Do you agree that Labour reforms, 1997–2005, have changed the British constitution profoundly? Why or why not?

2. Is it fair to say that the traditional British constitution of 1911–72 was marked by the characteristics of government secrecy, conventions of ministerial and Cabinet responsibility that often did not work, lack of government accountability and elective dictatorship?

3. Do you agree that Britain needs a written constitution? Why or why not?

Projects

1. Imagine that you are Home Secretary. How would you complete reform of the House of Lords and how would you change, if at all, the electoral system for general and local elections?

2. (For groups.) Each member of the group to take one of the following and discuss the respects in which it does and does not change the traditional British constitution of 1911–72: the Human Rights Act 1998; the Scotland Act and the Government of Wales Act 1998; the Greater London Authority Act 1999; Freedom of Information Act 2000; and the Regulation of Investigatory Powers Act 2000.

3. Do you agree with the claim that the House of Commons is totally unable to hold the executive to account on issues that matter?

Further reading

The best and most up-to-date introduction to the traditional constitution and recent changes is Anthony King, *Does the United Kingdom Still Have a Constitution?* (London: Sweet & Maxwell, 2001). A short recent book is K. Harrison and T. Boyd, *The Changing Constitution* (Manchester: The Politics Association, 2006). Recent assessments of British democracy are in I. Byrne and S. Weir, 'Democratic audit: Executive democracy in war and peace', *Parliamentary Affairs*, **57** (2), 2004, pp. 453–68; L. Maer *et al.*, 'The constitution: dragging the constitution out of the shadows', *Parliamentary Affairs*, **57** (2), 2004, pp. 253–68; and N. Forman 'The state and the people: Britain's changing constitution', *Talking Politics*, February 2004, pp. 26–8.

On party attitudes towards constitutional change see N. McNaughton, 'Constitutional reform in the United Kingdom', *Talking Politics*, April 2004, pp. 121–5. On referendums see M. McCartney, 'Oh referendum, where art thou?', *Talking Politics*, September 2003, pp. 19–22. M. Ryan, 'The House of Lords: Options for reform', *Talking Politics*, September 2003, pp. 29–31 discusses in detail the options presented to and rejected by the House of Commons and the House of Lords in 2003. Whether the UK is a liberal democracy is discussed in M. Garnett, *Talking Politics*, November 2005, pp. 24–6.

Useful web sites on the British constitution

Hot links to these sites can be found on the CWS at www.pearsoned.co.uk/budge.

For a comprehensive introduction to the core doctrines of the British constitution, see www.historylearningsite.co.uk/british_constitution.htm. There are also some sites containing information on the sources of constitutional authority. For example, the British Library offers an electronic version of Magna Carta at www.bl.uk/collections/treasures/magna.html and an interesting description of the 1689 Bill of Rights can be found at www.royal.gov.uk/output/ page100.asp. The main governmental sites with constitutional information are http://www.dca.gov.uk/constitution/reform/pubs.htm and the Parliament site, www.parliament.uk.

Academic commentary and analysis on constitutional issues are available from the Constitution Unit at University College London, www.ucl.ac.uk/constitution-unit. For careful and systemic evaluations of the state of British democracy, see www.democraticaudit.com and http://www.powerinquiry.org/report/index.php

For the implications of British EU membership on the constitution, see www.europa.eu.int and the Home Office at www.homeoffice.gov.uk. More specific information about the European Court of Justice is available from www.curia.eu.int/en/index.htm.

chapter 5

The Prime Minister, the Cabinet and the core executive

We have seen that the British constitution gives exceptional power to governments. Since the Prime Minister is the most powerful member of the Cabinet, and the Cabinet is effectively the governing committee of the country, this small group comprises the most powerful people in Britain. The way they work together and with a small core of other political influentials raises a host of important and controversial questions about the British system of government. Has the office of Prime Minister (PM) been transformed from the traditional 'first among equals' into a powerful political executive akin, in many ways, to a president? Or is the Cabinet still the effective centre of all important decision making? How do the prime ministerial styles of Thatcher, Major and Blair compare, and what effect does this have on the fate of their governments? How is the work of Prime Minister and Cabinet organised, and how do they relate to the broader apparatus of government?

The chapter is divided into seven main sections. They describe how the machinery of government works at this, the highest level of government, and how different officials and agencies interact in the decision-making process. The chapter focuses on:

- the Prime Minister

- the Cabinet

- the Cabinet, departments and joined-up government

- the eternal political triangle: departments, Cabinet and Prime Minister

- prime ministerial styles: Thatcher, Major, Blair

- prime ministerial versus Cabinet government

- the core executive.

The Prime Minister

Prime Minister

The head of the executive branch of government and chair of the Cabinet.

Since Britain has no written constitution, the powers and duties of the **Prime Minister** are neither clearly defined nor legally limited. They have evolved according to historical circumstances since 1721 when Robert Walpole started to create what is now regarded as the modern prime ministerial role. Since then there have been 51 prime ministers (post-war premiers are listed in Table 5.1), each exercising authority in different ways. Consequently, it is difficult to say exactly what the job of the PM is. As one incumbent (Herbert Asquith, prime minister 1908–16) remarked, it is 'what the office holder chooses and is able to make of it'. It is clear

Table 5.1 Post-war prime ministers

Prime Minister	Dates	Party
Clement Attlee	1945–51	Labour
Sir Winston Churchill	1951–5	Conservative
Sir Anthony Eden	1955–7	Conservative
Harold Macmillan	1957–63	Conservative
Sir Alec Douglas-Home	1963–4	Conservative
Harold Wilson	1964–70	Labour
Edward Heath	1970–4	Conservative
Harold Wilson	1974–6	Labour
James Callaghan	1976–9	Labour
Margaret Thatcher	1979–90	Conservative
John Major	1990–7	Conservative
Tony Blair	1997–	Labour

that the Prime Minister is the head of government at home (the monarch is the head of state), and the political representative of the country abroad, but this job description hides a multitude of responsibilities and powers. Among other things, the Prime Minister:

- Decides the number and nature of Cabinet and government posts and who is to fill them. This requires restructuring the Cabinet and its membership from time to time.

- Chairs Cabinet meetings, manages their agendas and discussion, calls on speakers, sums up discussion, and directs the writing of minutes.

- Decides the number and nature of Cabinet committees, subcommittees and ministerial groups, and appoints their chairs and members. Chairs some of the most important committees.

- Oversees the armed forces and security services.

- Manages relations between the Cabinet and the wider world of Parliament, the media, other countries, and international organisations – far and away the most important being the EU.

- Manages the flow of government information to the outside world.

- Answers formal questions in the House of Commons (Prime Minister's Questions – PMQs).

- Approves senior positions in the Civil Service and the diplomatic service. Recommends senior appointments in the Church of England, the judiciary, the Privy Council, quangos and other civil positions.

- Has a hand in the honours list.

- Dissolves Parliament before calling an election.

- Takes the lead in crises of government and the governing party.

- Leads the governing party and maintains contact with its MPs and party headquarters.

- Maintains contact with heads of other states as necessary.

- Keeps watch on the broad political agenda and the course of government.

BRIEFINGS

5.1 A day in the life of the Prime Minister

07.00	Wake
07.30	Family breakfast
08.00	Go over the day's diary with PM Office staff
08.30	Briefing meeting on political issue of the day
09.00	Meeting with No. 10 staff on education
10.00	Meeting on election reform
10.30	Briefing on PM Question Time
10.45	Visit the secretariat in the PM's Office
11.45	Briefing on freedom of information seminar
12.00	Seminar on freedom of information (Salad/sandwich lunch)
13.15	Interview with journalist
14.15	Seminar with policy advisers
15.15	Meeting with foreign head of state
16.00	Meeting with national politician
16.30	Meeting with top civil servant
17.00	Meeting with Cabinet colleague
17.30	Meeting with Cabinet colleague
18.00	Meeting about Cabinet committee business
19.30	Private dinner/family time
22.00	House of Commons vote/read official documents
23.00	Sleep

Note: Based on different sources.

Even this list, long though it is, does not capture the staggering range and responsibilities of the Prime Minister. Being head of government involves many tasks ranging from formal representation of the nation and crisis management at home and abroad, to guiding the daily work of the government and maintaining contact with senior figures in the government, Parliament and Civil Service at home, and senior statesmen abroad. This means constant travel, a ceaseless round of meetings, an endless chain of decision making, and incessant public appearances. The job is as demanding as it is difficult and as Tony Blair has put it: 'nothing prepares you for the difficulty of being prime minister'.

Margaret Thatcher, stormbird of British politics

It is clear, even from recent history, that prime ministers bring very different qualities, aptitudes and interests to the job. Margaret Thatcher was possibly the most memorable prime minister of the post-war period, unique in many respects. Though no feminist, she is the only woman to have held the post. But she was perhaps better known as a woman with a mission – to regenerate Britain – with a force and energy that stirred strong feelings of love or loathing.

From lower-middle-class origins (her father was a shopkeeper, but mayor of his town of Grantham) she went from the local grammar school to a chemistry degree at Oxford, followed by a law qualification. She was elected to Parliament in 1959, and within 11 years was minister of education in the Heath government of 1970.

Two events precipitated her break with the 'social democratic consensus' that had prevailed since the war. One was the election defeat of the Conservative government in 1974, following strike action by trade unions. The other, her conversion to free market policies on the grounds that government failure was due to 'overloading' the state with too much taxation and responsibility.

Winning the 1979 general election as the result of a general distaste for trade union action in the 'winter of discontent', she set out on a radical campaign to 'get government off the backs of the people' by cutting taxation and public services, reducing government regulation and privatising state enterprises. Her three successive general election victories (1979, 1983, 1987) had a lot to do with her forceful and dynamic politics, which seemed to make her political position impregnable, in spite of an increasingly autocratic style. When this led to the hugely unpopular poll tax (see Chapter 12) and open hostility with the Europhiles in her own party (see Chapter 8) her Cabinet dumped her for fear of losing the 1992 general election. She was the longest serving Prime Minister for 150 years and was replaced in No. 10 by John Major in 1990.

John Major: overreaction to Thatcher?

John Major came from a poor London family. The son of a circus performer and manufacturer of garden gnomes, he left grammar school at 16 with almost no qualifications, but rose rapidly through banking, a short period of local government experience, to election as a Conservative MP in 1979 – the year that Thatcher came to power. He was favoured by her during the 1980s precisely because he had no connections with the traditional Conservative grandees. Ten years after his election, Thatcher made him Foreign Secretary, and in short order he became Leader of the House, Deputy Prime Minister, and Chancellor of the Exchequer. He replaced Thatcher as Prime Minister in 1990.

Although a Thatcher supporter in the 1980s, he rapidly distanced his government from hers by abolishing the poll tax, taking up a more pro-European political stance, and adopting a radically different political style. He replaced the autocracy of the Thatcher era with something more collegial and unassuming. He succeeded in winning the 1992 election as a result but immediately ran into serious trouble when a mismanaged currency crisis forced the pound out of the European Monetary System. Government infighting over Europe, and a growing national concern over government 'sleaze' added to his reputation for being a weak and ineffective leader, and he was defeated spectacularly in the general election of 1997 by Blair and New Labour.

Tony Blair and New Labour

Blair and Major form a striking contrast in style and background: Major came from an underprivileged background, while Blair shares an exclusive background with many Conservative MPs. Born in Edinburgh in 1953, the son of a barrister and lecturer, Blair attended Fettes public school, went on to Oxford to study law and began a barrister's practice in London. He was attracted to Labour by his Christian Socialist beliefs and after winning his first parliamentary election in 1983 rose as fast as Major through his party ranks to a shadow Cabinet post in 1988. When John Smith, the Labour leader, died suddenly in 1994 Blair stepped into his shoes and immediately set about changing the Labour Party along lines already initiated by his predecessors Kinnock and Smith.

Under the slogan 'New Labour, New Britain', Blair led Labour away from its policies of nationalisation, high taxation, universal welfare benefits, alignment with the trade unions and 'Old Labour'. In their place he put centrist ('Third Way') policies – cautious economics, low taxation, a leaning towards free markets, and support for the EU. He loosened Labour's close ties to the unions, and introduced the most modern of public relations systems. He abolished Labour's Clause 4, which committed the party to public ownership, but emphasised the importance of high-quality education ('education, education, education'), and changed its image on law and order. As opposition spokesman on home affairs he caught the headlines and outflanked a startled Conservative government by claiming to be 'tough on crime, tough on the causes of crime'.

By taking the centre ground, he was able to maximise Labour's advantage over an unpopular and factious Conservative government in the mid-1990s, and was elected as Prime Minister by a landslide in 1997. Labour had been in opposition for 18 years. At 43 he was the youngest Prime Minister in almost 200 years, and the first to have a child born at No. 10 Downing Street for 150 years. Blair's goal in 1997, however, was not one term in office (five years) but at least three in order to complete his programme of reforms. New Labour started cautiously, adopting the outgoing Conservative government's budget, but engaged in an ambitious programme of constitutional reform (see the previous chapter). The result was another landslide win in 2001, and a more modest victory in 2005.

Freedom and constraint on PM power: hiring and firing

The great diversity of prime ministerial styles is not surprising given the lack of constitutional rules about their role and their wide range of powers. There is plenty of room to exercise their personal strengths and weaknesses. But personal characteristics are not the only thing that matter here. In their daily working life prime ministers are also limited by the force of circumstances. To illustrate this we will focus on the power to hire and fire members of the Cabinet and the government, partly because it is so important, and partly because it illustrates the powers and limitations of the office very well.

In theory, prime ministers have a free hand to decide how large or small their Cabinets are. In practice there are natural limits to Cabinet size. It is presently 23 strong, with another 1 'in attendance', but it has been as small as 16, and during the war Churchill's Cabinet had 10 members. For the most part, however, much less than 15 is too small to cover all the important aspects of modern government, and much more than 25 is too large for an effective committee. Most recent prime ministers have settled for a cabinet of 20–23.

In theory, prime ministers can merge or divide Cabinet posts in any way they want. The present Cabinet combines responsibility for Scotland with transport, and Wales and Northern Ireland go together. Culture goes with media and sport, and education is joined with skills. There is one post with no specific departmental duties (Minister without Portfolio). In practice, however, some Cabinet posts are more or less fixed – Chancellor of the Exchequer, Home Secretary, Foreign Secretary, and education, health, social services, transport, the environment, Scotland, Wales and Northern Ireland must be represented in one form or another.

In theory, prime ministers can fill Cabinet posts as they wish. In practice, they may be severely restricted in their choice:

- The convention is that most Cabinet members, and especially the most important ones, must be answerable to, and therefore members of, the House of Commons. This has 646 members.

- In single-party governments Cabinet members must be drawn from the majority party – usually between 330 and 400 individuals.

- Some powerful figures virtually select themselves for high office – Blair must find Cabinet places for Prescott, Brown and Straw.

- Other posts must be filled from a small pool of possibilities – the Welsh or Scottish offices are normally filled by Welsh and Scottish MPs.

- Some MPs are ruled out of holding government positions. Blair is unlikely to be able to reappoint Blunkett, Mandelson or Byers, if the question ever arose.

- The Cabinet should be a balance of men and women, maturity and promise, different political factions (left and right, Europhiles and Europhobes). The PM must take care to keep the government together and not leave out a potentially disruptive faction.

- Having filled Cabinet posts, the PM must fill more than 100 other government posts, most of them from a total pool of not much more than 300 members of the parliamentary party.

Once the political has-beens, the never-will-bes and those with difficult histories have been ruled out, the Prime Minister may be left with rather little choice. This is not to say that the PM has no room for manoeuvre. Some powerful political figures have been kept out of the Cabinet by their prime minister, or out of the Cabinet post they really wanted. Thatcher and Blair have contrived to put their own supporters into important government positions, and Cabinet sackings, promotions and reshuffles are fairly frequent as prime ministers try to balance the demands of political circumstances and groups jockeying for power. Equally, two very successful post-war prime ministers, Macmillan and Thatcher, seem to have signalled weakness rather than strength when they engaged in major Cabinet reshuffles in 1962 and 1989. Both were soon out of power.

In sum, the PM's powers to hire and fire government members are, as are many other functions of the office, a mixture of surprising freedom and constraint. There is often little choice, and some ministers choose themselves by virtue of their political position and stature. At the same time some PMs have juggled the careers of powerful people and have shaped governments to their own taste.

The Prime Minister's Office

We have emphasised the enormous number of prime ministerial tasks, and the extreme pressures of the job, but the PM does not carry this burden alone. He is supported by a staff of about 45–50 senior officials, and a total staff of over 200 in the Prime Minister's Office. Some are Civil Service appointments, others are purely political. Numbers in the Office are steadily rising and its organisation constantly changing, but the work centres around the following:

- The Policy Directorate, which has a staff of about 30, and includes the PM's private office (led by a Chief of Staff) and the Policy Directorate, which deals with short-term policy issues.

- The Strategy Unit, with a staff of 60 working on long-term issues of policy and implementation.

- Communications. Not just the Prime Minister's but *all* government press releases and briefing documents flow through this office. The Prime Minister's press secretary is very influential, therefore (think Alastair Campbell).

- Political operations – the management and development of the government's political strategy. This is directed by a Labour Party appointee who is paid by the party.

- Government relations – the management and development of the PM's relations with the government agencies of central, regional and local government.

The Prime Minister's Office works closely with the Cabinet Office (see below), and with the Whip's Office in Parliament (see Chapter 18), and has close and constant contact with all the main executive agencies and government departments in Whitehall, including the Deputy Prime Minister's Office, which was created in 2002 and has a staff of its own. Under Blair, the PM's Office, the Cabinet Office and the Deputy Prime Minister's Office have become, in effect, a single, centralised executive office.

The kitchen cabinet

Kitchen cabinet

The loose and informal policy advice group that prime ministers may collect around them, and that may include politicians, public officials and private citizens.

This is not the end of the story. Prime ministers often gather around them a collection of personal friends and advisers they can trust. They are often private individuals, not government officials, but they have direct access ('face time') to the PM. They are often resented by 'regular' politicians and civil servants, although one can appreciate the PM's need for advice he can trust from outside official circles. Thatcher and Blair seem to have made extensive use of their **kitchen cabinets**, but Major relied more on the official Cabinet. Being a closed and constantly informal circle of associates, friends and insiders, the composition of the kitchen cabinet is a matter of speculation and, in any case, it probably changes quite quickly according to circumstances.

The Cabinet

Cabinet

The committee of the leading members of the government who are empowered to make decisions on behalf of the government.

The **Cabinet** must not be confused with the government. There are usually 20–25 Cabinet members but more than 110 people in the government, including Cabinet ministers and others who attend Cabinet, junior ministers (27), parliamentary under-secretaries and private secretaries (37), whips (23) and law officers (3). Most Cabinet members are drawn from the House of Commons because of the convention that they should be accountable to the elected chamber of government, but some come from the Lords. Most Cabinet members are ministers who run Whitehall departments (Table 5.2).

The Cabinet, like the Prime Minister's Office, has changed over time. Churchill had only 10 members in his wartime Cabinet, and experimented with 16 'overlords' in 1951. The experiment did not last long and the Cabinet soon returned to its normal size. Whatever its size and composition, the Cabinet is the central committee of government. Its main purposes are as follows:

- to take major government decisions and approve government policy

- to reconcile the responsibilities of ministers to their individual departments with their responsibilities to the government as a whole

- to resolve any differences between ministers acting in their departmental capacities.

The Cabinet coordinates the policies of Whitehall departments and directs the work of government as a whole. As such it is the 'central committee' of the government executive, and it either discusses and makes important decisions, or ratifies the decisions of Cabinet committees. In doing so it is supposed to follow the principle of collective responsibility.

Table 5.2 Cabinet members, 5 May 2006

Name	Office
Tony Blair	Prime Minister, First Lord of the Treasury, and minister for the Civil Service
John Prescott	Deputy Prime Minister and First Secretary of State
Gordon Brown	Chancellor of the Exchequer
Margaret Beckett	Secretary of State for Foreign and Commonwealth Affairs
John Hutton	Secretary of State for Work and Pensions
David Miliband	Secretary of State for Environment, Food and Rural Affairs
Douglas Alexander	Secretary of State for Transport and Secretary of State for Scotland
Des Browne	Secretary of State for Defence
Jack Straw	Leader of the House of Commons and Lord Privy Seal
Patricia Hewitt	Secretary of State for Health
Alastair Darling	Secretary of State for Trade and Industry
Tessa Jowell	Secretary of State for Culture, Media and Sport
Jacqui Smith	Chief Whip (Parliamentary Secretary to the Treasury)
John Reid	Secretary of State for the Home Department
Peter Hain	Secretary of State for Northern Ireland, and Secretary of State for Wales
Hazel Blears	Minister without Portfolio and Labour Party chairman
Baroness Amos	Leader of the House of Lords and Lord President of the Council
Lord Falconer of Thoroton	Secretary of State for Constitutional Affairs and Lord Chancellor
Hilary Benn	Secretary of State for International Development
Alan Johnson	Secretary of State for Education and Skills
Ruth Kelly	Secretary of State for Communities and Local Government, and Minister for Women
Hilary Armstrong	Minister for the Cabinet Office and for Social Exclusion (and Chancellor of the Duchy of Lancaster)
Stephen Timms	Chief Secretary to the Treasury
Also attending the Cabinet	
Lord Grocott of Telford	Lords Chief Whip and Captain of the Gentlemen at Arms

Source: www.pm.gov.uk

Collective responsibility

> **Collective responsibility**
>
> The principle whereby decisions and policies of the Cabinet are binding on all members of the government, who must support them in public, to maintain a united front, or resign their government post.

As a collective decision-making body the Cabinet is bound by the principle of '**collective responsibility**'. It may be the centre of acute conflict in the privacy of the Cabinet room, but it must present a united front in public. As the nineteenth-century prime minister, Lord Melbourne, said: 'It doesn't matter what we say as long as we all say the same thing.' Cabinet discussions are secret (members sign the Official Secrets Act) and, to preserve the appearance of unanimity, the prime minister sums up the mood of the meeting, which adds to the PM's power. Votes in Cabinet are rare and usually reserved for special decisions, such as that of going to war with Argentina over the Falklands.

The nature of collective responsibility is changing. Originally applied only to the Cabinet, it now covers all government members. Between 1994 and 1997 the Labour Party also extended it to members of its shadow Cabinet. In contrast, the government suspended collective responsibility in 1975 and 1977 over the issue of the European Union. In 1994 a Cabinet minister, Michael Portillo, made thinly veiled criticisms of the Cabinet's European policy, but was not disciplined in public. Some ministers have also circumvented collective responsibility by leaking documents. The principle of collective responsibility, it seems, is now applied more broadly but also more weakly.

Cabinet committees

Established during the crisis years of the Second World War as a way of doing Cabinet work quickly and efficiently in small groups, Cabinet committees now play an important part in government. According to Cabinet Office information: 'Both Committees and Subcommittees act by implied devolution of authority from the Cabinet and their decisions therefore have the same formal status as decisions of the full Cabinet.' This means that committee decisions do not need Cabinet agreement or ratification.

The prime minister decides the number, terms of reference, membership and chairs of committees (Table 5.3). Most are composed of Cabinet members, but some include junior ministers and senior civil servants. There are five main kinds of committees dealing with Cabinet business in the present system:

- **Full Cabinet committees** dealing with the most important areas of government, such as defence and overseas policy, domestic affairs and schools policy. They are normally chaired by the prime minister or the Cabinet minister responsible for the area. In 2006 there were 30 full Cabinet committees.

- **Sub-committees** covering a narrower range of issues than their full committee. There were 18 of these in 2006.

- **Miscellaneous groups** concerned with specific tasks and usually having a short life span.

Table 5.3 Examples of Cabinet committees

Cabinet committees change over time, and miscellaneous groups often have a short life, but the following illustrates their work:

Committee on Constitutional Affairs – Chaired by the Lord Privy Seal and Leader of the House of Commons, this has 19 members, all drawn from the government. Its terms of reference are 'To consider strategic issues relating to the Government's constitutional reform policies including House of Lords reform and issues arising from devolution to Scotland, Wales and Northern Ireland.' It has three sub-committees covering electoral policy, freedom of information and parliamentary modernisation.

Committee on defence and overseas policy – Chaired by the Prime Minister with the Foreign Secretary as deputy chair, this has a membership of eight government members, with other ministers, the heads of the intelligence agencies and the Chief of Defence Staff invited to attend as necessary. Its terms of reference are 'To set strategies for the Government's defence and overseas policy.' It has four sub-committees covering international terrorism, protective security and resilience, Iraq, and conflict prevention and reconstruction.

Committee on European policy – Chaired by the foreign secretary this committee has 22 members, with other ministers and staff of the United Kingdom's permanent representative to the European Union (see Chapter 8) invited to attend as necessary. Its terms of reference are 'To determine the United Kingdom's policies on European Union issues, and to oversee the United Kingdom's relations with other member states and principal partners of the European Union.' It has no sub-committees.

Ministerial committee on influenza pandemic planning – A miscellaneous group chaired by the secretary of state for health with 16 government members, and other ministers and officials of the security and intelligence services, government communications, medical and scientific staff, and the devolved authorities of Scotland, Wales and Northern Ireland invited to attend as required.

Source: Government web sites

- **Consultative committees** are attended by Cabinet members and outside officials who meet to ensure a proper discussion of matters of common interest. Consultative committees are not bound by collective responsibility and they are consultative not executive bodies.

- **Official committees** shadow their Cabinet equivalents and are staffed by officials (mainly civil servants from Whitehall departments). They usually meet before their equivalents in order to identify possible problems and clarify key issues.

Committees, sub-committees and miscellaneous groups were much used by Thatcher to bypass formal discussion in her full Cabinet. She could fill them with her own nominees and so get her own way. John Major's more consensual style resulted in more discussion in full Cabinet. Blair comes between Major and Thatcher: on some matters he seems to push his own initiatives through ad hoc committees; on others he has used short meetings of his full Cabinet. One of the most interesting Blair initiatives was the Joint Consultative Committee with the Liberal Democratic Party (JCC). Although the work of the committee was suspended in 2001, it was important because it broke the constitutional convention that government committees were composed only of government members. It provided a political device to put pressure on traditionalists within the Cabinet who opposed change, as well as being a way of isolating the Conservative opposition.

The Cabinet Office

The Cabinet Office is a nerve centre of government. It supports and services the work of the Cabinet and its committees by timetabling meetings, preparing agendas and documents, drafting and circulating minutes, and following up decisions. The Office also plays a major part in coordinating the policies of government and Whitehall departments, analysing policy options, working out how best to deliver government policy, and then driving them through to the point of delivery. It consists of about 30 sections run by 50 senior officials and civil servants, and employs more than 2,000 staff. The secretariat is so important that its head, the secretary of the Cabinet, is the country's senior civil servant. The Cabinet secretary is in daily contact with the Prime Minister and Cabinet members, attends Cabinet meetings (although not for party political items) and some Cabinet committees. The Cabinet Office now works so closely with the Prime Minister's and Deputy Prime Minister's Offices that all three have become virtually one single operation.

The Cabinet, departments and joined-up government

The Cabinet has many responsibilities and roles. Politically, it must decide government policy and what legislation to put before Parliament. Administratively, it must ensure the efficient and effective functioning of government departments. Collectively, it must resolve disputes between departments, political factions and individual ministers. These functions overlap, of course, with those of the prime minister, which is why Cabinet and prime ministers and their respective Offices must collaborate so closely.

As the highest committee of government, the Cabinet is especially important for making final decisions that cannot be made elsewhere, either because they are so important or because they are points of acute conflict. Sometimes this conflict is a matter of ideology and principle (joining the euro, banning fox hunting, war in Iraq) and sometimes it is more organisational, involving the interests of the ministries and departments of government. The Cabinet is the place to resolve such conflicts, either in committee or around the large table in the Cabinet room.

Even if there is no conflict, policies still have to be coordinated, and coordination is extremely difficult to achieve in modern, large-scale government. On the one hand, the operations of the state are so huge that they must be broken up into manageable parts and organisations that are run by people with specialised abilities and knowledge. On the other hand no government service or policy area is an island on its own. All are related to others. Building a motorway affects the environment, has an impact on agriculture and consequences for other forms of transport, and costs money that could be spent on other services. One of the most difficult problems of government is being caught between the incompatible demands of departmentalisation and specialisation and the need to coordinate very complex policy issues across a large number of separate organisations. As the government machinery becomes larger, more complex and more specialised, the more important it is to create coordinated government, but the more difficult to do so.

Blair first used the term joined-up government when he launched the Social Exclusion Unit in 1997, as part of the Prime Minister's Office. Since then, joined-up government has risen and fallen in the political agenda. At first it was much discussed and different organisations and procedures were set up to achieve it, most of them within the Prime Minister's Office. Many have been subsequently reorganised, merged, downgraded or quietly dropped. The term 'joined-up government' is not often heard nowadays, either because it has become incorporated into standard thinking about public policy or, more likely, because it is a good idea that is extremely hard to implement. It is now mainly the responsibility of the Office of the Deputy Prime Minister. We will return to the subject in Chapter 7.

The eternal political triangle

Decision making within the Cabinet rests on three important principles, which often conflict with each other:

1. **Departmental autonomy** Whitehall departments are among the largest organisations in the country, and most ministers spend most of their time running them. This requires departmental autonomy, partly because different departments deal with different policy areas – education, defence, transport, health – and partly because they have their own practices, cultures and operating procedures. Ministers must defend their departments against other departments and fellow ministers. Indeed, the more effectively they do this, the greater their political reputation and the higher they are likely to rise up the greasy pole of politics. It is the job of the Cabinet to resolve inter-departmental disputes.

Cabinet collegiality

The feeling among Cabinet members that they must act closely and cooperatively together, even when they conflict over policy issues and departmental interests.

2. **Cabinet collegiality** At the same time the Cabinet must be a collegial body capable of resolving conflict and making collective decisions. Whatever their rivalries, Cabinet members must form a united front, and to do this they must have the chance of discussing issues.

3. **Prime ministerial authority** Prime ministers are leaders. Even the most powerful and ambitious ministers want the prime minister to lead the Cabinet, the party and the country. Besides, ministers are often so overburdened by their departmental duties that they have little time for general policy issues. The prime minister must try to hold all the many reins of government, rise above conflict in Cabinet, and settle disputes authoritatively. In this sense the PM is not a colleague of Cabinet members, but their boss.

The three principles do not always fit well together. Departmental autonomy clashes with collegiality when ministers fight, as they must, for money and their policies. Too little discussion and consultation undermines Cabinet collegiality. A dominant prime minister can easily undermine collegiality, and one who interferes with departmental affairs too much will erode autonomy. Conversely, a weak prime minister will not control departmental and personal rivalries. A good PM must know when to talk or listen, when to lead or follow, when to control or delegate. In short, a good PM balances the demands of autonomy, collegiality and leadership. It is an exceedingly difficult and delicate task, and there are recent examples of it going badly wrong, as we will now see.

Prime ministerial styles

Thatcher as Prime Minister

When Thatcher came to power in 1979 she seemed to be a strong and dynamic leader who could take charge of government and reverse national decline. The Falklands War strengthened popular belief in her leadership qualities. Yet when she lost power in 1990, as the longest serving Prime Minister of the century, she was widely seen as dogmatic and autocratic. For much of her time in Downing Street she dominated the government and stretched prime ministerial authority to its limits. She was an ambitious and driving force, but she also intervened too much in the departmental affairs of her ministers, and undermined Cabinet collegiality with her critical style.

The poll tax is a case in point. This policy to shift local taxation from a graduated property tax to a flat-rate tax on individuals was described as the worst idea in the world, and there was little government or even Cabinet support for it, but Thatcher pushed it through Parliament, forcing her colleagues to support it publicly against their own judgement. Its unpopularity was one of the more important factors leading to the Cabinet forcing her from office. Other examples of her leadership style are listed in Briefing 5.2. In general, Thatcher placed the principle of prime ministerial authority way above departmental autonomy and Cabinet collegiality – the eternal triangle was balanced on one corner, so it fell over.

Major as Prime Minister

Major adopted a more collegial and consensual style (see Briefing 5.3). Initially this succeeded in healing political wounds and unifying the government. He also came out of the Gulf War (1991) with much respect as a political leader. Yet after a while his quiet and unassuming style was described as 'grey', dithering and ineffective. His Cabinet was described as a collection of 'political chums', and was accused of being 'in office but not in power'. Intense conflicts about economic policy, social policy and the EU surfaced. The government appeared weak, divided and directionless. In the end, the eternal triangle of Major's Cabinet was balanced on departmental autonomy, so it toppled over.

Blair as Prime Minister

In the first years of his administration Tony Blair combined some of the best characteristics of Thatcher's dynamism and leadership with Major's informal and unassuming style. He managed to combine two contradictory tendencies:

BRIEFINGS

5.2 Prime ministerial style: Thatcher

- Ensured that 'dries' (right-wing free marketeers) dominated her Cabinets and committees.

- Sacked 12 Cabinet ministers, 1979–90.

- Reduced the frequency of Cabinet and committee meetings. Wilson's annual average of Cabinet meetings was 59, Thatcher's was 35.

- Greater use of ad hoc committees and the kitchen cabinet. It is said that some of her ministers knew nothing about some ad hoc committees, although they made important decisions.

- Intervened a great deal in departmental affairs.

- Publicly criticised some of her ministers, or used leaks against them, but strictly enforced collective responsibility.

- Started Cabinet discussions by stating her own views, rather than listening and summing up.

- Did not consult her Cabinets about some major policy decisions (e.g. the banning of trade unions from Government Communications Headquarters (GCHQ) in 1984).

- Appointed weak ministers who could be controlled.

- Kept some major issues off Cabinet agendas. Michael Heseltine claimed this as the reason for his resignation in 1986.

- Attended parliamentary debates less frequently than any other modern prime minister.

BRIEFINGS

5.3 Prime ministerial style: Major

- Made more use of the Cabinet, less of committees.

- More emphasis on Cabinet collegiality and consensus, less on leadership.

- A greater mix of opinion in the Cabinet, especially wets and dries, Europhiles and Eurosceptics.

- Greater openness in government.

- Less intervention in departmental affairs.

- Lapses of collective responsibility: Portillo's veiled criticism of the government in 1994 went publicly unchecked.

1. He has further centralised the Labour Party and imposed unprecedented discipline on it, reversing some traditional policies (Clause 4, public spending) with little debate and a great show of unanimity. He gradually appointed more of his supporters to senior positions. He reduced the number and length of Cabinet meetings, working (as did Thatcher) through Cabinet committees. He greatly increased the size and power of the Prime Minister's Office. His unprecedented popularity in the country, until Iraq, enhanced his leadership. In short, he is strong on prime ministerial authority.

2. In the earlier years he had the full support of the Cabinet on many of the most controversial policies, such as taxing and spending, and Scottish and Welsh devolution, and kept his Cabinet colleagues together by approaching some controversial issues (the EU, the euro, electoral reform) slowly and cautiously. Although said to be a control freak, he allows some of his senior Cabinet colleagues much autonomy – especially Gordon Brown on economic matters. In short, he has been strong on departmental autonomy and Cabinet collegiality.

Plate 5.1 The war on terrorism results in more power being accumulated in the hands of the government. Here 'King' Tony Blair receives a grovelling courtier

Source: Cartoon Stock

Until the early years of his second term in government, at least, Blair's Cabinet was generally a good balance of the three principles of prime ministerial authority, departmental autonomy and Cabinet collegiality. An extremely popular prime minister for an unprecedented period, Blair then gained a reputation for too personal a leadership style (the 'Tony Show') involving a few favoured advisers ('Tony's cronies') rather than wide discussion, and government by spin-doctor. He came to be personally identified with some unpopular policies (Iraq, close alignment with Bush, foundation hospitals, top-up fees and the Education Bill of 2006). The political triangle has shifted from a balance of elements towards too much prime ministerial authority.

BRIEFINGS

5.4 Prime ministerial style: Blair

- Took on major agenda and policy-setting powers of the government and made it clear that he would not tolerate dissent either from his Cabinet or from the Parliamentary Labour Party.

- Reduced the number, length and documentation of Cabinet meetings (it meets for about an hour) using committees and sub-committees more. The number and length of Cabinet meetings rose slightly in 2004–5, but is still low by historical standards.

- Employed increasing numbers of personal advisers. Major had 8. In 2005 Blair had 28.

- Had adopted an informal style of decision making ('sofa government') based on 'bi-laterals' (meetings between him and one other person). Policy on Iraq seems to have been largely formulated in private meetings with President Bush, and he promised a referendum on the EU constitution in 2004 without discussing it with Cabinet colleagues. The Butler Report (2004) on intelligence on weapons of mass destruction was critical of the 'informality and circumscribed character of Government procedures' and the risks it presents for informed, collective political judgement.

▶

- Spends even less time than Thatcher in the Commons, more and more on public speeches, press conferences and international high-level meetings.

- Allows considerable discretion to strong Cabinet ministers (Gordon Brown, Jack Straw and David Blunkett), provided their policies are broadly in line with government policy.

- Is careful to keep the Cabinet united on potentially divisive issues – Europe, the euro, electoral reform, Lords reform – but Iraq may have been an exception.

- Carefully cultivates his leadership image and places great importance on media management and 'message discipline' (centralising all government communications in his own Office and repeating the same theme many times).

- At the same time, he has an open and informal prime ministerial style – 'Call me Tony'; refusing to wear a morning coat at the Queen Mother's funeral.

Who governs: Cabinet or Prime Minister?

Prime ministerial government

The theory that the office of the Prime Minister has become so powerful that he or she now forms a political executive similar to that of a president.

A classic and long-running debate about British government revolves around the question of whether the power of the prime minister has increased relative to the Cabinet. It is said that the PM is no longer 'first among equals' but a dominant political executive, and the result is not Cabinet, but **prime ministerial government**. The Cabinet, once said to be the 'efficient secret of government' because it, and not the Commons, made decisions, is now a 'dignified' part of government that hides the real power of a presidential prime minister. This assertion dates back at least to Churchill's war government, but it surfaces again whenever forceful prime ministers emerge – Macmillan, Wilson, Thatcher and Blair. The 'controversy' that follows summarises some views on the matter.

Prime ministerial government

The argument that we have prime ministerial government is found in John Mackintosh's *The British Cabinet* and Richard Crossman's introduction to the 1960 edition of Bagehot's *The English Constitution*. Both claim that the British Prime Minister is now so powerful that the office is more akin to that of a president. Key decisions are made by the PM, plus a few powerful members of the Cabinet, the government and the kitchen cabinet. Key Cabinet committees are under prime ministerial control, with the Cabinet often only a rubber stamp, or not consulted at all. The prime minister directs the entire flow of government information and dominates relations between the Cabinet and the wider world. The overall result is said to be executive democracy or leadership democracy rather than parliamentary democracy.

Cabinet government

Cabinet government

The theory that the Cabinet, not the Prime Minister, forms a collective political executive that constrains the power of the Prime Minister to the role of 'first among equals'.

This school of thought argues that the political system limits the PM's power and ensures that the Cabinet forms a collective political executive. In the short run, PMs may be formidable, but in the long run they depend on Cabinet and party support, and most important matters will have to be agreed by Cabinet. Since the power of the Cabinet rests on the support of the majority party in the House of Commons it must, to some extent, reflect its political complexion. This, in turn, places constraints on the power of both the PM and the Cabinet, and ensures a degree of accountability of the political executive to the majority party in the Commons.

BRIEFINGS

5.5 Cabinet, Cabinet committees and other executive meetings, 1950–2000

Cabinet   Since the 1950s the number and duration of Cabinet meetings has steadily declined, from about 100 a year to about 40. Under Blair they rarely last for more than 60 minutes.

Cabinet committees   Between 1970 and 2000 the number of Cabinet committee meetings fell more than 50 per cent.

Other meetings   Since 1979, and especially under Blair since 1997, business has increasingly been handled by:

- ad hoc meetings of senior ministers
- kitchen cabinet meetings
- bilateral meetings between the PM and favoured friends and colleagues.

CONTROVERSY

Prime ministerial or Cabinet government?

Prime ministerial government

- The powers of the Prime Minister are considerable.
- There are no constitutional limits to the power of the Prime Minister.
- The fusion of the executive and the legislative branches of government gives the Prime Minister direct influence over both.
- One-party government and strict party discipline ensure the power of the Prime Minister over the governing party in Parliament.
- The apparatus of Whitehall government is hierarchically organised with the Prime Minister at the peak and in control.
- The office of the PM accumulates power over time, ratcheting up with each new incumbent. Wartime conditions gave Churchill special powers that were expanded by strong successors: Attlee, Macmillan, Wilson, Thatcher, Blair.
- The Prime Minister is at the centre of mass media attention. This gives the PM power over government colleagues.
- The Prime Minister represents the country in international meetings (often widely covered in the mass media).
- The Prime Minister's Office and the Cabinet Office are increasingly linked under the direction of the Prime Minister.
- All government communication with the media is increasingly controlled by the PM's Office.

Cabinet government

- Modern government is now so complicated and demanding that one person cannot possibly control all key decisions.
- Important political factions in the party need to be represented in the Cabinet if confidence in the Prime Minister is to be maintained.
- The Prime Minister has powerful and ambitious rivals for office. Some, but not all, may be ignored. Blair cannot keep Brown out of a senior Cabinet position.
- Ministers can use the weapon of resignation against the Prime Minister (Nigel Lawson in 1989, Sir Geoffrey Howe in 1990), although it may do the minister more harm than the Prime Minister in the short term.
- Politics is a hard and ruthless game. PMs need to be constantly watchful and careful, listening carefully to advice from all quarters – party whips, the Prime Minister's Office and advisers, commissions and committees of enquiry, Whitehall staff, the media, and especially friends and advisers who speak their minds.
- The media can be a powerful critic of the Prime Minister. Douglas-Home, Wilson, Heath and Major were weakened by a hostile press.
- Powerful PMs have been driven from office by Cabinet colleagues – notably Macmillan and Thatcher.

Cabinet or prime ministerial government?

There is no question that the British Prime Minister holds one of the most powerful political offices in the western world. What is not clear, however, is whether there is a trend towards greater prime ministerial power:

1. There is nothing new about powerful prime ministers – British history is full of them from the very first, Sir Robert Walpole, to Thatcher and Blair.

2. Strong prime ministers, such as Churchill, Macmillan and Thatcher, have often been followed by weaker ones, such as Eden, Douglas-Home and Major.

3. Relations between the Prime Minister and Cabinet members are largely secret, although surrounded by rumour and hearsay. It is difficult to know what really goes on, and difficult to draw firm conclusions about prime ministerial or Cabinet government.

4. It is often assumed that there must be rivalry and competition between the PM and leading Cabinet members, where there may actually be agreement and unity. Blair and Brown have often been presented (by the media looking for

---

CONTROVERSY

Prime ministerial or Cabinet government? What commentators say

It is no exaggeration to declare that the British premiership has turned not into a British version of the American presidency, but into an authentically British presidency.

M. Foley, 'Presidential politics in Britain', *Talking Politics*, **6** (3), 1994, p. 141

Cabinet does not make all the decisions but it does make all the major ones, and it sets the broad framework within which more detailed policies are initiated and developed.

M. Burch, 'Prime minister and cabinet: an executive in transition', in R. Pyper and L. Robins (eds), *Governing the UK in the 1990s*, London: Macmillan, 1995, p. 103

The prime minister is the leading figure in the Cabinet whose voice carries most weight. But he is not the all-powerful individual which many have recently claimed him to be. His office has great potentialities, but the use made of them depends on many variables – the personality, the temperament, and the ability of the prime minister, what he wants to achieve and the methods he uses. It depends also on his colleagues, their personalities, temperaments and abilities, what they want to do and their methods.

G. W. Jones, 'The prime minister's power', in A. King (ed.), *The British Prime Minister*, London: Macmillan, 2nd edn, 1985, p. 216

Centralisation of power in the hands of one person has gone too far and amounts to a system of personal rule in the very heart of our parliamentary democracy.

Tony Benn, 'The case for a constitutional premiership', in A. King (ed.), *The British Prime Minister*, London: Macmillan, 2nd edn, 1985, p. 22

The prime minister leads, guides and supports his team, but relies upon their energies and expertise, just as they in turn rely upon his leadership . . . The relationship is subtle and variable, but essentially it is one of mutual reliance. A strong prime minister needs strong ministers.

S. James, *British Cabinet Government*, London: Routledge, 1992, pp. 133–4

The more I've been here, the clearer it's become to me that Cabinet government is a reality; let's say that the power of departments and departmental ministers is strong . . . I should perhaps add that this is the way this prime minister, in particular, likes to work . . . He's a conciliator and therefore goes with the grain of the system of Cabinet government, rather than against it.

1993 interview with senior civil servant, quoted in C. Campbell and G. K. Wilson, *The End of Whitehall*, Oxford: Blackwell, 1995

trouble) as locked in battle. In fact, in the earlier years they often seemed to be close colleagues.

5. The memoirs of leading political figures, as well as commentators outside the system, are frequently contradictory.

In short, the controversy about whether we have prime ministerial or Cabinet government seems to be unresolvable. Consequently, political scientists have turned to a different way of analysing the political executive, using the concept of the 'core executive'.

The core executive

Frustrated by endless controversy about whether we have prime ministerial or Cabinet government, some political scientists have pointed out that both are embedded in a wider network of power relations that spread well beyond Downing Street and the Cabinet room. Increasingly during the twentieth century, and especially under Thatcher and Blair, the power of the political executive has been strengthened and centralised, and its tentacles of power have stretched out to other influential bodies, agencies, committees and individuals in Whitehall and Westminster. This network of power and influence at the apex of government has been termed 'the core executive'. It consists of the following:

- the prime minister, leading members of the Prime Minister's Office, and the more influential members of the prime minister's kitchen cabinet

- the Cabinet and its main committees, leading members of the Cabinet Office, and the more influential ministerial advisers

- the most senior officials in Whitehall departments, agencies and other bodies (e.g. the Bank of England and the main security and intelligence organisations)

- the individuals and organisations that circle around the Prime Minister, the Cabinet and those who serve them

- some members of the House of Commons and the Lords – government whips and a few chairs of Commons committees.

The advantage of focusing on the core executive is that it avoids the old and (some claim) sterile argument about prime ministerial versus Cabinet government to focus on the broader picture of decision-making power and influence. It sees power at the pinnacle of the British state less as the tip of a hierarchical pyramid formed by a few organisations, and more as a complex network of people and bodies in constant interaction and exerting mutual influences. However, the concept has three main problems as an analytical tool in political science.

Numbers

How many people are included in the core executive – 50, 100, 500, 1,000, 5,000, or more? The core executive most certainly includes the 'big beasts' of the Cabinet, but should we also include a few of the most influential junior ministers, and if so how many – 5, 10, or 20? Almost certainly the core executive includes the most important Cabinet committees, but should we also include some important subcommittees as well? Which ones and how many? Almost certainly the core executive includes the most influential people in the Prime Minister's Office, but is this 10, 20, 40, or 60 people? We should also include some of the most influential members of the kitchen cabinet, but who? Then there are the most important senior mandarins in Whitehall, but who? Discussions of the core executive are often rather vague about exactly which offices or people are involved and even about approximate numbers and offices.

Changing circles of power

The answer to the numbers problem is that a lot depends on the particular issue under discussion. The core executive may change its composition according to issues, circumstances and times. A small circle made strategic decisions about the Falklands and Gulf Wars, including senior military chiefs; a larger circle is likely to influence the decision on whether or not to join the euro (excluding military chiefs but including senior staff of the Bank of England and Treasury). Some people and institutions are involved in only one decision, others are involved in a few or many issues, but not all. A very few are involved in all major policy decisions. But this answer simply raises the problem: if different individuals and bodies are influential on different key issues, then the composition of the core executive will change from one issue to the next. If the head of the armed forces is involved in crucially important decisions about Iraq but not about the euro, the Education Bill, hospital trusts or constitutional reform, is he a member of the core executive or not? Or is he sometimes a member and sometimes not? In this case, is there any such thing as the core executive at all? Are we back to identifying the prime minister, the Cabinet, and a handful of senior staff members in the PM's Office and Cabinet Office as the inner core of power because it is involved in almost all key decisions, with constantly changing outer circles of lesser power circling around it? But if these are constantly changing and with lesser power, are they really part of the core executive – or only sometimes?

What does the concept of the core executive explain?

The concept of the core executive is useful in directing attention to the wide network of power and influence at the highest level of government, but it does not help much to answer important questions about who wields power, why, in whose interests, and to what effect? Why are some institutions, groups and individuals more powerful than others? And under what sorts of circumstances? How and why do they come to be powerful? How do they exercise their power, and in whose interests? Core executive theory does little to answer these questions and we have to turn to substantive theories such as class, pluralist, elite and bureaucratic theories as explanations, which is what we will do in following chapters.

Summary

- There is no question that the British Prime Minister has considerable power. A series of strong prime ministers since 1940 testifies to the fact.

- Neither is there much doubt that the Cabinet can be a powerful body. It reasserted its power over Thatcher in 1990, and it is not a body that even an authoritative leader such as Blair can take for granted.

- An effective political executive rests on the three principles of Cabinet collegiality, departmental autonomy and prime ministerial authority. If these are unbalanced the system will not work effectively.

- The power of the Prime Minister relative to the Cabinet has swung substantially from one prime minister to the next, and within the term of office of the same PM. Thatcher started in a more collegial mode than she ended. Major's Cabinet started collegially but ended divided. In his earlier years at No. 10 Blair managed to blend prime ministerial authority, departmental autonomy and Cabinet collegiality. Later his style emphasised prime ministerial authority more heavily.

- Consequently there is much evidence to support both the theory of prime ministerial government and that of Cabinet government.

- Some political scientists have stopped arguing about prime ministerial versus Cabinet government to focus on the much wider network of power and authority relations found in the core executive. There are many indications that the power of the core executive has been increased and centralised, especially under Thatcher and Blair.

MILESTONES

1721	Robert Walpole acknowledged as the first Prime Minister
1735	Walpole makes 10 Downing Street his official residence
1782	Resignation of the Lord North government on the principle that collective Cabinet responsibility links the Prime Minister with his Cabinet
1914–18	Lloyd George's wartime Cabinet has fewer than 10 members
1916	Lloyd George creates the Cabinet Office
1922	Prime Minister Bonar Law creates a peacetime Cabinet with only 16 people
1931	Appointment of the first Prime Minister's press officer
1937	First statutory reference to the Office of Prime Minister in the Ministers of the Crown Act
1940–5	Wartime emergency gives Churchill great powers as Prime Minister. The modern Cabinet committee system created. The wartime Cabinet had 10 or fewer members
1945–51	Attlee (Deputy Prime Minister under Churchill) continues as a strong leader
1951	Churchill's short-lived experiment with 16 'overlords'
1962	Macmillan's 'night of the long knives' – a Cabinet reshuffle that replaced almost half the members
1964	Wilson creates a Political Office in 10 Downing Street. Ministers allowed their own special advisers
1970	Central Policy Review Staff (CPRS) created by Heath. Super-ministries created: the Department of Trade and Industry, and the Department of the Environment
1974	Wilson sets up first PM's Policy Unit
1975	Collective responsibility suspended during the EC referendum. Collective responsibility again suspended over the issue of the voting system to be used in EC elections
1979	Thatcher starts process of expanding and strengthening the Prime Minister's Office. Gives special role to the PM's press secretary
1983	Thatcher abolishes the CPRS. Cabinet secretary becomes head of the Civil Service
1989	Thatcher shuffles 62 government positions. Lawson (the Chancellor of the Exchequer) resigns from government, criticising Thatcher's leadership and her economic advisers
1990	Sir Geoffrey Howe resigns from the Cabinet, criticising Thatcher's leadership. Thatcher's domination of the government contributes to her downfall. Major introduces a more collegial style of Cabinet government

▶

Milestones in British constitutional development continued

1992	Information about Cabinet committees made public for the first time
1994	Michael Portillo ignores the principle of collective Cabinet responsibility with criticisms of the government's EU policy
1994–7	Principle of collective responsibility applied to Labour's shadow Cabinet
1997	Blair's new Cabinet includes a predominance of strong party notables but marked by consensus on central policies. PM's Office expanded and strengthened
2002	Office of Deputy Prime Minister created
2002–5	The work of the Prime Minister's Office, the Deputy Prime Minister's Office and the Cabinet Office gradually merged to form an executive office.

Essays

1. Discuss the claim that Thatcher's period in office provides clear evidence of prime ministerial government, Major's clear evidence of Cabinet government, and Blair's clear evidence of both.

2. How useful do you find the concept of the 'core executive' in the analysis of British government?

Projects

1. Read this chapter carefully and pick out the bodies, agencies and offices that contribute most to the centralisation of executive power in British government. Explain how they do so, and say whether such centralisation is inevitable.

2. Read carefully through this chapter and make a note of the different bodies, agencies and committees that can help to produce joined-up government, and those which are more likely to produce fragmented government.

Further reading

A short up-to-date book is S. Buckley, *The Prime Minister and Cabinet* (Manchester: The Politics Association, 2006). Longer and older books are S. James, *British Cabinet Government* (London: Routledge, 1998) and G. Thomas, *The Prime Minister and Cabinet Today* (Manchester: Manchester University Press, 1998). A. King (ed.), *The British Prime Minister* (London: Macmillan, 2nd edn, 1985) is the classic collection of readings, and a useful collection of articles on the core executive is contained in R. A. W. Rhodes and P. Dunleavy (eds), *Prime Minister, Cabinet and Core Executive* (London: Macmillan, 1995). The most recent and complete study of Blair as prime minister is A. Seldon and D. Kavanagh (eds), *The Blair Effect 2001–5* (Cambridge: Cambridge University Press, 2005).

Recent articles include M. Burch and I. Holliday, 'The Blair government and the core executive', *Government and Opposition*, **39** (1), 2004, pp. 1–21; M. Rathbone, 'The British cabinet', *Talking Politics*, **16** (1), September 2003, pp. 36–9; M. Garnbett, 'Still first among equals?', *Politics Review*, **14** (4), April 2005, pp. 2–5; P. Riddell, 'Prime ministers and Parliament', *Parliamentary Affairs*, **57** (4), 2004, pp. 814–29.

The classic works on Cabinet and prime ministerial government are J. Mackintosh, *The British Cabinet* (London: Stevens, 1962) and R. Crossman, 'Introduction' to W. Bagehot, *The English Constitution* (London: Fontana, 1963).

Useful web sites on the core executive

Hot links to these sites can be found on the CWS at www.pearsoned.co.uk/budge.

Key sites for the core executive are those of 10 Downing Street (www.number-10.gov.uk) and the Cabinet Office (www.cabinet-office.gov.uk) and the Office of the Deputy Prime Minister at www.odpm.gov.uk.

The web sites for the key Whitehall departments within the core executive are the Treasury (www.hm-treasury.gov.uk), the Foreign Office (www.fco.gov.uk), the Home Department (www.homeoffice.gov.uk) and the Department for Constitutional Affairs (www.lcd.gov.uk). Others may be accessed through links within the Cabinet Office web site (www.cabinet-office.gov.uk).

In addition, three sites with information about Thatcher, Major and Blair as prime ministers is available on: www.margaret-thatcher.com; www.johnmajor.co.uk; and http://www.biogs.com/blair.

chapter 6

Ministries, ministers and mandarins: central government in Britain

Ministers in charge of government departments must work very closely with the civil servants who administer their departments. Ministers, of course, are elected politicians, but civil servants are non-political, permanent and appointed officials – bureaucrats, in other words. There are hundreds of thousands of civil servants, ranging from filing clerks to a small number of very senior administrators who are often referred to as 'mandarins', after the top civil servants of ancient China. The implication is that British mandarins are also highly trained, exceptionally able, totally dedicated and no less inscrutable than their Chinese counterparts. This chapter is concerned with the relationship between government ministers and the highest mandarin level of the Civil Service. The next chapter will look more broadly at the general workings of the administrative machinery of the state.

The relationship between ministers and top civil servants is crucial to the modern state. It is the government departments that actually produce public services – health, education, public transport, national defence – and it is the mandarins, not ministers, who have specialist knowledge and experience of how to run the huge organisations that deliver these services. In theory, ministers have the political function of making public policy, and mandarins the administrative task of advising on policy matters and implementing whatever ministers decide. In practice, it is impossible to draw such a simple distinction between the role of the minister and the top civil servants.

For this reason, the relationships between ministers and mandarins are both important and complex, and raise all sorts of issues. What is the proper relationship between ministers and mandarins? Should civil servants be responsible to the public, to Parliament, or only to their ministers? Should ministers be responsible for everything their civil servants do? Do civil servants really run the country? How has the relationship between ministers and mandarins changed since the Whitehall reforms of the 1980s and 1990s? What special features has New Labour brought to Whitehall operations?

This chapter examines:

- departments and ministries of Whitehall
- ministerial roles and responsibilities
- ministers and civil servants
- mandarin power?
- politicisation of the Civil Service?
- New Labour and the mandarins.

Departments and ministries of Whitehall

The central administration of Britain, like that of almost all other countries, is organised into separate departments or ministries (there is no real distinction between the two). There are about 70 of these. Cabinet ministers head 17 of the major ministries (Table 6.1).

Both the number and nature of ministries may change – just as Cabinet posts change – when the government reorganises departments. A huge ministry was created in 1997 dealing with regional and local government, housing and planning, social exclusion, and regeneration and neighbourhood development. But it was too large for effective coordination and was split up after the election of 2001. A department concerned with constitutional affairs is a new development, and in the latest Cabinet Welsh and Scottish affairs are combined with other jobs because the creation of the two regional authorities has reduced the workload in London.

The most important department is the Treasury, because it manages the national economy and controls the spending of other government departments. Its Comprehensive Spending Review (CSR – introduced by Gordon Brown) requires departments to justify their spending plans for a rolling three-year period. The Treasury used to have a limited coordination role, but the CSR gives it greater powers to control spending and direct future spending plans for Whitehall as a whole – another example of the centralisation of executive power and of the attempt to create joined-up government. The next CSR is planned for 2007.

BRIEFINGS

6.1 British central administration

Whitehall   The area of central London, close to Westminster, where the main ministries and their offices are located. Hence 'Whitehall' is often used as a symbolic term for central bureaucracy and the Civil Service.

Civil servant   A servant of the Crown (in effect of the government) who is employed in a civilian capacity (i.e. not a member of the armed forces), and who is paid for wholly and directly from central government funds (not by local government, agencies, nationalised industries or quangos).

Mandarin   A term given to the thousand or so top civil servants who have regular, personal contact with ministers and act as policy advisers. They are collectively known as the Senior Civil Service, and consist mainly of permanent secretaries (the senior civil servant in each department), under-secretaries and deputy secretaries. They constitute not much more than about 0.2 per cent of all civil servants.

Mandarin power   The theory that top civil servants exert a powerful influence over government policy making because of their ability, experience, expertise, training and special knowledge. One version of the theory claims that civil servants, not ministers, run the country.

Minister   There are more than 110 members of the government, including Cabinet ministers and those who attend the Cabinet, ministers of state and parliamentary under-secretaries of state (PUSS – or 'pussies' for short), down to the lowest rank of (unpaid) parliamentary secretaries. Collectively the last three are known as junior ministers. They usually look after the work of a particular part of their department, under the general direction of their senior minister. As government has grown so has the number of junior ministers – from 23 in 1945 to 89 in 2006.

Ministerial responsibility   The principle that ministers are responsible to Parliament for their own and their department's actions. In theory ministers take responsibility for administrative failure in their department, and for any individual injustice it may cause, whether they are personally involved or not.

Special adviser   Special advisers are not civil servants but political appointees who are either policy experts or general political advisers to ministers.

Table 6.1 Major departments and ministries of central government

Department	Main functions	Planned expenditure 2007/8 (£ million)	Web address
Department for Constitutional Affairs	Upholding justice, rights and democracy	3,856	http://www.dca.gov.uk
Department for Culture, Media and Sport (DCMS)	Museums, galleries, libraries, arts, sport, heritage, media, tourism, national lottery	1,668	http://www.culture.gov.uk
Home Department	The internal affairs of England and Wales (justice, crime and victims, security, passports and immigration, police, prisons, public safety, drugs, science research and statistics)	9,437	http://www.homeoffice.gov.uk
Department of Health (DH)	Health, welfare and well-being	92,621	http://www.dh.gov.uk
Foreign and Commonwealth Office	Foreign affairs and policy, relations with the Commonwealth	1,606	http://www.fco.gov.uk
Department for Transport (DfT)	The transport system	8,056	http://www.dft.gov.uk
Department for education and skills (DfES)	Education and training	23.8	http://www.dfes.gov.uk
Department of Trade and Industry (DTI)	Trade, industry, productivity	6,733	http://www.dti.gov.uk
Department for Environment, Food, and Rural Affairs (Defra)	Farming and fisheries, food and drink, horticulture, animal welfare, environment, rural affairs	3.4	http://www.defra.gov.uk
HM Treasury	The UK economy, tax, work, welfare, public spending and services, enterprise and productivity	Not appropriate	http://www.hm-treasury.gov.uk
Northern Ireland Office	Northern Ireland	8,391	http://www.nio.gov.uk
Privy Council Office	The exercise of prerogative powers, the affairs of chartered bodies (institutions, charities, companies), final Court of Appeal for the Commonwealth countries who choose to use it	724	http://www.privy-council.org.uk
Wales Office	Represents Welsh interests in Westminster, liaising with the devolved administration in Wales	8,766	http://www.walesoffice.gov.uk
Scotland Office	Represents Scottish interests in Westminster, liaising with the devolved administration in Scotland	17,644	http://www.scotlandoffice.gov.uk
Department for Work and Pensions (DWP)	Work, unemployment, disabled people, pensions	7,449	http://www.dwp.gov.uk
Department for International Development (DfID)	International aid and development	5,288	http://www.dfid.gov.uk
Ministry of Defence (MoD)	Defending the UK, international peace and security	33,457	http://www.mod.uk
Office of Deputy Prime Minister	Communities and local government	5,125	http://www.communities.gov.uk
Cabinet Office	Supports the prime minister and Cabinet, coordinating the policy and operations of government	2,154	http://www.cabinetoffice.gov.uk

Note: Because of departmental reorganisation not all figures are available.
Source: www.cabinet-office.gov.uk and HM Treasury *Public Expenditure Statistical Analysis 2005*, London, Table 4.1. Reproduced under the terms of the Click-Use Licence

Ministries are sometimes conglomerates of responsibilities that have grown up rather haphazardly. The most obvious example of this is the Home Department, which has retained all the activities of government that have not been hived off to more specialist ministries. Most ministries, however, focus on one policy area, such as foreign and commonwealth affairs, transport, health, trade and industry, defense, and education (see Table 6.1).

This focus contributes to the development of a 'departmental view', adding to the clash of views and adversarial nature of decision making in the Cabinet. Clearly, having a department charged with one service – transport, health or education – means that it will press its special interests and opinions. Departments have developed their own cultures and views of how best to do things over their decades of operations. Since no ministry has total control of everything it does, each has to cooperate or conflict with others from time to time according to circumstances, and there are often clashes between the departments with conflicting interests, particularly between spending departments fighting for a larger slice of the cake. If they cannot resolve their differences they may take their struggles right up to the Cabinet if necessary.

To understand the subtle and complex nature of this struggle for policy supremacy between ministers and departments we must first consider: (a) the general structure of ministries and departments; and (b) the enormous dependence of politicians on civil servants that this structure creates, a dependence that is quite notable in the British system, though not unique to it.

Ministry structure

Each major department is run by a senior minister or secretary of state, who usually holds a Cabinet seat. To try to keep pace with the huge increase in government work, post-war governments have appointed increasing numbers of junior ministers. In 2006 the Blair government consisted of the following:

- 23 Cabinet ministers (plus 1 more who attended Cabinet meetings), most of whom were department heads

- 27 ministers of state, who are usually responsible for specific aspects of their department's work

- 35 parliamentary under-secretaries of state, and parliamentary private secretaries (PPSs) who assist ministers.

The more important the department, the more senior and junior ministers it has. The Treasury has two Cabinet seats (the Chancellor and the Chief Secretary to the Treasury) and three ministers of state, but the Welsh Office has a Cabinet minister (shared with Northern Ireland) and a parliamentary under-secretary. Figure 6.1 shows the structure of a typical department. Many Cabinet ministers have served an apprenticeship by rising through the ranks of the government from parliamentary secretaries (unpaid ministerial bag carriers), often in a range of different departments.

Ministers are, legally speaking, powerful agents of government in the sense that most Acts of Parliament empower them – not the Prime Minister, the Cabinet, or senior civil servants – to do certain things. For this reason ministers are also formally responsible for what goes on in their department, and are answerable to Parliament for all that the department does in their name. Since government departments are among the largest organisations in the country, this is a huge responsibility.

Figure 6.1 Structure of a typical Whitehall department

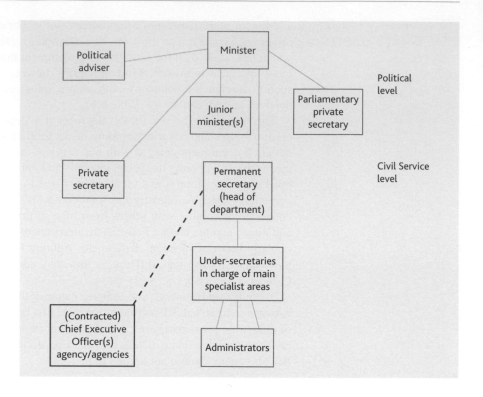

Plate 6.1 Aerial view of Whitehall looking towards the Houses of Parliament

Source: Alamy/Andrew Holt

Ministerial roles and responsibilities

Ministers have an incredibly busy and crowded schedule. In an average day a minister may meet with mandarins to talk about departmental matters, attend a press meeting, travel to a public function, be briefed about parliamentary business, receive a deputation from the public or a foreign government, attend a political meeting, a dinner, or a late-night sitting of the House of Commons, and then work late into the night on a dispatch box full of papers to be read in time for an early start the next day. Ministers also attend the Cabinet and its committees, travel to Brussels and to their parliamentary constituencies, and attend party meetings and conference. During the year they are likely to have to handle time-consuming departmental and political crises as well.

The daily workload of a minister is varied and crushingly heavy because it involves many different activities:

- **Administration**   Ministers are responsible for the daily operations of their department and for cases of maladministration.

- **Policy making**   Ministers set the policy of their department and are involved in general government policy making in the Cabinet and its committees. They are involved in many meetings with other ministers whose business overlaps with their own, and they have to fight for their department and its resources in the Cabinet.

- **Politics**   Ministers are accountable to Parliament, and attend its sessions to answer questions, speak in debates, vote and pilot legislation through Parliament. They also have party meetings and constituencies to nurse.

- **Public relations**   Ministers meet the media regularly to explain departmental policy and further their own careers. They keep up a demanding schedule of travel around the country to dinners, conferences, meetings and openings of various kinds. They meet deputations from interest groups, and receive a huge volume of mail.

- **The EU**   Many ministers read mountains of documents, attend innumerable meetings, and travel thousands of miles on EU business.

Ministers are mostly drawn from the approximately 300–400 people who get elected to Parliament for the majority party. In spite of the huge demands and complexity of their jobs, members of the House of Commons have no special background or training to prepare them for ministerial work. Not one of the members of the Labour government elected in 1997, and out of power for the previous 18 years, had ever held a government job.

Moreover, ministers usually spend little time in any one department before being moved in a government reshuffle. On average they spend two years in one job before switching to another. Between 1945 and 2003 there were 28 ministers of education, each lasting, on average, barely more than two years in office. One, Kenneth Clarke, was Chancellor of the Duchy of Lancaster, and secretary for health and then education, and home secretary, all within a six-year period, before becoming chancellor of the exchequer in 1993, a post he held until 1997. It is said to take over a year to master the work of a department, and at least another year to make any sort of impact on it, by which time ministers have often moved to another job.

Ministerial responsibility

Untrained and inexperienced though they may be, ministers are responsible to Parliament, and can be forced to resign if they or their departments perform badly.

BRIEFINGS

6.2 Ministerial responsibility: what they say

The individual responsibility of ministers for the work of their departments means that they are answerable to Parliament for all their department's activities. They bear the consequences for any failure in administration, any injustice to an individual or any aspect of a policy that may be criticised in Parliament, whether personally involved or not.

Central Office of Information, *The British System of Government*, HMSO: London, 1994, p. 42

The evidence of this study destroys the Crichel Down Affair as the key example of ministerial responsibility. The true convention regarding ministerial resignations is hang on for as long as you can. How long a minister can hang on depends upon his or her stock of political capital.

Keith Dowding, *The Civil Service*, London: Routledge, 1995, p. 169

Ministerial responsibility

The principle whereby ministers are responsible to Parliament for their own and all their department's actions. In theory, ministers are responsible for administrative failure in their department, and for any injustice it may cause, whether they are personally responsible or not.

According to convention they bear responsibility for administrative failure in their departments, for any injustices it may cause, and for general policy failures, whether or not they are personally responsible. In theory, ministers are responsible for everything that goes on in their departments. The classic example is the famous Crichel Down affair of 1954 when the minister of agriculture, Sir Thomas Dugdale, resigned because of departmental maladministration about which he knew nothing.

In theory, the convention of **ministerial responsibility** is a cornerstone of the British constitution because it is the basis of government accountability to Parliament, and hence the main mechanism for holding ministers responsible for their actions. In practice, however, ministerial responsibility does not work this way. Since the Second World War, no minister has resigned because of Civil Service mistakes. Table 6.2 shows that most ministers resign for personal reasons (sex scandals or drunken driving) or because of an error in their ministerial role (the Falklands in 1982, or salmonella in 1988). Even the much-quoted precedent of Crichel Down can be explained in terms of the minister losing backbench support, rather than taking responsibility for Civil Service errors.

There are many more recent examples of ministers hanging on to their posts in spite of departmental failures. To take just one small policy area as an example – that of prison escapes – we find four recent cases of ministers refusing to take responsibility for departmental failures: in 1983 (Secretary of State for Northern Ireland, James Prior), 1991 (Home Secretary, Kenneth Baker) and 1994 and 1995 (Home Secretary, Michael Howard).

There are six main reasons why the convention of ministerial responsibility is not always followed in practice:

1. Conventions are by definition not legally binding, but depend on the willingness of politicians to abide by them.

2. Ministers cannot possibly know everything about their huge departments or be held responsible for every one of its actions. It is estimated that they usually know little more than 1 per cent of departmental matters.

3. While ministers are supposed to resign because of 'failure' or 'injustice', or 'criticism' in Parliament, these are difficult terms to define. In any case, ministers are continuously criticised in Parliament, where there is a continual background of ritual catcalls for resignations.

Table 6.2 Some ministerial resignations and their causes

Year	Minister	Cause of resignation
1982	Nicholas Fairbairn (solicitor-general for Scotland)	Private life and handling of a departmental matter
1982	Lord Carrington (Foreign Secretary), Humphrey Atkins (Lord Privy Seal), Richard Luce (Minister of State, Foreign Office)	Failure to take due note of warnings that Argentina was planning a Falklands invasion
1985	Cecil Parkinson (Transport Secretary)	Private life, the Sara Keays affair
1986	Leon Brittan (Secretary of Trade and Industry)	Leaking official documents about the sale of Westland Helicopters
1986	Michael Heseltine (Defence Secretary)	Disagreement with Cabinet over sale of Westland Helicopters
1988	Edwina Currie (Under-Secretary of State, Health)	Claimed (correctly) that British eggs are infected with salmonella and forced to resign
1990	Patrick Nicholls (Under-Secretary of State, Environment)	Drunken driving
1992	David Mellor (National Heritage minister)	Private life and acceptance of hospitality from businessmen lobbying government
1993	Michael Mates (Minister of State, Northern Ireland)	Relations with Asil Nadir, businessman who jumped bail in a fraud trial
1994	Tim Yeo (Minister of State, Environment)	Private life and illegitimate child
1994	Lord Caithness (Minister of State, Transport)	Private life
1994	Tim Smith (Under-Secretary of State, Northern Ireland)	Accepted cash for asking parliamentary questions
1994	Neil Hamilton (Under-Secretary, Corporate Affairs)	Cash for questions
1995	Allan Stewart (Under-Secretary, Scotland)	Waving pickaxe at anti-road demonstrators
1995	Charles Wardle (Under-Secretary, Industry and Energy)	Opposition to government's immigration policy
1995	Robert Hughes (Parliamentary Secretary)	Private life
1996	David Willetts (Parliamentary Secretary)	Secretly directing Conservative members of Privileges Committee when he was a whip
1998	Ron Davies (Secretary of State for Wales)	Private life
1998	Peter Mandelson (Minister without Portfolio)	Conduct in office – undeclared personal loan from Paymaster-General, and Hinduja passport affair
1998	Geoffrey Robinson (Paymaster-General)	Conduct in office – personal loan to Peter Mandelson
2000	Peter Kilfoyle (Under-secretary of State, Defence)	Disagreement with government policy
2001	Keith Vaz (Minister of State for Europe, Foreign Office)	Misconduct (technically did not resign as a minister but was reshuffled out of office after suspension from the Commons for misconduct)
2002	Stephen Byers (Transport Secretary)	Various transport problems, especially Railtrack, plus behaviour of special advisers
2002	Estelle Morris (Education Secretary)	Various problems concerning schools' policy, especially controversy over A-level results – exacerbated by negative media coverage
2003	Robin Cook (Leader of the House of Commons) John Denham (Minister of State, Home Office)	Disagreement with government policy (Iraq)
2003	Clare Short (Minister for International Development)	Disagreement with government policy (Iraq)
2003	Alan Milburn (Health Secretary)	To spend more time with family
2004	Beverley Hughes (Immigration Minister)	Visa irregularities
2004	David Blunkett (Home Secretary)	Fast tracking nanny's visa
2004	Andrew Smith (Secretary of State for Work and Pensions)	To spend more time with work and constituency following rumours that he would be dropped from the Cabinet
2005	David Blunkett (Minister for Work and Pensions)	Not following procedures for former ministers taking private sector work

4. A minister who should resign may be protected by his or her Cabinet colleagues for political reasons, although in different circumstances the same minister might be sacrificed to public opinion for the same failing. Sometimes governments make a political gesture and find a scapegoat, and sometimes they close ranks to protect themselves.

5. The creation of Whitehall agencies with a degree of independence from ministers (Chapter 7) makes it more difficult to distinguish between the policy failures of ministers and the bureaucratic failures of agencies. Each side can blame the other.

6. When there is such a rapid turnover of ministers, is it fair to blame one for problems that may have been inherited from a predecessor?

As a result the convention of ministerial responsibility is vague, and mainly results in resignation where ministers have lost the support of their government colleagues and/or their party backbenchers.

Ministers and civil servants

Civil servant

A servant of the Crown (i.e. the government) who is employed in a civilian capacity (i.e. not a member of the armed forces) and who is paid wholly and directly from central government funds (not local government, nationalised industries or quangos).

Senior and junior ministers constitute a thin political layer of elected politicians superimposed on top of a large army of appointed **civil servants**. At the head of each army division is a permanent secretary who, as the equivalent of the chief executive officer of the department, oversees its daily administration, acts as a policy adviser to the minister, and as the channel of communication between the minister and the layers of officials below. In the post-war years permanent secretaries were powerful figures, and they still constitute an important part of the core executive. However, the Civil Service is now less hierarchical and more flexible than it was. Ministers have a much wider range of contacts and methods of working within their departments than before. So permanent secretaries may not be such powerful gatekeepers nowadays.

Nevertheless, British ministers are dependent on their career civil servants to a degree that is unusual in western democracies. In many countries incoming ministers bring with them a new team of political appointees to serve as senior administrators and policy advisers. This team may leave when a new minister takes over, especially if a new party or coalition comes to power. This is not how things work in the United Kingdom, where civil servants are permanent. Ministers have little control over the selection of the permanent officials with whom they have to work so closely. The idea is that British civil servants are professional and highly trained administrators who are appointed and promoted according to ability and experience, not according to their politics. Only if 'things don't work out' between a minister and his senior officials can the minister demand changes of staff, but there are limits to how many changes can be made. Ministerial dependence on permanent officials will be heightened if he or she is new to the department – as they often are when they are members of a new government, or when they have just been moved as part of a government reshuffle. To make things work effectively and efficiently between elected politicians and their top-flight permanent officials – the **mandarins** – both ministers and civil servants must play special and carefully defined roles in the policy making and administration of the state.

Mandarins

The comparatively small number (about 1,000) of very senior civil servants who have close and regular contact with ministers in their capacity as policy advisers.

Civil Service impartiality

The principle whereby civil servants should be politically neutral and serve their Cabinet ministers regardless of which party is in power and of what they may personally feel about their minister's policies.

The civil servant's role

The civil servant's role has four main features: **impartiality**, **anonymity**, permanence and confidentiality:

BRIEFINGS

6.3 Civil Service impartiality and anonymity

In the determination of policy the civil servant has no constitutional responsibility or role distinct from that of the minister. It is the civil servant's duty . . . to give the minister honest and impartial advice, without fear or favour, and whether the advice accords with the minister's views or not . . . When, having been given all the relevant information and advice, the minister has taken a decision, it is the duty of civil servants loyally to carry out the decision with precisely the same energy and goodwill, whether they agree with it or not.

Civil Servants and Ministers: Duties and Responsibilities, London: HMSO, 1986, pp. 7–8

The Civil Service as such has no constitutional personality or responsibility separate from the duly constituted Government of the day . . . The duty of the individual civil servant is first and foremost to the Minister of the Crown who is in charge of the department in which he or she is serving.

The Armstrong Memorandum, *Civil Service Management Code*, Issue 1, London: HMSO, 1993, paras 3–4 (Sir Robert Armstrong, Cabinet secretary, 1979–88, and head of the Civil Service, 1981–8)

Although my generation of civil servants has been brought up to regard every act taken by an official as an act in the name of the Minister, our successors may . . . have to be prepared to defend in public, and possibly without the shield of ministerial protection, the acts they take.

Sir D. Wass, 'The public sector in modern society', *Public Administration*, **61** (1), 1983, p. 12 (Sir Douglas Wass, Permanent Secretary at the Treasury, 1974–83, and joint head of the Civil Service, 1981–3)

- **Osmotherly Rules** A set of rules for the guidance of officials appearing before House of Commons select committees and designed to protect the principle of Civil Service impartiality, anonymity and confidentiality.

- **The Armstrong Memorandum** The official statement on the duties and responsibilities of civil servants, including their role in relationship to ministers.

Civil Service anonymity

Civil servants are the confidential advisers of ministers and must not be asked questions about politically controversial matters or the policy advice they give.

Osmotherly Rules

A set of rules, named after their author, Edward Osmotherly of the Civil Service Department, for the guidance of civil servants appearing before Commons select committees and designed to protect Civil Service impartiality, anonymity and secrecy.

1. **Impartiality** Civil servants must serve their political masters – their ministers – and be strictly impartial about party politics and ministerial policies. They must not enter the political fray. For their part, ministers must not ask civil servants to perform political tasks. Appointments and promotion in the Civil Service should not involve political considerations, or be affected by a change of government. According to the Osmotherly Rules, Commons committees must not ask civil servants 'questions in the field of political controversy'.

2. **Anonymity** Civil servants are anonymous. They should give their minister their best policy advice without fear or favour, but it is for the minister to defend department policy in public. The Osmotherly Rules state that parliamentary committees must not ask questions about the conduct of particular civil servants or about the advice they give to ministers.

3. **Permanence** Unlike the system in many other countries, top British civil servants do not change with a change of government. Impartiality and anonymity should mean they serve whichever party is in power to the best of their ability and whatever their own political opinions or department views.

4. **Confidentiality** The advice civil servants give their ministers is confidential, and the Osmotherly Rules and Armstrong Memorandum state that they cannot be asked to reveal their advice in public. Civil servants sign the Official Secrets Act.

Plate 6.2 The drive to reduce red tape and bureaucracy has, according to some commentators, resulted in an increase in red tape and bureaucracy
Source: Cartoon Stock

Events in the 1980s and 1990s, however, suggest that these four principles have been changed under the pressure of political events:

- **Impartiality and the Tisdall affair**   In 1983 the civil servant Sarah Tisdall was sentenced at the Old Bailey to six months in prison for leaking information about the arrival of Cruise missiles at Greenham Common. She believed her defence secretary was avoiding ministerial accountability. Her case raises the question of whether the Civil Service should carry out all ministerial directives, even those they feel are morally or legally dubious. Is their first duty to the public interest, or to their minister?

- **The Ponting affair**   Clive Ponting was a civil servant who was prosecuted in 1985 for releasing secret information suggesting that the battleship *Belgrano* was sunk during the Falklands War for political reasons, and not for military ones as claimed by the government. He argued that civil servants have a duty to the public interest that might, under certain circumstances, require them to 'go public'. The judge instructed the jury to find him guilty, on the grounds that ministers should judge what is in the public interest, but the jury acquitted him.

- **The 'arms to Iraq' affair**   The Scott Inquiry into the arms to Iraq affair (where the Conservative government had secretly relaxed the rules on exporting arms to Iraq in the 1980s) found that ministers had asked civil servants to help them misinform Parliament and the public, and that civil servants seemed to have colluded with them.

- **Anonymity**   An inquiry into the collapse of Vehicle and General Insurance in 1971 placed the blame on named officials. An inquiry following the Westland Helicopters affair in 1986 criticised five named civil servants for their role in leaking a letter, and another, Sir Robert Armstrong, the Cabinet secretary, for failing to take disciplinary action against them. In recent times the anonymity of civil servants has been increasingly difficult to maintain, as the media, political memoirs and official inquiries have publicised Civil Service and ministerial conduct. In 2006 a row blew up about the ruling of the information commissioner that the names of civil servants must not be deleted from documents released to the public under the Freedom of Information Act.

■ **Permanence**   Civil servants are also now less permanent than they used to be. The chief executive officers in charge of executive agencies are on fixed-term contracts (see Chapter 7).

In sum, the theory and practice of the Civil Service role are not the same thing, and the practice has changed in recent decades under the pressures of modern government.

Mandarin power?

In theory, ministers are the elected politicians who make public policy; civil servants provide policy advice and carry out ministerial orders and administer the decisions. Civil servants are 'on tap, but not on top', as the saying goes. In practice, it is impossible to draw a clear distinction between policy and administration. Policy inevitably involves administrative questions. For example, the poll tax, whether or not it was a good idea in principle, was difficult and expensive to implement and might have been rejected on administrative grounds alone. Administration often involves important policy issues, and policy involves important administrative matters. A series of administrative decisions about how to run a policy programme can easily affect its basic rationale.

Consequently, the roles of ministers and their Whitehall staff are blurred. Where the minister's job ends and the permanent secretary's begins is not at all clear. As Sir Humphrey, the caricature of the archetypal mandarin, says in the TV programme *Yes, Minister* with deliberate obscurity and ambiguity:

> I do feel that there is a real dilemma here, in that while it has been government policy to regard policy as the responsibility of ministers, and administration as the responsibility of officials, questions of administrative policy can cause confusion between the administration of policy and the policy of administration, especially where the responsibility for the administration of the policy of administration conflicts or overlaps with the responsibility for the policy of the administration of policy.
>
> J. Lynn and A. Jay, *Yes, Minister*, London: BBC, 1982, p. 176

Mandarin power/ dictatorship of the official

The theory that, no matter which party forms the government, civil servants will exert a powerful influence over government, or even control it, because of their ability, experience and expertise.

The overlap of policy and administration is not just of theoretical interest. It has important implications for the power potential of Whitehall mandarins.

According to the German sociologist Max Weber permanent officials, especially civil servants, hold the reins of power in the modern bureaucratic state. 'For the time being', he wrote, 'the **dictatorship of the official**, not that of the worker, is on the march.' His argument for making this claim was that permanent officials have the training, the ability and the experience that enables them to control or manipulate their nominal political masters. Officials are full time, experienced and highly trained professionals picked for their special ability; politicians are part time, often inexperienced amateurs who are elected from the general population.

There are many arguments for and against Weber's startling claim when we apply it to the British Civil Service. But for every argument in favour of **mandarin power** there seems to be another contradicting it. While the arguments do not necessarily cancel each other out, we have to turn to other ways of trying to resolve the controversy. One obvious way is to call on the evidence of insiders who know the Whitehall and Westminster 'village' well, and one obvious place to search is the growing body of political memoirs of ministers and mandarins who have written about their personal experiences. Unfortunately, these are also inconclusive. Not only is the evidence anecdotal and patchy, but for every minister – Benn, Castle,

CONTROVERSY

Mandarin or ministerial power? The theory

Mandarin power

Numbers

About 1,000 civil servants have a direct input into the policy-making process compared with about 60 ministers and junior ministers

Time

Civil servants are full time; ministers divide their time between many activities

Permanence and experience

Civil servants are permanent; ministers are temporary; civil servants often have many years' experience; ministers have few (if any)

Ability and training

Top civil servants are exceptionally able, usually with excellent educational qualifications. Ministers are untrained and not elected for their educational qualifications

Monopoly of advice and information

Ministers are heavily dependent on their civil servants for policy advice. This is a uniquely British situation, as elsewhere they take independent policy advisers in with them, as a matter of course

Tricks of the trade

Civil servants may use tricks of the trade: putting important documents at the bottom of the dispatch box; concealing major policy issues in long, complex reports; giving ministers little time for decisions; selective use of facts; getting other departments to intervene in matters of mutual interest

The departmental view versus vague party platforms

Departments have a comprehensive policy view; ministers have sketchy guidance from their party manifesto

Civil Service ambition

Those at the top of the Civil Service hierarchy are able and ambitious. Some ministers are weak, appointed because they can be controlled by Cabinet colleagues

Civil Service empire building

Civil servants are ambitious for their departments: they want to build empires

Evidence

It is not difficult to draw up a long list of ministers who were run by their departments

Ministerial power

The boss

Numbers may not count for much when ministers can use their legitimate power to overrule civil servants

Time is not the essence

It does not take a good minister long to come to grips with the essentials of policy decisions

Permanence and experience

Some ministers take charge of their department quickly: a few have much government experience if their party has been in power for some time

All amateurs

Civil servants are generalists, not specialists, and have no more professional training for their job than ministers. Some ministers are exceptionally able

Outside advice

Ministers are not totally dependent on civil servants or advice; they have their own (non-Civil Service) advisers, professionals, the party, pressure groups, academics and the media

Ministerial experience

It does not take ministers long to learn these tricks and ways of countering them. They have tricks of their own, and may be able to make life difficult for non-compliant civil servants

Cabinet and party backing

Ministers can use the party election manifesto and the weight of Cabinet opinion to force (if necessary) civil servants to accept a policy

Personality

Ministers are not famous for being shy and uncertain; many have great ambition, confidence and force of character to drive their will

Professional ethos

The Civil Service has a strong and well-developed ethos or ethic of serving ministers to their best ability

Evidence

It is not difficult to draw up a long list of ministers who ran their departments

CONTROVERSY

Mandarin or ministerial power? Some insider evidence

The trouble with the Civil Service is that it wants a quiet life. The civil servants want to move slowly along the escalator towards their knighthood and retirement and they have no interest whatsoever in trying to develop new lines of activity.

> Tony Benn, *Out of the Wilderness, Diaries 1963–1967*, London: Arrow Books, 1987, p. 195

I believe that civil servants like to be under ministerial control. There is nothing they dislike more than to have a minister whom they feel is weak, who does not know his mind and who wants to leave it all to them . . . What they like is to have a minister who knows a policy he wants to pursue.

> Edward Heath, quoted in Peter Barberis (ed.), *The Whitehall Reader*, Buckingham: Open University Press, 1996, p. 83

Even at the ODM [Ministry of Overseas Development] I remember Andy Cohen, the Permanent Secretary, trying to wear me down . . . He would be in my office about seven times a day saying, 'Minister, I know the ultimate decision is yours but I would be failing in my duty if I didn't tell you how unhappy your decision makes me.' Seven times a day. One person [the Minister] against the vast department.

> Barbara Castle, *Mandarin Power*, quoted in Barberis, op. cit., p. 66

Ministers set the policy agenda, often with help from officials, and make decisions within it. They seek, and officials offer, advice within the framework of the policy agenda.

> Lord Burns, permanent secretary of the Treasury, 1991–8, quoted in Kevin Theakston (ed.), *Bureaucrats and Leadership*, Basingstoke: Palgrave Macmillan, 2000, p. 40

I think the minister who complains that his civil servants are too powerful is either a weak minister or an incompetent one.

> Denis Healey, quoted in Barberis, op. cit., p. 81

Already I realise the tremendous effort it requires not to be taken over by the Civil Service. My Minister's room is like a padded cell . . . there is a constant preoccupation to ensure that the Minister does what is correct.

> Richard Crossman, *The Diaries of a Cabinet Minister*, vol. 1, London: Hamilton and Cape, 1975, pp. 21–2

Broadly speaking, I would say that it is quite untrue to believe that Whitehall, if you are firmly committed to anything, would try to stop you doing it.

> Richard Crossman, *Socialism and Affluence: Four Fabian Papers*, London: Fabian Society, 1967, p. 80

We concentrate on what *can* happen, not what *ought* to happen.

> Sir Brian Cubbon (permanent secretary of the Northern Ireland Office, 1978–88), 'The duty of the professional', in R. Chapman (ed.), *Ethics in Public Service*, Edinburgh: Edinburgh University Press, 1993, p. 10

Only bad ministers blame the Civil Service, because only bad ministers let themselves be dominated by the Civil Service.

> Gerald Kaufman, 'How to be a minister', *Politics Review*, **7** (1), 1997, p. 13

Crossman – claiming that civil servants were unhelpful or obstructive, there is another – Wilson, Carrington, Heath, Healey and Crossman – saying that they are professionals who can be controlled. Crossman appears to disagree with himself, so he appears in both lists.

If neither abstract argument nor insider evidence offers a conclusive answer to the controversy about mandarin power, perhaps the most significant evidence is provided by developments under Thatcher and Major. Their governments reformed the Civil Service structure and mode of operation in fundamental ways and, moreover, won big battles against determined opposition from almost all sections of Whitehall. This constitutes clear evidence that British civil servants can be brought under government control, if the government is determined to push its reforms through. Whatever may have been the case before 1979, Whitehall mandarins were not 'on top' in the 1980s and early 1990s when they had to submit to reforms they strongly disliked. In fact in this period, far from being too strong, civil servants were criticised at the time for being too weak and compliant, and giving in to ill-thought-out and hastily implemented government plans. Indeed it was even argued that the Civil Service had abandoned its traditional political neutrality to become a political tool of the government. The same complaint was raised a decade later by the Hutton Inquiry (http://www.the-hutton-inquiry.org.uk/index.htm) and the Butler Report of 2004 (http://www.butlerreview.org.uk), when it was asked whether the intelligence community was too sensitive to what the government wanted to hear and presented evidence to suit it.

Politicising the Civil Service: what price the code of ethics?

Since the 1980s the problem has not been that civil servants use their powers for their own purposes but, on the contrary, that the government has used civil servants for its own party political purposes. Critics argue that the Civil Service has been increasingly politicised by the Thatcher and Blair governments. There is some evidence for this view, although much of it is anecdotal and it is very difficult to know what actually has happened given the private and secret nature of most government business at this very high level. However, the Scott Inquiry (see above) showed that politicians had used civil servants to perform political tasks. It is also claimed that civil servants such as Sarah Tisdall, Clive Ponting and Dr David Kelly breached the Civil Service code by engaging in politics. After much pressure, the government accepted a formal code of ethics drafted by the Treasury and Civil Service Select Committee of the House of Commons dealing with the roles and responsibilities of civil servants. It came into effect in January 1996. An appeals procedure was set up for civil servants who felt under pressure to compromise their political neutrality, and a Propriety and Ethics Team was also created to give advice on ethical issues involving the Civil Service and the Cabinet.

There is continuing disquiet about dangers to the traditional role of the Civil Service. In 2003 the Committee on Standards in Public Life called for a Civil Service Act to place the Civil Service on a statutory footing. The Public Administration Committee of the House of Commons published its own draft Bill in 2004 and meanwhile the Civil Service Commissioners warned against the further politicisation of the Civil Service. With some reluctance, it seems, the government published a draft Bill in 2006 to regulate the appointment, duties and conduct of civil servants and special advisers.

New Labour and the mandarins

The Thatcher/Major Conservative governments were in power for 18 years. In that time they reshaped almost every aspect of government policy, appointed almost every senior civil servant, tried to remodel large parts of the Whitehall machinery, and did their best to instil a Thatcherite culture in Whitehall. As a result, some observers in 1997 suggested that the Blair government would need to clean-sweep the top levels of the Civil Service and replace it with its own people. No such thing happened, and the transfer of power from Conservative to Labour government was relatively uneventful, with the exception of a few minor 'hiccups'. Many top

Task forces

Task forces are usually small, official groups set up to do a particular and fairly limited job (write a report, investigate an issue or event), and dissolved when they have completed the task.

information officers (spin doctors) in Whitehall were replaced, but they held politically sensitive posts. In large part the Civil Service adapted to its new political masters. However, the Blair government has done two things to change working patterns in Whitehall: it has significantly enlarged and strengthened the role of special advisers, and it has created a large number of **task forces**.

Special advisers

The Civil Service once enjoyed a virtual monopoly as advisers to ministers. This was partly because British parties do little planning about how to turn their vague campaign promises into specific policies. For example, Richard Crossman, a new minister in 1964, noted with dismay in his diary that the file at Labour's headquarters on one of its longest standing policy commitments was almost empty. 'Think tanks' (outside centres providing policy advice) are relatively new in Britain, and limited in numbers and resources. Policy working groups in the main parties are relatively weak, and policy recommendations of parliamentary select committees (Chapter 18) often ignored. Thus, the first port of call for a minister in need of advice was, until recently, their senior civil servants. This has changed as governments become aware of their dependence on the mandarins, even though they did not appoint them in the first place.

A response to this has been the appointment of special advisers from outside the Civil Service. These are not new to British government, but their numbers have increased in the past 10–15 years. Compared with the 46 special advisers in Major's government there are now more than 75, with some 26 in the Prime Minister's and Deputy Prime Minister's Offices.

Special advisers are temporary civil servants and bound by the Civil Service code. But, unlike regular civil servants, they do not need to be appointed on merit or to be politically neutral. Most departments have no more than two special advisers but there are exceptions. The Department for Education and Skills and the Office of the Deputy Prime Minister have had more. Special advisers are paid out of public funds, and in 2004/5 cost £5.5 million.

There are two kinds of special advisers. The first are policy experts with specialist knowledge, and the second are political advisers (not a Civil Service function) who think generally about political tactics and strategy for their minister and the government. Many are on part-time or short-term contracts. As outsiders who are answerable only to the minister who employs them, they are independent of the civil servants. On the one hand, special consultants give the government a greater range of advice and greater freedom of action; on the other, they may undermine the traditional role of senior civil servants. Moreover, there has been a crossing of lines between the Civil Service, the government and the political parties, a trend further complicated by the fact that a few special advisers have the power to give orders to civil servants. This was part of the controversy about how one special adviser, Alastair Campbell, might have 'sexed-up' an intelligence report on Iraqi weapons of mass destruction.

The role and powers of special advisers continues to concern the Committee on Standards in Public Life, which points out that mixing special advisers' advice with that of civil servants effectively prejudices the objectivity and neutrality of civil servants. The advice of some special advisers has also been controversial. Jo Moore's email on the day of the 11 September 2001 attacks on the United States to her minister, Steven Byers, contributed to both of them losing their jobs. She wrote: 'It's now a very good day to get out anything we want to bury. Councillors' expenses?' This piece of special advice was followed by announcing two rather small changes to local government expenses.

Task forces

A second notable change in Whitehall since 1997 is the growth of task forces, ad hoc advisory groups and review bodies. Collectively these three fall into the broader category of non-departmental public bodies (NDPBs). They are appointed by ministers but work at arm's length with a degree of independence from government. They are usually appointed to carry out very specific tasks and have a limited lifespan. Members of the bodies are usually people in public, business and professional life, who are appointed for their specialist knowledge and skills. In 2005 there were 458 such groups in central government, ranging from the Food in Schools Management Group and the Employers Task Force on Pensions to the Expert Group on Mental Health in Prisons and the Music Industry Forum.

Such groups can ignore the traditional Whitehall approach to problems by getting outside experts to search for new and pragmatic solutions to government problems. For example, National Health Service task forces, composed of medical professionals and patients, can explore ways to improve the service. Other groups are set up because there is little expertise on a subject in Westminster or Whitehall, such as the group that reported on Near Earth Objects (asteroids and comets) that threatened the globe. Task forces are also good at cutting across departmental boundaries, and hence can help joined-up government, except that they add yet another layer and type of public body to the system, and hence can fragment it as well.

The problem with such groups is that they undermine the policy advice role of civil servants, and they bypass the traditional Whitehall structures of departmental and inter-departmental committees. There is such a large number and bewildering variety of them, and such a rapid turnover, that they are difficult to keep track of and are accountable only to their minister. They are yet another influence that encourages government to fragment and fly off in many directions.

Summary

- In theory, ministers are responsible for policy and civil servants for administration, but in practice no clear line can be drawn between policy and administration.

- In theory, ministers are responsible to Parliament for their own actions and those of their departments and civil servants. In practice, the principle of ministerial responsibility is often breached.

- In theory, civil servants are impartial, anonymous, permanent, and protected by secrecy. In practice, all four features of the civil servant's role have been undermined in recent years.

- The old controversy about mandarin power is unlikely to be resolved, because arguments are inconclusive and insider evidence is contradictory. However, it is clear that politicians wielded decisive power over their mandarins in the 1980s and 1990s when the Thatcher and Major governments implemented sweeping reforms of Whitehall.

- After much pressure, the government published its Civil Service Bill in 2006, but its increasing use of special advisers and task forces has tended to undermine the traditional policy adviser role of senior civil servants and bypass normal departmental methods of policy making.

- Critics of the Whitehall system claim that the doctrines which are supposed to regulate ministerial and Civil Service relationships are more mythical than real. They argue for clearer and firmer rules, especially on the role of Civil Service and special advisers, and for better procedures to protect civil servants from ministers who try to use them for political purposes.

MILESTONES

Milestones in relationships between ministers and mandarins in the post-war period

Nineteenth century	The modern principles of Civil Service permanence, neutrality and anonymity become established along with ministerial responsibility
1954	Crichel Down affair. Secretary of State for Agriculture, Sir Thomas Dugdale, resigns because of maladministration in his department. Later research suggests that he was forced from office because he lost backbench support
1955	Creation of junior minister posts (to fill in for ministers away from London)
1964	Junior ministers given specific departmental responsibilities. Named Ministry of Aviation officials blamed for excessive profits paid in defence contracts to Ferranti Ltd for Bloodhound missiles
1968	Foreign Office officials named by Commons select committee for failure to compensate British victims of the Nazis (the Sachsenhausen case)
1971	Collapse of Vehicle and General Insurance Co. A named civil servant is blamed, but the minister, John Davies, does not resign
1973	Cabinet Office sets up its European Secretariat to coordinate departmental policy on the EEC
1976	Publication of Osmotherly Rules, guiding officials and politicians involved in the proceedings of Commons committees
1983	Sarah Tisdall jailed for leaking documents about the siting of Cruise missiles on Greenham Common
1984–5	Ponting trial. Clive Ponting had leaked documents showing the political motives for sinking the Argentine cruiser, *Belgrano*, in the Falklands War with the loss of 700 lives. Acquitted by jury against judge's instructions
1985	Armstrong Memorandum on the duties and responsibilities of civil servants
1986–7	Westland Helicopters affair. Colette Bowes, a civil servant, publicly identified for leaking a secret letter on the instruction of her minister, Sir Leon Brittan, who then resigned
1987	A revised version of the Armstrong Memorandum
1995–6	Scott Report into 'arms for Iraq' (also known as the Matrix Churchill affair) finds that the government had used civil servants to try to suppress embarrassing information at a trial on grounds of 'national security'
1996	Civil Service code comes into effect
1997	Smooth transfer of power from Conservatives to Labour after May general election
1997–2005	Growing numbers of special advisers and task forces used in Whitehall
2004	Butler Report raises concerns about government decision making and the role of special advisers.
2006	The issue of Civil Service confidentiality clashes with Freedom of Information requirements about the release of official documents that name civil servants. Consultation on a new Civil Service code

Essays

1. Argue the case for and against a permanent layer of civil servants at the top of Whitehall departments.

2. In what ways, and for what reasons, has the role of Whitehall mandarins changed in the last 30 years?

3. Are ministers really responsible to Parliament in their departmental capacities?

Projects

1. Playing the roles of a minister and a permanent secretary, argue the case for and against special advisers and task forces in central government.

2. Find out what you can from newspaper reports about any cases involving ministerial responsibility (e.g. Sir Thomas Dugdale and the Crichel Down affair, 1954; Norman Lamont and the withdrawal of the pound sterling from the EMS in 1992; James Prior, Kenneth Baker and Michael Howard and prison escapes in 1983, 1991, 1994 and 1995; Stephen Byers, transport and the Millennium Dome, 2002; and Keith Vaz and misconduct, 2002) What, if anything, do these case histories tell us about ministerial responsibility?

Further reading

General accounts of the Civil Service can be found in R. Pyper, *The British Civil Service* (London: Prentice-Hall/Harvester Wheatsheaf, 1995), and K. Theakston, *The Civil Service Since 1945* (Oxford: Blackwell, 1995). Longer, but very readable, is P. Hennessy, *Whitehall* (London: Secker & Warburg, 1989), and a more advanced text is K. Dowding, *The Civil Service* (London: Routledge, 1995). For a useful set of insider views on the relationships between ministers and mandarins, see P. Barberis (ed.), *The Whitehall Reader* (Buckingham: Open University Press, 1996). The same book has a section on Civil Service loyalties, responsibilities and ethics. An excellent account of the decline of the Whitehall Model based on extensive interviews is Colin Campbell and Graham K. Wilson, *The End of Whitehall: Death of a Paradigm* (Oxford: Blackwell, 1995).

Shorter and more recent articles on the Civil Service are T. Butcher, 'The Civil Service under New Labour', *Politics Review*, **11** (3), 2002, pp. 29–31; R. Pyper, 'Ministers, civil servants and advisers', in J. Fisher, D. Denver and J. Benyon (eds), *Central Debates in British Politics* (Harlow: Pearson, 2003); and R. Pyper, 'Politics and the Civil Service' *Politics Review*, September 2005, pp. 17–21. For recent and general overviews, see K. Jenkins, 'Parliament, government and the Civil Service', *Parliamentary Affairs*, **57** (4), 2004, pp. 800–13 and A. Gray and B. Jenkins, 'Government and administration: public service and public servants', *Parliamentary Affairs*, **58** (2), 2005, pp. 230–47.

Useful web sites on ministries, ministers and mandarins

Hot links to these sites can be found on the CWS at www.pearsoned.co.uk/budge.

A good way to start your research on the structure of ministries and departments is to visit the Cabinet Office web site www.cabinet-office.gov.uk and the direct government web site on http://www.direct.gov.uk where you will find a comprehensive description of the ministerial network and the organisation of the Civil Service. Web site addresses for Whitehall departments are listed in Table 6.1.

The official reference point for the Civil Service is their home page www.civilservice.gov.uk. In addition there are various sites where the functioning of the Civil Service is scrutinised. The FDA is the trade union and professional body for Britain's senior public servants (www.fda.org.uk). Using their search engine enables access to a variety of reports and articles on the Civil Service. Useful information is also available on www.epolitix.com (here again we recommend you use their search engine) and the Study of Parliament Group at www.spg.org.uk.

chapter 7

The changing state: administrative reforms

While the previous chapter concentrated on relationships between politicians and bureaucrats at the very highest levels of the Whitehall machine, this one turns to the broader administrative operations of the state and to the many attempts to reform it, especially in the past 25 years. The traditional model of the Civil Service is examined first, then the ways the Conservative governments of Thatcher and Major changed the system between 1979 and 1997. The chapter finishes with an account of how New Labour has adopted, adapted or dropped Conservative reforms.

This chapter discusses:

■ the traditional model of British public **administration** and a radical critique

■ reforming the public services in the 1980s and 1990s

■ the spread of quasi-government

■ an assessment of public sector reforms in the 1980s and 1990s

■ New Labour and the public sector: joined up or gummed up?

The British Civil Service: the traditional model and the radical critique

The traditional model

The traditional model of the Civil Service operated between 1854, when the Northcote-Trevelyan Report drew up the blueprint for it, and the early 1980s, when the Thatcher governments started a sweeping programme of reforms. The main features of the traditional model are as follows:

Administration

Either (1) the process of coordinating and implementing public policy through the machinery of the public bureaucracy; or (2) another word for government – as in 'the Blair administration'.

■ a Civil Service staffed by qualified and experienced bureaucrats

■ a culture of public service

■ accountability of the Civil Service through ministers who are answerable to Parliament for all the actions of their departments

■ a centralised system for recruiting, training, promoting and paying civil servants

■ promotion according to experience and ability (a meritocratic public service)

■ a permanent, politically neutral, anonymous and confidential Civil Service, with no constitutional role or responsibility distinct from ministers (see Chapter 6).

The Fulton Report

In many ways the Fulton Report of 1968 represents the culmination of the traditional model. The report produced 158 recommendations for change, but the most important were the following:

- less dependence on gifted all-rounders (often Oxbridge graduates and generalists with no special training or qualifications) and more on highly trained specialists and graduates from a variety of backgrounds

- the creation of a single Civil Service career stream to encourage the advancement of the most talented from all grades

- the creation of a Civil Service Department responsible for all recruitment and a Civil Service College responsible for post-entry training

- the hiving off of some responsibilities to semi-autonomous agencies and departments.

Fulton's main concern was to create a more efficient and professional Civil Service, but in spite of widespread publicity only some of its recommendations were implemented. The Civil Service Department and the Civil Service College were created to centralise recruitment and training, and the top-level administrative class was nominally merged with the executive and clerical grades. However, a de facto administrative class remained. In any case, the economic problems of the late 1960s and the 1970s diverted government attention elsewhere, and the Civil Service was left to reform itself, which meant minor changes rather than major reform.

Nevertheless, it became increasingly evident that the civil service did not always work according to the traditional model. We have already seen, in the previous chapter, how the principles of neutrality, anonymity, permanence and confidentiality were breached. Besides, it was increasingly claimed that the system was inadequate for the demands of late twentieth-century society. Criticism of the Civil Service began to grow: right-wing politicians claimed that top civil servants were part of the liberal establishment and promoted their own interests by favouring a larger and larger state machine; left-wingers criticised it for being part of the 'conservative establishment' that obstructed left-wing policies. More important, perhaps, the growth of the state combined with increasing financial pressures in the 1970s and 1980s meant that the Civil Service came under increasing scrutiny. Attention switched from questions about the political power of civil servants to concern about the inefficient operation of the vast state bureaucracy.

The radical critique

By the late 1970s right-wing intellectuals in the United States and Britain developed a radical critique of public services. Drawing on the increasingly influential rational choice theory, they argued that the very organisation of public services provides officials with an incentive to maximise their own interests, not those of the general public. They claimed that the structure of public bureaucracies favoured ever-expanding government programmes and spending, not to benefit the public but in the interests of bureaucrats who would gain power, prestige and pay if their empires grew. At the same time the recruitment, composition and public service ethos of the British Civil Service, it was said, insulates it from modern and efficient management practices.

BRIEFINGS

7.1 Rational choice theory and politics

Rational choice theory (a slightly different version is known as public choice theory) assumes that all political actors (politicians, voters, officials, interest groups) are self-interested and seek to maximise their own benefits. Public officials try to maximise their budgets and increase the size of their empires in order to enhance their personal benefits of promotion, salary, prestige. As a result, there will be an overprovision of public service and, shielded from market competition, costs will be high.

Privatisation will, according to the theory, eliminate this problem. Where full privatisation is not possible, governments should change the institutional rules and procedures in ways that alter officials' incentives to maximise spending. This means creating agencies to provide public services that are run along commercial, not public service lines, with predetermined cost and performance targets.

These ideas were pioneered by a number of American economists, including William Niskanen and Gordon Tullock. They provided the basis for the influential book by David Osborne and Ted Gaebler, *Reinventing Government: How the Entrepreneurial Spirit is Transforming the Public Sector* (Reading, MA: Addison Wesley, 1992), which influenced reforming politicians in both the United States and Britain.

Rational choice

An approach to political science that treats politics as the outcome of the interaction between rational individuals pursuing their own interests.

Many government problems in the 1970s were said to be caused by government 'overload' (ever-increasing public demands for bigger and better services, escalating costs, a growing army of officials), and in some circles this argument was closely linked to self-serving civil servants. In effect, the public sector lacked the discipline that market competition forced on the private sector.

With this general approach to public management in mind, the Thatcher governments of the 1980s, and the Major government of the 1990s, set about changing and reforming the British Civil Service in order to achieve the following:

- reduce its size and costs

- improve value for money by improving competition (and hence efficiency), partly by privatisation and partly by introducing business culture and incentives into the Civil Service

- increase freedom to manage – giving organisations the resources and freedom to maximise efficiency, unrestricted by centralised Civil Service rules and regulations

- de-privilege Civil Service salaries, pensions and job security

- meet the demands of the consumers and customers of public service.

Reforming public services: a managerial revolution?

Margaret Thatcher applied these ideas as part of her campaign against big government, and immediately set about reducing the size of the Civil Service. As Figure 7.1 shows, civil servant numbers started to decline in 1977, but fell sharply after Thatcher's election in 1979. She curtailed many Civil Service privileges (pay rises, job security, pension schemes), and introduced performance-related pay. Secondments to and from the private sector were encouraged. Her policies provoked strike action by the Civil Service unions but she faced this down and

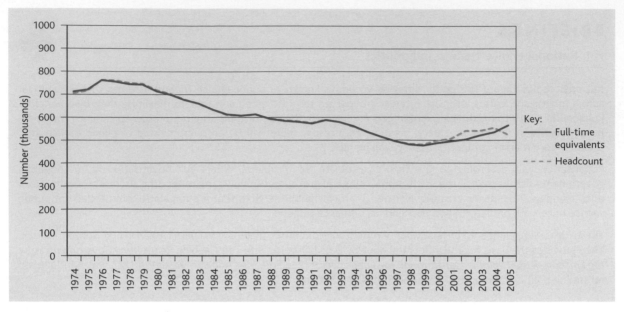

Figure 7.1 Estimated Civil Service numbers, 1974–2005

Source: Official Civil Service and National Statistics figures. Reproduced under the terms of the Click-Use Licence

they capitulated after 21 weeks. She later signalled her power over public service trade unions by banning them from the General Communications Headquarters (GCHQ). She also set about changing the structure of the Civil Service, starting with the abolition of the Civil Service Department, the key organisation protecting the traditional model (see Briefing 7.2).

These changes pale into insignificance compared with the total overhaul of Whitehall organisation that the government implemented in the 1980s, starting in

BRIEFINGS

7.2 Management of the Civil Service, 1965–2000

Until 1968 most of the personnel and training functions of the Civil Service were the responsibility of the Treasury. Indeed at that time the head of the Home Civil Service was also the head of the Treasury. In 1968 the Civil Service Department (CSD), responsible for all personnel matters, was created, along with a Civil Service College (CSC), responsible for training. However, the CSD was viewed with increasing hostility by the Thatcher government, which regarded it as a powerful and partisan supporter of Civil Service interests. So it was abolished in 1981 and most of its functions transferred to the Management Personnel Office (MPO) in the Cabinet Office, where it was under the immediate control of the PM.

In the late 1980s the MPO was transformed, reorganised and renamed several times, eventually becoming the Office of Public Service (OPS). In this guise it was the corporate headquarters of the Civil Service contained within the Cabinet Office. It was responsible for the overall implementation of Civil Service reforms, including the Efficiency Unit, **Next Steps** and the Citizen's Charter, as well as recruitment and training. It then disappeared as a separate entity for a time, being absorbed into the rest of the Cabinet Office, but reappeared in a new form in the Cabinet Office in 2001 as the Office for Public Sector Reform.

This example shows how rapidly units of government at the highest levels have been reformed, reorganised, renamed, abolished and revived, and all in the name of efficiency, managerial effectiveness and policy innovation, though to what effect is difficult or impossible to judge.

Next Steps

The short title of the Ibbs Report, *Improving Management in Government: The Next Steps* (HMSO, 1988), which identified serious management failure in the Civil Service and recommended far-reaching reforms in the shape of executive agencies.

1979 with the creation of the Efficiency Unit under the direction of Sir Derek Rayner. Significantly, he was not a civil servant, but a leading businessman who had been chairman of Marks & Spencer. The purpose of the unit was to identify areas where major savings could be achieved, including the abolition of unnecessary tasks. It made lightning visits to departments in search of savings for the remainder of the 1980s, producing in 1988 the most radical proposals for reform in its report *Improving Management in Government: The Next Steps*. Its tone was very different from Fulton. As one advocate of the reforms puts it:

> Next Steps is more like a report from a management consultancy firm than a traditional Civil Service review. It is glossy, bold and evangelical. The traditional mandarin style of drafting to avoid commitment has been replaced by a fresh passion for revitalisation and change . . . It is predicated on the belief that there is an important discipline of 'management' which has been traditionally and mistakenly overlooked by the Civil Service in favour of traditional 'policy skills'.
>
> Patricia Greer, *Transforming Central Government: The Next Steps Initiative*, Buckingham: Open University Press, 1994, p. 6

BRIEFINGS

7.3 Drive for efficiency, 1979–97

1979 Rayner's Raiders   Thatcher appoints Sir Derek (later Lord) Rayner as head of a new Efficiency Unit. Based in the Cabinet Office, the unit's brief was to improve efficiency by reducing costs and eliminating waste. Derek Rayner was replaced by Sir Robin Ibbs in 1983. By the early 1990s the unit was claiming savings of £1.5 billion.

1982 MINIS   As environment secretary, Michael Heseltine introduces Management Information Systems for Ministers (MINIS) to provide him with continuous and systematic information for the financial management of his department. No other department adopted MINIS in full, though some used watered-down versions.

1982 FMI   The Financial Management Initiative (FMI) required departments to identify clear policy objectives and to test performance in relation to these objectives. Managers within departments were given more control over their budgets or 'cost centres' and required to operate within cash limits. FMI was not fully implemented, mainly because it is difficult to identify clear objectives with some public services.

1988 Next Steps   The Efficiency Unit's *Improving Management in Government: The Next Steps. Report to the Prime Minister* proposes the separation of policy from management: the government to set policy; **executive agencies** with considerable operational and budgetary autonomy to be responsible for management.

1991 Market testing   The **White Paper** 'Competing for Quality' heralds the adoption of **market testing** throughout government.

1991 Citizen's Charter   Designed to make public services increasingly responsive to the needs of consumers (regarded as market customers rather than public service clients).

1992 PFI   The government launches the Private Finance Initiative (PFI) to encourage the private financing of public facilities. Private consortia raise capital and then, with contracts from the government, create facilities that generate income for them for a fixed period.

1994 *The Civil Service: Continuity and Change*   This White Paper gave executive agencies greater discretion on recruitment and pay.

1995 Annual efficiency plans   Departments required to plan for increased efficiency and to state how they would keep to their budgets.

1996 Benchmarking   Introduced to establish best practices for Next Steps agencies and to encourage them to learn from private management practice.

Executive agencies

Also known as 'Next Step agencies' – the semi-autonomous agencies set up to carry out some of the administrative functions of government that were previously the responsibility of Civil Service departments.

White Paper

Government document outlining proposed legislation in order to permit discussion and consultation of the policy. White Papers may be preceded by Green Papers, which are also consultative documents, but they outline various policy alternatives rather than the firmer policy proposals that the government sets out in its White Papers.

Market testing

The process of deciding whether a public service should be produced at all and, if so, whether it should be produced by the public sector, contracted out or privatised.

Benchmarking

The practice of measuring public sector cost efficiency against the standards of the private sector.

Next Steps: the theory

The main recommendations of Next Steps were as follows:

- To separate 'steering from rowing' or policy from management. Once the government has made a policy and set the targets, the management and delivery of services can best be done not by traditional Civil Service departments, but by separate bodies working under commercial contracts to agreed costs and targets.

- This decentralised system to be based on two main devices: semi-independent and specialised executive agencies to carry out particular functions; and by contracting out to commercial businesses.

- The heads of the agencies (chief executives) should have commercial contracts for a limited time according to an agreed business plan, and staff should be rewarded according to performance. Senior staff to be appointed in open competition.

- The centralised Civil Service should be decentralised into a series of executive agencies, each with its own powers (within the terms of the contract) to set the pay, recruitment and conditions of work.

Next Steps: the practice

The government accepted these recommendations with enthusiasm and immediately set about the business of setting up executive agencies. By 1993 there were 97 such agencies covering a vast range of public services from National Savings and the Royal Mint to Ordnance Survey and the Prison Service. There are no exact figures, but between 1979 and 1989 Civil Service numbers fell by about 238,000 and most of these people were transferred into executive agencies (see Figure 7.1). In 2005 there were 211 executive agencies employing 288,000 people. Many of these are small – in 2005 the National Weights and Measures Laboratory had 50 staff, as did the Foreign Offices Conference Centre at Wilton Park – but some are very large and involve important government functions. The Pensions Service employs 78,860 (see Table 7.1).

In 1991 the thinking behind Next Steps was extended to other areas of government by means of 'market testing'. Designed to explore whether value for money can best be achieved by contracting out to private producers – known, more

BRIEFINGS

7.4 Patricia Greer on contract government

One of the basic principles of Next Steps is that executive agencies are provided with the freedom and the tools to get on with their 'businesses' and that in return agencies must deliver certain outputs or standards of service within the available resources. This basic principle is enforced through a series of 'contracts' which essentially specify what freedoms an agency has, how much money it has and what ends the agency must achieve.

At a more detailed level agencies contract other agencies through 'service level agreements' to perform particular functions such as computer services, providing contribution record data or accommodation services. In other words, the 'contractor' becomes a 'client' organisation which must manage its dealings with other contract agencies.

Greer, op. cit., p. 60

Table 7.1 Top ten executive agencies, by number of staff, 2003

The Pensions Service	78,860
Forensic Science Service	43,210
Jobcentre Plus	11,120
Court service	9,520
HM Land Registry	8,180
Driver and Vehicle Licensing Agency	5,320
Warship Support Agency	5,140
Social Security (Northern Ireland)	4,845
Defence Storage and Distribution Service	4,480
Scottish Prison Service	4,450

Source: Cabinet Office, *Public Bodies 2005* (from the Public Bodies On-Line Directory), London, 2005. Reproduced under the terms of the Click-Use Licence

simply, as shopping around for the best service at the best price – market testing resulted in contracting out such things as the Inland Revenue's information technology service. By 1996 some £3.6 billion worth of services had been tested, with total savings claimed to be in excess of £700 million, although the figure involves some guesswork and perhaps some wishful thinking as well. Depending on the agency or service concerned, in-house bids from those already providing it could be included, and these won most of the contracts.

Various other experiments to introduce market or quasi-market forces into public services were also tried:

- Some services (notably the NHS) tried to create quasi- or 'internal' markets by separating the provider of a service from the purchaser – i.e. one part or department within a single organisation has to pay another for the services it provides.

- Some executive agencies, once established, were then sold to the private sector. In 1996: the Chessington Computer Centre (providing payroll, financial and accounting services) was sold for £15.5 million pounds; the Recruitment and Assessment Services (providing recruitment and personnel services) for £7.25 million; and Her Majesty's Stationery Office (HMSO) for £54 million.

- Voucher schemes were experimented with in nursery education.

- The Private Finance Initiative was launched in 1992 as a form of public–private partnership involving transferring some or all of the risks of public services to the private sector. Sometimes this involves private sector investment in public projects, sometimes private sector purchasing, and sometimes contracting out to the private sector.

Quangos

Quasi-autonomous non-governmental organisations financed by the government to perform public service functions but not under direct government control. Examples include the BBC and the Commission for Racial Equality (CRE).

Spread of quasi-government

Another change that swept through the public sector in the 1980s and 1990s was the growth of quasi-government. The government itself refers to the strange creatures that inhabit this twilight world as non-departmental public bodies. Academics and journalists usually call them **quangos** (quasi-autonomous non-governmental organisations), or extra-government organisations (EGOs). They are large in number and varied in function, but are all run by people appointed by the government, not by elected politicians or career civil servants. They are public bodies appointed by, but not immediately controlled by the government, and they perform public functions at 'arm's length' from the government.

BRIEFINGS

7.5 Quasi-government: The quango state

The government identifies four types of non-departmental public bodies:

1. Executive non-departmental public bodies. Established by statute to carry out public functions, they have their own staff and budgets.

2. Advisory NDPBs provide independent advice to ministers on particular topics. They do not usually have their own staff or budgets, but are supported by government departments.

3. Tribunals with judicial functions in specialised fields of law. They are usually provided with staff and money by government departments.

4. Independent Monitoring Boards – formerly known as Boards of Visitors or watchdogs of the prison system.

To this list must be added a number of other agencies that occupy the spaces between the pure public and private sectors, including opted-out schools and colleges, and housing action trusts (HATs). According to a report of the House of Commons Select Committee on Public Administration there were 8,466 quangos in Britain in 2002. Executive agencies are close to government departments or parts of them. But, like quangos, they are supposed to be distanced from government departments. In 1979 the Conservative government pledged itself to reduce the number of quangos, but actually increased them rapidly. New Labour has promised to open up public appointments to quangos by broadening the social and educational base of appointees.

Along with other democracies, Britain has long history of public or semi-public bodies that are distinct from the government. For example, the BBC was created to provide a public service that was not subject to political interference in news broadcasting. There was a rapid spread of quangos in the 1980s for two main reasons:

1. Central government found them useful because they bypassed normal political channels and institutions (often Labour controlled) and delivered particular services in line with its own policy. The government argued that they were less bureaucratic than other public sector organisations. Critics argued that they were run by largely unaccountable, hand-picked supporters of the government.

2. Privatisation led to the setting up of regulatory agencies – e.g. Oftel, Ofgas and Ofwat to regulate telephone, gas and water services.

Public sector reform: an assessment

The 1979–97 reforms, drastic and fundamental in their effects, were not the product of a thought-out master plan, but a piecemeal, step-by-step process that found its way by accident and experience. Nonetheless, reform in the United Kingdom was part of a much wider set of changes that occurred across many western states in the 1980s and 1990s, often referred to as 'the **new public management**'. Thatcher was a leading exponent of NPM, but by no means alone.

There were, inevitably, teething problems with the British reforms. For example, Group 4's contract with the prison service to transport prisoners brought public derision following a number of escapes. In the long run there have also been notable difficulties: the Child Support Agency (CSA) has lurched from one embarrassing problem to the next; those following rail privatisation; deregulation may have let in foot and mouth and mad cow disease; privately run government computer systems crashed; electricity blacked out, in spite of government bailouts of the industry. The long-term effects of the public sector reforms, however, are not at all clear and arouse great controversy. The outlines of the argument are

New public management (NPM)

The term applied to a mixed package of public sector reforms in many western states in the 1980s and 1990s, including the introduction of business management techniques and structures, the decentralisation and privatisation of public services, the deregulation of the private sector, and greater use of private–public and semi-autonomous agencies. Also known as 'reinventing government', it is said to have had the effect of 'hollowing out the state', that is, reducing its operations and transferring some functions to the private sector or other bodies.

CONTROVERSY

The Thatcher–Major public service reforms

For	Against
Efficiency With fewer employed and lower costs public services are more efficient	*Efficiency? Who can tell?* It is difficult to measure efficiency in the public sector and the government did not monitor performance anyway. Independent studies suggest that efficiency drives have not achieved their targets.
Quality Service standards are higher	*Quality? Who can tell?* There is no clear evidence about public service quality. This would be expected to rise over time without the reforms, in any case.
Decentralisation The rigid and centralised Civil Service has been replaced by flexible and decentralised agencies with modern management	*Fragmentation* Government bureaucracies are even more fragmented than they were, and joined-up government is even more difficult. Some quangos and executive agencies show no signs of modern management.
Responsiveness Helped by the Citizen's Charters, executive agencies are more responsive to consumer demands	*Unresponsiveness* Executive agencies are more responsive to market forces than client needs. If they respond it is to the most vocal and articulate groups – i.e. the educated middle class who can work the system.
Specialised skills Executive agencies develop specialised skills to perform their particular jobs	*Specialised monopolies* Skills lost to the public sector are not likely to be regained.
Competition Competition reduces costs	*Natural monopolies* Some privatised services are natural monopolies and others are not economically viable. The first will charge monopoly prices unless closely regulated (gas, water, electricity), the second will fail financially (railways).
Sweeping away bureaucracy Reforms replaced bureaucracy with more efficient market or quasi-market mechanisms	*Extra bureaucracy* Reforms in hospitals, schools and universities have created a huge extra bureaucratic burden.
Deregulation Removing red tape has set service providers free to do their jobs effectively	*Reregulation* Deregulation is inevitably followed by reregulation to prevent crises such as mad cow disease, foot and mouth, and railway disasters.
Separating steering from rowing Creating executive agencies leaves ministers and senior civil servants free to get on with policy making	*Policy making and administration* Policy making and administration are inseparable. Predictably, some ministers have interfered endlessly with agency administration.
Customers not clients Public service consumers should be treated as markets treat customers	*Clients not customers* Many public service core users (pupils and students, prisoners, hospital patients, children, the mentally ill) are not customers, and public service professionals (teachers, doctors, social workers) are not business or salespeople.
Accountability Ministers and agencies have clear lines of responsibility and accountability. Ministers 'steer', agencies 'row'	*Lack of accountability* Lines of ministerial accountability are more confused and weaker with semi-autonomous executive agencies.
Markets Market reforms have greatly improved public services	*Public service* The public service ethos, essential between the state and its services, has been severely damaged.

contained in the 'Controversy', but it is worth looking at three especially important government aspects of the reforms in greater detail – fragmentation, accountability, and efficiency.

Fragmentation

One of the major problems of British government in the post-war period – and quite possibly of *any* government in the modern world – is the fragmentation caused by the inevitable division of the state bureaucracy into separate departments and units. This tends to create overlapping, confusing, competing and incompatible policies and services. The reforms of the 1980s and early 1990s made the problem worse. The fragmentation of the public and quasi-public sector is now so great and confusing that it is difficult to obtain simple, reliable statistics even on something as straightforward as the number of organisations involved. But with an estimated total of more than 8,500 bodies, the quango state adds to the fragmentation of modern government.

Accountability

Fragmentation undermines accountability partly because it can be difficult to find out who is responsible to whom for doing what, partly because quasi-public bodies often work and take decisions in secret, and partly because many of them seem to be accountable to no one in particular. This is all the worse if, as often charged, the Thatcher and Major governments stacked quangos with their own party supporters, otherwise known as local notables, 'reliable chaps' and 'safe hands'. Although this was supposed to have been corrected by the creation of the Office of the Commissioner for Public Appointments (OCPA), in 2003 an official inquiry found that only one in six central government quangos were subject to OCPA regulation, and appointments to local quangos are not regulated at all. Many quangos are not accessible to the general public, and are not subject to full public audit.

The accountability problem of executive agencies is different but just as serious. It occurs when ministers, who remain responsible for the overall operation of their departments, pass the buck to chief executive officers when a problem arises. If 'operations' are separated from 'policy' then agency chiefs are responsible for maladministration. But, nonetheless, ministers are responsible constitutionally. This problem was graphically illustrated by the Prison Service Agency when, in 1995, the chief executive, Derek Lewis, was obliged to resign following a series of successful prison breakouts. The home secretary, Michael Howard, said it was an 'operational' and not a 'policy' problem, though he was accused by Lewis of interfering repeatedly in operational matters.

Efficiency

There are serious questions about the efficiency of some of the new bodies. Many quangos are not run by professionals or experienced managers, and devolving services to small, independent agencies can involve additional administrative costs and inefficiencies. The **Democratic Audit** found that clerical and accounting costs had risen rapidly in opted-out schools and hospital trusts, and that cost management in some bodies was defective. In 1994 the House of Commons' Public Accounts Committee found that the management standards of quangos, rather than rising, had fallen during the early 1990s. In some instances corruption, serious maladministration and waste of public money was uncovered, and the committee was 'seriously concerned', 'surprised' and even 'appalled' by the record of one regional hospital authority.

Democratic Audit

A private body that monitors and publishes regular reports on democracy and political freedom in Britain – see www.democraticaudit.com

One response to the problems of fragmentation, lack of accountability and inefficiency has been to add a new layer of regulation and inspection. A whole new industry of 'auditing' and monitoring has been created including the National Audit Office, the Prisons Inspectorate, the Office of the Commissioner for Public Appointments, the Office of Public Service Reform, the Better Regulation Unit in the Cabinet Office, the Benefit Fraud Inspectorate, the Commission for Health Improvement, and so on. The list runs to about 150 auditing organisations, spending close to £1,000 million, and probably incurring a roughly equivalent amount from the inspected and regulated bodies.

New Labour and the public sector

On coming to power, New Labour accepted many of the broad reforms of the Thatcher–Major governments. It took the following steps:

- declared the Next Steps agencies 'an integral part of the government machine'

- accepted Citizens' Charters and revived them in 1998 as *Service First*

- agreed to benchmarking and contracting out in both central and local government (see Chapter 12)

Plate 7.1 Superman Blair promises more and better public services than public private partnerships (PPP) can deliver, in spite of their cost

Source: Chris Riddell/The Observer 24th March 2002, Centre for the Study of Cartoons & Caricature, University of Kent

■ accepted the principle of selling central government assets (a majority stake in the Commonwealth Development Corporation was sold and, controversially, the National Air Traffic Services was privatised in 2001, and the defence firm, QinettiQ, was floated on the market in 2006, to the great profit of its US investors)

■ developed the practice of setting public policy targets, penalties and rewards, and using league tables

■ emphasised the importance of market, or market-like, competition between providers and choice in public services, especially education and health.

At the same time, New Labour has given some new twists to administrative reform. In its early years it created the People's Panel and emphasised joined-up government, and it has also pushed ahead with the Private Finance Initiative.

The People's Panel

A panel of 5,000 randomly selected people was used as a sounding board for opinion about public services, but the idea was quietly dropped in 2002.

Joined-up government

All modern governments wrestle with the intractable problem of departmental fragmentation in the modern, large-scale state. To some extent sprawling, specialised and competing public (and private) bureaucracies are inevitable. This makes joined-up government difficult, even impossible, to achieve. New Labour's concern with joined-up government was not new to British government: Churchill experimented (1951–3) with 16 'overlords' to coordinate the activities of Whitehall departments; Wilson (1964–70) tried merging departments to create 'super departments', such as Health and Social Security; and Heath created the Central Policy Review Staff in 1971 to give collective advice to ministers and overall direction to government policy. Blair gave this idea a vigorous new life in the early years of New Labour, setting up special bodies to try to integrate and coordinate policy in key areas such as education, health, social exclusion and electronic commerce. Often these were located in the Prime Minister's Office where he could keep a close eye on them.

Unfortunately, creating new units and agencies of government to foster co-ordination and integration may simply have added yet another layer of government and a new array of offices, units, departments, committees and task forces to the already fragmented and stratified structure, thereby making the problem of fragmentation even worse. Some observers of government under Blair have described it as 'congested' and not so much joined up as gummed up.

There is also an inherent tension between the government's drive to decentralise and offer local freedom of choice, on the one hand, and its top-down attempts at joined-up government and driving up the quality of public services on the other. New Labour has tried to reverse the inexorable trend towards a more and more highly centralised state. At the same time joined-up government and national performance standards for schools, hospitals and public service agencies rest on centralisation, hence many of the new units chasing joined-up government were located in the PM's or the Cabinet Office.

One can easily imagine Sir Humphrey, of *Yes, Minister*, explaining the latest agency for joined up to his befuddled minister in the following way: 'A new unit has been set up in the Cabinet Office to centrally co-ordinate the decentralised agencies that were created to monitor the central policy of the decentralised co-ordination of decentralisation. This replaced the policy of the previous government that created decentralised agencies to monitor the centralised policy of the decentralisation of centralisation within the ministries.' Perhaps this helps to explain why one now hears much less about joined-up government than in the early years of New Labour.

The private finance initiative

The private finance initiative (PFI) is a form of public/private partnership that encourages private involvement in public services at both central and local government levels. Unlike privatisation, PFI maintains a large role for the public sector that lays down the original specification of schemes to be designed, built, financed and operated by the private sector. The private contractors then lease back their products to the public sector in return for annual payments from the public purse over a 30–60-year period. The PFI scheme covers many hospital trusts, road building, the Channel Tunnel, schools, and all sorts of building projects for the Home Office and Ministry of Defence. In 2003 there were 570 PFI contracts and annual public costs in 2006 were estimated at £6,000 million.

PFI is strongly advocated by the government on the grounds that it offers value for money and injects capital and efficient management into public projects. But it has come under fierce criticism from many quarters on grounds of costs and effectiveness. The 2002 Labour Party conference voted against PFI, but the government has pressed on with contracts, controversially overruling the advice of an outside expert on how to fund London transport.

One of the main problems of PFI has been the rising and/or hidden costs of contracts, sometimes accompanied by large private sector profits. These have resulted in severe problems and financial difficulties (even collapse) in some agencies, including the Channel Tunnel, the Skye Bridge, council house repairs, the Passport Agency, the Inverness airport terminal, the Kidderminster Hospital, the Darent Valley Hospital in Kent, Norfolk schools, and the flagship of NHS PFI schemes, the Queen Elizabeth Hospital Trust in Greenwich. The PFI is said to transfer the risks of public services to the private sector. But when essential or politically sensitive projects are at risk, public authorities have sometimes bailed out the projects rather than have them fail. One problem with assessing PFI is that the government has never made known its total costs. Another is that it is simply impossible to know how PFI will eventually work out in financial, management or efficiency terms.

Summary

- The traditional Whitehall Model of the Civil Service presents it as a hierarchical, centralised, public service bureaucracy, with clear lines of responsibility from impartial civil servants to elected ministers and to Parliament. This has never been a precise portrayal of British public administration, although it has approximated the ideal in some respects.

- The public sector reforms of the Thatcher–Major governments, 1979–97, were intended to transform the traditional model radically by introducing market competition and business management in order to improve public service quality and reduce costs.

- The most important single innovation was the separation of policy making (steering) from management (rowing) by turning over many administrative tasks to more than 100 semi-autonomous executive agencies, run on commercial lines, and with chief executive officers on short-term contracts.

- Another change was the creation of a large quasi-government sector.

- There is much controversy about the effects of the 1979–97 reforms, and no clear-cut conclusions, although there is some evidence that government by quango lacks efficiency and accountability and goes against 'joined-up' government.

▶

- New Labour has accepted many Thatcher–Major reforms and added a few of its own, extending in particular the controversial PFI scheme.
- Most notably, New Labour has tried to create joined-up government, although success has been hard to achieve, particularly with 'hiving off' and privatisation.

MILESTONES

Milestones in administrative reform

1968	The Fulton Report aimed at a more professional Civil Service that recruited more widely
1968	Civil Service Department set up
1968	Civil Service College founded
1979	Efficiency Unit set up by Margaret Thatcher to review departmental performance
1981	CSD abolished. Management Personnel Office more closely linked to Cabinet Office
1983	Financial Management Initiative requires policy objectives to be specified and more managerial autonomy
1983	Cabinet secretary emerges as head of the Civil Service
1983	Privatisation of state-owned property and industry begins in earnest
1988	Efficiency Unit publishes *Next Steps*, proposing the separation of management from policy and creation of autonomous executive agencies in central government. Many such agencies created in the following years
1991	Citizen's Charter launched, specifying consumer rights in various areas
1992	Private Finance Initiative encourages private finance of government projects
1995	Office of Public Service succeeds CSD but remains under control of Cabinet Office
1997	New Labour government accepts the major administrative changes of 1979–97. Appoints more political advisers to Whitehall, and is criticised for continuing Thatcher's policy of politicising the Civil Service. Creation of the Social Exclusion Unit, the first of the attempts to create joined-up government. Government support for PFI announced in *Partnerships for Prosperity*
1998	White Paper, 'Modernising Government', and Wilson Report on Civil Service reform
1998	Comprehensive Spending Review by Treasury of three years' departmental plans introduced by Gordon Brown as regular feature of government
1999	Neill Committee on Standards in Public Life recommends a limit to the number of special advisers in Whitehall, and a code of conduct for them. White Paper on 'Modernising Government'
2000	First general statement on joined-up government produced by the government in *Wiring It Up: Whitehall's Policies of Cross-cutting Policies and Services*, produced by the Cabinet Office
2001	Blair second election victory prompts fresh attempts to reorganise the Prime Minister's Office and the Cabinet Office to promote joined-up government and to push through reforms
2001	National Air Traffic Services privatised
2002	Lyons report recommends relocating 20,000 civil servants outside the south-west of England, and Gershon Report says that 80,000 civil servants could be cut, saving £20 billion.

Essays

1. Which of the Thatcher–Major reforms of Whitehall has New Labour adopted, and which has it rejected? Why has it done so?

2. Why is joined-up government essential but difficult to achieve? What effect did the Thatcher–Major reforms have, and how successful are New Labour's attempts to create joined-up government likely to be?

Projects

1. (For class debate) What are the reasons for claiming or denying the idea that hospital patients, old people, young children, prisoners, the mentally ill and handicapped, and single parents are customers of public services? What are the implications of your answer for replacing the public service ethos with a market approach?

2. (For class debate) What are the reasons for believing that public service efficiency and quality have improved since 1979 as a result of reforms? Why is it so difficult to know?

Further reading

A vast literature exists on the organisation of British public services in general and recent Civil Service reforms in particular, but among the more useful of recent books are R. Pyper, *Britain's Modernised Civil Service* (Basingstoke: Palgrave, 2007); C. Pilkington, *The Civil Service in Britain Today* (Manchester: Manchester University Press, 1999); and D. Richards, *The Civil Service under the Conservatives 1979–1997* (Brighton: Sussex Academic Press, 1997). For a careful empirical study of the demise of the traditional Whitehall model, see Colin Campbell and Graham K. Wilson, *The End of Whitehall: Death of a Paradigm* (Oxford: Blackwell, 1995), and for an analysis of the policy-making role, see Edwards Page and Bill Jenkins, *Policy Bureaucracy: Government with a Cast of Thousands* (Oxford: Oxford University Press, 2005). Two useful collections of readings are P. Barberis (ed.), *The Whitehall Reader: The UK's Administrative Machine in Action* (Milton Keynes: Open University Press, 1996) and P. Barberis (ed.), *The Civil Service in an Era of Change* (Aldershot: Dartmouth, 1997).

A comprehensive review of recent developments is to be found in A. Gray and B. Jenkins, 'Government and administration: public service and public servants', *Parliamentary Affairs*, **58** (2), April 2005, pp. 230–47. Recent and useful reviews of the Thatcher–Major reforms and the New Labour record so far are R. A. W. Rhodes, 'New Labour's Civil Service: summing-up joining-up', *Political Quarterly*, **71** (2), 2000, pp. 151–66, and D. Kavanagh and D. Richards, 'Departmentalism and joined-up government: back to the future?' *Parliamentary Affairs*, **54**, 2001, pp. 1–18. Shorter articles are T. Butcher, 'The Civil Service under New Labour', *Politics Review*, **11** (3), 2002, pp. 29–31 and R. Pyper, 'The Civil Service under Blair', *Politics Review*, **9** (3), 2000, pp. 2–6; T. Butcher, 'The Civil Service: structure and management', in R. Pyper and L. Robins, *United Kingdom Governance* (Basingstoke: Palgrave, 2000); and M. Moran, 'The new regulatory state in Britain', *Talking Politics*, **13** (3), 2001, pp. 109–13.

Useful web sites on the changing state and administrative reforms

Hot links to these sites can be found on the CWS at www.pearsoned.co.uk/budge.

The web has much information concerning the British Civil Service and its transformation. A detailed account of changes between 1967 and 1997 can be obtained from the report of the Select Committee on Public Services at www.parliament.the-stationery-office.co.uk/pa/ld199798/ldselect/ldpubsrv/055/psrep03.htm. The British Council also offers interesting insights on the reform of the Civil Service (www.britcoun.org/governance). Since 1997, there have been major transformations in this area, for which the best source of information is the Cabinet Office web site www.cabinet-office.gov.uk and the Civil Service official site www.civilservice.gov.uk. A general overview of the reforms introduced by the Labour government in this area and others in the last five years can be found at www.politics.guardian.co.uk/fiveyears. A good deal of documentation on the renewal process can be obtained by using the search engine of the Archive of Official Documents web site at www.archive.official-documents.co.uk.

If you are interested in a comparative perspective on the reform of the Civil Service, visit the World Bank web site at www.worldbank.org/publicsector/civilservice.

There are also many sites offering information on the myriad quasi-autonomous non-governmental organisations (quangos). The first step is to visit the public bodies' web site at www.quango.gov.uk. You can also check the Office of the Commissioner for Public Appointments (www.ocpa.gov.uk). We suggest that you also visit the Committee on Standards in Public Life (www.public-standards.gov.uk) and the Local Government Association (www.lga.gov.uk). Academic analysis of public administration can be obtained from www.sourceuk.net/indexf.html.

The Parliamentary Commissioner for Administration (PCA) maintains a web site to address citizen grievances concerning the activities of government departments or agencies (www.parliament.ombudsman.org.uk). Her Majesty's Stationery Office (www.hmso.gov.uk) has full documentation on the Local Government Act 1992 and the Citizen's Charter. Visit the Council of Europe site (www.coe.fr/index.asp) for the full text of the European Convention for the Protection of Human Rights. Reports on the quality of British democracy in general can be found at www.democratic.org.uk. For comments and feedback on the public sector and its management, visit www.publicnet.co.uk.

PART 3

Sovereignty

chapter 8

Britain in Europe

As our discussion of central government, and even of the constitution shows, British politics have increasingly taken on a European dimension. The former European (Economic) Community (EC, EEC) changed its name to the European Union by the Treaty of Maastricht (1992). This symbolised the intention of the member countries, particularly France and Germany, to transform it into something more than an economic union. An important stage was marked by the adoption of a common currency, the euro, by 11 of these members in 1999. Britain stood aloof and clearly has no intention of joining in the foreseeable future.

'Europe' affects British politics in a number of ways. One is the role Britain plays as one of the major member states of the EU. That is the subject of this chapter. The other is the impact of the EU in Britain itself (Chapter 9), where the increasing integration of the country into European administrative structures means that British politics cannot adequately be described without the European dimension. The inseparability of European from domestic politics was shown in such an everyday but far-reaching matter as the specification in 1998 of a minimum wage following EU practice (despite Conservative opposition).

The fact that European bodies can now legislate for Britain independently of the government shows that national sovereignty is being eroded. By the same token a new entity, in which Britain constitutes just one unit, is clearly emerging.

This chapter describes the institutional development of the European Union and the British role within it. It covers:

- the nature and development of the European Union
- the British role
- the Single European Act, the Treaties of Maastricht, Amsterdam, Nice and the European Constitution; towards a European federal state?
- Europe as a crisis issue in British politics
- enlargement of the Union: how this affects Britain.

The European Union: origins and development

Britain is currently one of 25 member states of the European Union. It is not one of the founding members, however, since the Union originated in 1951 as the 'European Coal and Steel Community' (ECSC) grouping France, Germany, the Netherlands, Belgium, Luxembourg and Italy. Although severely functional in form and designed ostensibly to rationalise the continental iron and coal industry,

BRIEFINGS

8.1 The Council of Europe

The Council of Europe was an early attempt to integrate the European countries, set up in 1949 as an **inter-governmental consultative organisation** designed to advance cooperation between members and help encourage democracy and human rights throughout Europe. The Council meets in Strasbourg, France, and is made up of a Committee of Ministers, a Parliamentary Assembly and a Congress of Local and Regional Authorities. Meeting four times a year, the Assembly adopts resolutions and the Council then makes recommendations to members. In spite of this state-like structure, the Council of Europe has no legislative powers. Decisions are taken by consensus of all members. Until recently the most important function of the Council was the operation of the European Convention on Human Rights, which was created in 1954 and whose rules are enforced by the Court of Human Rights. Note that this Court, whose decisions are binding on members, is not an EU institution.

By 2005 the Council of Europe had 46 members. Since the fall of communism the Council's role as a forum for advancing democracy has increased substantially. A newly created European Commission for Democracy through Law advises emerging democratic countries on constitutional and other matters. In addition, membership of the Council is seen as a first step towards membership of the EU.

Inter-governmental consultative organisations

International organisations that allow national states to cooperate on specific matters while maintaining their national sovereignty.

the project actually masked political ambitions to integrate France and Germany so thoroughly that they would never be able to go to war again as they had in 1914 and 1939, provoking colossal destruction and 20,000,000 deaths.

While supporting this initiative Britain did not join it. In the 1950s British governments saw their interests in terms of three overlapping spheres of influence: the Commonwealth, the United States and Europe. The financial transactions of the City and its world trading relationships gave Britain stronger overseas links than with the continent.

Although British and continental attitudes to European cooperation have varied over the half-century since, the generally enthusiastic approach of the continentals to integration and the scepticism of the British have been constants throughout.

Plate 8.1 Vicky cartoon in the *Evening Standard*, 1962, showing Britain (personified by Harold Macmillan) caught in a dilemma between its Commonwealth commitments and a new European future

Source: Daily Express

"BUT MY DEAR, YOU KNOW — ALL THESE RUMOURS OF OUR BREAK-UP ARE RIDICULOUS!"

Underlying this contrast has been the British commitment to free trade and thus to a purely economic Common Market, as distinct from continental support for full-blooded political union.

The ECSC was important because it established the principle of functional integration – integrating specific industrial or economic sectors under a supranational institutional authority responsible for policing a European policy. It became the precursor of the European Economic Community created by the Treaty of Rome in 1957. In turn this was to develop into the European Union in the 1990s. From its very beginning the EEC opened up the possibility of evolving from a loose confederation of countries concerned only with integration in certain functional

Map 8.1 The enlargement of the European Union, 1957–2006

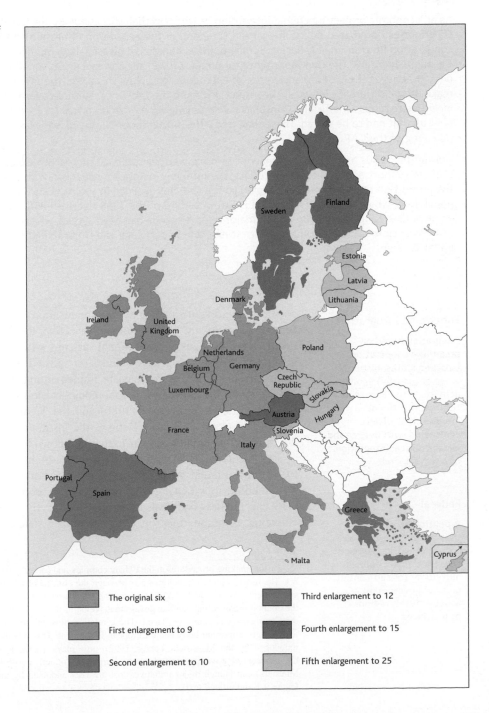

The original six	Third enlargement to 12
First enlargement to 9	Fourth enlargement to 15
Second enlargement to 10	Fifth enlargement to 25

BRIEFINGS

8.2 Functional integration and the Common Agricultural Policy

Following failures to create a European state directly after the war, continental leaders decided that **functional integration** would make the members of the EC interdependent economically and that this would encourage political integration. The reasoning was that, if countries shared common production and pricing policies in such essential goods as coal, steel, atomic power and agriculture, they would be locked into economic interdependence and would therefore have every incentive to cooperate on other matters (a phenomenon that social scientists have called spillover). This would then eliminate the sort of competition and conflict that led to the Second World War.

As an economic project functional integration proved less than successful. By the late 1950s national rather than EC priorities dominated policy in coal and steel and in the generation of atomic energy. Only in agriculture did cooperation flourish, mainly because of the political benefits of pleasing large numbers of small farmers in France, Germany and Italy. The Common Agricultural Policy (CAP) set artificial prices for all the major agricultural products. Whenever the world market price of a product fell below this price, the EC imposed tariffs on imports to make up the difference between the market price and the CAP price. Inefficient farmers were, therefore, given an incentive to remain inefficient. Consumers were paying above-market prices for food and in addition a surplus was built up that had to be stored. These surpluses – the 'butter mountains' and 'wine lakes' – resulted in a widespread ridiculing of the CAP.

During the 1980s and 1990s a number of reforms were initiated, all of which were designed to reduce the level of price support and eventually to replace the intervention price mechanism with direct income support. While the proportion of the EU budget devoted to the CAP has declined in recent years – as indeed has the agricultural population, which at around 5 per cent is just one-third of the 1958 figure – inefficiencies remain and constitute an obvious area for reform. By 2004 a major reform agenda had been agreed, which fixed subsidies independently of farm output, although some member states, and in particular the United Kingdom, considered that it did not go far enough.

Functional integration

Integration based on pragmatic cooperation between states in specific areas of (usually) economic activity. In the European context, functional integration is often contrasted with deeper and wider political integration of a federal kind.

Federal

A political structure that combines a central authority with a degree of constitutionally defined autonomy for sub-central units of government – usually states, regions or provinces.

economic sectors into a much tighter organisation resembling a loosely configured **federal** state. Aware of this ultimate objective, the founding fathers of the EEC created a comprehensive institutional structure which resembled that of a national government. The European Commission seemed very like a European government. Originally it was confined to implementing directives agreed by national governments. But powers of autonomous decision making were much expanded by the Single European Act (1986) and the Treaties of Maastricht (1992) and Amsterdam (1997). Figure 8.1 shows the institutional structure of the EU in the 2000s, which is broadly similar to that laid down in the Treaty of Rome of 1957.[1]

The Treaty of Rome set up a grouping of the original six members of the ECSC with a much greater range of functions and tasks than the original body. To symbolise this it changed its name to the European Economic Community. In particular the new body was to harmonise trade by removing internal barriers and enforcing common rules on all the member states; and to reform agriculture

---

[1] Decision-making procedures in the EU are complex and can only be provided schematically in Figure 8.1. The most important relationship is between the citizens of the individual member states, national governments, the Council of Ministers and the Commission. For major policy and political initiatives the Council representing national governments remains the key body. For the details of implementation the Commission is centrally placed. These relationships are shown in the figure. A secondary, but increasingly important body is the European Parliament. This, via the co-decision-making procedures introduced by the Maastricht Treaty (1992), now plays a role in a range of policy areas. Finally, the meetings of government leaders (the European Council, not to be confused with the Council of Ministers) can launch major initiatives that are later endorsed by the Council of Ministers (see also Figure 9.1 and related text).

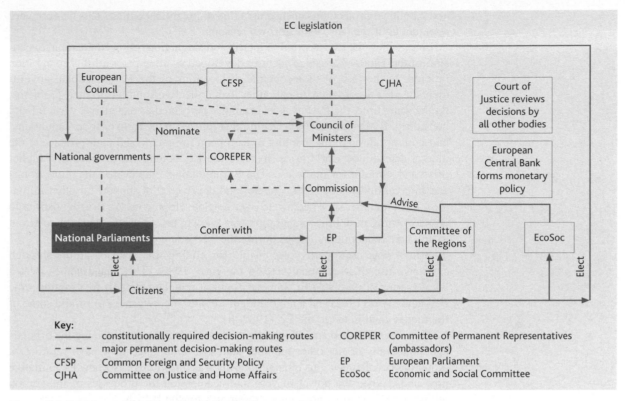

Figure 8.1 Decision making in the European Union

through the Common Agricultural Policy. This was a system of guaranteed price supports for the numerous farmers of France, Italy and other member states. CAP payments dominated the budget, which gave the EEC the reputation of a protectionist agricultural grouping rather than a promoter of free trade and open markets.

Despite this, economic activity among the six expanded enormously and they increasingly attracted British exports. By the early 1960s British trade was shifting from overseas towards Europe. The British were keen to share in community prosperity. Changes in both the Conservative and Labour parties encouraged a more pro-European position. Under the leadership of Harold Macmillan the Conservatives had become a modernising, centrist party committed to rapid economic growth and technological change. Similarly, the Labour Party under Harold Wilson was intent on modernisation. For both leaders participation in an economically dynamic Europe looked attractive. However, both the Conservative government's application for EC membership in 1963 and the Labour application in 1967 were vetoed by the French. Finally in 1973 Britain was admitted along with Ireland and Denmark.

Britain as a member state

In joining the EC Britain now acquired a voice in its affairs equal to that of each of the original 'Big Three' countries: France, Germany and Italy. However, the United Kingdom was only one among a number of members, and could always be outvoted by a coalition of the others. Given that Britain continued to view the EC primarily in economic terms while most other countries saw it as both an economic and a political project, this opened up a line of potential conflict. This was not very apparent until the late 1980s, for two reasons.

First, within the EC, a period of inertia and stagnation followed the rapid expansion of the 1960s. A crisis of identity developed as attempts at further integration faltered. In the face of the economic dislocations of the 1970s national governments tended to rely on national rather than collective solutions to their problems. At the same time, the CAP was increasingly perceived as expensive, wasteful and inefficient. By the late 1970s agricultural surpluses in the form of food 'mountains' had built up, through the inability of European farmers to sell their produce at the market-determined world price. Instead, the EC bought the produce at a higher price and stored it for future use. These 'mountains' emphasised the protectionist and interventionist side of EC policies and deprived it of support for other initiatives. Each member state had a veto over new developments. As British hostility to any deepening of political integration was known, this in itself acted as a deterrent to any non-economic initiatives during the 1970s and early 1980s.

Britain was itself partly responsible for ending this state of affairs through excessive use of its national veto in the early 1980s. Threatened vetoes over a whole series of unrelated EC policies secured reluctant support for Britain in the Falklands War (1982) and a large budget 'rebate', i.e. returning to Britain some of the money paid in tax to the EC (1982–4).

This all established an image of Britain as a 'bad European' among the officials and politicians of the other member states. Events since then have reinforced, rather than challenged, this reputation. This was unfortunate as a new EC initiative now undermined the power of veto and accelerated the processes of integration within the EC, thereby posing new dilemmas for the British.

The Single European Act and Maastricht: quantum leaps forward for the EC

Until the mid-1980s the EC was an inter-governmental organisation with responsibilities mainly in agriculture, environmental protection, regional and competition policy. For important decisions such as enlargement, or major budget and policy changes, a unanimous vote in the Council of Ministers was required. Although the European Parliament (EP) had been directly elected by voters since 1979, its powers were confined to approving or rejecting the EU budget as a whole. From 1985 to 1992 all this was to change as the EC evolved into an embryonic supranational state.

The impetus came from a growing perception that the member states could not compete successfully at world level unless they were truly integrated. In addition, the experience of the 1970s and the early 1980s had convinced many that national governments on their own would find it increasingly difficult to control inflation. The solution to these problems lay in a single economy with a single currency. Such arrangements would also require a degree of political integration so as to enforce them properly and to make European-wide institutions accountable to electors. Political integration was also seen, not least by Chancellor Kohl, the German leader, and François Mitterrand, the French president, as a way of binding an enlarged Germany into Europe, and preventing it from threatening its neighbours.

The first step in this transformation was the Single European Act. Signed in 1986 it was designed to achieve the original aim of the 1957 Treaty of Rome: the creation of a single market in goods, capital and labour. In addition, the Act strengthened the federal as opposed to inter-governmental nature of EC decision making. Unanimity in the Council of Ministers remained for major issues such as enlargement. But the details of implementation could be expedited through

BRIEFINGS

8.3 Inter-governmental and federal organisations

When discussing forms of international organisation it is common to characterise them in terms of a continuum ranging from loose organisations that have no power to impose rules or sanctions on members, to full-blown federal governments that can oblige a member (or constituent state) to adhere to legislation and punish it for non-compliance. One of the loosest inter-governmental organisations is the United Nations: members can leave at will and there are effectively no sanctions that the Security Council can impose on them.

Since the late 1980s the EU has developed into what might be called a 'strong' inter-governmental organisation. The Council of Ministers can, by majority vote, oblige members to follow certain policies (although on major matters, such as enlargement of the Union, unanimity is still required). Moreover, the EU has all the trappings of a state including a legislature, courts and a bureaucracy. Most scholars agree that, for a true federation to exist, the central government should have control over defence and macroeconomic policy. With its single currency, therefore, the EU has taken a significant step towards federalism – reinforced by the discussions on common defence set in motion by the Treaty of Amsterdam (1997). Note, however, that compared with other federations the EU has a weak central government. In countries such as the United States, Australia and Canada the federal government controls defence, the economy and a vast range of social policies. No one expects the EU to take on equivalent roles for many years, if ever, although proponents of a united Europe clearly want such a transformation. Note also that in the strongest federations the central government is often prepared to go to war to keep the federation together, as is the case with Russia's intervention in Chechnya. Membership of the EU is effectively voluntary: if a country wanted to leave, serious economic consequences might follow, but the other members would respect its decision. In this sense the EU resembles a confederation, where membership of the collection of states is voluntary, more than a federation, where membership is considered irreversible.

BRIEFINGS

8.4 The changed international situation during the 1980s and the impetus towards monetary cooperation

Competing theories exist to explain the acceleration of moves towards European union during the 1980s, but most agree that monetary cooperation is a key factor. From the 1970s most countries agreed to abolish exchange and other controls on the movement of capital across national borders. As a result, investors from around the globe could move their money to those countries that were likely to produce the best return. The key factors determining where to invest are the stability of exchange rates, level of interest rates and political and social order. With the internationalisation of capital movements, governments in all the EU countries had an incentive to keep their investment environments as attractive as possible. Previously they could literally stop money from leaving the country. But with the abolition of controls they had no power to do so. Moreover, during the 1970s and 1980s a number of governments (including Britain, Belgium, France and Italy) had been unable to stop the export of capital by raising interest rates and had been forced into humiliating devaluations. Thus opinion started to harden around the idea of pooling currencies in a European Monetary System that, through the operation of an Exchange Rate Mechanism, would oblige governments to keep their currencies within specified bands around a central rate. During the early 1980s the ERM did not work well, as many countries failed to keep within the specified bands. However, from 1983 to 1989 things improved so much that the ERM was increasingly viewed as a precursor to full monetary union. During 1992 and 1993, however, the system unravelled as the international markets decided that the currencies of the vulnerable economies (in particular Britain and Italy) were overvalued and ripe for mass selling. German unification had forced the Germans to raise interest rates to hold down inflation, so capital moved rapidly to Germany and out of other member states' currencies. Governments proved incapable of stemming the outward flow of capital and were forced to leave the ERM, effectively devaluing their currencies. This crisis destroyed public confidence in the Conservatives' capacity to handle economic affairs and thus helped lead to their election defeat in 1997.

▶

Since the events of the early 1990s, two schools of thought have emerged about monetary cooperation. The right wing of the Conservative Party sees these events as evidence of the folly of trying to link currencies together. It argues that a single currency is even more dangerous, because it removes an individual country's ability to devalue and leads to high unemployment and economic recession. Others argue that the problems with the ERM in 1992 and 1993 demonstrate the need for a single currency that stabilises all the European currencies at one level, with the euro (the new currency unit) forming a strong and highly sought-after international currency. These policy battles became less intense after 2004, by which time the comparatively good performance of the UK economy and the widely perceived risks involved in EMU membership led leaders in both the Conservative and Labour parties to postpone discussion of membership for the foreseeable future.

'qualified' majority voting (QMV).[2] The powers of the European Parliament were also strengthened, although not dramatically, and the Treaty made bold declarations on the need for greater political (i.e. defence) cooperation.

The British government enthusiastically supported the free market provisions of the SEA, but were critical of the political changes. Achieving a genuine common market in goods and services had long been an objective of Conservative governments. It was the marriage of this objective to political integration that was unacceptable to many members of the party.

Their objections paled into insignificance beside Conservative reactions to the Treaty on European Union (the Maastricht Treaty), signed on 7 February 1992. Maastricht represented a radical departure from preceding initiatives because of its ambitious economic and political objectives. The most important of these were the following:

- Creation of a European Union with a common citizenship.

- Creation of a single currency by 1999 under the control of a European central bank.

- Strict 'convergence criteria' for joining the currency.

- Acceptance of a Social Protocol (sometimes also known as the 'Social Chapter') on minimum working and social conditions for all citizens of the European Union.

- Creation of a Cohesion Fund to help the poorer states and regions adjust to economic change.

- Co-decision making between the Council and the Parliament in further areas so as to strengthen the role of the European Parliament. Decisions resulting from this procedure were subject to QMV in the Council of Ministers. The treaty also extended the number of policy areas subject to QMV.

---

[2] Each country represented in the Council of Ministers is given a weighting as shown in Table 8.1; for a measure to be adopted a total of 62 votes is necessary. The Single European Act and the Treaties of Maastricht, Amsterdam and Nice greatly extended the number of areas covered by QMV (they had previously required unanimity). Great controversy has surrounded the size of the blocking minority required under QMV. The British, in particular, are concerned that with enlargement the position of the bigger states would be weakened. From the very beginning the EC gave to smaller states a weighted vote greater than they would have been given in proportion to their populations. The present arrangement is a compromise. Following the 1995 enlargement the British wanted the blocking minority to be set at 23, whereas the final agreement was 25. In anticipation of further enlargement slightly more weight has been given to larger countries, in provisions which entered into force in 2004–5.

BRIEFINGS

8.5 Convergence criteria for European Monetary Union

To join the European Monetary Union a country has to demonstrate that it has achieved a 'sustainable convergence with the economies of the other member states'. This is because currencies cannot be united unless countries experience reasonably similar economic conditions and pursue similar economic policies. To qualify, therefore, countries have to meet the following criteria:

- price stability or a rate of inflation close to that of the three best performing states

- the achievement of a public sector deficit of not more than 3 per cent of gross domestic product in any year and not more than 60 per cent accumulated debt as a percentage of GDP

- stability of a member's currency in the ERM for two years with no devaluations within two years

- the achievement of a level of long-term interest rates as low as the average of the three best performing states in the EU.

These criteria proved very difficult to achieve in the 1992 to 1998 period, when many member states experienced economic recession. In both 1996 and 1997 the interpretation, if not the wording, of the criteria was loosened so as to accommodate the particular problems of Germany and Italy, neither of whom looked likely to meet the strict interpretation of the criteria by 1999, when EMU was scheduled to take effect. This demonstrates that EMU has a political impetus behind the economic measures. Similarly the economic 'tests' proposed by the Labour government to determine whether joining EMU would be good for Britain were interpreted partly in terms of political considerations and popular reactions to such a move.

Table 8.1 Arrangements for qualified majority voting (QMV) in the EU

Country	Weighting	Population (millions)	Country	Weighting	Population (millions)
Germany	29	82	Finland	7	5.2
UK	29	60	Lithuania	7	3.7
France	29	59.4	Ireland	7	3.7
Italy	29	57.6	Latvia	4	2.4
Spain	27	39.7	Slovenia	4	2.0
Poland	27	38.6	Estonia	4	1.4
Netherlands	13	15.8	Cyprus	4	.8
Greece	12	10.6	Luxembourg	4	.4
Czech Republic	12	10.3	Malta	3	.4
Belgium	12	10.2	Total votes	321	
Hungary	12	10.0	Qualified majority	232*	
Portugal	12	9.9	Veto votes	90†	
Sweden	10	8.9			
Austria	10	8.1			
Slovakia	7	5.4			
Denmark	7	5.3			

* Number of votes needed to approve a measure in the Council.
† Number of votes needed to block a measure in the Council.

Plate 8.2 Anti-Euro sentiment reached a peak during 1999–2003
Source: Cartoon Stock

The Conservative prime minister, John Major, eventually signed the Treaty in 1992. But he did so only after extensive negotiations that secured an opt-out for Britain from the final stage of the single currency, which is still in force. British objections were partly political and partly ideological. Major was vulnerable to the vociferous and significant minority of 'Eurosceptics' within the parliamentary Conservative Party, convinced that a single currency would end British sovereignty.

The then Conservative leadership assumed a more pragmatic line: that membership would be in Britain's interests 'when the time was right', particularly in terms of keeping inflation down. If there has been a constant in British economic policy since 1979 it has been a commitment to keeping inflation low. The debate created deep divisions within the Conservative Party. Labour and the Liberal Democrats supported the Treaty, particularly its Social Protocol, which guaranteed limited working hours and a minimum wage.

Europe as a crisis issue in British politics

As the controversies over recent treaties show, EU policies now affect many aspects of British economic and social life. However, for most of the population the Union remains remote. In their everyday lives people feel more directly affected by the activities of local councils, regional executives and the Westminster government. This is confirmed by the large number (one-quarter in 2002) who continued to hold 'no opinion' about membership of the EU. British antipathy to Europe is among the highest in the EU (Table 8.2). Moreover, at

Table 8.2 Public opinion on membership of the EU in constituent countries

Country	1973			1980			1990			1994			1998			2002		
	Good	Bad	No opinion/ no reply	Good	Bad	No opinion/ no reply	Good	Bad	No opinion/ no reply	Good	Bad	No opinion/ no reply	Good	Bad	No opinion/ no reply	Good	Bad	No opinion/ no reply
Belgium	57	5	38	57	2	41	69	5	26	56	10	36	47	9	43	56	25	19
Denmark	42	30	28	33	29	38	49	25	26	53	26	21	56	20	25	72	19	10
Germany	63	4	33	65	6	29	62	7	31	50	12	38	48	11	40	44	34	22
Greece				42	22	36	75	5	20	64	9	27	67	9	25	78	14	9
Spain				58	5	37	65	8	27	50	14	36	63	7	30	60	20	21
France	61	5	34	51	9	40	63	7	30	50	13	37	52	12	36	53	25	22
Ireland	56	15	29	52	19	29	74	8	18	72	7	21	79	4	17	90	5	6
Italy	69	2	29	74	3	23	75	3	22	68	5	27	68	5	26	57	19	24
Luxembourg	67	3	30	84	3	13	72	8	20	71	9	20	77	6	18	71	19	10
Netherlands	63	4	33	75	3	22	82	3	15	77	5	18	75	6	19	67	18	15
Portugal				24	6	70	62	4	34	54	13	33	58	9	33	73	13	15
UK	31	34	33	21	55	24	52	19	29	43	22	35	37	22	41	36	39	26
Austria													38	19	43	46	37	17
Finland													45	21	29	39	49	12
Sweden													35	36	29	31	54	15
Averages	56.5	11.3	32.2	53	13.5	33.5	66.6	8.5	24.9	59	12.1	28.9	54.1	12	34.2	52	27	21

Source: Commission of the European Communities, *Eurobarometer*, Brussels, various issues

37.6 per cent in 2004, British turn-out in the European parliamentary election was dramatically below the 2005 general election figure of 61.3 per cent and was one of the lowest in the EU.

There are, therefore, deep divisions over Europe in many sections of the public and in particular among British political leaders, the deepest of which used to exist between the Conservative and Labour parties. This derived from a broader cleavage between internationalists and nationalists. The former see Britain's future as an active but by no means dominant partner in a multicultural Europe. The nationalists see Britain essentially as an independent economic and political force in an increasingly complex global economy. While this division is discernible within both main parties it was, until 2004, associated with differences between them. It was a division that underlay attitudes towards EU institutions and in particular the European Parliament. The internationalists accept the interdependence of Britain with Europe and the rest of the world, and adopt an essentially pragmatic stance towards the increasing power of supranational institutions: they agree with them if they bring concrete benefits. For the Eurosceptics, any attempt to strengthen EU institutions is a direct affront to parliamentary **sovereignty** and must be resisted at every turn.

The 'Controversy' at the end of the chapter puts the arguments for and against further integration of Britain with the European Union. The depth of these divisions and the continuing impetus within the EU to ever closer union meant that the European question dominated British politics until the general election of 2005.

Sovereignty

The exclusive right to wield legitimate power within a territory. A sovereign state has complete control over its own affairs.

BRIEFINGS

8.6 The transformation of Labour's position in Europe

Between 1979 and 1997 the position of Labour was transformed from deep hostility to warm acceptance. This reflected the transition of the party from socialism under its then leader Michael Foot in 1982 to 'Third Way' capitalism under Tony Blair in 1997.

> We aim to develop a Europe which is democratic and socialist, and where the interests of the people are placed above the interests of national and multinational capitalist groups, but within which each country must be able to realize its own economic and social objectives, under the sovereignty of its own Parliament and people.
>
> Labour manifesto, 1979

> On taking office we will open preliminary negotiations with the other EEC member states to establish a timetable for withdrawal; and we will publish the results of these negotiations in a White Paper.
>
> Labour manifesto, 1983

> Labour's aim is to work constructively with our EEC partners to promote economic expansion and combat unemployment.
>
> Labour manifesto, 1987

> European integration should be used to promote Britain out of the European second division into which our country has been relegated by the Tories.
>
> Labour manifesto, 1992

By 1997 the transformation was complete. The New Labour manifesto of that year was highly positive on Europe, proposing that Britain should stay in the EU but also play a leading role. In addition, and in contrast to 1987 and 1992, the manifesto devoted much more space to the European issue (248 words compared with a mere 62 in 1987).

This was amply demonstrated in the aftermath of the Labour victory in the 2001 general election. In the ensuing Conservative leadership election the pro-European candidate, Kenneth Clarke, was decisively defeated by Iain Duncan Smith. Deeply hostile to the EU his first act as leader was to appoint only Eurosceptics to the shadow Cabinet.

The Labour Party in the meantime has found itself increasingly comfortable in the EU. It agreed to tightening integration in the Treaties of Amsterdam (1997) and Nice (2001). Formally it accepts the position negotiated by the Conservatives at Maastricht in 1992, that it will join the EMU 'if and when the time is right'. However, Labour decided in 2003 not to join the monetary union until after the next general election – really an indefinite postponement.

While 'Europe' remains an important issue in British politics, events during the 2003–5 period were to change both public perceptions of Europe and the salience of the issue in British politics.

The first of these was the rejection by the Swedes in 2003 of EMU membership. This seemed to confirm in the minds of policy makers that the future would see a 'two-speed' Europe with Sweden, Denmark, Britain and many of the new EMU states remaining outside the single currency. This sentiment was compounded when the chancellor, Gordon Brown, announced in 2003 that only one of the five economic tests for British membership had been met. Together with the comparatively good performance of the British economy relative to 'Euroland' these events effectively postponed British membership, and a possible referendum, into the indefinite future. This was confirmed by the fact that the EMU was hardly an issue in the 2005 general election.

The second major change came with the publication in July 2003 of a draft treaty on a new European constitution. This was seen as necessary to accommodate the expansion of the EU to 25 states in 2003. After some amendments the heads of state and government signed the treaty on 29 October 2004. There then followed a period of ratification, where the approval mechanisms were to be decided by member states. In some, parliamentary approval was sufficient, in some judicial assent was necessary and in others the final ratification would be decided by national referendums. In 2004 Tony Blair announced that Britain would hold a referendum on the draft constitution. Michael Howard and the Conservatives vehemently opposed ratification while the Blair government supported it.

However, much to everyone's surprise, on 29 May 2005 the French voted in a national referendum to reject the EU constitituon by 55 per cent to 45 per cent. A few days later, on 1 June the Dutch rejected the constitution by an even great margin of 62 per cent to 38 per cent. If two of the six founding members of the original European Community rejected the new treaty, then it was effectively dead – something that Jack Straw was to acknowledge on 6 June when he announced that legislation to introduce the referendum bill would be postponed indefinitely.

By 2006, therefore, the whole question of Britain's status in the EU had been transformed. Both EMU membership and the ratification of the constitution were postponed indefinitely. The Tory Party under David Cameron remained decidedly 'Eurosceptic'. But then in many ways so did Blair and the prime minister-in-waiting, Gordon Brown. Britain continued to champion open markets and the free movement of labour. Indeed the United Kingdom was one of the very few member states that allowed the free movement of labour from the new accession states after 2004. But both the main political parties – although not the Liberal Democrats – remained doubtful about the benefits either of EMU membership or the draft EU constitution.

This said, the historical fault lines inspired by the issue run deep and, any time in the future, the issue could re-emerge as a major cleavage in British politics.

CONTROVERSY

Should Britain agree to closer European union?

The case for Britain strengthening and deepening the EU

The danger from Germany

The EEC transformed Franco-German relations but Germany – especially a united Germany – is still the dominant economic power in Europe. Any possible threat from this is best thwarted or pre-empted by locking Germany into closer political union with the rest of Europe.

The danger from outside

The collapse of the Soviet Union and the increased uncertainties of the post-Cold War era mean that Europe needs to meet any new threats or challenges that might emerge from international terrorism, Asia, the Middle East or from an unstable eastern Europe. Europe needs to move towards a common foreign and defence policy, which can only be achieved by strengthening the central institutions of the European Union. At the same time, the EU should be enlarged to include most of the former Communist states of eastern Europe.

The democratic deficit

EU policy makers are subject to very limited popular control. The Council of Ministers is not answerable to the European Parliament and the unelected and largely unaccountable Commission has far greater decision-making autonomy than any national Civil Service. The way forward therefore must involve the strengthening of democracy in the EU, which means making central institutions stronger and more accountable directly to the people of Europe.

The bicycle analogy

Unless the EU keeps moving forward – towards ever closer integration – it will atrophy.

World economic competition

Changes in technology are creating an increasingly competitive global economic system. Deepening the EU in economic and financial terms will enable European producers to compete more effectively in the internal EU market and strengthen the European Union's bargaining position in world markets more generally.

The case for Britain resisting EU federalism

Dangers of a common currency

It is too risky to have a common currency when real economic convergence has not occurred among the economies of the EU's member states. The Maastricht convergence criteria (inflation, interest rates, debt/GDP ratios) are inappropriate. The real criteria are employment rates, economic activity and growth rates. Without convergence on these poor areas will remain depressed, because they will be unable to devalue themselves into activity and the EU will not possess sufficient central funds to stimulate economic activity there.

The democratic deficit

EU integration needs to proceed at a rate that has the overwhelming majority support of electorates in the member states. 'Real democracy' may be impossible in such a large and diverse community and the adoption of an EU constitution could increase the democratic deficit.

The dangers of judicial legislation

Judicial legislation (judges in effect creating new law by interpreting established legal principles or commitments in the light of new situations) is dangerous because the judiciary are not accountable to electors. This applies particularly to the European Court of Justice, which has been very assertive in the EU.

Injustices in EU rule operation

Uneven rule implementation in different member states means Britain loses out by having an efficient administration. Such losses will increase with enlargement and stoke up massive popular resentment.

Foreign and defence policy

A common EU foreign and defence policy really means lack of agreement, inaction and impotence – witness European ineffectiveness in the continuing Middle East crisis.

Fortress Europe versus global market

The real market of the future is the global market. An insulated EU market – economic fortress Europe – will atrophy.

Flexibility

British interests, as in the past, are best served by retaining maximum strategic flexibility in terms of trade patterns and political–military alliances. Circumstances constantly change. The EU will be too unwieldy to respond effectively to new economic, political, ecological and military challenges.

Summary

- Britain has traditionally been sceptical about European integration, because of its stake in world markets and its links with English-speaking countries overseas. It suffers from a structural and cultural dilemma which other countries do not have and that have caused it to be seen as a 'bad European'.

- However, it did support the Single European Act (1986) creating a single market in goods, labour and capital, but was suspicious about moves towards fuller political integration.

- 'Eurosceptics' took over the Conservative Party in the 1990s, but the issue has since been defused following the ratification failure of the EU Constitituon and Labour's decision to postpone EMU membership.

- New Labour is reasonably united around a pragmatic attitude to Europe: they support it if there are clear benefits. This is far removed from the political commitment of the Continental states to union, and traditionally has weakened the British bargaining position within the EU. However since enlargement to 25 Britain has championed the extension of open markets to the new member states.

MILESTONES

Milestones in the development of the EU

1951   Treaty of Paris. Belgium, the Netherlands, Luxembourg, France, Italy and West Germany (the Six) set up the European Coal and Steel Community

1957   Treaty of Rome. The Six set up the European Economic Community and the European Atomic Energy Authority (Euratom)

1962   Common Agricultural Policy created. The EEC regulates farm prices and decides on agricultural priorities right across the community

1966   The French president de Gaulle establishes the right of national veto (the 'Luxembourg Compromise')

1967   Creation of the European Communities by the merger of EEC, ECSC and Euratom under a Commission and Council of Ministers

1968   Creation of European Customs Union

1973   Denmark, Ireland and the UK join the EC

1974   Heads of government meet as European Council. The Regional Fund created to help poor or declining regions inside member states

1979   First direct elections to the European Parliament. The European Monetary System with its Exchange Rate Mechanism and European Currency Unit created

1981   Greece joins the EC

1985–6 The Milan Summit and the Single European Act amend the Treaty of Rome to introduce the principle of qualified majority voting in areas related to the single market, and take the first steps towards a common foreign policy

1986   Spain and Portugal join the EC

1992   Treaty on European Union (Maastricht Treaty) amends the Single European Act and presents a plan for economic and political union. The Treaty covers cooperation on political, economic, defence, social, environmental, cultural and legal matters. Britain and Denmark opt out of the Social Chapter on welfare and regulation of working conditions, and reserve decision on European Monetary Union

1992/3 Maastricht Treaty narrowly approved by all member states

1992   The UK is forced by a currency crisis to withdraw from ERM and EMS, to be followed in the next few months by many other EU currencies

▶

Milestones in the development of the EU continued

1993	Single internal market inaugurated
1995	Austria, Finland and Sweden join the EU
1997	Treaty of Amsterdam strengthens defence and foreign policy cooperation, extends qualified majority voting in the Council and establishes common rules on immigration and citizenship
1999	Single currency zone set up inside 11 (later 12) countries of the EU. Britain announces it will decide on membership later. Series of scandals produce resignation of the Santer Commission in face of censure by European Parliament. This greatly increases the power of the European Parliament. The new (Prodi) Commission takes more power over the nomination and resignation of its members, limiting the power of member states in this regard. It thus enhances its position as an autonomous EU government responsible to the European Parliament
2001–2	Treaty of Nice effectively codifies failure to agree on extensive institutional reform in advance of enlargement. It was rejected in Irish and Danish referendums, although Ireland held a second referendum in which it was accepted
2003	Sweden votes to reject membership of EMU
2004	Enlargement in central and eastern Europe takes EU membership to 25. Britain opens its doors to workers from the new states
2005	In national referendums the French and Dutch vote to reject the draft European constitution, rendering it effectively dead

Essays

1. Account for the transformation of the European issue in British politics since 2003.

2. Account for the transition of Labour from hostility to Europe to enthusiastic supporter between 1979 and 1997.

3. In what sense is Europe a federal state rather than a mere supranational organisation?

4. What have been the political and economic consequences of enlargement of the EU to 25?

Projects

1. Which countries are likely to be included in the next wave of EU enlargement? What criteria will be applied to determine membership?

2. What are the five economic tests laid down by Gordon Brown for joining the EMU. In what respect are the tests political as well as economic?

3. Analyse British public opinion on the EC (later EU) since 1970s? How do you account for the trends?

Further reading

Anthony Forster and Alasdair Blair, *Britain's European Foreign Policy* (London: Macmillan, 2001) and Stefano Falla, *New Labour and the European Union* (London: Ashgate, 2002) are up-to-date analyses of British inability to choose decisively between the United States and the European Union. Lively, up-to-date accounts of British–European relationships are: J. Baker, 'Britain and Europe: more blood on the Eurocarpet', *Parliamentary Affairs*, **55** (2), 2002, pp. 317–30; S. Kettell, 'Why New Labour wants the euro', *Political Quarterly*, **75** (1), 2004, pp. 52–9; D. Baker and P. Sherrington, 'Britain and Europe: the dog that didn't bark', *Parliamentary Affairs*, **58** (2), 2005, pp. 303–17. On the role of the EU in British elections, see David McKay, 'The reluctant European: Europe as an issue in British politics', in John Bartle and Anthony King (eds), *Britain at the Polls, 2005* (London and Washington DC: Congressional Quarterly, 2006).

Useful web sites on Britain in Europe

Hot links to these sites can be found on the CWS web site at www.pearsoned .co.uk/budge. The amount of information on the European Union in general, and the role Britain plays in it, increases almost on a daily basis. There are certain web sites that can be regarded as thresholds for entering into this debate.

The Labour Party (www.labour.org.uk) sets out what is essentially the government's view and the pro-integration lobby is exemplified by the views of organisations such as the European Movement at www.euromove.org.uk and the coalition known as Britain in Europe (www.britainineurope.org.uk); you can also visit the Young European Movement at www.yem.org.uk.

The Conservative Party (www.conservative-party.org.uk) reflects the views of the 'Eurosceptic' position. Other groups on this side of the debate provide material at www.eusceptic.org, Youth for a Free Europe (www.free-europe.org.uk), the Bruges Group (www.brugesgroup.com), the Democracy Movement (www. democracy-movement.com), the Libertarian Alliance (www.libertarian.co.uk) and www.no-euro.com. Material on Eurosceptics across Europe can be accessed at www.keele.ac.uk/socs/ks40/eurocrit.htm.

For excellent media coverage of the debate, see the *Guardian*'s special reports on Britain and the EU (www.politics.guardian.co.uk/eu), Britain and the euro (www.politics.guardian.co.uk/euro) and the more general report on European integration (www.guardian.co.uk/eu). Daily news reports and comments on European affairs are available from www.euobserver.com. You might also want to visit www.europolls.co.uk for information on opinion polls. The official EU website is www.europa.eu.int.

chapter 9

Europe in Britain

Chapter 8 looked at the part Britain plays within the European Union. This chapter will examine the other side of the coin: the impact of the EU on government and politics within Britain. It will discuss the decisions British governments have to take about Europe, the constitutional effects of membership up to the present, how the EU itself makes decisions and what effects this has in Britain. In addition we shall see how membership of the European Union has affected the machinery of government and the ways in which public policy is made inside Britain. The chapter will also address the problem of the 'democratic deficit' of the EU and tackle the question of 'subsidiarity': that is, which level of government is best equipped to deal with particular responsibilities.

This chapter discusses:

■ the centrality of the EU to contemporary British politics

■ the EU and the British constitution

■ how the EU is governed and Britain's part in this

■ how British civil servants interact with their EU counterparts

■ how British interest groups deal with EU policies

■ how the EU affects public policy

■ the nature of the 'democratic deficit'

■ subsidiarity: which level of government should be responsible for which policy area inside Britain.

Union or secession?: the British dilemma

Some of the most important decisions the British government has to take in the next decade are about its relationship with Europe. This is not just a matter of foreign policy, for such decisions will crucially affect Britain's own power and standing inside the national territory, what is commonly termed its 'sovereignty'. What the government has to decide is how far it is prepared to become a constituent part of an ever more integrated European Union. A European government in Brussels, only partly elected from Britain, would decide aspects of British social policy, for example, and largely regulate the economy. Perhaps it might even direct foreign policy and deal with matters of peace and war involving British lives. In these respects the European Union might come to resemble a loose **federation** rather than a supranational organisation.

Federation

A political organisation in which power is divided between a central authority and other units, usually geographical, that retain some independent authority in the system. The term is a controversial one in Britain because it can either mean a fairly centralised form of government (e.g. a United States of Europe) or a loosely organised one, in which the member states retain much autonomy.

Eurosceptics in Britain see no benefits from this, since their ideal is an autonomous British state regulating all its own internal and external affairs. Pro-Europeans, by the same token, see the loss of autonomy as a price worth paying for the influence British governments and individuals can exert in a much larger political unit. Better to be part of a new superpower, they argue, than an independent third-class state on the fringe of world developments. They cite the new opportunities available for finance and industry within the European Union, and claim that economic and social development will be faster and smoother within a more dynamic economy, in which British financial expertise, for example, is joined with German industrial strength.

The pro-Europeans believe that loss of political autonomy would be balanced by the British share in electing a European Parliament and government. European institutions would not be 'foreign' but representative of European citizens in Britain as much as they would be of European citizens in Spain, France, Italy and Scandinavia. Only if one thinks of the British Parliament and government as the sole bodies authorised to represent the British people can one regard a wider European democracy as threatening.

This is, of course, exactly what many Conservative Eurosceptics do think. Many groups in Britain, however, are positively attracted by Europeanisation. Scottish, Welsh and Irish nationalists see it as a way of easing the stranglehold of the British state on their own countries (see Chapter 10). The Labour Party is reassured by the social protection the European Union offers to vulnerable groups such as low-paid workers. From the trade unions' point of view, undermining Conservative reforms might be no bad thing. Employers' competitiveness is their employees' poverty. Constitutional reformers see in the guarantees offered by the European treaties a protection for the civil liberties threatened by British governments. Even Conservatives such as Kenneth Clarke, one of the unsuccessful contenders in the party's leadership election of 2005, see Europeanisation as a necessary step to consolidating Britain's world trading position, rather than as a threat to it.

These issues are not theoretical ones likely to affect us only later. The European Union already operates in Britain, parallel to but independently of the British

CONTROVERSY

European federalism

Federalism has a clear meaning in political science, but in public discussion it takes on different meanings according to who is using it and for what political purpose. In political science, a federal state combines a central authority (the federal government) with a degree of constitutionally defined autonomy for sub-central units of government – usually territorial units of government such as states, regions or provinces. In other words federal government is a form of decentralised government that guarantees some autonomy for units of government below the central state. It contrasts with unitary and centralised states, such as Britain has been traditionally.

In Britain, however, the term 'federal' is sometimes used by politicians as a codeword for a highly centralised 'European superstate' – for rule by a centralised

bureaucracy in Brussels, with all the red tape, rigidity and loss of sovereignty this implies for Britain. Europhobes often use the word 'federal' to imply centralisation, which they hate. British objections to the use of the word 'federal' to describe the European Union in the Maastricht Treaty led to the term being removed. Nonetheless, the federal nature of some EU institutions remained, and were actually supported by the British government.

For others in Britain, 'federal' means decentralised government that preserves substantial rights of member states to administer their own territory in their own way. These rights are protected by the principle of subsidiarity (see later). Hence, Europhiles often use the term 'federal' to describe a degree of decentralisation in the EU, which they like.

BRIEFINGS

9.1 Subsidiarity and its possible consequences in Britain

The principle of **subsidiarity** states that public policy should be made and implemented at the lowest appropriate level of government compatible with efficiency and accountability: that is, at the point closest to ordinary citizens. Only decisions that have to be taken at the European level should be made there; all others should be made by national, regional or local government.

One reason for doing so is to make decision making more open and accessible to those whom it affects. In the (clumsy and vague) words of Article 3B of the Maastricht Treaty:

> In areas which do not fall within its exclusive competence, the Community shall take action, in accordance with the principle of subsidiarity, only if and insofar as the objectives of the proposed action cannot be sufficiently achieved by the Member States, and can, therefore, by reason of the scale or effects of the proposed action, be better achieved by the Community.

The subsidiarity principle therefore protects the interests and powers of nation states where there is no good reason to take decisions at the European level. However, it can easily be extended within member states to relations between the centre and the regions or localities. It is therefore something of a two-edged sword so far as protecting existing state power is concerned and may serve to empower Scotland or Wales, for example, in relation to the United Kingdom as a whole.

Subsidiarity

The principle whereby decisions should be taken at the lowest possible level of the political system that is compatible with policy efficiency.

government and Parliament. On a range of questions British courts take their precedents from the European Court in Luxembourg, just as British civil servants and local councils follow directives from Brussels. The EU does not have (and is not likely to have) its own administration in Britain to enforce decisions directly. It relies on British institutions to do that. But, as the example of the courts shows, they can be quite effective in enforcing European interventions.

This chapter looks at the way in which EU institutions operate in Britain and the way in which their interventions have already changed British political practices and structures. We may expect more changes as the Labour government in principle supports closer integration and federal union. Having said that, the EU will always rely more on indirect rather than direct means of intervention. Thus, what we can expect is continuing adaptation by the British Civil Service and local government to the European dimension, rather than any immediate administrative restructuring to meet EU needs. Adaptation has already gone a long way, as we shall see when we examine the European presence in Britain more closely.

Europe and the British constitution

Practical and parliamentary sovereignty

The main constitutional issue raised by membership of the European Union concerns **parliamentary sovereignty**. In Britain, legal sovereignty is vested in Parliament. The concept of parliamentary sovereignty means that Parliament can pass any law it wants. In effect, as we saw in Chapter 4, this gives extensive and undefined powers to the majority government.

Parliamentary sovereignty

The power of Parliament to make or repeal any law it wishes.

From the mid-nineteenth century until 1973 parliamentary sovereignty was one of the cornerstones of the British constitution. Joining the European Community – and therefore accepting the 43 volumes of legislation and more than 3,000 regulations and directives already passed – changed all that. British law must now be consistent with European law, and British courts must both accept and enforce European law. In cases of disagreement the European Court of Justice in Luxembourg has the final word, and British citizens may directly approach the European Court if they believe the British government is acting unlawfully. The British government may even have to compensate citizens for actions judged by the European Court to exceed its powers. It was clear that European law would take precedence over British law when Britain joined the EC, but the principle was underlined strongly by the *Factortame* case of 1991. This required British law to fall into line with European law on the registration of shipping, a matter that had been jealously controlled by the sovereign British state for centuries. More recently, in 1996, the Conservative majority in Parliament was forced by decisions of the European Commission and the Court to accept the right of employees to opt for a 48-hour week, even though the government resisted this strongly and had in fact declared it would not accept it. This clearly involved a loss of sovereignty.

In a practical sense, Britain has long since ceased to have exclusive and total control over its own affairs (if, indeed, any country ever does have total control). Joining the North Atlantic Treaty Organisation or signing the General Agreement on Tariffs and Trade on free trade, for example, requires agreement with other nations and the loss of some national autonomy. To this extent practical sovereignty is limited in even the most powerful modern state.

But the question of constitutional sovereignty and the EU is more complicated than this. Membership of the EU limits practical sovereignty, but it also legally limits parliamentary sovereignty. This makes the issue supremely important in the minds of some politicians.

Others contend that this legal loss of sovereignty is neither final nor absolute. They argue that Parliament could, if it wished, revoke membership of the EU tomorrow, so regaining its old sovereign status. The process of leaving the EU would, of course, be long, messy, disruptive and expensive. Thus for all practical purposes it may be impossible. To the extent that British secession remains theoretically possible, however, Parliament has not lost its legal sovereignty. To the extent that it is in practice unlikely, absolute parliamentary sovereignty no longer exists in Britain.

Judicial review under the EU

Judicial review is the power of courts to invalidate parliamentary legislation or government actions on the grounds that they infringe some higher body of law, such as a constitution (see Chapter 19 for a more extensive discussion). English judges have traditionally not asserted such a right (Scots ones occasionally have) – partly because there is no clearly defined body of constitutional law in the UK (Chapter 4), and partly because their licence to interpret common law and the 'real' meaning of legislation gives them extensive powers anyway.

However, the overriding nature of the EU Treaty obligations, and the authority of the European Court of Justice to lay down binding interpretations of them, do mean that British courts now have written standards against which to evaluate parliamentary legislation and government decisions. This has substantially reinforced their willingness to intervene in the administrative process even at detailed levels of decision, most notably in defence of immigrants' rights to a fair process and hearing.

This tendency has been strengthened by the European Court of Justice's adoption of the European Convention for the Protection of Human Rights as the practical standard for evaluating human rights in the EU, and its direct incorporation into

English and Scots law by the New Labour government in 1998–9. This provides a body of written 'higher' legislation defining individual rights in relation to government, just as the EU treaties delimit areas in which the British government cannot act, or act only in certain ways. Both set clear limits on unlimited parliamentary sovereignty, which has been the legal basis for effective government autonomy.

Nowhere is this clearer than in immigration appeals. Partly because of the EU's abolition of internal barriers to mobility the number of foreigners from outside its area seeking permission to reside in Britain has increased enormously (144,500 individuals from outside the European Economic Area[1] were given the right to settle in the United Kingdom in 2004). Many applications are, however, refused, and such 'administrative' decisions may have enormous implications for individual and family safety. So the courts have shown themselves quite prepared to consider appeals against government decisions. The number of appeals in all areas increased more than ten times between the start of the 1980s and 2004, and continues to rise rapidly. The European Court itself now considers cases initiated by individual citizens. The title of a booklet issued to civil servants – *The Judge Over Your Shoulder* – clearly underlines the extent to which the courts are involved in decision making at all levels, from the most general to the most detailed. It is clear that membership of the EU has accelerated this process, which was however already underway (for more detail, see Chapter 19).

European parliamentary elections and voting reform

From 1979 the European Parliament in Brussels has been directly elected by the citizens of the EU. Elections have been held simultaneously across Europe within the member states. Currently the United Kingdom elects 87 out of 626 Members of the European Parliament (MEPs). Depending on their political affiliation the elected members join different party groups within the EP: Conservatives, the European People's Party (although in 2005 the new Conservative leader David Cameron pulled the party out of this grouping); Labour, the Socialists; Liberal Democrats, the Liberal Group; Greens and Welsh and Scottish Nationalists, the one entitled Group of Greens/European Free Alliance. MEPs tend to be more pro-European than their home parties, and of course integrated into their pan-European groups, so there is often some tension between the Brussels and Westminster party line. This is aggravated by the Euroscepticism of the British Conservative Party.

A weakness of the trans-European parties however is that they have no grass-roots organisation in any country and depend on the local party apparatus to select candidates, campaign and organise the vote. British Euro-elections are run by the British parties (Table 9.1). The latter regard the elections primarily as a national popularity contest, in which the British government record and domestic issues play the major part. Europe is an issue in Britain of course. But instead of competing on what the EU should be doing about the current problems facing it, the debate continually looks back to whether the EU should be tackling them at all and whether Britain should be in it.

All this weakens the claims of MEPs and of the EP itself to have a popular mandate comparable to that of the Westminster Parliament. Elections usually go against the British party currently in national office. Euro-voting is a cheap way to express dissatisfaction with the EU, carrying none of the consequences for a change of government that general elections would. This also explains why turnout in European elections is so low in Britain – a mere 24 per cent in 1999, although this recovered to 38.2 per cent in 2004.

---

[1] The European Economic Area includes the EU plus associated states such as Norway.

BRIEFINGS

9.2 Britain and the European Convention on Human Rights

The European Union is not the only body in Europe with an influence over British government and politics. The Human Rights Bill passed by the Blair government in 1998 originates in the European Convention on Human Rights signed by 15 west European countries in 1950. The Convention is implemented by the European Court of Human Rights in Strasbourg. This is not to be confused with the EU's European Court of Justice in Luxembourg, which, however, uses the convention as its reference point. The EU's Charter of Fundamental Human Rights, approved at its 2000 Nice Meeting, also draws heavily on the Convention.

Main provisions of the Convention

- the right to life (Article 2)
- freedom from torture and inhuman or degrading punishment (Article 3)
- freedom from slavery or enforced labour (Article 4)
- the right to liberty and security of the person (Article 5)
- the right to a fair trial (Article 6)
- freedom from retroactive criminal accusations and punishment (Article 7)
- the right to respect for private and family life (Article 8)
- freedom of thought, conscience and religion (Article 9)
- freedom of expression (Article 10)
- freedom of assembly and association (Article 11).

Britain and the ECHR

Britain was the first country to sign the Convention in 1950 but did not make it part of its own law, claiming this was unnecessary because the rights were already part of common law. Consequently it was not possible for individual British citizens to bring a case against the British government to the ECHR until 1966, when the law was changed.

ECHR cases against Britain

The decisions of the ECHR have had a considerable impact on British government. Between 1966 and 1998 some 100 cases were brought against the British government and in 50 of these the ECHR found the government guilty of breaching the Convention. The cases include:

- **GCHQ (1984)**   The government's ban on trade unions at GCHQ was upheld by the Court.
- **Prevention of terrorism (1993)**   The power of the Secretary of State for Northern Ireland to detain terrorist suspects for up to seven days without charges was upheld.
- **Death on the Rock (1994)**   The British government was ordered to pay £38,000 towards the legal costs of those who brought a case about the killing of terrorist suspects in Gibraltar.
- **Age of homosexual consent (1996)**   British law about different ages of consent for heterosexuals and homosexuals was upheld by the Court.
- **Juvenile murders (1996)**   The Home Secretary (Michael Howard) was found in breach of the Convention when he decided on special terms of imprisonment for juvenile murderers.
- **Patrick Finucane (2003)**   The Royal Ulster Constabulary and the British army were found guilty of colluding in the murder in Northern Ireland of Patrick Finucane.

Incorporation into British law

In 1998 the Labour government incorporated the Convention into Scots and English law through the Human Rights Act (HRA). Britain has thus acquired a written body of fundamental law – a major innovation in the constitution – which provides a strong basis for judicial review of administrative acts.

BRIEFINGS

9.3 Relations between British MEPs and MPs

The British Conservative Party is predominantly Eurosceptic. They hate the loss of national sovereignty involved in membership, and even if they are not advocates of total withdrawal at least want to wrest back many powers from Brussels to London. They dislike the social dimension of EU policy (the Social Chapter, for example), and claim that Brussels stands for the remote and stifling bureaucracy of a European superstate. On the Labour side, some feel that the EU is a club for wealthy countries, while others also resent the loss of sovereignty. The fact that both main parties have their pro- and anti-Europe wings makes the issue difficult for them to handle, and the issue being so highly charged increases the problem. Only the Liberal Democrats are united, having always been strongly pro-European. In short, Europe has been a source of rancorous conflict both within and between the two main parties for three decades, and the conflict shows no sign of going away.

Relations between the party groups in the European Parliament and in Westminster are thus not particularly good, especially on the Conservative side. Conservative Members of the European Parliament are allowed to attend the Backbenchers' Committee in Westminster (the 1922 Committee) but there are few other direct connections. There are stronger ties on the Labour side: MPs and MEPs meet frequently, and the latter have rights and powers within the national organisation. For example, the leader of the Labour group in the European Parliament sits on the party's National Executive Committee, and Labour MEPs may vote in the national leadership elections.

Table 9.1 Results of UK elections to the European Parliament, 1979–2004

PARTY	1979 % vote	1979 MEPs	1984 % vote	1984 MEPs	1989 % vote	1989 MEPs	1994 % vote	1994 MEPs	1999 % vote	1999 MEPs	2004 % vote	2004 MEPs
Conservative	48.4	60	38.8	45	33.0	32	27.0	18	35.8	36	26.7	27
Labour	31.6	17	34.7	32	39.0	45	42.6	62	28.0	29	22.6	19
Liberal Democrat	12.6	0	18.5	0	6.2	0	16.1	2	12.7	10	14.9	12
Green					14.5	0	3.1	0	6.2	2	6.3	2
UKIP									7.0	3	16.1	12
SNP	1.9	1	1.7	1	2.6	1	3.0	2	*	2	1.4	2
Plaid Cymru	0.6	0	0.7	1	0.7	0	1.0	0	*	2	1.0	1
Democratic Unionist	1.3	1	1.6	1	1.0	1	1.0	1	*	1	*	1
Ulster Unionist	0.9	1	1.1	1	0.8	1	0.8	1	*	1	*	1
SDLP	1.1	1	1.1	1	0.9	1	1.0	1	*	1	*	1
Sinn Fein											*	1
BNP									1.0	0	4.9	0
Socialist Labour									0.9	0	0.4	0
% turnout	31.6		32.6		36.2		36.4		24.0		38.2	

* Due to changes in the electoral system, voting figures for the United Kingdom are not given.
Source: European Parliament UK Office, *Election Facts*, August 2005; accessed via
http://www.europarl.org.uk/guide/Gelectionsmain.htm

One consequence is that small or new parties have a better chance to make an impact in the European elections and even to gain seats, as the Greens did with

6 per cent of the vote and two seats in 1999. As the EP still has very limited powers results are however marginal to the mainstream of British politics.

Where Euro-elections have an important impact is in the constitutional sphere – on the conduct of general elections to the Westminster Parliament itself. These are the central mechanism of power distribution in the United Kingdom, deciding which party will form the government for the next five years. As we shall see in Chapter 15, the method of translating party votes into seats in Parliament, which then determines who forms the government, is biased in several ways at the moment. It favours Labour over the Conservatives and both over all the other parties. This is because individual MPs are elected in small constituencies with a plurality of the vote: that is, if they receive more votes than any single rival (often only one-third of the total) they win. The system favours parties with concentrated regional support over those such as the Liberal Democrats who receive fairly equal support from all parts of the United Kingdom.

The European elections were originally held on this basis in the United Kingdom. But from 1999, under pressure from the EU, they have been held in large regional constituencies under a proportional system, which makes the seats received by a party list of 10–15 candidates proportional to the votes they get. This is why the Greens in 1999, with 6 per cent of the vote, got two seats – whereas in 1989 with over 14 per cent of votes they got no seats under the small constituency plurality system.

The Euro-elections thus offer an outstanding example of how British elections could be made fairer to small parties. The change to European proportional representation was in fact one of the constitutional reforms carried through by the Labour government when it came to power in 1997, along with semi-proportional elections in Scotland, Wales and London. Indeed, all national and regional elections in Britain are now more proportional than general elections. This creates an increasing pressure for the latter to be reformed, although the two large parties, which would lose by it, will resist any real change.

Any move towards proportional general elections would change the current 'elective dictatorship' into a coalition government in which the Liberal Democrats would decide to govern either with a Labour or Conservative partner. Whether this is regarded as a good or bad thing there is no doubt it would introduce enormous changes into the way Britain is run. Thus the role of the Euro-elections in demonstrating the feasibility of PR in Britain and setting up pressures for changing to it have important constitutional implications.

Executive power

Just how important this could be is illustrated by another, contrary, tendency of EU membership – an increase in the political power of the government and Cabinet. This is because the main centres of power in the EU are no more accountable to the British Parliament than to the European, or to other national parliaments for that matter. The Council of Ministers, the main **executive** body in Brussels, is composed of representatives of national governments. It cannot become embroiled in the domestic politics of its member states. Thus any influence the British Parliament brings to bear on the Council must pass through the British government. And this, of course, gives the government a crucial role.

Parliamentary approval is not required for EU legislation. On the contrary, the British Parliament may only scrutinise legislation on a 'take note' basis, and even then may only deal with proposed, future legislation. 'Taking note' means recording legislation and the action it requires, but doing nothing to change it in any way. Officers of the EU do not attend parliamentary meetings, and neither explain nor

Executive

One of the three branches of government (with the legislative and judiciary). The executive is concerned with making government decisions and policies rather than the legislative function of law making. In Britain the executive is, in effect, the Cabinet or the prime minister.

BRIEFINGS

9.4 Scrutiny of European legislation by the House of Commons

The best that Parliament can do to control EU legislation is to exert control over the British government's nego-tiating position within the European bodies. In practice this has been difficult. The various committees of the House of Commons charged with examining European legislation have had extremely limited powers once they received the documents, usually sending them on rather than discussing their substance. With 30–40 documents arriving every day there have been few that could be given further consideration.

Once an issue is earmarked for debate there remains the problem of how Parliament is to influence the govern-ment's Council negotiating position. No specific amendments are allowed to be made to Commission proposals, and the House or standing committee may only debate on a 'take note' motion. During parliamentary vacations even less can be done. A statement by the supposedly radical Michael Foot, then Labour Leader of the House, sums up procedures nicely:

> Ministers will not give agreement to any legislative proposal recommended by the Scrutiny Committee for further consideration by the House before the House has given it that consideration, unless the Committee has indicated that agreement need not be withheld, or *the minister concerned is satisfied that agreement should not be withheld for reasons which he [sic] will at the first opportunity explain to the House.*

The italicised section emphasises the almost unlimited freedom of action that the British government has been able to reserve for itself. The House of Commons reorganised its procedures in 2000. The European Scrutiny Committee now considers all proposed legislation and refers matters needing further scrutiny to one of two standing committees. They report to the House of Commons, but parliamentary approval is still not required for European legislation. The government may note parliamentary opinion but may also ignore it if it wants.

Legislative

The law-making branch of government. In Britain it is the Queen in Parliament – the Queen, the House of Lords and the House of Commons.

justify their actions to Parliament. Parliament can only advise ministers about the policy they should adopt and await the outcome. Ministers may take note of par-liamentary opinion, but they may also ignore it if they please.

Other aspects of the constitution

Membership of the EU has so far had little effect on other aspects of the British constitution. The three-tier structure of government (central, regional and local) has been retained, as has the same set of central ministries. The highest court in the land remains the House of Lords and there is still no fully written-up constitution. The same rules of parliamentary procedure apply and much the same parliament-ary timetable is followed. In these respects EU membership has changed British practice very little.

How the EU is governed

Before seeing how the EU has affected government in Britain we need to see how it manages itself. The most important EU institutions are located at Brussels in Belgium (see Map 8.1), about an hour's flight from London. The European Court sits further away in Luxembourg, and the European Parliament is located even fur-ther away at Strasbourg on the French–German border (but its committees operate in Brussels close to the other centres of EU power).

Figure 9.1 identifies the central institutions of the EU and British participation in them. Decision making in the EU is complicated by the fact that it has two exec-utives and governments rather than just one.

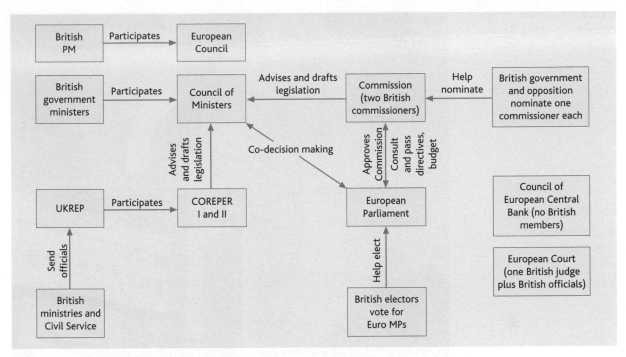

Figure 9.1 British participation in the central European Union institutions

The body that might become the European government if the EU becomes a truly federal state is the European Commission. This is a body of 25 politicians nominated by each member country. The Commission as a whole is scrutinised and approved by the European Parliament at the beginning of its term of office.

This procedure emphasises that Commissioners' loyalties are not to their home country but to the EU. The Commission has increasing powers to act autonomously in implementing the Single European Market and the general industrial and trade policies of the EU. We have already seen how action under its work, health and safety powers, in allowing workers to opt for a 48-hour minimum week, cut across Conservative government policy in 1996. The Commission runs the EU's central bureaucracy, divided into 38 directorates-general. These resemble the functional ministries of member states that act in each separate policy area (Table 9.2).

However, the Commission and its Civil Service are not autonomous. In many areas their function is to prepare policy proposals for decision by the Council of Ministers. The latter is the parallel, second and in most respects more powerful organ of the EU. Because it consists of representatives of national governments it is easy to think of the Council as an executive. In fact, however, as the ultimate source and approver of policy initiatives, the Council performs many of the functions carried out by legislatures in other political systems.

The Council consists of a General Affairs Council and various technical councils. The foreign ministers of member states meet in the General Affairs Council, while ministers for particular policy areas such as agriculture meet in the technical councils. Associated with the ministerial councils is the Committee of Permanent Representatives (COREPER in EU jargon). COREPER I 'shadows' the foreign ministers and consists of the national ambassadors to the EU, while COREPER II consists of the deputy ambassadors. There are numerous committees and working parties of appropriately qualified national civil servants associated with it. All these bodies carry out detailed preparatory work for the meetings of corresponding ministers.

Plate 9.1 European
Parliament building, Brussels
Source: Alamy/Image State

Thus the Council of Ministers also has a Civil Service working for it, which in many respects overshadows the permanent 'Eurocrats', just as the Council overshadows the Commission. Most new initiatives come from it or from the European Council (not to be confused with the Council of Europe), which is the meeting of prime ministers and heads of governments of the member states that often has to take decisions over matters on which the Council of Ministers cannot agree. Any major new initiatives or proposals for the extension of EU powers have to be agreed here. It is only the ministers who can commit national governments to courses of action not already agreed in the founding treaties, particularly in foreign and defence policy.

Because of the powers of the Council of Ministers and of the European Council it has often been said that the EU is more of an inter-governmental than a truly federal structure. Decisions have to be negotiated and agreed between the governments of the member states rather than autonomously by the supranational bodies. It is here that the British government can hold out for what it considers to be British interests.

Table 9.2 Directorates and services of the European Commission

Policies	External relations
Agriculture and rural development	Development
Competition	Enlargement
Economic and financial affairs	EuropeAid – Cooperation Office
Education and culture	External relations
Employment, social affairs and equal opportunities	Humanitarian Aid Office – ECHO
Enterprise and industry	Trade
Environment	**GENERAL SERVICES**
Fisheries and maritime affairs	Communication
Health and consumer protection	European Anti-Fraud Office
Information society and media	Eurostat
Internal market and services	Publications Office
Joint research centre	Secretariat-general
Justice, freedom and security	**INTERNAL SERVICES**
Regional policy	Budget
Research	Bureau of European Policy Advisers
Taxation and customs union	Informatics
Transport and energy	Infrastructures and logistics – Brussels
	Infrastructures and logistics – Luxembourg
	Internal audit service
	Interpretation
	Legal service
	Personnel and administration
	Translation

Source: European Commission

This was reinforced by the original practice of taking decisions in the Council unanimously. Every country had a veto, so by withholding its consent any national government could block any proposal. This is how British governments would have liked the situation to continue, so that they could veto any action affecting Britain with which they did not agree.

Since the Single European Act of 1986, however, and even more under the Treaty of Maastricht (1992), qualified majority voting has been introduced into the Council of Ministers for all but very major policy decisions such as the enlargement of the EU. Under this procedure not even two of the larger countries, acting together, could block proceedings. This put the initiative – even in the intergovernmental Council of Ministers – into the hands of France, Germany and the smaller countries, which wanted to speed up integration. Increasingly in the 1990s, therefore, an anti-federalist British government found itself isolated even on the body that might have been expected to protect its interests. Its position was also undermined by the decisions of the European Court, which tends to support the Commission. Since enlargement, however, the majority voting formula has changed and provided more opportunities for groups of countries to form coalitions to block initiatives. In addition, and following the ratification failure of the EU Constitituon, unanimity decision making remains in place for a range of key issues including enlargement.

Meanwhile the European Parliament has also proved itself pro-integrationist. It has often carried with it not only British Labour and Liberals but also British Conservative 'Euro MPs', who have thus found themselves at loggerheads with their own party at Westminster.

Of course, as Figure 9.1 also shows, stand-offs between British and European institutions are not a simple matter of 'us' versus 'them'. This is because British MPs and civil servants participate in EU institutions and shape EU policy just as much as any other national group. In fact, as one of the leading member states in the EU, the British play a disproportionate part compared with most others. This was particularly true of the framing and implementation of the Single European Act (1986) with its free market principles, which the former Conservative Commissioner Leon Brittan pushed through with the help of British economic advisers.

The EU and the British Civil Service

In spite of spreading integration, membership of the EU has had little impact on the way government actually works in Britain. The EU has no direct administration of its own within member states. Instead it relies on the existing national machinery to carry through its directives and legislation.

Thus no special ministry has had to be created in Britain to look after EU affairs. Instead, the European Secretariat of the Cabinet Office and the Foreign and Commonwealth Office (FCO) coordinate the work of Whitehall ministries, and of the British staff in Brussels through a constant round of inter-departmental meetings. Whitehall departments that are most deeply embedded in European affairs – the Treasury, Department of Trade and Industry (DTI), Department for Environment, Food and Rural Affairs (Defra) – have special European divisions within them. The rest deal with matters on an ad hoc basis as required. Where they are affected, regional governments and ministries are brought in.

The implementation of EU policy is thus handled by central ministries and departments, very much as is the implementation of national policy. This is because it is now national policy, even if decided by European bodies. What has called for more of an administrative effort is the fact that Britain, through its membership of the Council of Ministers, and its associated committees (COREPER I and II) is now heavily involved in the process of preparing and passing European legislation in the first place.

Such legislation is not wholly, or even largely, 'political' in nature. However, the fact that policy is decided through negotiations between national governments, and that there is, on occasion, considerable controversy, pervades the entire policy formulation process. The British government has to define and defend its interests in relation to the EU as a whole and to the other member states. The result is that the FCO, which traditionally represents British interests abroad, has become the central coordinating ministry for EU policy. It organises the UK Permanent Representation in Brussels and acts as the link between the home civil servants based in Brussels and their counterparts in the Whitehall ministries. The European Communities Section in the FCO is responsible for most of the coordinating work. It consists of several sub-departments covering different EU policy areas.

Although the FCO plays a coordinating role in formulating Britain's EU policy it does not have the technical expertise to determine that policy by itself. The specification for an industrial product, for example, is hardly within its competence. So there is considerable reliance on the functional ministries that do possess such expertise. Departments closely involved in formulating British EU policy in their areas of competence are the Treasury, Defra, the DTI and the Department of Communities and Local Government, most of which have EU sections coordinating their involvement with the EU. Departmental representatives liaise with the FCO, but also participate directly in meetings of specialists held under the aegis of the Commission, in the working parties and associated committees of COREPER, and also in ad hoc British Civil Service committees shadowing European Council meetings. The functional departments also play a major role in the preparation of briefs for Council meetings.

Coordination of British policy is achieved for the most part through a series of informal contacts among officials from interested government departments. But there is also a committee system through which EU policy can be discussed. At a basic level, there are a series of inter-departmental committees in the major policy areas. There are also temporary committees, bringing together the people most immediately concerned with a particular policy issue, and usually organised at the instigation of one of the functional departments. Their composition varies widely. A committee meeting on shipbuilding subsidies, for instance, would be chaired by a representative from the DTI and include officials from the Treasury, the DTI, the FCO, and possibly the Welsh, Scottish or Northern Irish administrations. Only the FCO would be represented on every committee. Above the specialist policy committees is a European Union Committee that oversees the preparation of briefs for the Permanent Representation and the Council meetings, and is generally responsible for the coordination of Britain's EU policy.

In its capacity as a central coordinating body the Cabinet Office also plays a significant role in the formulation of British policy. Officials from the Cabinet Office attend the regular committee meetings of the EU and are very closely involved in the more controversial issues. They also play a mediating role in ironing out differences between British government departments. Such a mediating role is especially important in the European context, where the government tries to present its views in terms of a national consensus.

Besides all the inter-departmental Civil Service committees concerned with formulating Britain's EU policies there are also political inter-ministerial committees. These include a Cabinet committee, composed of the ministers most affected by EU activities, which regularly discusses EU issues and is chaired by the foreign secretary.

Many of these arrangements for coordinating policy form an extension of inter-departmental committees and negotiating sessions inside Britain itself. What is new is the central coordinating role of the FCO, and the opportunities for civil servants from different ministries to work closely within the same organisation in Brussels, at the UK's Permanent Representation to the EU (UKRep).

Indeed, the major effect of the EU on the British Civil Service is the addition of a major European dimension to every civil servant's work. Most departments are involved one way or another with European policy matters, and most home civil servants have to keep a careful eye on developments in Brussels. Many have to attend the London meetings or travel regularly to EU meetings, apart from being seconded to UKRep. This means that many civil servants have to incorporate the European dimension into their daily working lives, and attend frequent training or refresher courses to keep them abreast of developments.

This creates a huge workload for politicians and civil servants. Every week tons of documents arrive from Brussels, Strasbourg and Luxembourg. Almost every week there is a high-level EU meeting involving the Prime Minister and/or other ministers. Apart from the Council of Ministers there are many other political meetings, and civil servants may spend as much time in Brussels as in London. There is also a meeting every week or so of the Cabinet EU Committee. Even without the EU, pressure on senior politicians and civil servants is enormous. With it, demands on their time and energy are even greater.

The EU and British pressure groups

Pressure groups

Private, voluntary organisations that wish to influence or control particular public policies without actually becoming the government or controlling all public policy.

Pressure or interest groups are organisations representing bands of people with some condition or activity in common that might be affected by politics. The most obvious of these are trade unions, grouping manual workers, craftspeople or white-collar workers. But there are thousands of others: churches, sports and professional organisations, animal and environmental protection groups and many more. Almost any activity or interest one can think of has an organisation to protect or advance it.

Politics inevitably affects these aspects of life. Any proposal for regulation or intervention affects somebody who either wants intervention to take an advantageous form or to be left alone. In either case groups exist or are formed to influence the political outcome.

Traditionally, interest groups in Britain have enjoyed close relationships with particular ministries. The extent to which they have enlarged their 'lobbying' in Brussels is a good indication of how far British policy is now being decided there rather than in London.

Among the pressure groups whose interests are affected by the EU, the larger ones are now organised at both national and international levels. They operate in Brussels, as in London, maintaining offices in both places in order to keep a close watch on policy developments and to lobby for their interests. At the European level groups act mainly on the Commission and Parliament, both of which are fairly open to outside interests. However, both also try to simplify life by dealing with only one or two large organisations in the same policy field. Therefore British pressure groups look for close working relations with their European partners. They are more likely to get a hearing if they act together, and more likely to be successful if they pool resources and speak with one voice. For example, the National Farmers' Union is part of the Committee of Professional Agricultural Organisations (COPA), which maintains a strong presence in Brussels; so also do other umbrella groups such as the European Trade Union Confederation (ETUC) and the Union of Industries of the European Union (UNIEU).

Public policy

Policy development in pursuit of European integration has often been patchy, and implementation of policy erratic, as the budget and the bureaucracy of the EU are relatively small. The budget is fixed at under 2.007 per cent of the combined gross national product (GNP) of member states. The EU employs approximately 25,000 people in Brussels and Luxembourg, which is smaller than a medium-sized department of central government in Britain or the administration of a large city such as Amsterdam or Barcelona. Nevertheless the EU already has an enormously powerful and wide-ranging policy impact, covering almost everything from the routines of daily life all the way up to the grand issues of monetary union and foreign policy. Every year the EU issues more than 12,000 legal instruments in the form of regulations, directives, decisions, recommendations and opinions.

Economic affairs – the euro

This is probably the most important single area so far as national policies are concerned. The Single European Act, passed in 1986 and implemented patchily in the 1990s, encourages free movement of goods, services, capital and people

BRIEFINGS

9.5 How policy is implemented by the EU

Decisions in the EU are implemented by means of five types of 'legal instruments', as follows:

1. Regulations are general and, since they have the force of EU law, they are directly binding on all member states.

2. Directives are more frequently used than regulations and, similarly, are binding on all member states. Unlike regulations, however, directives leave it open for member states to decide how best to achieve the desired goal.

3. Decisions are binding on all those to whom they are addressed.

4. Recommendations have no binding force, and are sometimes not defined as 'legal instruments'.

5. Opinions have the same characteristics as recommendations.

throughout the EU. Among other things this means the free movement of university students (promoted by programmes that pay the extra expenses). Many technical specifications in manufacturing and services have been standardised (the EU term is 'harmonisation'). And since the EU itself is funded by each nation paying a proportion of its receipts from value added tax, VAT rates have also been partly standardised. The EU would like the whole tax structure in member countries to be standardised across Europe, a logical complement to the idea of a unified market.

The most ambitious, difficult and controversial part of the whole agenda (certainly in Britain) has been the introduction of a common currency, the euro, now functioning in 12 states of the European Union. Britain is the major member state holding aloof from this, with a corresponding marginalisation of its influence in the EU that we have already discussed. Decisions about financial (and hence implicitly economic) policy for the EU are taken by the Council of the European Central Bank on which Britain is not represented, though decisions to increase or slow down European economic activity inevitably affect the United Kingdom.

The problem for a Labour government, which might be generally disposed to go in, is that any decision to do so involves calling and winning a referendum campaign against impassioned Conservative opposition. The government will not initiate this if it gets in the way of its internal political agenda, particularly winning the next general election. It has thus taken refuge in a formula. It will recommend joining the eurozone if their economic 'tests' are met. Unlike the EU's own conditions for joining the European Monetary Union, the British criteria stress economic convergence rather than financial considerations. However, they are both vague and highly technical and can probably be interpreted to favour whatever conclusion the government wants, once it decides what the political circumstances dictate. Under the mask of economic debate most decisions about the EU are political ones. The real question for Britain in the monetary debate is how best to reconcile the economic and the political consequences of EMU membership. The Chancellor, Gordon Brown, partly answered this question in 2003 when he announced that only one of the five economic tests (the impact on UK financial services) had been passed. This in effect postponed EMU membership for the foreseeable future.

Other aspects of EU harmonisation

These have been less controversial. National governments are no longer permitted directly to subsidise industries. But the EU provides money for industrial

BRIEFINGS

9.6 British economic 'tests' for joining the European Monetary Union

Gordon Brown, New Labour Chancellor of the Exchequer (i.e. Minister of Finance), postponed controversy in October 1997 over a decision to adopt the euro by laying down five economic tests that had to be met for a decision to be made. These were:

1. sustainable convergence between the United Kingdom and the economies already using the euro

2. sufficient flexibility to cope with economic change

3. positive effect on investment

4. impact on British financial services

5. impact on employment.

Compared with the EU's criteria for whether a country is capable of adopting the euro (see Briefing 8.5) the British tests stress economic rather than purely financial considerations – would the British economy integrate well with the Continental ones or not? However, they are more vague.

Of course, in a world boom (or recession) the economies would show convergence but at other times might be out of kilter. So all depends on when the campaign is initiated. What is flexibility? If the test were seriously applied to the northern industrial and southern financial service economies within Britain itself they would probably show non-convergence and lack of flexibility in the north. But should the United Kingdom be split up politically as a result? Few politicians outside the Scottish National Party would argue so.

All this implies that the British tests, like the EU's own convergence criteria, are a front for decisions that have to be taken on political grounds – does Britain wish to integrate with the EU or not? It may remain as it is and occupy a half-way house, but this will in the long run deprive it of influence within the wider Europe.

restructuring and technological development, offering loans at special interest rates through the European Investment Bank. The basic principle is that public subsidies should be distributed on an EU basis to strengthen the EU economy, and not by national governments in a way that interferes with a free market. There are also rules about public procurement. Public bodies, such as governments, are obliged to seek tenders for large contracts on the open market across the EU. Finally, attempts have been made to regulate conditions of work, including minimum pay, employment laws, and such things as the enforced use of tachographs (monitoring machines) in the cabs of long-distance trucks, a measure the European Court forced on an unwilling British government in 1979.

By and large the EU has been successful in creating a single, integrated market, although its difficulties and failures have often attracted more attention than its successes. Examples of problems involving British interests are: the banned export of British meat to France (blocked on health grounds after the mad cow and foot and mouth scares); ending the practice in some countries of favouring home-produced spirits, a decision that helped the Scottish whisky industry. Once again these examples show how deeply EU policy reaches into national economic affairs. EU authority is supreme in competition policy (the EU policy of encouraging free competition between firms in the same sector and discouraging monopoly practices), although few mergers or acquisitions of note have been blocked by the Commission. Similarly, although the Maastricht Treaty speaks optimistically about a free labour market, linguistic, cultural and other barriers have resulted in low levels of mobility between member states.

Regional aid

Britain receives substantial grants from the European Regional Development Fund, created in 1975 to help poor or industrially run-down areas. Of the 50 million people in the EU living in such regions (prior to enlargement to 25 members in 2004), 20 million are in Britain (Wales, Scotland, Northern Ireland and the north of England). The standard of living in Britain as a whole is almost exactly the pre-enlargement EU average, but only in the south-east of England is it higher (by about 20 per cent), while in Northern Ireland it is 25 per cent lower. The special regions of Britain benefit from funds and policy initiatives aimed at building up small businesses and the tourist trade, retraining workers in declining agricultural areas, restructuring industry and retraining workers, rebuilding urban infrastructure and revitalising the economy in areas of industrial decline. Merseyside alone now receives about £1.3 billion from London and Brussels.

Consumer affairs

Common standards for the labelling and selling of foods have been adopted. Well-publicised examples in Britain involve the production of ice cream, sausages and beer, but EU regulations cover a large proportion of the goods sold in shops. The EU has ruled that tobacco products must not be advertised on television, and it carefully regulates the amount and the timing of television advertising. Recently it cleared British meat after the foot and mouth epidemic of 2001, and took judicial action against the French government for continuing to ban it.

Agriculture and fishing

The Common Agricultural Policy is the largest single item on the EU's annual budget, accounting for almost half the total, although it used to be three-quarters. It is intended to give some economic security to the large number of poor farmers and agricultural communities in western Europe. Although British farmers benefit very substantially from the CAP the country as a whole pays more than it gets because British farms are relatively large and efficient. Currently the EU's fishing policy is even more controversial because, in trying to preserve fish stocks, it has affected the livelihoods of fishing communities in Britain.

Environmental policy

The EU has developed a wide range of policies to protect the environment involving, among other things, forests, birds, plants, animals, drinking water, waste disposal, bathing beaches and recreational areas. Many of these have caused difficulties for the British government: substandard water supplies and bathing beaches, inadequate industrial pollution controls, new roads that fail environmental impact norms (the M3 at Twyford Down, for example), and new conifer forests inconsistent with EU standards. In 1993 Lancashire County Council successfully prosecuted the British government in the European Court for its failure to clean up three bathing beaches. EU policy in these matters may be embarrassing for the government but serves to protect British consumers.

Social policy

The EU has enacted a broad range of social measures. For example, industrial training has been financed by the European Social Fund since 1972. Some policies have attracted much publicity, such as the case of *Smith* v. *Macarthy*, in which the European Court forced a British employer to observe equal pay rules. The controversial Social Chapter of the Maastricht agreement laid down a broad range of regulations on, among other things, social conditions, working hours, minimum wages and health and safety standards. The Chapter was not signed by the Conservative government of the time, but has been accepted by the Labour government.

Justice and home affairs

This is an area where the member states jealously guard their own autonomy, so common European policies on policing and internal security have to be arrived at by inter-governmental negotiations and unanimity or not at all. In some cases such as the Schengen agreement to abolish frontier controls inside the EU, some states have agreed to go in together leaving others including the United Kingdom outside. Free internal mobility within the EU poses problems for frontier controls as it is more difficult to exclude aliens who have already been admitted to another EU country. This particularly affects the British concern to exclude purely 'economic' immigrants to the country. Under the terms of the Treaty of Amsterdam (1997) the EU is now able to act more directly in the area of justice and home affairs.

Foreign affairs and security

On foreign economic policy the EU has been relatively successful in framing a common European policy. It now acts for its members in the vitally important GATT negotiations, and appears alongside the most powerful nations in world economic meetings. But on diplomatic and defence matters its success is limited. Some member states, including Britain, jealously guard the power to decide their own foreign and defence policies, or else prefer to work through NATO. Consequently Europe failed to provide international leadership during the various crises of the 1990s and has been unable to formulate a common response to the US 'war on terrorism' or the continuing Middle East crisis.

Two points should be noted about the impact of the EU on public policy. First, some of the rules and regulations that exist on paper are only partially enforced, if at all, in some member states. There are many ways of breaking, bending or ignoring them. This means that many areas of public policy remain largely unaffected by EU directives and law (law and order, for example). Also unaffected are all those very important areas – agriculture apart – where the nation state provides direct cash payments for individuals: pensions, social and unemployment benefits. In other words EU competence is mainly confined to regulation rather than the direct distribution of benefits. This may, of course, change with further integration and monetary union and consequent pressures to redistribute across countries and regions to help adjustment. Figure 9.2 shows the budget of the EU in 2006. Note the continuing importance of agricultural subsidies and of cohesion funds used to help poorer regions 'catch up' with the more affluent regions. The category 'the EU as a global partner' refers mainly to economic aid to Third World countries that have historical associations with the member states under the Suva Convention.

The rules on public procurement are complex, and can easily be twisted and evaded. Britain has a good record of compliance with EU directives. In 1991 only Denmark, Luxembourg and the Netherlands were found to be more compliant, and some countries were much worse. Figure 9.3 shows the degree of compliance with single market laws in the mid-1990s and the number of complaints against countries for flouting the trade rules. Again, Britain's performance is relatively

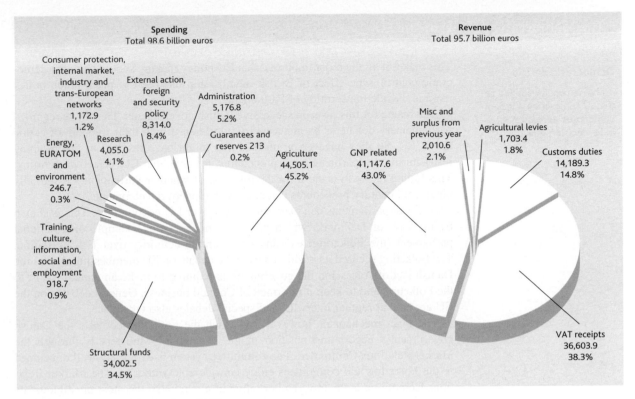

Figure 9.2 European Union budget, 2006

Source: Public finance figures of the European Union from the web site
http://europa.eu.int/comm/budget/library/publications/budget_in_fig/dep_eu_budg_2006_en.pdf

Figure 9.3 Single market
laws enacted by national
governments, 31 December
1995, and complaints
against countries for rule
violation, 1995

Source: European Commission

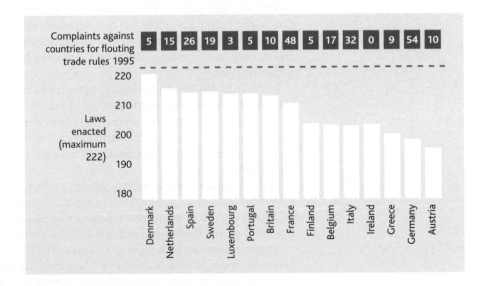

good compared with many member states, in particular Germany. However, Britain continues to have the worst ice cream and the best beer in Europe, despite EU attempts to change both!

Whatever the actual impact of EU policy, the fact remains that many of the policy areas previously controlled by national governments are now partially or even wholly in the hands of European decision makers. To this extent it is certainly true that EU policy has an important and expanding effect on daily life in Britain.

The 'democratic deficit' of the EU

Democratic deficit

A phrase usually applied to the EU to describe a lack of democratic accountability in its decision making.

This makes it all the more important that EU policy making should be under democratic control. One effect of British membership has been to place much policy making outside the scrutiny of Parliament.

The blame for this rests on successive British governments. They have regarded parliamentary debate as an unnecessary interference with their freedom of action in the EU. So they have given no lead that might have resulted in a substantial restructuring of parliamentary procedures to give the EU effective scrutiny. This failure raises in acute form the question of whether Parliament's essentially nineteenth-century procedures can cope with modern developments.

National parliaments can exert real power over EU negotiations. This is shown by the case of Denmark, which provides an interesting example of a national parliament (the Folketing) exerting considerable authority over EU legislation. The Folketing secured its position during the debate on EU membership. Under the Danish Act of Accession the government is required to make an annual report to the Folketing and to keep it informed of Council business. General debates on the EU are held at regular intervals, and special debates also take place.

The main mechanism, however, by which the Folketing controls the Danish government's negotiating position in the Council of Ministers is through the Market Relations Committee. The committee system is extremely well developed in the Folketing and committees enjoy considerable authority. The Market Relations Committee is the most authoritative of all and also the most prestigious: its 17 members, elected proportionately from the various political parties, include many former Cabinet ministers. Under the rules of procedure the government is committed to consult with the Market Relations Committee on all Council business. The Committee meets weekly and may question ministers and civil servants involved in EU policy. The government is obliged to seek mandates from the Committee before important Council decisions. In many Council sessions Danish ministers have had extremely narrow mandates and on some occasions they have had to seek new mandates from the Committee before reaching agreement on a particular issue.

In the light of Danish experience, the inability of the British Parliament to control its government's negotiating position may be part of a general decline in its power, attributable to the dominance of a single party in government at any one time, government control of the parliamentary agenda, and the poor access of MPs and peers to information. In Chapter 18 we shall consider the general question of parliamentary power.

In the European area, however, there is another body that might be able to hold governments to account: the directly elected European Parliament itself. It holds its legislative meetings in the French city of Strasbourg, far away from the real centres of power in Brussels, and meets in full session for only one week a month.

This indicates that its influence is limited. The EP is the least weighty of the four major European bodies (Council of Ministers, Commission, Court, Parliament). However, it is not quite so limited as its peripheral position and short legislative sessions might suggest.

For one thing, it does most of its work in specialised committees, and these meet in Brussels where they cross-question Commissioners and European civil servants on all aspects of European policy. Increasingly these meetings receive press coverage, especially when they uncover frauds or anomalies in EU policy.

The EP has also been given increased powers in every revision of the original treaty (Treaty of Rome, 1957), so it can reject the budget or national nominees to the Commission (but only as a whole). The EP has to be consulted on a

BRIEFINGS

9.7 The European Parliament

Since 1979 the EP has been directly elected every four years. Seats in the EP are allocated among member states in rough proportion to their population.

While the EP is charged with the duty of supervising the Commission and the Council of Ministers it lacks power and has mainly a secondary and advisory role. Although its jurisdiction has expanded, the European Parliament is still primarily a delaying or amending body with limited powers of veto, especially on budgetary matters. It is logistically and bureaucratically hampered by having to meet in Brussels for committees and in Luxembourg and Strasbourg for plenary sessions. Moreover, the main secretariat is located in Luxembourg. Business is conducted in all the official languages of the EU, which imposes a huge burden of translation.

The European Parliament is increasingly flexing its muscles, however. In 1998 it forced the resignation of the European Commission en bloc, after the publication of a damning report on corruption on the part of some Commissioners.

whole range of social and economic policy (Single European Act, 1986) and it has positively to approve policy, or at least not reject it, in other areas, under the Treaties of Maastricht (1992), Amsterdam (1997) and Nice (2000). Under the draft EU Constitution the European Parliament would have received further enhanced powers. But the rejection of the Constitution by referenda in France and the Netherlands has effectively killed off any prospect of ratification for the foreseeable future.

The weakness of the European Parliament is that it mainly controls the Commission. The body it really wants to control is the Council of Ministers, since that is where initiatives on most EU matters originate. Until it can affect the Council's decisions, or until the latter's governmental powers are mostly transferred to the Commission, much of what the EP does seems like shadow boxing. It really has no desire to punish or hamper the Commission when it is its ally in campaigning for a transfer of power from national to EU level.

This fact also mutes party conflict within the European Parliament. MEPs are organised into six main party groups: Communists, Socialists (with British Labour included), Greens, Liberals (including British Liberal Democrats), European People's Party (Conservatives – although not the British Conservatives – and Christian Democrats) and Democracies and Diversities. The major groupings are Socialists and Populars, who compete for parliamentary control with each other. However, most politicians who get themselves elected to the EP are naturally Europhile and federalist. Hence party conflict is muted, rendering parliamentary proceedings rather dull as well as often irrelevant to core decision making.

The European Parliament's significant asset is that it is the only elected European body. Direct elections are held every four years, more or less simultaneously across all the countries of the EU. Hence it can claim to have more of a democratic, popular mandate for what it says than can the Commission or the Court.

However, the Council of Ministers can also claim that its members, chosen to represent their country by their respective national governments, owe their position ultimately to popular election. In Britain, general elections are clearly regarded as more important than Euro-elections, as evidenced by the fact that they attract almost double the number of voters.

Indeed, as campaigning in Euro-elections is in the hands of the British parties rather than an all-European Socialist or Conservative organisation, they often appear as a pale reflection of the general election. European issues only enter in a negative way (e.g. 'resisting Brussels bureaucracy') and elections are fought mostly on issues of domestic politics. It is difficult, therefore, for British members of the European Parliament to claim a very convincing mandate for wresting power from the Council of Ministers, when they have been elected on the basis of (or as a protest against) the British government's domestic record.

The powerlessness of the British Parliament in European affairs is not counter-balanced, therefore, by any greater authority or effectiveness of the European Parliament. The latter has only marginally greater power of scrutiny over European legislation and no greater control over the Council of Ministers. This detracts even from its direct election, by lowering its visibility to electors and ulti-mately their turn-out. The EP has the potential for democratic control should the EU become a real federation. Until that day, however, it remains the weakest of the European institutions and the most limited in its functions.

Subsidiarity and local government

This 'democratic deficit' might be made up within the structure of the EU – at least to some extent – by implementing the idea of 'subsidiarity', which is frequently talked about and is even written into the Treaty of Maastricht as a vague commit-ment. 'Subsidiarity' has been seen by 'Eurosceptical' countries such as Britain as a way of limiting future transfers of power from London to Brussels, or even of getting some powers back. This hardly guarantees democratic control, given the weakness of parliamentary scrutiny.

A better idea might be to go all the way and transfer some European and cen-tral powers to local and regional governments, the third set of directly elected bod-ies in Britain. They have the advantage of being much closer to their electors than either the European or British governments and parliaments.

Traditionally, many 'personal' services that were centralised in other European countries – education, police, public health – have been controlled by local author-ities in Britain. The tendency under governments from 1976 onwards however has been quite the opposite. Such services have either been taken over by central gov-ernment or given to unelected 'quangos' nominated by the government – the only exception being the 'hiving off' of these services in Wales and Scotland to elected regional executives. Centralisation has been justified in terms of controlling pub-lic expenditure, benefiting from the 'economies of scale' of larger, if non-elected, units, and of introducing competition. An unstated reason, arising from the elec-tion cycle in Britain (which ensures that most local councillors are elected at the government's mid-term, when its popularity is low), is that councils are often con-trolled by opposition parties. Governments have often found it easier to work with nominated bodies whose members were more likely to be 'one of us' (in Margaret Thatcher's phrase).

This erosion of local democracy has been one factor stimulating demands for local autonomy in Scotland, Wales and Northern Ireland. We shall discuss these regions and their local nationalist parties in the next chapter. Here we need only note that regional elected assemblies are also boosted by the doctrine of subsidiar-ity. There are few tasks outside foreign affairs and defence that government at this level would not be fit to do. Even if Scottish and Welsh independence became an option it would be easier to contemplate within the single market and the structure of the EU. Hence, the Scottish National Party uses the slogan 'Scotland in Europe' to indicate that an independent Scotland is viable. Paradoxically, the centralisation of western Europe under the EU helps its decentralisation, a point noted in the next chapter.

Quite apart from the possibility of carrying 'subsidiarity' to its logical conclusion, the EU has already had an effect on the British regions and local government. The EU has substantial regional funds and many of its policies have a direct impact on local services. As a result a large and increasing number of local and regional bodies have built their own special links with Brussels. Some maintain an office and staff there to keep a close watch on events, to try to influence European bodies and to raise money. Others employ consultants in Brussels to act on their behalf. Some authorities group together to form consortia, but the larger ones act separately.

It often suits both local interests and Brussels to work directly with one another, thereby short-circuiting the government in London. This is consistent with subsidiarity, but it is also a convenient political device that allows the localities and Brussels to build political alliances independently of national governments. This is notably true for Britain, where the government has the reputation of being the 'awkward partner'. Thus the EU strengthens the position of local and regional government as against the central government in London. This is a concrete example of centralisation in Brussels developing hand in hand with the decentralisation of power to the local and regional levels, something that is taken up within the context of regionalism in the next chapter.

Summary

This chapter has examined the impact of the European Union on government and politics in Britain. The effects have been deep and profound but they also vary considerably, as follows:

- Constitutional effects have been limited, with the single and major exception of parliamentary sovereignty. Parliament must accept EU law, and cannot change, repeal or even debate it. Legal sovereignty in relevant policy areas has therefore shifted from Westminster to the EU. With this important exception, the British constitution has changed little as a result of membership.

- Much policy, particularly in economic, social and environmental matters, is now made in Brussels rather than London. The common currency poses a dilemma for British policy makers, which they will have to confront at some time.

- In terms of the machinery of central government the United Kingdom has adapted existing structures rather than changed them. There is no special Ministry for European Affairs, as there is in many countries. Instead, European affairs are handled by a series of inter-departmental committees, coordinated by the Cabinet Office, and by the Foreign and Commonwealth Office. Nonetheless, the sheer volume of EU work has added enormously to the pressures on leading politicians and civil servants. They have also had to develop a European awareness in almost everything they do.

- Pressure groups whose interests are affected by the EU have responded by moving into Brussels, where they have replicated their London lobbying activities and organisations. They often join forces with other European partners to form 'umbrella' organisations that represent many national organisations with similar interests. It is estimated that about 500 'Eurogroups' are recognised by policy makers in Brussels, and that over 3,000 full-time lobbyists operate in the city. British groups are fully involved with both.

- Local governments and regional organisations have followed suit and made direct contact with European decision makers in Brussels. The advisory 'Committee of the Regions' gives them an institutional basis inside the structures of the EU.

- The impact of the EU varies considerably in different policy areas. In some its effects are pervasive, in others less so. But EU policies now affect many aspects of daily life in Britain, and their influence is likely to grow.

Essays

1. Why did the European Union issue decline in importance in British politics after 2003?

2. What impact has membership of the EU had on the ways in which policy is made in Whitehall and Westminster? Has it made the business of government more or less difficult?

3. What have been the legal consequences of British membership of the European Union? Answer with specific reference to decisions of the Court of Justice.

Projects

1. Compare and contrast the ways in which Conservative and Labour governments have incorporated EU affairs into the policy-making process. Which party has been most sympathetic to the EU in the policy context?

2. Imagine you are the leader of a major European pressure group. How would you try to influence EU policy on a matter of interest to your group? Answer with reference to:

    (a) agricultural policy

    (b) environmental policy

    (c) labour market policy.

3. Has membership of the EU had a different impact on government in Scotland compared with England? Are any differences attributable to the ways in which institutions operate in the two countries?

Further reading

For the fullest account of the impact of the European Union on the government, politics and policy of the United Kingdom, D. Watts and C. Pilkington, *Britain in the European Union Today* (Manchester: Manchester University Press, 3rd edn, 2005), Janet Mather, *The European Union and British Democracy* (London: Palgrave-Macmillan, 2000) and J. A. Cygan, *The UK Parliament and EU Legislation* (Dordrecht: Kluwer, 1998) are very useful. Recent articles are: H. Macmillen, 'Political responsibility for the administration of Europe', *Parliamentary Affairs*, **52** (4), 1999, pp. 703–18; N. Kinnock, 'Accountability and reform of internal control in the European Commission', *Political Quarterly*, **73** (1), 2002, pp. 21–8; A. Menon, 'Britain and European integration: the view from within', *Political Quarterly*, **75** (3), 2004, pp. 285–317; P. Stephens, 'Britain and Europe: an unforgettable past and unavoidable future', *Political Quarterly*, **76** (1), 2005, pp. 12–21.

Useful web sites on Europe in Britain

Hot links to these sites can be found on the CWS at www.pearsoned.co.uk/budge.

The impact of the European Union in the design and implementation of governmental policies in Britain cannot be underestimated. In our previous chapter we focused on the conflicts that such influence may engender with the United Kingdom. Now we can suggest some useful web sites on the structure and functioning of the European Union and its impact on Britain.

The inevitable first step is to visit the EU official web site at www.europa.eu.int/index_en.htm, where you can find links to the European Parliament, the Council of Ministers, the European Commission and other relevant institutions. A comprehensive analysis of the historical evolution of the European Union after the Maastricht treaty is available at www.europarl.eu.int/code/maastric/default_en.htm. Detailed information on the political outcomes of the Amsterdam Treaty can be found at www.europa.eu.int/abc/obj/amst/en/. We suggest you consult the European Committee of the Regions (www.cor.eu.int/home.htm) and the European Economic and Social Committee (www.esc.eu.int/pages/en/home.htm). Reliable statistical data on the EU is available at www.europa.eu.int/comm/eurostat. The official publications of the EU can be accessed from www.euros.ch. There are critical voices within the European Union structure itself: you can find them at www.europarl.eu.int/edd.

For official British policy towards Europe, visit the Foreign and Commonwealth Office site (www.fco.gov.uk). For UKRep (the UK's Permanent Representation to the EU) see www.ukrep.fco.gov.uk. You might also want to visit the European Foundation at www.europeanfoundation.org.

An excellent source for academic approaches to the EU is the European Research Papers Archive (www.eiop.or.at/erpa/). Visit also the Centre for European Reform (www.cer.org.uk) and the working papers of the Jean Monnet Programme (www.jeanmonnetprogram.org).

chapter 10
Disuniting the Kingdom: Ireland

Besides Europe Britain is embroiled in another set of territorial relationships affecting its sovereignty – in Ireland. The whole of Ireland was once part of the 'United Kingdom of Great Britain and Ireland' – up to 1922. Then the south and west broke away after a violent armed struggle to form the independent Republic of Ireland. Britain is the only member of the EU to have lost part of its territory through twentieth-century violence. Its current territorial sovereignty as the 'United Kingdom of Great Britain and Northern Ireland' is threatened by developments there, which may also set precedents for Scotland and Wales.

This chapter covers:

■ nationalism and state building in western Europe – is the United Kingdom really the unified nation it claims to be?

■ how relationships with the British state worked out in Ireland

■ Northern Ireland: origins of the 'Troubles'

■ the 'Troubles', 1969–97: rival claims of nationhood

■ the 'Peace Process', 1997–2005

■ the Northern Irish Assembly, keystone of the political settlement

■ prospects for a lasting peace.

Minority nationalism and state building in Britain and Europe

Britain is unique among the countries of western Europe in having had part of its national territory secede in a violent struggle for independence. The present-day Republic of Ireland broke away from the United Kingdom in 1922 by force of arms. Irish nationalists have continued the guerrilla war in Northern Ireland and on the British mainland up until recently. Only Spain among the member states of the EU has experienced anything similar to this, in the form of Basque terrorism. Islamic terrorism has so far been much more limited than Irish.

Minority nationalism, putting peaceful demands for political autonomy on the part of cultural or religious minorities is common throughout western Europe. Belgium has effectively split between Dutch-speaking Flemings and French-speaking Walloons; Italy and Spain have granted extensive powers to regional minorities; and Bavaria has its own political party inside Germany.

BRIEFINGS

10.1 England, Britain, Great Britain, the United Kingdom and the British Isles

There is often confusion between the terms England, Britain, Great Britain, the United Kingdom and the British Isles. This is partly because geographical entities get mixed up with political ones. The largest geographical entity, the British Isles, consists of the two main islands and many smaller ones. The larger island, Great Britain, contains England, Wales and Scotland, and the smaller one, Ireland, comprises Northern Ireland and the Republic of Ireland. The largest political entity is the United Kingdom of Britain and Northern Ireland, which consists of England, Scotland, Wales and Northern Ireland. This is often shortened to the UK. The largest part of the UK is England, often confused with Britain or even the UK by the English. The Republic of Ireland was part of the UK until 1922 when it broke away after the War of Independence.

BRIEFINGS

10.2 State nationalism and minority nationalism: are nation states really nations?

'State' is another word used to describe a 'country' or 'polity'. It refers first to a territorial unit governed by a single supreme (or 'sovereign') authority and second to the military and administrative institutions which defend and organise that unit. In the context of international relations the idea of an autonomous territorial unit is usually uppermost. References to the activities of the 'state' inside Britain usually mean the executive and its administrative apparatus.

The British state was consolidated by English kings and rulers, based around London, who conquered the outlying regions of England from 800–1200, then Wales and Ireland. They tried but failed to conquer Scotland, which was, however, incorporated by negotiation through the dynastic Union of the Crowns in 1603, and the Union of Parliaments in 1707. Southern and western Ireland broke away violently from the British state at the end of the First World War (1919–22) and set up a separate state, the Republic of Ireland. The 'six counties' of Northern Ireland are still disputed between the British and Irish states and sporadic violence continues. The Scottish Nationalist Party (SNP), which gained 22 per cent of the Scottish vote in the 2003 Scottish Parliament election, advocates Scottish independence through peaceful means. Welsh Nationalists organised in Plaid Cymru want more autonomy inside Britain.

The growth of independence movements stems from the influence of **nationalism**. This is the idea, which originated in the nineteenth century, that each 'people' defined by a particular language and culture should have its own state. In practice, this argument was often reversed by the dominant group as each existing state imposed its own language and culture on the minorities, claiming that as there was one state it ought to have a unified people. 'Unionists' often claim that Britain is a nation state, as most 'Britons' speak English and have a common culture. Welsh, Scottish and Irish nationalists oppose this, arguing that the existence of a separate culture in their country justifies an independent state for them. Nationalism is thus a two-edged sword. Depending on what groups are identified as important, it can be used either to argue for the legitimacy of the existing 'nation states' such as the United Kingdom, or for the right of secession of the Irish, Scots and Welsh.

Nationalism

The belief that the people identified as belonging to a national community should form their own sovereign state.

Irish (and Scottish and Welsh) nationalism are thus not anomalies on the European scene; on the contrary, they are a familiar phenomenon. That is in part why the EU has created its advisory 'Committee of the Regions' to represent minority groups, bypassing the claims of the existing member states to be homogenous nations.

Indeed, there are some European federalists who advocate a 'Europe of the Homelands' (*Europe des Patries*), which would cut out existing states altogether and base a European federation on the traditional regions. One does not have to go this far to see that regional aspirations might be a useful ally in attempts by Brussels to take power away from the member states.

The reason why so many regional minorities exist goes back to the very formation of the European states. Most were created by powerful rulers expanding from their fortified capital to seize surrounding territories. Sometimes these were inhabited by people speaking the same language and sharing a similar way of life to the original subjects, but sometimes they were very different. Whatever the case, they could be taxed and used to support an even more powerful army for further territorial expansion.

The traditional state tried to impose the same religion on all its subjects but did not concern itself with their culture or language. After the French Revolution, however, the idea that the state should be 'one and indivisible' – all citizens should be equal to each other but also similar – gained ground. This was the origin of nationalism, according to which every people or nation should have its own state. Universal education gave those in control of existing states an opportunity to create a corresponding nation by imposing the state language on all schools and educating all children in it. The growth of a mass press, and later radio and television – all using the majority language – aided this process.

State attempts to impose a single language provoked resistance from minorities who saw their own culture and language disappearing under state pressure. Their remedy was to create their own political institutions in order to sustain, rather than depress, their culture. Thus they too found support in the ideas of nationalism. One only had to recognise the minority as a separate nation to argue that it should have its own state. However, minority secession or even autonomy was resisted by the majority, who saw this as splitting 'their' nation, and redoubled their attempts at assimilation of the minorities. What these conflicts call into question is what constitutes the nation: the region, or the state in which it has become embedded?

These conflicts have worked their way through British politics. The core of the British state is formed by south-east England, which conquered or assimilated the other parts of the islands in a process lasting 1,000 years (up to the parliamentary union with Ireland in 1801).

In some respects state formation in Britain was more permissive than in other European countries. Because of its island position it had less need to exert an iron control over its borders – it could afford to leave local leaders in charge (in mainland Britain at least). Provided they paid taxes and kept order they could do more or less what they wanted within their own region or county. Nineteenth-century political reforms were aimed at freeing local initiatives rather than promoting centralisation. It was, for example, native Scottish educationalists, and not a London government, who tried to replace both Gaelic and Scots with standard English as their language.

In Ireland, however, the British government – because the island was a potential area of military weakness – acted much more like an imperial power towards a colony, planting settlers and ruling through an alien bureaucracy. Differences were exacerbated by the fact that four-fifths of the population were Roman Catholic in a largely Protestant British state. Doctrines of nationalism thus found fertile ground among the Catholic Irish of the south and west in the nineteenth century. Like many such European nationalist movements the struggle for independence fused with movements for political emancipation, social advancement and cultural autonomy. These sparked off a century-long series of revolts against British rule (1798, 1848, 1867–8, 1879–83, 1919–22). The last of these succeeded in establishing an independent state, now the Republic of Ireland, in the south and west of Ireland.

The Irish example illustrates the ambiguity and interchangeability of the concepts of nation and minority, region and state. It all depends on whether a territorially concentrated group has state institutions of its own or whether its area is run by a state in which a larger group dominates. Ireland was a region of Britain and

Plate 10.1 The aftermath of the Easter Rising in Dublin, 1916, which initiated the violent secession of Southern Ireland from the United Kingdom

Source: Empics

is (mostly) now a separate state. The same could conceivably happen in Scotland and Wales and may well happen in Northern Ireland over the next 20 years.

Northern Ireland illustrates another phenomenon, however, which is equally characteristic of nationalist movements. The nationalist struggles set off reactions not only from the state majority but also from other minorities or from representatives of the state majority within their own region. In the case of Ireland the Protestants, a local majority in the north, strongly opposed Irish nationalism and upheld the union with Britain. The Irish War of Independence was also a civil war between largely Catholic nationalists and largely Protestant unionists. When Irish independence was granted the latter retained their own territory in the north as part of the British state.

Like Russian dolls, however, such territorial solutions always reveal another minority lurking underneath. Northern Ireland contained a substantial nationalist, Catholic minority who supported a takeover by the Republic. This led to continuing guerrilla warfare and terrorism (1919–23, 1936–41, 1956–63, 1969–96) in mainland Britain as well as in Northern Ireland.

Plate 10.2 Ulster Protestant volunteers take on the Republicans: preliminaries to the Irish Civil War, 1920–2
Source: Empics

BRIEFINGS

10.3 Guerrilla warfare, terrorism and freedom fighters

Nationalist groups frustrated with constitutional procedures for expressing their demands may turn to violence, often calling themselves 'freedom fighters' or a 'liberation front'. The main example in Britain was the Irish Republican Army (IRA). The mainstream Welsh and Scottish nationalists are dedicated to non-violent ways of expressing their claims for self-determination, but fringe groups in both cases have used violence. (The most notable example is the burning of English-owned holiday homes in Wales.) Nationalists may be tempted to follow such tactics because they are minorities within the British state, where the inbuilt English majority can always vote them down. The danger in resistance to all claims for autonomy is that the frustrated nationalists may turn to violence.

One group's terrorism is another group's liberation struggle. The very definition of the situation was one element in the conflict between the IRA and the British state. The latter has infinitely more soldiers, weapons and resources than the IRA. The 'freedom fighters' or 'terrorists' thus have to adopt hit and run tactics, killing individual members of the armed forces or leaving bombs that will injure or kill civilians indiscriminately. Through these actions they hoped to provoke the authorities into indiscriminate action against Catholics as a whole, thus provoking general resentment and providing recruits to their own movement. Once 'guerrilla warfare' of this kind starts it can generate its own grievances and become self-perpetuating, as the example of Ireland (and currently Iraq) shows.

Devolution

A way in which compromises might be achieved between a minority and the central state is also suggested by Northern Ireland. From 1922 to 1972 it had a provincial Parliament and government largely responsible for internal affairs. Its record was marred by discrimination against Catholics. But in other respects the

Northern Irish administration modernised the province and vastly improved social conditions.

The Northern Irish case provides a precedent for the way Welsh and Scottish demands for more autonomy have been met, without breaking up the British state. A more sweeping form of '**devolution**' to Northern Ireland, with equal power sharing between Protestants and Catholics, has formed the basis of Labour's 'Peace Process' in the troubled province.

Devolution is not a curious British anomaly. Most member countries of the EU have self-governing arrangements for culturally distinctive regions. The argument that any grant of political devolution will break up the United Kingdom is mistaken. Indeed, by compromising with local nationalists before they become totally frustrated, devolution may prevent an Irish situation developing. However, devolution clearly does have constitutional implications, which we shall explore in this chapter and the next.

> **Devolution**
>
> The delegation of specific powers by a higher level of government to a lower one.

Northern Ireland: origins of the 'Troubles'

Historical and social background

Northern Ireland had no history as a separate political entity before 1922. It was created at that time out of the six counties of Ireland that had a Protestant majority. These were set up with a separate Parliament and government as part of the Government of Ireland Act (1922), which effectively recognised the remaining 26 counties as a separate state.

The British government believed that the new unionist entity of 'Northern Ireland' would not be viable without a respectable territory. Hence it included many areas where Protestants were in only a tenuous majority, or were actually a minority. Substantial numbers of Catholic nationalists were thus incorporated against their will in this 'Protestant state for a Protestant people' as Viscount Craigavon, its first Prime Minister, described it. Thus there is a major division inside Northern Ireland between the Protestant heartland of North Down and Ards – on the east – and Armagh and the counties of Fermanagh, Tyrone and

BRIEFINGS

10.4 Northern Ireland, Ulster and the 'six counties'

The largest concentration of Protestants in Ireland was in the north-east around the industrial town of Belfast. They thinned out towards the north-west of the island, although there was a concentration in the town of Derry (or Londonderry). In the 'Troubles' of 1919–22 the Protestants, supported by the British army, gained the upper hand in this part of Ireland. When the British government decided on partition between a Catholic-dominated free state (the future Republic of Ireland) and the Unionist–Protestant north as the only stable solution to the Irish conflict, they carved out the largest area Protestants could dominate within the historic province of Ulster, following county boundaries. They left out the three western and southern counties of the historic Ulster because these had Catholic–Nationalist majorities. The remaining 'six counties' had no previous tradition as a political unit and Derry, in particular, was cut off from its natural hinterland. Because it comprised the bulk of the historic province of Ulster the region was often referred to, loosely, by that name. However, the official term was 'Northern Ireland' (even though the tip of Donegal, in the Republic, lies further north!). This is the entity that had full internal Home Rule from 1922 to 1972, with its own Parliament and government based at Stormont, near Belfast.

Table 10.1 Regional disparities within Northern Ireland

	Belfast and district	Rest of east	West and south
Percentage of unemployed, 2002	4.2	4.5	5.7
Average weekly earnings of full-time workers (£), 2002	401.0	335	341
Religious groups, 2001			
Percentage Catholic	37.4	31.6	59.6
Percentage Protestant	58.3	65.0	38.4
Percentage other	0.7	0.3	0.2
Percentage no religion	3.7	3.6	1.8

Source: Northern Ireland Office Statistics Research Agency. Reproduced under the terms of the Click-Use Licence

Londonderry, in the west. This division is not only a religious one, but a social and economic one too, as Table 10.1 shows.

The western part of the province is more rural and less developed. Such east–west differences exist in the Republic of Ireland too. They were exacerbated in Northern Ireland, however, by the tendency of the Protestant-dominated 'Stormont' government (1922–72) (so called from the suburb of Belfast where it was located) to concentrate investment in Antrim and Down.

Religious divisions

Practically the whole of the politics of the province can thus be traced back to the Protestant–Catholic religious division. This extends to voting too. Nowhere else in the United Kingdom, not even in Scotland, does a person's religious affiliation so emphatically determine their vote. The parties themselves are founded on the basis of such divisions. Sinn Fein is the Irish nationalist party associated with the

Map 10.1 Northern Ireland, showing local government districts shaded according to religious affiliation

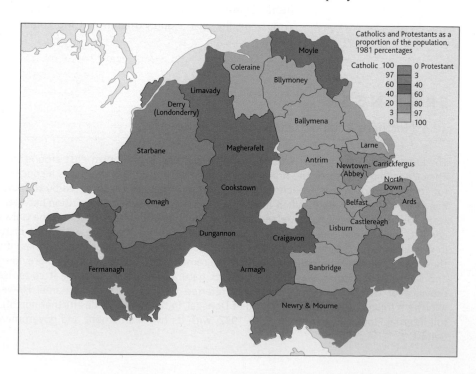

Plate 10.3 Stormont Castle, Northern Ireland: seat of the Northern Irish Parliament, 1932–72, and now of the power-sharing Assembly and Executive

Source: Topfoto

underground Irish Republican Army, while the Social Democratic and Labour Party (SDLP) is the representative of moderate Catholics. The Alliance Party attempts to bridge the sectarian divide and attract both Protestant and Catholic votes from the working class. The various Unionist groupings represent Protestants of varying degrees of extremism. As their name suggests, they advocate 'no surrender' to Catholic nationalist demands and support continuing union with Britain.

This pervasiveness of religion in politics is not surprising. Northern Ireland was created on the basis of the politico-religious division in Ireland. Its continuing existence perpetuates this unless a way can be found to accommodate the demands of both sides within it. However, such a settlement would have implications for both the territorial integrity and sovereignty of the existing British state, as we shall see.

Outsiders, including the English, cannot understand why religion should be such an explosive force in the province. In the rest of Britain it is regarded as an individual matter, having nothing to do with politics and certainly not party politics. To understand why religion goes to the root of personal and political identity in Northern Ireland one must go back into Irish history and Irish relations with the rest of the British Isles.

In the course of the seventeenth century the Gaelic-speaking Catholic tribes of Ireland were colonised by Protestants from Great Britain, just as happened to the Algonquian-speaking tribes of North America. Settlements were planted, and the natives converted, massacred or driven out in Ireland just as they were in New England or Virginia. The native Irish managed to survive better than the native Americans, but only as an exploited peasantry with no political rights.

It was in north-eastern Ireland that colonisation succeeded best in driving the natives out because of the continual flow of poor Protestant settlers from south-west Scotland (only 30 miles away). The growth of Catholic Irish nationalism in the nineteenth century was seen in the north-east as threatening the very existence of the 'Protestant people'. It provoked a popular resistance to nationalism unparalleled

BRIEFINGS

10.5 The Orange Order

In the eighteenth century Catholic resistance to the 'Protestant ascendancy' in Ireland often took the form of secret societies (Whiteboys, Defenders) that took reprisals against obnoxious landlords. These continued in the south during the nineteenth century (the Fenian Brotherhood). As Protestants began to feel threatened they formed their own secret societies, most notably the Orange Order, which took its name from William of Orange (William III) who established the Protestant ascendancy with his victory at the Battle of the Boyne (1690).

Widespread at one time on the British mainland and among army officers, the Orange Order came to have its main strength in Ireland, particularly the north. Modelling itself on the Freemasons, with which it had many links, it has a strong local organisation of 'lodges', and an overall hierarchy of Grand Masters, lodgemasters and so forth. What gave it a unique force was its ability to unite the Protestant governing elite with a strong grassroots working-class organisation.

The Orange Order does not get directly involved in conflict itself. But it forms a recruiting base and communications network for paramilitary groups. Its elaborate symbolism and annual marches to commemorate Protestant victories can be a provocation to violence and confrontation with Catholics during the 'marching season' (most of the summer). There are also Orange lodges and marches in central Scotland and Liverpool. However, their activities are muted in comparison.

in other parts of Ireland where Protestants were thin on the ground. Semi-underground movements, above all the Orange Order, were created to oppose it, with violence if necessary.

Northern Ireland, 1922–72

The local Unionist politicians joined the Conservative Party in Great Britain to defeat any concession to Irish nationalism, such as Home Rule, up to the First World War. The settlement of 1922 was a defeat for the Northern Unionists, because their object was the preservation of British rule (and support for Protestants) everywhere in Ireland. Instead they found themselves partitioned off in the north, while a Catholic nationalist republic was built up in the rest of the island.

However, the Protestants did have a secure majority in Northern Ireland. The region had been created expressly to ensure this: Protestants constituted 60 per cent of the population. The Unionist leaders organised their built-in majority to control the Northern Irish Parliament and government for 50 years (1922–72). The British Parliament and government were content to turn over the internal running of the province to them, incidentally making nonsense of the claim that such a delegation of powers subverts the constitutional sovereignty of the British Parliament. No constitutional difficulties arose during the existence of the 'Stormont' Parliament and government.

Unionist policy was aimed primarily at ensuring the viability and stability of Northern Ireland as a territorial unit separate from the Republic of Ireland. They could count on British armed support, but they also built up their own paramilitary Protestant militia, the 'special' police. This was sufficient to deter open opposition from the minority for most of the time.

No lasting settlement, however, could be built on armed force alone. Politically the Unionist government had to balance three groups. These were the Protestant working class, anxious to protect their jobs and differentials against Catholic competition; the Protestant middle class with something of the same anxieties, but also a concern with modernisation and development, who would be alienated by too open a display of sectarianism; and the Catholic population, who had to have some concessions if they were not to pose a constant threat of disorder.

A major Unionist achievement was to get the British government to agree in 1936 to parity of social provision between Northern Ireland and the British mainland. Thus the post-war Welfare State operated fully in Northern Ireland, providing the unemployed and sick with infinitely better payments and facilities than they had before. This appealed to all segments of the population, and it was a powerful argument for Catholics to put up with political discrimination in return for better living conditions. The other major concession to the Catholic Church was state support for Catholic schools, again carrying over practices on the British mainland.

Both these measures enabled the Protestant middle classes to convince themselves that Northern Ireland was as tolerable a solution to bigotry and violence as could be found in Irish conditions, and preferable to living under the domination of a reactionary Catholic Church in the Republic. Throughout its existence the Stormont government pursued an active policy of modernisation of the traditional agricultural and industrial economy, thus creating more middle-class jobs in management and administration.

These activities also demonstrated to the Protestant working class that the government was trying to conserve their jobs and improve their living conditions. Where Protestants faced the most severe job competition, in the depressed west of the province, local councils and government agencies actively discriminated in their favour. The Orange Order, a semi-secret society dedicated to maintaining Protestant supremacy, enrolled the working class as its rank and file while keeping control firmly in the Unionist leadership's hands. Anti-Catholic rhetoric and rituals contented the membership while keeping it out of real policy making.

Until 1965 Northern Ireland functioned in this way without major difficulties. Successive British governments, Conservative and Labour, saw no need to intervene in its internal affairs. The Unionist MPs affiliated to the Conservative Party (at that time called the 'Conservative and Unionist Party'). When the British Conservative government of 1951–5 depended on their votes for its majority the Labour opposition did not object. Nobody saw any anomaly in Northern Ireland MPs voting on domestic English and Scottish legislation when MPs from these regions could not vote on Northern Irish affairs, although this is a question raised about Scottish MPs today.

The 'Troubles', 1969–97

The old system collapsed because of the rise of a new, educated Catholic middle class that organised a non-violent civil rights movement inside Northern Ireland to protest against discrimination and sectarianism (1967–9). Their peaceful protests provoked violent Protestant reactions, culminating in armed attacks by the 'specials' on the Catholic areas of Belfast and Londonderry in 1969. A new factor was the television reporting of these conflicts, rendering it impossible for the old tactics of repression to be quietly employed.

The riots and publicity forced a British military intervention to separate the two sides. They finally led to the abolition of the devolved Parliament and government, in an attempt to create a new power-sharing settlement. The disorder provided an opening for both extreme Irish nationalism and extreme Protestant loyalism. The first is represented by the Provisional Irish Republican Army (the 'Provos' or IRA), the second by the Ulster Defence Association (UDA) and Ulster Volunteer Force (UVF) and smaller groups. Over 28 years both sides carried out regular attacks on each other, on the British Army and on the Northern Irish police, as well as indiscriminately against anyone of 'the wrong sort'. The IRA also engaged in terrorism on the British mainland, mainly with explosives and bombs.

The 'Milestones' section at the end of the chapter summarises events from the creation of Northern Ireland in 1922. Since 1970 its history has been dominated by political violence, on the one hand, and attempts at political settlement, on the other. The most important of these were the arrangements for inter-governmental negotiations between Britain and the Irish Republic from the mid-1980s on, which recognised that the heirs of the Irish independence struggle had a legitimate interest in the territory.

The 'Peace Process', 1997–2005

The last Conservative government made a determined effort to resolve the political situation by negotiations with all sides to the conflict in 1995–6, which produced a cessation of violence for over a year. Its insistence on the IRA surrendering its weapons before they could join a constitutional conference proved a demand that the political leadership could not get their rank and file to accept.

Hardly had New Labour got into power than they initiated further meetings with all sides to the conflict. The government tried to break through previous deadlocks by involving not just the parties and paramilitaries of the province itself but also the Irish and even the US governments (Irish-Americans are the main financial backers of the IRA).

These negotiations produced the 'Good Friday' agreement in April 1998 on:

1. keeping Northern Ireland as a separate political entity

2. which would however have an autonomous power-sharing Parliament and government where action could be taken only with the agreement of representatives of the two communities

3. the province would remain part of the United Kingdom

4. but the Irish government would have a right to be consulted on everything the UK government did in the province and in effect exercise a veto over policy.

Both communities made considerable concessions in the agreement – Nationalists stopping short of incorporation into the Republic but Unionists tolerating its formal right of intervention in the province. Not surprisingly the agreement split both sides but the Protestants most seriously, almost down the middle. In a referendum on whether to accept the agreement slightly over 70 per cent of the total population voted to accept it (May 1998). In an election for the new Assembly in June the Ulster Unionists and smaller Protestant parties supporting the agreement got enough votes to form a power-sharing executive with the Social Democratic and Labour Party, representative of moderate Catholics, and Sinn Fein representing militant Catholic Nationalists.

The Assembly and the projected executive managed to survive the summer 'marching season' when extreme Protestant groups sought to provoke violent confrontations and riots. They foundered, however, on the IRA refusal to make even a token surrender of its arms in the following year. The negotiated compromise had included the understanding that no group linked to paramilitaries could take its place in the Assembly or executive without its allies surrendering their arms. Sinn Fein protested it was independent of the IRA. But nobody believed it, least of all Protestant Unionists. They refused to participate in the Assembly until arms began to be surrendered.

This stalemate lasted for the best part of a year, constantly threatened by riots and confrontations between the communities, atrocious murders and reprisals by extremist groups outside the settlement, by paramilitaries asserting claims to control their own areas, by punishment beatings and shootings of alleged social deviants and drug dealers. A major effort by the British and Irish governments in November 1999 produced a fudged compromise. The IRA declared an intention to review arms and the Unionists agreed provisionally to go into the executive subject to reviewing progress.

The 12-member executive that emerged comprised representatives of all parties in the Assembly, including the Democratic Unionists hostile to the agreement. It was thus hardly in a position to agree any policy initiatives, far less controversial ones. This is beside the point, however. The executive's major achievement was to exist at all, as a concrete symbol of peace and compromise between the warring factions.

This achievement was threatened in February 2000 as a result of reiterated IRA refusals to make even symbolic surrenders of arms. In turn this led to a threatened Unionist withdrawal from the executive. To avert this the British government suspended it again, after less than three months of life (February 2000). Concerted pressure by the Irish and US governments on Sinn Fein and the IRA and British reform of the Protestant-dominated Royal Ulster Constabulary produced promises of IRA arms inspection by international representatives that the Unionists could live with. The executive was therefore reconstituted in May 2000. Further suspensions have followed up to the present, leading the IRA to make surrenders of arms and a formal ceasefire to conciliate the Unionists.

One may expect similar cliff-hangers to continue. What the history of the peace process indicates however is that a large-scale return to guerrilla action and bombings by any of the main groups is unlikely. Disputes will be conducted through words and symbolic gestures using the still suspended Assembly as the focus. In a sense both sides have got what they want – Catholic Nationalists now feel they are under the (admittedly very) extended jurisdiction of an Irish government, while Unionists have preserved the separateness of the political order in the north.

The Northern Ireland Assembly: key to power sharing

The Assembly and executive that sporadically occupy the old seat of government at Stormont, near Belfast, are of prime importance as the symbol and guarantee of power sharing, the basis of the peace settlement. On this they can work with inter-governmental bodies, such as the North–South Council, with the Irish government, and the British–Irish Council consisting of the Westminster government and all the devolved administrations in Britain. The executive can also participate in the Joint Ministerial Council with the British, Welsh and Scottish administrations on immediate practical matters such as EU negotiating stances on agriculture, fisheries, environment and social affairs.

Almost permanent suspensions of the Assembly mean that policy making falls into the hands of the British Secretary of State for Northern Ireland, a member of the British Cabinet at Westminster. (S)he may enforce controversial reforms such as those of the police, which local politicians are reluctant to take responsibility for. But these would never be pushed through without their tacit consent, and support from the Irish government in Dublin.

Just to describe the diffuse nature of policy making in Northern Ireland illustrates how tenuous the idea of national sovereignty has become, especially as the existence of the EU renders the strict demarcation of national boundaries increasingly irrelevant. In Ireland there has long been free movement of people and goods across the unpoliceable border. Natives of Northern Ireland are simultaneously British and Irish citizens owing to the claim of both states to the territory. Carrying anomalies even further, Irish citizens resident in the United Kingdom may vote in local and national elections – a relic of the old union between the countries.

The all-incorporating political structures of Northern Ireland may have been driven by the need to get a settlement by sharing power. But they clearly have constitutional implications for the general relationship between regional administrations and the centre within the United Kingdom. If the still very centralised British government can cede all its powers in Northern Ireland, why not also in Scotland, Wales and even the English regions? The Northern Irish situation with its mutual vetoes clearly cuts across the doctrine of absolute parliamentary sovereignty that lies at the base of the unwritten British constitution (Chapter 4).

Workings of the Assembly

When in existence the Assembly consists of 108 members, 6 from each of the 18 constituencies. These are grouped into parties. As Table 10.2 shows, the balance of power among these has shifted. The second Assembly elections of November 2003 made the Democratic Unionists the largest party on the unionist side (30 seats). Its strong opposition to Nationalism meant that its gains make the reinstatement of the Assembly difficult, as do those made by Sinn Fein (24 seats) on the Catholic Nationalist side. The latter have replaced the Social Democratic and Labour Party (18 seats) as the main Catholic standard bearer. On the Protestant Unionist side, the Ulster Unionists (27 seats) who provided the First Minister David Trimble for the first five years have been substantially weakened. Various other small groups complete the Assembly, the most important of which is the non-sectarian Alliance Party, which has traditionally advocated political compromise.

The power-sharing institutions are designed among other things to prevent any one party having sole power over anything. Thus the Unionist, Protestant, First Minister – David Trimble from 1998–2003 (occupying that position because Ulster Unionist support was essential to buttress the agreement) – had to do everything with his SDLP Deputy First Minister, representing the then largest (Catholic) party. In practice, the few decisions that were made through the Assembly mechanisms were taken by the 12-person executive and endorsed in the Assembly.

Executive posts have been shared out among all the parties in the Assembly in proportion to their seats. The Opposition – notably the Democratic Unionists, who are against the power-sharing agreement as a whole – were represented on the

Table 10.2 The strength of the parties across Northern Ireland: voting in the British general election, 2005

	Belfast %	Rest of East %	West and South %	Northern Ireland %
DUP	33.4	40.6	21.1	33.7
UUP	15.6	23.4	9.6	17.7
SF	27.9	14.5	39.5	24.3
SDLP	16.5	14.6	21.9	17.5
APNI	4.9	5.9	0.0	3.9

Note: Party abbreviations: UPP Ulster Unionist Party; SDLP Social Democratic and Labour Party; DUP Democratic Unionist Party (some candidates also stood as United Unionists or similar labels); SF Sinn Fein; APNI Alliance Party of Northern Ireland. *Source*: Calculated by authors from figures supplied by Cain Web Service, 5 May 2005. http://cain.ulst.ac.uk

Table 10.3 Policy areas covered by executive ministries and Assembly committees in Northern Ireland

Agriculture and rural development
Culture, arts and leisure
Education
Employment and learning
Enterprise, trade and investment
Environment
Finance and personnel
Health, social services and public safety
Regional development
Social development

executive when it existed, in nominal control of ministries like its other members. Even so they often boycotted its meetings.

Each executive 'minister' is in addition responsible to a specialist Assembly Committee, chaired by party members from the opposing side of the religious–political divide. Thus the Sinn Fein Minister of Education, Martin McGuiness (1998–2003), faced a Committee chaired by a Democratic Unionist, assisted by an Ulster Unionist. Table 10.3 gives the policy areas in which the ministers and committees have operated. These spell out the broad social and economic matters over which the Assembly and executive will have autonomous powers. The Westminster government retains responsibility for constitutional and security issues, including courts, law and prisons. If the Assembly could agree on requesting the transfer of such 'reserved' powers it would get them. In that sense 'rolling devolution' exists in Northern Ireland, but the real problem is getting agreement between two sides who trust external governments more than they trust each other.

Towards a lasting peace?

The results of the regional election – confirmed by the results of the general election of 2005 in the province, shown in Table 10.2 – have again thrown politics into the melting pot. Relentless appeals to sectarian fears coupled with intimidation and social pressures have made the extreme parties on both sides of the political divide dominant both in terms of votes and Assembly seats. As the precedent is for the First Minister and his deputy to be chosen from the two largest parties this creates immediate problems for devolved government in the next few years. A Sinn Fein presence at the top would be unacceptable to most Protestants while the Democratic Unionists have the same effect on Catholics. The result is likely to be stalemate and continued suspension of the Assembly.

The ingenuity already shown in cobbling together institutional compromises plus international pressures on the participants may bridge the gap. The peace settlement has survived long suspensions before and neither the executive nor the Assembly are really essential for governing the province. The important thing is to have them in being as a concrete guarantee of power sharing.

In the long run, with Catholics and Protestants now almost equal in numbers, this is the only tolerable solution that can be reached. The alternative is the previous violent stalemate that neither side can win. The Nationalists have shown there can be no peace without including them. But it is equally clear that the Unionists cannot be bombed into a united Ireland – which is also the last outcome that the government of the Republic would want anyway.

The overwhelming majority of English opinion would accept any solution agreed inside Ireland. The latter has never been regarded as part of the Union in the same way as the countries of mainland Great Britain. It is the Northern Irish Protestants who want to continue the Union, not the British public as a whole. It is therefore the internal constraints that hinder a lasting settlement and of these the main one is the mutual suspicion of the two communities. This may in the end bring the peace process down. But that remains the best way of enabling Catholics and Protestants to live tolerably together.

That said, the solution will not be a comfortable one. High-level political conflict may diminish but in parts of the province the rule of law has broken down altogether. Normal policing continues in town centres, middle-class suburbs and in much of the countryside. The working-class areas and housing estates are however dominated by paramilitary groups. These have lost much of their original impetus and degenerated into criminal gangs. The IRA seeks to substitute its own administration for that of the state in the areas it dominates through impromptu courts, punishment beatings and shootings. It has turned the social control it exerts to political ends, pressuring voters to support Sinn Fein in its drive to replace the SDLP as the main representative of the Catholic community. So far its tactic of 'guns and ballots', now leaning towards ballots, seems to have succeeded. However, frustration among poor urban protestants led in autumn 2005 to the worst rioting in Belfast for years. The stability that has been achieved is always under threat.

All this makes Northern Ireland a difficult place to live in, although it has to be said that the presence of the army and the high proportion of the population employed on security have given a boost to the economy it would not otherwise have enjoyed. It is a chastening thought that the British state, usually regarded as a model of stability and peaceful resolution of conflicts, has accommodated a near civil war for 30 years and now finds parts of its territory beyond control. The peace process may survive this situation but it will not properly resolve it for a very long time.

Summary

This chapter has shown the following:

- The United Kingdom, like most European states, was formed out of different territories with divergent histories and cultures.

- From the seventeenth century Ireland was treated more like an overseas colony than an integrated part of British territory.

- This provoked a Catholic Nationalist movement that used violence to create a separate state – a Republic of Ireland – in the south and west of the island (1919–22).

- The Protestant Unionists who dominated the north-east formed a separate statelet, Northern Ireland, which had a devolved government inside the United Kingdom.

- Protestant domination in the north was challenged first by a Catholic Civil Rights movement (1967–9) and then by the shootings and bombings of the Provisional IRA (1970–97), which extended to the British mainland.

- The 'Peace Process' (1997–2006) produced a compromise in which the Nationalist parties accepted the status of Northern Ireland as part of the United Kingdom, and Protestant Unionists accepted power sharing within it, in the shape of a devolved Assembly and executive.

- Endemic disorders and grassroots violence threaten the peace settlement, already weakened by the IRA–Sinn Fein drive towards total dominance in the Catholic community. Power sharing is, however, likely to continue in some form as there is no viable political alternative to it.

MILESTONES

Milestones in Irish history, 1922–2006

Northern Ireland ('six counties', 'Ulster')		Republic of Ireland ('Irish Free State', 'Eire')	
1922	Government of Ireland Act effectively divides Ireland between Northern Ireland in the north-east and the Irish Free State (Eire), covering the south and west		
1922	Special Powers Act gives Northern Irish government exceptional powers to maintain order	1923–7	Civil war followed by extensive disorder over whether to accept partition and dominion status within British Empire. Pro-treaty side (later Fine Gael Party) wins
		1926	Fianna Fàil founded to contest treaty by non-violent means. This splits it off from Sinn Fein and IRA, which remain committed to violence
1929	Abolition of proportional representation in Northern Ireland parliamentary elections		
1932	Unemployed in Belfast hold non-sectarian demonstrations and riot	1932	Fianna Fàil wins general election and forms government
		1933–8	'Economic war' with Britain
1935	Serious sectarian riots in Belfast renew old religious hostilities		
1936	British government agrees to equality of social support between Northern Ireland and (mainland) Great Britain		
		1937	New constitution whittles away British treaty rights and entrenches position of Catholic Church
		1938	British return treaty ports (where they had had naval bases) to Irish Free State
1939–40	IRA bombing campaign in England	1939–45	Irish Free State stays neutral in Second World War
1940–43	German bombing of Belfast and (London) derry		
1940–5	Northern Ireland forms base for allied air forces protecting Atlantic convoys		
1943–63	Sir Basil Brooke (Lord Brookeborough), NI Prime Minister, maintains system of strict Unionist monopoly of power based on inbuilt Protestant majority	1948–51, 1954–7	Fine Gael forms coalition governments with smaller parties
1949	Bitter Northern Irish election reaffirms Unionist domination	1948	Eire becomes Republic of Ireland and leaves Commonwealth
1956–63	IRA border attacks mostly fail	1959–72	Modernising Fianna Fàil prime ministers, Lemass and Lynch
1963–9	O'Neill succeeds Brookeborough as Unionist Prime Minister. Rhetoric favours Catholics but does nothing practical on discrimination		
1967–9	As a result civil rights movement formed to press for reform. TV shows non-violent protests broken up by Protestant militants and police		

▶

Milestones in Irish history, 1922–2006 continued

Northern Ireland ('six counties', 'Ulster')		Republic of Ireland ('Irish Free State', 'Eire')	
1969	Special police and Protestant militants attack Catholic areas of Belfast and Derry. British troops intervene to protect them		
1970–2	IRA provokes army into indiscriminate internment and shooting of nationalists ('Bloody Sunday' 1972)		
1972–4	British attempts to introduce power sharing between Protestants and Catholics thwarted by Protestant general strike. Unionist Party splits into small groupings		
1972	Joins EU as part of the United Kingdom	1972	Joins EU along with the UK
1974–98	Direct rule: province run by Northern Ireland Office as part of British government		
1974–95	IRA, UDA, UVF mount terror campaign (extended by IRA to mainland Britain): killings and bombings, often indiscriminate	1973–7	Coalition government of Fine Gael and Labour
		1977–81	Fianna Fàil government
1982	Elections to a new Northern Ireland Assembly. 'Rolling devolution': Assembly can take over whatever powers it agrees on, but no agreement between Unionists and Nationalists	1981–92	Various short-lived minority governments or coalitions alternate
1985	Margaret Thatcher and Fine Gael Prime Minister, Garrett Fitzgerald, sign Anglo-Irish Agreement providing for joint consultation of two governments on Northern Ireland. These continue and intensify up to present		
		1986	Referendum rejects divorce
		1992–8	Stable coalitions of both major parties with Labour
1994	Downing Street Declaration sets out plans for talks between British and Irish governments and all parties in Northern Ireland. In response IRA and Protestant ceasefires declared		
1995–6	Talks stalled and blocked by Unionists on whom British Conservatives increasingly depend in British Parliament	1995	Referendum legalises divorce by narrow majority
1996	Renewed IRA bombings in mainland Britain. Violent Protestant marches in Northern Ireland	1995–2006	Sustained economic boom, active partnership of Irish government with British in 'Peace Process'
1997	New Labour government in Britain announces accelerated talks: start of 'Peace Process'		
1997	New IRA and Protestant ceasefire		
1998	Agreement for a political settlement between Irish and British governments approved by referendums on both sides of the border	1998–2006	Fianna Fàil–Progressive Democrat – right-wing coalition government
1998	Power-sharing Assembly elected		
1998–9	Assembly only elects executive at end of 1999 because of IRA refusal to give up any arms		
2000	Power-sharing executive suspended, then reinstated as IRA makes symbolic concessions on arms	2001	Referendum rejects EU Treaty of Nice because it might liberalise social relationships

Milestones in Irish history, 1922–2006 continued

Northern Ireland ('six counties', 'Ulster')		Republic of Ireland ('Irish Free State', 'Eire')	
2001–2	Further political confrontations and suspensions force IRA to put some arms caches 'beyond use' under independent verification	2002	Referendum closes last loophole for abortion in the constitution Catholic Church indemnified by government against lawsuits over child abuse
2002	Reform of Royal Ulster Constabulary (RUC): changed to NI Police Service	2003–6	Sinn Fein increases electoral support in the Republic
2002–6	Suspension of NI Assembly over allegations of Sinn Fein–IRA spy ring within it		
2003	The November Assembly elections give extreme parties (Democratic Unionists and Sinn Fein) pluralities in the Assembly		
2004	December talks between NI parties and British and Irish governments fail to agree on reinstating Assembly		
2005	Northern bank robbery attributed to IRA		
2005 Jan–June	Internal pressure on IRA after local officials accused of murdering a Catholic man and covering it up		
2005 May	General elections confirm political dominance of Democratic Unionist Party and Sinn Fein		
2005 July	IRA announces formal end to its armed campaign		
2006	International arms decommissioning commission confirms most IRA arms have been destroyed		
2006	New Assembly convened and meets under deadline of September to produce executive		

Essays

1. Distinguish between the British Isles, Great Britain, the United Kingdom and England. To what extent is the United Kingdom a unitary state?

2. What are the main political groupings in Northern Ireland? What accounts for the differences between them?

3. In what politically related ways are the Irish, as an ethnic group, different from Afro-Caribbeans?

4. To what extent does the blueprint for devolution in Northern Ireland offer lessons for the rest of the United Kingdom?

Projects

1. Describe the various institutions now involved in governing Northern Ireland and how they relate to each other.

2. Compare and contrast the ideologies of Irish Nationalism and Northern Irish Unionism.

3. Assess how far the 'Peace Process' in Northern Ireland has been successful.

Further reading

The Irish background is reported in T. P. Coogan, *The Troubles: Ireland's Ordeal 1966–1995* (London: Hutchinson, 1995). The Northern Irish dilemma is discussed in J. Loughlin, *The Ulster Question since 1945* (London: St Martin's Press, 1998), Paul Dixon, *Northern Ireland* (London: Palgrave, 2001) and D. Norris, 'Northern Ireland: the long road to peace', *Talking Politics*, **11** (1), 1999, pp. 34–6. See also Jonathon Tonge, *Northern Ireland: Conflict and Change* (London: Pearson, 2nd edn, 2002). Short discussions on aspects of the Northern Ireland situation can be found in Barbara Lomas, 'The Good Friday Agreement', *Talking Politics*, **14** (1), 2000, pp. 28–31 and Stephen Hopkins, 'General Election 2001: Northern Ireland, a place apart', *Politics Review*, **11** (2), 2001, pp. 22–5.

Lively and informed comment on the workings of devolution and constitutional reform is provided by *Monitor*, published quarterly by the Constitution Unit, University College London, which also maintains a web site (see below).

Useful web sites on Ireland

Hot links to these sites can be found on the CWS at www.pearsoned.co.uk/budge.

Specific sites on Northern Ireland are Northern Ireland Government (www.nio.gov.uk); Official Documents (www.hmso.gov.uk/acts/acts1998/ 19980047.htm); CAIN web site (http://cain.ulst.ac.uk/) and the Mitchell Report (www.irishnews.com/mitchell.html). See also the Constitution Unit web site (www.ucl.ac.uk/constitution-unit).

chapter 11

Devolution: Scotland, Wales and the English regions

Devolution is the delegation of powers by a state to units within its territory. It differs from a federal set-up in two ways. The state can (at least in constitutional theory) take powers back when it wants. And the powers delegated to different units may differ quite considerably. Devolution is a common arrangement in western and southern Europe and has always existed in Britain (in the Isle of Man, Channel Islands and Northern Ireland 1922–72). From 1998 it has again operated sporadically in Northern Ireland, as we have seen, and also in Scotland, Wales and Greater London.

This chapter asks:

■ why is devolution now being implemented in Britain?

■ to what extent is it due to regional differences that make it more efficient to run diverse areas differently?

■ how far is it a political response to Welsh and Scottish nationalism, as it certainly is to Irish nationalism?

■ how does the devolution of powers actually work in Scotland and Wales?

■ is London a model for what may happen in other English regions?

■ what are the prospects in general for regional government in England?

■ what are the constitutional implications for parliamentary sovereignty and the centralised state?

Nationalism and devolution

Chapter 10 showed the British government had little choice about setting up a Northern Ireland Assembly if it wanted to get even an uneasy peace in the province. The driving force in events there has always been violent Irish nationalism (confronted by an equally violent Protestant sectarianism). Even the Unionists, however, were used to the idea of devolution, which they had had themselves for 50 years (1922–72).

At its nearest point the Scottish mainland is only 18 miles from Ireland, with which it shares much of its traditional culture and history. It is not surprising therefore that from the late nineteenth century Scottish nationalist sentiment was stimulated by events there and advocated 'Home Rule all round' – that is, devolution not only for Ireland but also for Scotland and Wales. Scottish nationalism differed from Irish, however, in basing itself on the Protestant rather than the Catholic traditions of Scotland and having an obvious focus on the institutions surviving

Plate 11.1 With a cost overrun of £400 million, this expensive new building at Holyrood for the Scottish Parliament has caused great controversy

Source: Empics

from its period as an independent state – primarily the Scots language and law, Gaelic and the (Presbyterian) Church of Scotland. It was also different in deploring violence and working through peaceful and constitutional routes to change. These paid off when the Scottish Nationalist Party consolidated its support at 20–30 per cent of the Scottish electorate, threatening Labour's strong base in Scotland and pushing it into supporting devolution. (The SNP, however, wants full independence.)

Welsh nationalism has developed along the same lines as Scottish – peaceful, constitutional and moderate, to the point where it has accepted devolution as an acceptable substitute for independence – provided the Welsh Assembly gets legislative powers. Much more than Scottish, Welsh nationalism is focused on the need to protect and extend the native language and consolidate its social base.

The reason why Welsh and Scottish (and Irish) nationalism are such powerful forces within their own countries goes back to the state-building process discussed in the last chapter. In conquering and consolidating their territories the European states incorporated areas with different languages and cultures to those of the majority population. The natural attachment of such groups to their own culture caused them to resent the state imposition of schooling in the majority language and discrimination in its favour (e.g. by making access to top jobs dependent on speaking it). Such minorities have felt more and more threatened by developments such as a mass English-language press, radio and television; widespread emigration of their native population because of economic decline; and English immigration to take over businesses, top jobs, land and housing.

These processes are going on throughout Europe. The solution as nationalist parties see it is to have sovereign political institutions to protect their culture and society against takeover. A compromise, by states that want to resist breakup, is often to give the territory devolved political institutions to handle most domestic matters, keeping security, and economic and foreign affairs, in central hands.

Scottish and Welsh (not to mention Northern Irish) devolution can be seen as this kind of compromise, borrowed from other west European countries such as Belgium and Spain. It is politically difficult for any British government to admit it is compromising with Welsh and Scottish nationalism, however, since its official stance is that what unites the British is much stronger than what divides them. Hence official devolution rhetoric has stressed themes such as subsidiarity (having problems dealt with at the level most appropriate for them), local democracy, efficiencies from producing solutions tailored to regional characteristics, 'bringing government closer to the people' and so on. There are arguments in favour of all of these, which as a result of regional devolution have now come to the forefront. Clearly these apply just as well to the often very distinctive English regions as to Scotland and Wales. As a result English **regionalism** is now being discussed to an unprecedented extent and serious consideration, almost for the first time, has been given to the prospect of a (more limited) devolution of power within England.

> **Regionalism**
>
> Regions are geographical areas within a state, and regionalism involves granting special powers and duties to regional representatives.

Regional disparities in Britain

One paradox of the previous discussion is indeed that we have concentrated on Scotland, Wales and Ireland without mentioning the English regions such as Merseyside or the north-east. In terms of their social and economic profile these areas are almost as distinctive as Scotland and Wales. However, they do not possess the cultural and institutional differences that act as a focus for separatism or nationalism. All these regions have as good a claim to be 'English' as the London area. Social and regional deprivation has fuelled political reactions, but these have taken the form of overwhelming support for the Labour Party in its struggle for central power. Discontent was therefore expressed in support for Labour at the centre rather than for autonomy and Home Rule for the region itself.

Labour and, to a lesser extent, the Liberal Democrats have attracted disproportional support in Scotland and Wales for the same reasons. The support of the peripheries makes Labour a territorially rather than a class-based party. The difference is that in Scotland and Wales it has to compete internally with the local nationalist movements, which explains its definite commitment to devolution in these areas compared with its vague rhetoric about greater political freedom for English regions.

The major force behind movements for regional autonomy are feelings of distinctiveness. But they are also fuelled by perceptions of relative deprivation in relation to London and south-east England. Table 11.1 shows a whole series of figures, covering wealth, living conditions and health, that illustrate this point. The varying levels of regional unemployment, a central factor underlying other disparities, were shown in Figure 1.2. As Chapter 1 noted, the underlying reason for regional disparities is that nineteenth-century industrialisation took place in the north and Midlands. Its attendant problems of rapid and unplanned urban development, slums, badly paid repetitive work, crime and poverty were most keenly experienced there and linger on to the present day – exacerbated by the collapse of manufacturing at the end of the twentieth century. Attempted solutions (such as rehousing and relocation in vast featureless housing estates on the outskirts of cities) in turn created fresh social problems.

Table 11.1 Disparities between different areas of the United Kingdom

	% of workforce with a degree	Average weekly earnings (£)		GDP per head (UK = 100)	Mortality rate per thousand births	% of households with no car
		Male	Female			
Scotland	14.1	423	316.1	77	5	34
Northern Ireland	12.8	393.3	307.3	96	6.4	n/a
Wales	12.3	400.5	313.7	81	6.4	27
England	15.6	459.2	341.5	102	5.7	28
North-east	10.4	398.9	306	77	5.5	38
North-west	12.9	428.6	312.8	87	6.6	30
Yorkshire	12.2	409.9	308.8	88	6.2	31
East Midlands	12.6	407	301.1	94	6.1	26
West Midlands	11.9	425.3	311.2	92	6.9	28
East	14.4	455.5	333.8	116	4.9	21
London	25	593	434.3	130	6	36
South-east	17.8	482.1	353.1	116	4.8	23
South-west	15.5	418.2	309.8	91	4.6	23

Source: ONC Regional Trends, **36**, 2001, and ONC Social Trends, 2001. Reproduced under the terms of the Click-Use Licence

The area around London, in contrast, always benefited from greater government and consumer spending. When industrialisation came in the 1930s, with light engineering and service industries, it was cleaner and paid better wages. The planning and welfare measures discussed in Chapter 3 ensured that living conditions were also better.

Apart from modern industrialisation, south-east England has always benefited economically from the overspill of wealth from London. Government employment has created a disproportionately large middle class that has sustained the largest and most concentrated consumer market in Britain. The end beneficiaries of foreign wars and conquests were the financial interests and markets of the City of London, which reinforced middle-class political and economic dominance of the region.

Foreign wars and Empire did provide markets for industry in the peripheries, particularly for coal, steel and shipbuilding. They also provided jobs, but not at home. Emigration to the colonies provided an outlet for the restless and ambitious, supplemented by posts in the colonial administration. The army and navy recruited disproportionately in the more deprived areas: between a quarter and two-fifths of the nineteenth-century army originated in Scotland and Ireland, far in excess of their share of the British population.

Such outlets for the surplus populations can be seen in two ways. They can be viewed positively, as providing economic and social opportunities that would never have been available otherwise; or they could be judged negatively, as a haemorrhage of the brightest and best. Had they been able to stay at home, they would have provided an indigenous regional leadership otherwise lacking.

Whatever one's judgement on this, 'economic' emigration certainly helped maintain social stability in the peripheries. During the single decade of the 1950s, for example, a third of a million – out of a total population of $5\frac{1}{4}$ million – emigrated from Scotland, about 6 per cent of the population, mostly young and disproportionately better educated. Half went to (south-east) England, and half abroad. As a result of emigration the Scottish population remained static while south-east England grew. Increased emigration in the 1990s meant the Scottish population actually declined.

Map 11.1 Counties and regions of England and Wales

The loss of Empire and reduction of military commitments in the 1960s may have contributed to regional discontent by reducing job opportunities. Certainly they helped concentrate attention on domestic rather than foreign problems. Among the more obvious domestic problems were the decline of traditional industries – coalmining, steel making, heavy engineering, shipbuilding and textiles – and the centralisation of the firms that remained in London. Branches in the peripheries, remote from the main consumer markets, tended to be closed first. This applied even to the new industries that found their way there. Meanwhile, British economic management was focused on the south-east. The price of credit and loans was raised when financial markets reacted to 'overheating' in the south at times when the north had barely warmed up. 'Stop–go' economic policies have thus hit particularly hard in the peripheries: from the point of view of peripheral industry it was all stop and no go. The Monetary Policy Committee of the Bank of England has raised and lowered interest rates under New Labour in response to London and financial needs. It has ignored the decline of manufacturing in the rest of the country as a result of expensive credit and the strong pound, which depresses exports and encourages imports.

Social conditions are poorer and health is worse among the larger numbers of the working class in the outlying regions (Table 11.1). This means that direct government expenditure on social benefits and the health service is greater in these areas than in the more prosperous south-east. Maintenance of roads and infrastructure in large, thinly populated areas, such as the Highlands of Scotland, also costs more. Hence the figures for direct government expenditure show more state money being spent per head in Scotland, Wales and Northern Ireland than in England (Table 11.2). British 'unionists' (i.e. those who favour retaining the existing United Kingdom) use this to underline the benefits these regions get from being in the British state. Local nationalists say it simply shows that conditions are worse, owing to disparities that can only be eliminated by regional autonomy or independence. They also argue that figures for directly attributed expenditure conceal what happens with indirect expenditures (research and development, military, administration), which go almost exclusively to south-east England.

Overall comparisons between the constituent countries of the United Kingdom can be misleading. Within England, some of the most deprived British regions exist in the north and the west. Similarly, inside Wales, there is a great difference between south, east and north-west. And in Scotland, Edinburgh, Aberdeen and their regions are in many ways as prosperous as the London area and contrast greatly with the deprived Glasgow conurbation and the declining industrial city of Dundee.

Table 11.2 Direct government expenditure per head in the United Kingdom

(a) Identifiable public expenditure per capita as a percentage of UK identifiable expenditure per capita (UK = 100)

	1989/1990	1990/1991	1991/1992
England	95.8	96.1	96.8
Scotland	119.1	118.2	114.6
Wales	107.8	109	106.8
Northern Ireland	151.1	141.5	137.0

(b) Public spending and GDP per head, regions of the UK 1999–2000 (£)

Region	Public exp/head on 'devolved' services	GDP per head
South-east	2,281	15,100
East Anglia	2,386	15,100
Greater London	3,367	16,900
South-west	2,395	11,800
West Midlands	2,504	11,900
East Midlands	2,403	12,100
Yorkshire and Humberside	2,481	11,400
North-west	2,701	11,300
North	2,783	10,000
Wales	3,069	10,400
Scotland	3,406	12,500
Northern Ireland	3,870	10,100

Source: (a) D. Heald, 'Territorial public expenditure in the UK', *Public Administration*, **72**, 1994, pp. 147–75; (b) I. Maclean and A. McMillan, 'The fiscal crisis of the United Kingdom', *Nuffield College Working Papers in Politics*, 2002, W10, http://www.nuff.ox.ac.uk/Politics/papers/

We shall explore these internal differences further when we consider Scotland and Wales. What should be noted here, however, is that minority nationalism is not solely social or economic in character. Its basis, whatever the issues it raises, is cultural and derives from feelings of national or regional distinctiveness. Moreover, even if some peripheral areas are prosperous, most are not, and it is their situation that fuels the grievance. This emerges more clearly from the individual cases considered in this chapter.

Territory and ethnicity

Ethnicity

A combination of different social characteristics (which may include race, culture, religion, or some other basis of common origin and social identity), that give different social groups a common consciousness, and which are thought to divide or separate them in some way from other social groups.

There are of course many ethnically and culturally distinctive groups in Britain, as noted in Chapter 1. The most distinctive are recent immigrants from the Caribbean and particularly the Indian sub-continent, who are distinguishable racially and, in the case of Sikhs, Hindus and Muslims, by language and religion as well. Accommodating them may raise political problems from time to time, especially when the group suffers from high unemployment, poverty, poor living conditions and social breakup. Riots, crime and delinquency tend to spread under these circumstances, and they have been linked with internal terrorism.

However, one thing immigrant groups do not do is threaten the sovereignty of the British state. This is because they do not constitute a local majority in any city or region where they have settled. Demands for better treatment or recognition therefore are channelled through all-British institutions, through national parties such as Labour and the Liberal Democrats, or through London-based pressure groups.

The Welsh, Scots and Irish are less culturally distinctive than immigrant groups. Over the last two to three centuries they have evolved within the British context and many of their cultural patterns and institutions mark them out as British. Paradoxically, however, they still pose more of a threat to the integrity of the British state than more obviously 'different' groups, because they occupy a distinct territory within which they constitute a local majority. Their demands, mainly for greater regional autonomy, thus become bound up with their territorial distinctiveness. The British state is nothing if not a territorial unit subject to a central political authority. Thus the territorial demands voiced by the Scots, Welsh and Irish constitute more of a threat to it than the demands of more distinctive groups that can be met without territorial concessions. We start by looking at post-devolution Scotland and Wales, with a particular focus on how the new political arrangements work there, before going on to their constitutional implications for the British state as a whole, and the English regions.

Scotland: some cultural but more institutional distinctiveness

Historical and social background

Scotland covers the northern third of Britain but has a population of just over 5 million. Most Scots live in the central lowland area between the two major cities of Glasgow and Edinburgh, and on the eastern coastal plain stretching through Dundee and Aberdeen. Most of the country consists of mountains and islands that are very thinly populated. Unlike Wales, however, the various regions of Scotland are more accessible from each other than from England.

Map 11.2 The regions of Scotland

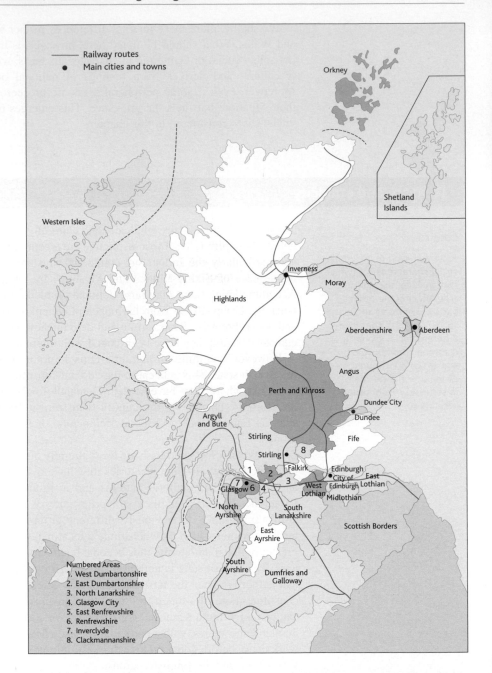

Historically, the differences between the Highlands and Lowlands of Scotland were just as great as those between Scotland and England. The Highlands (the Grampian Massif, west coast and western islands) hosted a tribal, pastoral society speaking a Celtic language (Gaelic). The Lowlands were a feudal, arable society speaking Scots, a form of northern English. The assimilation of the Highlands through internal (often forced) emigration, improved communications and compulsory schooling in English has eliminated the cultural gap. Gaelic remains an important symbol of national distinctiveness but is spoken only by 60,000 people, mostly in the remote Western Isles. Scots has also been eroded by universal education in standard English. Like Gaelic, however, it has an important literature and experienced a cultural revival (the 'Scottish Renaissance') in the mid-twentieth century.

Scottish nationalism and devolution

Cultural distinctiveness clearly provides local nationalism with a focus, as in Wales. Unlike Wales, however, the negotiated union with England in 1707 preserved the distinctive institutions that Scotland had developed as a sixteenth- and seventeenth-century state. These were first a State Church, organised on Presbyterian and not Episcopalian lines (that is, governed by elders and not bishops), and therefore sharply distinguished from the Church of England. Second, the separate body of Scots law, with supporting courts, was retained. Scots law differs from English in basing itself on Roman civil law rather than precedent. The retention of the supreme courts in Edinburgh meant that Scotland had a separate legal elite, which provided a high-level career outside London.

The Church's responsibility for education and social welfare, and the judiciary's for internal order and policing, passed over to other governmental bodies in the nineteenth century. Their initial organisation on a Scottish basis meant that Scottish bodies based in Edinburgh emerged to handle them (eventually grouped together as the contemporary Scottish Office). The separate legal code made this a logical development. It also fostered the emergence of a Scottish banking system more closely meshed with local commerce and industry than its English counterpart.

In contrast with Wales, which was integrated administratively with England, all regions of Scotland focused on Edinburgh. The Scottish institutions, however, were emanations of the British state, more intent on enforcing London's wishes in Scotland than in pushing Scottish interests in the corridors of power.

However, Scottish institutions *do* function separately and they *are* based in Scotland. They thus provide the basis for another Scottish difference: the existence of a distinctive mass media. Press and radio in Britain are generally very centralised. London-edited papers have a national circulation and there are remarkably few morning newspapers based in the 'provinces' (see Chapter 14). Scotland is the major exception, with local mass-circulation newspapers dominating readership

BRIEFINGS

11.1 The Scottish media

In an age of mass communication, control of the media – particularly of newspapers and television – is often the major factor influencing cultural identities and the political agenda. Generally, the centralisation of the British media on London serves to depress regional self-consciousness and focus attention on the 'glittering scene' in the capital.

Scotland and Northern Ireland, in part because of their distance from London, are the major exceptions here. Moreover, Scotland has enough autonomous institutions, both political and cultural, to provide something of an alternative focus to London. This has resulted in Glasgow and Edinburgh each having a quality local paper (the *Herald* and the *Scotsman*), which contain all local as well as national and international news, and hence are almost a necessity for middle-class reading. The mass circulation *Record* and *Scottish Sun* are based in Glasgow, with 50 per cent Scottish content. Dundee and Aberdeen have local papers that transcend the quality/mass divide (the *Courier*, and *Press and Journal*).

The BBC has always had a strong Scottish regional unit with an autonomous council. The independent television companies (Borders, Scottish, Grampian) have developed Scottish and local programming over the last 20 years. The Glasgow-based Scottish Media Group owns Scottish Television. Scottish programmes provide employment for Scottish actors, musicians and artists as well as writers, who in turn contribute to a distinctive cultural voice.

Thus developments towards deregulation and competition have in this case strengthened the bases of Scottish identity rather than eroding them. The new Scottish Parliament provides even more of a focus for a distinctively Scottish media.

in the big cities. Regional programming of radio was strong even under the BBC (British Broadcasting Corporation) monopoly and is stronger now. Television in Britain has been regional since the emergence of independent television. Scotland has its own independent television companies, some of which, such as Scottish Television (STV), have developed into media conglomerates.

The Scottish media face two ways, as do other Scottish institutions. On the one hand, much of their comment and reporting is of British affairs, and differs little from the London-based media. On the other, their location and the nature of their public mean that they have a particular interest in Scottish news. The coverage may have little to do directly with politics but certainly supports the idea that Scotland is different. From this it is a short step to thinking of it as a cultural and social entity that ought to have its own political institutions.

This sounding board from which to address the whole of the (potential) nation perhaps accounts for the most salient feature of the Scottish National Party, its tendency to argue the case for independence in economic and material, rather than cultural, terms. The main plank of the SNP platform is that Scotland would do much better economically outside the United Kingdom than by staying inside – for example by setting its own business tax at a lower level; taking over the oil revenues in its sector of the North Sea; or securing direct subsidies from the European Union. This position was summarised in the slogans 'It's Scotland's oil' and 'Scotland in Europe'.

Clearly Scottish cultural distinctiveness offers a focus and a basis for the SNP. Anyone with a strong sense of Scottish identity is likely to be susceptible to its appeals. To gain power in Scotland, however, the party needs to win over a substantial block of Labour supporters. These identify themselves as Scottish but have massive material problems – which they share with the other British peripheries – such as unemployment, poor housing and bad health. To gain their votes the SNP has to convince them that they are not just 'Tartan Tories' but committed to social redistribution and welfare. The SNP has therefore become one of the most left-wing minority nationalist parties in Europe, lauding political radicalism as an essential element in the Scots character.

Opinion polls and election results suggest that about one-third of Scots support total independence (Table 11.3). Opposing them are about one-tenth hostile to even moderate devolution. In between there are 50–60 per cent who support devolution. Other survey evidence shows that this group also favours giving more power to the Scottish Parliament within the United Kingdom – the referendum of September 1997 showed that this was favoured by a convincing majority of Scottish voters. Devolution got a majority in all areas of the country, unlike Wales.

Regional divisions inside Scotland

The main political division inside Scotland is between the Glasgow conurbation, which contains about half the population and is overwhelmingly Labour, and the rest of the country, where Labour is challenged by Scottish Nationalists, Liberals and Conservatives, in more or less that order. The 'service' cities of Edinburgh and Aberdeen give less support to Labour and more to other parties. In the Highlands the Liberal Democrats run equally with Labour and the Nationalists. These political differences are based on considerable social and economic differences, which are not without some cultural reinforcement, as Table 11.4 shows.

Scotland as a whole does not appear to differ significantly from south-east England in terms of most social indicators (Table 11.1). The regional figures show that this is due to the relative wealth of Edinburgh and Aberdeen. This prosperity contrasts with severe deprivation in Glasgow and Dundee, both of which have had

Table 11.3 Support for Scottish independence and devolution

	1. Independence %	2. Devolution %	3. Neither %
1990	34	44	17
1991	33	43	19
1992	34	42	21
1993	34	45	18
1994	35	45	16
1995	32	44	21
1996	30	43	23
1997	28	44	25
1998	47	40	4
1999	36	43	14
2000	30	55	12
2001	29	57	11
2005	46	39	

Note: Figures to 1999 from MORI opinion polls. The question wording for earlier years is 'Do you favour . . . 1. An independent Scotland that is separate from England and Wales but part of the European Community? 2. Scotland remaining part of the United Kingdom but with its own devolved Assembly with some taxation and spending power? 3. No change from the present system?' After 1997 the wording was somewhat changed. Respondents were asked: 'In the long term would you prefer a devolved Scotland within the United Kingdom, or a fully independent Scotland, or neither?' Figures for 2000 and 2001 are taken from political surveys funded by the Economic and Social Science Research Council. In 2005 an opinion poll for TNS System 3 asked: 'Do you support or oppose Scotland becoming a country independent from the rest of the United Kingdom?' Figures do not total 100 per cent because 'don't knows' have been excluded.

Table 11.4 Social and economic differences between Scottish regions, 2001

	% with degree-level qualification	% unemployed	GDP per head	Average weekly wage (£)
North-east	30	2.2	121	391.6
Eastern	23.8	3.7	99	383.2
West	22.4	4.7	90	389.9
Highlands and Islands	28	3	74	374.5

Note: Percentage with degree and average wages for Orkney, Shetland and Western Isles n/a. The regions include: North-east – Aberdeen City, Aberdeenshire, Moray; Eastern – Angus, Dundee, Borders, City of Edinburgh, Falkirk, Perth, Kinross, Stirling, West Lothian, Fife, East Lothian, Midlothian, Clackmannan; West – East and West Dumbartonshire, Dumfries & Galloway, Ayrshire, City of Glasgow, Renfrewshire, Lanarkshire, Inverclyde; Highlands and Islands – Western Isles, Orkney, Shetland, Argyll & Bute, Highland. *Source*: GDP, Office for National Statistics regional accounts; Scottish Executive Economic Advice and Statistics Division. Reproduced under the Click-Use Licence

to cope with the social legacy of early industrialisation followed by later industrial collapse. It is this heritage, shared with other deprived peripheries such as northern England and south Wales, that pushed them into fervent support for trade unions and the Labour Party.

An additional factor fostering such support in Scotland is religion. The core of Labour Party support is the Roman Catholic vote. Catholics in Scotland are descendants of immigrant groups, mostly Irish, who came in the nineteenth and early twentieth centuries to take the jobs nobody else wanted. Their poverty was compounded by the large families that the Church encouraged. Once the Church

Plate 11.2 Bill McArthur cartoon in the (Glasgow) *Herald*, 25 July 1997. The biggest change in Scotland's links with the rest of Britain for nearly 300 years was heralded as the Blair government proposed an Edinburgh Parliament to raise taxes and make many of its own laws

Source: Glasgow Herald

"Freedom, son? ...it's the right to vary income tax by 3p in the pound."

accepted that the Labour Party was not hostile to it the social circumstances of Catholics pushed them overwhelmingly into voting Labour. At the same time their religious ties made them less susceptible either to Conservative appeals to support the (Protestant) British state or to nationalists harking back to the traditions of a largely Presbyterian Scotland. The concentration of Catholics in the populous west of Scotland makes the habit of Labour voting hard to break there and Labour is, as a result, the dominant party in Scotland.

However, Labour in its turn has had to safeguard itself against nationalist appeals by going part way to meet them, with its proposals for devolution. We

CONTROVERSY

Alex Salmond MP, National Convener, Scottish National Party: why I believe in Scottish independence

Scotland is one of the longest established countries in Europe; her culture, law and institutions preserve her identity as a modern, outward-looking European nation. Yet Scotland has no effective democratic voice. Westminster has misrepresented us with its isolationist attitude to Europe.

The House of Commons doesn't have time or enough interest to meet the real political needs of Scotland. This will change now we have our own Parliament devoted to getting the best deal for Scotland and giving us a real say in the running of our country.

One of the positive actions the Parliament has taken is to introduce fair voting at local government level. With fair voting, no one political party will have absolute control. All politicians will have to co-operate in the best interests of the whole country. This will also sweep away the scandals which have resulted from one party's domination of Scotland's councils.

While it is not as powerful as I would like, Scotland's Parliament is still able to abolish Skye Bridge tolls, end the feudal system of land ownership, fight the creeping privatisation of the health service and the galloping privatisation of all our universities and colleges.

The independent Parliament that I seek would put even more power in Scotland's hands. It would be able to remove Trident from the Clyde, demand Scotland's share of the oil revenues and speak up for Scotland in Europe.

Personal statement

CONTROVERSY

Sir Teddy Taylor MP: devolution

As regards devolution, I believe it could lead to the break-up of the United Kingdom because the Scottish Parliament has limited powers and the funding available to it is limited. My fear is that the new Assembly will simply become a complaints department about alleged inadequate financing and provision of power from London and this will lead to continuing disputes.

The same problems could arise with devolution in Northern Ireland, without the additional problem of the policies of a devolved Parliament being interpreted as being biased in a particular direction.

I do believe European integration to be a greater danger to democracy and international integrity than devolution of Scotland and Wales. The devolved parliamentary proposals can, of course, be changed by a future national Parliament if it is found to be utterly unacceptable. However, as far as Europe is concerned, all the power we hand over is wholly and permanently without the control of democracy.

Personal statement

(Sir Teddy Taylor was first elected in 1964 to a seat in Glasgow, was appointed as a junior minister in the Scottish Office and resigned this position because of opposition to the membership of the European Community. He voted against the Treaty of Rome and against all subsequent European treaties. He lost his Glasgow seat in 1979 and was re-elected for a seat in Southend, Essex.)

have noted at various points that Labour is as much a coalition of British peripheries against the centre as a class party. Nowhere is this aspect of Labour's character more marked than in Scotland, where it tries to maintain its claim to be the major exponent of Scottish interests against rival claims of the Scottish Nationalists.

Scottish devolution in practice

The first Scottish Parliament in almost 300 years was elected on 6 May 1999. It differentiated itself in two ways from the British Parliament:

1. **Electoral arrangements** The new voting system gave top-up seats to party lists of candidates within regions in addition to the seats parties had been able to win individually within 73 constituencies. This system was deliberately designed to produce a more proportional representation in the Parliament than would have been secured by 'first past the post' in constituency voting on its own. This would have resulted in a permanent Labour majority, unacceptable to the other parties. The balance of seats in the single chamber after the May 2003 elections is Labour 50, SNP 27, Liberals 17 and Conservatives 18. With an overall membership of 129 this means that no party has a majority. To form the executive two parties have to go into coalition. A Labour–Liberal one has existed since 1998.

2. Related to the absence of a single-party majority are arrangements for more consensual and informal policy making within the chamber, and closer involvement of all members (MSPs) in executive decision making. The executive of 11 ministers including a First Minister is shadowed by parliamentary committees with broadly comparable coverage of ministerial assignments. These give a good idea of the policy areas in which Scotland can act on its own. Broadly speaking these are detailed domestic matters. Parliament's remit does not include general decisions about the nature of economic or social policy, still less foreign or constitutional affairs (see Table 11.5).

Table 11.5 Policy areas covered by executive ministries and parliamentary committees in Scotland

Executive ministries	Parliamentary committees
Justice	Justice 1, Justice 2
Education and young people	Education, culture and sport
Enterprise and lifelong learning	Enterprise and lifelong learning
Environment and rural development	Rural development: transport and environment
Finance and public services	Finance: audit, local government
Health and community care	Health and community care
Parliamentary business	Procedures: standards, public petitions, subordinate legislation
Social justice	Equal opportunities, social justice
Tourism, culture and sport	Education, culture and sport
	European scrutiny

The emphasis on consensual decision making reflects the precedent set by Northern Ireland on power sharing. But there are not the same compelling reasons to share power in Scotland (or Wales). As a result Scottish Labour, the dominant partner in the executive, has imposed important decisions on the Parliament despite strong opposition. Thus it decided to build an expensive new building to house it, which has proved a permanent provocation for the Scottish press. Massive cost overruns contributed to the impression that Parliament is more concerned with its own accommodation, working conditions and pay than with the general well-being of the country.

Labour's high-handed behaviour has been prompted partly by British government attempts to use party mechanisms to keep control of the devolved arrangements. There is still a Secretary of State for Scotland with a seat in the British Cabinet whose remit is to 'manage' Scottish affairs. Symptomatic of this is British Labour's concern to get an acceptable nominee as First Minister. A financial scandal however pushed their preferred candidate (Henry McLeish) out of office, to be succeeded by the more independent-minded Jack McConnell, the current First Minister.

The episode reflected resentment among even Labour MSPs at London's interference. If the party link between Edinburgh and London ever breaks down (e.g. through a British Conservative election victory) we could expect to see more open confrontations over policy.

One symptom of covert London influence to date is the somewhat thin legislative programme, which has been concerned with useful but uncontroversial measures. Controversial proposals in line with general Labour policy have been the abolition of restrictions on what school teachers may say about homosexuality, and of fox-hunting within Scotland. The two areas where the Lib–Lab coalition has managed to break away from the straight Labour line has been when they exempted Scottish students from having to pay top-up fees to universities, and demanded free personal care (financed by general taxation) for the elderly.

In 2002–3 by far the most potent, symbolic and potentially explosive Scottish issue was confronted – the land question. More than half of Scotland, and two-thirds of the Highlands, is composed of vast (largely sporting) estates owned by wealthy outsiders. These are run to foster grouse or deer for autumn shooting, often to the detriment of the environment and local economic development. The legacy of the 'crofting wars' of the late nineteenth century, and of the 'clearances' of natives off the land, make the question of its control and ownership a highly symbolic issue. The Land Reform Bill passed in February 2003 took a first step to dealing with it by consolidating open access to all land (except for very special

Single transferable vote (STV)

This is the electoral system now introduced for Scottish local governments and used in Ireland (both north and south). Voters record their preferences over all the candidates standing in a multi-member constituency. 'Surplus' votes for successful candidates and 'wasted' votes for failed ones are then redistributed in line with preferences until the constituency 'quota' of elected candidates is reached.

reasons) and giving crofters the right to buy their own land if they want to. These measures do not tackle the complex question of overall ownership but they give the promise of doing so in the future.

Land reform possibly reflects Liberal Democrat influence within the executive coalition. It is important to their credibility at British level to be seen in government. Their major reform – of the constituency-based plurality voting that gave Labour permanent control of almost all local governments in the west of Scotland, and many elsewhere – was agreed in coalition negotiations after the second Assembly elections in 2003. By breaking one-party Labour dominance in the west and centre it will benefit Liberals as much as nationalists and provide a general boost to public life by freeing it from the dead hand of local Labour oligarchies. An agreement to do this forms part of the present coalition arrangement.

The results of the Scottish elections of May 2003 show that the SNP has been unable as yet to capitalise on the relative moderation of the executive and Parliament. They are still far from replacing Labour as the dominant party in Scottish politics. Until they do they will be unable to advance very effectively their agenda for Scottish independence. In the meantime, however, there is strong public support (66 per cent) for increasing the powers of the Parliament, which is a useful intermediate step from a nationalist point of view and one on which they could make common cause with Liberals and some Labour. Nobody wants to cooperate closely with the Conservatives. This, together with their limited number of parliamentary seats, renders them ineffective within the Scottish four-party system (Table 11.6).

Table 11.6 List voting in Scottish parliamentary elections, by region

1999	Labour %	SNP %	Lib Dem %	Conservative %	Other %
Highlands & Islands	25.5	27.7	21.4	14.9	6.3
North-east	25.5	32.3	17.5	18.3	3.9
Mid-Scotland and Fife	33.4	28.7	12.7	18.6	4.9
Lothians	30.2	25.7	14.4	15.8	11.8
South	39.2	27.8	6.2	9.2	12.0
Central	38.5	26.0	11.0	15.7	4.5
Glasgow	43.9	25.5	7.2	7.9	11.2
West	38.5	26.0	11.0	15.7	4.5
Scotland	38.8	28.8	14.2	15.6	2.3
2003					
Highlands & Islands	22.3	23.4	18.8	16.0	19.1
North-east	20.2	27.3	18.8	17.4	16.3
Mid-Scotland and Fife	25.3	23.0	12.0	17.6	21.3
Lothians	24.5	16.2	11.0	15.1	22.8
South	30.0	18.4	10.3	24.2	16.9
Central	40.4	22.5	5.9	9.2	22.0
Glasgow	34.7	19.1	7.3	7.5	31.3
West	32.6	19.6	12.3	15.4	19.6
Scotland	29.1	20.9	12.1	15.3	21.2

Note: Votes are the ones cast for party lists in regions, which give a better idea of the parties' overall standing. Percentages add across rows, although not in all cases to exactly 100 per cent because of rounding. 'Other parties' are the Scottish Socialist Party, Socialist Independents, Socialist Labour and Greens – all on the left of the political spectrum and generally supporting full independence.

Wales: cultural distinctiveness and territorial fragmentation

Historical and social background

Wales is arguably the part of Britain with the most distinctive popular culture. Like the other non-English areas it emerged from Celtic kingdoms that held out against the invading German tribes after the collapse of the Roman Empire. However its rugged geography, with high mountains protecting it against invasion but hindering internal communications, meant that it was not united under a single political authority before its incorporation into the English administrative structure in 1536.

This mattered less than its cultural and religious distinctiveness. Almost all the Welsh population spoke a separate Celtic language until the last quarter of the nineteenth century. In common with other 'submerged' European languages Welsh experienced a cultural renaissance in the nineteenth and twentieth centuries. However, its popular base was concurrently eroded through universal education in English, exposure to English language mass media, and massive immigration of English speakers into eastern and industrial south Wales. Although there is a special Welsh-language TV channel and schools that encourage bilingualism, Welsh is now spoken by only half a million people (20 per cent of the population), mainly located in north and west Wales (Table 11.7).

Another nineteenth-century development, however, reinforced Welsh distinctiveness. This was religious revivalism, spearheaded by Methodists and Congregationalists, radical Protestant denominations opposed to the torpor and worldliness (as they saw it) of the Anglican State Church. The Nonconformist Churches used Welsh as their medium and penetrated every village and town of the country. They demanded the 'disestablishment' of the Anglican Church and loss of its special privileges, especially in education within Wales.

This was a uniquely Welsh demand, met in 1920. By that time, however, religious passions had started to ebb. While the Nonconformist tradition still gives Welsh life a particular flavour it is not especially influential in contemporary Wales, where only 12 per cent of the population attend church regularly.

Nonconformity and the call for disestablishment did, however, give Welsh voters a push towards radical politics as they were enfranchised in the late nineteenth and early twentieth centuries. This expressed itself in support for

Table 11.7 Differences between regions inside Wales

	West	North-west (Gwynedd and Dyfed)	North-east (Clwyd and Powys)	South (Gwent and Glamorgan)
Percentage of households with no car	23.7	25.5	24.3	31.8
Average weekly earnings	354	353	368	387
GDP per head (UK = 100)	70.0	71.5	82.0	92.0
Percentage with higher educational qualifications (A-level or equivalent)	22.0	17.0	18.3	21.8
Percentage Welsh speaking	44.9	68.4	23.5	9.7

Note: 'Welsh Wales', the north-west, has the highest percentage of Welsh-speaking people and is therefore culturally the most distinctive. It is also, with the west, the poorest region.
Source: Computed by authors

progressive liberalism and subsequently for Labour and nationalist parties in the north and west.

The English-speaking south suffered all the evils of early industrialism: slums, overcrowding, bad health, precarious employment. This too generated votes for reforming liberals in the nineteenth and early twentieth centuries. The political party that really gained, however, was Labour, the defender of working-class interests against the free market. South Wales became one of the earliest trade union and Labour strongholds, and from there Labour spread out to the rest of Wales. In the 2005 general election, Labour held 29 out of 40 Welsh seats, the Liberal Democrats 4, Plaid Cymru (PC, the Welsh Nationalist Party) 3, and the Conservatives 3.

The Welsh regions

The overall figures mask a marked regional variation inside Wales. Labour predominates everywhere but particularly in the industrialised south, traditionally home to a militant working class. 'English Wales' – the border area of the east – provides the highest level of support for the Conservatives. The strongest support for nationalism comes from the north-west – centred on Gwynedd, the Welsh kingdom that held out longest against English domination. This is the predominantly Welsh-speaking area where the influence of nonconformity lingers. Its economic base is mainly farming and tourism, a fragile means of livelihood. The extractive industries, slate and stone, which supported the population from the mid-nineteenth to the mid-twentieth centuries, have now substantially disappeared. This may explain why the nationalists have not opted for a separate Welsh-speaking entity in this area, leaving the English-speaking regions to themselves. Another reason is that west Wales (with the exception of South Pembroke) is culturally similar to the north.

Attracting support in the rest of Wales is difficult for the nationalists. Unlike the Scottish Nationalist Party, Plaid Cymru is predominantly a cultural defence organisation. The party wants separate political institutions to protect and extend the Welsh language, together with a better economic and social base to support the Welsh-speaking population. This gives it a strong appeal in the north and west. Its problem, however, is how to appeal to the English-speaking borders and south Wales, whose voters are opposed to the extension of the Welsh language, which most do not speak.

Regional political differences are heightened by geography. Most of the regions of Wales are difficult to reach (the reason the Welsh were able to survive in the first place); but each of them is more accessible from the neighbouring part of England than it is from the rest of Wales. This fact of geography has been underpinned by the building of railways and roads from east to west, rather than from north to south. It is easier for all-Welsh bodies to meet in Shrewsbury, an English town – or even in London – than in far southern Cardiff, the official capital.

Rural west Wales (the coastal strip and its hinterland down to Carmarthen on the Bristol Channel) is linked to the north historically and politically. Here support for the nationalists is strong. The regions over the mountains to the east, bordering on England, are the most anglicised, and here nationalism attracts little support. These differences are almost perfectly illustrated in the referendum votes for a separate Welsh Assembly, shown in Map 11.3. The north and west supported devolution and the east was totally opposed. The south was split between the old mining valleys (for) and the coast (against).

Map 11.3 The three Wales: voting in the devolution referendum, 1997

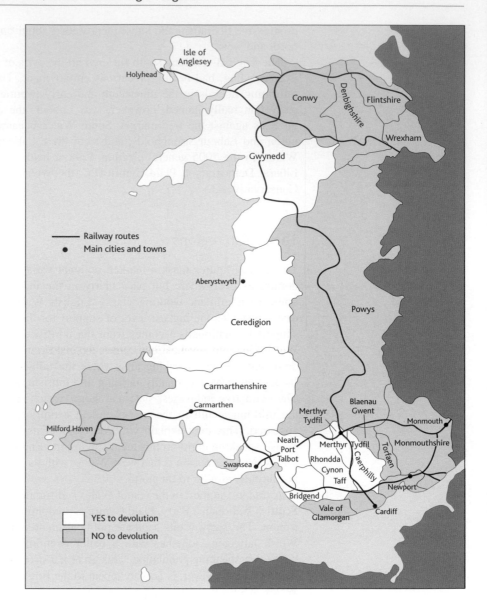

South Wales (the triangle of Cardiff, Swansea and Merthyr Tydfil) is the most populous area of the country and the classic heartland of industrial working-class Wales, the country of trade unions and Labour. Labour has controlled all of local government and most of the constituencies of south Wales for generations.

Welsh devolution

In many ways this consistent support for Labour has defined Welsh politics better than sporadic upsurges of nationalism. Support for Labour, the national 'Opposition party', can be seen as the main political expression of Welsh distinctiveness. Labour, in its turn, can be seen as a representative of peripheral protest against the centre in Britain, as much as a class-based party. In south Wales both fuse because the region itself is defined by its working-class nature.

Welsh Labour MPs may express political demands for their region but some have been bitter opponents of nationalism inside Wales, denouncing it as a distraction from the real task of improving living standards and getting jobs. The Cardiff area's relative proximity to London (200 miles) makes it a favoured location for new industrial development, provided it remains well integrated into Britain.

The opposition of many Welsh Labour MPs to a Welsh Assembly ensured the high vote against it in the Welsh referendum of September 1997. The furthest Labour had gone in the past in terms of devolution was the creation of the Welsh Office in Cardiff in 1965, on the model of the well-established Scottish Office. The Welsh Office is a regional ministry that administers culture, environment, local government, housing, social affairs, agriculture, infrastructure and economic development in Wales. It thus groups administrative areas that in England (and in Wales until 1970) were handled by separate functional ministries from London.

Having a separate administration in these areas means that the Welsh Assembly charged with overseeing it has been set up with relatively little difficulty. The creation of the Assembly was urged on democratic as well as nationalistic grounds, given that the British Parliament has little time for specifically Welsh business. Its specialist committee on Welsh affairs has little power, and is dominated by the party that won most British votes, not necessarily by the parties preferred by Welsh voters.

This was the reason given by New Labour for having put the proposal for a Welsh Assembly to a referendum in Wales, this time with Labour more united in support. From the viewpoint of stimulating local democracy the argument is clearly correct. Labour-dominated councils, particularly in the south where they face little challenge, have often been accused of corruption and nepotism. The Welsh Assembly is open to wider influences and more party competition, so it has brought a breath of fresh air into the closed Labour politics of south Wales.

The new Assembly

This promise was borne out by the results of the first Assembly election on 6 May 1999. Plaid Cymru obtained an unprecedented 28 per cent of the Welsh vote compared with its 10 per cent in the British general election. This could not have been achieved without massive support in south Wales. Large switches from Labour to PC were also recorded in the concurrent local council elections in the southern valleys. With the Conservatives rejected and the Liberals unconvincing, Plaid Cymru emerged as the natural political opposition to Labour throughout Wales.

This status was also reflected in the new Assembly, where the party controlled 17 out of 60 seats, the Conservatives 9 and the Liberals 6. Labour, although the largest party, was short of an absolute majority with 28 seats. These results were achieved, as in Scotland, through an election system where top-up seats distributed through proportional representation in large areas supplemented the traditional first past the post constituency-based results. The result is a much more proportional system of representation, where parties have to win a majority or near majority of votes to get a majority of Assembly seats, unlike the British Parliament.

After the election Labour decided to form the Welsh executive on its own, with the tolerance of the other Assembly parties. This tolerance did not extend to a Labour proposal to give wide discretionary powers to the executive outside the supervision of the Assembly. A majority administration would have been able to

Plate 11.3 The Welsh Assembly in session. Note the informality in contrast to the House of Commons
Source: Alamy/Photolibrary Wales

force this through in the tradition of the elective dictatorships at Westminster, or of the Welsh local councils. In face of the reality of divided power at Cardiff Labour had to drop the proposal, which indeed consorted badly with its own calls during the election campaign for a more inclusive and consensual politics.

The power of the other parties in the Assembly has been reinforced by splits within Welsh Labour's own ranks, notably between New and 'old' Labour. This, together with the fact that the Assembly's main powers relate to supervising Welsh administration and not to legislation, means that much of its work is done through all-party committees rather than through ministries and departments, unlike the Westminster government. In turn this focuses decision making within the Assembly itself rather than within the executive.

The party stand-off has given considerable potential for influence to the central policy committees of the Assembly. These cover economic development, health and social services, agriculture, environment and higher education. Only two of these are chaired by Labour. Plaid Cymru has two and the Liberal Democrats and Conservatives one each (Table 11.8).

The legislation setting up the Assembly subordinates it much more to the British government and Parliament than is the case with the corresponding Scottish body. The British Secretary of State for Wales may sit in the Assembly (but not vote). This well underlines his/her directing and guiding role. In particular, the Welsh Assembly lacks legislative powers, even in areas of prime concern. They allocate funds provided by the British Treasury, and develop and implement policies initiated by the London Parliament and government.

Table 11.8 Policy areas covered by ministries and Assembly committees in Wales

Ministries	Assembly committees
Rural development and Wales abroad	Agriculture and rural development: European and external affairs
Culture and sports	Culture
Economic development	Economic development
Education and lifelong learning	Education and lifelong learning
Environment	Environment, planning and transport: planning decisions
Health and social services	Health and social services
Finance, local government and communities	Local government and housing: audit
Assembly business	Business: standards
	Equality of opportunity
	Subordinate legislation
	Regional committees (mid, north, south-east, south-west Wales)

The pro-devolution parties (Labour, Liberals and Plaid Cymru) have all felt hampered by these restrictions on their power. In 2005–6 a Government of Wales Bill was introduced at Westminster with provisions for: legal separation of the National Assembly from the Assembly government, primary legislation to be passed by the Assembly within framework legislation passed by Westminster, and changes in the election system (to the single-transferable vote). As the election changes affect both MPs and parties they are unlikely to be passed, but acceptance of the other provisions in the Bill would certainly enhance the standing of the Assembly and Welsh executive.

The Assembly has already taken some independent political stands, despite its limited powers. In early 2000 the failure of the executive to secure aid from London to 'match' European aid, and the consequent risk of losing it altogether, sparked a political crisis. This failure was seen as part of a supine, do-nothing attitude on the part of Labour ministers headed by Tony Blair's nominee for Labour leader and First Secretary, Alun Michael. On the one hand, he adopted an autocratic attitude to the Assembly, while on the other doing nothing that might offend the British Labour government. A vote of no confidence proposed by Plaid Cymru was carried in February 2000, resulting in Michael's resignation and the succession of the 'Old Labour' Rhodri Morgan to his post. Morgan promised a more consensual and consultative approach in politics, working in partnership with the Assembly. His election was certainly an assertion of independence from London, as Blair had strongly opposed him in the earlier leadership campaign. It was followed by a formal coalition with the Liberals and more vigorous Welsh initiatives at Brussels. In May 2002 the Assembly went completely against British government policy by voting for free personal care for the elderly. It also took up Plaid Cymru concerns about excessive English immigration driving up house prices and eroding Welsh-speaking communities.

Shared powers and interdependent decision making between Wales and London are clearly a recipe for continuing tensions and quarrels. Plaid Cymru has denied that it ever sought full independence for Wales (Table 11.9). But it is committed to seeking full legislative powers in the areas covered by the Assembly and has already pushed the other Welsh parties in the same direction. However, PC lost ground in south Wales as well as in other areas in the election of 2003. With the decline in its vote and its policy moderation the party does not pose much of a threat to the territorial integrity of the British state, which is more likely to emerge in Scotland and above all in Northern Ireland.

Table 11.9 List voting in Welsh Assembly elections, by region

1999	Labour %	Plaid Cymru %	Lib Dem %	Conservative %	Other %
North	34.2	32.3	10.3	19.4	1.7
Mid and west	24.6	38.6	16.7	14.4	5.8
South-west	42.3	30.4	11.1	12.6	4.7
South Central	36.9	27.0	14.4	16.2	5.6
South-east	4.5	24.3	12.2	16.8	3.5
Wales	37.6	28.4	13.5	15.9	4.3
2003					
North	31.6	23.8	10.0	22.0	10.8
Mid and west	25.2	28.3	16.4	19.3	10.9
South-west	41.6	17.2	12.7	15.0	13.0
South Central	41.1	15.4	13.8	18.5	11.3
South-east	45.1	12.6	10.4	20.2	11.4
Wales	36.9	19.6	12.7	19.0	11.5

Note: Votes are the ones cast for party lists in regions, which give a better idea of the parties' overall standing. Percentages add across rows, although not in all cases to exactly 100 per cent because of rounding. 'Other parties' are the Socialists and Greens – both on the left of the political spectrum.

BRIEFINGS

11.2 Clientelism, corruption and patronage

Whatever happens in general or regional elections Labour always dominates the local governments of south Wales, often as the only party. Freed from effective accountability, the ruling group of councillors can in these circumstances favour their own supporters and friends in matters over which they have local control – jobs, minor building contracts, priority on public housing lists etc. Patronage of this kind can be used to favour party supporters ('clientelism') and can slide over into corruption if money is given in exchange for favours.

Remarkably little overt corruption has been uncovered in British local government, either in Wales or out of it. Rumours of a 'Taffia' in local politics are widely believed, however. Probably the best solution is more transparency in government (helped by the Welsh Assembly, and challenges to Labour predominance by other parties).

It is noteworthy that Plaid Cymru has made most headway in south Wales as a challenger to Labour predominance on local councils, culminating in its 28.4 per cent share of the Welsh vote in the 1999 Assembly election. If a more proportional voting system were introduced in Welsh local governments that would very much help its political position there. The Scottish reforms of local government elections due to come into force in 2007 may add to the pressure for a similar Welsh reform.

Extending devolution to the English regions?

The islands of Man, in the Irish Sea, and Guernsey and Jersey in the English Channel, have always had independent parliaments and governments with full control over their domestic affairs – more so than Scotland, in fact, since they control their own budgets and taxes. Even with devolved government in these areas and in the other countries of the British Isles, five out of six of the UK population living in England are directly under the control of central government.

BRIEFINGS

11.3 Traditional autonomy in the Isle of Man, Jersey and Guernsey (the Channel Islands)

The Isle of Man, Jersey and Guernsey (the last two are part of the Channel Islands off the coast of France) have always had their own parliaments and government. This is because they owed feudal allegiance to the English Crown but were not juridically part of England or under the control of the English (later British) Parliament. In practice, British governments handle their foreign and defence policy, leaving domestic matters to the locals. Autonomy extends to taxation (with income tax set very low to attract wealthy residents). Jersey and Guernsey even issue their own coinage, which is, however, related to the British. This is typical of the political compromise on which the islands are run. Most British domestic legislation is automatically accepted by the local parliament and applied. Only occasionally are modifications made to accommodate local preferences. The best known was Man's retention of flogging and birching as criminal punishments until it was struck down by the European Court of Human Rights in the 1970s – even though the island's exact status within the EU is somewhat uncertain.

These little autonomous areas were regarded as an irrelevant anomaly until recently. With the growth of interest in English regionalism they may come to be regarded as working models of how some regional relationships with the centre might be organised, particularly in Cornwall and similar areas.

It would thus be quite feasible to 'hive off' the more troublesome peripheries while consolidating central control over England. This has indeed seemed to be the strategy of New Labour in regard to English local government.

Contrariwise, the official justification for Scottish and Welsh devolution has always been its greater efficiency, transparency, democracy and ability to 'bring government closer to the people'. What is sauce for the goose is sauce for the gander, and such arguments apply equally well to the regions inside England as to the other countries of the United Kingdom. So it is not surprising that there has been increasing discussion and even concrete moves towards setting up regional assemblies and administrations in England.

Of these initiatives the most important has been the reconstitution of Greater London as a political entity. Because of its political differences with the Labour-controlled Greater London Council (GLC) in the mid-1980s, the then Conservative government abolished it outright, leaving only a lower tier of urban government, the London boroughs, in place. The lack of even a planning authority for Greater London as a whole made it difficult to make integrated decisions for the whole region, and it became increasingly obvious that this was necessary, particularly for transport and planning.

New Labour set out to remedy this but in a novel way – by having an executive mayor elected directly by the whole area, overseen by a small council. This 'presidential' arrangement is completely different to the assembly-dominated systems that operate in Wales and Scotland and in local government. Labour has been urging change to directly elected executive mayors on other local governments. But referendums have mostly defeated the proposals.

Further difficulties were created by events in Greater London. The new arrangements, which took effect in May 2000, set up the most powerful directly elected politician in Britain, the choice of 7 million London voters. The actual events of the Greater London campaign in which 'Red Ken' Livingstone, defeated as Labour nominee by Tony Blair's hostility, then ran as an independent and won, show that the post could become a potent centre of opposition to government policies. Livingstone has already fought partial privatisation of London transport all the way to the courts and has charged all private cars entering London a flat daily fee, to relieve congestion.

BRIEFINGS

11.4 Turn again, Livingstone, twice Mayor of London

'Red Ken' Livingstone came to political prominence in the early 1980s when he used his position as Chairman of the Labour-dominated Greater London Council (GLC) to institute a number of innovative policies and thumb his nose at Mrs Thatcher at a time when the Labour Party was at a low ebb. The GLC operated in County Hall, a massive stone building directly across the Thames from the Houses of Parliament. Typically, Livingstone put up a vast notice recording increases in the unprecedented level of unemployment under the Conservative government, so it could be seen every day by MPs from their own terrace on the river bank opposite.

His impish gestures enlivened what were, at bottom, serious alternatives to Conservative individualism and free market policies. He distributed money to minority groups, particularly Afro-Caribbean ones, at a time of serious racial tensions. This provided them with non-violent political outlets for their activism such as the London carnivals, local liaison groups and neighbourhood councils. He masterminded London Labour's 'Fare's Fair' transport policy whereby cheap flat rates were introduced by the Transport Board with revenues being made up by the London rates if they fell short. Actually the policy was a great success and very popular. Passengers and revenues boomed until the policy was struck down by the Law Lords on appeal by a Conservative borough council.

Livingstone's attitudes caused difficulty both with a Labour leadership anxious to shed its 'loony left' image and with the Conservative government. Mrs Thatcher abolished the GLC in 1986 primarily to deprive him of a platform. County Hall was sold to the Japanese as a private hotel (another piece of highly symbolic politics!).

Livingstone declined to be an ordinary backbench MP until Labour's decision to reconstitute Greater London as a political entity with an executive mayor. Running for the Labour candidacy he was so violently opposed by Tony Blair that he had a good justification for standing as an independent when the party rejected him. In an unprecedented result he beat the official party nominees on a low turn-out, and used this as a basis to fight New Labour's partial privatisation of London transport all the way through the courts (where he lost). The prospects for Labour's transport policy are not good and Livingstone should benefit politically – which may counterbalance some of the hostility stemming from his proposal to charge each car entering London a flat rate for the privilege. The initial introduction of the 'congestion charge' in February 2003 proved quite successful, once again confirming Livingstone's potential for creative policy innovation. For the second London mayoral elections he was finally accepted as the official Labour nominee.

None of this creates good precedents, from Labour's point of view, for regional bodies elsewhere. This was however one of the few policy areas left to John Prescott, the Deputy Prime Minister, reduced to Blair's shadow after the 2001 election. He was able to make his own mark on the structure of government in Britain with a White Paper published in May 2002, containing official proposals for elected English regional assemblies with some important powers – economic development, European funding, local housing and strategic planning, as well as oversight over other regional bodies. The model for this was presumably the Welsh Assembly – a high-level elected body with administrative rather than legislative functions. Financially, the assemblies were to have a block grant from the government, rights to tax local authorities in the region and a power to borrow – putting the English regions in as favourable a situation as Wales and Scotland in this respect.

All these proposals came to nothing with their defeat in a referendum in north-east England in November 2004. On a low turn-out, the proposal for a regional government with unitary local authorities was defeated. This was highly symbolic, since the north-east was the area with the strongest pressure group for regional autonomy (the North-east Constitutional Convention) based at Newcastle – the English city furthest from London and with one of the highest levels of social deprivation. The 'No' campaigners' most potent symbol was an inflatable white elephant – a reference to the cost of the new Scottish Parliament building – which they carried around with them from meeting to meeting. This forms a concrete illustration of the knock-on effects of autonomy in one region on autonomy in others.

The north-east defeat means that plans for elected regional assemblies have been abandoned by Labour and would hardly be taken up by Conservatives. In spite of this the administrative regionalisation of England has proceeded apace. Strategic health authorities, ambulance trusts and police authorities are all likely to be reorganised on a regional basis. Regional spatial strategies are being formulated through consultations between central and regional bodies, with implications for housing targets. The (nominated and co-opted) Regional Assembly for South-East England is developing in 2006 into a coherent lobby group for lower building numbers than is wanted by central government. Not coincidentally it is dominated by Conservatives, illustrating again the potential veto points being built into the British political process by regional autonomy.

Whatever final arrangement may emerge, devolution in England is likely to follow the same pattern as in the United Kingdom as a whole, with different regions having different powers and different relationships with the British centre. Areas without a distinct regional identity and at least some grassroots support for autonomy are likely to have less power, if it ever comes at all. The prospects for devolved government in England do, however, look brighter than before, and may

Plate 11.4 The Liverpool town hall. In terms of their social and economic profile, regions such as Merseyside and the north-east are almost as distinctive as Scotland and Wales. Regional civic pride, epitomised in the architecture of grand Victorian town halls, diminished under the centralising Conservative governments of 1979–97. New Labour has maintained tight control over English local government

Source: Alamy/Topix

compensate in terms of local autonomies for the central controls increasingly imposed on local government. More space to voice local opinions and reactions would inevitably make decision making more complex and less of an 'elective dictatorship' in Britain. But if it also becomes more consensual and inclusive of regional interests that might be no bad thing.

Constitutional implications

Traditional constitutional theory has stressed parliamentary sovereignty as the basis of the British constitution – whatever the majority of the nationally elected House of Commons decides is conclusive. In practice this meant that the government, with its Commons majority, could not be challenged in policy terms until the next election.

Devolution, as does membership of the EU, substitutes a more pluralist conception of politics and policy making. Many more groups will have formal powers that enable them to veto or at least substantially modify central decisions. This will make it essential for the British government to have genuine consultations with regional bodies rather than simply issuing directives for them to carry through. A foretaste of this is given by the Joint Ministerial Committee, which brings together ministers from the Northern Irish, Welsh and Scottish executives and the UK government to discuss matters of common concern.

Northern Ireland is an extreme example of where the UK government is involved in a mesh of institutions and processes that require it to consult at all times, not just with the NI executive itself but with the Irish government and – through the British–Irish Council – with all the devolved administrations down to the Isle of Man and the Channel Islands! If English regional governments come into being there is hardly going to be any domestic decision that does not involve consultation with another governmental body and often with many – at a variety of levels, from the European to the local.

The need for consultation is going to be greater because the electoral calendar affecting regional bodies, local governments and central government will be different. Local governments even now are chosen on the basis of annual elections. These only occasionally coincide with general elections. There is thus a tendency for electors to register their dissatisfaction with the party in power at the centre by voting for opposing parties locally – and now also regionally. The same obviously happens at the European elections. The result is that parliaments and assemblies at the different levels are almost bound to be dominated by opposing parties. In the future the government will not be able to rely, as New Labour has, on manipulating party ties to secure consent. Instead it will have to compromise with opponents to ensure that action does not get blocked. The prospects are for a much more 'consensual democracy' in Britain in place of confrontation between an all-powerful government and an effectively powerless opposition.

All this could be seen as subsidiarity – the doctrine that decisions should be made at the lowest level of government appropriate for them – in action. However, in an increasingly interdependent world it is unlikely that many decisions can actually be isolated from their broader context and made on their own by only one government. For example, roads and other transport projects in any one region are going to affect the contiguous ones and either facilitate or hinder British and European planning. All interests need to be consulted and aggregated. Perhaps subsidiarity should be reinterpreted as a prohibition on higher levels of government being able to steamroller their decisions through regardless of their impact on lower levels.

BRIEFINGS

11.5 New systems of voting – will they create pressures to reform general elections (and local ones)?

Devolved legislatures on the British mainland are all elected on the additional member system or supplementary vote system. Constituency-based first past the post or plurality voting, where the candidate with the most votes wins, still takes place for the majority of members. But party preferences are separately aggregated within larger areas and used to elect MPs for parties that did badly in the constituencies compared to their overall vote. This produces a more proportional representation. The Northern Irish system of voting, where all the Assembly members are elected on the basis of the single transferable vote, is even more proportional. In addition, elections to the European Parliament are now purely proportional: electors vote for party lists of 10–15 candidates in large regions and the seats are distributed on the basis of the party vote.

In contrast, general and local elections still take place in one-candidate constituencies with plurality voting. This notoriously favours parties with concentrated local support, primarily Labour but in the south-east the Conservatives. The result is to distort representation in favour of big parties, leading to 50 years of Labour dominance in many local governments. In both Wales and Scotland the other parties are pressing for change in local election procedures towards a more proportional system and in Scotland STV will be used from 2007. The same argument applies to the House of Commons, however. Why should Labour and Conservatives have an inbuilt bias in their favour while Liberals are artificially under-represented? Tony Blair's counterargument is that a proportional reform of voting would deprive all parties of an overall majority and put power in the hands of the minority Liberals, who would decide between a coalition with Conservatives or a coalition with Labour. Opponents of the 'elective dictatorship' of a single-party majority government might not object to this, however. If proportional representation is good for Europe and the regions, why should it not be good for the United Kingdom too? That is a hard position to oppose, so moves towards greater proportionality are likely to come both at local and British level in the next 10 years, probably in the shape of an additional member system.

This is just what has happened in the past under traditional interpretations of parliamentary sovereignty. As we will see, Parliament itself needs more real sovereignty, as its fictive legislative omnipotence has in practice been used to justify the 'elective dictatorship' imposed by single-party majority government. Paradoxically, devolution may end by giving the Westminster Parliament more time and opportunity to scrutinise and challenge central government.

As Chapter 4 indicated, this is still a long way in the future. The British Labour government has given devolution to Scotland, Wales and London with one hand while, with the other, seeking to maintain control through internal Labour Party manipulation. One suspects that it regards the Joint Ministerial Committee as a way of letting devolved governments know what it has decided or for persuasion and arm-twisting, rather than as a venue for genuine consultation. This parallels its attitudes to English local government, increasingly subjected to central control under both Conservative and Labour administrations, as we shall see in the next chapter.

Summary

This chapter has discussed:

- the forces promoting devolution in Britain, primarily Welsh and Scottish nationalism

- regional differences, which play some part in supporting the idea that local problems require local solutions, even in England

▶

- the workings of devolution in Scotland and Wales, together with the internal politics of these countries

- prospects for devolution in the English regions

- constitutional implications of devolution, primarily the undermining of the 'elective dictatorship' of the UK government based on its control of a parliamentary majority, and the need for more extended consultations over its decisions.

MILESTONES

Milestones in Scottish and Welsh devolution

Scotland		Wales
1886–1924	Home Rule all round, devolution for Ireland, Scotland and Wales advocated by Liberal and Labour parties but abandoned by Labour after 1924	
1888	Scottish Office created as a separate administration for Scotland	
1886–94	Crofters' land agitation in West Highlands met by new land tenure arrangements	
1896–1900		'Young Wales' movement. Lloyd George agitates for Home Rule within the Liberal Party
1920		Disestablishment of the Anglican Church in Wales
1928	Scottish National Party founded	Plaid Cymru (the Welsh Party) founded
1930–55		Protests and demonstrations against flooding Welsh valleys to provide water for England
1938–9		Sanders Lewis (major Welsh poet) imprisoned for burning RAF buildings
1944	SNP wins first parliamentary seat in by-election	
1945–50	Tom Johnston, charismatic Secretary of State for Scotland, institutes massive social and economic reform programmes	
1948–51	Scottish Covenant Association gathers 1 million signatures in favour of Home Rule	
1960–74	Some bank raids used to finance 'Scottish Liberation Army'	'Wales Liberation Army' burns English holiday homes and posts letter bombs
1965		Welsh Office created to take over administration for Wales
1974	SNP gains unprecedented one-fifth of the vote in Scotland	Plaid Cymru gains three Welsh seats
1978–9	Devolution for Scotland gains slim majority of Scottish vote in referendum but fails to meet parliamentary requirement of a majority of all electors	Devolution gains only a minority of Welsh votes in a referendum
1980–2		Gwynfor Evans (ex-PC leader) fasts to secure Welsh-language TV channel
1992, 1997	SNP regains one-fifth of the Scottish vote in general elections	PC consolidates vote in north and west Wales

Milestones in Scottish and Welsh devolution continued

Scotland		Wales
1997	New Labour government holds Scottish and Welsh referendums that approve devolution	
1999	First election to Scottish Parliament results in Lib–Lab coalition. SNP vote increases to nearly one-third	First election to Welsh Assembly results ultimately in Lib–Lab coalition. PC vote increases to nearly one-third
2003	Land Reform Law consolidates right to roam and gives crofters right to buy own land	
2003	Second Scottish parliamentary election consolidates Lib–Lab coalition	Both Labour and Plaid Cymru lose votes in second Assembly election
2004–5	Substitution of STV for first past the post in local elections from 2007 undermines Labour single-party dominance of local councils	

Essays

1. To what extent is the United Kingdom still a unitary state?

2. In what ways is the government of Scotland distinct from that of England?

3. What are the main differences between federal and devolutionary arrangements? Which is better for the United Kingdom?

Projects

1. Write a historical account of the incorporation of Wales and Scotland into the United Kingdom. To what extent do the problems of these territories today have their roots in history?

2. Write a new constitution for the United Kingdom providing for the full representation of all the peoples of the country.

3. Choose some area of devolved policy making in Wales or Scotland and trace in detail how a particular policy decision is made.

Further reading

Comprehensive analyses of Scottish politics are Peter Lynch, *Scottish Government and Politics* (Edinburgh: Edinburgh University Press, 2001) and Gerry Hassan and Chris Wadhurst, *Anatomy of the New Scotland* (Edinburgh: Mainstream, 2002). Jo Murkens *et al.*, *Scottish Independence: A Practical Guide* (Edinburgh: Edinburgh University Press, 2002) explores the viability of an independent Scotland. Welsh politics is analysed in John Osmond, *Welsh Politics in the New Millennium* (Institute of Cardiff Affairs: Welsh, 1999). On English regionalism see H. Armstrong, 'What future for regional policy in the UK?', *Political Quarterly*, **69**, 1998, pp. 200–14. On 'constitutional implications', *Political Quarterly*, **70**, 1997–9 contains much discussion, including Vernon Bogdanor, 'Devolution: decentralisation or disintegration?', *Political Quarterly*, **70**, 1999, pp. 185–94. See also Ben Plimlott and Nirmala Rao, *Governing London* (Oxford: Oxford University Press, 2002). Lively and informed comment on the workings of devolution and constitutional reform generally is contained in *Monitor*, published quarterly by the Constitution Unit, University College London. Almost every issue of the journal *Scottish Affairs*, published by the Unit for the Study of Government in Scotland, Edinburgh University, contains discussions of Scottish politics and the devolution arrangements for Wales and the English regions as well as Scotland.

Useful web sites on devolution

Hot links to these sites can be found on the CWS at www.pearsoned.co.uk/budge.

The question of devolution and regional politics in the United Kingdom has become a central component of the political agenda. There are many sites covering aspects of this process. At a general level, official information on the devolution process can be obtained from www.cabinet-office.gov.uk/constitution/devolution/devolution.htm. Insights on governmental policies on the regions are accessible from the Office of the Deputy Prime Minister (www.regions.odpm.gov.uk/index.htm), official documentation is available at www.regions.odpm.gov.uk/governance/whitepaper/index.htm. The Campaign for the English Regions (CFER) is a national organisation campaigning for devolution to the regions of England: you can find them at www.cfer.org.uk. You can also visit the Regional Policy Forum at www.rpf.org.uk. Highly valuable information and feedback on devolution can be found at www.devolution.info, www.devolve.org. For an excellent source of academic research on devolution and constitutional change, see www.devolution.ac.uk. You might also be interested in media coverage; if so, visit www.guardian.co.uk/Devolution.

Specific sites on Scotland

Government: www.scotland.gov.uk

National Archives of Scotland: www.nas.gov.uk

Institute of Governance – University of Edinburgh: www.institute-of-governance.org

Scottish affairs: www.scottishaffairs.org

Campaign for Scottish Independence: www.standupforscotland.com

Scottish Independence web server: www.forscotland.com

Specific sites on Wales

Government: www.wales.gov.uk

General: www.gjwwales.co.uk

Wales official legislation: www.wales-legislation.hmso.gov.uk

Political parties and movements: www.cymru1400.com and www.independentwales.com

Specific sites on England

Campaign for an English Parliament: www.englishpm.demon.co.uk

English petition online: www.petitiononline.com/engfree/petition.html

Specific sites on Northern Ireland

Government: www.nio.gov.uk

Official documents: www.hmso.gov.uk/acts/acts1998/19980047.htm

CAIN web site: http://cain.ulst.ac.uk/

Mitchell Report: www.irishnews.com/mitchell.html

Specific sites on the Greater London Authority

Information about the mayor and other aspects of the work of the Greater London Authority can be accessed via the comprehensive web site at www.london.gov.uk. For example, material concerning City Hall, the purpose-built centre for the authority, can be found at www.london.gov.uk/gla/city_hall/ and data on the authority and its members can be accessed directly via www.london.gov.uk/assembly/.

chapter 12

Local democracy?

For the last 100 years local government has had a dual function in the British political system and still has in England. The first is to serve as one of only two levels of democracy in the political system, alongside central government; the second is to provide public services in an effective and efficient manner. Local authorities are democratically elected in their own right and they should be accountable to their local citizens. At the same time local government is also the creature of central government and must, by law, comply with its decisions. Central government often has different ideas about public services that come into sharp conflict with local government's.

The resulting conflict between two layers of government, each with its own democratic legitimacy, has been sharpened by the fact that central government is largely dependent upon local government for the delivery of some of its most important and most expensive public services – education, environmental health, local transport, social services, fire, police, housing, and many others. Consequently, central government has kept tight control over local authorities in order to keep them in ideological line with its own policies. Central government also intervenes constantly in local government business to ensure national service standards, equality of service provision between areas, and to keep down local taxes and expenditure. To complicate matters still further, local government and central government are often in the hands of different parties, which have differing ideas about government and politics.

This dual function of being the lower layer of a democratic system that is overshadowed by central government, and a local service provider under the control of central government, creates an inherent tension and a good deal of political conflict between central and local government. In the 1980s Thatcher governments reduced local powers and financial capacities, and introduced the poll tax. As a result, a good many health warnings were issued at the time about local government being 'in turmoil', subject to 'massive upheaval' and enmeshed in 'endless futile reform'.

To understand how and why local politics has become such an intense subject of national controversy we will, first, set it in the overall context of the British system of government, then look at its structure and mode of operation, and finally, consider its role in democracy.

This chapter accordingly covers:

- local politics in context
- territorial and functional reorganisations
- how local councils function
- parties, political control and local politics
- money and power in local government
- councillors and officers
- local government, democracy and 'revolution'
- New Labour: local democracy revived?

Local politics in context

To understand local government in England we also have to understand the nature of the British state. Effective power is concentrated in central government by the constitutional doctrines of the unitary state, which enables national government to change local government boundaries, powers and functions, and finances, at will. Yet, in spite of these draconian powers, central government does not have its own local agents to execute its orders. There is nothing in Britain that remotely resembles the French prefect, a civil servant posted in a locality to implement national legislation directly. Central departments in Britain mostly lack this kind of 'field administration', as it is called, and therefore rely heavily on local governments and quangos to execute their policies. Responsibilities are laid on local authorities either by legislation (requiring them to carry out its provisions) or by central 'circulars' or 'directives' from government departments.

In other European countries the responsibility for service provision is more usually shared between different levels of government, and local discretion over both services and local taxation is greater. This helps to explain why, in the United Kingdom, the overwhelming part of local government income comes from central government in the form of grants, and more than half of all public employment is at the local level. In effect, central government pays for public services and uses local government as its administrative arm to deliver them.

Central control over English local authorities is ensured by two important legal principles, *ultra vires* and *mandamus*. This effectively places them in a straitjacket designed by central government; they must do what the law requires of them, and they must not do anything else. This means that most service activity is initiated centrally, not by local government, although in some ways local government is still accountable to its local electorate for what it does and does not do. Central government is dependent upon local government because it has no means of producing or delivering services itself. It has to: (1) somehow force the locality to comply, directly or by controlling its supply of money; (2) abolish it; or (3) transfer its powers to other bodies. All these strategies have been pursued by governments in the last 25 years, often creating intense controversy and conflict in the process.

Controversy and tension in local politics are thus paradoxically caused by the following:

- The close mutual dependency of local and central government. Local government depends on the centre for revenues, central government depends on the localities for many public services.

- Their shared democratic status, the fact that both are elected and have a 'mandate' from their respective electorates to pursue their own policies, which have often conflicted.

- The constitutional latitude that central government has to bludgeon local governments into submission – by abolition, legal action, 'capping', regulation and inspection – combined with the limited 'blocking' ability of local politicians if they do not wish to comply.

None of this makes for a happy relationship, and the potential for conflict is likely to continue, because it is built into the structure of central–local relationships. This is especially because, unlike many countries, local (and regional) governments do not have a constitutionally protected position. Instead their fate depends on the unwritten constitution and the majority party in Parliament.

Ultra vires

The legal doctrine stating that local authorities may only do that which the law expressly allows them to do.

Mandamus

The legal doctrine stating that local authorities must carry out the duties imposed on them by law.

Territorial and functional reorganisations

Two-tier local
government

Where the functions of
local government are
divided between an
upper level (counties,
for example) and a lower
level (boroughs or districts,
for example).

Unitary system

Where local functions are
controlled by only one
layer of local government.

Nowhere is the centre's legal power shown more clearly than in its ability to abolish or create local authorities. Parliamentary sovereignty and the constitutional traditions of a unitary state (Chapter 4) mean that central government can change local areas and functions more or less at will, something that it has done with great frequency since the modern system was established in the early industrial era.

The basics of the current system of local government were created by the 1888 Local Government Act that extended the franchise for local elections, established county councils for the rural areas and created a **two-tier system** in local government. County councils, the higher level, ran services affecting broad areas (planning, education and police) while lower units nested within them ran local and more personal services (housing, health and local amenities). The lower units (urban or district councils) also had elected councils and their own administration. London was organised as a county, with a second tier of boroughs beneath it. But other large cities were '**unitary**': that is, they had a single-tier city council responsible for all services. Outside England and Wales, Scotland and Ireland were organised on broadly similar lines but with differences in some of the structural detail.

This two-tier system has remained more or less intact since 1888, although it has been tinkered with, in recent times most notably in 1972, 1984–7 and 1995–6.

1972   The Local Government Act of that year rationalised and simplified the somewhat ad hoc changes implemented in 1888, but with special arrangements for Greater London and six of the larger metropolitan areas outside London.

1984–7 The Thatcher government abolished the Greater London Council and the six metropolitan counties in the largest urban areas of England, arguing that this would cut local government expenditure by high-spending city councils. It was said at the time that this was a political move designed to undermine a power base of the Labour Party rather than an administrative reform. It was also said that it would be necessary, sooner or later, to recreate a special authority to run London, and the Greater London Authority Act of 1999 duly did this.

1995–6 Local government in Wales and Scotland was reorganised into 22 and 28 unitary authorities respectively. Since the Conservatives had little to lose politically the new structure was imposed without much consultation and largely ignored local objections. In England, where the Conservatives had their own electoral base they could not afford to ignore local opinion, and local objections had to be entertained seriously. New unitary authorities emerged only where local feelings favoured them. So far as these reforms had an organisational logic, rather than a political and electoral agenda, it was to give more autonomy to certain areas on the fringes of existing counties that were in themselves strong local communities needing all-purpose local governments.

The present system of local government is outlined in Figure 12.1 and Map 12.1. In outline these look much like the figures and maps showing the local government system of 1888. A few new unitary units have intruded here and there, but there is still fragmentation of powers, not least because of special authorities for health and police, and the expansion of ad hoc bodies and quangos (see Chapter 7). Overall the picture still supports the comment made by an exasperated MP in 1871: 'The truth, sir, is that we have a chaos as regards authorities, a chaos as

Map 12.1 The new territorial organisation of local government in England, 1995

Source: HMSO

The 46 new unitary authorities

Greater London and the metropolitan counties

Two-tier authority areas

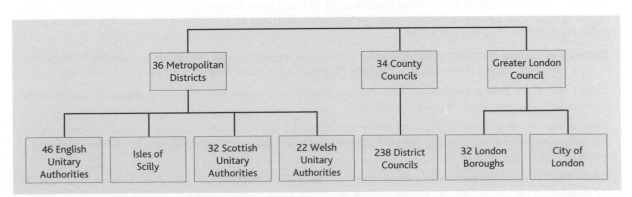

Figure 12.1 Local government structure in England, Scotland and Wales

regards rates, and a worse chaos than all as regards areas.' This is because the system has been created by ad hoc and incremental change mixed with as much political 'fixing', manipulation and boundary drawing as the government of the day thought it could get away with. Criticisms of the 1995–6 reforms were particularly bitter. They were variously described as inept, an unequivocal failure, shameless and shameful politics, a costly farce and a messy compromise. None of this helps democratic accountability and representation in the localities, dramatically shown by the confusing distribution of functions between tiers and types of local government unit shown in Table 12.1.

In retrospect, the reforms of 1972–96 were more important for what they did not change than for what they did change. In particular, the legislation failed to address three vital areas that dominate most of the debate on the shortcomings of local government in Britain today: first, the organisation of local government as a layer

BRIEFINGS

12.1 Local government reorganisations in England and Wales, 1800–2000

1800 and before   Unelected borough councils (or corporations) were gradually established by Royal Charter for some cities. Benches of magistrates and parish 'vestries' appointed by local notables provided rudimentary government in other areas.

1835 Municipal Corporations Act   Established elections (with limited suffrage) for town (borough) councils. The City of London retained its medieval corporate privileges.

1888 Local Government Act   Established the principle of a two-tier local government system with the creation of counties, with urban and district councils beneath them, all directly elected. The London County Council (LCC) was responsible for education and transport. By 1899 28 metropolitan boroughs became the lower tier of government within the London area.

1894 Local Government Act   Two-tier principle extended with the creation of urban and district councils for cities and small towns. Parish councils retained residual responsibilities in small villages.

1963   The Greater London Council was created to accommodate the continuing growth of London. The two-tier principle remained, with Greater London embracing 32 London boroughs. The GLC was responsible for transport and planning, while the Inner London Education Authority (ILEA) was retained with jurisdiction over the old LCC area.

1972 Local Government Act   The major change was the creation of 6 metropolitan counties and 36 metropolitan districts for major urban areas. In addition, the number of counties was reduced to 39 and urban and district councils replaced with 296 district councils. The two-tier principle was retained and strengthened.

1984–7   The Conservative government abolished the GLC and the metropolitan counties. Responsibilities were devolved to London boroughs, district councils (outside London) and to a variety of quangos. The two-tier principle was abandoned for large urban areas.

1995–6   A number of unitary authorities were created, but the old two-tier structure remained in many areas. In Wales the two-tier structure was abolished and replaced with 22 county and county borough councils.

1996 Local Government (Scotland) Act   Further wholesale changes involved the abolition of the regional councils and the creation of 29 unitary councils.

1999–2000   1999 Greater London Authority Act creates a new London Assembly with an elected mayor following a referendum in which 72 per cent of London voters approve the government's plans. Plans for elected mayors in other cities drawn up.

2000   New London Assembly with elected mayor is responsible for strategic planning and a range of services in the Greater London area. Ken Livingstone elected as London's first mayor.

Plate 12.1 City Hall, headquaters of the Greater London Authority and of its mayor and Assembly, was built to replace County Hall, which sold when the GLC was abolished in 1986
Source: Alamy/Simon Stanmore

Table 12.1 Local authority services in England, Scotland and Wales

	England metropolitan		England non-metropolitan		London		Scotland, Wales and England	
	Joint authorities	Boroughs/ districts	Counties	Districts	Boroughs	GLA	Joint/special authorities	Unitaries
Social services		*	*		*			*
Education		*	*		*			*
Libraries		*	*		*			*
Museums and art galleries		*	*	*	*			*
Housing		*		*				*
Planning								*
– strategic		*	*			*		
– local		*		*	*			
Highways		*	*	*	*	*		*
Traffic management		*	*		*	*		*
Passenger transport	*		*			*	*	*
Sport		*	*	*	*			*
Parks		*	*	*	*			*
Refuse collection				*	*		*	*
Refuse disposal	*	*	*		*	*	*	*
Consumer protection		*	*		*	*		*
Environmental health		*		*	*	*	*	*
Police	*		*			*	*	
Fire	*		*			*	*	

Source: T. Byrne, *Local Government in Britain*, London: Penguin Books, 2000, pp. 84–5

of the democratic system; second, the arrangements for local government finance; and third, provisions for regional government. Having looked at the last in Chapters 10 and 11, we now turn to the other two in more detail.

Local councils and how they function

The mode of operation of local government has changed in the last two decades. For much of the twentieth century it was based on council committees composed of elected members of the local council, usually in proportion to the elected strength of the parties on the council and usually controlled by the majority party or ruling coalition. These committees focused on managing various departments of the authority, such as housing, parks, libraries, local transport and social services, and they were intimately involved with both policy making and daily administration. They worked closely with their permanent staff, known as 'officers' to distinguish them from elected members. As the powers and functions of local government were reduced in the 1980s, and as much of their property and service provision was privatised, so the role of local councils changed. They turned increasingly from direct producers of services to facilitators who mapped out policies and brought together the various bodies, organisations and commercial companies involved in producing the services.

Under New Labour the system changed yet again, this time to replace the old council committees with forms of executive power based on mayors or council leaders, and cabinets. Table 12.2 shows a typical set of committees and panels for Colchester, an urban council within the administrative county of Essex.

Table 12.2 A local council: cabinet, committees and council in Colchester, 2006

The council	Consisting of 60 elected councillors (one of whom is appointed to be the politically neutral mayor) the council establishes certain policy guidelines and approves the budget.

The cabinet	Formed by the council leader, the cabinet (or executive) is responsible for daily decision making and controls virtually all the policy-making powers previously held by the committees of the council. These powers are exercised by the cabinet within the council's agreed policies. The cabinet (Conservative in this case) consists of the following roles and functions:
	Chair: the Leader of the council who also holds the strategy portfolio
	Deputy Chair: Deputy Leader also holding the regeneration and partnerships portfolio
	Members: Street services and waste portfolio
	            Business, tourism and leisure portfolio
	            Planning and transportation portfolio
	            Housing and community services portfolio
	            Communications and rural issues portfolio
	            Assets and resources portfolio

Committees and panels

Finance and Audit Scrutiny Panel	Chair and 8 members
Licensing Committee	Chair and 13 members
Local Development Framework Panel	Chair and 7 members
Policy Scrutiny Panel	3 members plus outside members and representatives
Strategic Overview and Scrutiny Panel	Chair and 8 members
Planning Committee	Chair and 11 members
Standards Committee	Chair and 3 members

Local democracy, like parliamentary democracy, is also party democracy. If one party holds a majority of council seats, policy may be decided at a party meeting. Party discipline will generally ensure that party decisions are voted in as council policy, even if individual councillors disagree with them. The cabinet is formed by the council leader, much as the Prime Minister forms the Cabinet in national government.

The cabinet structure of local councils is, of course, roughly similar to that of national government. The difference at the local level is that competition between three or more parties often results in coalitions, or in no overall party control. Table 12.3 reports the distribution of party control across England and Wales, showing the extent to which coalition or minority government has become the usual state of affairs in many local authorities.

Where there is a coalition, committee chairs are distributed between the parties. In some cases they are also given to minority parties to get their support, in which event the meetings of the separate parties are necessarily less effective in determining policy. It then tends to be decided by inter-party negotiations on central coordinating committees. The absence of a majority party, therefore, makes the council as a whole more important, as it would Parliament (Chapter 18).

Corresponding to each main local function there is an administrative department of local government with a chief officer, who usually attends council and committee meetings and takes instructions from them. Depending on their area of responsibility, local officials are often professionally trained with specialised qualifications and experience. Public health requires a medical person, and public works requires architects and engineers, although the shift from service providers to service 'facilitators' makes this less important now than it used to be.

Traditionally, administrative coordination was handled by a town clerk who was usually a solicitor, but most councils now have a chief executive officer or manager with business experience and qualifications in administration, who leads the permanent staff of the council. This reflects general tendencies in society towards more training and experience in the methods of modern administration. We should not assume, however, that local government is only about administration. Its history over the past 100 years and more is, in large part, the history of the growth of local politics.

Table 12.3 Councillors and parties in local government, 2006

Councillors			
England	19,894	Scotland	2,219
Wales	1,268	Northern Ireland	582
		Total	23,963

There are another 80,000 councillors in the town and community councils of England and Wales.

Parties in England and Wales		
	Councillors	Councils controlled
Conservative	8,069	156
Labour	6,014	79
Lib. Dem.	4,568	31
Independent	2,133	12
Plaid Cymru	173	1
No overall control		131
Total	20,957	410

Parties and political control

Local government has become steadily more party political since the Conservatives started building local organisations to get out the vote after the 1884 Reform Act. But the process was accelerated in the 1990s when two things happened:

1. The Conservative governments from 1979 to 1997 cut financial support for services, forcing local councils to make highly political decisions about if and what to cut.

2. The parties excluded from power at the centre became more radical in the localities and, where they took power, sometimes chose to oppose central government cuts outright, thereby sparking off unprecedented confrontation and crisis.

It was the Liberals who first built themselves up locally with a form of community politics that concentrated on local issues and grievances that sometimes provoked confrontation with bureaucratic and unresponsive Labour councils. This tactic gained the Liberals widespread local support, which stimulated Labour to base their national recovery on local politics. Labour and Liberal successes were also helped by the fact that local elections were held annually and their results often reflected popular discontent with the party in power in central government (the mid-term effect). Thus councils became increasingly Labour and Liberal dominated from 1979 to such an extent that only 6 per cent were left in Conservative hands in 1997. The result was that the party divisions in national politics were increasingly found in local politics as well.

The spread of party politics across local government has rather important consequences for national government, which also underline the close association between national and local:

■ The decline of party membership has been counterbalanced by the emergence of a body of some 23,000 locally elected party politicians who sit on the councils of local government.

■ Party activists have often been thought of as idealists and ideologues whose lack of first-hand political experience causes them to be more extreme, pure, and impractical in their political views. In reality, local activists are often fully immersed in pragmatic local politics, and they constitute an important group both among New Labour and Liberal Democrats in Parliament: two-thirds of New Labour MPs and 70 per cent of Liberal Democrats in the 1997 Parliament had been local councillors with hands-on experience of the practicalities of local government.

Money and power in local government

Money was at the centre of the battle between central and local government in the 1980s. Up until then local revenues were traditionally based on the 'rates', a tax based on the notional rental value of residential and commercial property. For many years the rating system worked moderately well, but the tax raised less than half of local income, and the shortfall was increasingly made up by central government grants, known as the rate support grant (RSG). This was designed to equalise the financial resources of rich and poor authorities, and did so to some degree according to a complicated formula that took account of the wealth and needs of authorities.

During the 1970s pressure grew in some circles to abolish the rates because:

- There was a widespread myth that they were unfair because only the property-owning middle classes paid them. In fact, tenants paid them indirectly, but 'invisibly' as part of their rent. And far from being unfair to the property-owning middle class, the rates were actually a mildly **regressive form of taxation** in which the poor paid proportionately more.

- The size of the RSG grew as local government costs increased. In the late 1930s the RSG stood at around 30 per cent of total local spending, but by 1977 it was closer to 60 per cent. The Conservative government of the 1980s claimed this encouraged councils to overspend money they did not have to raise.

- Adjusting the rates to pay for a larger proportion of local services was politically difficult. With inflation and house prices rising rapidly, adjustments resulted in *apparently* sharp increases in the rates – although, in fact, the real costs barely rose at all as a percentage of disposable household income.

Between 1979 and 1989 central government used its power of control over the RSG to reduce local spending. It employed more and more draconian measures to force local authorities to comply, including grant cuts, punishing authorities that exceeded their centrally determined spending ceilings by clawing back more in grants than the authority overspent, and **rate capping**. In the end, some members of the left-wing Liverpool City Council refused to comply with government directives and were personally bankrupted.

These extraordinary events strengthened the government's conviction that fundamental reform was needed of the local government finance system. From a number of alternatives, however, the government chose the one that was the least effective, the least efficient, and the most likely to arouse opposition: the **community charge or 'poll tax'** as it was generally known. The idea behind the poll tax was simple: every individual adult living in a particular area would pay a flat charge to the local council. The charge would be reduced for the poor and the disadvantaged, but the vast majority of people would pay the same amount, whether owners of a stately home or tenants of a slum flat.

Defenders of the tax argued that the poll tax, though initially very unpopular, would attract support for the following reasons:

- its high visibility would make a clear connection between the cost of local services and paying taxes for them

- it would apply to all residents, and therefore force everyone to weigh up the cost of local services against taxes

- it would make councils more accountable for their policies and therefore force spending down.

Critics of the tax – most of the population – argued that the poll tax was 'the worst idea in the world', because:

- it was unworkably difficult and expensive to collect

- it was highly regressive and unfair

- it had been abolished in all civilised countries centuries before

- it would discourage people from voting because the poll tax list was widely believed to be the local electoral registration list, and some people would avoid getting on to the poll tax list.

Regressive taxation

Where lower income groups pay proportionately more in taxation than higher income groups.

Rate capping

The practice introduced in the 1980s whereby central government set a maximum rate level for local government in an attempt to control their expenditure.

Community charge or 'poll tax'

The local tax that replaced the rates (or property tax), in which every adult resident of a local authority paid the same amount. It came into operation in 1990 and was replaced by the council tax in 1993.

BRIEFINGS

12.2 What is the best system of local government finance?

Type of tax system	For	Against
Rates (up to 1989 in Scotland, 1990 in England and Wales)	Well established (until abolition) and easy and cheap to collect	Subject to *apparently* large increases during periods of inflation. Falls only on residential and commercial property owners. Difficult for central government to control
Community charge (poll tax) 1989–93	A flat rate tax everybody has to pay. Simple and highly visible so should provide an electoral check on high-spending local authorities	Proved very difficult and expensive to collect. Very regressive. Highly unpopular
Council tax (1993 onwards)	Relatively simple and easy to collect. Levied on households, but the amount paid is determined by the value of the properties, which are placed in value bands. It assumes a two-person household, but rebates are available for single people, the poor and the disadvantaged	Banding can be arbitrary. May prove as unpopular as the rates during periods of inflation. Progressive element is linked to property values rather than income or ability to pay
Uniform business rate (effective since 1990/1)	Easy to collect and to understand. Linked to property values as with the old rating system	Not really a local tax at all as the revenue goes to the central government, which then redistributes it to localities. Unpopular with small businesses. Can be regressive as it is unrelated to the profit or turnover of business
Local income tax	Easy to collect and to adjust. Strongly progressive and linked to the ability to pay. Highly visible and accountable	Could be inflationary and encourage spending. Not amenable to control by central governments and therefore unlikely to be adopted in Britain outside Scotland, where the Scottish Parliament has limited powers to raise income tax for the whole of the Scottish jurisdiction
Local sales tax	Could be hidden in prices (such as VAT). Its 'invisibility' makes it less unpopular than more visible taxes. Easy to collect	Highly regressive and unrelated to ability to pay. Its invisibility reduces accountability. As with income tax, highly unlikely to be adopted because central government cannot control spending levels

Council tax

The local tax that replaced the community charge in 1993 in which, like the rates, payment is related to property values and levied on all occupants of property.

The critics proved right: the introduction of the community charge was one of the most disasterous policy mistakes in British government in the twentieth century. It was expensive to collect (in some poorer areas collection costs exceeded revenues), was socially unjust, and became so unpopular as to provoke widespread protests and serious civil disturbance. It was also a major cause of Thatcher's downfall. When John Major became leader, a new local tax was the first priority of the government.

What emerged was the **council tax** and the uniform business rate. The former is similar to the old rating system. Every property is rated in one of seven (later eight) bands of property value (A to H), and the tax falls on the current occupant of the property. Rebates are available for the poor and the disadvantaged. The tax has worked without too much public attention or adverse publicity, it has proved easy to collect and an element of fairness was incorporated into the banding system by weighting the tax towards the occupants of more expensive properties. Part of its success is also due to the simple fact that it accounts for a smaller and smaller proportion of local expenditure.

In retrospect it is difficult to understand the whole poll tax business. It was based on political myths about the old rating system that were easily destroyed; it chose the worst from the list of available options; it was forced on the country by a tiny minority against the better judgement of a huge majority of politicians and financial experts; it proved, as widely predicted, to be a hugely expensive and wasteful disaster; and it was replaced by something close to the old rating system. After all the organisational turmoil, costs and civil disturbance, the country went back to pretty much where it started.

Councillors and officers

Elected councillors

As elected representatives local councillors are involved in local policy making, the administration of services, the representation of interests, and in community and political leadership. They are not paid for this, although they receive expenses and attendance allowances for approved duties. A complicated electoral system exists whereby county councillors are elected every four years, but the timing of district council elections can be varied. Districts can hold elections concurrently with county council elections, or at the mid-term of county elections, or by thirds, that is, one-third of district councillors elected every year that there is no county council election. All elections are held on the first Thursday in May. Eligibility is different from national elections: Commonwealth citizens may vote, as may citizens of the EU.

Council members are not typical of the population. They are:

- generally older than the general population, with an average age of almost 58 in 2004, when 87 per cent were aged 45 or older, compared with 54 per cent of the population

- mostly male, although there are proportionately more women in local councils (29 per cent) than even the highest level in the House of Commons (20 per cent in 2005)

- more middle class, and more likely to be professionals, employers or managers (about two-thirds)

- disproportionately drawn from the white majority, with 3.5 per cent drawn from ethnic minorities compared with 8.4 per cent of the population

- better educated, with about half having higher and further education qualifications (NVQ Level 4 and above)

- disproportionately retired people – 39 per cent of councillors compared with 23 per cent of the population.

The unrepresentative nature of councils probably has a lot to do with the fact that councillors are not paid. Therefore the job attracts either those who are retired, not in the labour market (10 per cent), or self-employed (about one in six) who can organise their day around council meetings. Councillors are more professional and politicised than before, with the average councillor spending more than 21 hours a week on council and political work, leaders and chairs putting in an average of 25 hours. The average councillor has served for eight years. The 1986 Widdecombe Report into the conduct of local authority business recommended pay for councillors and a formal recognition of the role of political parties, but the government rejected these suggestions.

Officers

Elected council members are supported by a full-time, paid professional and managerial staff. There are about 750,000 of them in local government (amounting to rather more than a quarter of all local government employees), and in many ways they are organised along the same lines and perform the same kinds of jobs as the national Civil Service. The senior ranks are professionally qualified and highly experienced, and they have a national career structure with a tightly integrated set of organisations that helps the rapid communication of information about technical and policy matters (see Chapter 7).

Chief executives and chief officers

Like permanent secretaries in their Whitehall departments, local government has chief officers such as the chief fire officer, director of social services, education officer, chief financial officer, a registration officer (for elections) and (most usually) a chief executive officer (CEO), who also acts as the 'head of paid service' and often acts as a 'monitoring officer' who is responsible for reporting any illegal or improper council activity. There were 407 chief executives and 7,187 chief officers in England and Wales in 2005.

Political impartiality

Like the Civil Service, local government officers are required to be politically neutral, and serve whichever party or coalition is in power. By convention they refrain from open support of parties, and under the Local Government and Housing Act 1989 senior officers are not allowed to stand for political office or engage in party political activity.

Professional management

Many local services are of a highly technical nature – education, health, refuse collection and disposal, traffic management etc. – so local government officers have long been more specialised and professional than the generalists of the Civil Service. In recent years they have also become caught up by the new public management language and practices: mission statements and visions, best practice, loose–tight structures, leadership competencies, ongoing and additional efficiencies, comprehensive performance assessments, enhancement, new burdens procedure, capacity building and multi-project scheduling are the order of the day.

Dictatorship of the official?

Like civil servants (see Chapter 6), the chief officers of local government are sometimes accused of running the show, using their professional training, experience and ambition to dominate their nominal political masters – the part-time, amateur and untrained elected councillors. Officers are also accused of being lazy, time-serving, incompetent and old-fashioned bureaucrats. Both these stereotypes are rejected by analysts who argue, more plausibly, that council officers and councillors depend upon each other and form a joint elite.

Local government and democracy

Most democratic theorists agree that local democracy is an essential part of the system of government for several reasons:

- **Size and subsidiarity** Other things being equal, small-scale democracy is better than large-scale democracy. Participation is easier, knowledge of local issues is greater, and the gap between voters and leaders is smaller. This is similar to what the EU calls the principle of subsidiarity (Chapter 9).

- **Efficiency** Local people with a knowledge of special local conditions are likely to make more sensible and efficient decisions than central bureaucrats. In any case, there is no reason for a Whitehall office to make decisions about the opening time of public libraries in Cornwall.

- **Training ground for democracy** Local government is a democratic training ground that gives citizens first-hand experience of how to organise public affairs.

- **Experimentation** It is easier to experiment with services on a small local scale: failures are not large and expensive, and successes can easily be transferred to other authorities.

- **Pool of talent** Local government provides a pool of experienced political talent that can be recruited into national politics.

- **Pluralism** Many different political arenas, and a fragmentation of political power between different levels of the political system is a democratic virtue.

Nevertherless, the scope for local democracy in Britain in the twentieth century seems to have shrunk progressively over the years. The usual complaint is that every government claims that it will decentralise and democratise when it comes to power, but then centralises and undermines local government with a fresh wave of reforms. The result is that in spite of the protestations of national governments, Britain has become one of the most highly centralised political systems among all the western democracies (at least so far as England is concerned). What explains this strange pattern? It seems to have a lot to do with technical matters relating to size and efficiency, and with ideological matters of party politics.

The division of functions, and size and efficiency

One of the most enduring debates in democratic theory concerns the proper division of powers between different levels of government. It is generally agreed that central government should be responsible for such things as national defence, macroeconomic planning and European Community policy, while local government should handle local services such as parks, street lighting and refuse. In between, however, there are a large number of services that can be assigned to either national or regional or local government, or run jointly by any combination of these. Services that might be shared are education, health, housing, social welfare, public transport, highways, police, regional and local development, and planning. In most democratic countries responsibilities of these kinds are normally shared between two or more levels of government.

BRIEFINGS

12.3 Division of functions among different levels of government

With the growth of powers of the European Union, and the devolution of power by central governments to regional and local governments, the debate about which level of government should do what has received fresh impetus in recent discussions about subsidiarity. Unfortunately, which level is best at doing what is usually a matter of tradition or political expediency rather than efficiency or fairness. As long ago as 1861 the political philosopher John Stuart Mill argued that there are three levels of responsibility:

■ the purely local, where such tasks as street cleaning, lighting and refuse collection should be performed

■ those where because of 'spillovers' to other areas, such as education or policing, the central government should administer policy

■ those areas such as sanitation and welfare where the central government should set minimum standards but localities should administer and pay for the services.

Writing in the US context, the political scientist Paul Peterson has argued that:

■ central government should play a major role in redistributive policies such as income support (welfare), pensions, health and housing

■ lower levels of government should provide what he calls developmental policies – such things as sanitation, transport, education and utilities.

In fact this division is not so very different from that which prevails in Britain today, except that successive governments have privatised or centralised many of the developmental policies.

One thing is for sure: debate over the proper division of responsibility, including which level of government should pay for what, will continue for many years. There is no simple, uniform or rational solution. Circumstances change, making it necessary to change the allocations of function. The debate will probably intensify following Scottish and Welsh devolution and the possible creation of regional governments in England.

At this point a second set of arguments are introduced about the most efficient size of local authorities. It is usually assumed that small is beautiful so far as local democracy is concerned, but there is inconclusive debate about size and economic efficiency because there are different factors to consider.

1. Some services are efficiently produced on a small scale (parks, refuse collection, libraries), others on a larger scale (refuse disposal, higher education, police).

2. Services are not isolated from each other – housing has to be related to transport, schools and shops – and there is a need for a body that can plan and integrate them.

3. Local authorities should have a tax base adequate for their purposes, and it is unwise to cut off the inner city from its suburbs when suburban commuters and visitors make heavy use of city services.

4. Allowance should be made for local geography (mountains, rivers), traditions and history.

These points suggest that we need general-purpose authorities to plan and integrate local services in a sensible way, but that there is no optimum size for general-purpose authorities given the range of services they should plan and integrate, and the different technical circumstances applying to each of them. To make things worse, circumstances change as technology develops, and as residential and business patterns change.

This explains why there is no optimum size for general-purpose authorities, and why local government has been reformed so often in an attempt to square the circle of optimality. Given the lack of any clear-cut answers to technical and economic questions, ideology and party interest has generally filled the vacuum to guide many of the reforms of the twentieth century, especially those of 1979–97.

Local government revolution, 1979–97

Local government changed in the first part of the twentieth century in response to changing social, economic and political circumstances. As cities grew to form larger and larger continuously built-up areas, so the number of local authorities was reduced to cover them. Important service functions were removed from local authority responsibility (health, police, water) and given to larger special bodies, while central government imposed stricter controls over the financing and provision of the services that were left at the local level. These processes of consolidation and centralisation characterise practically the whole of the twentieth century, but they moved further and faster than ever in the 1980s and 1990s:

1. **Financial centralisation**   Local taxing powers were cut, and central grants increased, so giving central government more power of the purse over local government. This was intended to cut local spending significantly, and local current expenditure fell from its all time high of 8.6 per cent of total national domestic expenditure in 1975/6 to 7.6 per cent in 1993/4. Capital spending was under almost total central control and fell much faster. Total local government employment (including teachers, police officers, firefighters and social service workers) fell from 2,360,000 in 1979 to 1,971,000 in 1998.

2. **Privatisation and deregulation**   Many services previously provided by local governments were privatised or opened up to private competition. Bus and rapid transit systems, street cleaning and refuse collection, and the care of parks (among many others) were privatised. Compulsory competitive tendering (CCT) became obligatory for a range of services in 1988 and extended to almost all services in 1992. It compelled councils to put some services out to competitive, private sector tendering, and for the councils' own workforce to compete with them if they were to win contracts.

3. **Council house sales**   Between 1980 and 1996 2.2 million dwellings previously owned by local authorities were sold to sitting tenants or housing associations.

4. **Educational reform**   Local authority responsibility for education, easily the most expensive local service, was reduced or eliminated. Polytechnics (now universities) were removed from local control, the management of schools (including decisions over hiring and firing and resource allocation) were devolved to school governors, and schools were given the opportunity to 'opt out' of local government funding altogether in favour of direct financing from the central government. The opt-out rate has been low, but has tended to involve higher-status secondary schools. The introduction of the National Curriculum, testing for standards of both teachers and pupils, and the publication of performance tables, all tightened the central grip on education.

Implications for local democracy

These changes were enormously controversial, some arguing that local democracy had been emasculated, others that it became modern, efficient and responsive to citizens. The changes were not necessarily bad in themselves and some, such as the sale of council houses, have been popular in some circles, although they have highly adverse consequences for the poor and homeless. There is no doubt, however, that they have changed the nature of local government. Instead of providing national programmes and tempering them to the needs of the locality, they have become purchasers of local services and thus constrained by the guidelines laid down by central government (cheapest bids) and the alternatives offered by the market.

There are two opposing views about the effect of these changes on local democracy.

Enabling or facilitating role of local democracy

The first view is that it has changed the role of local governments from providers of public services according to local needs and demands to enablers or facilitators of a range of policies decided on by central government or by the market. By enabling is meant the assessment of needs, and the organisation and purchase of services to meet them, rather than the direct provision of services by local authorities themselves. At best, the 'enabling authority' is the central player that coordinates formal and informal networks of organisations (government bodies, quangos, businesses and voluntary organisations) that think imaginatively about local problems and the public services to solve them. At worst, enabling means reducing the political power of local authorities and degrading the quality of local services by turning them over to the cheapest supplier. It may also cause the further erosion of the link between citizens and local services.

Some commentators argue that the link between local citizens and local government was already weak because local authorities are little more than an agent of

BRIEFINGS

12.4 Politicisation of local government in Britain

Party politics were introduced into local government by the Conservatives who organised themselves locally after the 1867 and 1884 Reform Acts in order to try to capture the vote of the newly enfranchised population. For the first half of the twentieth century, however, local government in Britain was relatively free of party politics. Elections in the large urban areas were organised along party lines and councillors organised into party groups, but many councillors in the smaller and rural authorities were labelled 'independents', 'ratepayers' or 'homeowners', although they were often Conservatives in all but name. Many seats in local elections were uncontested, and many councillors were willing to serve the community provided they were spared the embarrassment of an election. From the 1960s onwards more seats were contested, and candidates increasingly stood as representatives for the main national parties. Majority parties (sometimes coalitions) took control of committees and the leadership of the council.

The politicisation of local government reached new heights in the 1980s, which saw fierce battles between opposing party groups over such contentious issues as council house sales, secondary education and the poll tax. Some left-wing inner city councils also became associated with a variety of issues (gay rights and nuclear policy), which infuriated the Conservative government. It reacted with the abolition of the Greater London Council and the six metropolitan authorities, and the progressive reduction of local government responsibilities and taxing capacity.

At the 1984 Conservative Conference the government announced that the Widdecombe Committee would look into the conduct of local councils. It recommended a number of reforms to strengthen local democracy, but these were generally passed over by the government. Instead it banned the use of local authority resources for politically motivated publicity and advertising.

central government and the provider of its national services. The link is also weak because local elections are no longer fought primarily on local issues but depend on the popularity or unpopularity of national governments.

Some on the political right go further and claim that market provision of services is the best guarantee of quality and value for money, so there is little need for elected local government at all. The job of the enabling authority might simply be taken over by a skilled negotiator who would arrange for the best services to be delivered by private companies at the lowest cost. Such a perspective is difficult to reconcile with the fact that the vast majority of the public do regard a range of services as best provided by a government that is directly accountable to its citizens, and that local provision is the best guarantee of public accountability. Whether it is market forces or political accountability that matters, it is worth noting the striking fact that emerges from most surveys on the matter – most citizens are well satisfied with their local government services (Briefing 12.5).

In many western democracies accountability is maintained by a close link between locally raised taxes and the provision of local services, ensuring that the public knows what it is paying and what it is getting for its taxes. In Britain this link has been eroded by ever-increasing central control over local government finance and by central grants accounting for an ever-increasing proportion of local expenditure. As a White Paper on local government finance concluded in 1986: 'Local accountability depends crucially on the relationship between paying for local services and voting in local elections. As this link has been evaded, so local democracy has been weakened.'

An expanding role for local democracy?

The second view of the changing role of local government concentrates attention on democracy, not public services. The role of enabler and facilitator is not at all trivial, for it gives councils some power to decide from whom to purchase services, how best to deliver them, and at what quality, quantity and cost. It also releases them from the large-scale, routine administrative tasks of having to provide services themselves. Local councils can now concentrate on their relations with local citizens, who are the customers for services.

BRIEFINGS

12.5 Satisfaction with local services?

It is certainly true that local services have been subjected to strong criticism in certain instances, and service quality may have suffered during the poll tax years, but generally speaking most people seem to be satisfied with their services most of the time:

1. The **Audit Commission**: 'The best of local government is better than the private sector and much better than the NHS or Whitehall at delivering services.'

2. The **Consumers' Association**: two-thirds thought local services good value for money and 80 per cent were satisfied overall.

3. The **Widdecombe Committee**: more than 70 per cent of respondents were very or fairly satisfied with the performance of their councils.

4. The Audit Commission's **Comprehensive Performance Assessment** of all single-tier and county councils in 2005 found that over 70 per cent of councils had improved strongly or well since the previous assessment in 2002, and that more than two-thirds of them performed consistently well in all parts of the evaluation.

In contradiction to this line of argument it might be said that the enabling authority in Britain is essentially a weak one that is not in a good position to provide democratic government. On the one hand it is subject to the stringent controls of the centre, and on the other it is the prisoner of market forces and competing private businesses. It has little power in taxing matters, and little discretion over important decisions about services. In such a straitjacket it can scarcely be held accountable for most of what it does, and hence local democracy and political accountability is largely, though not wholly, symbolic.

When New Labour was elected to government in 1997 it was concerned about both the quality of local services and the quality of local democracy, and set about implementing policies intended to improve both.

New Labour: local democracy and service quality

New Labour accepted many of the Thatcher–Major reforms of local government, as it did with central administration (Chapter 7). It is revealing to list the things it left in place:

1. **Boundaries and structure**   The old local government boundaries have been left intact, and the old structures largely so (see Figure 12.1).

2. **Powers**   Local government was left with pretty much the same list of service responsibilities as before.

3. **Finance**   Central government continued to control local spending and kept its rate-capping powers for authorities thought to be overspending.

4. **Central control**   New Labour showed little enthusiasm for lifting central government controls over local government, on the contrary by setting performance targets it tightened them.

Nonetheless, New Labour came to power with cogent and thought-out plans for local government reform, centring on the dual concerns of improved service quality and the renewal of local democracy. These were implemented through the Local Government Acts of 1999 and 2000.

New organisation   The Local Government Act 2000 gives local authorities a choice of four new forms of government (see Briefing 12.6). The great majority chose the system with an indirectly elected leader/mayor (usually selected by the majority party), a cabinet, and a council and committees with monitoring and scrutinising powers. This is similar in many ways to the Westminster system of Prime Minister, Cabinet and elected House of Commons, and not so very different from the old local government system of a council with a council leader and committees. Supporters of the reform argue that this encourages modern political management, opponents that it simply creates a new and smaller local political elite.

Best value options   The 1999 Act replaced compulsory competitive tendering with best value options, which allowed local authorities either to choose the best private sector offer (not necessarily the cheapest) or to deliver the service itself. Either way it had to produce a performance plan, showing that it has chosen the 'best value' option, and have this plan approved by the Best Value Inspectorate, which is part of the Audit Commission. Councils failing to meet national standards may lose their service powers. Hackney and Leeds have had some education transferred to private direction for this reason.

BRIEFINGS

12.6 New Labour's council constitutions

1. **Leader and cabinet**   The leader is elected by the council, and the cabinet is either appointed by the leader or elected by the council from a single party or a coalition of parties. The great majority of councils (82 per cent) have chosen this option.

2. **Directly elected mayor and cabinet**   The mayor is directly elected by the population for a four-year term of office, and selects a cabinet from among the members of the council who belong to a majority party or a coalition. Ten councils (4 per cent) have chosen this option.

3. **Mayor and council manager**   Imported from the United States, this system has a directly elected mayor who is similar to a non-executive chairperson in a business, and a manager who is a powerful chief executive with responsibility for both policy and management. Only the city of Stoke-on-Trent has chosen this option.

4. **Alternative arrangements**   Available to councils with a population of less than 85,000, or those that have rejected a referendum for an elected mayor, this system creates a council with greater policy-making powers and a smaller committee system. Fifty-nine councils (15 per cent) have chosen this option.

Services   The Local Government Act 2000 gives local authorities the power to promote the economic, social and environmental well-being of their communities. Authorities that are judged to perform well in these and other services areas can be awarded 'beacon' status, which gives them some extra autonomy from central government and some extra taxing capacity.

Local strategic partnerships   With the shift from service provision to facilitating, and from local government to local governance, local authorities are now supposed to enter into partnerships to produce public services with public agencies and quangos, businesses and voluntary organisations. In Tony Blair's words their 'distinctive leadership role will be to weave and knit together the contribution of various stakeholders', rather than directly to deliver all these services themselves. Public/private partnerships (PPPs) and private finance initiatives are to be the main instruments of local governance.

London government   Reform of London government has had a lot of media attention, partly because a directly elected mayor and 25-member Assembly are genuinely radical innovations, and partly because the unofficial Labour candidate, Ken Livingstone, easily saw off his Conservative and Labour opponents in the first election (2000), to the embarrassment of the Labour government – forcing it to accept him back as an official Labour candidate for the second election (2004).

Electoral systems   The Greater London Authority, the Scottish and Welsh Assembly, and directly elected mayors are elected by the supplementary vote system, not the first past the post system (see Chapter 15).

Devolution   The creation of the Scottish Assembly with powers to restructure local government has resulted in reforms, particularly in the electoral system (to STV). The Welsh Assembly has more limited powers to amend but not make primary legislation about local government.

As with its national constitutional project, Labour seemed to have lost its reforming way for local government after the general election of 2001. This was partly because of the failure of plans for English regional authorities following the rejection of a referendum in the north-east of England in 2004.

More concrete and more specific is New Labour's recent pursuit of choice in public services as a way of getting them to respond to consumer demands rather

Plate 12.2 Ken Livingston, Leader of the Greater London Council (GLC) 1981–86, Member of Parliament, 1987–2002, and Mayor of the Greater London Authority (GLA), 2000 to the present day. Known as 'Red Ken' because of his outspoken left-wing views, Livingston is a controversial political figure whose position in the old GLC and the current GLA has given him national visibility

Source: Nicola Jennings/ The Guardian

than what a few service-producing professionals regard as desirable. All too often, it claimed, public services are of the 'one size fits all' kind. The word 'choice' became politically important as the government argued that people should be able to choose their school, their hospital and their doctor, among other public service providers. The problem with so much emphasis on choice, critics argued, is that it is only one of a range of features that people look for in their services – quality, accessibility, accountability and social justice are also important. Asked about choice in social surveys, many citizens respond that they do not want a choice of railway companies, schools, hospitals or refuse disposers, they just want good services. There is not much advantage in having choice if the best hospital or school is 30 miles away and difficult to get to.

Labour's new big idea for local government, announced in 2006, is 'double devolution'. This means devolving from central government to local government, and devolving from local government to community government. This form of 'new localism' involves recognising that there are many more centres of local life than the local authority, including schools, hospitals, water and bus companies, as well as thousands of quangos, special-purpose authorities, and public/private partnerships. The general idea is that these services and organisations should be democratised and made accountable to their users by directly electing boards and committees. The experience of elected boards for the new hospital trusts in 2004 was not a great success, however, because few signed up to be members and even fewer voted.

The question is whether these accumulated changes will do much for local democracy when the basic structures of service delivery inherited from the 1980s and early 1990s are left in place. Reviving local democracy would seem to call for a fairly radical reform that gives local government real control over local taxes and services. This means a tax that is capable of raising real money, if that is what local people want, and less central control over the general contours and small details of services. It means making thousands of local quangos more accountable to the public, and it also means changing the top-down and highly centralised policies of

CONTROVERSY

Improving local democracy

The problem

Local election turn-out is lower in the United Kingdom than in almost any other western democracy, and falling; local government units are larger than in almost any other western democracy; local government has fewer financial powers than most other western democracies; and local government is subject to closer control by national government than in most other western democracies.

Some solutions?

1. Create smaller authorities to encourage local democracy. The problem is that local election turn-out is not closely related to local authority size. Turn-out in the London mayoral election in 2004 was just under 37 per cent, substantially higher than turn-out in the much smaller district elections of 2003.

2. Change the voting system to one that is more proportional. This may increase local election turn-out, but not a lot. However, it would break one-party (largely Labour) dominance of councils.

3. Allow local authorities to create small area committees (as the Local Government Act, 2000 does) to encourage community participation. The problem is that community and parish councils do not arouse great participatory enthusiasm.

4. Create directly elected mayors and cabinets. Executive mayors may attract local interest (e.g. Ken Livingstone). The danger is that they may make local decision making less democratic by creating a strong executive and a weak council which does not attract active or high-calibre members. Concentrating attention on mayors may also erode interest in the lower tier of city government.

5. Create unitary authorities because the two-tier system is confusing and lacks direct accountability. The problem is that election turn-out in unitary authorities is not much different from two-tier authorities.

6. Give local authorities more power, so that electors know that serious decisions are taken at the local level. Most know that local government does not count as much as central government and so few take much interest or know much about local affairs. Surveys show that if something went wrong with council decisions citizens are as likely to turn to their MP as their local councillor. There are various ways of giving local authorities more power:

- Give more discretion over local taxation. Central grants would still be necessary, to ensure equalisation of financial capacity between rich and poor areas. But they could be reduced considerably if local authorities were given greater tax-raising powers.

- Give local government more service responsibilities, so reversing the trend of the last 70 or 80 years.

- Remove the dead hand of *ultra vires*, giving local authorities more discretion.

- Reduce central government's regulation, monitoring and control of local services. New Labour is currently making the central regime tighter, not looser.

It seems that the most effective way of improving local democracy, participation and election turn-out is to give local government more power over taxes and services. The problem is that while most post-war governments have paid lip-service to more local autonomy, they have actually tightened central control. There is, however, a last option, which should not be forgotten.

7. Forget about local democracy, and concentrate on improving local service quality and efficiency. Repeated surveys show that citizens are generally quite satisfied with local services. Perhaps one way ahead is simply to recognise that local democracy is not particularly important in the British system of government, and concentrate instead on raising service performance to a still higher level? This may be difficult because the indications (see the Audit Commission's Comprehensive Performance Assessments) are that local government is already performing to a high standard and getting better, and there may be limited room for still more improvement.

joined-up government and target setting, so that local organisations are set free to deliver their own services in their own way. At the moment, local government is scheduled by the Gershon efficiency review to contribute some £6.5 billion to the public expenditure cuts by 2007–8. It is not easy to see how this fits with new localism and double devolution.

Summary

- Conflict and tension is built into the very structure of central–local government relations in Britain, partly because both have a democratic legitimacy and partly because central government is heavily dependent upon local government for the delivery of services but has its own ideas about how best to do this. As the 'creature' of central government, local authorities are accountable to their citizens but must conform to the tight and exacting requirements of the centre.

- The local government system has been subjected to ceaseless change, reform and restructuring by central government, which has tried to square the circle of an optimum size for local efficiency and democracy.

- The most recent rounds of reform from the 1970s onwards have turned local authorities from the providers of public services to facilitators who plan and coordinate service delivery.

- New Labour has devolved power to new regional authorities in Scotland, Wales and London but it has maintained tight control over other local authorities by means of financial powers, target setting, auditing and best value financial arrangements. It has put much effort into improving local service quality, but been less successful in strengthening local democracy.

- It is unlikely that local government will be given new taxing powers. For this reason the close accountability linkage between local voters, local taxation and local policies, which is the essence of local democracy in many countries, is unlikely to develop in Britain.

MILESTONES

Milestones in local government in Britain

1888 and 1894	Local Government Acts create the local government structure that prevails until the 1970s
1966	Creation of the Greater London Council
1967	Redcliffe-Maud Commission on Local Government
1972	Local Government Act rationalises the system of local government and creates metropolitan counties and districts
1975	Local government reorganised in Scotland
1976	Local Government and Planning Act: overspending curbed, sale of council houses compulsory
1984–6	GLC and metropolitan counties abolished. Local transport subsidies curbed
1986	Widdecombe Report recommends major changes to role of political parties in local government. Only minor changes made in the ensuing legislation
1987	Central government grants are fixed to expenditure
1988	Government announces abolition of rates, creation of community charge and uniform business rate, plus other measures including the opting out of schools
1989	Poll tax (community charge) introduced in Scotland

Milestones in local government in Britain continued

1990	Poll tax introduced in England and Wales
1991	Government announces phasing out of poll tax and introduction of a replacement council tax
1994–6	Two-tier local government systems abolished in Scotland and Wales. Some unitary authorities created in England
1997	Referendum in Scotland produces a four to one majority for the creation of a Scottish Parliament and three to one majority for the Parliament to have tax-raising powers. Referendum in Wales produces a very small majority for a Welsh Assembly. Plans for devolution to English regions in doubt
1998	Referendum on directly elected executive mayor for London. Local Government Act introduces best value system
1999	Local Government Act replaces CCT with best value
2000	Local Government Act introduces directly elected mayors and cabinet. Representation of the People Act – directly elected mayors elected by the supplementary vote system. Independent candidate Ken Livingstone elected as first Mayor of London
2001	White Paper on *Strong Local Leadership: Quality Public Services*
2002	First election for directly elected mayors outside London
2004	A referendum in the north-east of England rejects a proposal for a regional authority. Government discussion paper on *The Future of Local Government: Developing a 10-year Vision*
2006	Plans for double devolution revealed.

Essays

1. 'The revival of local democracy calls for radical reform of the tax and service powers of local authorities. Anything else is not likely to have much effect.' Discuss.

2. Is there a proper place for politics, including party politics, in local government?

3. 'The truth, sir, is that we have a chaos as regards authorities, a chaos as regards rates, and a worse chaos than all as regards areas.' Is this still true of British local government?

Projects

1. Playing the role of an expert consultant who has been called in to advise the Minister of State for Local Government and the Regions, lay out the arguments for the different systems of local taxation outlined in Briefing 12.2.

2. (For class discussion) Divide the class into small working teams, each to formulate its own plan for dividing different public services between central and local government. Make sure that you consider national defence, macroeconomic planning, education, health, housing, transport, EU affairs, parks, police, fire and libraries. Come back together in the class to compare your plans.

3. Imagine your local authority is to have a referendum on the three forms of local mayor/leader and cabinet government outlined by the Local Government Act 2000. Which would you vote for and why?

Further reading

Useful and recent books on British local government include: G. Stoker, *Transforming Local Governance: From Thatcher to New Labour* (Basingstoke: Palgrave Macmillan, 2003); G. Stoker and D. Wilson (eds), *British Local Government in the 21st Century* (Basingstoke: Palgrave Macmillan, 2002); D. Wilson and C. Game, *Local Government in the United Kingdom* (4th edn, Palgrave Macmillan, 2006); and most recent of all, S. Leach, C. Game, and D. Hall, *The Changing Role of Local Politics in Britain* (Bristol: The Policy Press, 2006).

For shorter articles see L. Pratchett and S. Leach, 'Local government: choice without constraint', *Parliamentary Affairs*, **57** (2), 2004, pp. 366–79; S. Leach and L. Pratchett, 'Local government: a new vision, rhetoric or reality?', *Parliamentary Affairs*, **58** (2), 2005, pp. 318–34; G. Stoker, 'New localism, progressive politics and democracy', *Political Quarterly*, **57** (2), 2004, pp. 117–29.

Useful web sites on local democracy

Hot links to these sites can be found on the CWS at www.pearsoned.co.uk/budge.

Although Britain has a highly centralised form of government, local councils offer a fundamental channel of representation for citizens. The first step is to visit the Local Government Association (www.lga.gov.uk) and the New Local Government Network (www.nlgn.org.uk). The Central and Local Government Information Partnership was set up to enable central and local government to work together to develop an efficient and effective infrastructure for policy development, implementation, monitoring and reporting – visit their web site at www.clip.gov.uk. The Improvement and Development Agency was established by and for local government in April 1999; its mission is to support self-sustaining improvement from within local government – visit them at www.idea.gov.uk.

The Local Government Association Parliamentary Monitoring and Intelligence Service provides specialist coverage of the activities of Parliament as they affect local government; you can find them at www.pamis.gov.uk. The local government ombudsman (www.lgo.org.uk) investigates complaints of injustice arising from misadministration by local authorities and certain other bodies. The Institute of Local Government Studies (University of Birmingham) provides valuable academic insights into the problems arising in relation to local government and administration. Visit also the National Association of Local Councils at www.nalc.gov.uk.

There are also a number of independent associations engaged in the expansion of local democracy; a good example is Localis (www.localis.org.uk). For direct access to data about local government elections, visit the Local Government Chronicle's specialist web site maintained by the University of Plymouth at www.politics.plymouth.ac.uk/lgecentre.

PART 4

Popular Participation

chapter 13

Pressure groups

Although we often read about 'public opinion', there is no such thing. There are a great many public opinions because society is divided into a great many social groups, each with its own set of opinions. Opinions can vary according to age, gender, ethnicity, class, education, religion, region, occupation, history, culture, and social and political values. In order to realise its own rather special set of opinions and goals, each group organises itself into voluntary associations that represent its interests and speak for it on matters of political substance. Since there are a huge variety of social groups and interests there is also a huge variety of voluntary organisations and associations, including charities, community associations, social clubs, youth clubs, churches, educational, scientific and cultural associations, sports clubs and occupational groups for businesspeople, trade unionists and professionals.

Voluntary associations such as these play a vital role in society and politics. They constitute what is often termed 'civil' or 'pluralist' society – an organised sector of society that is outside government and not controlled by it. They are important because they help to give people a sense of belonging and social involvement, and they are a way in which individuals can cooperate with each other to achieve collective goals, whether these are to protect wages and salaries, ban fox-hunting, promote genetically modified foods, play football or grow roses. They are also one of the most important ways that citizens can express their democratic rights to be heard and influence government. Most ordinary citizens do not have any political influence as individuals. To have an impact on politics they must join with others and form pressure groups.

This chapter looks at the role and influence of voluntary organisations and pressure groups in British society and government. It is divided into six main sections:

- civil society and social capital
- voluntary associations, pressure groups, parties and social movements
- how groups operate: tactics and targets
- the impact of groups
- Thatcher, Blair and pressure groups
- pressure groups and democracy.

Civil society and social capital

The idea of **civil society** was important in the classical political theory of the seventeenth and eighteenth centuries, when absolute monarchy was strong and democracy in its infant stages. Its basic claim was that there should be a large area of private and social life which was independent of the state and its rulers. Private groups and associations would provide the foundations for a free society and the

Civil society

The aspects of social and economic life (primarily voluntary associations and private organisations) that are outside the immediate control of the state. A strong civil society based on a large number and wide variety of private associations and organisations is thought to be the basis for democracy.

basis for organised opposition to political tyranny. One of the first things dictators do when they come to power is try to gain control of voluntary organisations, knowing they may be centres of a struggle for freedom and democracy.

The term civil society has come back into common use recently, particularly to describe the social foundations necessary to sustain democracy in central and eastern Europe where, under communism, citizen organisations and associations were closely controlled by the state. Civil society is no less important in established democracies, which are based, it is claimed, on a great diversity of active voluntary associations that are outside the immediate control of the state, even though many of these have little to do with politics most of the time. However, they provide the organisational basis for civic involvement, social participation and forms of collective action that are not regulated by the state.

Some of the basic ideas about civil society are repeated in social capital theory, which also has a long history, going back to the classic work of the French writer Alexis de Tocqueville in *Democracy in America*, published in the mid-nineteenth century. His writings have been reformulated in a more powerful form by the American political scientist Robert Putnam, in his recent research on social capital. Social capital is a mixture of three things:

1. **Trust**   Trust between citizens is a powerful social glue that binds society together and makes social, political and economic life easier and more efficient. Those who are socially trusting, it is said, also tend to trust their political leaders and to have confidence in their institutions of government. Social trust between citizens is said, therefore, to be a key to understanding political life.

2. **Norms**   The norms of social capital are the cultural expectations of reciprocity (mutual help and respect), civic and community engagement, cooperation and a common appreciation of the public interest. Once again, social life is claimed to have a strong connection with political life.

3. **Social networks**   Joining with others (who may be very different socially) in voluntary associations brings people into close relationships with fellow citizens and leads to mutual understanding and tolerance. Networks of civic engagement that develop cooperation and trust help to produce social integration and stability, and a much more efficient and cooperative social and political system.

The bottom line of social capital theory is that a decay of social trust, a decline of voluntary associations and an erosion of community participation and involvement will have a profound effect on political life, causing election turn-out and party membership to fall, political alienation and cynicism to rise, and a mood of low confidence in the institutions of government. In other words, declining social capital, especially voluntary organisation membership, will cause support for politicians, governments and democratic institutions to fall.

We will return to this claim at the end of the chapter when we have looked more closely at the world of voluntary organisations and pressure groups in Britain, how pressure groups are organised, how they work, how they acquire political influence and how they have been treated by recent governments under Thatcher and Blair.

Voluntary associations

Voluntary associations have roots that are deep and widespread in British society. Statistics about them tend to vary from one research report to another, because they depend on how voluntary associations are defined and counted, but most studies show the following:

■ Britain has a high density of voluntary associations by western European standards, though by no means the highest (Table 13.1).

■ A large proportion of British citizens (40–50 per cent) belong to at least one voluntary association, and a large minority (20 per cent) belong to two or more. According to one recent survey there are about 18 million voluntary group members, 11 million participants and 4 million volunteers (see Table 13.2).

■ There are few signs that overall voluntary activity is declining (see Table 13.3), and more signs that it is increasing. While some groups are shrinking, others are growing.

■ The number and variety of associations is extremely large and varied. Table 13.4 lists almost 5,800 formally organised voluntary associations in one city alone, and there are likely to be many more that could not be tracked. They cover almost every conceivable sort of human interest and activity. The largest of

Table 13.1 Voluntary associations membership, western Europe, 2002

| | (Percentages of population aged 15 and over) | | | | | |
	France	Germany	Italy	UK	Sweden	Portugal
Sports	32	38	19	36	50	13
Cultural	28	24	15	25	30	6
Consumer	6	29	8	33	38	2
Religious	11	25	11	21	19	12
Trade unions	11	15	14	17	56	7
Humanitarian, social, aid	15	21	15	14	33	7
Social	14	18	8	21	22	7
Environmental	10	15	9	17	14	3
Business	4	9	13	15	10	4
Science	11	9	5	13	14	4
Political	3	6	6	4	10	5
Other	10	9	4	11	13	10

Note: The table shows figures for the four largest countries of western Europe, plus Sweden and Portugal, which tend to be at the high and low ends of organisational membership.
Source: European Social Survey, http://www.europeansocialsurvey.org/

Table 13.2 Voluntary activity

	Percentage	Number (millions)
Member	41	18
Participant	25	11
Volunteer	10	4

Source: C. Pattie, P. Seyd and P. Whiteley, 'Civic attitudes and engagement in modern Britain', *Parliamentary Affairs*, **56**, 2003, p. 625

Table 13.3 Non-members of voluntary associations (percentages)

1959	1977	1983	1987	1990	1998
52	46	42	47	39	47

Source: K. Aarts, 'Intermediate organisations and interest representation', in H.-D. Klingemann and D. Fuchs (eds), *Citizens and the State*, Oxford: Oxford University Press, 1995, p. 232, and Table 13.1

Table 13.4 Voluntary associations in Birmingham, 1970 and 1998

	1970	1998
Sports	2,144	1,192
Social welfare	666	1,319
Cultural	388	507
Trade associations	176	71
Professional	165	112
Social	142	398
Churches	138	848
Forces	122	114
Youth	76	268
Technical and scientific	76	41
Educational	66	475
Trade unions	55	42
Health	50	309
Other	–	75
Total	4,264	5,771

Source: William A. Maloney, Graham Smith and Gerry Stoker, 'Social capital and associational life', in Stephen Baron *et al.* (eds), *Social Capital*, Oxford: Oxford University Press, 2000, p. 220

them are sports clubs, social clubs, consumer groups (especially the AA and the RAC) and churches, but there are also highly specialised associations for science, the arts, hobbies and business interests.

■ Although membership is fairly widely spread in society, 'joiners' tend to be concentrated among the educated, middle and upper class, middle aged and male sections of the population.

Most groups are tightly linked into a pyramid structure, with local branches at the bottom, area and regional associations in the middle and national and international bodies at the top. Cricket clubs, for example, belong to local leagues, which join regional associations, which are brought together by national and international associations. At the same time many local groups are also integrated into a parallel structure of umbrella associations, also in a pyramid that reaches from local associations to national and international headquarters. Cricket clubs are affiliated to local sports councils, which can cover a hundred or more activities

BRIEFINGS

13.1 Political participation in Britain

The most authoritative study of the extent to which people undertake political action shows that, apart from voting, most action is stimulated by social groups. About 14 per cent of adults take part in informal group activity and 11 per cent in organised group activity to do with politics (such as writing letters or distributing leaflets to express concerns). Twenty-one per cent had contacted a local councillor and almost 15 per cent had attended meetings to protest against some policy. Sixty-three per cent had signed a petition.

Most people do not do these things very often: three or four of them are undertaken in a five-year period. When they do, however, it is generally at the prompting of a group that organises the action in the first place. (The percentages are from Geraint Parry, George Moser and Neil Day, *Political Participation and Democracy in Britain*, Cambridge: Cambridge University Press, 1992.)

from angling to yoga, and these also have regional, national and international structures. This complex network of horizontal and vertical links between the same and kindred activities is found among trade unions, professional associations, business associations, charities, churches, sports, women's organisations and environmental groups.

The result of this extensive, overlapping and interlocking network of organisations is twofold: on the one hand, the network helps to integrate and stabilise society; on the other, it can be a formidable and highly organised force if it mobilised politically.

Voluntary associations, pressure groups, political parties and social movements

Pressure groups

Private, voluntary associations that wish to influence or control particular public policies, without actually becoming the government or controlling all public policy.

Many voluntary associations are not at all political. In fact, most organisations try to avoid politics because they are divisive and conflictual, and because they were not formed for political purposes in the first place. They were created so that people could play football, sing in choirs, drink real ale or provide help for the less fortunate. This means that we must distinguish carefully between voluntary associations and pressure groups. Voluntary associations may have any purpose or goal, including political ones, and pressure groups are voluntary associations acting in a specifically political manner. Pressure groups are a type of voluntary association, therefore.

The surprising thing is that a remarkable number of normally non-political voluntary associations become politically involved when their interests are affected. The Football Association is not normally political but the issues of football hooliganism, stadium safety, EU rules on the transfer market and the new Wembley stadium have drawn it into politics on quite a few occasions in recent years. The Rum Importers Association is not political, but became so briefly when the government proposed changes to the weights and measures regulations about the sale of food and drink in 2004. The Violin Teachers Association was not political until public expenditure cuts caused heating in school halls to be turned off early, making it too cold to teach children to play the violin. Government now affects the daily lives of so many people that thousands (if not tens of thousands) of groups are likely to be politically active in national and local politics at any given time.

Political parties are one special kind of voluntary association and similar in important respects to pressure groups. How, then, are we to distinguish between pressure groups and parties? It is not easy because they overlap to some extent, but they also differ in four ways:

1. Parties want to become the government, pressure groups only want to influence government. Action on Smoking and Health (ASH), for example, wants to influence a part of government policy, but does not want to become the government.

2. Parties have broad policy interests, pressure groups generally have narrow ones. The Countryside Alliance has a fairly broad array of interests, but even so it is not involved in most aspects of public policy.

3. Parties are primarily political, many pressure groups are not. The Ramblers' Association becomes involved in politics only when issues arise that are dear to its heart.

4. Parties fight elections, most pressure groups do not because they want to influence not become the government.

There is no clear distinction between parties and pressure groups. Some groups have broad policy interests, for example the Trades Union Congress and the

Plate 13.1 Opposition to the war in Iraq brought together many different groups and organisations to demonstrate in 2003

Source: Topfoto

New social movements

The broad and loose-knit organisations that emerged strongly in the 1970s to influence public policy on such issues as the environment, nuclear energy and weapons, peace, women and minorities. They have wider policy interests than most pressure groups, but are more loosely knit than political parties.

Confederation of British Industries (CBI). Some (e.g. Friends of the Earth, Fathers 4 Justice) are closely tied to politics because they were set up as pressure groups with a political agenda. Some groups fight elections, and a few even win (the Independent Kidderminster Hospital and Health Concern won parliamentary elections in 2001 and 2005), and some sponsor party candidates (the TUC, the National Farmers' Union (NFU)). One thing is clear, however: while there are few political parties, the range, diversity and number of pressure groups is enormous. Although they sometimes overlap we can usually tell the difference between them.

New social movements (NSMs) are another kind of political voluntary organisation. How, then, are we to distinguish them from parties and pressure groups? This is also not easy because all three overlap to some extent, although they also differ in four ways:

1. *Organisationally* they are less bureaucratic and hierarchical than traditional parties and pressure groups, consisting of loose-knit networks of networks. They have been called rainbow alliances.

2. *Ideologically* they often have broader objectives than most pressure groups, but narrower ones than the parties.

3. Their *methods* are often innovative, direct and designed to catch media attention: the opponents of the Newbury bypass who lived in trees and underground tunnels to obstruct building work; Greenpeace, which has sailed its boats into nuclear test zones and the path of whaling ships. They often emphasise direct political action and community involvement.

4. Their *membership* often cuts across normal social divisions of class and left–right politics, bringing together different social groups. 'Crusties' of the anti-road movement have combined with the 'Land-Rover and green welly' country set to defend the countryside.

There is nothing particularly new about 'new' social movements. The most famous in British history is probably the Chartist movement of the mid-nineteenth century, which brought together a broad alliance of liberal, working-class and left-wing interests to press for political reform. However, it is the movements that emerged in the 1970s and 1980s that attract attention now, especially those concerned with women's rights, the environment, peace, minorities, the anti-nuclear movement and animal rights. It was claimed that the new movements would undermine the centralised, hierarchical and bureaucratic parties and pressure groups of conventional politics, so destabilising democracy. New social movements were said to be better adapted to the fluid and fragmented social groupings of postmodern and post-industrial society. This idea was strengthened when the membership of conventional parties and trade unions began to decline in the 1980s and 1990s.

Plate 13.2 Protests against the war in Iraq are still going on in 2006

Source: Alamy/Dominic Burke

However, the old parties and many of the old pressure groups proved more resilient than this and responded to the NSM threat. Some had been advocating new social movement goals for a long time (women, peace, minority rights), and they simply responded by making these more prominent in their political agenda and adopting others. Most parties and groups had grassroots organisations and a mass membership already (see Chapter 16) and tried to strengthen them. In fact, community organisation in Britain was not pioneered by new social movements but by the Liberal Party in Birmingham. Its leader in the 1960s, Wallace Lawler, placed a high priority on party organisation in the localities. In the 1990s New Labour tried with some success to forge a new and broad alliance of interests on which to build its revival. There is no doubt that the NSMs have had an impact on British politics, but they have been added to the old system, and changed it rather than transformed it. They operate alongside the parties and pressure groups but have not replaced them.

A last comment on the term 'pressure group' should be made here. Some dislike the term because they think it implies the use of sanctions, coercion, or even illegitimate pressure. They prefer the term 'lobby' or 'interest groups'. Nonetheless, the collective term 'pressure groups' is used for good reasons:

1. Pressure does not necessarily entail illegitimate pressures or sanctions. It may involve nothing more sinister than information or advice.

2. Strictly speaking the term 'interest group' applies to a special kind of pressure group (see Briefing 13.2).

3. The term lobby derives from the idea that pressure groups congregate in the lobby of the House of Commons where they can whisper in the ears of MPs. In fact few pressure groups go near the lobby of the Commons. They use entirely different methods – as we will shortly see.

The pressure group world

The group world has three main features: huge numbers, great diversity and a dense network of groups.

Numbers

There are so many groups that it is virtually impossible to count them. Some are set up for political purposes and continuously active. A few are set up for very specific political purposes and disappear when the issue is decided. A good many are sporadically active in politics when circumstances demand. Between them, they crowd the political arena, pushing and pulling at each other and the government to try to influence public policy.

Diversity and competition

There is a huge variety of pressure groups covering almost every conceivable interest and organised in almost every conceivable way. They are large and small, loose knit and highly organised, strong and weak, rich and poor, conventional and radical. Some support each other, some fight. The Countryside Alliance, the League Against Cruel Sports, the anti-hunt saboteurs and the hunts themselves are all involved in the political struggle about fox-hunting. Similarly issues such as abortion, gun control, road building, joining the euro and Scottish and Welsh independence are fought out between opposing groups and coalitions. It is not true to say that all issues involve two or more opposing groups, but many do.

BRIEFINGS

13.2 Types of pressure group

Pressure groups come in so many shapes and sizes that any attempt to classify them inevitably runs into trouble. For example, interest groups (e.g. the NFU) are primarily concerned with the occupational interests of their members, and cause groups (e.g. the Countryside Alliance) promote a wider range of concerns and values. The problem is that the NFU wants to preserve the rural way of life, as does the Countryside Alliance (a cause group). The concerns of interest and cause groups in the same sector often overlap. Nor is the distinction between trade unions and parties clear in the case of trade unions that are closely aligned with parties. Similarly, the distinction between insider and outsider groups is blurred when some outsider groups move towards the inside (environmental groups). Consequently none of the following categories is watertight but, nevertheless, they are generally helpful in the analysis of the pressure group world.

Interest groups Interest (or sectional) groups represent the interests of occupational groups, mainly business organisations, professional associations and trade unions. Major examples include the Institute of Directors, the British Medical Association, the Transport and General Workers Union, and the National Union of Students (NUS). They are mainly (not exclusively) concerned with material and economic interests.

Cause groups Cause groups (promotional or attitude groups) promote a general cause or idea. Membership is not limited to particular occupations, and the range of interests covered is very wide – religion, education, culture and art, leisure, sport, charity and welfare, community, social, youth and science. Major examples include the Royal Society for the Protection of Birds (RSPB), Shelter (a housing action group), the Consumers' Association, animal rights' groups and hunt protesters, and Amnesty International.

New social movements These have broader concerns than most pressure groups, but are more loosely knit than political parties.

Episodic groups These are not normally political, but become so when circumstances require (e.g. the Football Association).

'Fire brigade' groups These are formed to fight a specific issue, and dissolve when it is over (e.g. the Anti-Poll Tax Federation).

Peak associations Peak associations are 'umbrella' organisations that coordinate the activities of different pressure groups in the same area of interest. Examples include the Confederation of British Industry and the Trades Union Congress, but equivalents exist for many other areas of activity. There are also European peak associations in Brussels (see Chapter 9) and international peak associations (Save the Children, Amnesty International, the Red Cross, the International Labour Organisation) that operate around the world.

Insider groups Groups with access to government officials and decision makers. Sometimes called established groups, they usually speak for legitimate and mainstream interests in society. Most professional associations have an official standing in policy-making bodies and many are legally entitled to be consulted, for example the National Farmers' Union in the annual farm prices review. Insider groups pay for their privileged status by playing the rules of the Whitehall and Westminster game, which means not being too critical of ministers, and behaving 'responsibly'.

Outsider groups Outsider groups do not have (easy) access to officials or decision makers. They are kept at arm's length because of who or what they represent. Examples include the Campaign for Nuclear Disarmament (CND), the Animal Liberation Front, and Fathers 4 Justice. Not all groups want greater insider status, because they do not want to become 'domesticated' by being too closely involved with government. Sometimes groups move from outsider to more of an insider status, as environmental groups did in the late 1980s.

Crossbench groups Some groups are inevitably aligned with a particular party, but most try to maintain party neutrality, knowing that they must deal with whichever party is in power. They are called crossbench groups after crossbench (non-party) members of the House of Lords.

Pyramids of power

Many pressure groups are organised into pyramids in the same way as voluntary associations, with a broad base of local groups, all the way up to a single international peak association. Trade unions, business and trade associations, churches

Plate 13.3 Anti-hunt protestors launch a balloon during the Liberty and Livelihood march, which was organised by the Countryside Alliance in 2003

Source: Topfoto

and professional organisations are notable in this respect but it applies no less to many other kinds of pressure group. Such a tight and well-organised structure can make pressure groups a formidable political force. How powerful they are, however, depends on the tactics they adopt and the targets they are able to aim at in their political campaigns.

How groups operate: tactics and targets

There are two general rules for pressure group operations. First, get into the policy-making cycle as early as possible, when options are being considered, before government takes a position and the political parties draw public battle lines. Second, work at the highest possible level of the political system to which you have access, because that is where the least effort has the greatest influence. These two general rules means there is usually a preferred set of pressure points in the political system.

Civil servants

Much pressure group activity does not concern great policy issues, as many assume. A good deal of group work concerns detailed and technical matters that are usually handled by Whitehall officials. In any case, the policy cycle often starts and ends with the civil servants who draft the early documents and implement final decisions, so successful 'insider' groups develop close working relations with their opposite numbers in Whitehall, and on any given issue are likely to start off a campaign by talking to them. The relationships are sometimes very close indeed because both need each other: groups provide civil servants with technical information and practical advice; civil servants provide groups with inside political information, and channel information to ministers. Early consultation may avoid much trouble later on.

Ministers and the Cabinet

Civil servants cannot 'deliver' their ministers, any more than ministers can guarantee their proposals being accepted by the Cabinet. If an issue is already politicised, as many are, then groups may have to go to Westminster to press their case. They will start with ministers if they can, because this is where the power lies. Insider groups may have access to this high level, where much may be accomplished by small, private meetings in committee rooms or London clubs. Outsider groups do not have such access, so use other methods that tend to be more expensive, time consuming and uncertain.

Westminster

Groups that have no access to high government circles, or cannot convince it of their claims, may turn to the House of Commons, although this is a larger and more uncertain arena than the Cabinet or Whitehall offices. Nevertheless, many pressure groups approach Parliament, and most MPs get mountains of pressure group mail every day. Wealthier groups may employ professional lobbyists with contacts and experience. Groups with a sympathetic MP have been able to take advantage of

BRIEFINGS

13.3 Affecting the detail of legislation

In 1996 a very detailed measure requiring water to be supplied to caravan sites was being considered in a parliamentary standing committee.

It was uncontroversial and the need was not disputed by the parties. The Country Landowners' Association (CLA), however, was concerned about whether landowners or water companies would be responsible for the costs. The CLA was extremely active, using both professional lobbyists and interested MPs (some were members of the association) to influence the committee decision. The water companies had, of course, spotted this possibility, and they also employed consultants and lobbyists. However, more MPs were landowners than shareholders in water companies, so the CLA had the advantage.

This case illustrates several points:

- Even very technical legislation or administration will have consequences for group interests.

- Groups benefiting will often be opposed by groups that might lose, resulting in the push-and-pull of pluralist politics.

- However, the group with more resources has the advantage.

- Given the network of connections between MPs and some pressure groups, there is a very thin line between legitimate 'lobbying' and corruption. There has been a series of scandals in recent years involving MPs, professional lobbyists and personal interests.

private members' bills in the Commons (the laws on abortion and homosexuality have been changed this way), and some well-connected groups can influence legislative details. Some groups can present their views to parliamentary committees, others can influence party backbench committees.

Political parties

Groups with strong links to a political party will use them to try to influence party policy. Trade unions used to be closely connected to the Labour Party and business and trade associations with the Conservatives, but most groups try to maintain a crossbench status so they can work with whichever party is in power.

Local councils

Many pressure groups have purely local objectives: opposition to a new road, support for parking restrictions or traffic controls, better schools. In such cases the natural target is the local council. Even if the issue is a national one, it pays to get the local council on your side. As a democratically elected body it has a legitimate claim to represent local opinion, and resources and expertise to access policy-making circles in central government, even if it does not have much influence. Councils have taken an increasing number of cases to the courts in the 1980s, even as far as the European Court.

Public campaigns and the mass media

Public campaigns are often the last resort of pressure groups, but less so than they were, given the ability of some groups (Greenpeace, Animal Rights Groups, GM opponents, Stop the War in Iraq) to mobilise supporters or attract attention. But in spite of modern mail-shot and advertising techniques, public campaigns tend to be expensive, time consuming and unpredictable. Some groups use advertising firms – also costly – and most try to develop close contacts with journalists. Some groups try to get media coverage by the headline-hitting methods of demonstrations, protests, petitions, sit-ins, civil disobedience or violence against people or property. Email and web site campaigns are increasingly used.

Courts

Some groups have taken their cases to court (equal pay, the abolition of corporal punishment in Scottish schools), including the EU's Court of Justice in Luxembourg and the Council of Europe's Court of Human Rights in Strasbourg. Legal action is often costly and uncertain.

The European Union

The EU is so important that many groups have turned their attention to it, especially to the Commission, and Brussels is now stuffed full of pressure group organisations. Most of them operate in one of four ways. The simplest is to set up an office in Brussels, but this is expensive and often groups look around for partners to share the cost. Second, they can combine with similar interests in other EU states to form a Eurogroup. The EU encourages and officially recognises over 1,000 of them, but they tend to be rather weak and fragmented. Third, groups can form a European pressure group drawing support from EU countries. Fourth, groups can try to work through the British government, or regional governments, which takes us back into the kinds of action outlined earlier.

Policy networks and policy communities

Groups often use a combination of targets, but the most prestigious insider groups work smoothly and quietly with their high-level contacts. Outsider groups have to use the noisier methods of public campaigns. Paradoxically, the quieter the group the greater its influence is likely to be; the more noisy and obstructive its tactics the less influential it is likely to be. In some cases contacts between pressure groups and government are so tight that they form what is known as a **policy community**. The members of such communities are in close and constant contact with each other, and generally agree on the main issues in their policy arena. Policy communities have been formed around food and drink policy, farming, technical education and water privatisation.

> **Policy communities**
>
> Small, stable, integrated and consensual groupings of government officials and pressure group leaders that form around particular issue areas.

The biggest and most powerful policy community in Britain probably centres on the financial interests of the City of London, which reach into the heart of the government through the Treasury and the Bank of England, and into the heart of the national economy through companies and investment. The need to protect the national currency and London's position as a leading financial centre is so obvious to government that the City needs to do little to ensure that its case is heeded by the government.

Sometimes the relationship between Whitehall departments and pressure groups in a policy community is so close that there is a fear that department officials are taken over by the group – the officials 'go native'. This is a danger, of course, because governments and the civil servants are supposed to protect the interests of the public at large, not those of a sectional group. Although it is difficult to say if this actually happens, if only because policy communities are closed circles of influence, the accusation has sometimes been made about decision making in farming, business, the defence industry, the legal system and some areas of health policy. Equally, there is the reverse danger that groups will be 'domesticated' by close and constant contact with government officials. Group leaders are supposed to represent the interests of their members, but if they live in the pockets of officials they may come to lose their autonomy and sell out on group interests.

> **Policy networks**
>
> Compared with policy communities, policy (or issue) networks are larger, looser, less integrated and more conflictual networks of political actors in a given policy area.

The twin dangers of domestication and going native are less likely to beset **policy networks**, which are looser, more open and more conflictual than policy communities. Policy networks include not just government and core insider groups, but also a larger and wider range of groups, sometimes even outsider groups. Because a wider variety of opinions is included in networks there is more disagreement, and decision making is more pluralist, spilling over from Whitehall and Westminster into public arenas. Being a group member of a policy network means that groups can retain their autonomy, but equally it also means that they are likely to have less influence over their area of policy interest.

Growth of direct and radical action

The above account emphasises conventional forms of pressure group politics that concentrate on the formal and traditional institutions of government. In recent years the new social movements have used more radical and unconventional forms of direct action. Direct action has a long history, going back at least to Boadicea's attack on the Roman invaders and to Wat Tyler's Peasants' Revolt of 1381. It includes the mass demonstrations of the Chartists (1848), suffragette action later in the nineteenth century, the Jarrow march against unemployment in 1936, and the pitched battles between Fascists and Anti-Fascists in the streets of East London in the same year. The Campaign for Nuclear Disarmament organised its first Aldermaston March in 1958, and peaceful anti-nuclear civil disobedience was organised by the Committee of 100 in the 1960s. Mass direct action by students, workers and intellectuals spread across large parts of the western world in 1968, and in the 1970s the anti-apartheid movements disrupted sports events against South Africa.

Since the huge publicity given to the demonstrations of 1968, groups seem to have turned increasingly to direct political action in the form of marches, sit-ins, petitions, occupations, civil disobedience and occasional violence. Such methods often get a lot of publicity. Recent examples include:

- **Groups and movements**   The peace movement, environmental groups, women's groups, hunt saboteurs, the anti-poll tax movement, animal rights groups, anti-capitalist groups, People's Fuel Lobby, Farmers for Action, Fathers 4 Justice, Greenpeace, anti-road movements and the Countryside Alliance

- **Forms of direct action**   These include petitions, marches, protests, boycotts, strikes, occupations and sit-ins, most of it peaceful, legal and democratic but sometimes illegal and violent. Greenpeace sailed its boats into nuclear test areas and into the path of whaling ships. The Fathers 4 Action threw purple powder into the debating chamber of the House of Commons and, dressed as Father Christmas, Batman and Spiderman, climbed a balcony of Buckingham Palace, the London Eye and a giant crane. The Countryside Alliance brought an estimated 400,000 people to a protest march in London in 2002, and there 1–2 million demonstrated against a war in Iraq in 2003. Anti-road protestors lived in trees and tunnels to prevent work starting on Twyford Down, poll tax protestors demonstrated peacefully in large numbers (and a few rioted violently), animal rights protestors have demonstrated and petitioned, and some have issued death threats.

Although not new and still not very common, direct and unconventional action is increasing. It has been argued that radical groups and new social movements challenge the traditional structures and organisation of government and tend to destabilise, even threaten, democratic politics. It can also be argued that radical groups may strengthen conventional groups and procedures because, faced with radical action from outsider groups, the government may open negotiations with more conventional and moderate groups to resolve the issue. This is exactly what happened when the Blair government, faced with radical action from farmers, road hauliers and taxi drivers, set up the Fuel Forum in 2000 to solve the fuel tax issue. Direct and radical political action by groups may undermine conventional politics in some ways, but strengthen it in others.

This leads naturally into the questions of the impact of pressure groups, and how and why some are more influential than others.

Impact of pressure groups

So many factors affect the issues surrounding pressure group campaigns that it is difficult to unravel the reasons that lead to groups being successful or unsuccessful. For example, have anti-smoking groups been the power behind the ban on smoking in public places? Quite possibly, but so also might the government take credit, MPs in the new Parliament, scientists who uncovered the link between smoking and passive smoking and cancer, public opinion (which has changed substantially in a few years), foreign governments that have already enacted the same laws, the EU (which banned TV adverts for cigarettes) and the mass media, and quite possibly the poor political tactics of the smoking lobby. How much influence one assigns to anti-smoking pressure groups depends on how much weight you give to the other possible influences that have changed and developed over time. The problem is that so much is going on during pressure group campaigns that it is virtually impossible to be sure about what the causes and effects are.

While it is impossible to pin down the exact influence of any particular group, their political power seems to depend partly on their own group characteristics and partly on the characteristics of the political environment in which they operate.

Group features

- **Membership size and type** Groups with a large membership can raise money through subscriptions and contributions. With over a million members, a staff of more than 1,300, a gross annual income of £81 million and net assets of £103 million, the Royal Society for the Protection of Birds runs a network of offices and shops around Britain. In 2000 it contributed half a million signatures to a petition to maintain EU bird protection laws.

- **Money** Some groups are wealthy because of the people and interests they represent. The National Farmers' Union has 132,000 members, an income of £23 million and assets of almost £71 million. Friends of the Earth has total revenues of £5.5 million, net assets of £0.5 million and 2,000 'active' volunteers in the United Kingdom, though 1.5 million members worldwide. This is fairly typical of the difference between many interest and cause groups.

- **Organisational advantages** Some groups are easier to organise than others. Interest groups are often easily organised at places of work. Cause group sympathisers are often scattered, and potential members difficult to identify and contact. For this reason producer and occupational groups are easier to organise than consumer and cause groups. Doctors are easier to organise than patients, producers easier than consumers, and teachers easier than pupils.

- **Membership density** A group representing practically all its possible members (e.g. the British Medical Association (BMA) with 100 per cent density) is in a stronger position than a trade union with 50 per cent density.

- **Divided membership** The BMA speaks for almost all doctors; miners were crucially divided between competing unions in the 1980s. The NFU used to be the only farmers' organisation, but now it competes with Farmers for Action, a more militant group.

- **Internal structure** Interest groups are often centralised, making political action easier. Cause groups are often more decentralised and participatory, making it more difficult to respond quickly and effectively.

- **Sanctions** Some groups have powerful sanctions: capital can move easily, labour cannot; professional bodies can withdraw cooperation; some organisations can call on public sympathy. Other groups have few sanctions: the homeless cannot strike, withdraw cooperation or move their investments.

- **Leadership** A charismatic leader is an asset – e.g. William Wilberforce and the Abolition Society (one of the first pressure groups, and concerned with the abolition of slavery) in the late eighteenth century, and Frank Field (Child Poverty Action Group), Des Wilson (Shelter), and Jonathan Porritt (Friends of the Earth) in recent times.

The political environment

Features of the political environment that might affect the impact of pressure groups include the following:

- **Public opinion**   A group with public support is more likely to get a sympathetic hearing; the poor image of students hinders their negotiating power. But public opinion is not always potent; nurses seem to get a more sympathetic hearing in public than in committees that decide their pay.

- **Legitimacy**   A group that is thought to speak for legitimate interests – doctors, lawyers, teachers, business – is likely to get a better reception than one which does not – drug addicts, the unemployed, ex-criminals.

- **Insider status**   Insider groups are more likely to be successful than outsider groups – but not always.

- **Technical and policy issues**   Groups can have more influence on technical issues and details than basic policy matters. On hot political topics they usually have less room for manoeuvre, because the battle lines for these are often fixed.

- **Opposing groups**   Some groups operate alone in their field of interest, especially on technical matters that attract little public or political interest. On moral and value issues such as fox-hunting, smoking, abortion and the Iraq war the arenas are crowded with competing groups and attitudes are often inflexible.

- **Institutionalised power**   'Institutionalised power' occurs where the interests of a group are implicitly built into the very structures and cultures of decision making, so that the group often has to do very little to protect its interests. Feminists argue that such an institutional bias results in male supremacy, ethnic minorities talk of institutional racism and workers and trade unionists refer to the 'capitalist system'. The provinces often complain of a built-in bias that favours London.

Because there are so many factors affecting pressure groups' success, it is difficult to estimate their influence in the political system or compare their relative power. The best we can say is that a combination of factors is likely to be important in any given case. Groups with a variety of resources (an insider status, a large bank balance, a mass membership, effective leaders, sympathetic public opinion) are likely to have an advantage in the group struggle. However, things change, and the whole nature and background of pressure groups politics has shifted markedly in the last 25 years in Britain, as we will see now.

Thatcher, Blair and pressure groups

In the earlier post-war era of consensus politics both Conservative and Labour governments cooperated with business and labour organisations to solve economic problems. The National Economic Development Council (NEDC) was created in 1961 in order to institutionalise this three-cornered relationship to take joint action on economic policy. Many similar bodies were created in the 1960s and 1970s, and the practice of officially including insider groups in consultative and decision-making processes was widespread in central and local government. Some writers describe this period as '**corporatist**', though others argue that Britain was never a corporatist state in the way that Austria and Switzerland were. They prefer the term '**tripartite**' to refer to the much looser British system of three-cornered consultation between government, business organisations and trade unions (often described pejoratively as 'beer and sandwiches at No. 10').

Corporatism

A system of policy making in which major economic interests work closely together within government structures to frame and implement public policies. Corporatism requires a formal government apparatus capable of concerting the main economic groups so that they can jointly formulate and implement binding policies on their members.

Tripartism

Tripartism is a looser, less centralised and hierarchical system than corporatism. It brings together three main interests (government, business, unions) to make economic policy. It is a consultative method rather than a binding method of policy making.

Thatcher and pressure groups

The 'winter of discontent' of 1979 effectively brought the tripartite era to an end. When Margaret Thatcher came to power she dismantled or weakened most tripartite practices and institutions. According to her, close cooperation between government and pressure groups was neither democratic nor functional, giving too much political power to private, narrow interests and interfering with the efficient operation of the market. She insisted that her government had been democratically elected to run the country, not private, factional, self-interested pressure groups.

Thatcher confronted many pressure groups, not just trade unions. Business interests, teachers, lawyers, civil servants, doctors, local government, universities, the BBC and the Church of England all felt the roughness of her tongue and the iron of her determination. Official advisory bodies were cut by one-third, and the influence of the rest was reduced. Groups were excluded from the early stages of policy formulation, though less often from the final implementation stages, where cooperation is important for effective policy. In short, the close association between groups and government was broken in the 1980s, and pressure groups often found themselves out in the cold.

Blair and pressure groups

New Labour has tried to establish warmer working relationships with leading groups, but without returning to the old tripartite system:

■ It tried to work with the CBI.

■ It started quarterly meetings with the TUC in 2000, but these soon came to an end.

■ It co-opted group members on to task forces and quangos, although in an ad hoc manner, and as individuals rather than group representatives.

■ When a crisis occurred over increases in fuel taxes, it created the Fuel Forum with representatives of the Road Haulage Association, the NFU and the Federation of Small Businesses. This showed a willingness to consult and co-operate with organised groups in order to solve an urgent political problem.

In short, Blair did not try to pick fights with interest groups. But then neither did he encourage them or invite them into the heart of his government. In large part Thatcher and Blair's treatment of groups rests on their different conceptions of democracy – a topic we will take a closer look at now.

Pressure groups and democracy

Thatcher viewed pressure groups as a potential danger to parliamentary democracy. Are they? In theory, groups play an important part in democracy:

■ They are an important means of political participation and influence, especially for minorities.

■ They collect and sort out group opinions to produce an agreed position (interest aggregation), and argue their case in the political arena (interest articulation).

■ Groups inform and educate their members about political issues, and act as channels of communication between citizens, and between citizens and political elites.

- They mobilise citizens politically.

- They serve as pools of talent for recruitment to political office.

- They provide governments with aggregated opinion, technical expertise and practical advice.

In practice, the role of pressure groups has been hotly disputed by competing **pluralist**, elitist and New Right theorists. All democrats agree that freedom of association is crucial, and that rights to assembly and free speech are the hallmarks of democracy, and many would argue that groups have the right to be consulted, at least, on matters affecting their immediate interests. But not all democrats agree on how much power or influence groups should have. Critics of pressure group politics, both left and right wing, point out the following:

- Pressure groups are narrow, sectional, self-interested actors. Governments are democratically elected and accountable to citizens. Therefore governments, not groups, should make policy.

- Too much group power results either in domination by factional interests or in fragmented, confused and unaccountable decision making, what is sometimes called 'hyper-pluralism'.

- Groups can fragment public policy, destroying its unity and any government sense of direction.

- In pursuing its own interest each group forces up public expenditure and expands the scope of public services.

Nonetheless, too little group power means that government is too autocratic. The difficulty, of course, is knowing what is 'too much' and 'too little' power. This seems to be a matter of judgement about the correct balance – too much for some is too little for others.

Whatever conclusion one might reach about the correct role of pressure groups in government, however, there remains the claim that voluntary organisations in general and pressure groups in particular are an essential social basis for democratic politics. This chapter outlined theories of civil society and social capital in the first section, and will return to them now in the last section, since we understand so much more about the group world and how it works in Britain.

Social capital and support for government

There is little doubt that Britain, as do many other western nations, suffers from the same sorts of political malaise that concern social capital theorists so much. Election turn-out and party membership are declining, trust in politicians and confidence in political institutions are at a record-breaking low level, and larger numbers than ever believe that the democratic system is not working well and needs reform. Many are alienated and dissatisfied with British politics and the system of government, and the issue of declining trust is generally acknowledged to be a serious issue.

Is the erosion of civil society and the decay of social capital responsible for declining political support? It seems not. There is little evidence that membership of and activity in voluntary associations has decreased in recent decades, and some evidence that it has increased. Some organisations have declined, it is true, but others have grown. Women's organisations, trade unions and churches have found it difficult to keep their numbers up, but environmental groups, aid and charity organisations and pre-school play groups have expanded. There is no clear sign that

---

Pluralism

According to pluralist theory, political decisions are the outcome of competition between many different groups representing many different interests.

CONTROVERSY

Are pressure groups good for democracy?

The pluralist case

- The greater number and diversity of groups ensures political struggle and competition. As a result (nearly) all issues are contested by competing groups.

- Groups look for allies in the political struggle, which forces them to compromise.

- All groups have some resources to fight battles: money, members, leadership skills, public sympathy or access. Group resources are not distributed equally, but the inequalities are not cumulative. No group is powerless, none all powerful.

- Power is distributed between many different groups. There is no fixed 'power structure'; it depends on circumstances.

- Groups that fail in one arena (Parliament) may succeed in another (the courts, local government, the EU).

- Groups cannot get everything they want. They compromise to get something.

- Many groups have veto power – they can rule out proposals they don't like.

- Pluralist democracy is not perfect, but it works reasonably well, 'warts and all'.

The elitist case

- Group resources are often distributed with cumulative inequality. Just as power in society is unequally distributed, so some groups have few resources, others many.

- Some interests are unorganised, some rely on others to protect them and some are poorly organised – minority groups, children, the mentally ill, the homeless, the poor.

- The group world is dominated by educated, wealthy, middle- and upper-class 'joiners'.

- Groups fight their battles within a political structure and according to rules of the game, which are systematically loaded in favour of middle- and upper-class interests or even a particular sector, such as the City of London.

- Organisations are internally oligarchic. Group leaders are often unelected and unaccountable to members.

- A small national elite controls all important decisions, but leaves smaller issues to pluralist competition.

- The group world reflects and reinforces the political power structure in which the wealthy dominate.

The New Right case

- Groups represent narrow sectional interests; governments are elected by citizens to represent the public good.

- Groups, especially trade unions, distort market operations but so also do professional bodies and some business groups. Their power should be reduced to ensure market competition.

- Groups fragment policy making and prevent government developing a coherent programme.

- In protecting their sectional interests groups slow economic growth, and cause unemployment, inflation and high public expenditure.

- Groups create 'hyper-pluralism' – too many economic and political demands on government. This undermines good economic policy and democracy and creates 'ungovernability' and 'democratic overload'.

- Group leaders are often unelected and unaccountable to their members.

- Government may consult and groups may advise, but government should hold the reins of power.

the number of people belonging to voluntary associations has increased since the 1950s (see Table 13.2). If anything the proportion of non-members has decreased.

A survey by the Institute for Volunteering Research (www.ivr.org.uk) shows that 44 per cent of the adult population was engaged in formal voluntary activity over a 12-month period in 1981, 51 per cent in 1991 and 48 per cent in 1997. The equivalents for informal voluntary activity were 62 per cent, 76 per cent and 74 per cent. This means that about 22 million people were formally volunteering in 1997, and about 33 million were informally volunteering, and that the figures have been fairly stable over a 16-year period. This picture of a generally strong and, if anything, gently rising level of volunteering activity is confirmed by a survey of

40,000 charities carried out by the National Council for Voluntary Associations (www.ncvo-vol.org.uk). It finds evidence of a real growth in the number of organisations and in the number of large charities with incomes of over £1 million. The income of the whole charitable sector increased by £1 billion to £26.3 billion between 2002 and 2003, and it employed 488,000 full-time equivalent staff in 2003. Just under two-thirds of all adults gave money to charities in 2003, and the average monthly donation was £12.32. All these figures suggest a strong voluntary and charitable sector, and one that is growing rather than declining.

It seems that decaying civil society and social capital is not responsible for declining levels of political support in Britain. We have to look elsewhere for an explanation, and one of the prime suspects is the mass media, the topic of the next chapter. Meanwhile we can conclude with some confidence that social capital generated by voluntary associations is not responsible for declining levels of political trust, confidence and support in the United Kingdom.

Summary

■ The dense network of voluntary associations in the United Kingdom creates a pluralist or 'civil' society, with indirect and direct consequences for democracy.

■ The distinction between pressure groups, new social movements and parties is not clear-cut, but groups usually have a narrower range of policy interests than parties, and want to influence the government, not replace it. New social movements usually have broader interests than groups, but narrower ones than parties, are often more loosely organised and often favour direct action and community organisation.

■ The main targets (pressure points) for groups are: top civil servants, ministers and the Cabinet, Westminster, political parties, the mass media and the public, local councils, the courts and the European Union.

■ Group influence is impossible to measure but depends on group characteristics (membership size, type and density; income; ability to recruit members; ability to respond quickly to political change; ability to use sanctions; group unity; insider status) and outside factors (public opinion; legitimacy; insider status; whether their issue is politicised; and the power of opposing pressure groups).

■ The period of tripartite cooperation in the 1960s and 1970s was ended by Thatcher, who was more inclined to confront and exclude groups from government consultation. The Blair government has tried to work more closely with groups, but has not recreated a tripartite system.

■ Pluralist theory places great emphasis on the role of groups in democracy, but elite theory claims that group politics reinforce elite or class power. The New Right argues that groups produce hyper-pluralism, ungovernability and overload.

MILESTONES

Milestones in the development of British pressure groups

1950s	British pressure groups 'discovered' by British and American political scientists
1961	National Economic Development Council set up
1965	Confederation of British Industry formed
1966	Devaluation of the pound postponed for a year by the Labour government because of financial pressures from 'the City'
1968	Demonstrations and direct action by students, workers and intellectuals spread across the western world

Milestones in the development of British pressure groups continued

1969	Trade union pressure forces the Labour government to abandon plans for trade union reform ('In place of strife')
1970s	Rise of the 'new social movements'
1971	The Conservative Industrial Relations Act reduces trade union powers
1974	The Prime Minister (Heath) calls an election, as a result of the miners' strike, and loses
	The Labour government's 'Social Contract' with the trade unions agrees to social legislation and repeal of the Industrial Relations Act in return for a 'prices and incomes policy' but no agreement is struck with business or professional organisations about prices, salaries or profits
	Manpower Services Commission (a tripartite agency for jobs and training) created, followed by 1975 Health and Safety Commission, and 1976 Advisory, Conciliation, and Arbitration Service (ACAS) to deal with industrial relations disputes
1979	Thatcher begins to dismantle the machinery of 'tripartism' and begins a long series of confrontations with a wide range of organised interests and groups
1982	CBI Director-General, Sir Terence Beckett, threatens to 'get the gloves off' with the Thatcher government over its financially orthodox economic policy
1984–5	Miners' strike, the most bitter and prolonged industrial dispute since 1926, lost by miners
1980, 1982, 1984, 1988, 1989, 1990	Employment and Trade Union Acts reducing powers and rights of trade unions
1988	Edwina Currie, Junior Health Minister, is forced out after her statement that eggs are widely infected by salmonella angers egg producers and the NFU
1988–90	Anti-poll tax protests, culminating in demonstrations and riots across the country in 1990
1992	NEDC abolished
1994–6	Payments to MPs and other incidents of sleaze involving pressure groups and lobbyists prompt Nolan Committee to investigate MPs' interests
1997–8	Stronger regulation of MPs' interests by House of Commons
1997	Blair tries to establish working relations with major interest groups, but not under the old tripartite system
1997	The start of a long series of protests by farmers. Countryside Alliance organises demonstration attracting 300,000 people
1998–2000	Destruction of GM crops by Greenpeace
1999	Anti-capitalist and World Trade Organization rallies in London and Seattle become an annual event
2000	Fuel tax protest
2002	Countryside Alliance attracts 400,000 participants in London demonstration. Student protests against top-up fees
2003	Anti-(Iraq) war coalition attracts 1–2 million demonstrators in London

Essays

1. 'Elite theory claims that pressure groups merely reflect and sustain the power structure of modern society.' Discuss.

2. Why do some analysts attach so much importance to civil society, and is Britain such a society?

3. 'Once powerful in Britain, pressure groups have been weakened to the point of powerlessness since 1979.' Is this true?

Projects

1. Collect what information you can from books, articles and newspaper reports about the fuel tax protests of 2000, the campaign against genetically modifed food and the Countryside Alliance. What does this information tell us about the conduct of modern pressure group campaigns?

2. Make a list of all the groups mentioned in this chapter and classify them into their different types listed in Briefing 13.2. What do you learn from this exercise?

3. Carefully read a good national daily newspaper for one week, and list all the pressure groups and pressure group issues mentioned in the news reports. What does this tell you about the pressure group world in Britain?

Further reading

A recent comprehensive book is W. Grant, *Pressure Groups and British Politics* (Basingstoke: Palgrave, 2000). Slightly older is R. Baggot, *Pressure Groups Today* (Manchester: Manchester University Press, 1995). A good study of environmental pressure groups and movements is G. Jordan and W. Maloney, *The Protest Business* (Manchester: Manchester University Press, 1997). On business groups, see W. Grant, *Business and Politics in Britain* (London: Macmillan, 2nd edn, 1993) and, on trade unions, D. Marsh, *The New Politics of British Trade Unions and the Thatcher Legacy* (London: Macmillan, 1992). A good account of European pressure groups is found in S. Mazey and J. J. Richardson, *Lobbying in the European Community* (Oxford: Oxford University Press, 1993).

A review of pressure group politics in 2004 is to be found in W. Grant, 'Pressure politics: a politics of collective consumption?', *Parliamentary Affairs*, **58**, (2), 2005, pp. 366–79. H. Margetts, 'Political participation and protest', in P. Dunleavy *et al.* (eds), *Developments in British Politics* (Basingstoke: Palgrave, 2002) discusses protest politics. Other useful and recent articles include N. Jackson, 'Pressure group politics', *Politics Review*, September 2004, pp. 2–5 and G. Jordan, 'Groups and democracy', *Politics Review*, February 2004, pp. 20–3.

Useful web sites on pressure groups

Hot links to these sites can be found on the CWS at www.pearsoned.co.uk/budge.

Before visiting specific pressure groups' web sites, you might want to log on to www.historylearningsite.co.uk/pressure_groups.htm where you can find basic answers to questions such as: What are pressure groups? How do they influence democratic performance? What is pluralism?

There are tens of thousands of pressure groups in Britain, many of them with web sites, and some with excellent and innovative ones. In the following list you can find samples of those with particularly good web sites and those mentioned in the chapter. Each site will provide basic information about the group, such as its history, objectives, activities and the ways in which you can become involved.

Action on Smoking and Health: www.ash.org

Amnesty International: www.oneworld.org/amnesty/index.html

Animal Concerns: http://animalconcerns.netforchange.com

Black Information Link: www.blink.org.uk

British Medical Association: www.bma.org.uk

Campaign for Nuclear Disarmament: www.cnduk.org

Campaign for an Independent Britain: www.bullen.demon.co.uk

Charter 88: www.charter88.org.uk

Child Poverty Action Group: www.homelesspages.org.uk

Chronicle World (changing Black Britain): www.chronicleworld.org

Commonwealth Foundation: www.commonwealthfoundation.com

Compassion in World Farming: www.ciwf.co.uk

Confederation of British Industry: www.cbi.org.uk

Conservation International: www.conservation.org/xp/CIWEB/home

Country Landowners' Association: www.cla.org.uk

Countryside Alliance: www.countryside-alliance.org

Friends of the Earth: www.foe.co.uk

Greenpeace: www.greenpeace.org/homepage

International Council for Local Environmental Initiatives: www.iclei.org

League Against Cruel Sports: www.league.uk.com

Local Government Association: www.lga.gov.uk

Mind: www.mind.org.uk

National Farmers' Union: www.nfu.org.uk

National Society for the Prevention of Cruelty to Children: www.nspcc.org.uk

National Trust: www.nationaltrust.org.uk

Nexus: www.netnexus.org/nexus

Press for Change: www.pfc.org.uk

Royal National Institute for the Blind: www.rnib.org.uk

Royal Society for the Protection of Birds: www.rspb.org.uk

Shelter: www.shelter.org.uk

World Conservation Monitoring Centre: www.unep-wcmc.org

World Council of Churches: www.wcc-coe.org

chapter 14

The mass media and pluralist democracy

The mass media have a strategic position in politics because they are the main way in which governments, pressure groups, parties, politicians and voters talk to and learn about each other. In this sense they are not just another actor in the political system, but an over-arching actor that reports and comments on all the others. The mass media inform millions of voters every day about politics and politicians, and they inform politicians about politics and voters. In fact, the political content of the mass media is of obsessive interest to politicians.

Nor are the mass media merely channels of communication. They are also significant political actors in their own right: they help to create news as well as report it; they give the news their own slant and interpretation; they push some issues and interests and not others; they pursue economic interests; and they support some parties and groups against others. Is all this good or bad for democracy? The answer seems to depend heavily on answers to a series of related questions. What impact do the mass media have, if any, on political life and public opinion? Can the mass media manipulate public opinion, or do they simply reflect it? Are the mass media biased in their reporting of political news, and if so in what way and why? Do the mass media form a free and competitive market, as pluralist theory says it should, or is it, rather, controlled by an oligopoly of economic interests that shape the daily news according to their own wishes? Should the mass media be controlled in the public interest, or should it be left to market forces in the same way as, say, washing powder or motor cars? What impact has the new e-media had on all this, if any?

This chapter, therefore, examines the nature and impact of the mass media, and its role in democracy. It covers:

- who uses what medium for what purpose
- the impact of the mass media
- media bias
- public service and commercial media systems
- commercialisation of the electronic media
- ownership and control
- the political consequences of market change
- e-media: digitopia or dystopia?

Who uses what medium for what purpose?

We take the modern media for granted in many ways, because we are totally immersed in them. Just as fish will be the last life form on earth to discover water, because they are completely surrounded by it and know of nothing else, so we find it difficult to imagine what life would be like without TV, the radio and the daily paper. A few contrasts between 1945 and modern times will help make the point:

- In 1945 there was no TV in Britain. The BBC resumed its post-war broadcasts in 1946 with the 25,000 viewers who happened to live close enough to Alexandra Palace to receive its signals. Now virtually every household in the kingdom has at least one TV set, with more than a hundred channels to choose from, some operating around the clock. On average, British adults now spend over 26 hours a week watching TV, and half the population watches TV news seven days a week.

- In 1945 politicians communicated with voters mainly by newspapers, public meetings and the radio. Newspapers were very thin, had very little in-depth analysis of politics, and little commentary. There were no opinion polls. Reporting of parliamentary debates was limited. Modern papers are fat and glossy, their political content is vastly larger, and they are far more critical and party political than in 1945. Total national daily newspaper circulation in the United Kingdom is 12.3 million, and Sunday circulation is 13.4 million (Table 14.1). About three people read every newspaper sold, which means that some 37 million read a daily paper, and 40 million read a Sunday paper.

- In 1945 about 10 million households had a 'wireless', but political broadcasting was limited, and there was little coverage of the 1945 election. Now there are over 750 radio stations in the United Kingdom, including 69 student stations. Many stations have regular news updates.

- In 1945 the terms 'spin doctor', 'photo opportunity', and 'sound bite' had not been invented. The government had a small handful of press departments and officers, but nothing like the scale of modern operations. Spin doctors are now power players in government.

All this means that the mass media are now vastly more important in politics. But what exactly is their role and impact on British democracy? To answer this seemingly simple question we must first examine the main sources of political news and commentary – TV and the papers – to see what sorts of people use what sorts of mediums for what sorts of purposes.

Tabloids, broadsheets and TV

It has been said with some truth that all statements about the media are wrong: there are different mediums and different people use them for different purposes. There is a world of difference between the electronic mass media (radio and TV) and the print media, and a big difference again between the **tabloids** and **broadsheets**. We must be careful to distinguish between these different kinds of media and not talk loosely about them as if they were a single entity.

Broadsheet readers are usually better educated and more middle class. They spend more time with their paper than tabloid readers, trust their paper more than tabloid readers, and know more about politics. Conversely, tabloid readers spend less time with their paper and more with the TV, although their TV diet is mainly entertainment and sports programmes, rather than news and current affairs.

Tabloids

Less serious (popular) national daily and Sunday papers, so called because of their smaller size. To confuse matters, the broadsheets now publish in a tabloid format, but are still known as broadsheets, or quality papers.

Broadsheets

Serious (quality) national daily and Sunday papers, so called because of their size. Daily broadsheets are *The Times*, the *Daily Telegraph*, the *Guardian*, the *Independent* and the *Financial Times*.

Table 14.1 Main national newspaper circulation per issue, 2006

Daily broadsheets	Sales (million)	Sunday broadsheets	Sales (million)
Daily Telegraph	0.90	*Sunday Telegraph*	0.68
The Times	0.69	*Sunday Times*	1.37
Guardian	0.38	*Observer*	0.44
Independent	0.26	*Independent on Sunday*	0.21
Financial Times	0.43		
Total of all daily broadsheets	2.80	Total of all Sunday broadsheets	3.02
Total number of titles	7	Number of titles	7
Average sales	0.40	Average sales	0.43
Daily tabloids		**Sunday tabloids**	
Sun	3.26	*News of the World*	3.72
Daily Mirror	2.17	*Sunday Mirror*	1.51
Daily Express	0.83	*Sunday Express*	0.86
Daily Mail	2.36	*Mail on Sunday*	2.29
Daily Star	0.84	*People*	0.92
		Sunday Star	0.41
Total of all daily tabloids	9.46	Total of all Sunday tabloids	10.41
Total number of titles	6	Number of titles	8
Average sales	1.58	Average sales	1.30
All national dailies		**All national Sundays**	
Total sales	12.26	Total sales	13.43
Number of titles	13	Number of titles	15
Average sales	0.94	Average sales	0.89

Source: Audit Bureau of Circulations and National Readership Survey

However, because they watch so much TV (Table 14.2), they also watch a lot of TV news. In fact they watch *more* TV news than broadsheet readers, and they trust TV news much more than their tabloid paper (see Tables 14.2 and 14.3). But they are less interested in politics, and know less about them.

As Table 14.1 shows, more than three times as many tabloids are sold as broadsheets. But the tabloids have less political news and analysis, and tend to be more party political. Some media analysts argue that good newspapers are, in principle, better at conveying political news and comment than TV, which by its very nature tends to be superficial and entertaining. As a result, those who spend time with a good newspaper are usually better informed than those who watch TV news. But it is not always clear whether this is due to the inherent properties of different media or to the education of those who use them.

Social scientists refer to this growing division between tabloid and broadsheet readers as the '**knowledge gap**'. Educated people and those interested in politics read quality newspapers and magazines, listen to serious radio and watch serious TV, and talk more about politics with their friends, thereby accumulating a broader and deeper understanding of politics. Less well-educated people, who read the tabloids and watch a lot of entertainment TV, are likely to know less and understand less about politics. In other words there is a tendency for the information rich to become information richer. But whether this is due to media impacts, or to the characteristics of those who use different media for different reasons, is the subject of a good deal of dispute, as we will see now.

Knowledge gap

The result of the process whereby those with a good education and high status acquire knowledge faster than those with a poorer education and lower status.

Table 14.2 Different media, different uses, 1996 (%)

| | Educational qualifications | | |
	O-level/GCSE or less	A-level	Further or higher
Newspapers			
Irregular readers	43	47	43
Regular tabloid	54	41	31
Regular broadsheet	4	13	27
(Total)	(101)	(101)	(101)
Television hours per week			
Up to 3	28	46	58
3–4	41	39	32
5 or more	30	15	9
(Total)	(99)	(100)	(99)
TV news hours per week			
3 or less	27	32	28
4–6	14	24	22
Every day	59	44	50
(Total)	(100)	(100)	(100)

Note: Columns total more than 100 per cent because respondents mention more than one source. Broadsheet readers mention more than tabloid readers.
Source: British Social Attitudes Survey, 1996, as reported in R. Jowell et al. (eds), *British Social Attitudes*: *The 14th Report*, Aldershot: Dartmouth, 1997, p. 156

Table 14.3 Main sources of political information, 2003 (%)

	National news	World news
TV	73	78
Papers	13	10
Radio	10	7
(Total)	(96)	(95)

Source: Ofcom, *The Public's View Survey Results*, 2004

Impact of the media

Some claim that the effects of the mass media are strong and self-evident, but others argue, with equal conviction, that the media have minimal direct effects of their own. In spite of these strong views on both sides it turns out to be remarkably difficult to demonstrate media effects, even more to measure them. There are three main problems:

1. It is difficult to untangle the effects of the media from other influences, such as family life, education, work or the community. The media are only one set of influences among many, and sorting out their distinctive impact is a tricky matter.

2. It is not possible to generalise about 'the impact of the media' when there are different kinds of media pushing and pulling in different directions and with different kinds of effects on different kinds of people. The evidence is that most people are exposed to different media influences because they scan different news sources.

Table 14.4 Newspaper politics and voting intentions of readers, 2005 (%)

Paper	Editorial endorsement	Voting intention of readers		
		Con	Lab	Lib. Dem.
All voters		34	39	20
Daily Express	Conservative	44	29	20
Daily Mail	Conservative	57	24	14
Mirror	Labour	13	66	15
Daily Telegraph	Conservative	64	14	18
Financial Times	Hesitant Lab	36	34	23
Guardian	Labour	7	48	34
Independent	Lib. Dem./Labour	11	38	43
Daily Star	None	17	53	13
Sun	Labour	35	44	10
The Times	Labour	44	27	24

Note: The political position of each paper is determined by the party it recommended readers to vote for on the morning of the election. This generally reflects its partisan colour during the campaign.
Source: MORI Polls, 1st quarter, 2005

3. There is an acute problem of establishing causes and effects. People pick the sorts of media that suit their tastes and opinions – they self-select themselves. At the same time the media shape themselves to appeal to particular sorts of people and markets, so they reflect rather than create the views of their audiences. This makes it difficult to know whether the chicken or the egg comes first.

Consider the simple figures in Table 14.4. They show that people who read Conservative papers generally identify with the Conservative Party, compared with those who read Labour papers who generally identify with Labour. This is scarcely surprising, but which causes what? Do papers create the party sympathies, or do people usually select a paper to suit their politics? Or is it a bit of both? And what do we make of the *Financial Times* and *The Times* that gave Labour their qualified support, but had a heavy preponderance of Conservative voters, and the *Daily Star* which endorsed no party but had a very heavy preponderance of Labour voters? A quarter of the *Mail*'s readers intended to vote Labour even though their paper was strongly anti-Labour.

Given these difficulties it is scarcely surprising that experts disagree about the impact of the newspapers on politics, and more generally about the impact of the mass media on politics. There are four main schools of thought on the subject: reinforcement theory claims minimal effects; agenda-setting theory and framing theory claim indirect effects; and media impact theory claims direct, though not necessarily strong, effects.

Reinforcement theory and minimal effects

Reinforcement theory (media effects)

Argues that the media do not create or mould public opinion so much as reinforce pre-existing opinion.

Reinforcement theory argues that the media can only reinforce attitudes that already exist. It does so for two main reasons:

1. **Markets** In a competitive market the media are forced to give consumers what they want, just as supermarkets sell what their customers demand. The commercial media seek out tastes and try to appeal to them by reflecting and satisfying them. The modern media are bound by the golden chains of the market. Moreover, the media market is competitive. It presents a great diversity of political opinions, allowing customers to pick and choose what suits them.

2. **Personality** Research shows clearly enough that individuals have a strong propensity to preserve their core beliefs, even if they are forcefully challenged. They start by picking the media that best suit their predispositions (self-selection), and if unwanted messages get through they then tend to ignore, forget, distort, misinterpret or simply refuse to believe them. Even if the mass media tried, they cannot shift entrenched opinion.

Reinforcement theory argues that individual psychology, on the one hand, and consumer sovereignty in a competitive market, on the other, renders the media all but powerless to influence mass political opinion. Media effects are minimal.

Reinforcement theory does not fit all the facts about the British media, however. First, the British media do not operate in a free competitive market. As we will see, radio and TV are regulated in non-market ways, and the print media form an oligopoly rather than a free, competitive market. Second, individuals may adhere strongly to their core values – religion and morality – and to attitudes based upon their own experience, but politics are fairly remote for most. Few have first-hand experience of, say, the Iraq War, EU affairs or economic policy. They may be more open to media influence on these particular issues.

Agenda setting

Agenda-setting theory

Argues that the media cannot determine what people think, but can have a strong influence over what people think about.

Agenda-setting theory claims that the media cannot determine what we think, but they can strongly influence what we think about, and so they help set the public agenda. In recent years in Britain we have seen waves of media interest (sometimes short lived) in such things as football hooliganism, road rage, dangerous dogs, the monarchy, Princess Diana's death, and a more or less permanent focus on crime. By focusing on crises and catastrophes the media help to create 'moral panics' about such things as crime, famine in Ethiopia and bird flu. Political issues highlighted by the media include:

- the foundation of the Social Democratic Party
- Labour's tax plans in the 1992 election campaign
- Conservative government sleaze, 1992–97
- immigration
- terrorism.

Widespread media attention to these topics has helped, it is claimed, to concentrate public attention on them.

Early agenda-setting theory tended to assume a pliant public that responds to the media's agenda. Some even claimed that the media barons could keep serious politics off the popular agenda by feeding the general public with an endless stream of distractions in the form of soap operas, game shows, Hollywood films, sport, gossip, trivia and sensationalism. Critics of the theory argued that most issues will get a hearing in a pluralist system, and that there is much more about politics in the mass media than there ever used to be. At any rate, later agenda-setting theory now accepts that the public has its own agenda, while claiming that the media can still influence its priorities, especially on matters about which the public knows little.

Framing effects (of the media)

The argument that the media can exercise a subtle but strong effect on how public opinion thinks about political issues according to how it presents (frames) the issue in the first place.

Priming and framing

Framing theory goes one step further than agenda-setting theory and argues that the *way* in which the modern mass media present politics has a strong influence on how citizens see them and evaluate them. It is not the news content that is so important, but the mass media's basic approach to the news:

■ **Framing**   Some media stories present issues in a general way, while others present it in human interest terms. For example, the issue of homelessness can be analysed with the help of statistics and explained in terms of social forces such as unemployment, the housing shortage and mortgage interest rates. Or else it can be made into a human interest story by interviewing homeless individuals about their life stories. In the former, political and social forces are foremost, especially government policy, but in the latter, the homeless are more likely to be held individually responsible (laziness, drunkenness, stupidity).

■ **Priming**   Parties and candidates are usually strong in some areas of politics, weaker in others, and simply by focusing on a strong or a weak area a news report can help or hinder their campaign. In most post-war elections the Conservative Party has been thought more competent on the issue of law and order, whereas Labour has had a better rating on unemployment. By concentrating on one or other of these issues, the mass media can prime people to think about a party's strong or weak points.

Plate 14.1 Some critics argue that the dumbing down of tabloid news, as well as of tabloid TV, is responsible for the decline of literacy and for poor knowledge and understanding of politics
Source: Cartoon Stock

Direct effects

The most recent school of thought argues that the mass media can and do directly influence attitudes and behaviour, including voting behaviour. Direct effects include:

Videomalaise

The attitudes of political cynicism, despair, apathy and disillusionment (among others) that some social scientists claim are caused by the modern mass media, especially television.

■ **Bad news**   The mass media concentrate on bad news about disasters (tsunamis, earthquakes, famines, air crashes, terrorism) crime, conflict, violence, scandal and incompetence, which sell papers and hold TV audiences. The focus on a 'mean world' is said to create '**videomalaise**' – cynicism and disillusionment with politics, distrust of politicians and fellow citizens, low confidence in political institutions, and political apathy.

- **The 'fast-forward' syndrome**   In Victorian times political events and news about them moved slowly. Nowadays the mass media are constantly searching for the latest story to attract the public's attention. News is a perishable commodity, and the news media make sure they are constantly abreast of the breaking news. As a result, the public is increasingly bewildered by a ceaseless and ever-changing flow of unconnected events, which is not explained and not understandable.

- **Personalisation and trivialisation**   The mass media concentrate not on policies or issues, but on personalities and appearances. Election campaigns are not presented as a struggle between party policies, but as a horse race between party leaders, illustrated by the sound bites and photo opportunities of the spin doctors. Many politicians now go to TV 'charm schools' that train them to speak, smile and dress correctly. Packaging and presentation, not content, is what matters.

- **Social capital and political support**   TV pulls people out of their communities and isolates them in their living rooms where they are fed a junk-food diet of bad news, sensationalism, crime, violence, and political corruption and incompetence. The result, it is said, is videomalaise that causes voting turnout to decline, political trust to fall, alienation to rise, and undermines confidence in the institutions of democratic government.

Reinforcement

Reinforcement occurs where political forces push in the same direction – e.g. where someone with Labour sympathies reads a Labour paper.

Concerns about media effects are sharpened by parallel concerns about political bias. If the mass media are politically powerful and if they are also politically biased, then they may well be able to maipulate public opinion in a way that is not democratic. Therefore we next look at the issue of media bias.

CONTROVERSY

Conflicting theories of media effects

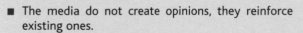

Reinforcement theory

- The media do not create opinions, they reinforce existing ones.

- Market competition ensures that the mass media adapt to their audiences and give them what they want.

- In a pluralist system, many views have a way of making their voice heard.

- Different media with different messages compete. There is no single or dominant voice.

- Individuals select their media to suit their opinions and tastes. They tend to suppress, distort, forget or misinterpret what does not suit them.

- The effects of the modern mass media are minimal, they confirm what people already believe rather than creating or influencing political life and attitudes.

Agenda-setting theory

- The media cannot exercise much influence over what people think, but they can influence what they think *about*.

- Only a few issues can be important at any one time and the media play an important role in sifting and sorting issues for public attention.

- Different media often focus on the same events or issues. Journalists live in echo chambers (they talk among themselves most of the time) and indulge in 'feeding frenzies', taking cues from each other about what is important and topical.

- Concentrating media attention on a few issues at a time pushes them up the political agenda.

Framing politics

- The way in which the modern mass media treat politics subtly, but strongly, affects political life, and

▶

how people view it. This is a matter of presentation not content.

- By concentrating on bad news (wars, deaths, disasters, conflicts, incompetence and corruption) the media give politics a bad name, and so create alienation, political cynicism and distrust.
- The 'fast-forward' syndrome speeds up political life, and makes it difficult to understand.
- In order to provide human interest the media tend to trivialise and personalise politics. They emphasise style and appearance, sound bites and photo opportunities, rather than policies and programmes.
- By focusing on particular issues the media favour the politicians and parties that 'own' those issues ('priming' effects).
- Reports that concentrate on episodes, particularly individual human interest stories, tend to emphasise individual causes. News that deals with themes tends to emphasise 'the system' and the actions of governments.

Direct effects

- Reinforcement theory was mainly a product of 1950s' social science before the creation of the powerful modern media, especially TV, so it underestimates media impacts.
- The mass media now saturate society. In particular many people now spend a large proportion of their leisure time in front of the TV.
- TV has powerful effects: it encourages passivity (the 'couch potato'), it entertains rather than explains or informs, and it isolates people socially.
- Media effects go beyond agenda setting, priming and framing. The media influence the way in which people think about politics – the videomalaise thesis.
- There is some evidence that newspapers influence the voting patterns of their readers. Allowing for the effects of background characteristics and political attitudes, readers of Conservative papers are more likely to vote Conservative than readers of Labour papers, and vice versa.

Media bias?

Many people are convinced that the media are biased. The problem is that right-wingers are convinced that the bias is left wing, and left-wingers are equally convinced that it is right wing. British governments of all persuasions usually feel that the press is unfair to them. We are unlikely to get far with any discussion of media bias unless we go back to a few basics.

Bias in the mass media is most likely to originate in two sources: political authorities, especially the government, and the news media themselves.

Government bias

The government is only one source of political information, but it is a particularly important one that can try to shape the news in two different ways:

1. **The suppression of news?**   On the one hand, freedom of information is rather weakly protected in the United Kingdom and, on the other, the Official Secrets Act is powerful. Compared with many democracies, these two together give British governments rather more room for manoeuvre in controlling news flows and information, and keeping things secret. In addition, the governments of the 1980s were strongly critical of both the BBC and ITV for their treatment of some political issues, and there were whispers that this might affect both the renewal of the BBC Charter in 1994 and again in 2003, and the cost of the TV licence (the BBC's main source of income), which the government controls.

2. **The manipulation of news?**   The government provides a large proportion of the daily news through its press releases and tries to shape the news ('give it a spin') in its own interests. The government's efforts to market itself increased

substantially in the 1980s under Thatcher and again in the late 1990s under Blair. The Government Communication Network, a 'virtual' group to link all those working in government communication, now has 3,500 members and central government is one of the largest advertisers in the land. At the same time both journalists and voters alike have become suspicious and cynical of attempts to manipulate the news. Trust in politicians has declined accordingly (see Briefing 14.1).

BRIEFINGS

14.1 A question of bias? The BBC and the 'sexed-up' dossier about weapons of mass destruction.

Shortly after 6 am on 29 May 2003 the BBC's morning news programme on Radio 4 broadcast a report by Andrew Gilligan alleging that the government had deliberately exaggerated the military capabilities of Iraq in order to build its case for war. In his first live and unscripted broadcast that morning Gilligan said that an expert but confidential source told him that the claim that Iraq could deploy biological weapons in 45 minutes was 'wrong' (later changed to 'questionable'). Gilligan repeated his claim in an article in the *Mail on Sunday*, adding that the Prime Minister's Director of Communications, Alastair Campbell, was responsible for the exaggerations. Furious at the allegation that the government had 'sexed up' its document, Campbell demanded a retraction and an apology from the BBC. The BBC stood by Gilligan and refused to divulge his expert source of information. But the name of Dr David Kelly, who had been a United Nations weapons inspector in Iraq, was leaked as the person responsible.

These events created an enormous political storm and Kelly, Gilligan and the BBC came under enormous political pressure, especially from the government. Kelly was found dead in a wood near his home shortly after appearing before a House of Commons committee and the government's Intelligence and Security Committee. The government immediately set up the Hutton Inquiry into events leading up to Kelly's death. This largely exonerated the government and Alastair Campbell of wrongdoing and as a result Gilligan and the BBC's Director-General and Chairman, Greg Dyke and Gavyn Davies, resigned.

The affair of the BBC and its reports on Iraqi weapons of mass destruction is enormously complex. Almost every aspect of it is the subject of great controversy and disagreement, but there are several points of interest for an understanding of the media's role in British politics.

The BBC took the full brunt of the government's wrath, and the Gilligan article in the *Mail on Sunday* was overlooked, suggesting that the public service nature of TV news and the commercial nature of the newspaper may have caused them to be treated in different ways for presenting essentially the same news. This may explain why ITV, and especially the BBC, have been taken to task by previous governments for their news reporting over the past quarter of a century (see Chapter 21).

Governments and journalists define good news reporting in different ways. Reporters are on safe ground with governments if they faithfully repeat their messages – a form of accurate reporting – but not so when they probe behind the scenes with investigations – a form of balanced and impartial reporting.

The BBC is trusted as a source of information more than the government. A YouGov poll of Feb/March 2003 found that more than 80 per cent of the public placed a great deal/fair amount of trust in ITV and BBC journalists to tell the truth, but 25 per cent placed the same trust in ministers in the Labour government.

Partly for this reason perhaps, there was a widespread feeling that the Hutton Inquiry, although it was the work of a distinguished former Law Lord, was a government whitewash and unfair on the BBC.

It is ironic that the BBC suffered greatly for telling what many observers thought to be very largely the truth about weapons of mass destruction in Iraq, whereas the tabloid press is rarely held to task for printing stories that are more dubious.

In the end it may be politicians and the government itself that suffer most from a growing sense of distrust. 'Videomalaise', it seems, may have less to do with distrust of the mass media than of politicians who attempt to manipulate the mass media in order to manipulate public opinion.

Media bias: newspapers

When considering the political bias of the media it is essential to distinguish between print and electronic media. Electronic media are required to be politically balanced and impartial, while newspapers can be as partial and partisan as they like. We will deal first with the easier case of print media. There are four main reasons why British newspapers have had a particular ideological leaning for most (but not all) of the post-war period:

1. The press (and commercial TV) is owned and controlled by multimillionaires and multinational companies, often (not always) with the same economic and political interests.

2. Generations of British press barons have pursued not money, but power. They have frequently controlled the editorial policy of their newspapers, and even written the editorials themselves: Northcliffe, Rothermere, Astor, Beaverbrook, Thompson, King, Matthews, Maxwell, Rowland, Black and Murdoch have all followed this practice.

3. Newspapers and commercial TV rely heavily on advertising income, and are unwilling to bite the hand of the business interests that feed them.

4. Since the late 1950s the British press has tried to carve out a media market that is distinct from television's. TV is required to be balanced and impartial, so the tabloid press has increased its party political bias, and the quality press has increasingly presented in-depth commentary and analysis of the news.

The result is that much of the national press in Britain is strongly party political compared with most other western countries, and for much of the post-war period (1945–92) it has been heavily Conservative. As Figure 14.1 shows, the circulation of Conservative newspapers outnumbered Labour or Liberal papers 1951–97, and from the 1970s to 1997 they dominated. During these decades a large majority

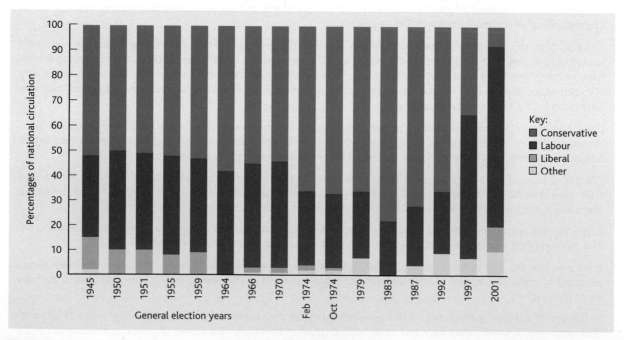

Figure 14.1 Party politics of the press: percentages of national circulation

Source: Calculated from figures provided by C. Seymour-Ure, *The British Press and Broadcasting since 1945*, Oxford: Blackwell, 1992, pp. 196–7 (1945–87); Audit Bureau of Circulations for more recent elections

of people read a Conservative paper including about 70 per cent of the working-class people who traditionally provide Labour with most of its support. Three of the largest circulation mass tabloids (*Sun*, *Mail*, and *Express*) were strongly Conservative, and the fourth (the *Daily Mirror*) offered Labour only lukewarm support at times.

In the 1997, 2001 and 2005 elections the scene was totally changed. The Conservative government of the 1990s came under increasing attack and criticism, to such an extent that by 1997 the *Sun*, strongly Conservative in the 1980s and early 1990s, switched support to Blair. For the first time, Labour had a newspaper advantage. Not only that, but *The Times*, *Telegraph* and *Financial Times* were not as staunchly Conservative as usual. By the election of 2001 the balance had swung even more to Labour. In that election the Tories were supported by only one national Fleet Street daily paper (the *Telegraph*). In 2005 it was rejoined by the *Daily Express* and the *Daily Mail* in the Conservative camp, but Labour still led comfortably in the circulation battle.

Did this contribute to Labour's three victories? We do not know. Labour scored a remarkable win in 1945, and won again in 1964, 1966 and 1974, all with most papers against it. Besides, do newspapers influence the voting of their readers or, on the contrary, do voters pick their newspapers to suit their own politics? In 1997 the *Sun* switched its support to Labour, most *Sun* readers voted Labour, and Labour duly won the election by a landslide. Does this prove that 'it was the *Sun* wot won it'? Probably not. It has been estimated that about 60 per cent of *Sun* readers would have voted Labour in 1997 whoever the paper backed. But from the paper's point of view it is bad commercially to run against the grain of your own readers, and it is not good to be on the losing side. In any case, so many people had firm voting intentions of their own in 1997 and 2001 that the newspaper effect may well have been small, if it existed at all.

Media bias: radio and TV

The electronic media are an entirely different matter. Commercial TV is legally required to be politically neutral and balanced (particularly in its handling of election campaigns), and the BBC voluntarily follows the same code of conduct. As a result, a large majority of viewers (more than two-thirds) trust both BBC and ITV news, and a declining minority believe they are biased. In 2003, 15 per cent believed BBC 1 had a political bias, 5 per cent said the same of BBC 2 and ITV 1, and 2 per cent and 1 per cent perceived a C4 and C5 bias. Trust in TV is much higher than in radio, and newspapers are trusted the least, especially the tabloids.

Nevertheless some research argues that TV news is systematically prejudiced. The Glasgow Media Group (GMG) has published a series of books (the main ones are *Bad News*, *More Bad News*, *Really Bad News* and *War and Peace News*) claiming there is a pervasive elitist and conservative bias in the BBC's news. The Glasgow team has been criticised, in turn, by those who argue that their work is sometimes wrong or exaggerated, and ignores contradictory evidence. The controversy about broadcasting bias continues and is likely to generate more heat than light for some time to come.

We can summarise this section on mass media bias by saying that it is exceedingly difficult to establish a political bias in TV or radio, but easy to show a clear but changing party political leaning in the national press. However, whether newspaper bias has a strong effect on public opinion and voting behaviour is an entirely different matter, and also one that is exceedingly difficult to establish. To this extent it seems that we have to keep open minds on the matters of bias and the political impact of the mass media. Nevertheless, bias and impact are not the only things that worry media watchers. There is also the issue of the ownership and control of the media and its implications for a pluralist democracy.

Pluralist democracy and the mass media

The mass media are an essential part of modern democracy. The reasons are easy to understand. Democracy requires, at a minimum, informed and politically educated citizens who can make decisions for themselves. In turn, they need balanced and reliable news and access to a wide variety of opinion so that they can make informed and sensible choices.

At the same time, most of us have to rely on the media for our news and opinion because we have little first-hand experience of politics – we know few politicians personally, and we rarely hear their speeches for ourselves or witness political events with our own eyes. Most citizens have neither a detailed knowledge nor a deep interest in politics. Most rely on the media to keep them informed, mainly TV news (Table 14.3). Indeed, the great merit of television is that it brings political leaders and events into our own living rooms where we see and hear them for ourselves, and form our own judgements.

The first democratic requirement of the mass media, then, is to provide us with a full and fair account of the news and opinion so that we can play our role as informed citizens in a democracy. The news media, however, are far more than mere channels for the communication of facts. We expect them to comment, analyse, criticise, investigate and evaluate – to tell us what is really happening, not just what politicians tell us is happening. For this reason the mass media are sometimes described as 'the fourth estate of the realm', or 'the watchdog of the constitution'. The problem is that the media role is a demanding and complex one, which requires them to perform a number of tasks, some difficult to achieve and others not easily combined:

- The news must be accurate, but it is often difficult to get facts right in the rushed world of news deadlines.

- The media must present a full account of the news, but they cannot possibly report all the news. There is just too much of it, so the media must select and impose their judgement about what is important.

- It is impossible to be completely neutral about political news. Facts do not speak for themselves; they must be interpreted, and the language we use is sometimes loaded, especially about dramatic political events.

BRIEFINGS

14.2 Pluralist democracy

Pluralist democracy is based on the idea that modern societies contain all sorts of competing groups, interests, ideologies and ideas, which have a right to be heard and to defend themselves in the public arena. Democracy is seen as a peaceful struggle between political interests, ideas and values – often expressed by parties, pressure groups and social movements. The best arguments will win the day if there is a genuinely 'free marketplace of ideas' (J. S. Mill).

This is an attractive ideal. Unfortunately Britain, along with other modern societies, may fall short of providing a free market of ideas. Powerful groups and interests – including the party in power – may try to control the channels of communication and manipulate the news so that their views tend to shape discussion. Consequently, there is a controversy between those who want (a) market competition for the mass media, and (b) media regulation to protect the public interest.

- The news should be objective and detached, but also critical and engaged: it should report what politicians say in their own words, but also be hard hitting and dig beneath the surface (investigative journalism).

- The news media should present a wide variety of opinion, not just the views of government leaders. But it is quicker and easier to rely on neatly packaged government press releases than hunt for alternative views and information.

- The news media must resist the pressures of spin doctors who want to manipulate the news, but in doing so they are often attacked by political leaders who feel they have been unfairly reported.

- Democracy requires the media to provide a full and comprehensive coverage of the news, but research shows that citizens are sometimes bored by this. TV news audiences are falling and in 2001 got more news of the election campaign than they wanted. The media are trapped between the demands of democracy and the market.

For these reasons alone it is clear that the mass media would have a tough job playing their proper role in democracy, even in an ideal world, but the world of the British media is also far from a pluralist ideal, as we will see.

Pluralist theory and the media

It is clear that no single newspaper or TV news programme can possibly cover all news and opinion. What is important is that the news media as a whole present the important news and a diverse range of opinion, so that citizens can choose in a free market of ideas and opinions. This places great importance on a diversity of news sources that cover the news from different political perspectives.

In the late nineteenth century the newspaper market roughly met these conditions. It was relatively easy and inexpensive to publish a paper or newssheet to serve small, local markets, and there was competition between different publications advocating different political positions. The industry was fragmented and run by different people with different political positions, several of them independent of large political parties and major economic interests.

Nowadays the news media are entirely different. On the one hand, there are many more forms of communication – not just the papers and pamphlets of Victorian times, but radio, television, films, videos, tapes, CD-Roms, DVDs, email and the web. In this sense the media are more pluralist because there are many more forms of communication. On the other hand, the modern media are now a capital-intensive big business with worldwide markets. The question is whether they still represent a pluralist and competitive market.

The print media

In theory anyone can set up a newspaper or a magazine, especially in the age of desktop publishing. In theory there is no limit to the number of producers who can compete in this market. Thus there is no more theoretical need for state regulation of the print media than there is, say, for soap powder. Moreover, it can be argued that the principle of freedom of speech means that the less regulation of publishing there is the better. Therefore the print media should not be subject to any political controls: they should print the news as they see fit, and publish whatever editorials and political advertisements they wish.

Since 1945, and the lifting of wartime restrictions, the State has intervened in the newspaper industry only in exceptional circumstances when market failure has threatened competition. In this sense the newspaper market is the same as any other that attracts the attention of the Competition Commission when there is a danger of market failure.

In practice, however, the British newspaper industry has long shown strong oligopolistic tendencies towards concentration of ownership in the hands of a few big publishing companies. Attempts to prevent further concentration have been no more than half-hearted. The national press in Britain does not show the pluralist market structure that is required for democracy.

In recent years another problem has become more visible, namely the content and standards of tabloid journalism, including bias, inaccuracy, sensationalism, cheque-book journalism and invasion of privacy. Press standards have been a long-standing source of complaint in Britain, but they seem to have fallen to a new low.

Because the principle of a free press is so strong, governments have been unwilling to impose outside regulation, and have placed their faith instead on self-regulation by the industry, in the shape of a code of practice drawn up by newspaper editors, and adjudicated by the Press Complaints Commission. The Commission has little power and few sanctions. The Calcutt Report (1990) and the Calcutt Review of the Press Complaints Commission (1993) recommended stronger action, but this was rejected by the government. Tabloid press standards remain a difficult and unresolved issue. Few outside the newspaper industry believe that self-regulation has worked. But state regulation is a minefield of political problems.

The electronic media: regulation and the public service model

Until quite recently, radio and television markets were entirely different from newspaper markets. Because of spectrum scarcity the electronic media were natural monopolies quite unlike the theoretically open market of the print media. Spectrum scarcity meant that the airwaves were regarded as a public good, and closely regulated by the state in the public interest (see Briefing 14.3).

In the early years of radio and TV the British Broadcasting Corporation had a monopoly of broadcasting, which it used according to 'the **public service model**' as 'the voice of the nation'. Funded by a licence fee set by the government and paid by radio and TV owners (later TV owners alone) it did not have to make a profit, and consequently was able to provide high-quality news and entertainment for the nation as a whole. The public service model of television operated from 1946 (when the BBC resumed its post-war TV broadcasting) until 1955, when commercial TV went on the air. The BBC's monopoly of radio lasted from 1926, when the BBC was founded, until commercial radio was legalised in 1971.

Radio and TV broadcasting is still carefully regulated in Britain by an alphabet soup of agencies (Briefing 14.5), and news and current affairs programmes are closely regulated in order to achieve balance, accuracy and impartiality. As a result, most people believe that the BBC and ITN (Independent Television Network) are reliable and impartial sources of news. Whereas about two out of three trust BBC and ITN 'a great deal', and about half say the same of their broadsheet newspaper, fewer than one-third of tabloid readers trust their newspaper.

Given the convergence of the TV, radio, phone and computer communications sectors, a single new regulatory body (OFCOM) was created in 2003 that merges

Public service model

The idea that radio and TV should not be commercial but used in the public interest to educate, inform and entertain.

Spectrum scarcity

The shortage of broadcasting frequencies for radio and TV caused by the fact that the wavelengths available for public broadcasting on the spectrum are limited.

BRIEFINGS

14.3 Market and content regulation of the electronic media

Market regulation

Because broadcasting wavelengths are limited in number (**spectrum scarcity**), the state controls the electronic media. Initially it gave the British Broadcasting Corporation a monopoly over radio and TV, but as technology developed more channels became available and commercial TV and radio stations were legalised. There are still only a few terrestrial broadcasting wavelengths, so the state continues to control broadcasting licences.

In order to prevent monopoly or oligopoly emerging in the limited market the state also regulates cross-media ownership of TV, radio and newspapers. **Market regulation** is found mainly in electronic media, but it is also supposed to apply to the print media. In Britain, however, market regulation of the print media has not been conspicuously successful, and market regulation of all media has been relaxed considerably, starting in 1993.

Content regulation

Because the airwaves are public property it is argued that they should be used in the public interest. For example, the number and the content of TV and radio commercials is controlled, and programmes unsuitable for children are not broadcast until the late evening. News and election programmes are closely regulated by the Television Act of 1954, which established independent (commercial) TV, and that was amended by the Broadcasting Act of 1981:

- Political and religious advertising and editorialising are banned.
- Political programmes are required to maintain 'proper balance . . . accuracy and impartiality'.
- Election candidates and parties must be treated fairly and impartially.
- Party political programmes and election broadcasts, made and financed by the parties, are broadcast free of charge, with time allotted to parties in proportion to their voting support.

The BBC is not legally bound by the 1954 or 1981 Acts, but voluntarily observes their codes of practice.

Content regulation by the European Union

The European Union has also begun to regulate the media and advertising. It has banned cigarette advertisements on TV, and controls other advertising. The advertising of alcohol and products aimed at children are also regulated. Other press, advertising and broadcasting restrictions are being introduced, and the EU is likely to play a bigger role in the regulation of broadcast content in the future.

Market regulation

Regulation of the media market by public bodies.

Content regulation

Regulation of the content of the media by public bodies.

the ITC, BSC, Oftel, the Radio Authority and the Radiocommunications Agency into one body charged with regulating all branches of the UK communications industry.

Friends of the BBC point out that it is widely admired throughout the western world for its high-quality broadcasting, especially its news and current affairs programmes. Critics say that it is elitist or paternalistic, giving people not what they want but what the BBC thinks they should have. Perhaps because it is neutral and impartial in its political reporting the BBC has also acquired many political enemies, besides the free marketeers who dislike it because it is a public service. Since commercialisation, however, the BBC has had to pay more careful attention to its audience ratings, and 'backdoor commercialisation' is the result. The public service model of political reporting still applies to all radio and TV, but commercial pressures have changed almost everything else. Commercialisation of the media has been a fiercely controversial issue in British politics and it is likely to remain so for some time to come.

BRIEFINGS

14.4 The public service model

The main aim of the public service model of broadcasting is not to use the media to make money in a commercial market, but as a national resource for the public good. Lord Reith, the founding father of the BBC, saw it as 'the voice of the nation' with a duty to 'educate, inform and entertain', in that order of priority. The main features of the British public service model are as follows:

- **Market regulation**   As natural monopolies the electronic media are regulated by the state, which issues broadcasting licences under specific conditions.

- **Content regulation**   If broadcasting wavelengths are public property then they should be used for the public good: programmes should appeal to a wide range of tastes, majority and minority; news and election programmes should be balanced, accurate and impartial; political advertising and editorialising are not allowed.

- **Accountability**   The electronic media should be accountable to the public, not to market shareholders or the government.

- **Self-regulation by quango**   To avoid the dangers of state interference the media should be controlled and regulated by their own bodies or quangos.

- **National broadcasting**   Broadcasting should serve the entire nation, including remote areas, not a particular territory or section of the population.

- **Public funding**   Broadcasting should be financed mainly from public funds, not commercial sources. Public funds may take the form of general subsidies from the government, or licence fees, or some combination of the two.

BRIEFINGS

14.5 The alphabet soup of media agencies

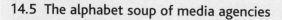

BBC (British Broadcasting Corporation)   Established in 1926 as a public radio monopoly, the BBC now runs local, national and international radio and TV channels, as well as the largest web site in Europe. The Home Secretary appoints its board of governors, which appoints the director-general, who has day-to-day authority. Its charter is periodically renewed, the last time in 1994 until 2006. It is funded mainly from the TV licence fee, which is set by the government.

ITC (Independent Television Commission)   The Broadcasting Act of 1990 created the ITC in place of the previous controlling body (the Independent Broadcasting Authority). The ITC licenses and regulates commercial TV stations, which have been auctioned since 1990. Commercial broadcasting is funded by advertising revenue.

BSC (Broadcasting Standards Commission)   The Broadcasting Act of 1996 replaced the Broadcasting Complaints Commission with the Broadcasting Standards Commission. The BSC is the statutory body dealing with codes of practice, standards and fairness, and complaints for all forms of broadcasting in the United Kingdom – BBC and commercial, text, cable, satellite and digital broadcasting.

The Radio Authority   The Radio Authority licenses and regulates all independent radio in accordance with the Broadcasting Acts of 1990 and 1996.

Oftel   Oftel was set up in 1984 to regulate the UK telecommunications industry when British Telecom (a nationalised industry) was privatised.

Radiocommunications Agency   This is an executive agency of the Department of Trade and Industry that manages the non-military radio spectrum and keeps it clean of unauthorised users.

OFCOM (Office of Communications)   Created by the Communications Act 2003.

CONTROVERSY

Public services versus free media markets

Public service model

- There is no market for ideas or for political news as there is for soap powder or motor cars. News programmes cannot be put to the same tests as consumer durables, neither can political ideas be subject to the same sorts of tests as soap powder.
- The market does not ensure that truth will prevail, or even that the best ideas will survive, only that popular demands are satisfied. If people want sound bites, gossip, trivia, racism, sexism, prejudice, chauvinism, that is what the market will deliver.
- The news is far too important to be left to commercial forces that are only interested in profits. Only public regulation can ensure balance, accuracy and impartiality.
- State control of the electronic media (market and content) should remain as long as there is no competitive market in the electronic media as there is, in theory, in the print media.
- There are dangers in the state regulation of the media, but these are avoided in some western countries where there is no state control or influence over the political content of the media.
- In the commercial media the bad drives out the good, and market competition forces the best to adopt the standards of the worst.
- The state has to step in when the market fails and the media market shows clear signs of oligopoly, not pluralistic competition.
- Media oligopolies are increasingly driven by conservative ideologies, which render their content politically biased.
- The state will have to continue its regulation of such things as pornography, racism and children's programmes.
- Self-regulation of the newspapers has produced low journalistic standards, cheque-book journalism, sensationalism and the invasion of privacy.

- Probably the most commercial media market in the western world is in the United States, which also has one of the worst news services.

Free market model

- There is no difference, in principle, between the market for goods and services and the market for news and ideas. We should turn news and ideas over to the market, as we do other goods and services.
- The market ensures that people get what they want, which is more democratic than BBC directors broadcasting what they think people need.
- Regulation of the media is inconsistent with free speech, and government by quango still gives the government too much influence. The media should be completely independent of the government.
- Cable and satellite TV, local radio and the convergence of media sectors have virtually eliminated spectrum scarcity, and there is little difference between the markets for electronic and print media. State control is no longer necessary.
- Some claim that market competition between ideas will ensure that the 'truth will out', others that truth is relative, and only media competition will deliver a multiplicity of truths.
- The state can regulate cases of media market failure as it does other cases of market failure, but this means occasional intervention, not control.
- Content regulation of the media should go no further than dealing with the conditions for public order and the protection of those unable to protect themselves, especially children. Libertarians even argue that the state should not regulate pornography.
- Low journalistic standards are better than repression or manipulation by governments.

Commercialisation of the electronic media

Post-war Conservative governments were persuaded by technical developments in radio and TV broadcasting to introduce commercial radio and TV, so ending the BBC monopoly and progressively diluting the public service model. The Television Act of 1954 created commercial (independent) TV, which went on the air a year later, the first in western Europe. Then, pressured by pirate radio (illegal commercial radio broadcast from ships outside territorial waters), commercial radio was authorised in 1971. A second commercial TV Channel (Channel 4) was set up by the Independent Broadcasting Authority Act of 1979, and it went on the air in 1982. Meanwhile, cable TV was introduced in 1972, and satellite TV (first broadcast in 1962 from Telstar) expanded rapidly in the late 1980s, vastly increasing the total number of TV stations.

The arguments for commercial radio and TV, as against the public service model, are complex and many sided, but ultimately they are political rather than technical or economic. Advocates of the market claim that only full commercialisation can guarantee pluralist competition, and the absence of state regulation that freedom of speech demands. They argue that the British media can only compete with the main European players, never mind the giant media corporations of the United States, if media ownership restrictions are lifted. Defenders of public service media point out that the media market is an oligopoly, and likely to become more so. They fear that commercialisation will produce the worst kind of 'tabloid TV', just as the print market has produced the worst kind of newspaper journalism. Further commercialisation may result in US-style media that deliver poor news and current affairs coverage.

Although the British government may well introduce more commercialism into the media in the future, state regulation of broadcasting is not likely to disappear altogether:

- The European Union wants to impose greater regulation on the media market and its content.

- Those who most strongly advocate a media market are often most strongly opposed to some of its free-market and highly commercial products: violence and pornography on TV and the web, for example.

- The requirements of balance, accuracy and impartiality for TV and radio news are still in place, as are the restrictions on election campaigning and reporting.

In other words the commercialisation and deregulation of the electronic media may well create pressures for some reregulation. At the same time there is concern about the democratic role of the mass media (print and electronic) that derives not only from its content but also from the structure of its ownership and control.

Ownership and control of the British media

The history of the British mass media in the twentieth century is marked by five related features:

1. concentration around a national press
2. a declining number of newspaper titles
3. concentration of ownership and control
4. the growth of multimedia conglomerates
5. internationalisation.

Centralisation

Britain is a small, densely populated and highly centralised country, so it is not surprising that the media have a centralised and nationalised market centred on

London. There are still many local and regional daily and Sunday papers, but two-thirds of the adult population regularly see a national daily paper, and 70 per cent a national Sunday paper. As a result, the national newspaper market in Britain is very large by most standards. In round figures 90 million newspapers are sold every week. The national dailies have a total circulation of 12.3 million a day, and the national Sundays sell 13.4 million. Since each paper is read by about three people the readership of the national dailies is around 36 million, and of the national Sundays around 40 million. All national newspapers have their headquarters in London, even if some print regional editions in Manchester or Scotland.

Radio and TV are also highly centralised, with a few national organisations dominating the market. ITV is based on regions, and there has been a rapid expansion of local and community radio stations. But most viewers and listeners still tune to national programmes and national news broadcasts.

Declining number of newspaper titles

In the same way that the market for cars has produced an ever-increasing need for capital investment, and so an ever-decreasing number of mass manufacturers, so the newspaper market has less and less room for competing titles. In 1900 there were 21 national daily papers, now there are 11 main titles (including the *Financial Times*). In 1923 there were 14 Sunday papers, now there are 9. In the 70 years after 1920 the number of provincial morning papers declined from 41 to 18, of provincial evening papers from 89 to 76, and of national and provincial Sunday papers from 21 to 9. There were about 1,400 local and regional daily and Sunday titles in 1947, only 637 on sale in 2006. In 1975 18 per cent of British towns had competing papers run by different owners, half the percentage of 1921. In 1900 London had 11 evening papers; now it has 1.

Concentration of ownership and control

Concentrated ownership and control of the British newspaper business is by no means new. In 1910 the biggest press magnate of the day, Lord Northcliffe, controlled 39 per cent of national daily circulation. In 2003 his modern equivalent, Rupert Murdoch, has 35 per cent of the daily and almost 40 per cent of the Sunday market. However, in 1910 the three best-selling national dailies accounted for two-thirds of total circulation, whereas in 1983 the biggest three (Murdoch, Maxwell and Matthews) took 75 per cent. In that year the five biggest companies accounted for 84 per cent of national daily and 96 per cent of national Sunday sales. By 2006 the big five were controlling 91 per cent of the national daily circulation.

The big five have also increased their control of the local and provincial press. In 1947 they had 44 and 65 per cent of provincial evening and morning circulation. By 1983 the figures had risen to 54 and 72 per cent respectively. Over the same period they increased their share of the local weekly market from 8 per cent to almost one-third. In 2006, the biggest owner of local and regional papers was Trinity Mirror with 230 titles and a weekly circulation of 14.4 million.

The policy of regulating the market to preserve competition has not been effective. The Royal Commissions on the press of 1949, 1962 and 1977 all expressed concern about increasing concentration of ownership and control. As a result of a recommendation of the 1962 Commission it was decided in 1965 that large companies should get the consent of the Secretary of State for the Department of Trade and Industry before acquiring more newspaper holdings. Between 1965 and 1977 50 such applications were made. Not one was refused. In 1981 Rupert Murdoch

was allowed to buy *The Times* and *Sunday Times*, increasing his share of national daily sales to 30 per cent, and of national Sunday sales to 36 per cent.

In 1990 Murdoch's Sky company merged with its main rival, British Satellite Broadcasting (BSB), to form a satellite monopoly, BSkyB, although this was inconsistent with the 1990 Broadcasting Act. The companies did not consult the Independent Broadcasting Authority before the merger, but the IBA approved it after the event. In 1992 there was a moratorium on mergers of commercial TV stations, following the first franchise auction of the previous year. Nonetheless Yorkshire Television absorbed Tyne Tees Television and the Independent Television Commission agreed to the merger.

The concentration of ownership and control is likely to speed up over the next decades, because of economic pressures and because controls were loosened in 1993 by allowing companies to hold two licences, which some promptly did. In 1995 controls of **cross-media ownership** were further loosened, although large newspaper groups continued to have restricted rights to TV ownership.

Multimedia conglomeration

What makes the current situation different from the earlier times of press barons, such as Lords Northcliffe and Rothermere, is that the concentration of ownership and control now extends far beyond the press to publishing and other media forms. The largest multimedia conglomerates now include newspapers, journals, books, films, recording, radio, TV and entertainment. They also extend into commerce and finance of other kinds, such as property, banking, insurance, oil, transport and computers. As the Press Commission of 1977 wrote: 'Rather than saying that the press has other business interests, it would be truer to argue that the press has become a subsidiary of other interests.' This is even truer now. In short, the media have been absorbed into the general world of business and finance.

Cross-media ownership

When the same person or company has financial interests in different types of mass media – radio, TV, newspapers, magazines, films, recording etc.

Multimedia conglomeration

When the same company has financial interests in different media and (usually) in a range of other economic activities as well.

BRIEFINGS

14.6 Media moguls

Robert Maxwell

When Maxwell died in mysterious circumstances in 1991 his newspapers (*Mirror/Daily Record*, *Sunday Mirror*, *Sunday People* and *Sporting Life*) sold close to 12 million copies a week, accounting for one-quarter of the daily tabloid market. Maxwell also had financial interests in TV (Central, Border, SelecTV, MTV and Rediffusion Cable), books (EJ Arnold and Pergamon Press), magazines and journals, computer software, transport and plastics.

Rupert Murdoch

Rupert Murdoch, an Australian with US citizenship, owns newspapers and TV stations on three continents. In Britain his companies own the *Sun*, *News of the World*, *The Times*, *The Sunday Times* and *The Times'* supplements with sales of over 10 million copies, including one-third of the daily and Sunday tabloid market and almost half the Sunday broadsheets. His financial interests have included London Weekend TV, BSkyB (the largest satellite company in Britain), cable TV, films (Metromedia and Fox), recording, magazines and journals, general publishing (Collins, Fontana and Granada Books), the Reuters news agency, property, land and air transport (TNT trucking), computer software, gas and oil, and shares in Manchester United, Leeds United and Chelsea football clubs.

Lord Matthews

The main Matthews company, Trafalgar House, ran the Express Group (sold to United Newspapers in 1985), which published, among others, the *Daily Express*, *Sunday Express*, *Star* and *Standard*, and 11 local papers (a circulation of over 7 million). At various times his companies have had interests in TV-AM, Capital Radio, publishing houses in Britain and abroad, Cunard shipping and hotels, and in property and insurance.

Lord Rothermere

Rothermere's Associated Newspapers publishes the *Daily Mail*, *Mail on Sunday* and *Weekend*, which have a circulation of around 5 million. It also has financial ties with Northcliffe Newspapers in companies on three continents that cover publishing, broadcasting, theatre, oil, transport and investment finance.

United Newspapers

When United Newspapers (Lord Stevens) absorbed the Express Group it controlled one-quarter of daily tabloid and 10 per cent of Sunday tabloid circulation. In the 1990s it published 8 regional dailies, over 100 weeklies, and controlled two large publishers of magazines and directories as well as the Extel news agency.

Internationalisation – the borderless world

Multimedia moguls and corporations now span not just countries but continents. The most conspicuous examples include Time Warner, AT&T and General Electric in America, Sony in Japan, Berlusconi in Italy, the Bertelsmann and Springer groups of Germany, and Rupert Murdoch, with companies in Australia, Asia, Europe and the United States. While newspapers usually cater for national (that is, specific language) markets, they are increasingly controlled by multinational companies, and some journals and magazines are increasing their international circulation (the *Financial Times*, *The Economist*, *Time*, *Newsweek*). The inherently international nature of films and TV is being strengthened by the spread of cable and satellite, which is helping to create a global and borderless television network. The result is that a few international news channels, such as Cable News Network (CNN) and BBC World TV, are chasing the global news market hard.

There are two dangers in increasing ownership and control, and of growing multimedia, multinational conglomerates. First, such companies are increasingly beyond public accountability or regulation, and represent growing power without responsibility. Second, by controlling large market shares they weaken media competition that pluralist theory says is essential for democracy.

Political consequences of market changes

Changes in the media market seem to have contradictory consequences for news and current affairs reporting.

Smaller media: specialisation and diversity

As ownership and control of the mass media becomes increasingly consolidated and centralised, so the mass media become progressively homogeneous. At the same time technology also makes it possible for the smaller media to become increasingly specialised and varied. Local TV and radio, satellite and cable TV, the increasing number of magazine titles, and the communication possibilities of the World Wide Web and email are a few examples of media differentiation. However, a closer look at these media sectors reveals a more complex situation of progressive consolidation of mass markets, and increasing fragmentation of minority markets.

Magazines

A visit to any high street newsagent will reveal a pluralist heaven of magazine titles catering for a huge diversity of tastes. A closer look shows that many of the big circulation magazines in Britain are published by a few of the largest companies. Between 1966 and 1974 over half of the new consumer magazines with sales of 30,000 or more were launched by four major publishing groups. The largest, the International Publishing Corporation, has over 200 titles.

Newspapers

New computer methods of newspaper production have not weakened the Fleet Street empires, as they were predicted to do. It is true that two new national papers were launched between 1960 and 1985, whereas eight were created between 1986 and 1992, but few survive. The *Independent*, also launched in 1986, was the first successful new national daily in the country since 1873, but with daily sales of around 259,000 (barely more than 2 per cent of the national total), it has hardly disturbed the mass-circulation papers.

TV

BBC had a monopoly of TV with its single channel in 1955. Now it fights with an ever-growing number of terrestrial, cable and satellite channels. In spite of this fragmentation of the market, however, the BBC keeps a 34.6 per cent share of mainstream viewing. Moreover, following the auctioning of commercial TV licences in 1990 and the weakening of market regulation, three companies (Granada, United News and Scottish Media Group) now control 10 of the 15 regional channels, and Murdoch's BSkyB has a large share of satellite broadcasting. A large number of small channels account for a small percentage of the total TV market.

Sensationalism and investigative journalism

Commercialisation means that profit and dividends for shareholders have become an overriding imperative. This has two effects on news content; sensationalism and **investigative journalism**. These are different sides of the same coin, in the sense that both are intended to attract readers and viewers in a commercial media market. The tabloids turned to more cheque-book journalism and sensationalism in the 1960s and 1970s, partly to combat TV competition. TV, faced with commercial pressures, has increasingly 'dumbed down' its programming and cut its news and current affairs coverage.

At the same time both newspapers and TV have turned to more investigative journalism. It could be argued that the media now do a much better job of questioning leading politicians than Parliament. The trend, started by Robin Day in the 1970s, has been sharpened by John Humphrys and James Naughtie on radio, and Jeremy Paxman on TV. Paxman once asked the Home Secretary, Michael Howard, the same question 14 times, to make it clear that he could not get a straight answer. Newspapers, for their part, are increasingly involved in investigative journalism (sometimes called 'attack' journalism), which is said to contribute to videomalaise.

> **Investigative journalism**
>
> In-depth and often critical journalism that involves research which is usually time-consuming and expensive.

Less politics and current affairs?

Whether because of citizen political fatigue or commercialisation, or both, there are signs that political and current affairs reporting has been cut in recent years.

Plate 14.3 Alasdair Campbell, Tony Blair's chief spin-doctor from 1994 to 2003, tries to distract from the 'clash' between the Ministry of Defence (MOD) over the issue of weapons of mass destruction (WMD). See Briefing 14.1

Source: Chris Riddell/The Observer, 27th August 2003, Centre of the Study of Cartoons of Carcatures, University of Kent

The tabloids showed rather little interest in the election campaign of 2001 and not a great deal more in 2005 (perhaps because the campaigns were rather dull and the results a foregone conclusion), ITV cut its news programmes compared with 1997, and it was left largely to the BBC to do its public service duty. Nevertheless its viewing figures for the election night programme fell from 6.5 million in 1997 to 4.9 million in both 2001 and 2005. The best and most extensive election news tended to be 'ghettoised' in the specialised news channels, often in the late evening with small audiences. In other words, the political content of the mass media may be declining, but that of the more specialised media is increasing. The government has been concerned about rising levels of political distrust and falling levels of political interest, especially among the young, and has tried to use the new electronic communications technology to reverse the trends.

E-media: digitopia or digital dystopia?

By the start of the new millennium, technical change had already transformed the electronic media market, and is set to revolutionise it again within another decade or so. Digital broadcasting means the convergence of media sectors (TV, radio, newspapers and computer communication) so that sound, pictures and words can be transmitted and received across communication sectors, blending them into one. Broadband technology allows the communication of multiple signals at the same time, and speeds up the whole process. The potential of the 'wired nation' with information superhighways, smart buildings and smart cards will introduce cheaper and more accessible communications with more competition and variety.

Some regard this as a huge potential benefit to democratic politics. The new technology multiplies the number of channels of communication and hence creates a more pluralist system capable of delivering more information from different sources to more people. It also enables us to develop cheap and easy forms of electronic voting, polling, discussion and communication, and therefore raises the possibility of direct democracy at the click of a mouse. Others regard it is a threat, making it easier for global business empires to consolidate their control of communications technology, enhancing the cultural imperialism of US corporations, widening the knowledge gap and creating new information inequalities, and further commercialising and dumbing down the mass media.

It is certainly the case that new media in the shape of the World Wide Web and email have spread like wildfire. There were 50 web sites in the world in 1992 but an estimated 30 million of them in 2001, and growth is exponential. By 2006 two-thirds of the adult population of the UK (30 million) had internet access, using it mostly for buying goods and services, but also for web searches, sending emails and posting messages to newsgroups or chat rooms. Acutely conscious of this, New Labour has set up special units within government to promote both e-government and e-commerce, but the results have not been encouraging. The difficulty is not technology or knowledge but social attitudes and adaptability. As a result developments in e-politics and e-government show a variety of different and contradictory trends.

- **MP web sites and email** Members of Parliament themselves have not always been quick to set up their own web sites or email connections. Almost a third (30 per cent) did not have web sites in 2006 and, more seriously, another 16 per cent had no email. Some of the web sites are dull, unimaginative, unprofessional, or do not work properly.

- **E-government** The government's plans to exploit the technology for e-government and e-commerce have not progressed rapidly. Some experiments have been cancelled, others delayed. Electronic voting in the 2006 local elections was abandoned, and instead the government accepted 16 local authority plans to experiment with new ways of voting and vote counting.

■ **E-elections**   Limited use of the new technology was made for electioneering in 2001 and 2005. All the large parties now have web sites, and text messaging and emails were used to target selected groups of voters, but few attempts have been made to exploit the full potential of the new technology. It has been used for information sending rather than interaction – talking at rather than with the voters. There were election campaign weblogs by voters and politicians (including parodies), some instances of cybersquatting and some interesting web sites. Not much more than 3–5 per cent of the population have used the net or email for election purposes.

■ **Vote swapping**   In 2001 and 2005 web sites were set up to help vote swapping between tactical voters in marginal seats. It is difficult to know how much they were used or how much impact they had on results in marginal seats.

■ **Pressure group campaigns**   Some groups have made good use of the technology to sign up members, to campaign and inform, and to interact with the public. Groups include the Countryside Alliance, the RSPB, Age Concern, Oxfam, Greenpeace and the NUS (whose web campaign against top-up fees attracted a 90,000 signature petition and 50,000 faxes to MPs.)

■ **Using mobiles to coordinate protest action**   Truck drivers used their mobile phones to coordinate road blocks to protest against increased fuel tax in 2000, and 'crusties' did the same to peacefully occupy Stonehenge at dawn one midsummer day.

■ **Mass media web sites**   The mass media have their own web sites, not least the BBC's full reporting of the news and its superb coverage of elections.

Most research on e-government and politics concludes that we are destined for neither digital utopia nor dystopia, at present anyway. For the most part it is business as usual. There are some innovative pressure group sites, but few parties or government departments have exploited the interactive potential of the new electronic media. Few people use the new technology for political purposes, and most of those who do are the wealthier, better educated, and middle- and upper-class sections of the population who are already firmly plugged into the traditional news mediums. The new media have a clear tendency to widen the information gap rather than bridge it. The one exception to this general rule is that the young are more e-literate and active than the old, which may change the scene when they grow older and form a larger percentage of the population. The problem is that the present younger generation is noted for its political disinterest and uses the new communications technology for largely non-political purposes.

Summary

■ The mass media have been transformed out of all recognition since 1945, and now play a hugely important role in British politics. We are in the 'media age', but exactly what this means is a controversial matter.

■ Different people use different media for different purposes. Well-educated people tend to read a broadsheet, and watch comparatively little TV. Poorly educated people tend to read a tabloid and watch a lot of TV, including TV news. The result is a growing 'knowledge gap'.

■ It is exceedingly difficult to pin down what sort of medium has what sort of impact on what sorts of people. The four main opinions on this topic are: reinforcement theory/minimal effects; agenda-setting theory; framing theory, which claims indirect and direct effects; and direct effects theory.

▶

- The matter of media bias is also highly controversial, but content regulation reduces party political bias in the electronic media that, as a result, is trusted much more than the tabloid press. Until 1997 Fleet Street leaned heavily towards the Conservatives.

- Spectrum scarcity in the past resulted in both market and content regulation of the electronic media, and the BBC conformed closely to the public service model, but technological developments in broadcasting have changed this, and commercialisation and deregulation of the electronic media have followed.

- The result is conflicting patterns in the media market and its coverage of politics: (a) concentration of ownership and control of the mass market; (b) greater variety in the specialised media; (c) the growth of sensational and of investigative journalism; but (d) a decline of political coverage in the mass media and an increase in the specialist media.

- For all the speculation about them, e-media seem to have had little impact on politics so far.

MILESTONES

Milestones in British media history

1945–6	BBC Radio resumes normal peacetime broadcasting with the Light Programme, the Home Service and, in 1946, the Third Programme
1946	BBC TV starts again
1950	First TV coverage of general election results. First political programme on TV (*In the News*)
1951	Beveridge Committee on broadcasting recommends public service TV similar to radio
1953	First edition of BBC *Panorama* programme. Press Council set up
1954	Television Act establishes commercial TV (ITV)
1955	ITV goes on the air
1956	Anthony Eden makes first prime ministerial TV broadcast (about Suez). Labour opposition insists on a reply
1959	First TV election campaign coverage
1962	First Telstar TV satellite broadcast
1964	BBC 2 goes on the air, as does Radio Caroline (pirate radio)
1967	First colour TV (BBC 2). First BBC local radio station
1969	Rupert Murdoch (News International) buys the *Sun* and *News of the World*
1970s	Investigative journalism spreads as a feature of all newspapers and television
1971	Commercial local radio authorised
1972	First cable TV
1974	First election phone-in on radio
1975	Trial radio broadcasts of the House of Commons
1979	Independent Broadcasting Authority Act gives Channel 4 to IBA
1981	Murdoch buys *The Times* and *Sunday Times*
1982	First Channel 4 broadcasts
1983	Breakfast TV on BBC and ITV
1984	Maxwell buys Mirror Group
1985	Lord Stevens (United Newspapers) buys Express Group
1986	Peacock Report on financing the BBC recommends only minor changes. BSB wins contract for direct satellite broadcasting. Eddie Shah launches *Today*, then sells to Lonrho ('Tiny' Rowland). The *Independent* launched

Milestones in British media history continued

1987	*Daily* and *Sunday Telegraph* bought by Conrad Black
1988	Broadcasting Standards Council established to regulate radio, TV and video standards. Rupert Murdoch announces Sky TV (satellite TV)
1989	House of Commons televised
1990	Commercial TV franchises auctioned amid much criticism. Sky TV merged with BSB to form BSkyB. BBC Radio 5 Live launched
1991	BBC launches World TV. Press Council transformed into Newspaper Press Complaints Commission with stronger powers
1992	Classic FM goes on air. Mirror Group passes to creditor bank when Maxwell dies. The *Sun* claims it won the election for the Conservatives
1993	Channel 4 sells airtime. TV ownership rules relaxed to make multiple ownership possible
1994	BBC Charter renewed until 2006
1995	Increasing concern about press invasion of privacy and 'cheque-book' journalism
1996	Murdoch establishes monopoly over digital TV, but required to provide access to other broadcasters
1997	Channel 5 TV goes on the air
1997	The *Sun* switches support to Blair
1997	New Labour expands news management (spin doctor) staff in Downing Street and Whitehall
1998	*News at Ten* ends. Digital widescreeen TV starts. The ITC fines Carlton TV £2m for breaches of its code
2000	*News at Ten* reinstated. The Political Parties, Elections, and Referendums Act imposes tighter restrictions than ever on election spending and campaigning
2001	Fleet Street continues its strong support of New Labour. The BBC wins contract for new, 28-channel digital terrestrial TV
2003	The Communications Act creates OFCOM. Director-General and Chairman of the BBC resign after the Hutton Report, which largely exonerated the government of charges of 'sexing up' its weapons of mass destruction report.
2004	Downing Street press and public relations system changed after the Phillis Report.

Essays

1. The British media are often said to be biased. Explain how and why this bias may reach beyond simple party political bias in the shaping of the news.

2. What impact have the new means of communications (notably the World Wide Web and email) had on British government and politics, particularly on election campaigning?

3. What has been the impact on news reporting of the commercialisation of the British media?

Projects

1. Playing the role of a national newspaper editor, explain how you would reconcile (a) your democratic obligations to inform your readers fully and fairly about politics, and (b) the demands of your shareholders to maintain your circulation figures.

2. (Class project) Debate the merits and deficiencies claimed for public service and commercial broadcasting.

Further reading

The best account of the historical development of the political media is C. Seymour-Ure, *The British Press and Broadcasting since 1945* (Oxford: Blackwell, 2nd rev. edn, 1996), and comprehensive recent work on the topic is R. J. Curran and J. Seaton, *Power Without Responsibility: The Press and Broadcasting in Britain*, London: Routledge, 5th edn, 2003 and J. Watts, *Political Communication Today* (Manchester: Manchester University Press, 1997).

On the role of the political media in the 2005 general election, see J. Bartle, 'The press, television, and the internet', *Parliamentary Affairs*, **58**, (4), 2005, pp. 699–711. Good accounts of the impact of the new media are in S. Ward, R. Gibson, and W. Lusoli, 'Online participation and mobilization in Britain: hype, hope and reality', *Parliamentary Affairs*, **56**, (4), 2005, pp. 652–68 and C. Di Gennaro and W. Dutton, 'The internet and the public: online and offline political participation in the United Kingdom', *Parliamentary Affairs*, **57**, (2), 2006, pp. 299–313.

Useful web sites on mass media

Hot links to these sites can be found on the CWS at www.pearsoned.co.uk/budge.

There is sound evidence of the enormous influence that mass media has on every aspect of contemporary British politics. In this section you will find links to Britain's most important media sites as well as links to academic and professional associations engaged in the analysis of the effects of mass media in contemporary Britain. The government's Office of Telecommunications is the United Kingdom's regulator for the telecommunications industry (www.oftel.gov.uk). There are other web sites for Britain's chief media regulators; these include the Broadcasting Standards Commission (www.bsc.org.uk), the Advertising Standards Authority (www.asa.org.uk), the Information Commissioner (who is responsible for data protection and freedom of information) (www.dataprotection.gov.uk), the Independent Television Commission (www.itc.org.uk), the Internet Watch Foundation (www.iwf.org.uk) and the Press Complaints Commission (www.pcc.org.uk). OFCOM's new site is www.ofcom.org.uk.

There are also independent associations aimed at improving the quality of media coverage, some of them include the Campaign for Freedom of Information (www.cfoi.org.uk), the Campaign for Press and Broadcasting Freedom (http://keywords.dsvr.co.uk/freepress/index.html), the Community Media Association (www.commedia.org.uk), the Different Voices Network (www.differentvoices.org.uk), the Presswise Trust (www.presswise.org.uk), Indymedia (www.uk.indymedia.org) and Media UK (www.mediauk.com). Some of the unions representing media workers include Unison (www.unison.org.uk), the National Union of Journalists (www.nuj.org.uk) and BECTU (www.bectu.org.uk).

You also might want to visit www.newscorp.com where you can find useful information on media ownership in the United Kingdom. Interesting insights are also available from the Press Association (www.pa.press.net). At www.cultsock.ndirect.co.uk/MUHome/cshtml/ you can find an impressive number of links and resources for all issues related to mass media.

A very comprehensive and fully updated list of Britain's newspapers, magazines, TV and radio stations can be found at www.rapidtree.com.

chapter 15

Elections and voting

Although we may be unclear about the details of media influence, few would deny that it plays a role in shaping the outcomes of elections, and thus the control of the government by one party and ideological tendency of another. Recent general elections have changed the face of British politics by substituting a Labour government for the Conservative one that had ruled for 18 years. After its third election victory in 2005 it looks as if Labour may last almost as long. Television and newspapers derive their power from the influence they are commonly assumed to have over political opinions, which ultimately get translated into votes. As governments have to face elections every four or five years, everything that might affect their chances of winning or losing is important, and that gives them a strong motivation to control journalists or to seek the support of newspaper proprietors.

However, many factors in addition to the media shape election results. Before an election is ever called voters are influenced by their experiences as members of social groups, together with their enduring party loyalties, values and attitudes. After an election is called they may be influenced by the policies they are offered, together with their evaluations of the parties and leaders. The campaign strategies adopted by the party leaderships may therefore have some effect on the outcome.

The exact number of votes a party receives may be less important than the way these votes are 'converted' into parliamentary seats by the counting rules of the electoral system. British governments depend on being able to control Parliament by means of an overall majority of seats in the House of Commons, not on winning a majority (50 per cent) of the popular vote. Labour's historic third victory in 2005 was built on a mere 35.2 per cent of the vote (and just one in five of all eligible voters).

This chapter will review the factors affecting election results. Accordingly it will:

■ provide an overview of elections since 1945

■ examine the political effects of the current 'first past the post' system for Westminster elections and alternative electoral systems

■ analyse the long-term factors that predispose some voters to support the same party and which provide the two major parties with their 'core support'

■ analyse the short-term factors that cause votes to change between elections

■ explore the reasons for declining turnout in elections and 'disengagement' from the political process.

Table 15.1 Election results, 1945–2005

Elections	Conservative Seat nos	Conservative Seat %	Conservative Vote %	Labour Seat nos	Labour Seat %	Labour Vote %	Liberals Seat nos	Liberals Seat %	Liberals Vote %	Others Seat nos	Others Seat %	Others Vote %	Total number of MPs
1945	210	32.8	39.6	393	61.4	48.0	12	1.9	9.0	25	3.9	3.4	640
1950	298	47.7	43.4	315	50.4	46.1	9	1.4	9.1	3	0.5	1.4	625
1951	321	51.4	48.0	295	47.2	48.8	6	1.0	2.6	3	0.5	0.6	625
1955	345	54.8	49.7	277	44.0	46.4	6	1.0	2.7	2	0.3	1.2	630
1959	365	57.9	49.4	258	41.0	43.8	6	1.0	5.9	1	0.2	0.9	630
1964	304	48.3	43.4	317	50.3	44.1	9	1.4	11.2	0	0.0	1.3	630
1966	253	40.2	41.9	364	57.8	48.0	12	1.9	8.6	1	0.2	1.5	630
1970	330	52.4	46.4	288	45.7	43.1	6	1.0	7.5	6	0.9	3.0	630
1974 (Feb)	297	46.8	37.9	301	47.4	37.2	14	2.2	19.3	23[a]	3.6	5.6	635
1974 (Oct)	277	43.6	35.8	319	50.2	39.2	13	2.0	18.3	26	4.1	6.7	635
1979	339	53.4	43.9	269	42.4	36.9	11	1.7	13.8	16	2.5	5.4	635
1983	397	61.1	42.4	209	32.2	27.6	23[b]	3.5	25.4	21	3.2	4.6	650
1987	376	57.8	42.3	229	35.2	30.8	22[b]	3.4	22.5	23	3.5	4.4	650
1992	336	51.6	41.9	271	41.6	34.4	20	3.1	17.8	24	3.7	5.9	651
1997	165	25.0	30.7	418	63.4	43.2	46	7.0	16.8	30	4.5	9.3	659
2001	166	25.2	31.7	413	62.6	40.7	52	8.0	18.3	28	4.2	9.3	659
2005	198	30.7	32.3	356	55.1	35.2	62	9.6	22.0	30	4.6	10.5	646

Notes: [a] Northern Irish MPs are counted as 'others' from 1974; [b] In 1983 and 1987 'Liberal' includes the SDP/Liberal Alliance.

Elections and parties since 1945

Electoral system

A set of procedures for translating votes received by party candidates into shares of parliamentary seats.

British elections register support for the parties, using an **electoral system** that usually, though not inevitably, enables the party with a 'plurality' of the vote (i.e. the largest single vote) to win an absolute majority of seats in the House of Commons and thus form the government on its own. The next chapter will discuss how political parties came to dominate elections in the first place. For the moment, it is important to note that elections involve a choice between party alternatives, not between individual candidates or leaders. In Britain, where one or other of the two main parties normally wins a majority of the seats, elections focus on whether there will be a Conservative or a Labour government. Generally speaking, the Conservatives favour less government intervention in the economy and Labour favours more, so the party choice has implications for policy: do voters want freer markets, more social inequality, lower taxes and lower public spending; or more state intervention, redistribution, taxes and public spending? This is the main ground on which the elections listed in Table 15.1 have been fought.

Elections to Parliament: first past the post

British elections are the result of contests fought in hundreds of different seats from St Ives in Cornwall to Caithness and Sutherland in Scotland (see Map 15.1). In each seat electors cast their vote by placing a cross next to the name of their chosen candidate. In order to win a seat under the **'first past the post'** system a candidate simply needs one more vote than the nearest other candidate. This

Map 15.1 The electoral map of Britain is a common feature of most textbooks but greatly distorts perceptions of party strength (marginal constituencies and safe seats look the same and the Conservative blue in rural seats dominates the map). (Northern Ireland is not shown on this map)

Source: Reproduced with permission of Ordnance Survey. © Crown copyright

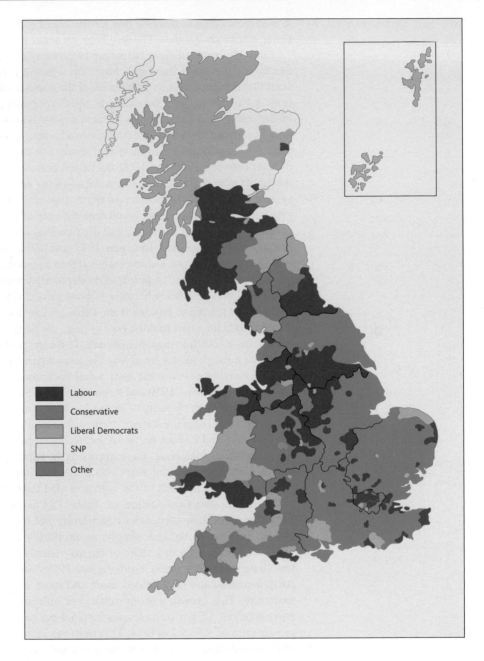

Labour
Conservative
Liberal Democrats
SNP
Other

First past the post

Also known as the single-member simple plurality system (SMSP), this translates votes into seats by awarding each seat to the candidate who gets most votes (a plurality) inside a small constituency.

'plurality' rule means that if there are just two candidates contesting a seat the winner would always gain a majority (50 per cent plus 1). If there are more than two candidates, however, a candidate could win with far less than 50 per cent of the vote. In a three-cornered contest a candidate might be elected with 34 per cent of the vote if the other candidates receive 33 per cent each. In a four-sided contest, a candidate could win with as little as 26 per cent.

These are more than mere theoretical possibilities. In the 2005 election only 220 out of 646 (just 34 per cent) of all MPs gained more than 50 per cent of the vote in their constituency!

The plurality rule also has important consequences for parties, the party system and the nature of British politics. The most important consequence for the moment, however, is that it makes it difficult to predict how vote shares are translated into seats in Parliament. Much depends on the distribution of votes across the country.

It is quite possible to imagine that a party could gain a majority even though it has fewer votes than another. The key is to get votes in the 'right' places.

Table 15.1 sets out the relationship between seats and votes since 1945. Several features of this table stand out. First, the winning party has won a proportion of seats that is higher than its proportion of the popular vote. In each of the four elections from 1979 to 1992, for example, the Conservative Party won over 50 per cent of the seats – and thus enough to form a government by itself – even though its vote never rose above 44 per cent. Second, small changes in vote share can produce very significant changes in seat share. For example, the Conservative share of seats between 1979 and 1992 fluctuated between 51.6 and 61.1 per cent, even though its vote share held steady at 42 to 44 per cent. This shows how, under this system, a party's parliamentary strength depends not only on how many votes it gets but also on how its vote – and how the vote of other parties – is spread across constituencies. Small shifts in these distributions can produce large fluctuations in parliamentary majorities. Between 1987 and 1992, for example, the Conservatives' majority fell from a comfortable 100 to a slender 21 even though its share of the vote fell by a mere 0.4 points. The electoral system translated a ripple of votes into a tidal wave of losses because Labour gained votes in the 'right' places.

The third feature to emerge from Table 15.1 is that, despite the distortions produced by Britain's first past the post system, the party that wins the most votes normally wins an outright majority of seats. In this respect the electoral system usually dispenses a rough justice by giving the largest party a bonus of seats large enough to form a stable government over a full parliamentary term. In the 15 elections since 1945 only two – 1950 and February 1974 – have failed to provide the winner with a large enough majority of seats to sustain it in office for a full term. And only two – 1951 and, again, February 1974 – produced the 'wrong' result, in which the Conservative and Labour parties respectively won slightly more seats but slightly fewer votes than their rival. The capacity of the current system to convert a plurality of votes into a majority of seats was illustrated dramatically in the 2005 general election when 35 per cent of the vote provided Labour with 55 per cent of seats.

The fourth and final feature of Table 15.1 is the way in which the Liberal Democrats and their successors consistently fail to receive a 'fair' share of seats (where fairness is defined simply as proportional). In the 1950s the Liberal Democrats obtained a tiny share of the vote (partly because they did not then contest all parliamentary seats). From the late 1950s onwards, however, support for the party increased and they fielded more and more candidates. This further boosted their vote. This growth was, however, not reflected at Westminster. In 1983 the party received 3.5 per cent of seats for 25.4 per cent of the vote, producing a seat to vote ratio of 3.5:25.4 or 0.14. This ratio has increased in recent years, as a result of increased targeting of seats by the party and tactical voting by non-Conservative voters. In 2005 the ratio rose to 9.6:22.0 or 0.44. Nevertheless the Liberal Democrats are still unfairly rewarded (any ratio less than 1 is 'unfair'). As we shall later demonstrate, moreover, the fact that the Liberal Democrats (and other 'national' minor parties) are unlikely to win seats may deter people from voting for those parties in the first place. The current system, therefore, may artificially suppress support for minority parties and increase support for the two major parties.

The bias in the first past the post system

The British electoral system translated Labour's modest 3-point lead (or 'plurality') over the Conservatives into a comfortable majority of 66 seats because it is currently biased towards Labour. This does not mean that the system is rigged either by or on behalf of the Labour Party. It simply means that the system mechanically operates in Labour's favour.

Proportional representation

A voting system that uses an allocation formula (of which there are many) for distributing seats among parties in proportion to their vote.

BRIEFINGS

15.1 Plurality and proportional electoral systems

Free elections are essential to modern democracy. Although at first sight they appear to be a simple matter – expressing a preference for one party over others – they are in fact complex affairs. There are two main types of electoral system (or procedures for translating votes into seats): simple plurality voting and proportional representation.

Simple plurality systems

First past the post (or SMSP)

'First past the post' (FPTP) or 'single member simple plurality' only requires the winning candidate to obtain more votes than any other candidate, no matter how many candidates there are, and no matter how small the winner's share of the total vote is. In a three-way contest the winner may get little more than one-third of the total and, in a four-way contest, little more than one-quarter. Simple plurality voting is usually linked with single-member constituencies (though multi-member constituencies are used in some local elections). In Europe FPTP is used only in the United Kingdom, and outside Europe in the United States and Canada.

Both the act of voting and the method of determining a winner are simple. Locally, the system encourages MPs to serve local constituents in order to build up a 'personal vote'. Nationally, the system invariably produces 'strong' (single-party) government capable of carrying out its 'mandate' and of making 'tough' decisions (in contrast with coalitions, which are supposed to be unable to agree). Thus the link between elections and forming a government is relatively direct. It produces results, however, in which the proportion of seats in the Parliament won by each party does not match the proportion of votes it won in the election. FPTP unfairly penalises some minority parties, including large minority parties such as the Liberal Democrats, which have widespread rather than concentrated geographical support.

Second ballot system

The second ballot system tries to avoid the worst flaws of first past the post by requiring the winning candidate to obtain an absolute majority (50 per cent + 1) of the votes cast in the first round of elections. Failing this, a second (run-off) election is held for the strongest of the first-round candidates. This system is currently used in France for both its parliamentary and presidential elections. It does, however, require voters to go to the polls twice (and turnout is already low under the less demanding SMSP system!).

Additional member system (AMS)

Again this attempts to redress extreme disproportionality in the results from first past the post. Two types of MPs are elected. First, constituency MPs are elected by first past the post. Second, 'top-up' MPs are elected from a 'regional list' in a way which favours parties that lose out in the constituency-based voting. The larger the proportion of list seats the more proportional the overall result. This system preserves the direct link between some MPs and constituencies. It is the system used in Germany for elections to the Bundestag. In the United Kingdom it is used for elections to the Scottish Parliament and Welsh and London Assemblies, where it has reduced but not eliminated the bias in favour of Labour.

Alternative vote system

Another variation on the simple plurality system allows voters to indicate their first and subsequent preferences among candidates, so that if no candidate receives a majority of first preferences second (and subsequent) preferences may be brought into play in second and subsequent counts. The Jenkins Committee on electoral reform (which reported in 1998) recommended a modified version of this system for Westminster elections (called 'AV-plus'). But the Labour government declined to follow their advice.

Proportional representation systems

Proportional representation is not itself an electoral system but a principle by which different electoral systems can be judged. The principle is that the distribution of seats between parties in the elected legislature should correspond to the national distribution of votes cast for the parties in the election. In other words, minorities as well as majorities should be represented in proportion to their voting strength. The main ways of doing this are the party list system and the single transferable vote.

▶

Party list system

This is the simplest way of ensuring that seats are proportional to votes. Parties draw up a list of candidates in order of preference, and the candidates are elected in proportion to the number of votes their party receives in the nation as a whole (as in the Netherlands) or in large regions, starting from the top of the party lists. The party list system is highly proportional. The need for a national list puts a lot of power into the hands of the party leadership, who decide where candidates are ranked (and who is likely to be elected). The system produces no incentives for MPs to serve specific constituents. It is used in most European countries and in UK elections to the European Parliament. In some countries parties must pass a 'threshold' (e.g. 5 per cent of the vote) before they obtain any representation. This is designed to penalise small 'extreme' parties.

Single transferable vote

This system is used in the Irish Republic and for the Northern Irish Assembly and is preferred by the Liberal Democrats for the United Kingdom. It requires multimember rather than single-member constituencies. Voters rank order their preferences for all the candidates, so that their second, third or subsequent preferences can be taken into account. A minimum quota of votes for election to the Parliament is calculated (the quota depends on the number of votes cast divided by the number of members to be elected for the constituency). The first preferences are counted in the initial round of counting. Those candidates who exceed the quota are elected. In the second round the 'surplus votes' (those over the number required by the quota) obtained by candidates elected in the first round are redistributed according to the second preferences of voters for unelected candidates. Once the redistribution of surpluses ceases to elect any further candidates the votes of the least preferred candidate are redistributed according to second and subsequent preferences. Counts continue in this fashion until all seats are filled. There are many minor variations on STV, and different ways of calculating the final result, but the system usually leads to close proportionality at the national level, especially if most of the multimember constituencies elect five or more Members of Parliament. Because voters can rank order all the candidates they do not regard a vote for a minor party candidate as wasted. This system will be used for local elections in Scotland from 2007.

Commentary

The debate about electoral reform is complicated. However, some of the issues can be resolved by careful examination of the evidence. Research into the effect of new electoral systems in the United Kingdom, for example, suggests that there are more spoiled ballots under other systems than under first past the post. But the differences are not very large. Comparative studies across the world suggest that turnout is higher in proportional systems, presumably because voters know that their votes are not 'wasted'. There is, moreover, a great deal of research suggesting that coalition governments can be as stable as single-party governments and deliver more of what voters want. However, in proportional systems the link between elections and the formation of the government is often indirect. In Norway in 1989, for example, the Conservatives lost one in four of their votes and yet managed to move from opposition to government all the same!

The debate about electoral reform, however, may boil down to this: 'Do we want [power] concentrated under the winner-takes-all system of first past the post, or do we want it spread between parties as is probable under any proportional system?' (The Independent Commission on PR, p. 12). Put quite simply, does the greater risk come from a coalition government that is unable to take 'tough but necessary decisions' when needed or a 'strong' government that is all too ready to act by passing hasty, ill-thought-out, ineffective or illiberal legislation?

Since the future is uncertain there is no right or wrong answer to this question. Moreover, one's answer might depend on the way the choice is 'framed'. Someone committed to constituency representation might reject the party list system but accept either AMS or STV (which both preserve the link while ensuring greater proportionality).

The extent of the pro-Labour bias can be illustrated by calculating a 'reverse result' for the 2005 election. The actual result was: Labour 35.2 per cent, Conservatives 32.3 per cent, Labour overall majority of 66. But if the result had been: Labour 32.3 per cent, Conservatives 35.2 per cent, then – assuming a uniform swing – Labour would still have won 62 more seats than the Conservatives (though it would have been 15 seats short of an overall majority).

There are several reasons why the system is biased towards Labour:

- Labour wins many seats with small majorities ('efficiency bias').

- Labour constituencies are smaller (67,000 voters) than Conservative ones (around 73,000). It therefore needs fewer votes to win a seat.

- Labour constituencies have lower turnouts (58 per cent in 2005) than Conservative (65.4 per cent). Labour again needs fewer votes to win seats.

- Liberal Democrat wins come largely at the expense of the Conservatives.

The current electoral system produces a significant advantage for Labour and a serious obstacle to the Conservatives. They do not simply need to win more votes – they need to win more votes in the right places. This can be briefly illustrated by considering the effects of a uniform **swing** (where the swing is the same in every constituency). If there is a swing of 1.5 points and the party draws level with Labour at the next election, Labour will still have 115 more seats than the Conservatives and an overall majority of 24 seats. If there is a swing of 4.8 points and a lead over Labour of some 7.1 per cent, the Conservatives will become the largest party in a **hung parliament** and have some claim to form a government (though Labour may still be able to stay in power with Liberal Democrat support). This sort of swing has been achieved only twice by the Conservatives in the post-war period (in 1970 and 1979). In order to gain a slender overall majority of 1 seat (not enough to survive for more than a few months in government) they need a swing of 7.4 points and a lead of 11.9 per cent. This sort of swing has been achieved only twice; both times by Labour (in 1945 and 1997). If history is any guide to the future the Conservatives will have their work cut out to win the next election outright.

Targeting seats

The predictions about the sort of swing that the Conservatives need to win an election made above assume that there is a uniform national swing. If recent experience is any guide swing is unlikely to be uniform. Not only do voters in different constituencies behave in different ways, parties behave in different ways in different seats too. In particular, the current system provides incentives for parties to identify those seats that might swing from one party to another and focus their campaign activity on them. If the Conservatives were able to secure a large enough swing in just the most 'marginal' seats, they might be able to win an election with a much smaller swing and a smaller lead over Labour.

Well before each election the main parties assess the electoral battleground and focus their campaigns on **'target' seats**, ensuring that they regularly contact voters in person, by mail or by telephone. Senior party figures regularly visit the targeted constituency in order to gain the attention of local media and raise the party's profile. In the formal campaign itself, moreover, party workers will be directed to these seats in order to mobilise their potential vote and win the seat.

Targeting of seats is important in an era when party membership is in decline, since parties cannot afford to run a full campaign in every constituency (see Chapter 16). In recent years Labour and the Liberal Democrats have been particularly successful at directing resources (workers, posters and so on) to where they are needed most. Both Labour's traditionally centralised organisation and the Liberal Democrats' focus on 'community politics' have naturally lent themselves to effective local campaigning. By contrast the autonomy (or parochialism) of many Conservative local associations frustrated attempts to direct campaigners to where they were most needed. In 2005 the Conservative campaign was more effective than before. Individual donors were encouraged to support Conservative

---

Swing

The simple sum of the change in two parties' share of the vote divided by two. Thus, in 2005 the Tories gained 0.6 points and Labour lost 5.5 points, resulting in a swing of (0.6 + 5.5 = (6.1)/2) 3.05 points to the Conservatives.

Hung Parliament

A situation in which no single party has a majority over all other parties in the House of Commons. In the current 646-member Parliament a party needs 324 seats to gain an overall majority. If no party gains 324 seats there is said to be a 'hung' Parliament.

Targeting seats

The process by which parties identify marginal (vulnerable) seats and focus their campaign resources in order to gain or hold that seat.

associations in marginal constituencies and a telephone canvassing operation was put in place that targeted seats. However, the party was still unable to win some highly marginal seats such as Dorset South, which was Labour's most vulnerable seat that year.

Of course all the parties are likely to focus their activities on the marginal seats and the partisan effects are likely to cancel out to some extent. Targeting may, however, have the unintended consequence of reducing turnout in safe seats. If only swing voters in marginal seats (so-called '**golden voters**') are made to feel as if they 'count', core voters in safe seats may be less likely to turn out to vote. In some cases recent election campaigns may have simply bypassed many constituencies. Little wonder then that turnout slumped badly in Labour's safest seats in the north and the inner cities in 2001 and 2005.

Golden voters

Swing voters in marginal constituencies. Shifts in their behaviour are amplified by the first past the post system, producing dramatic shifts in the parliamentary strength of the parties.

Boundary reviews

The process of redrawing constituency boundaries in order to ensure constituencies are approximately the same size.

Boundary reviews

A special feature of the first past the post system is the importance of constituency boundaries. The 2005 election was (with the exception of Scotland) fought on boundaries introduced in 1995 and without exception based on census data collected in 1990. Changing the boundaries – which is necessary to keep up with shifts of population – can deprive the sitting member by excluding districts with concentrations of supporters or including new districts with concentrations of opponents. The precise boundaries are so important that responsibility for drawing them up is given to an independent Boundary Commission, which is now a special section of the Electoral Commission (see Briefing 15.2).

According to the relevant legislation constituencies should 'as far as is practicable' be of equal size. There is a different notional quota for seats in each of the four parts of the United Kingdom, but it is currently largest in England and Scotland than in Wales, so the latter is 'over-represented at Westminster'. However, the Boundary Commission has to take into account local government boundaries and local ties. This means that it has to strike a balance between these goals. An assistant commissioner, therefore, chairs hearings, receives submissions from the parties and then makes a recommendation. The very public nature of this system largely avoids changes of 'gerrymandering' (altering boundaries to one party's advantage). The final decision on whether to act on these recommendations, however, is made by Parliament itself. In the late 1960s Labour postponed changes that would have lost it seats but still lost the 1970 election!

There is a separate Boundary Commission for Scotland. It advised on the drawing up of new boundaries for the 2005 general election, when the number of Scottish seats was reduced from 72 to 59 in order to reflect the fact that Scotland now has a great deal of autonomy as a result of devolution. This had the effect of reducing the number of Labour MPs by 10, Liberal Democrats by 1 and Scottish Nationalists by 1.

The next Boundary Commission review for England and Wales is due in 2007. There are no plans to reduce the number of seats in Wales, so this will advantage Labour. The review will almost inevitably abolish some of the smaller urban and northern seats in England (held by Labour) and create more rural, suburban and southern seats (which are more Conservative). These changes will probably deprive Labour of about 10 seats; enough to reduce – but not eliminate – Labour's majority.

The impact of new electoral systems

Electoral systems have important consequences for parties, the party system and the culture of politics. The Labour government has introduced new electoral

BRIEFINGS

15.2 The Electoral Commission

The Electoral Commission is an independent body created as a result of the Political Parties Elections and Referendum Act 2000. It was established partly as a result of recommendations contained in the fifth report Committee for Standards in Public Life and is accountable to Parliament via a committee chaired by the Speaker of the House of Commons.

The Commission has responsibilities for the following:

- registering political parties (and party symbols, such as Labour's red rose)

- registering major donations to political parties (all donations above £5,000 must be registered, spending by third parties is regulated and foreign donations are banned)

- regulating election campaign spending (limited to around £19 million in the 2005 election)

- reporting on the conduct of elections

- reviewing electoral law

- advising government on changes

- advising those involved in the regulation of elections and referendums (returning officers and the Association of Electoral Administrators)

- promoting awareness of electoral systems

- reviewing constituency boundaries.

The Commission has produced a series of reports on electoral matters, including postal voting, young people and participation, social exclusion and political engagement. It has powers relating to monitoring and investigation of elections, but electoral cases are still dealt with by the courts. (In 2005 several Birmingham Labour councillors were prosecuted for electoral fraud. The judge declared, 'Anybody who has sat through the case I have just tried and listened to evidence of electoral fraud that would disgrace a banana republic would find this surprising.')

The Commission can merely advise the government on changes and may be ignored. In 2004 the government did not accept its recommendation that postal voting should take place in two rather than three regions for the European Parliament, as the government wished. Many believed that Labour declined to accept these recommendations because it believed that a higher turnout in those regions would produce a partisan advantage.

systems in each and every one of the new, devolved authorities (see Table 15.2). By the time of the 2005 general election, everyone in the United Kingdom had been provided with the opportunity to use a system other than first past the post on at least two occasions in elections to the European Parliament. If they lived in the devolved areas of Scotland, Wales and London, they had the experience at least twice more. Voter and party behaviour has already changed as a result, but is likely to alter still further as both respond to new incentives. Across the United Kingdom several large scale experiments in a new form of politics are taking place.

The electoral system had consequences for the relationship between votes and seats. In the European elections of 1994 the Liberal Democrats obtained 17 per cent of the vote but just 2 out of 84 (2.4 per cent) of seats when these were fought under FPTP. In 1999 their vote fell to 13 per cent, but they gained 10 out 84 (12 per cent) seats. In 2003 they got 15 per cent of the vote; but they obtained 12 out of 78 seats (15.4 per cent) under the party list system. The AMS system used in Scotland has had similar results. In the 1997 general election the Conservatives obtained around 18 per cent of the vote north of the border, but did not return a single Scottish MP to Westminster under FPTP. In the elections to the Scottish Parliament held under AMS the party received just 16 per cent of first and second

Table 15.2 Electoral systems in use in the United Kingdom

System	Body elected
Single member first past the post	House of Commons
	Some English/Welsh and all Scottish local authorities until 2007
Multiple member simple plurality	Some English/Welsh local authorities
Additional member system	Scottish Parliament
	Welsh Assembly
	London Assembly
Single transferable vote	Northern Ireland Assembly
	Scottish local elections from 2007
Regional party list	European Parliament
Supplementary vote	London mayor

Source: David Denver, *Election and Voters in Britain*, p. 169

votes, but won 18 out of 129 (14 per cent) seats. The system worked in a similar way in 2003. AMS in Scotland saved the Conservatives from a wipe-out, yet the Conservative Party seems the most hostile to the new systems. It operated in a similar way in Wales.

The same system clearly did *not* benefit Labour in Scotland. The party would probably have won a substantial majority under first past the post, but emerged as merely the largest single party under the AMS system in elections held in 1999 and 2003. It has governed in coalition with the Liberal Democrats since 1999. In Wales Labour was deprived of a majority in the first election, governed as a minority until 2000 and then went into coalition with the Liberal Democrats until 2003. AMS had a similar effect in London, which now has two Green and two UKIP members of the GLA.

The impact of the new electoral systems on voters has been fairly consistent: it has reduced support for the major parties and increased support for the smaller parties. In the 2004 European elections Labour received just 23 per cent of the vote, compared with 35 per cent in the general election less than a year later. Similarly, the Conservatives received just 27 per cent in 2004 compared with 32 per cent in 2005. The party list system allowed voters either to cast a vote according to their real preferences or to experiment with minor parties in relatively unimportant ('**second-order**') **elections**. Support for UKIP in the 2004 Euro-elections (fought under the party list system) rose to 16 per cent, compared with a mere 2.2 per cent just one year later. The AMS system has similarly allowed voters to split their vote in order to reflect their preferences. Around one in five voters appears to have split their votes by voting for one party in the first past the post section and another in the regional list. This has increased the number of minor parties represented at Holyrood; with the Scottish Socialist and Green parties picking up seats that they would not have been allocated under first past the post. In Wales the level of split ticket voting was slightly lower, but still significant.

While first past the post encouraged voters to think of elections as a choice of government between Conservative and Labour, the new electoral systems encourage voters to think more carefully about their preferences and either vote for a minor (or less established) party or split their vote. These developments may have had small 'carry over' consequences in the recent general election. Some of the 1 per cent rise in the vote for minor parties in 2005 may be a 'carry over' from other elections. Voters may be getting used to voting for other parties and, in an era when the major parties appear to be converging, are less worried about the consequences of wasting their vote even under first past the post. These developments

Second-order election

An election to a body other than the national legislature.

will undoubtedly lead some within both major parties to reject any moves to introduce more proportional systems at Westminster. Electoral reform may unleash the 'latent pluralism' and reveal that most voters are 'multi-party' at heart.

A hung Parliament: from first past the post to proportional representation?

Some analysts believe that Labour will continue to lose support at the next general election, either as a result of an economic downturn, failure to improve the public services or as a result of the 'costs of ruling' (see Briefing 15.4). Nevertheless, the electoral system is currently biased in their favour and it seems unlikely that the Conservatives will make enough gains to obtain an overall majority. It is quite possible that the next election will result in a 'hung parliament' in which the Liberal Democrats hold the balance of power and could choose to form a coalition with either of the main parties.

A hung parliament is a real possibility even if the Liberal Democrats lose a substantial portion of the 62 seats they won in 2005. Its parliamentary leadership has suggested that, in these circumstances, they would only be prepared to enter into a coalition on condition that the electoral system for elections to Westminster is reformed. This position is likely to be reinforced by their experience after 1997, when Labour reneged on a manifesto promise to hold a referendum on reform for elections to Westminster. This experience will not necessarily bias the Liberal Democrats against entering into coalition with Labour, but it will almost certainly mean that they will expect legislation on reform of the electoral system to be enacted in the first year of the new parliament.

Given the possibility of a hung parliament, both major parties are likely to cosy up to the Liberal Democrats. Labour will probably stress their commitment to social justice and their record of successful cooperation with that party in Scotland. The Conservatives will stress their belief in freedom and the free markets, their willingness to decentralise the government and the danger of prolonging the Labour government. It remains to be seen, however, whether either Labour or the Conservatives will think it worth taking the risk of introducing a new (more proportional) electoral system. As elections to the European Parliament and devolved institutions make clear, new electoral systems could unleash a dynamic that would destroy their duopoly at Westminster forever.

Explaining individual votes and electoral success

In this section we examine why one party rather than another manages to win more votes. What explains why the Conservatives led Labour by 42 to 35 per cent of the national vote in 1992 but trailed Labour by 32 to 35 per cent in 2005? So many factors can influence voting that the task of selecting the most important to explain the overall result seems almost impossible. However, they include the following:

- long-term social factors (age, race and gender, social class, neighbourhood, religion, housing tenure and so on)
- long-term political factors, party loyalties and values
- short-term 'campaign' issues, policies, evaluations of party competence etc., party and leadership images
- tactical voting considerations.

BRIEFINGS

15.3 Why not ask the voters?

It might be supposed that it would be a good idea to ask voters themselves to explain their own behaviour. Unfortunately, however, there are reasons to be cautious about voters' own explanations.

One problem with 'open-ended questions' ('Why did you vote that way?') is that some voters, particularly the less educated, sophisticated or articulate may not be able to express their reasons. Many may simply respond 'Don't know' because it seems better than embarrassing themselves by making a grammatical mistake or using the wrong word. Yet even if voters are asked 'closed-ended questions' ('Which of the following reasons best explains why you voted?') there are reasons for doubting whether their responses will reveal much:

- Voters may genuinely not know why they vote as they do. Most people are not usually required to explain their actions and may have given them little conscious thought. They may be able to rationalise their behaviour (i.e., tell a plausible story or choose a plausible option) but that may have little to do with the real causes.

- Voters' own explanations will be biased. In particular, they are likely to emphasise the 'immediate' causes of their vote (a campaign event or particular leader) rather than 'deeper' reasons (such as family loyalties or values).

- Voters may be unwilling to reveal to others that they are motivated by socially undesirable (selfish or racist) motivations.

- Voters may not even be willing to reveal to themselves that they are motivated by socially undesirable considerations and may suppress such feelings.

- Voters may be similarly unable to judge the importance of specific factors in their vote decisions.

Most analysts believe that the best way to find out why people vote as they do is to examine the statistical relationship between various social, psychological and political characteristics using responses to structured questions.

A vast amount of research has been done on the relationship between social, economic and political factors and the actual election result. This has identified the central processes that explain both individual vote decisions and the overall election result.

Long-term factors and the vote

Core voters

Those voters who are strongly predisposed to support a party election after election. Parties do not need to persuade their core voters that they are the best party, merely to turn out and vote.

Swing (or floating) voters

Those voters with either weak or non-existent predispositions to support any particular party.

Election outcomes are the result of a large number of decisions arrived at for a large number of reasons. A useful way of thinking about voters, however, is to distinguish between those who support the same party time and time again ('**core voters**') and those who vote for different parties ('**swing voters**').

Core voters provide the major parties with 'all-weather' support. Even in the dramatic landslide election of 1997, some 61 per cent (of all those who voted in 1992) supported the same party as five years previously. Moreover, in the year running up to the 1997 election, fully 82 per cent of those who intended to vote supported the same party. More strikingly still 57 per cent of those who gave a vote intention in each of five successive interviews between 1992 and 1997 indicated support for the same party. For many people at least, political preferences are stable and apparently resistant to change.

One of the main reasons why voters are stable is that they belong to social groups that have developed links with parties. Since these characteristics change only slowly, so do party loyalties.

There are three reasons why groups influence voting behaviour:

1. *Social-psychological*. People seek to understand the world about them. They naturally attach labels to both themselves and the people they meet. They also tend to value people like themselves and seek to gain the acceptance of fellow group members. Membership of a social group, therefore, gives rise to certain 'norms' or 'expectations'. Members of the Church of England are expected to vote Conservative, trade union members to vote Labour and so on.

2. *Rational interests*. Those who share certain characteristics may share similar interests. Public sector workers generally have an interest in increased public spending, while private sector workers have an interest in lower taxes.

3. *Information biases*. Political information is produced in a social context. Members of trade unions are exposed to 'pro-Labour' information, while inhabitants who live in a Conservative area are exposed to 'pro-Conservative' information in their everyday lives.

Table 15.3 briefly summarises the sorts of characteristics that have been associated with Conservative, Labour and Liberal Democrat voting. By far the most important of these characteristics historically has been social class (partly because one party, the Labour Party, styled itself as a class party). Put simply, the middle class have voted Conservative and the working class have voted Labour. In contrast with the rest of Europe, however, religion has played a lesser role in British voting behaviour. There is a tendency for members of the Church of England to vote for the Conservatives – presumably as a result of their association with traditional features of British society, including the monarchy. Catholics are more likely to vote Labour as a result of that party's policies on Ireland and the fact that many Catholics are working class.

Younger voters tend not to vote Conservative. In 1997 they were overwhelmingly Labour, but in 2005 they provided a great deal of support for the Liberal Democrats, possibly because of their opposition to the Iraq War. Black voters,

Table 15.3 Social characteristics associated with party vote

Characteristic	Conservative	Labour	Liberal Democrat
Middle class	X		
Working class		X	
Young voters		X	?
Old voters	X		
Black		X	
White	X		
Church of England	X		
Catholic		X	
Nonconformist		X	X
Higher education			X
High income	X		
Low income		X	
Public sector		X	
Trade union membership		X	
Home owner	X		
Council tenant		X	
Car owner	X		
Reliant on state benefits		X	
England	X		
Scotland		X	
Wales		X	

moreover, provide Labour with strong support. They are more working class and more likely to live in Labour areas. But also Labour has generally been more welcoming of immigrants and supportive of measures to promote equality. Someone with all the characteristics indicated in the Labour column, such as a young, black, working-class, uneducated council tenant, working for a local council and a member of a trade union, is highly likely to be a Labour voter because group norms, material interests and exposure to biased information all push them in one direction.

One thing that stands out from Table 15.3 is that the Liberal Democrats fail to attract the support of any particular group. The only possible exceptions are those who have been in higher education and nonconformists. But these groups spread their support relatively evenly between the parties. Moreover, since neither of these groups is particularly large, the Liberal Democrats have only a small core vote and rely on attracting the temporary support of many voters.

Analyses of voting behaviour usually begin with the relationship between social characteristics and vote for several reasons. First, social characteristics are obvious prior causes of the vote and – unlike political attitudes, opinions and evaluations – are not consequences of vote decisions. (The fact that someone has voted for X might lead them to report 'pro-X' opinions that they do not hold; the fact that someone has voted for X does not alter their race, gender, social class or job!). Second, as we see in Chapter 16, parties develop programmes and policies with certain 'target groups' in mind. Third, analysing social trends enables us to predict whether the size of a party's core vote is increasing or decreasing. The contraction in the size of the working class, trade union membership, the size of the public sector and the number of council tenants in the 1980s, for example, all reduced the size of Labour's core vote and made it necessary to broaden the party's appeal.

Though group memberships influence voting behaviour, they do not determine it. Most people are members of more than one group. This ensures that they are subject to conflicting norms, guided by conflicting interests and exposed to many sources of information. In recent years, moreover, the proportion of the population with either 'pure Conservative' or 'pure Labour' group memberships has fallen dramatically, leaving voters less firmly anchored in the parties and more open to the appeals of others. This has been accentuated by changes in the parties' appeals that have weakened the relationship between group and party. 'New Labour', for example, played down its appeals to the northern industrial and unionised working class in order to attract the expanding middle classes in 'middle England'. Not surprisingly, therefore, social characteristics are poorer and poorer predictors of voting behaviour.

Although these relations tend to endure, the relationship between social characteristics and vote can thus vary over time. This is perhaps best illustrated by exploring how the relationship between social class and party has changed in the post-war period.

Class dealignment

Social class has traditionally been the most significant social influence on the vote in Britain. In the post-war period the Labour Party has invariably attracted the support of somewhere around two-thirds of the 'working class' (those in manual occupations) and the Conservative Party has received the support of a similar proportion of the 'middle class' (those in non-manual occupations). As Figure 15.1 shows, on this simple index of class voting around two-thirds of all voters supported the 'correct' class party in 1945 and 1970 (a degree of 'class alignment' that was very strong by international standards).

From the early 1970s onwards the association between class and vote weakened considerably. Sections of the working class became more prosperous and more

Figure 15.1 Class and voting, 1945–2005

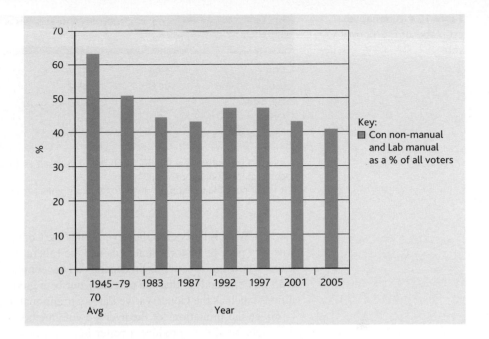

likely to work in the private sector. The middle class became unionised and more likely to work in the public sector. Hence more people were exposed to conflicting norms, interests and less biased sources of information. Thus, as Figure 15.1 shows, by 1979 just 51 per cent of all voters supported the 'correct' class party and by 1987 a mere 44 per cent. This decline in class voting occurred well before the 1997 election, suggesting that 'New Labour' was more of a response to class dealignment than a cause. Although the index increased to 47 in 1997, by 2005 it had fallen to 41 (largely as a result of the greater swing away from Labour to the Conservatives among the working class). Social class has not ceased to be an influence on vote, but its influence has diminished.

Party loyalties

It is widely thought that voters have loyalties to a political party and come to think of themselves as 'being Conservative' or 'being Labour'. These 'party identifiers' tend to support 'their party' in most circumstances and provide their party with 'all-weather' support even when it is undergoing serious internal problems.

One way of estimating a party's 'core' or 'normal' vote is simply to average their vote over a number of elections. Such calculations enable us to judge whether a party's vote is higher (or lower) than average and, accordingly, whether it is likely to fall (or rise) at the next election, other things being equal. While this strategy is simple the problem is that there are many 'averages' that can be calculated and no way of telling which is correct. Table 15.4, for example, shows three possible averages for Labour. The first for 1945–70 is almost 47 per cent. This seems inappropriate because this relates to a period of two-party competition when the centre party almost ceased to exist. The second for 1974–92 at 35 per cent is more plausible. The third average for 1997–2001, however, is 42 per cent and this seems plausible too. Labour's share of the vote in 2005 was 35 per cent. Viewed from the perspective of the earliest and latest period, Labour's performance is poor and seems likely to rise. Viewed from the perspective of the middle period Labour's performance is average and may rise or fall. Thus the average vote method does not produce firm predictions about what is likely to happen to Labour at the next

Table 15.4 Alternative estimates of the 'normal' vote

	Average vote estimate			
	1945–70	1974–1992	1997–2001	2005 Survey[1]
Con.	44.8	41.7	31.2	27.9
Lab.	46.8	35.2	42.0	36.8
Lib. Dem.	7.1	20.0	17.8	13.1
Other	1.3	3.1	9.3	5.1
Floating voters	N/A[2]	N/A	N/A	17.1

Notes: [1] 'Generally speaking do you think of yourself as Conservative, Labour, Liberal Democrat, Nationalist or what?'
[2] It is not possible to estimate swing or floating voters from vote shares.

election. What is fairly clear, however, is that the Conservatives' performance in 2005 was very poor by historic standards and the Liberal Democrats better than average (though how much better again depends on the comparison used). Another problem with this 'method' is that the past may not be a guide to the future if crucial conditions (such as the Conservative Party's traditional thirst for power) have altered.

Given the limitations of the average vote method it is tempting to suggest that we might be able to produce a better indicator of the parties' normal votes if we ask voters directly about their loyalties. It is, however, difficult for voters to distinguish between how they usually think of themselves and how they have actually voted. Different questions produce different indications of core support. (In particular, there is a tendency to bring reported identity into line with vote.) The estimate of the 'normal vote' in the final column of Table 15.4 must, therefore, be treated with caution. Nevertheless, they suggest that in 2005 some 37 per cent of voters 'thought of themselves' as Labour, 28 per cent as 'Conservative' and a mere 13 per cent as 'Liberal Democrats'. Since the actual vote share was 35, 32, 23, Labour seems to have polled under its normal vote, while the Conservatives did slightly better and the Liberal Democrats much better than their normal vote. (This analysis makes the dubious assumption that non-identifiers do not vote.) According to this evidence, however, short-term factors were operating strongly in the Liberal Democrats favour and, to a much lesser extent, the Conservatives.

Further analysis reveals just how complex were the forces influencing vote in 2005. Labour was clearly less good at motivating its potential voters than the Conservatives. Just 75 per cent of Labour identifiers turned out to vote in 2005, compared with 83 per cent of Conservatives. Had Labour been as successful as the Conservatives at mobilising its support its share of the vote would have increased by about 0.6 points. It may be that recent losses in Labour membership, coupled with the reduced enthusiasm on the part of activists in safe Labour seats and the ruthless targeting of marginal seats by the party organisation, contributed to a failure to mobilise Labour's potential vote in 2005 (see Chapter 16).

When they actually bothered to vote Labour identifiers were as loyal to their party as Conservatives were to theirs. However, fully 11 per cent of all Labour identifiers voted Liberal Democrat: some for tactical reasons and many as a result of policy disagreements (Iraq, tuition fees and Blair's unpopularity). It seems likely that many of these votes will return to Labour if the short-term forces that pushed them away (Iraq, the tuition fees controversy and Tony Blair's personal unpopularity) have gone.

Labour won more votes than the Conservatives for the following reasons:

■ It had around a 9-point advantage in terms of party identification.

■ It polled better among non-identifiers (28 to 24 per cent).

- The party attracted 15 per cent of Liberal Democrat identifiers, compared with just 6 per cent who voted Conservative. Many of these were undoubtedly tactical voters in marginal seats (see below).

The Liberal Democrats received many votes from those who did not think of themselves as belonging to any party. This group made up one in five of all the party's voters and Labour identifiers a further 15 per cent. The Liberal Democrats resemble a small hotel with a high turnover. It has few permanent residents and quite a few temporary visitors.

The main implication of this is that the 2005 election may have concealed Labour's long-term advantage over the Conservatives. However, these loyalties do not represent an insurmountable obstacle to Conservative victory since some loyalists can be persuaded to 'defect' from their normal party. The Conservatives are capable of winning enough votes if the conditions are right (though they may find it difficult to translate these votes into seats!). There has, moreover, been a general weakening of party loyalties, which may work to the Conservatives' advantage.

Partisan dealignment and its consequences

Party loyalties vary in intensity. Some people feel 'intensely' Conservative or Labour while others feel a less intense commitment. This intensity of feeling is itself a predictor of some types of behaviour. Stronger identifiers are more likely to turn out and vote, to vote for their party and be immune to the appeals of other parties. It follows that any decline in the intensity of partisan feeling, other things being equal, will increase the likelihood that voters will temporarily abandon their party if short-term factors are sufficiently strong. As Figure 15.2 shows, long-term party loyalties have weakened. In 1964, 44 per cent of voters thought of themselves as 'very strong' identifiers. By 2005, however, this had fallen to a mere 10 per cent. By this time fully 48 per cent of all electors either felt themselves 'not very strong' Conservative, Labour or Liberal Democrat or had no party loyalties

Figure 15.2 Strength of party loyalties, 1964–2005

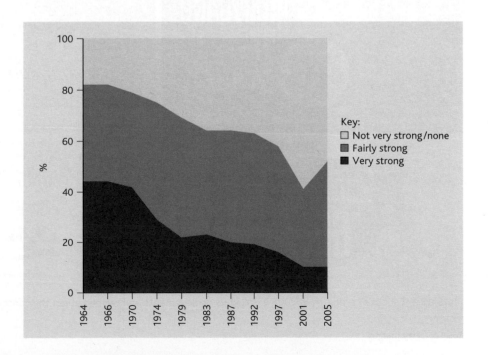

at all. In 1964 a mere 10 per cent of all voters did not think of themselves identifying with any party. By 2005 this figure had risen to 17 per cent.

Figure 15.2 shows that over the course of the last 40 years the pool of weakly aligned or totally uncommitted voters has increased. More and more voters are up for grabs and 'volatile' (i.e. changeable). Whether or not such voters do swing between the parties depends on the success, or otherwise, of their campaign appeals. We therefore now examine the impact of short-term factors.

Electoral volatility

Large and rapid changes in voting behaviour from one election to another.

Short-term factors and the vote

Political parties can do little to alter the social composition of the electorate or their long-term loyalties in the short term. They must take these factors as 'givens' for any particular election. They can, however, seek to appeal to voters by advocating popular policies, projecting an image of competence, creating a favourable image and persuading people that only they can defeat the least preferred party. (This is why the parties spend so much time and energy creating good relations with the media; they want newspapers, television and radio to carry 'good news stories' about them.) These 'short-term' factors are of great and increasing importance in the determination of the vote.

Policies and positions

Political parties spend a great deal of time formulating policies and drawing up their manifesto proposals in the hope of attracting votes. Yet while some people may take careful note of proposals on issues of particular concern to themselves, their family and group, individual policies rarely have much impact on election

Plate 15.1 Labour's campaign in 2005 extolled its achievements and warned about the consequences of a Conservative victory

Source: Getty Images

BRIEFINGS

15.4 The costs of ruling

One of the most well-corroborated findings of modern voting behaviour research is the tendency of all governing parties to lose support almost irrespective of their performance in office. This finding appears to hold across time and countries. Most calculations suggest that governments lose somewhere around two to three points at each election net of all other factors.

It is possible to treat this as a purely empirical generalisation without worrying about why this phenomenon comes about. However, there are several possible explanations as to why governments lose support:

■ **Frustrated expectations** Voters have high expectations of governments and are inevitably disappointed by the reality. (Frustrated expectations may be a consequence of the fact that governments have to make inconsistent promises to different groups in order to win elections.)

■ **Ideological distance** Governing parties tend to pursue their own ideological predispositions. Left-wing parties spend more to reduce unemployment and increase the size of the state, right-wing parties spend less to keep inflation and taxes down. By definition these positions are either to the left or the right of the typical voter. The longer they govern the more distant from the average voter they become until they eventually lose. Public opinion thus acts as a 'thermostat', ensuring that governments do not pursue extreme policies.

■ **Asymmetrical impact of performance** Voters punish governments for 'bad times' but do not reward them for 'good times'. Evaluations therefore slowly chip away at support for the governing party.

The costs of ruling is an intriguing idea. It suggests that governments will eventually lose elections no matter how good things are: thus democratic competition is sustained. These 'swings' and 'roundabouts' perhaps explain why some politicians adopt a fatalistic approach to elections.

The 'costs of ruling' idea is actually an old one. In the 1960s commentators spoke of 'pendulum politics', referring to the expectation that parties would alternate in office.

outcomes. In 2005 Labour's plans for university 'top-up fees' undoubtedly cost the party some votes among students, first-time voters and some parents of students (or potential students). In general, however, it is the overall direction of policy that seems to have most influence on votes. Whenever one of the major parties has become regarded as 'extreme' they have been punished. In 1983, for example, the Labour Party advocated massive increases in nationalisation, taxation and public spending, withdrawal from the European Union and unilateral nuclear disarmament; policies that were unpopular even among its own voters (see Chapter 17). The party's share of the vote was forced well below its normal vote and it went down to its greatest defeat since 1918.

Performance

Voters are influenced not only by the policies advocated by the parties or the general direction they wish to take the country, but also by judgements of how capable the parties are in achieving consensual goals such as a strong economy, peace and high standards of public life. This is especially true where the parties have converged at 'the centre' and are not offering a radical change. It is generally thought that evaluations of economic competence are particularly important in vote decisions. ('It's the economy, stupid' was a campaign slogan for Bill Clinton in the 1992 presidential election in the United States.) Certainly a government that presided over high unemployment or inflation could expect to be punished, other things being equal. However, the impact of economic conditions might be reduced if the electorate thinks that the government is either not responsible for those

Plate 15.2 The first past the post electoral system makes for exciting election nights as it transforms tiny movements in vote share into dramatic changes in parliamentary representation
Source: Cartoon Stock

conditions (e.g. because they are a result of international factors) or if they think the opposition would do even worse if it were in power.

There is evidence that evaluations of a party's ability to manage the public services (NHS, education and transport) are also of some importance. Moreover, in the wake of the 9/11 attacks in New York and 7/7 attacks in London, it is probably the case that national security considerations are of increasing importance (see Chapter 20). In the 2005 election Labour was given high marks for its management of the economy, but poor marks for its record on the public services and disastrous marks for its record on managing immigration and asylum. These latter issues may have hurt Labour particularly among working-class voters (who swung more heavily to the Conservatives than the middle class).

Assessments of future competence are based in large part on past performance. The Conservative Party was, for example, historically regarded as a competent manager of the economy, while Labour was regarded as incompetent. This made some sense, since Conservative governments were generally associated with economic stability, while Labour governments had been associated with economic crises in the 1930s, 1960s and 1970s. These evaluations were subsequently revised as a result of real events. First, the ERM crisis in September 1992 shattered the Conservatives' reputation for competence. Second, New Labour's adoption of orthodox fiscal and monetary policies, together with its successful management of the economy between 1997 and 2005, did much to revise estimates of Labour's competence. By the time of the 2005 general election 58 per cent of voters thought that Labour would best manage the economy compared with 33 per cent who thought the same of the Conservatives. It was probably this factor, together with Labour's lead in terms of party loyalties, which contributed most to its victory. If Labour were to lose this reputation in the future it might find it very hard to win another election.

Party image

The appeal of political parties is based largely on the appeal of their policy platform and apparent ability to manage the economy and public services. However,

Plate 15.3 The ideal politician might need the personal appeal of Santa and the ability to shower gifts on the electorate
Source: Cartoon Stock

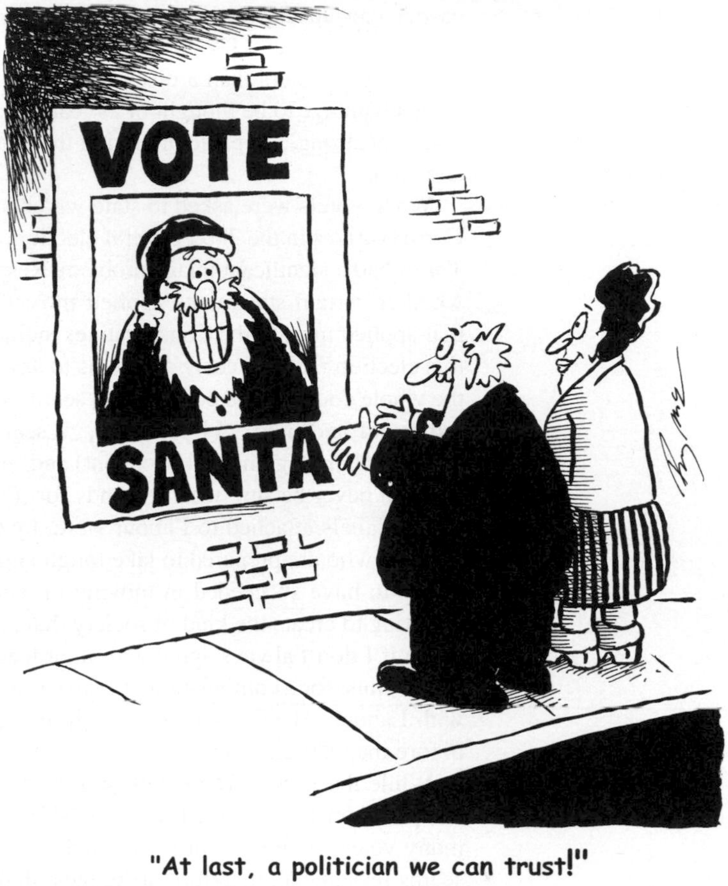
VOTE
SANTA
"At last, a politician we can trust!"

Plate 15.4 Elections are not necessarily a choice between goods; sometimes voters take the 'least worst' option
Source: Cartoon Stock

"Let's try voting for the greater of the two evils this time and see what happens."

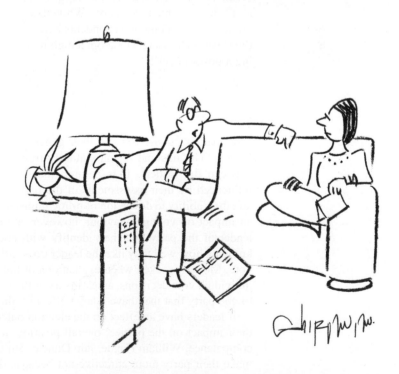

parties can appeal to voters in other ways by projecting a favourable image or otherwise creating a favourable impression. A united party, for example, is more appealing to voters than a disunited party (other things being equal). Similarly, it is an advantage to be thought of as 'caring' rather than 'not caring', 'strong' rather than 'not strong', 'capable of uniting the country' rather than 'dividing the country' and so on.

When voters were asked to state which statement applied most to Labour or the Conservatives in the 2005 general election, voters' responses left no doubt that the Tories had a significant image problem. Respondents in Yougov surveys were asked whether certain statements applied most to the Conservatives or Labour. Those that applied most to the Conservatives included 'it has very little chance of winning this election' (63 per cent), 'it seems to appeal to one section of society rather than the whole country' (48 per cent), 'it seems stuck in the past' (45 per cent), 'it seems rather old and tired' (44 per cent), 'it seems to want to divide people instead of bringing them together' (41 per cent) and 'it seems to chop and change all the time: you can never be sure what it stands for' (35 per cent).

The labels attached to Labour were, by contrast, more positive. They included 'leaders who are prepared to take tough and unpopular decisions' (42 per cent), 'it seems to have succeeded in moving on and left its past behind it' (42 per cent), 'wanting to create the kind of society that is broadly what I want' (40 per cent) and 'even if I don't always agree with it, at least its heart is in the right place' (40 per cent). Thus, for a combination of reasons, most voters simply felt more comfortable with Labour. The Conservatives will undoubtedly wish to alter these perceptions before the next election.

While the Liberal Democrats attracted some voters with their commitments to scrap tuition fees, council tax and NHS targets, they did not seem to convince many voters on important issues such as crime, immigration and the economy. It seems reasonable, therefore, to suggest that part of their appeal lay in their image as a 'nice' and moderate party. While this may be true, it is worth noting that fully 66 per cent of Yougov respondents agreed with the proposition that 'it is easy for the Liberal Democrats to adopt a high moral tone as they have no chance of forming a government'!

Leaders

Most parties choose to build their general election campaigns around their party leaders. The national media similarly treat the election as a gladiatorial contest between the leaders. It is natural, therefore, to assume that many voters are influenced by their assessments of the party leaders (their likeability as a person and their ability to do the job of prime minister). The evidence that leaders do have an impact on voting behaviour, however, is mixed. Most people tend to like the leader of the party that they identify with and/or think the more competent, so knowing how well they like the leader does little to improve our prediction of their vote. Moreover, even when evaluations of the party leaders do have an effect on individual vote decisions, assessments of the party leaders are rarely so favourable to one party that they have a large effect on the election outcome.

If leaders have an effect on the election outcome it is more likely to operate via their impact on the parties' overall position, its policies and evaluations of party competence. William Hague, Iain Duncan Smith and Michael Howard all failed to make their party more attractive not because they were unattractive personalities and implausible prime ministers, but because they failed to reposition their party and craft an attractive image for it.

BRIEFINGS

15.5 Voter Vault

In 2005 the Conservative Party invested £250,000 in a computer programme called Voter Vault to help them identify 'target voters'. The programme used census data, together with 'lifestyle' and credit information, to predict votes and to tailor campaign material that might cause voters to switch.

Liam Fox, the then Tory co-chairman, said: 'This is potentially very significant. In the 2002 mid-term elections in the US, Voter Vault helped the Republicans increase their vote by 4 per cent. This is politics of the margins but this is where elections are won.'

Although great claims are made for such technology it is unlikely that any computer program would have a major impact unless the party also has appeal. In the era of mass membership party local activists would have kept information about the preferences of voters in their heads! Nevertheless, parties are likely to continue investing in such databases in future.

Source: See Nicholas Watt and Julian Borger, 'Tories reveal secret weapon to target voters', *Guardian*, 9 October 2004

Tactical voting

Social characteristics and party loyalties predispose voters to support a particular party most of the time. Short-term factors may lead a voter to prefer one party rather than another in this particular election. The particular strategic position in a constituency, however, may lead someone who prefers A to vote B in order to prevent the least preferred candidate C from winning the seat; especially if that least preferred alternative is intensely disliked. In 1997 and 2001 this factor conspired to deprive the Conservatives of a large number of seats and helped generate some of the 'bias' in the electoral system we have already noted.

The degree of **tactical voting** should not, however, be exaggerated. The majority of voters with an opportunity to vote tactically choose not to do so, either because they are unaware of the tactical situation or because they choose to vote positively for their party of first preference, however hopeless its prospects. Moreover, tactical voting only occurs on a significant scale where supporters of two parties feel much closer to each other than they do to the third. In 2005 around 12 per cent of voters were 'tactical voters', and many voters still thought of Labour and the Liberal Democrats as close to each other. It appears that voters either failed to take account of disagreements between the parties over Iraq or regarded their socio-economic policies as broadly similar. Whatever the case, tactical voting again benefited both Labour and the Liberal Democrats in 2005. It may well be that as intense dislike of the Conservatives declines the motivations for tactical voting may also decline. But that point was not reached in 2005.

Tactical voting

The practice of voting for a candidate who is not one's first preference in order to keep out a less preferred candidate.

Electoral turnout

The vote share received by the political parties is all very interesting but it tells only part of the story about elections. For not only have the major parties received a smaller and smaller share of the vote, fewer and fewer people have bothered to turn out and vote at all. This decline in participation has caused increasing anguish among the political classes. They feel that they need to boost turnout in order to legitimise their actions.

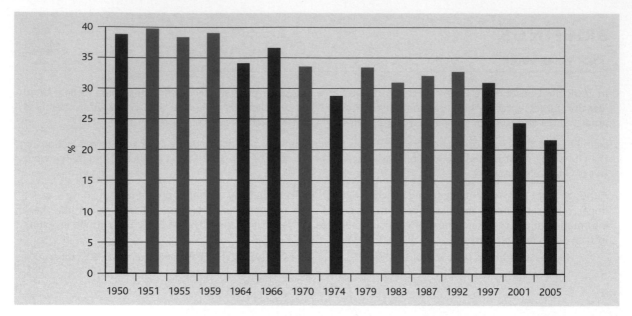

Figure 15.3 Percentage of electoral votes won by governing party, 1950–2005

Table 15.5 Turnout in general elections, 1945–2005

Election	Turnout in UK	Change in turnout
1945	75.5	–
1950	83.6	+8.1
1951	84.0	+0.4
1955	76.8	−7.2
1959	78.7	+1.9
1964	77.1	−1.6
1966	75.8	−1.3
1970	72.0	−3.8
1974 (Feb)	80.9	+8.9
1974 (Oct)	72.8	−8.1
1979	77.9	+5.1
1983	72.7	−5.2
1987	75.3	+2.6
1992	77.7	+2.4
1997	71.4	−6.2
2001	59.4	−12.0
2005	61.4	+2.0

Source: House of Commons Research Paper 05/33
http://www.parliament.uk/commons/lib/research/rp2005/rp05-033.pdf

The low share of the vote won by Labour in 2005 coupled with low turnout means that the proportion of the electorate (including non-voters) which supported the winning party stood at just over one in five of all voters. Moreover, as Figure 15.3 shows, this figure has fallen from around 40 per cent in the 1950s.

The raw data about electoral turnout is displayed in Table 15.5. This shows that the willingness of people to turn out and vote has drifted down from around 84 per cent in the early 1950s to around 60 per cent in the early twenty-first century. Presented in this way the decline does not appear to have been continuous. There were some unusually sharp declines between 1951 and 1955, February and October 1974 and between 1997 and 2001.

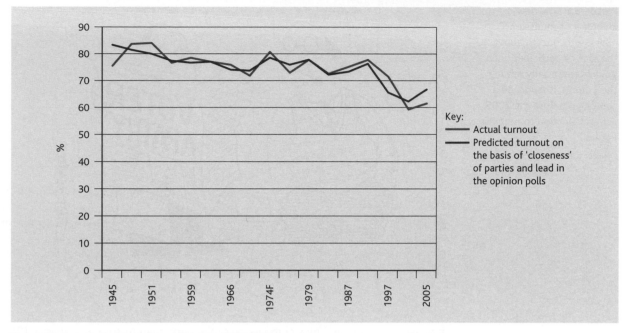

Figure 15.4 Actual and predicted turnout, 1945–2005

Figure 15.4 provides a visual representation of the same data. This strongly suggests that there is an underlying trend downwards in turnout , but that there is some variation around the trend. Thus, any explanation of turnout may have to account for both a long-term trend and short-term deviations from the trend. One obvious cause of variations is the extent to which people think that their vote 'matters'. In particular, the closer they feel the election will be and the greater the difference between the parties, the more likely they are to vote.

It is possible to measure both these factors by gathering data on the 'lead' in the polls prior to the election and the distance between the parties on the left–right

Plate 15.5 While Labour got only 35 per cent of the vote in 2005 they obtained 55 per cent of the seats, partly as a result of tactical voting by 'anti-Conservative' votes

Source: Manchester Evening News

Plate 15.6 The new Electoral Commission expressed concern about the lack of participation in politics (especially among the young). It launched a campaign before the 2005 general election to mobilise voters

Source: Cartoon Stock

"I see disinterest rates are up again".

dimension as estimated by a comparison of the party manifestos (see Chapter 17). It is also possible to capture any long-term effects by including a variable representing the number of years since 1945. Statistical analysis suggests that the following equation provides the best fit to the data:

Turnout = 79.8 − 0.39 (Lead) + 0.12 (Distance) − 0.22 (Years from 1945)

This simple model 'explains' about 70 per cent of the variation in turnout and all three variables contribute to our understanding of trends. The linear trend contributes most powerfully, the further we move from 1945 the lower turnout is. By 2005 this factor alone contributed a 13-point drop in turnout ($60 \times 0.22 = 13.2$). This suggests that there are powerful long-term social and political changes that are reducing turnout. There are, of course, a large number of possible explanations for this trend:

- The decline of social organisations such as the churches and trade unions, which previously mobilised people to vote.

- The increasing cynicism of the media.

- The physical replacement of older cohorts who were socialised into participation and their replacement by increasingly apathetic younger voters. (Older voters valued democracy more because they fought for it between 1939 and 1945!)

The equation also suggests that overall turnout does increase when votes 'count' for more. For example, if Labour's lead had been 10 points rather than 5 in the polls (a difference of 5 points), turnout would have declined by 2 points ($5 \times −0.39 = −1.95$). Distance also had an impact. In 2005 the parties were 8 points further apart from each other than in 2001. Thus, if the parties had been just as close on the left–right scale as they had been in 2001, turnout would have been ($8 \times 0.12 = 0.96$) or 1 point lower. The slight divergence in party positions between 2001 and 2005 boosted turnout marginally.

In 2005 turnout was around 6 points below the level that could have been expected given where the parties stood and Labour's lead in the polls; all of which underlines the fact that 'other factors' were at work in both 2001 and 2005. These may include:

- increased cynicism about the tendency of parties to 'spin'

- the unusual conjunction of small differences in party positions and widespread expectations of a Labour victory

- an Iraq War effect (which may account for the lower turnout among Labour loyalists) (see above)

- increased targeting, which bypassed many voters (see above).

Solutions

Elections are the essential institution of democracy in fulfilling its central purpose of making public policy conform to popular preferences. If fewer than half the people vote, however, the real popular preferences may get distorted or lost. Low turnout may be a sign that many people do not value democratic processes and may be disinclined to defend them if they are threatened. For both these reasons there has been much discussion of how to encourage more people to vote in forthcoming elections. Long-term solutions include:

- increased civic education in schools

- reforming the electoral system to make votes count more

- making it easier to vote (e.g. via the internet or texting).

These measures will probably all help but not enough to raise turnout to over 70 per cent again. The controversial extension of postal voting in 2005 had only a marginal impact on voting. It appears to have allowed committed voters to express their commitment by voting early rather than encouraging non-voters to vote at all.

Political circumstances are likely to play a part – above all if the parties seem to have major policy differences and the election outcome carries important consequences for public policy. Both the major parties' strategies seem to go against this. Labour under Tony Blair (and Gordon Brown) and the Conservatives under David Cameron appear to be playing down differences and seeking to make non-controversial stands. Thus we should not really expect any dramatic rise in turnout in the near future.

CONTROVERSY

Turnout and compulsory voting

One way to stop worrying about turnout percentages would be to legislate for compulsory voting. This might be opposed on the grounds that it restricts freedom of choice. Just as we have to pay taxes however the act of voting could be seen as a civic duty we owe to the democracy we live in. It would not restrict voting choice once we got to the polling booth (or signed in electronically). We could even spoil our ballot paper! But we would have expressed our preferences, which is essential to democracy.

Geoff Hoon, who became Leader of the House of Commons after the 2005 general election, has advocated this for the United Kingdom. He argued that 'international experience points to compulsory voting being the most effective way to increase turnout '. He claimed it was 'the most obvious way to bring those who feel alienated into the political process and the best means to enhance civic participation' and 'bring back the sense that we can all work together'.

Source: See Patrick Wintour, 'Hoon calls for compulsory voting', *Guardian*, 4 July 2005.

Summary

In seeking to explain the results of recent general elections, and the underlying pattern of voting behaviour, this chapter has:

- shown that Britain's FPTP system has the advantage of usually producing an overall majority in Parliament but the disadvantage of unfairly penalising small parties with widely distributed support, such as the Liberal Democrats

- pointed out that this makes for strong government but also means that the majority of voters actually vote for other parties than the one which gains office, which may produce cynicism and reduce turnout

- examined the way other electoral systems work

- examined the impact of 'long-term' factors that shape the core vote for Labour and Conservatives

- explained the impact of 'short-term' factors that cause votes to shift between one election and another

- suggested that the main reasons for the exceptionally low turnout s in 2001 and 2005 were that these elections were foregone conclusions and there seemed to be little at stake.

This chapter's account of elections and voting has focused on the question of which party wins most votes and why. Part of the explanation lies in the parties themselves. In the next two chapters we look directly at the parties and the ways they seek to organise and define themselves, so as to attract voters and members.

MILESTONES

Milestones in post-war elections

1945	Labour wins landslide, helped by army votes, on the basis of an ambitious programme of social reconstruction and promise to demobilise the forces
1950, 1951	Conservatives accept most of Labour's social and economic reforms, including the Welfare State. On this basis, they reduce Labour majority to 6 in 1950 and take over government with majority of 17 in 1951
1955	Conservatives consolidate their majority on the slogan 'Conservative freedom works'
1959	Under Harold Macmillan the Conservatives win a substantially increased majority of 100. In a campaign speech he says, 'Let's face it, you've never had it so good.' The Liberals reorganise and put forward a programme of social reform, doubling their vote. Labour tries to abandon large-scale nationalisation as a policy
1964, 1966	Under its new leader, Harold Wilson, Labour wins a small majority in 1964 and increases it substantially in 1966, with promises of planning for the 'white heat of technology'
1970	Rising price inflation enables the Conservatives under Edward Heath to win the election unexpectedly, with promises of regulating trade unions and letting the 'lame ducks' of industry go bankrupt
1974	Conservatives fight February election in midst of a miners' strike and power shortages (the three-day week) on the slogan 'Who governs Britain?' Inflation, however, is the more important issue for voters. In a hung Parliament Labour forms a minority administration on a promise of 'getting Britain back to work'. In the October election Labour wins small overall majority, promising a 'social contract' with the unions. Liberals and Scottish Nationalists win unprecedented support but few seats
1979	'Winter of discontent' – strikes and industrial unrest – lose election for Labour. Mrs Thatcher becomes Conservative Prime Minister
1983	A Conservative landslide victory of 144, helped by the Falklands War, economic recovery and a divided opposition. Disunited under its left-wing leader, Michael Foot, Labour proposes full-blooded socialism, unilateral nuclear disarmament and withdrawal from the European Economic Community. Its support plummets to a little over one-quarter of the vote. The Liberal/Social Democratic Alliance takes 25 per cent of the vote (but only 23 seats), the best third-party performance for half a century

Milestones in post-war elections continued

1987	Labour's new leader, Neil Kinnock, achieves internal reform but pushes up the Labour vote only marginally. Alliance vote slips slightly. Conservatives retain their vote on the basis of an economic boom and the taming of the trade unions
1992	Conservatives present themselves as a totally new government under John Major and attack Labour as a high-tax party. Labour's attempt to concentrate election campaign on welfare fails. However, they increase their vote to 34.4 per cent while Liberal Democratic support falls
1997	New Labour wins a massive parliamentary majority of 177 with 43.2 per cent of the vote. Conservatives reduced to their lowest share of the vote since 1832. Liberal Democrat seats double to 46, their largest number since 1929, as a result of tactical voting
2001	The results of 1997 are repeated, owing to economic prosperity and irrelevance of Conservative campaign on the euro. Liberal Democrat seats rise to 52. Turnout falls to less than 60 per cent
2005	Labour is returned to office on a sharply reduced share of the vote, as a result of disillusionment with its performance on public services and the Iraq War. The Conservatives make a modest recovery in terms of seats but hardly improve vote at all. Liberal Democrat seats rise again to 62 in a smaller House of Commons. Turnout barely increases despite relaxation of rules on postal voting

Essays

1. Consider the following questions: (a) Why did Labour win the 2005 election? And (b) Why did the Conservatives lose the 2005 election? Are the answers to these questions identical? If not, why not?

2. Is Britain's first past the post electoral system fair?

3. How much do election campaigns affect an election result?

Projects

1. In the light of its three successive defeats what advice would you offer the Conservative Party on how to win the next general election?

2. Write a brief report to either the Labour or Conservative Party leader explaining what the effect of proportional representation might be if it were adopted for elections to Westminster. Where would you gather evidence to support your conclusions? Would reform be an 'unwelcome leap in the dark' or a 'golden opportunity'?

3. Assume that you are a market research company engaged by the Electoral Commission to find out how voters can be persuaded to vote. How would you go about devising your campaign?

Further reading

By far the best book on British voting behaviour is David Denver, *Elections and Voters in Britain* (Basingstoke: Palgrave Macmillan, 2003). Other very useful books on elections are Paul Webb, *The Modern British Party System* (London: Sage, 2000) and Dick Leonard and Roger Mortimore, *Elections in Britain: A Voter's Guide* (Basingstoke: Palgrave, Macmillan, 2005). The best single-volume comparative study of voting in the United Kingdom, United States, France and Germany is Russell J. Dalton, *Citizen Politics: Public Opinion and Political Parties in Advanced Industrial Democracies* (Washington: CQ Press, 2005).

On electoral systems, see David Farrell *Comparing Electoral Systems* (London: Prentice Hall/Harvester Wheatsheaf, 1997); David Denver, 'Whatever happened to electoral reform?' *Politics Review*, **13** (1), 2003, pp. 8–10. On the impact of the new electoral systems see The Independent Commission on PR, *Changed Voting: Changed Politics: Lessons of Britain's Experience of PR since 1997* (London: Constitution Unit, 2003). For an assessment of systems outside the United Kingdom, see Sarah Birch, *Electoral Systems and Political Transformation in Eastern Europe* (Basingstoke: Palgrave Macmillan, 2003).

The 2005 election is reported in Dennis Kavanagh and David Butler, *The British General Election of 2005* (London: Macmillan, 2005) and Pippa Norris and Christopher Wlezien (eds) *Britain Votes 2005* (Oxford: Oxford University Press, 2005). John Bartle and Anthony King (eds), *Britain at the Polls, 2005* (Washington: CQ Press, 2006) contains a useful series of commentaries. Peter Kellner, 'Clearing the fog: what really happened in the 2005 election campaign', *Political Quarterly*, **76** (3), 2003, pp. 323–32 is particularly useful; John Curtice, 'Historic triumph or rebuff', *Politics Review*, **15** (1), 2005, pp. 2–7 and Neil McNaughton, 'The 2005 general election', *Talking Politics*, **18** (2), 2006, pp. 12–15 are also useful. On voting turnout see Pippa Norris, *Democratic Phoenix: Reinventing Political Activism* (Cambridge: Cambridge University Press, 2002).

Useful web sites on elections and voting

Hot links to these sites can be found on the CWS at www.pearsoned.co.uk/budge.

We strongly recommend that you visit the government's Electoral Commission web site (www.electoralcommission.gov.uk). Among other important aspects here you will find an ongoing consultation on the way elections are financed. The UK Politics site (www.ukpol.co.uk) has over 200 pages on election-related material. The British Elections site (www.club.demon.co.uk/Politics/elect.html) maintains coloured maps of Britain depicting its partisan composition across a range of national, local and European elections. The Election Page (www.election. demon.co.uk) offers thorough coverage of all British elections with additional links. As the next general election approaches all the political parties will publish their manifestos on the web (see Chapters 16 and 17 for site details, or consult Richard Kimber's Political Science Resource Pages at www.psr.keele.ac.uk). The Democratic UK site (www.democratic.org.uk) has information on alternative electoral systems, including online election demonstrations for the devolved assemblies.

For more general information on British voting behaviour and public opinion, see Market and Opinion Research International (MORI) (www.mori.com), which includes a digest of polls published by other companies, ICM (www.icmresearch.co.uk) and Yougov (www.yougov.co.uk).

For data sets on British attitudes and public opinion, see the British Election Study (www.essex.ac.uk/bes) and the UK Data Archive (www.data-archive.ac.uk), both at the University of Essex, and the Inter-university Consortium for Political and Social Research (ICPSR) at the University of Michigan (www.icpsr.umich.edu).

For comparative information about elections, voting patterns, electoral systems and electoral administration in other countries, consult the excellent web site of the Institute for Democracy and Electoral Assistance (IDEA) (www.idea.int). See also www.pippanorris.com for papers and data on many aspects of elections and links to other sites, and www.electionworld.org for information on elections in many countries.

http://dodgson.ucsd.edu/lij/, the web site of the Lijphart Election Archive at the University of California, San Diego, has information about elections in 26 countries.

For Scottish elections results and analysis, visit http://election.scotsman.com; for Northern Ireland, www.ark.ac.uk/elections; and for Wales, www.wales.gov.uk.

There are also many sites engaged in analysis and proposals for electoral reform, including Direct Democracy Campaign (www.homeusers.prestel.co.uk/rodmell/index.htm) and Direct Vote (http://myweb.tiscali.co.uk/voter/).

Representation

chapter 16

Political parties and party factions

The parties, particularly the Conservatives and Labour, link together all the political processes and organisations we have examined up to this point. Their influence is obvious in elections, where they provide the alternatives for voting and stimulate popular participation. But they also form a central focus for the media, which they continuously try to influence to their advantage. The ultimate aim of parties is to control the government, so as to inject party policies and personalities into the decision-making process. In government the parties interact with civil servants, business and pressure groups in the ways already described.

The parties' external relations with other political institutions are the subject of almost every chapter of this book. Here we concentrate on the parties' internal structures and relationships, leaving party ideology to Chapter 17.

We look at internal relationships because we cannot take party unity and discipline for granted. Parties have to unite to win elections and run the government. But as the deep Conservative divisions on Europe have shown, internal disputes can give rise to factions and tendencies within a party. For most of the time these groups can live together; otherwise they could not form a **party**. If disagreements become too extreme, however, disaffected factions may split off to form a new party. This is far from being a remote possibility. It has happened in recent memory. In 1981 former Labour MPs founded the Social Democratic Party (SDP) and fatally split the vote on the centre-left.

We consider the history of party factionalism in this chapter, along with the ways in which party organisations and structures have adapted to counter it and put overall control in the hands of the leadership.

This chapter therefore covers:

- the functions of political parties
- the evolution of the modern parties
- factions and factionalism within the parties
- how they are organised.

Functions of parties

The evolution of modern parties cannot be understood without an appreciation of their general role. Democratic parties are associations of generally like-minded people who, by means of election, compete for state power to further their common goals. A unique characteristic of parties is that they serve the dual function of government and representation. As instruments of the government they form an

Party

An organisation of ideologically like-minded people who come together to seek power – often to fight elections with a view to gaining representation in decision-making bodies.

executive that seeks to steer the state. They recruit and train politicians, they implement policies and they mobilise popular support. As instruments of representation they promote the interests and values of sections of the electorate, translate their demands into policies and give them a sense of place within the wider society. Most important of all, they form the government or the opposition, the 'ins' or the 'outs', thereby rendering the government ultimately accountable to the electorate. In elections voters can choose to either 'kick the rascals out' or 'give them another chance to put things right'.

As instruments of the government and representation the major parties therefore perform a third function: political integration. To win elections parties must attract support from many different groups. By aggregating distinct group interests parties identify and create consensus across large segments of the population. They must also respond to expectations or persuade electors to modify them, by altering ideas about what government can do. Horizontally, parties link many groups; vertically, they act as a link between citizen and state and are one of the few instruments for public education about what the government can achieve.

Parties have to concern themselves with interests and needs beyond those of their core voters, because they need to attract other voters. They also aim to form governments that will make policy for the country as a whole. They cannot just pursue a narrowly sectional programme but have to reach out to many groups by varying their appeals. The need to adapt to new circumstances and new challenges, however, makes internal disputes an ever-present possibility. To be national and representative parties have to be coalitions of interests; but political interests invariably conflict. We can see how this has worked out by looking at the growth of British parties from the mid-nineteenth century onwards.

Party unity and internal dissent: Conservatives, Liberals and Labour, 1868–1979

Emergence of modern parties: Whig and Tory, Conservative and Liberal

Like most other political institutions in Britain parties took on their modern form in the mid-nineteenth century. The shift produced by the Second Reform Act of 1867–8 from a small, restricted electorate to a large one numbered in millions meant that local 'notables' could no longer rely on their own resources to secure the election of themselves or their nominees. Central party organisations emerged that fostered local organisations in every constituency and provided supporters for local campaigns. Members were no longer drawn into these organisations by personal ties to a candidate but by support for the national party's principles and policies, which local MPs pledged to support in Parliament. Soon it became immaterial whether the candidate was a local person or not. Just about anyone pledged to the national leadership and policy was acceptable because the job of an MP was to support and serve the party. MPs thus owed their election to their endorsement by the central organisation and were dependent on leadership approval for (re)election. This became a powerful factor enforcing party discipline in Parliament.

The newly emerging Conservatives defined themselves as defenders of traditional institutions such as the Crown and Church, and as supporters of the empire. At the same time they cast themselves as social reformers concerned to improve the lot of the poor. Both these goals were justified by appeals to national unity but also served to attract the votes of the newly enfranchised working class.

The Liberals emphasised free trade at home and abroad, and were not much interested in the empire. They advocated political reforms, particularly those opening careers to the expanding lower middle class, Nonconformists and Roman Catholics. Since most Catholics originated in Ireland, the Liberals sought an alliance with the Irish Nationalist Party in Parliament, which led them to advocate 'Home Rule' (a form of devolution) for Ireland in 1886. This measure split the party, driving out manufacturers who saw it as a step to dissolving the empire and old Whig aristocrats who viewed it as an attack on Irish property rights.

The early twentieth century: Conservative, Liberal and Labour

The Conservatives suffered a split in 1905 when the new influx of Unionist businessmen supported tariffs to protect British markets. The Liberal Party united around the Irish Home Rule project and a programme of social reform, aiming to attract Catholic working-class voters and their political representatives, the Irish Nationalists and the Labour Party. With their support the Liberals passed legislation setting up a rudimentary Welfare State; the power of the House of Lords to delay legislation was limited to three years, and Irish Home Rule was pencilled in for 1914. The latter was largely overtaken by the First World War, which split the Liberals over military strategy. A section of the party, led by David Lloyd George, formed a coalition with the Conservatives (1916–22). The resulting split in the Liberal Party was never completely healed.

Liberal divisions provided an opportunity for the new Labour Party, which had struggled to make an impact. Unlike the other parties, Labour was not formed by parliamentarians seeking a mass base, but by bodies outside Parliament seeking parliamentary representation. The trade unions allied with existing socialist parties, which had a constituency-based organisation, to form the Labour Representation Committee in 1900. This became the Labour Party in 1906. From its very beginning Labour was a coalition of ethical (largely Christian) socialists who wanted to abolish capitalism and replace it with a society based on cooperation rather than competition, the Fabians who were pragmatic reformers who wanted to replace capitalism with a more rational system and trade unions who simply wanted to improve the lot of their members. The party attracted many – though by no means all – in its 'natural' working-class constituency, further eroding the Liberals' electoral base. In 1918 Labour adopted an explicitly 'socialist' commitment to public ownership. The weakening of both Liberal and Conservative parties resulting from continuing divisions between 'coalitionists' and 'anti-coalitionists' helped Labour form minority governments in 1923–4 and 1929–31 and establish itself as the main opposition to the Conservatives.

The 1929–31 Labour government coincided with the financial crisis of 1931 caused by the world depression. The Labour Party split over the question of cutting unemployment benefit as part of a package of orthodox financial measures to restore confidence. Four members of the Cabinet, including the Labour leader Ramsay MacDonald, joined a national government dominated by the Conservatives and supported also by a Liberal **faction**, the 'National Liberals'. MacDonald's actions were regarded as betrayal by the majority of the party and haunted Labour throughout the 1930s.

The national government introduced policies to ameliorate the worst effects of the depression in the 1930s, including trade protectionism and increased government intervention in the economy. The outbreak of the Second World War in 1939, however, required the government to intervene even more extensively. The political mood shifted decisively leftwards: favouring collective (state) action, government intervention and the provision of welfare.

Labour's participation in the coalition from May 1940 onwards provided many within the party with experience of government and this helped Labour appear less dangerously radical. The party secured a sweeping electoral victory in 1945

Factions

Enduring (and often organised) groups within parties that share common attitudes or place particular emphasis on certain parts of a party's core beliefs.

and carried out many radical reforms: creating the National Health Service, founding the Welfare State along the lines advocated by the Beveridge Report (1944), experimenting with Keynesian policies to sustain high levels of employment and nationalising many industries (including coal, gas, electricity). Most of these policies were accepted by their Conservative opponents. In just six short years the terms of political debate had altered: all the major parties accepted that the state would act to solve economic and social problems.

Post-war developments: Conservative, Labour and Liberals 1945–79

While Labour remained reasonably united on its social reforms, it became increasingly divided by two issues during the 1950s. The first was the building of British nuclear weapons (a decision taken by the 1945–51 Labour government). A left faction wanted Britain to engage in 'unilateral nuclear disarmament', chiefly for moral reasons. A right faction, on the other hand, argued that the deterrent should not be surrendered without multilateral agreements. The second issue related to 'nationalisation'. Clause 4 of the party's constitution committed Labour to the public ownership of industry, but left the precise scope of the commitment unclear. The 'Keep Left' group, led by Aneurin Bevan, wanted to extend nationalisation to large parts of private enterprise. The **social democrats** on the right, such as Tony Crosland, wanted to play down the party's commitments to public ownership and focus on promoting equality.

Social democrats

'Moderate' socialists who emphasise the pursuit of equality rather than nationalisation as the goal of the Labour Party

Labour divisions in the 1950s were exacerbated by Conservative electoral success. The popularity of the Labour government's reforms gave the upper hand within the Conservative Party to the 'one-nation' tendency in the Conservative party led by R. A. Butler and Harold Macmillan, who argued that national unity and stability depended on reasonable living conditions for the lower classes, through government intervention if necessary. This led to acceptance and extension of the Welfare State, though the party was less keen on nationalisation and returned some enterprises to the private sector in the 1950s (later known as 'privatisation').

The limited privatisation that took place under the Conservative government (1951–64) was not enough to challenge the 'social democratic consensus' that existed between the dominant factions in both major parties, and among the Liberals. Harold Wilson, Labour Prime Minister 1964–70 and 1974–6, papered over his party's divisions by extending economic planning and promising to harness technology to solve Britain's problems. Labour's experiment with planning, however, proved a failure. In 1967 it was forced to 'devalue' the pound and this badly damaged its reputation for economic competence. Its faith in technology also proved misplaced. Many technological projects, including the supersonic Concorde aircraft, either failed or proved too costly.

The Wilson governments, followed by the Callaghan administration (1976–9), lapsed into pragmatic crisis management; especially after the recessions produced by the oil price shocks of the early 1970s. Inflation and unemployment grew rapidly and the government's attempt to control both via a prices and incomes policy, negotiated with the unions, failed. Many workers sought large pay rises in the expectation that inflation would erode their value. The number of strikes, particularly unofficial strikes called without a ballot, increased rapidly. The various crises came to a head in 1978–9, the so-called 'winter of discontent', when a series of strikes led to shortages of basic products and rubbish piling up in the streets. Labour's reputation as the party that could control the unions and govern competently was left in tatters and not restored for many years.

Plate 16.1 The Winter of Discontent. A series of strikes in the winter of 1978/9 led to Mrs Thatcher's election in 1979 and shattered Labour's reputation of economic competence

Source: Empics

BRIEFINGS

16.1 The social democratic consensus, 1950–79

This covers the ideas that the mainstream sections of all parties broadly shared between 1950 and 1979. Factions of both major parties always stood outside this consensus and, even where there was agreement by the parties on fundamentals, disagreement remained on details and emphasis. The consensus consisted in:

■ acceptance of a 'mixed economy', consisting both of private companies and of nationalised industries (especially where there was a 'natural monopoly' of supply as in the electricity and gas industries)

■ a Keynesian economic policy aimed at striking the right balance between inflation and unemployment

■ acceptance of the powers and roles of the main pressure groups (particularly business and trade unions)

■ acceptance of the steady expansion of the Welfare State and the National Health Service

■ a managed withdrawal from colonies and overseas territories

■ support for NATO in the Cold War with Russia, while seeking to reduce confrontation (détente).

The 'New Right' under Mrs Thatcher broke dramatically with aspects of the consensus in the 1980s. However, even after 18 years in power the proportion of national income in the public sector (NHS, Welfare State and education) had not altered dramatically. Mrs Thatcher failed to wean the public off their reliance on the state.

The New Right

Comprise both Neo-Conservatives who are concerned to preserve order, authority and discipline and Neo-Liberals who emphasise a free market economy.

One Nation Conservatives

Moderate Conservatives who emphasise the need for pragmatic policies to promote social stability rather than adherence to any ideological (particularly free market) principles.

The Conservative Party was also divided by the mid-1970s. The defeat of the 'one-nation'-dominated party in the election of 1964 prompted a reassessment of its ideas. The Heath government (1970–74) briefly experimented with radical right-wing policies; removing government subsidies for 'lame duck' companies and introducing legislation to reduce union power. When unemployment grew and the trade union legislation failed, however, Heath proved just as pragmatic as Wilson. In a dramatic 'U-turn' his government bailed out struggling companies and tried to engage trade union and business in planning the economy; actions that many on the right regarded as a betrayal.

The oil price shocks of the early 1970s dramatically increased the power of the unions. In 1974 the miners called a strike to increase their pay and industry was limited to a 'three-day week'. This strike precipitated, and contributed to, Heath's defeat in the February 1974 election. Shortly after, Margaret Thatcher successfully challenged Heath for the leadership. Her supporters became known as 'the dries' or '**the New Right**'. They included Neo-Liberals (associated with the Adam Smith Institute, the Institute of Economic Affairs or Centre for Policy Studies) who advocated the free market and a reduction in state power and Neo-Conservatives, who were concerned about the erosion of order and self-discipline and wished to reassert the authority of the state. The dries were initially outnumbered by '**One Nation Tories**' or 'wets' (associated with the 'Tory Reform Group', which was formed in 1975), who were sceptical about New Right solutions.

Factions and factionalism since 1979

Although many wets hoped that their new leader would prove more pragmatic when in office, they were disappointed. Instead, the 1979 general election became one of the few 'watershed' elections of the twentieth century and marked an end to the presumption that the state would automatically intervene to solve social or economic problems.

Margaret Thatcher's governments prioritised the control of inflation ahead of unemployment, introduced strict controls on government spending, privatised many state industries, introduced laws to control unions, cut local government spending and reduced the size of the Civil Service. She faced down opponents in the Falklands War (1982) and the miners' strike (1984–5). Defeat of the miners, as did the defeat of the Argentinians, had enormous symbolic importance for Mrs Thatcher. She took it as an indication that only a 'resolute' approach would solve Britain's problems.

Although Mrs Thatcher and her supporters were in a minority in both Cabinet and party, she was often able to get her own way and obtain reforms more radical than her colleagues thought were wise. The Cabinet was sometimes 'bounced' into accepting radical policies. She also appealed over the heads of colleagues for the support of party members at Conservative conferences. At other times she publicly committed the government to contentious policies. Many wets were appalled at the massive increase in unemployment, social divisions and riots in the inner cities, but at a loss to know what to do. If they removed her, they risked dividing the party and letting the Labour Party (socialists) in. Moreover, many of their own preferred solutions had been discredited under Heath. The 'wets', therefore, largely failed to mobilise. 'One Nation' groups such as Centre Forward, founded by Francis Pym, a former Foreign Secretary, had little impact. Most of the parliamentary party were, moreover, loyalists and concerned with ensuring election victory. Her run of election successes gave her the prestige and authority to rid herself of some of the 'wets' from her Cabinets and win over others. Thus, by the end of the 1980s the 'wet–dry' opposition had been largely superseded. Most Conservatives accepted

Plate 16.2 Matthew Pritchett cartoon from the *Daily Telegraph*, 21 April 1997. In 1996, scientists bred Dolly the sheep, a clone of her mother, but in the 1990s no two Tories could agree about Europe

Source: Daily Telegraph

'Scientists think they might one day be able to produce two Conservatives who agree about Europe'

the principle of the 'free market and strong (but slimmed-down) State' that Thatcher proposed.

Though she largely won the party over on economic policy, Mrs Thatcher began to lose support as a result of her increasingly hostile attitude to Europe. In 1986 her Neo-Liberalism led her to sign the Single European Act and accept an end to the British veto over large swathes of policy. Later, however, her Neo-Conservativism, and in particular her belief in the nation state, led her to express concerns about social and political integration. She made an increasing number of speeches or off-the-cuff comments that either cast doubt on or simply contradicted Cabinet policy. In a famous speech at Bruges she linked her belief in markets with a desire to preserve the nation state, 'We have not successfully rolled back the frontiers of the state in Britain, only to see them reimposed at a European level with a European super-state exercising a new dominance from Brussels.' It was her refusal to accept further European integration, coupled with her association with an unpopular new system of financing local government (the poll tax) that brought about her downfall in 1990. Sir Geoffrey Howe, the Deputy Prime Minister, resigned in protest at her attitude to Europe and called on someone to challenge her leadership. Michael Heseltine, a leading wet, stood against her. Abandoned by many Cabinet colleagues, she resigned and was replaced by John Major who tried to unite the party in the run-up to the next election.

The Conservative Party's election victories in the 1980s were due as much (if not more) to splits within Labour as to the attractions of New Right policies. It won only around 42 per cent of the vote in the 1980s. Its large parliamentary majorities were a result of a divided opposition and the 'first past the post' electoral system (see Chapter 15). The split in Labour occurred because the left, led by Tony Benn (a former minister), claimed that Labour governments had failed to implement socialist policies. The left succeeded in persuading many of the trade unions who dominated the party to support proposals, including massive increases in spending and taxation, withdrawal from Europe without a referendum, the repeal of the Conservatives' 'anti-trade union' laws and unilateral nuclear disarmament. These proposals were incorporated in the party's manifesto for the 1983 election – known as 'the longest suicide note in history'! At the same time, groups such as the Campaign for Labour Party Democracy and the Labour Coordinating Committee campaigned for reforms to the party's constitution to increase the activists' control of the Parliamentary Labour Party and ensure that a future Labour government would not renege on its commitments.

The right of the Labour Party felt threatened by these developments. Uneasiness with policy extremism, the power of left-wing activists and the shift in trade union support for left-wing policies provoked a major split involving some of the most prominent figures on the right of the party including Roy Jenkins (a former Chancellor of the Exchequer), Shirley Williams, David Owen and Bill Rodgers. This 'Gang of Four' founded the Social Democratic Party (SDP) in 1981. The new party aroused enthusiasm for its commitment to a reformed social democratic consensus as an alternative to the dogmatic policies of the left and right. The new SDP was a natural ally of the Liberals who, after 20 years of drift, gradually recovered from 1959 onwards with a non-doctrinaire but radical reform programme. The 'SDP-Liberal Alliance' formed between the two parties gained a quarter of the vote in 1983, driving Labour down to 27.6 per cent.

The Alliance held on to most of its ground in the election of 1987, winning 22.6 per cent of the vote to Labour's 30.8 per cent. By that time, however, bitter clashes between the leaders and disagreements about policy, coupled with electoral failure, led many in both parties to conclude that it was time to merge and create a new party, the Liberal Democrats, in 1988. After initial hiccups, the new party inherited the mantle of the Alliance and many, though not all, of their former supporters.

The Social Democratic secession, and the miserable performance of the party in the 1983 election, prompted a reappraisal among many on the left of the Labour Party. The 'soft left', many of whom – like Gordon Brown and Tony Blair – were members of the Tribune Group, cooperated with right-wing Labour MPs who were members of another group called Solidarity to elect a compromise leader with a left-wing past, Neil Kinnock (1983–92) and a deputy leader with right-wing (social democratic) credentials, Roy Hattersley (1983–92). In time the old distinction between left and right was replaced by a division between the parliamentary leadership and a small and weak left faction, organised around the Socialist Campaign group.

Kinnock was convinced that the only way for Labour to recover was to offer moderate policies and assert strong leadership. The party slowly shed left-wing policies and accepted many of the reforms introduced by the Thatcher governments. It dropped its proposals to leave the European Community and subsequently became an enthusiastic pro-European party (something made easier by Mrs Thatcher's increasing hostility to Europe). After a long internal struggle it also abandoned unilateralism. Strong internal leadership was also seen as a necessary element of party 'modernisation'. The party introduced reforms to purge itself of 'entryists' such as the hard-left Militant Tendency and shifted the balance of power from activists and trade unions to ordinary party members. Although this strategy was successful Labour gained votes only gradually. The party received 30.8 per cent in 1987 and 34.4 per cent in 1992.

These disappointing results were seen as pointing towards even further moderation in terms of accepting financial and, above all, fiscal orthodoxy, with restraints on government spending and direct taxation. After its fourth consecutive defeat in 1992 Labour elected John Smith as the new leader. Smith sought to consolidate Kinnock's reforms and wait for the Conservative Party to make mistakes. His death in May 1994 led to the election of Tony Blair as leader and a reappraisal of Labour's strategy.

Blair's approach was very different from that of Smith. In a bold first step he launched a campaign to drop its commitment to public ownership and replace it with an updated statement of beliefs. This was accepted in a ballot of the membership in 1995. 'New Labour' essentially sought to reassure voters that Labour no longer represented a risk to their standards of living. Working closely with his colleague, Gordon Brown, Blair continually emphasised the importance of a market economy and his reluctance to intervene in it. There was a new emphasis on education and

Plate 16.3 Tony Blair's New Labour learned many lessons from Mrs Thatcher's governments (1979–90)

Source: Empics

training to equip people for the global economy and a desire to reform the Welfare State to encourage people to work. In order to help expunge memories of the 'winter of discontent' Blair warned the trade unions that they could expect 'fairness, not favours' from a Labour government. In order to further reassure middle-class voters in England ('middle England') that Labour no longer constituted a threat, Gordon Brown announced in 1997 that there would be no increases in the basic or top rates of income tax. These changes, coupled with commitments to increase spending on the NHS, helped transform Labour into a modern social democratic party that largely left the market to produce wealth, but accepted that the state would modestly redistribute it via public spending.

The party also adopted an increasingly 'tough' approach to law and order issues, promising to marry a concern for social justice with a determination that everyone should play by the rules. This approach was summarised by Blair's soundbite that Labour would be 'tough on crime, tough on the causes of crime'. This shift in emphasis not only appealed to voters in 'middle England' – it also appealed to the authoritarian instincts of many of its working-class voters.

'New Labour' neatly avoided many of the difficult issues associated with wealth redistribution and government intervention in the economy. The party's electoral successes in 1997 and 2001 were undoubtedly aided by the Conservative Party's weaknesses, but gave Blair great personal authority. Large parts of his party, however, remained committed to more 'Old Labour' policies and wanted the government to spend more and be more sympathetic to the trade unions. Labour remained an uneasy alliance of disparate groups, welded together by history and a desperate desire to win.

Thatcher's legacy to the Conservative Party was to leave it more ideological than it had ever been before, especially in relation to Europe. The tensions between the free European market and national sovereignty came out into the open and produced a confrontation between '**Eurosceptics**' and '**Europhiles**' and led both to organise into factions. Eurosceptics, such as members of the Bruges Group and Fresh Start, believed in defending British sovereignty, either by limiting the powers of the EU to what they were in the early 1980s, before the Maastricht Treaty or the SEA, or if necessary by withdrawing altogether. Europhiles, who were members of the Centre for Europe and the Positive European Group, believed that it was in the national interest to remain at the heart of Europe. They maintained that Britain

Eurosceptics

Those who are not generally well disposed to the further integration of Europe, at least within the framework of the European Union.

Europhiles

Those who are generally well disposed to the further integration of Europe within the framework of the European Union.

THE ONE COMMANDMENT

Plate 16.4 Tony Blair's New Labour demonstrated a determination to win that was uncharacteristic of the old Labour Party
Source: Daily Telegraph

could not stand aside from currency union because it was already so heavily involved in the single market (a position that agreed with many of the business interests that have traditionally supported the Conservatives). The Major government (1990–7) steered an uneasy course between these extremes, but was continually denounced by both sides.

The role of the European issue in Mrs Thatcher's downfall also soured relations within the party. Those who admired her could never forgive the parliamentary party for removing her from office and saw every subsequent treaty as a betrayal. A small group of MPs were suspended from the parliamentary party for refusing to support the government on a vital vote on the Maastricht Treaty in 1993. In 1995 Major tried to resolve the conflict by resigning the leadership. In the subsequent election he defeated the Eurosceptic John Redwood, but even this did not stop open warfare. Many activists joined the Referendum Party, which fought the 1997 election demanding a referendum on British membership of the European Union. Others joined the United Kingdom Independence Party (UKIP), which proposed that Britain leave the European Union.

After the 1997 general election the Europhiles found themselves in an increasing minority in the party. Three successive leaders: William Hague, Iain Duncan Smith and Michael Howard were all confirmed Eurosceptics. In order to resolve the European issue Hague proposed that Britain stay out of the single currency for two parliamentary terms. This policy was overwhelmingly supported in a ballot of members in 1998. In the 2001 election the Conservatives campaigned to 'Save the Pound', but went down to yet another defeat. Polls suggested that, although most voters opposed the single currency, the issue was not very important to them and the party appeared 'obsessed' with the issue. Duncan Smith and Howard, therefore, played down the European issue.

While Europe most obviously divided the Conservative Party at the start of the twenty-first century, it also remained divided about other aspects of the Thatcher inheritance, especially the role of the public sector. Neo-liberals wished to continue with a tax-cutting agenda and extend the market to the public services by using the private sector. 'One Nation Tories' wished to reassure voters that the public services would be safe in their hands by matching Labour's spending commitments. In 2001 and 2005 the party fudged the issue by promising to fund tax cuts by reducing waste; a proposition that voters found difficult to believe and which made it easy for opponents to accuse them of secret plans to cut services.

The Conservatives remain divided on moral issues. 'Modernisers', including many Neo-Liberals, wanted the party to be less critical of those who lived alternative lifestyles (single-parent families, homosexual couples and so on) and more supportive of women who wanted to work. They were concerned that the party's emphasis on 'traditional' families (married, heterosexual couples) made them appear to be hostile to increasing sections of the public (unmarried couples, single-parent families and homosexual couples). Neo-Conservatives, on the other hand, opposed civil partnerships for homosexual couples and other policies that undermined 'family values'. They also supported immigration controls. Though such policies were not necessarily motivated by racism, they did little to encourage ethnic minorities to join the party.

On becoming leader, David Cameron appeared to advocate a 'compassionate' conservatism and accept parts of the New Labour agenda. He played down tax cuts and sought to reassure voters that the party would spend as much as Labour on the key public services: especially the NHS and education. Cameron has also tried to re-position the party by focusing on issues such as the environment and global poverty and also by welcoming those who had alternative (chiefly homosexual) lifestyles.

Plate 16.5 David Cameron, the new Conservative leader, is trying to re-position the party at the centre and foster a new image

Source: Empics

More traditional Conservatives, such as Norman Tebbit, expressed outrage but their influence in the party appears to have waned as a result of successive defeats.

'New Labour' represented both a threat and an opportunity for the Liberal Democrats. Labour's moderation attracted many former supporters. But the apparent ideological closeness of the two parties also made it easier for both party supporters to cooperate to keep the Conservatives out. 'Tactical voting' in 1997 and 2001 increased the centre party's haul of seats, even though its vote hardly altered. Disillusion with Labour added to their vote in 2005.

In Labour's first term, the Liberal Democrats cooperated in introducing Labour's constitutional reform package; but were disappointed by the failure to hold a referendum on electoral reform. In the second term, the Liberal Democrats became more critical of the government, especially in relation to Iraq, civil liberties and reform of the public services. Despite their continued success in 2005, there were calls for their leader, Charles Kennedy, to stand down. The immediate cause of concern was Kennedy's personal performance as leader and, in particular, his self-confessed drinking problem. There were deeper tensions, however. Those MPs who followed the old Liberal tradition believed that the party had become too 'statist' in its attempt to appeal to disappointed former Labour voters. They were concerned that the more socially liberal Conservative Party which appeared to be taking shape under David Cameron would attract many former Liberal Democrats. In the event, Kennedy was forced to stand down and Sir Menzies Campbell became leader. Many in the party expected that the next election would produce a 'hung Parliament', which might provide them with an opportunity to achieve electoral reform (see Chapter 15).

The Labour Party has also had to face internal problems in recent years. Just as in the 1950s the divisions have related to both domestic and foreign policy. 'Old Labour' MPs opposed some of Blair's plans to reform the public services; in particular contracting out, self-governing hospitals and schools reform (see Chapter 18). It was Blair's decision to support the 'war on terror' and to go to war in Iraq, however, that most bitterly divided his party. Blair's commitment to fight terrorism at home by increasing police powers and introducing national identity cards also alarmed many libertarians. In late 2005 the government was defeated in the Commons on proposals to detain suspects for up to 90 days.

Plate 16.6 The Liberal Democrats faced strategic difficulties after their success in the 2005 general election. They replaced Charles Kennedy with Sir Menzies Campbell

Source: Empics

By the end of 2005 all the major parties appeared to be competing on the 'centre ground'. It remains to be seen whether David Cameron can broaden the Conservative Party's appeal, whether Menzies Campbell can forge a new position for the Liberal Democrats and whether a new Labour leader, such as Gordon Brown, can succeed in appealing to both 'middle England' and Labour's core voters.

Party structure and organisation

Factional disputes are capable of destroying parties' hopes of election victory. They are obviously situations leaders would like to avoid. One way of controlling or dampening confrontations is through organisation. We have already noted how Kinnock and Blair rooted out 'extremists' in constituency Labour parties by tightening central control. In this section we examine how British party organisations usually enable the party to function and how they allow leaders to exercise control.

BRIEFINGS

16.2 Michels and McKenzie: The iron law of oligarchy and British political parties

In 1911 the German sociologist Robert Michels published *Political Parties* (New York: Dover Publications, 1959), in which he formulated the 'iron law of oligarchy'. This states that mass organisations cannot be democratic, by their very nature, and will always be controlled by a small elite group ('the oligarchy'). There are two reasons for this. First, leaders know all the business of their organisation. They control internal communications and have greater political skills than ordinary members. Second, the 'masses' are incompetent. Few know much about policy matters, or turn up to meetings. Most feel the need for 'direction and guidance' provided by leaders. A culture of deference is thus encouraged.

According to Michels leaders develop their own particular interests and goals, which differ from those of members. They control organisations, and use them for their own purposes, not those of the members. Leaders of mass movements inevitably become members of the power elite.

Robert McKenzie applied Michels' analysis to the Conservative and Labour parties in the 1950s in his classic *British Political Parties* (London: Heinemann, 1955). He began by noting that the Conservative Party was not formally democratic and vested a great deal of power in the leader. The Labour Party, on the other hand, liked to think of itself as democratic, in that the party conference was the sovereign body of the party and the leader merely a 'servant' of the conference. McKenzie argued, however, that for most practical purposes power was distributed in the same way in the two parties. One reason was simply that the trade unions sided with the leadership in their battles with their activists in local parties. He also argued that leaders were accountable to the wider electorate rather than their 'members'. In short, Michels' general argument was correct because the British constitution trumped the Labour's Party's constitution.

Things changed after McKenzie's book was written. The left reduced the power of the leader by making MPs subject to regular reselection by local activists. It was hoped that the threat of 'deselection' would make them more sensitive to the activists and less concerned to please the leader. The left also obtained reforms of the method of electing the leader, giving the trade unions and constituency activists a share of the vote in an electoral college. They failed, however, to make the National Executive Committee (NEC, a body elected by annual conference) responsible for drafting Labour's election manifesto. Had they succeeded, the leadership would have been severely constrained and have found it very difficult to 'modernise' its policies, as eventually happened under Neil Kinnock's leadership.

Under Kinnock's (1983–92) and John Smith's (1992–4) leadership the principle of one member one vote was extended to election of the party leader and selection of candidates in an effort to bypass the activists. Just as Michels suggested, this group was more likely to defer to party leaders. Thus, while formal power appeared to pass to members, in reality it returned to the parliamentary leadership.

'Iron law of oligarchy'

The proposition that mass organisations cannot, by their very nature, be democratic, and will always and of necessity be controlled by a small elite – the oligarchy.

As we shall shortly demonstrate, party organisations reflect both the origins and the ideologies of the parties. However, since the ultimate purpose of most parties is to gain power and since elections are a competitive business, they often learn from successful parties both at home and abroad. (New Labour learned a great deal from observing Bill Clinton's New Democrats in the United States.) It is hardly surprising, therefore, that the party organisations resemble each other.

The organisational ladder contains four main rungs:

1. At the top is the leadership, a group of 20–30 MPs occupying, or hoping to occupy, senior government positions as Cabinet ministers. Their primary interest is in winning the next election.

2. A little further down is the parliamentary party of elected MPs and members of the House of Lords, from whom the leadership is drawn. They too place enormous importance on electoral success, but their priorities are subtly different from the leadership. Most MPs represent safe seats and have more to fear from deselection by local parties or from an unfavourable redrawing of their constituency boundaries than from an adverse national swing against the party.

3. Much further down the ladder is the party in the country – the unpaid officers and active members of local associations – many of them elected councillors on the local authority. For most activists the reward is not career advancement – indeed there are no tangible rewards at all – but furtherance of the party's broad goals, on which they tend to take a more principled stand than leaders and MPs.

4. On the bottom rung is the 'party in the electorate': stalwart supporters (or 'party identifiers') who, while not formally members, can be relied on to vote for the party in elections and to accept the party line on most political issues.

All major parties can be examined in these terms. However, the precise nature of the party organisation depends on their origins and ideology.

The impact of origins and ideology

The Conservative Party began in the nineteenth century as a party formed in Parliament; after the extension of the franchise it organised in the country in order to mobilise support. It was always assumed, however, that the members would defer to their parliamentary leaders. Historically there has been little pretence that Conservative party members 'decide' policy or that the party is democratic. Members have simply wanted their leaders to win in order to keep their (socialist) opponents out!

Federal party

A party in which power is located in different bodies that affiliate to the party organisation.

The Labour Party, on the other hand, was formed in order to gain greater working-class representation in Parliament. It was part of a wider 'labour movement' that consisted of an 'industrial' and a 'political' wing' (the trade unions and the party respectively). Since the unions provided most of the money, personnel and organisation, they insisted on having formal rights over policy, but reserved the right to govern their own affairs according to their own rule books. Labour is a **'federal' party**. It was the union organisations, rather than individual union members, that affiliated to the party. Trade union members paid a 'political levy', which went to a 'political fund'. The union executive decided how many members should be affiliated to the party. The more members the unions affiliated, the more votes they acquired at conference. These votes were, moreover, cast in a single **bloc** to maximise their impact, rather than divided in order to reflect divisions of opinion within the union. From its birth through to the early 1990s the unions had around 90 per cent of votes at conference and dominated its committees. Not surprisingly, critics called Labour a 'wholly owned subsidiary' of the unions.

Bloc vote

The practice whereby the trade unions used to cast their votes in a single bloc at the Labour conference in order to maximise their impact. Thus, even if a union executive voted 51 per cent for A and 49 per cent for B, all its votes would be cast for A.

Modernisation

A loose term describing the process of reforming policy, organisation and presentation by which parties seek to gain office.

These differences in origins were accentuated by differences in ideology. Conservatism regards leadership and deference from members to leaders as natural. Socialist ideology, on the other hand, claims that all are equal and have an equal right to be listened to in policy making. The very idea of leadership is, therefore, often regarded with suspicion by socialists. These differences have important implications for party competition. The Conservatives have a natural impulse to allow the leader enough policy discretion to win elections. Labour's equally natural impulse is to constrain the leader and reduce their discretion.

The concentration of power in the hands of the Conservative Party leader has helped it continually adapt to changing circumstances. In the Labour Party, by contrast, the dispersion of power in its affiliates and continual demands for wider participation in policy making has made it more difficult for the party to adapt. The Conservatives have historically tended to be both less 'ideological' and more pragmatic than Labour. The party has, therefore, been able to adapt more quickly to changed circumstances. Labour, on the other hand, has continually struggled to reconcile '**modernisation**' with its core principles and has agonised over what these core principles were. In recent years these roles have arguably been reversed. New Labour has been less ideological (some would say unprincipled) while the Conservatives have been more ideological (some would say dogmatic), especially in relation to Europe.

The leadership

At the apex of the party organisation stands the party leader or, since political parties are teams of like-minded politicians, the leadership. The leaders of both parties were, until 1983, elected by fellow MPs. From 1983 the Labour leader has been elected by an electoral college consisting of MPs (and MEPs), the trade unions and ordinary party members. From 2001 the Conservative leader has been elected by party members in a national ballot after the parliamentary party has whittled a field of candidates down to two. (There was no national ballot in 2003 because Michael Howard was the only candidate.)

The leader of the Conservative Party has enormous powers over policy and senior appointments. Indeed the leader is the only person with formal responsibility for policy; a position that was unaltered when the party adopted a new constitution in 1998. The Conservative leader nominates a colleague to write the party's manifesto (in 2005 Michael Howard appointed David Cameron). The leader can also appoint members of the shadow Cabinet, a party chairman (who is responsible for the operation of Conservative Central Office), deputy chairmen, the party treasurer and several members of the party's board of management, which assumes responsibility for party organisation reviewing the annual accounts, appointing senior staff, administering the national membership list, maintaining a list of approved candidates and resolving disputes.

The leader of the Labour Party, by contrast, has far fewer powers. The party's constitution declares that the annual conference is the 'sovereign body', which implies that it can both change the constitution and make policy. According to that constitution, the Labour manifesto is drawn up by a joint committee of the Cabinet (or shadow Cabinet) and the National Executive Committee (NEC). The leader and deputy leader of the party are ex officio members of the NEC. Historically, the NEC itself also had a policy-making role between party conferences and often produced policies that were at odds with the parliamentary leadership. When in opposition there are annual elections among Labour MPs to select members of the shadow Cabinet and the leader must appoint these in his first Cabinet. The party's general secretary is appointed by the NEC, while the party treasurer is elected by annual conference, as is the NEC itself.

Labour's penchant for elections had one unintended (and undesirable) consequence: together with the ideological pluralism that characterises the party, it encouraged organised groups to emerge in order to compete for office. Conflict within the party became 'institutionalised'. Party members were just as likely to view 'politics' as a battle between one Labour faction and another as they were to think of it as a competition with the Conservatives. The annual conferences in the 1970s were the scene of heated debates between the factions. The Conservative Party, by contrast, allowed the leader to make such appointments as (s)he deemed necessary to achieve a 'balance' between the various parts of the party. Conservatives were, moreover, less ideological. While there were policy differences between individuals in the leadership, these were less intense and did not become the focus of elections. The Conservative Party was, therefore, a party of **tendencies** rather than *factions*. Not surprisingly, it used to be said that 'unity' was the Conservatives 'secret weapon', but it could equally have been said that 'disunity' was Labour's not so secret handicap.

> **'Tendencies'**
>
> Individuals who share common attitudes or place particular emphasis on parts of a party's ideology but who are not organised.

On paper the Conservative leader appears to be far more powerful than the Labour leader. Yet the formal 'powers' set out on paper are not the same as 'power', defined simply as the ability to get one's way. The power of the leader depends, among other things, on the positions of other senior colleagues (or 'big beasts'), the party's position in the polls and the leader's political skills. Edward Heath (1975), Margaret Thatcher (1990) and Iain Duncan Smith (2003) were all ousted from office when they lost the confidence of colleagues.

Leaders have more time, resources and expertise than most other figures in the party. They can, in addition, usually rely on party members to defer to them. In recent years, both parties' leaders have appealed to members over the heads of the leadership and activists by holding referendums. Success is not inevitable, however. Conservative activists failed to provide the two-thirds support Michael Howard required to abolish their role in the election of the leader in 2005.

In practice Labour leaders have often been in just as strong a position as their Conservative counterparts, since they could invariably rely on the support of the trade unions. Indeed, it was only when Labour leaders lost this support that they became much weaker than their Conservative counterparts and more constrained. Once a Labour leader became prime minister, he acquired all the powers of that great office, including extensive powers of appointment, control of honours and so on. Tony Blair is a good case in point.

The parliamentary parties

All members of the Conservative Parliamentary Party who take the Conservative whip are members of the 1922 Committee, which meets once a week to discuss all matters affecting the party. This committee elects a chairman (who has formal responsibility for organising the parliamentary round of the leadership election) and an executive committee.

When the Conservative Party is in government ministers regularly attend meetings of the 1922 Committee to exchange views with their backbenchers. A failure to impress the audience may have an adverse effect on a minister's career and even lead to resignation. The Conservative Parliamentary Party is capable of exhibiting great loyalty to the leader. Even those 'wet' MPs who were privately bitterly critical of Mrs Thatcher in the 1980s couched their criticism in moderate language. Yet as more and more MPs have become professional politicians and the personal cost of losing elections has risen, deference has weakened and the pressure on leaders to produce electoral success increased. Backbench MPs became more restless under John Major in response to concerns about developments in Europe and lingering bitterness about Mrs Thatcher's removal from office.

The Parliamentary Labour Party (PLP) is organised in a similar way to that of the Conservative Party. It has its own standing orders, which were revised before the party came to power in 1997 to give it greater power to discipline MPs. The chairman of the PLP is elected by MPs and chairs its weekly meetings. Labour MPs did not rebel much in the first term, but became much more likely to do so in the second term (see Chapter 18).

Both parliamentary parties have a team of 'whips' who are responsible for MPs from certain regions. They relay information from the front to the backbenches, try to ensure that the party's vote is maximised and monitor the performance of MPs and ministers. Occasionally, they try to get an MP to follow the official party line by threatening to write to the local Conservative association or Constituency Labour Party (CLP) accusing them of disloyalty. Local parties, however, are sometimes immune to such pressures and reward MPs for taking an 'independent' line. Attempts to make sure that MPs stay 'on message' by providing them with pagers and mobile phones have often failed because MPs switched them off! Party cohesion in Parliament depends much more on instinctive loyalty than threats of deselection and the patronage of the Prime Minister. A backbench MP, who has good relations with his local party and does not want high office or honours, is unlikely to be successfully bullied by the party hierarchy.

The national headquarters

Conservative Central Office and Labour Party headquarters serve several functions:

- keeping national membership lists (vital for membership ballots and financial appeals)
- advising the local parties on policy
- providing training for campaigns
- providing advice on regulatory matters
- producing campaign materials (standardised leaflets)
- commissioning party election broadcasts
- supplying the parliamentary party with additional research.

The Conservative chairman is appointed by the leader and regarded as the leader's man (or woman) in Central Office; Labour's general secretary is appointed by the National Executive Committee and regarded as a servant of the party. In practice, however, the general secretary forges a close working relationship with the leader.

The party in the country and party conferences

Local parties

The major British parties are organised in similar ways at a local level. A Conservative association or CLP exists in each parliamentary constituency on the mainland and, where support is strong enough, in each ward making up the constituency. In the 1950s local parties served a social function and many joined them to get access to sporting facilities or simply to meet people. As leisure opportunities have increased the parties have lost this function and membership has declined dramatically. Their main function now is to contest elections by raising campaign

BRIEFINGS

16.3 Why has party membership fallen?

Party membership has fallen dramatically in recent years. In the mid-1950s the Conservative Party claimed over 2 million members and Labour around 800,000. By 2005 membership stood at around 320,000 for the Conservatives, 215,000 for Labour and 75,000 for the Liberal Democrats. While there have been occasional increases in membership (there was a net increase of 100,000 Labour Party members when Blair became leader) there has been a general decline. There are a number of possible reasons for this:

■ Some of the decline is more apparent than real. Historically, membership records were inaccurate and local parties tended to 'over-claim'. Conservative associations often included many of those who attended Conservative clubs for social reasons rather than those who paid subscriptions, while CLPs had to pretend that they had at least 1,000 members in order to send delegates to conference. Rule changes and computerisation has improved the accuracy of records.

■ Increased leisure opportunities. People no longer need to join parties for social reasons.

■ Organisations closely associated with the parties have declined. (The trade unions in the case of Labour and the Church of England in the case of the Conservatives.)

■ The real cost of party membership has increased.

■ Ideological convergence. The sharp divisions between the parties have been much reduced. There is less incentive to join parties.

■ The decline of 'tribal' loyalties. More people have mixed characteristics that weaken party attachments.

■ Politics is structured around new issues (such as the environment) that are less relevant to the major parties, which were based on class and left–right ideological divisions.

■ Parties do not need members as much. National elections are fought on television and do not need campaigners (except in marginal seats).

■ The leadership of parties can often raise funds by appealing directly to the public or a few rich individuals.

■ Voters are smarter. They realise that they have little influence over party policy and are not taken seriously by the leadership.

The decline in membership may matter. Research has demonstrated that local campaigns do influence voters. A party without 'foot soldiers' may be unable to mobilise its vote on election day. The decline in membership may also lead a party to rely on a few rich individuals for finance. (It is easier to ask one individual for £10 million than a million members for £10 each!) Unless this money comes with 'no strings attached' there is a risk that rich individuals will gain excessive influence.

funds, engaging in electioneering and, most important of all, selecting the candidate who, in the safe seats, will become the MP. In most parties political agreement is taken for granted and politics is not discussed much!

Conservative associations have traditionally enjoyed autonomy over their own affairs (electing their own officers, having their own finances, selecting their own candidates, fighting campaigns and imposing discipline). Although some associations are enormously wealthy, they are reluctant to make contributions to Central Office, accusing it of waste and bureaucracy. They also jealously guarded their rights to select candidates and resisted attempts to select more socially representative individuals (women, ethnic minorities and openly homosexual candidates have not found it easy to be selected for 'safe' seats).

This autonomy has been eroded in recent years, though members have acquired the right to elect members of the board of management, the right to expect a certain level of service and the right to participate in the election of the party leader. Each local association used to have its own constitution. The new constitution adopted in 1998 produced 'model rules' and made it clear that every association is subject to national rules and the authority of the leader. Local associations are required to report regularly on their activities and forward subscription money to Central Office. Members can also now join the party nationally. Money is automatically deducted before being forwarded to the constituencies, making it much easier to fund the central organisation. In addition, there is a national membership list, so leaders can now communicate directly with members without relying on local associations. There are even provisions for the national party to take over those local parties that do not meet performance criteria relating to recruitment and campaigning. The constitution also introduced a new Ethics and Integrity Committee that has the power to expel members for conduct likely to bring the party into disrepute. In February 2002 the committee expelled Jeffrey Archer, after his conviction for perjury.

The new constitution did not alter the method by which candidates are selected. Central Office keeps a list of approved candidates and offers training to potential candidates. Attempts to influence the type of candidate have met with little success. In late 2005 it was announced that a 'priority list' would be drawn up consisting of a wider range of the 'best' in British society and that associations will be encouraged to involve non-party members in the selection process. It remains to be seen whether this will make the parliamentary party more representative of the party as a whole. In the past associations have resisted attempts to produce a 'politically correct' list of candidates.

Constituency Labour Parties have always been subject to a great deal of central control by the NEC, who were anxious to keep their left-wing activists in check. In the 1970s and 1980s the general management committees of the CLPs, which dominated the local parties, became dominated by left-wing activists. The NEC has extensive powers to interfere in the operation of CLPs and impose candidates. The party experimented with 'all women' short-lists before the 1997 election, but this was declared illegal by the courts. The *Sex Discrimination (Candidate Selection) Act, 2002* made the practice legal for a short time. The tactic backfired spectacularly in Blaenau Gwent in 2005 when Peter Law stood as an independent, defeating the official female Labour candidate.

Annual conference and policy making

Conservative associations have the right to send members to attend the annual conference that takes place in the autumn of each year. Those who attend act as representatives and are expected to make up their minds in light of the debate. Unlike the Labour equivalent, the conference has no formal policy-making powers, rarely votes and often does little more than provide senior party figures with a platform for expressing their current thinking. The conventional wisdom, therefore, has been that while Labour conferences decide, Conservative conferences confer.

The conventional wisdom probably underestimates the influence that Conservative members have over policy. Although most attention is focused on the annual conference there is a thriving conference system with special conferences for women, youth sections, councillors and the Welsh and Scottish parties. The Conservative leadership is often sensitive to the mood in the party and is anxious to please members. Certainly there is a great deal of evidence that senior party figures take their conference speeches seriously, not just because they wish to address the nation but because they wish to please the 'party faithful'.

It is difficult to measure influence with precision because there are so few votes. Most of the influence undoubtedly takes place in private meetings outside the conference halls. There are, however, clear cases of influence. In the 1950s the Conservative conference pressured the leadership to increase targets for house building, while in the 1970s the conference persuaded the party to adopt a more restrictive immigration policy. Such influence does not always produce popular policies, however. In the late 1980s ministers were persuaded to introduce the massively unpopular poll tax as a result of pressure from the grass roots, who wished to avoid increases in the old tax (domestic rates). The results were disastrous and the new tax was both introduced and abolished in the 1987–92 Parliament!

The Labour Party's constitution declares that the annual conference is the 'sovereign' body of the party; suggesting that it is the place where all the great matters are decided. It provides its members (the trade unions, constituency parties and other affiliated organisations) with formal voting rights. Those attending conference are 'delegates' who are mandated (instructed) how to vote on each motion or proposal. This makes it less easy for the party to achieve a compromise at the conference. Delegates have, however, enjoyed some discretion because motions produced by various parts of the party on the same issue have had to be collected together in 'composite' motions, which – by definition – cannot have been discussed beforehand.

Traditionally the large trade union delegations would get together before conference and cut deals that were mutually beneficial to their members and supportive of the leader. Labour leaders looked to the unions and their bloc votes to protect them from the CLPs. Yet as the unions moved to the left in the 1970s the Labour leadership found itself increasingly at odds with both conference and the NEC. Harold Wilson and James Callaghan regularly ignored conference decisions or invoked the rule that since a motion had not been carried by a two-thirds majority it could not be put in the party's programme for office and could not be included in the manifesto. This continual flouting of the spirit of conference decisions caused resentment and led to demands to increase the constraints on the leader and make him the servant of the conference. In the late 1970s the CLPs launched a successful campaign to introduce an electoral college for the election of the Labour leader. This was made up of trade unions (40 per cent of vote), CLPs (30 per cent) and MPs (30 per cent). The unions, however, were not obliged to ballot their members and most general secretaries or executives took it on themselves to decide how their bloc vote would be cast without consulting their members. The initiative in leadership elections, therefore, lay with a few union leaders who could provide any candidate with momentum by promising their votes. In effect a few union leaders decided who would be the Labour leader in 1983 (Kinnock) and 1992 (Smith). At around the same time a system of 'mandatory reselection' was introduced that obliged parties to hold a reselection meeting and made it more likely that the MP or candidate would be deselected. Unsurprisingly, the leadership felt compelled to accede to the demands of the conference and the 1983 Labour manifesto contained many of the policies the left wanted. Perhaps equally unsurprisingly, the party went down to its worst defeat since 1918, gaining just 28.6 per cent of the vote.

The road from the 1983 manifesto to the New Labour landslide of 1997 was a long one because the leadership had to carry the case for organisational and policy 'modernisation' to each and every part of the party. Neil Kinnock, in particular, devoted a great deal of time and energy to persuading the unions to support change. Continued electoral failure added to the pressure for the unions to cede power. In 1993 their share of the vote in the electoral college was reduced to just one-third and they were required to ballot their members in Labour leadership elections. This reform meant that the initiative shifted back to the PLP. A candidate could build momentum by securing the support of MPs (who could announce their intentions without consulting anyone if they wished). The unions' share of votes at conference was reduced from 90 to 70 per cent in 1993 and to under 50 per cent in 1995 and they were allocated a smaller proportion of seats on the NEC. Both these changes were designed to counter claims that Labour was 'in the pockets of the unions'. Both, however, carried another risk. As the unions lost their share of the vote, the CLPs gained accordingly. Unless something was done to change matters, the conference and NEC might shift to the left.

In order to prevent this the leadership also acted to reduce the power of the NEC and annual conference. The NEC was increasingly required to focus on organisation and campaigns rather than policy. The annual conference was neutered by reforming policy making. This process had actually begun in the late 1980s when the party used joint committees of the shadow Cabinet and NEC to formulate policies, thus increasing the leadership's ability to control decisions. In the mid-1990s Labour introduced more new policy-making mechanisms. A National Policy Forum (NPF) was established, made up of around 180 members elected by the various party 'stakeholders' (unions, CLPs and socialist societies). This meets two or three times a year behind closed doors and out of the media spotlight. Labour's divisions have, as a direct consequence, become much less evident. Beneath the NPF are around six policy commissions covering specific areas. These are required to formulate policy over a two-year period, taking evidence from all parts of the party, commissioning research papers and producing draft reports that are circulated among the various parts of the party. The policy commissions are jointly chaired by a member of the NEC and ministers. Informal consultations are usually chaired by specially trained facilitators at regional conferences. The whole policy process is guided by a Joint Policy Committee (JPC), chaired by the Prime Minister and comprising the NEC and members of the government.

The new policy-making process is designed to be more 'deliberative' than in the past and increase the role of the leadership. The briefing papers are often produced by the leadership, ministers and their advisers. Policy papers are discussed, comments collated and revisions drafted. The final proposals do not formally become party policy until they are voted on at conference. Formally, conference remains 'sovereign'. It is very difficult, nevertheless, for opponents of the leadership to mobilise opposition at this late stage. Annual conference has, in effect, become a mere rubber stamp, a 'showcase' for the leadership and an opportunity to project a new 'modern' image to the electorate.

Labour conferences are less entertaining than in the past, but there is little doubt that the conference system (comprising the NPF, JPC and Policy Commission) is more effective at making electorally popular policy.

The party in the electorate

The Conservative Party has traditionally been attentive to the needs of the wider electorate and largely eschewed a narrow ideological approach to politics. In the 1950s it claimed a massive membership of around 2 million that could not only be relied on to vote and sometimes to campaign for it, but also to provide a useful gauge of public opinion. This may have been one of the factors that allowed it to rapidly accept the social democratic consensus from 1945.

Ironically the Labour Party, the self-styled 'People's Party', has often been inattentive to the wider electorate and has instead turned in on itself, focusing on internal battles rather than the need to reach out to voters. The party often pursued an ideological approach to politics that made it difficult to 'modernise'. Since it has always been able to rely on the trade unions to provide affiliated members, moreover, it has never had a genuinely mass membership and its members are politically unrepresentative of both its voters and potential voters.

The principal architects of New Labour were all too aware of the party's tendency to turn in on itself and focus on internal battles rather than focus on the battle with the Conservatives. They eagerly used opinion polls and focus groups to keep in touch with popular opinion. The process began in the early 1980s but speeded up under New Labour, which invested heavily in such methods. Philip Gould, Blair's focus group 'guru', produced streams of memos, keeping the leadership informed about what ordinary people were saying and advising them what words to use in making their appeals. Such research also found its way into the new National Policy Forum and various Policy Commission discussions. Revealingly, one party document warned that, 'for the government to stay in tune with the party, the party must stay in tune with the nation' (the Labour Party, *Partnership in Power*). In 2003 the party also launched the so-called 'Big Conversation' in which it canvassed members' and voters' opinions on a range of subjects.

Some regarded the use of such techniques as anti-democratic, since they diminish the role of party members and vastly increase the power of the strategic community of professionals around the leader who have responsibility for collecting such data. Others cast doubt on the usefulness of the information, alleging that the findings were inevitably distorted to comply with the leadership's positions. It could be argued, however, that market research methods improve democracy by making parties more responsive to the wider electorate. As party membership continues to fall members are likely to become increasingly unrepresentative of the electorate as a whole. It is essential that all parties listen to the wider electorate if they are to adapt or modernise. The danger, however, is that if ordinary party members feel that their opinions count for just as much (or less) than focus group members, there is less incentive for them to join. Some have seen the new techniques of political marketing as contributing to a massive drop in party membership.

Summary

Commentators sometimes depict political parties as disciplined armies moving in perfect order on the political battleground. The reality could hardly be more different. As with all voluntary organisations, people join with dissimilar objectives and protest or quit if these are not met. Parties have an inner life, marked by ideological divisions, personal rivalries and tensions between the leadership and members. All parties are uneasy coalitions.

This is clearly evident in the recent struggles within both Conservative and Labour parties and goes back a long way, as shown by our earlier discussion and by the Milestones section that follows. We have emphasised not only party divisions, however, but also the way in which leaders can use their organisational advantages to pull the party together and stake out a winning position that endures over a considerable period of time. Besides covering internal disputes this chapter has charted the overall development of the parties and their internal structure. Specifically it has discussed:

■ inner tensions and ideological developments from 1868 to 1979;

■ factional and leadership initiatives of the 1980s and 1990s;

■ the way in which parties link grass roots and leadership through their organisational structures;

■ the leverage this gives to party leaders in pulling the party together.

MILESTONES

Milestones in the development of British political parties

Conservatives	Liberals	Labour
1867–8 Second Reform Act transforms franchise from a small, propertied basis to a mass electorate		
1870s Primrose League promotes mass organisation of party, with a branch in every constituency. Party promotes Empire, monarchy and social reform	Joseph Chamberlain and the 'Birmingham Caucus' pioneer a mass party organisation emulated in other parts of Britain	
1868–86 Alternation of Conservatives and Liberals in government		
1886 Accession of Liberal Unionists initiates 20-year dominance of Conservative Party in national politics	Gladstone's First Home Rule Bill for Ireland splits Liberal Party	
		1900 Labour Representation Committee brings together socialist parties and trade unions
1905 Under influence of Liberal Unionists, party advocates imperial preference and protection, is defeated in the general election, and remains divided	**1905–14** Liberal governments introduce social reforms and push for Irish Home Rule Parliament Act 1911, National Health Insurance Act 1911, Irish Home Rule Bills 1912, 1913, 1914	**1905–14** Labour supports reforming Liberal governments
		1914–18 Labour internally divided over whether Britain should fight First World War
1922 Break-up of coalition. Bonar Law propels Conservatives to office	**1922–9** Liberals split between 'Lloyd George' and 'Asquith' Liberals	**1923–4** First minority Labour government legislates for public housing programmes
		1929–31 Second minority Labour government
1926 General strike broken by Conservative government with implicit support of Liberals and Labour		
1931 Financial crisis related to world slump leads to split in Labour and Liberal parties, and formation of Conservative-dominated 'national government'		
1932 Government intervenes to impose protection, tariffs, industrial mergers and rudimentary planning	Split between mainstream opposition and 'National Liberals' who are absorbed by Conservatives	**1932** Split between mainstream Labour and 'National Labour' who are absorbed by Conservatives
1940–5 Wartime coalition government, in which Labour basically runs home affairs		
1946–51 Conservatives accept Welfare State and most nationalisations	Liberals drift without clear leadership	Reforming Labour governments establish 'Welfare State', nationalise large industries and decolonise India
1951–59 They win elections of 1951, 1955 and 1959 on basis of abolishing controls and freeing economy	**1959** Grimond provides strong leadership that reverses vote decline	**1951–64** Party divides increasingly between left and right

▶

Milestones in the development of British political parties continued

Conservatives		Liberals		Labour	
1962–4	Government shifts to idea of indicative economic planning	1964	Gain votes with advocacy of electoral reform, civil rights and European integration	1964–6	Wins 1964 and 1966 elections on basis of 'making planning work'. Devaluation of sterling leads to financially orthodox policies. Trade union reform fails. Strengthening of the left
1965–70	Shift to the right – support for free market and trade union reform				
1970–4	Heath government imposes legal framework on trade unions and joins European Union				
1973–4	'Three-day week' and miners' strike precipitate election, which brings government down	1974	Liberal vote increases to 18–19% at the two general elections that year	1974	Wins elections but with reduced vote. Wage and price controls lead to trade union revolt in 1979 ('winter of discontent'). Loses 1979 election
1975	Margaret Thatcher wins party leadership election on a 'New Right' programme				
1979–90	Margaret Thatcher wins a series of elections on a programme of financial orthodoxy, privatisation of state industry, strict regulation of trade unions, cuts in public expenditure, a cautious attitude to EU and full support of NATO	1983–7	Alliance with Social Democrats nets one-quarter of the vote in general elections of 1983 and 1987	1979–83	Ascendancy of 'hard left'. Alternative economic programme and internal reforms lead to breakaway Social Democrat Party and to heavy election defeat in 1983
				1983	Election of Neil Kinnock as leader. Centralising reforms and adoption of 'Neo-Liberal consensus' fails to avert election defeats of 1987 and 1992
1990	Thatcher ejected as leader to avert election defeat				
1992–7	Split between 'Eurosceptics' and 'pro-Europeans' weakens party by continual controversy. Series of financial and sexual scandals. Go down to record defeat in 1997			1992	Kinnock resigns as party leader
				1992–4	John Smith carries on internal reforms as party leader
				1994	Tony Blair elected party leader, imposes strong central discipline, abolishes Clause 4, loosens ties with the trade unions and evolves image of 'New Labour', which wins 1997 election
		1997	Liberals win 46 seats in Parliament, their largest number since 1929	1997	Government initiates programme of political reform starting with devolution. Cautious pursuit of 'Neo-Liberal consensus' aids stability and economic prosperity

Milestones in the development of British political parties continued

Conservatives		Liberals		Labour	
1998	System for electing party leader changed to include party members	1998–9	Coalitions with Labour in Scotland and Wales		
2001	Eurosceptic, right-wing leader William Hague loses election. He is replaced by the very similar Iain Duncan Smith	2001	New leader Charles Kennedy increases vote and seat numbers	2001	Landslide victory in general election consolidates Tony Blair's leadership
2002	Main party division shifts to efficiency and delivery of public services				
2003	Michael Howard replaces Duncan-Smith				Serious internal dissent over Iraq War
2004					Blair announces intention not to stand for further re-election after 2005
2005	Suffer third consecutive defeat. Howard stands down and is replaced by David Cameron, begins shift to centre		Party makes modest progress but disappointed by results		Labour re-elected for third successive time Government hit by series of revolts in Parliament over plans for new laws on terrorism and education reform
2006			Kennedy is forced to resign and is replaced by Sir Menzies Campbell		

Essays

1. How far are British political parties 'umbrella' organisations covering a loose alliance of factions and tendencies, and how far are they basically united?

2. Does Michels' 'iron law of oligarchy' still hold for British political parties?

3. Are party activists inevitably more extreme than party leaders? Why or why not?

4. In what sense, if at all, is the use of market research and focus groups to inform policy anti-democratic?

Projects

1. Document with examples the major ways in which either the current Conservative or the current Labour leader control their respective parties.

2. Update Robert McKenzie's analysis of power relationships within the Conservative and Labour parties.

3. Imagine that you are asked by a party leader to find out why people do not join their party. How would you go about providing an explanation? What do you think are the most important reasons for the decline in membership?

Further reading

Valuable historical material is contained in R. T. McKenzie, *British Political Parties* (London: Mercury, 1964). The leading book on parties today is Paul Webb, *The Modern British Party System* (London: Sage, 2000). On the Labour Party see Thomas Quinn, *Modernising the Labour Party: Organisational Change since 1983* (Basingstoke: Palgrave Macmillan, 2004). On the Conservative Party see Philip Norton, 'The Conservative Party: is there anyone out there?', in Anthony King (ed.), *Britain at the Polls 2001* (Chatham, NJ: Chatham House, 2002). On the Liberal Democrats see Andrew Russell, *Neither Left nor Right?* (Manchester: Manchester University Press, 2005) and David Denver, 'The Liberal Democrats in constructive opposition', in King, *Britain at the Polls 2001*.

The best account of the internal democratisation of parties is in Paul Webb, 'Parties and party systems: modernisation, regulation and diversity', *Parliamentary Affairs*, **54** (2), 2001, pp. 308–21.

On the Conservative Party see Gillian Peele, 'Towards new Conservatives? Organisational reform and the Conservative Party', *Political Quarterly*, **69** (2), 1998, pp. 141–7; Richard Kelly, 'Farewell conference, hello forum: the making of Labour and Tory policy', *Political Quarterly*, **72** (3), 2001, pp. 329–34; Jennifer Lees-Marshment and Stuart Quayle, 'Empowering the members or marketing the party? The Conservative reforms of 1998', *Political Quarterly*, **72** (2), 2001, 204–12.

On Labour see Thomas Quinn, 'Block voting in the Labour Party: a political exchange model', *Party Politics* (2002), 207–26 and Thomas Quinn, 'Leasehold or freehold? Leadership eviction rules in the British Conservative and Labour Parties', *Political Studies*, **53** (4), 2005, pp. 793–815.

Also see Mark Rathbone, 'The future of the Liberal Democrats', *Talking Politics*, **18** (1), 2005, pp. 14, 16–19 and Peter Joyce, *Realignment of the Left? A History of the Relationship between the Liberal Democrat and Labour Parties* (Basingstoke: Macmillan, 1999); Neal Lawson and Neil Sherlock, *The Progressive Century: The future of the Centre-Left in Britain* (Basingstoke: Palgrave, 2001).

Useful web sites on political parties and party factions

Hot links to these sites can be found on the CWS at www.pearsoned.co.uk/budge. (For further study aids on this subject, please see the self-assessment test for this chapter on *The New British Politics* web site at www.pearsoned.co.uk/budge.)

The main political parties in Britain include, in alphabetical order:

Conservative Party: www.conservative-party.org.uk

Democratic Unionist Party: www.dup.org.uk

Labour Party: www.labour.org.uk

Liberal Democrats: www.libdems.org.uk

Plaid Cymru: www.plaid-cymru.wales.com

Progressive Unionist Party (NI): www.pup.org

Provisional Sinn Fein: sinnfein.ie/index.html

Scottish National Party: www.snp.org.uk

Social Democratic and Labour Party: www.sdlp.ie/sdlp

Ulster Unionist Party: www.uup.org

United Kingdom Unionist Party: www.ukup.org

Other web sites of interest include:

Conservatives: The 'moderate Conservatives' in Conservative Mainstream (http://core1.conservativemainstream.org.uk), the Tory Reform Group (http://core2.trg.org.uk), the Bow Group (www.bowgroup.org), the Eurosceptic Bruges Group (www.brugesgroup.com), the right-wing Monday Club (www.conservativeuk.com).

Labour: The Fabian Society (www.fabian-society.org.uk), the *Tribune* newspaper (http://www.tribweb.co.uk), the *New Labour Renewal* journal (www.renewal.org.uk), the left-wing Campaign Group (www.poptel.org.uk/scgn), Campaign for Labour Party Democracy (http://home.freeuk.net/clpd), the far-left Militant (www.militant.org.uk).

Liberal Democrats: The Liberator (www.liberator.org.uk).

chapter 17

Party ideologies

Parties are at the heart of British politics not only because of the role they perform but because of what they stand for. The last chapter showed how their organisations bridge the various levels of British society, linking members and electors to leaders who form the government or the government-in-waiting.

Parties do not, however, simply seek to run the country for its own sake. They seek to run it along certain lines, either as a free market economy or as a 'mixed' system, in which market competition is regulated and the state intervenes to protect losers. This is only one of the issues that divide the two main parties, but it has been a central one over the past 20 years, and it has deep historical roots.

Other policy differences exist, notably over the European Union. However, parties do tend to shift positions on these issues from time to time. Labour was split on the European Union in the 1970s but is much more supportive today, while the Conservatives totally changed from support to opposition between the mid-1970s and the late 1990s.

On central questions such as the management of the economy, the pursuit of equality and the emphasis on stability, the parties are more consistent in the policies they adopt. This is partly because their position is embedded in their very identity and ideology, as well as in the expectations of its core voters and members. The Conservatives would not be the Conservatives, for example, if they were not sceptical about the extent to which governments can or should directly help people.

This chapter will accordingly:

- examine the concept of 'party families' and the development of party ideologies
- explore the idea of 'left' and 'right' in British politics
- examine party programmes and see how these reflect left–right distinctions
- ask whether ideology is still as important as it was in the past and whether differing party ideologies give voters a real choice
- question the importance of political parties in Britain and ask whether there is an alternative way of running the country.

Party families

Party families

Groupings of parties with similar beliefs and support groups, even though they operate in different countries.

British political parties are the second oldest in the world (the Americans had them first). But they are not wholly unique. Labour falls into the general 'family' of socialist and social democratic parties, the most numerous of all party families. The Liberals belong to the rather small family of radical liberal parties. In recent years the Conservatives' natural home has been the conservative–liberal, free market grouping.

Even the smaller British parties have counterparts in other countries with whom they form a broad transnational grouping. The Greens, for example, resemble environmental parties elsewhere; and parties such as Plaid Cymru (the Welsh nationalists) and the Scottish Nationalist Party belong to a broad range of minority nationalist parties. The Northern Irish Social Democratic and Labour Party can be classified with the Christian party family, given their roots in Catholicism. Ulster Unionists are in the rather unusual position of being a regional party upholding the central state. Their belief in the indissolubility of the Union groups them with straight Conservative parties elsewhere in Europe.

BRIEFINGS

17.1 Ideology and the concept of 'party families'

'Ideology' is a slippery term that means different things to different people. For present purposes, however, it can be said to be a system of ideas and assumptions that help us understand and interpret the world. It is a set of values and beliefs, factual assumptions and ideas, which indicates the appropriate action to take in given circumstances. The term is often restricted to a fairly explicit, coherent and elaborate set of ideas: a general theory about how the world *is*, how it *should be* ('core beliefs') and how to get from how it is to how it should be ('action principles' or 'predispositions').

Few people have ideologies in this sense, even among the political leadership. But many do subscribe to looser and less explicit ideologies such as liberalism, conservatism or socialism. Parties are built around a few political principles that are roughly compatible (though they may conflict at various times). Moreover, parties in different countries share a similar ideology and can be grouped together as a 'party family' because they share the same beliefs, principles and policies and often win support from the same groups.

Table 17.1 shows the general 'family' to which each British party belongs. It summarises which groups their supporters come from, what their core beliefs and action principles (or policy commitments) are and where they stand on the extent of government intervention in the economy and society, which is the central issue in left–right differences. 'Families' are roughly ordered in left–right terms (**the left–right continuum**), from radical environmental groupings to socialists and radical liberals to conservative liberals devoted to the free market and as little governmental intervention as possible.

State intervention versus the free market is not the only way in which to think of '**left**' and '**right**'. The terms are also used to distinguish between internationalist and nationalistic outlooks in foreign and defence policy and between libertarian and authoritarian outlooks on regulating private behaviour. Parties (and individual politicians) can be on the left on one dimension but in the centre or on the right on another. New Labour and Tony Blair, for example, might be described as left of centre on the social and economic dimension but right of centre on many issues touching on the libertarian–authoritarian dimension, such as the introduction of 'tough' anti-terrorism legislation and punishing the use of hard drugs.

British party politics in the twentieth century, however, have largely revolved around the roles of the state versus the market in economic and social affairs. It is, therefore, in these terms that 'left' and 'right' are usually defined. Of course, a summary table like this inevitably simplifies reality. The divisions within British parties have already been described in greater detail in Chapter 16. Nevertheless, the comparison shows what a lot in common they have with European parties, where the same groupings appear.

Table 17.1 European 'party families' and their British members

'Family' ideology	Support groups	Core values	Characteristic policies	Attitudes to government intervention	British 'family member'
Ecological and communitarian	Young, well educated	Environment participation, peace	Encourage sense of community, protect environment, help minorities, disarmament	Support more intervention to achieve objectives	Green Party
Socialist	Workers, public employees in social and service sectors, intellectuals	Equality of wealth and opportunity	Extend welfare protection (health and pensions), regulation of capitalism, peace	Government provision in all areas where market does not provide	Labour Party
Minority nationalist	Territorial minorities	Cultural diversity, regional devolution, autonomy	Decentralisation, devolution and autonomy	Intervention necessary to uphold minority cultures in the modern world	Scottish National Party, Plaid Cymru
Radical liberal	Anti-authoritarian elements of the middle classes, religious minorities, some peripheral regions	Liberty and a minimum standard of living to enjoy it	Safeguards for political and social rights	Against 'big' government but favour intervention to safeguard weaker sectors	Liberal Democrats
Christian democratic	Churches, especially the Catholic Church, the Catholic middle class, country and small towns	Fraternity, community, human dignity	Strengthen traditional morality and family, extend welfare, mixed economy	Intervention where necessary to ensure welfare and family stability	Social Democratic and Labour Party (Northern Ireland)
Conservative	Traditionalists of the State Church, upper and middle class, 'loyal' members of working class, country and small-town areas	Order, security, social hierarchy	Uphold established state structures and national boundaries, maintain armed forces	Intervention as and when necessary to ensure stability	Ulster Unionist Parties, British Conservatives 1868–1979
Conservative (Neo)Liberal	Business and professional middle classes	Liberty, individualism	Freedom from controls, free markets, efficient limited government	Government limited to upholding free market	Conservative Party (post-1979)

Plate 17.1 Advocate of the free market or equality? Tony Blair, like many politicians, combines different ideas
Source: Cartoon Stock

The left–right continuum

A straight line (or dimension) on which it is often convenient to locate parties. It stretches from the left-wing parties that believe in radical or revolutionary change, through the socialists and centre parties, to parties of the moderate right that oppose change, and on to extremist parties espousing a Fascist or Nazi ideology.

The left

Those who generally advocate change in the direction of greater social, political and economic equality. They include Communists, Socialists, Social Democrats, together with some Liberals and Greens.

The right

Those who generally oppose change in the direction of greater social, political and economic equality. They include Fascists, Conservatives and (in the United States) most Republicans.

Party ideologies

The three major British parties clearly differ in terms of all the factors listed in Table 17.1. Labour traditionally drew its members and core supporters from the working class, trade union members and public employees. It elevated 'equality' into a core value and advocated welfare programmes to ensure this. These policies were played down in 'New Labour' manifestos in 1997 and 2001 in favour of 'fairness' or 'equality of opportunity' in order not to scare voters in 'middle England'.

The Liberal Democrats, who are quite radical and reformist by general European standards, come close to Labour on government intervention but are more inclined than Labour to set limits on what governments do. They also have a more enduring concern for protecting individual civil liberties.

The Conservative Party traditionally drew its support from the middle class, members of the Church of England and country-dwellers. It emphasised order, security and the preservation of traditions (including social hierarchy). The legacy of Margaret Thatcher, Conservative leader from 1975 to 1990, was to shift the

Conservative Party decisively. She emphasised the principles of economic freedom and individualism, as represented by the free market, rather than social stability. Traditional Conservatives had often accepted the need for social welfare and economic intervention to maintain political and social order. Mrs Thatcher, however, tried to reduce what she saw as 'dependence' on the state and was prepared to risk creating conflict in order to achieve that goal.

Recent years have thus seen political and ideological shifts on the part of both the New Right and New Labour. How significant are these changes? Are they likely to last? And do they mean that the parties are coming together? Are we seeing both convergence and an end of distinguishing party ideologies?

Ideologies and political cleavages

To answer these questions we need to put today's ideologies in historical perspective. All parties date to the beginning of the twentieth century or earlier and many of the traditional differences between them also derive from that time. Parties adapted their ideology to the needs of particular supporters, both building on and emphasising certain political 'cleavages' in the country. Seeing how they did this helps us appreciate how fundamental **ideology** is to the study of British politics.

The Conservative and Liberal parties trace their origins to the parties (so-called 'cadre' parties) that operated under the very restricted franchise from 1832 to 1867 (when the Second Reform Act enfranchised large parts of the working class). From today's perspective the differences between the leading figures of these two parties do not seem very great. Many (including Gladstone, the dominant figure of nineteenth-century Liberalism) switched between them. Starting from the effective introduction of free trade in 1846–7, however, the Liberals gradually developed more progressive policies, pressing for political reforms and the extension of the franchise. Liberal thinkers, such as T. H. Green (1836–82), began to think of liberty not in terms of 'freedom *from*' monarchical rule, arbitrary government or the tyranny of the majority but 'freedom *to*' develop one's individuality. It was realised that markets failed to provide a clean environment, adequate education

> **Political ideology**
>
> A system of ideas, assumptions, values and beliefs that help us to understand the political world: how it *is*, how it *should* be and how to get from one to the other.

BRIEFINGS

17.2 Social and political cleavages

A political cleavage is made up of three elements:

1. A persistent social (or group-based) division that produces differences in interests, lifestyle and material advantages. Such divisions may be based on differences in class (workers v. employers), religion (Protestant v. Catholic) or geography (urban v. rural).

2. The presence of a set of values common to that group.

3. Party programmes designed to appeal to those group values.

Historically, the franchise was a controversial issue. A first step to the creation of cleavages was often to enfranchise a group so that it could cast votes in favour of a party. Political parties and organisations are, therefore, as important in the creation of cleavages as the objective social divisions themselves. An illustration of this is the fact that the division between town and country never turned into a cleavage in Britain, because all parties lined up with urban interests in accepting free trade after 1850.

For more information on the relationship between cleavages and parties in Western Europe read Seymour Martin Lipset and Stein Rokkan (eds), *Party Systems and Voter Alignments* (New York: Free Press, 1967).

BRIEFINGS

17.3 Classical liberalism

The essence of liberalism (with a small 'l') is the belief that individual rights should be protected by maximising freedom of choice and by limiting the powers of the government. Historically, liberalism represented a rejection of the absolute powers of a monarch, or other ruler, and sought to establish limited government, tolerance and freedom under the law. In Britain classical liberalism was built on the writings of John Locke (1632–1704) and John Stuart Mill (1806–73). In *Two Treatises of Government* (1690) Locke defended the Glorious Revolution of 1688 that established the dependence of the monarch on Parliament and was thus a first step towards limited, constitutional government. In his *Letter Concerning Toleration* (1693) Locke made the case for freedom of religious conscience, and so laid out the case for freedom of thought and belief, which is a fundamental tenet of liberal theory. In *On Liberty* (1859), Mill argued that the only justification for government interference with the liberty of individual citizens is to prevent them doing harm to others (the famous 'harm principle'). His great fear was that majority rule could threaten individual freedom no less than paternalistic or authoritarian government. Classical liberalism was, therefore, opposed both to the despotism of the monarchy and the 'tyranny of the majority'.

Classical economic liberalism is expounded by Adam Smith (1723–90) in his book *The Wealth of Nations* (1776), which argues that the 'invisible hand of the market' succeeds in making individual economic self-interest work for the common good. In this way Smith lays out the arguments for capitalism, individualism and free trade.

BRIEFINGS

17.4 Neo-liberalism

In the twentieth century some of the ideas of classical liberalism have emerged in 'neo-liberal', or 'New Right', form as a reaction to the growth of the state. Neo-liberals place supreme importance on the freedom of the individual and on rolling back the frontiers of the state. They argue that market competition is the best way of guaranteeing both political freedom and economic growth. *In The Road to Serfdom* (1944), for example, F. A. von Hayek (1899–1992) argues that socialism and the Welfare State inevitably lead to loss of individual freedom. The 'Chicago School' of economics, led by Milton Friedman in the 1970s and 1980s, similarly rejects Keynesianism in favour of a form of classical economics that favours competitive markets and low public expenditure. The main economic function of government is to regulate the money supply (monetarism) in order to control inflation. The ideas of Hayek and Friedman influenced Margaret Thatcher. Two right-wing think tanks, the Centre for Policy Studies (established in 1974) and the Adam Smith Institute (established in 1977), produced a steady stream of research arguing that the state was just as (or even more) likely to 'fail' as the market. Such reports provided the intellectual case for reducing the scope of state activity (**'state failure'**).

State failure

The proposition that state intervention in the economy or society invariably leads to a less good social outcome than if the market were left to operate.

and essential needs such as healthcare. It was further argued that state intervention might rectify market failures; though few liberals advocated public ownership. The Liberals' new policies attracted the support of minority groups who felt disadvantaged under the old system: the Scots, the Welsh and religious Nonconformists (both Protestant and Irish Catholic).

With the actual achievement of a mass franchise it became even more important for the Liberals to attract the votes of these groups to gain power. To do so they took up the causes dear to them: removal of state support from the Anglican Church in Ireland and Wales; and wider political reforms, particularly of the patronage system in government appointments and of the Church's hold on education. Representing above all the Nonconformist middle classes of Wales, Scotland and northern and western England, the Liberals could not, however, appear as effective defenders of the working-class interest. This created an opportunity for the Conservatives and the new Labour Party formed in 1906.

BRIEFINGS

17.5 Conservatism

Conservatism (with a small 'c') is a general tendency in politics (or 'a way of thinking') rather than a clearly worked-out ideology such as Marxism. It believes in preserving what is best in traditional society and opposes change (particularly radical change) unless it is vital.

Conservatives believe that society is naturally hierarchical and should be regulated by a strong state. The classical British work of conservative theory is Edmund Burke's *Reflections on the Revolution in France* (1790). This cast great doubt on the capacity of people and governments to plan an ideal society and therefore argued for slow change rather than radical transformation. Old institutions and practices, wrote Burke, often have great, though hidden, virtues, and should be allowed to adapt slowly to changing circumstances. This did not mean, however, that conservatives should resist all change. Conservatives have realised that yielding to reform may prevent revolution. Many Conservatives regarded it as their duty to ward off socialism, but they also regarded it as inevitable. Until the late twentieth century, therefore, most adopted an essentially defensive strategy.

Conservatives have accepted change where necessary and where no change would represent a greater threat to the social fabric. British conservative thought has, therefore, varied over the years. It was strongly opposed to socialist ideas in the first half of the twentieth century, but accepted the 'social democratic consensus' that allowed the National Health Service and Welfare State to expand. The social democratic consensus eroded under the Labour government led by James Callaghan in 1976–9, which introduced policies designed to control the growth of the state. The Conservative government led by Margaret Thatcher in the 1980s was inspired by 'neo-liberal ideas' and tried to reduce both the size of the state and the public's reliance on it to solve problems. Her governments had mixed success in relation to achieving the first goal and little success in the second.

Market failure

The proposition that the market, left to its own devices, fails to produce socially optimal outcomes, 'public goods' (e.g. defence, water), to incorporate social costs (e.g. pollution) or to respond to needs (e.g. healthcare).

In the mid-nineteenth century the Conservatives, as did other such parties in Europe, defended the traditional state structures – monarchy, army and Church – against reformist Liberals. With the advent of the mass male franchise in 1867–8 they developed an appeal to the new working and lower middle class that built on the themes of national unity, military strength and Empire. The Conservatives consolidated their new support, above all in the south-east and Midlands of England, after the Liberals backed Home Rule (a form of devolution) for Ireland in 1886. The crisis over Irish Home Rule, which the Conservatives opposed, also alienated another traditional group of Liberals (the former Whigs). This left the Liberals more than ever a party of nonconformists on the geographical peripheries and in the urban areas of northern England. While classical liberalism emphasised freedom from arbitrary monarchical government and freedom from the tyranny of the majority, the 'New Liberalism' of the late nineteenth and early twentieth centuries emphasised freedom as the ability to realise one's potential. Many 'New Liberals' began to advocate an enhanced role for the state in order to correct '**market failures**' (such as environmental protection). They also advocated modest redistribution of wealth from the rich to the poor in order both to promote 'national efficiency' and reduce extreme poverty. Liberal governments emphasised the importance of education and promoted 'equality of opportunity' as an alternative to socialist 'equality' of outcome.

The economies of the peripheries were based on manufacturing and so were dominated demographically by the urban working class (Chapters 1 and 2). This left the Liberals vulnerable to a class-based party that could put the interests of this group first, as Labour did from 1906. The final straw for the old Liberal Party, however, was the First World War, which divided the party between those who supported 'total war' and those who clung to more liberal ideals. In the post-war years, the Liberals suffered from a double haemorrhage, losing working-class support to Labour, while the business classes fled to the Conservatives, who offered stronger opposition to demands for greater welfare and trade protection.

The consequences were as follows:

- A steady decline in Liberal importance.
- Labour became the main party of opposition to the Conservatives (and attracted many of the 'New Liberals' who favoured an increased role for the state).
- The Conservatives became divided between traditionalists, who were disposed to concede welfare demands for the sake of national unity, security, hierarchy and order, and the ex-Liberal supporters of free trade and the free market.

The ex-Liberals became progressively more influential in the Conservative Party. Of course, free markets depend on the state maintaining order and security. These two sides could compromise on the need for both. But in terms of political priorities, order and security began to take second place to economic freedom, both at home and abroad.

The Labour Party, unlike the Liberals, has always been ambivalent about free trade, and often wanted protection for workers secured by government intervention. It parted company with the Liberals (now Liberal Democrats) on this point. Liberal thinkers developed the argument that to take advantage of economic freedom people needed the resources to implement their choice. To have a choice of medical services, for example, is of no benefit if one cannot afford to buy any of them. However, unlike 'old' Labour, these New Liberals did not see state intervention as a good in itself but as a means to giving individuals economic freedom. As in the case of the other two parties, these ideas spring out of older concerns, modified to fit modern conditions. The question asked later in this chapter is, how far have their older ideas been modified?

First, however, we should comment on the relationship between cleavages and ideologies. The two intermesh because parties aim their appeals at certain social groups in order to gain their support. It is easier to target social groups with identities and interests in common. Trying to appeal to the electorate as a whole on the basis of their common interests is difficult because of the uncertainty about what common interests actually are. Having identified a distinctive social group, politicians can communicate with their leaders who can, in turn, advise their followers to support a particular party.

Of course this is a two-way process because, by appealing to group interests, the party is helping to define them. The working class was much more conscious of itself as a group with distinct and sometimes conflicting interests from other sectors once the Labour Party was launched. The Labour Party also helped develop other organisations to represent them: for example, by strengthening trade unions.

In the books, articles and pamphlets that set out the Labour and working-class case, a systematic analysis of the position of workers in contemporary society appeared, linking together the appeals for more welfare, housing, minimum wages and equality that Labour made at elections. As did other European socialist parties, Labour had the advantage of being able to draw on the work of Karl Marx, who wrote from the mid-nineteenth century onwards, and his intellectual followers; but it drew much more on other traditions, in particular religious nonconformity and radical liberalism such as the Chartism of the 1840s.

Marxist theory sees all events in terms of the class struggle. Nationalism, religion and individualism are simply bourgeois weapons to create 'false consciousness' and delude the workers about where their real interests lie. These are in essence to struggle against their employers, and eventually to overthrow the capitalist system that allows the latter to control the means of production such as factories and land. Their monopoly over the means of production enables them to exploit workers by forcing them to sell their labour (their only resource) very cheaply and thus creates gross inequalities in society.

BRIEFINGS

17.6 Marxism and socialism

The ideology developed by Karl Marx in the mid-nineteenth century is still the best-known political ideology. In contrast with many other socialist parties, however, the British Labour Party was only intermittently influenced by Marxist ideas.

Although it has developed a bewildering number of different branches, Marxism essentially states that economic relations, particularly those between the classes created by the system of production, determine all forms of political and social life. In the late capitalist system there are only two classes of political importance: the capitalists (or property owners or bourgeoisie), who are increasingly rich; and the workers (or proletariat), who are increasingly impoverished. Economic conditions and an informed political leadership encourage workers to develop a revolutionary class consciousness, overthrow the system and, after a period of state socialism, establish a society without either state or property.

According to Marx, history can only be understood in terms of class, and capitalist politics can only be understood as a constant struggle between the bourgeoisie and the proletariat. Other ideas, such as religion or nationalism, might seem important, but are actually manifestations of class interests, which are used by the ruling class to mask political reality and create the false consciousness that conceals the real class struggle. A Marxist, therefore, reacts to events by asking whose class interests are being served. Foreign wars, for example, may appear unconnected with the class struggle but, according to Marxist theory, they are actually a means of promoting capitalist interests.

Few parties in contemporary Europe support all of Marx's arguments. Many in the Labour Party may agree that class relationships are the most important and that the central issues in politics are those concerned with the distribution of resources between classes. But they would argue that the working class – as do others – has an interest in preserving peace and stability. Redistribution achieved through negotiation and argument is much better than imposed solutions supported by force because these can always be reversed by greater force.

Within a broad acceptance of democracy, party ideologies differ from each other in terms of which groups are considered to be the important ones in society and how their interests should be served. Are classes so pervasive and central that the interests of the workers should always come first? Or are workers' interests only part of the national interest, as 'bourgeois' parties tend to argue, and hence better served by strengthening the free market that will create more wealth for all? Or, on the contrary, is economic growth the force that is destroying the natural world in which we all have a common interest, as Greens argue, and so should it be resisted? Should economic growth be resisted because through uncontrolled development it ravages the countryside and threatens the culture of minority groups, which need to be defended by setting up their own institutions, as in Scotland and Ireland?

There is thus rich ground for controversy and argument among the adherents of different ideologies. This is particularly so because no one can say, objectively, which ideology is right. Assertions that class is the most important of social relationships, or that the world would suffer an irreparable loss if Welsh ceased to be spoken, are not subject to decisive proof. They spring out of an identification with or immersion in a particular group in society. One function of an ideology, indeed, is to buttress that identity, as most people belong actually or potentially to many different overlapping groups. For example, is a Polish-born secretary working in north-east England primarily a worker, British, English, Polish, European, Catholic, an immigrant or a woman? In a situation of multiple individual identities parties struggle to make one identity predominant and thus to mobilise support for their policies and general point of view.

Ideologies are thus important not only in telling leaders what to do but in telling voters who they are and so making them receptive to leaders' diagnoses of the

BRIEFINGS

17.7 British socialism and social democracy

British socialism takes from Marxism the ideas of class interest, equality and the Welfare State. It differs from Marxism, however, in maintaining that change can and should be achieved by means of peaceful reform rather than revolution. The Labour Party is a social democratic party, as are the mainstream labour movements in most of Europe.

The Labour Party's 'socialism' drew on a range of traditions, all of which were critical of nineteenth-century industrial capitalism. Ethical (also often Christian) socialists, such as R. H. Tawney (1880–1962), thought that the capitalist system promoted greed and 'uncharitable' behaviour and wanted to replace it with a utopian society. This group brought an evangelical passion to the party. (Less usefully, they also established Labour's reputation as a party of 'bossy do gooders'!) Fabians, on the other hand, stressed that capitalism was inefficient and could be replaced with a more rationally planned system. Sidney Webb (1859–1947), Beatrice Webb (1848–1943) and George Bernard Shaw (1856–1950), believed that the state could act as 'universal problem solver', identifying market failures and removing them by planning, regulation and taxation. With the ethical socialists they believed that revolution was undesirable and that a gradual change to a socialist society was inevitable. The most important influence on Labour's socialism, however, was the trade union movement. While the ethical or Christian socialists supplied Labour with its passion and fervour, the Fabians with its analysis and policy prescriptions, the trade unions supplied the organisation, personnel, resources and its essential pragmatism. Many unions were in no sense socialist, since they wished to improve the lot of their members. The skilled unions, in particular, wanted to maintain 'differentials' with less-skilled workers. The unions ensured that Labour remained focused on practical problems.

Ironically, however, it was John Maynard Keynes (1883–1946), a self-professed Liberal, who had one of the strongest influences on Labour policy. In his book *The General Theory of Employment, Interest, and Money* (1936) Keynes advocated government economic intervention in order to achieve economic stability, growth and full employment. 'Keynesian' demand management and a mixed economy replaced classical 'laissez-faire' (liberal market) economics as the economic orthodoxy between 1945 and 1975. Many claimed that Keynes 'saved capitalism' and that, in accepting his doctrines, Labour had become a party which ameliorated the worst aspects of capitalism rather than a party with a different (socialist) vision of a good society.

In the 1960s British socialist thought went through a period of change under the influence of Anthony Crosland's book, *The Future of Socialism* (1956). This argued that socialist goals of freedom and equality require some government economic planning but a large measure of private economic activity. State control and regulation of key sectors of the economy was necessary, but not further nationalisation. In the 1970s Labour moved sharply to the left as first the activists and then the unions were radicalised by economic failures. The party later moved back to the centre from 1983 onwards eventually abandoning nationalisation (see Chapter 16).

political situation. Ideology is particularly important for political parties, which have to operate across different levels of society. It helps to link up often complex governmental decisions with the broadly defined interests of a party's supporters and voters.

'Left' and 'right' in British politics

Specific party ideologies can be distinguished in terms of how far they are to the 'right' or to the 'left'. This is because differences over the extent of government intervention in society – whether to leave things to the free market or to limit its often disruptive workings – are a central and apparently permanent issue in modern societies. Intervention is sought by all sorts of groups that feel themselves weak in social and economic terms: not just the working class but also ethnic minorities, women and environmentalists. They want the government to restrict the power of the purely economic interests privileged by the market.

BRIEFINGS

17.8 The aims and objectives of the three major parties

The preamble to the Liberal Democrat Constitution (1988)

The Liberal Democrats exist to build and safeguard a fair, free and open society, in which we seek to balance the fundamental values of liberty, equality and community, and in which no one shall be enslaved by poverty, ignorance or conformity. We champion the freedom, dignity and well-being of individuals, we acknowledge and respect their right to freedom of conscience and their right to develop their talents to the full. We aim to disperse power, to foster diversity and to nurture creativity. We believe that the role of the state is to enable citizens to attain these ideals, to contribute fully to their communities and to take part in the decisions that affect their lives. [Continues.]

Conservative Party's proposed aims and objectives (2006)

Our aims:

To improve the quality of life for everyone through:

A dynamic economy, where thriving businesses create jobs, wealth and opportunity.

A strong society, where our families, our communities and our nation create secure foundations on which people can build their lives.

A sustainable environment, where we enhance the beauty of our surroundings and protect the future of the planet.

Our values:

The more we trust people, the stronger they and society become.

We're all in this together – government, business, the voluntary sector, families and individuals. We have a shared responsibility for our shared future.

Clause 4 of the Labour Party Constitution (1995)

The Labour Party is a democratic socialist party. It believes that by the strength of our common endeavour we achieve more than we achieve alone, so as to create for each of us the means to realise our true potential and for all of us a community in which power, wealth and opportunity are in the hands of the many and not the few, where the rights we enjoy reflect the duties we owe, and where we live together freely, in a spirit of solidarity, tolerance and respect [Continues.]

These differences appear in attitudes to foreign affairs as well as inside Britain. The left-wing parties (Greens, Labour, Liberals) are generally more sympathetic than the right towards supranational bodies such as the EU and UN, designed to regulate what states and multinational corporations do (although the Labour left opposed NATO and the European Economic Community, as it then was, in the 1980s). They tend to be 'idealists' in international terms, with a strong belief in the possibility of peaceful cooperation at the international level and a commitment to building institutions to encourage this.

The fact that all parties take a position on these questions allows us to place them on a single line running from left to right, as shown in Figure 17.1.

Left–right differences are not the only ones that exist between parties, and probably not the most important ones for minority nationalists, for example. They are central to British politics, however, so it is interesting to look at them across the whole political spectrum.

The point that leaps out from Figure 17.1 is that the three main British parties are not, on average, so very distant from each other in terms of the full range of ideological difference that could exist. Labour does *not* want to regulate everything and the Conservatives do *not* want to leave everything to the free market or

Realism

The view of politics, especially international relations, that emphasises the role of self-interest as a determinant of state policies, and hence the importance of power in these relations.

BRIEFINGS

17.9 Left–right differences in British politics

The terms 'left' and 'right' originated from the location of supporters and opponents of political change in France at the end of the eighteenth century. Supporters of reform sat on the left of the legislative chamber while supporters of the Crown and established institutions sat on the right. The 'left' today advocates change in the direction of greater political, social and economic *equality*, while the right oppose it. (Note: the right-wing parties often introduce greater changes than left-wing ones but these do not promote equality.)

In the twenty-first century the core distinction is defined in terms of support for more government intervention, on the left, and opposition to it, on the right. Left-wing parties want to extend the Welfare State and increase regulation of the economy. Right-wing parties want the government to refrain from interfering in society and the economy as far as possible, in order to extend individual freedom of choice. However, they do support strong government measures to guarantee law and order and national security. Thus they advocate a strong, but limited, state. In contrast left-wing parties want peace through international cooperation. Left-wing positions have generally developed out of some variant of Marxist ideology.

Centre parties tend to mix these positions and support limited government intervention in most policy areas, but specifically oppose the Marxist analysis of society.

The 'right' adopts '**realist**' views, seeing the international arena as a free market, where states and firms pursue their own interests and maximise their well-being. To prevent the pursuit of national interests getting out of hand, however, strong military alliances are necessary to create a 'balance of power' where no one side can dominate. The Cold War of 1948–89, when the US and Soviet alliances confronted each other, was an example of such a balance, where each side deterred the other from taking over the world. Now that the Russians have accepted capitalism and free markets new threats may arise, such as Islamic fundamentalism, which make continuing military preparations necessary. The left tend to be '**idealists**' who would be much happier seeing the old alliances dismantled and substituted by supranational bodies.

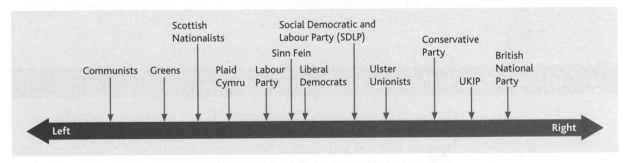

Figure 17.1 Location of UK political parties on the left–right ideological spectrum

(internationally) to only what can be agreed through inter-state negotiations. The Liberals are the most centrist of all, seeking to balance the general efficiency of the free market with government intervention in favour of weaker groups.

The positions set out in Figure 17.1 summarise what the parties have said and done over the 60 years from 1945 to 2005. Of course it is more interesting to ask how they have changed recently: have they moved closer together or drifted further apart? We analyse more precisely what has happened and whether these left–right differences still remain in subsequent sections.

It is also worthwhile looking at the smaller parties' position in these terms. Smaller parties are often thought to be more extreme because they are more 'pure' ideologically than the big parties can afford to be in case they put off voters. However, none of the regional parties takes positions very far (in left–right terms) from those of the main parties. The Scottish Nationalists are a little to the left of Labour. This is a good strategic position to take in Scotland where voters are more

Idealism

The view of politics, especially international relations, that emphasises the role of ideals and morality as a determinant of state policies, and hence the possibility of peaceful co-operation.

sympathetic to state intervention. Plaid Cymru is less radical, partly because it is the Welsh-speaking middle class who form its core voters. The Northern Irish SDLP are even more centrist than the leftist Sinn Fein, and (in left–right terms) are not too far from their local opponents, the Ulster Unionists. The last are traditional Conservatives who believe in order, security and the integrity of the British state. But they support financial aid and government-directed development in Northern Ireland. Further to the right are small single-issue British nationalist and racist parties. The United Kingdom Independence Party defines British nationalism in terms of independence from the European Union and the British National Party in terms of extreme hostility to immigrants and to their descendants, especially Asians and Afro-Caribbeans.

The most extreme left-wing parties are those that have a 'cause' and no regional base, the Communists and the Greens (the party that wants government intervention to save the environment). Both are small parties with limited political support.

The prospects for a genuinely left-wing party have looked dim ever since the downfall of the Soviet Union. The Communist Party of Great Britain has long ceased to contest elections. In 2005, however, a leftist party, RESPECT ('Respect, equality, socialism, peace, environmentalism, community and trade unionism'), contested 26 seats, retaining nine deposits (i.e. obtaining 5 per cent or more of the vote). Its most prominent member, George Galloway, was elected as MP for Bethnal Green. The party owed its limited success to its vociferous opposition to the Iraq War and its appeal among Muslim voters. It seems unlikely to be a permanent feature of British electoral politics. In Scotland, however, the Scottish Socialist Party has gained growing support from traditional Labour supporters disillusioned with New Labour's shift to the centre. In addition, the steady deterioration of the environment, both in Britain and the rest of the world, may well provoke a crisis that will give the Greens more votes and influence. At the moment they are electorally weak, although they won two seats in the 1999 European elections, two seats on the Greater London Assembly in 2004 and environmentalist pressure groups have been effective on many issues (see Chapter 23).

Left–right differences in the major parties' ideologies

In Britain it is the three traditional parties that are the real contenders for power. The next sections examine how they have changed their policies and ideologies over the post-war period. Have they moved closer together recently, or moved further apart, or all moved in the same direction? Seeing how the main parties have changed from election to election, in terms of the left–right differences illustrated in Figure 17.1, provides a way of answering this question.

It is true, of course, that such a 'single-line' representation provides only a very summary idea of the full range of party policies. There is more to political life, and ideology, than just left and right. As Table 17.1 showed, parties on the left have significant differences of opinion among themselves, on the importance of devolution for example, or the primacy of environmental issues. These do not show up in simple left–right terms.

Left–right differences thus do not cover all of British politics. But they are central to them for the following reasons:

- *Political discussion – in the press, on television, in Parliament – is structured in terms of left and right.* Commentators always ask whether a party is moving towards the centre or the extremes, particularly in the context of elections. A party that has 'seized the centre ground' is usually considered to have a better chance of winning the election, as most electors are thought to be in the 'middle' (somewhere between the left and right poles).

- *The question of how far governments should intervene – in welfare and the economy above all – is and always has been central to British politics.* Chapter 2 showed how it defined politics in the late nineteenth century and it has remained the crucial dividing line between the major parties ever since.

- *Because of their centrality, the positions parties take in their election programmes on this range of issues are more likely to carry through into actual government policy than others.* This is important because the measure we use to trace left–right ideological shifts in party positions is derived from the party manifestos.

Elections, manifestos and programmes

A major feature of each general election in Britain is the programme published by each party at the beginning of its campaign (around one month before the election). This is the **party manifesto**. In this document the parties set out their views on how society should develop and how the country should be run for the next parliament. Only parties set out a reasonably detailed overall plan for national development and this distinguishes them from all other political organisations.

A manifesto's practical use is that it gives electors an indication of what would be done if the party were elected as the government, and thus enables voters to choose between them on policy grounds. Manifestos enable voters to exert influence over which policies the incoming government will pursue. The ability of electors to influence government in this way is, however, dependent on the existence of parties with alternative programmes.

If elections simply involved selecting individuals who came together in Parliament after the election in order to form a government, nobody would know in advance what their policy would be and electors would lose their opportunity to influence government policy. It is no coincidence, therefore, that the slow extension of democracy over the last century and a half has been bound up with the consolidation and growth of parties and the intensification of their competition for office.

Party manifesto

The document parties publish at the start of election campaigns outlining the policies they intend to implement if elected to government.

Plate 17.2 Parties are often accused of promising the same things time and time again and failing to deliver
Source: Cartoon Stock

Plate 17.3 Michael Howard launches the Conservative manifesto in 2005
Source: Empics

Democracy in Britain is indissolubly linked to the political parties; and electoral influence over public policy is linked to the programmes the parties offer.

Manifestos are usually prepared under the direction of party leaders (see Chapter 16). But many of the documents on which they are based have been approved by party conferences and other official party bodies. They thus constitute a unique and authoritative policy programme to which the party as a whole is publicly committed.

Despite their importance in setting out a national five-year plan, and offering a choice, party manifestos are not widely read by electors. Their contents are, however, extensively reported in the newspapers and on the television and radio and so they are known to voters, although at second hand. Electors who want to choose between parties in terms of their policies will, in the course of the campaign, be able to acquaint themselves with the main policies the parties lay out.

What do the manifestos actually say? On first reading they seem rather woolly and far from offering a precise programme for government. New Labour was exceptional in 1997 and 2001 in making precise pledges about Scottish and Welsh devolution and about limiting tax increases. Usually the manifesto makes precise commitments in only a few peripheral areas, such as Labour's 1997 commitment to restore trade union rights for employees at GCHQ (the government's intelligence-gathering organisation).

Much of the document consists of rambling discussions of various topics such as 'youth', 'unemployment', 'the economy' and so on. Topics such as these constitute its main sections. Typically the sections state how important the problem is and

Plate 17.4 Tony Blair launches what he promised would be his last manifesto in 2005

Source: Empics

provide an analysis of past developments and of the present situation, stressing party concerns and achievements, but not committing it to very much. This vagueness is due to a well-founded fear by leaders that tying themselves down to specific actions might give too many hostages to fortune. Changed circumstances or a financial crisis might result in their not being able to do what they promised, and thus lead to accusations of bad faith and to their loss of credibility.

From the viewpoint of parties it is better to emphasise the importance of a particular policy area rather than state what exactly it is they will do about it. This does not render the manifesto valueless as a statement of future policy. Its main purpose is to set priorities for action rather than to tie the government in advance to specific things it must do. Talking a lot about a particular area such as 'youth' implies that the party would do more and spend more in the area, without saying exactly what it would do or how much it would spend. Setting priorities in this way makes it easier for electors to choose between the parties on broad policy grounds, rather than having to decide on the feasibility of particular courses of action in areas where they have no expert knowledge.

There is often scepticism about the extent to which parties carry through their programmes in government. Many feel that promises made at the election are simply not kept once the party takes office. Research by Hans Dieter Klingemann *et al.* (*Parties, Policies, and Democracy*, Boulder, CO: Westview, 1994) has shown, however, that not only are the majority of pledges carried through by the winning party but also that the priorities stressed in the manifesto are strongly related to subsequent government expenditure in the different policy areas. Electors choosing between parties on the basis of their policy priorities can thus have some confidence that they will try to put them into effect in government. To paraphrase a recent television advertisement for wood varnish: 'The manifesto [largely] does what it says on the tin'.

Party manifestos and party ideology

Manifestos are programmes for government action so it follows that they are strongly influenced by party ideology. This is apparent from the manifestos issued by different parties at the same election. These often give such dramatically opposed accounts of the situation that one would think they were talking about two quite different countries! Thus in 2005 the Labour manifesto painted a glowing picture of a Britain with an expanding economy and improving public services, while the Conservative document talked of hospital bugs, uncontrolled immigration and excessive regulation stifling private enterprise.

Such differences occur in part because ideologies lead parties to focus on different groups and developments. The Conservative reference point is the English middle class, in particular in the south-east, with their concerns with financial markets, order and opportunity. In recent years Labour has also tried to appeal to 'middle England' while providing something for the peripheries and their problems of economic stagnation, bad housing and health.

Differences in the party programmes also occur because the parties' ideologies and history make them 'proprietors' of different issues. A voter who wants free markets and an emphasis on individual opportunity and law and order knows from what the Conservatives have done and said in the past that it is more likely to provide these than any other party. If these issues are what people think important in an election more are likely to vote Conservative. Education and welfare, however, are 'Labour issues'. Those who think these issues are most important will support that party.

Issues such as these become important partly because of developments outside the political arena. But the parties can also try to focus on them by emphasising 'their' issues in the manifesto and in their campaign. Differences in emphasis thus arise partly from the imperatives of competition, but also build on pre-existing ideological differences between parties and their reputation for competence in different, ideologically defined, issue areas.

Measuring left–right ideology in manifestos

The fact that party programmes stress different kinds of issues according to their ideology gives us an opportunity to measure the ideological distance between them at each election, by assessing the amount of attention each document pays to the characteristic issues of the left and right. The party's position between left and right is not the whole of a party's ideology but it is a major part of it. It covers the most central issues in British politics and the ones on which electors are most likely to assess parties, and governments to take action.

The emphasis parties give to different issue areas can be measured very simply and directly, by counting the number of sentences in each manifesto devoted to each issue area. Table 17.2 shows how the parties differed on the 'top ten' issue areas in the 2005 election, that is, the ten most often mentioned categories in each party manifesto, to which most sentences were devoted. This analysis reveals some agreements and also some differences. After two terms of Labour government it is hardly surprising that all the parties devoted substantial portions of their

Table 17.2 Top ten issues, 2005

Policy areas	Labour		Liberal Democrat		Conservative	
Demographic groups	1	10.2	2	10.7	4	7.3
Health and welfare positive	2	9.9	4	6.0	6	6.1
Government effectiveness	3	9.2	1	15.8	1	18.3
Education positive	4=	9.0	–	–	2	11.0
Law and order	4=	9.0	7	4.5	3	7.6
Culture	6	6.4	–	–	–	–
Internationalism positive	7	4.5	8	4.4	4	7.3
Decentralisation positive	7	4.5	8	4.4	4	7.3
Technology	9	4.2	10	3.8	7	4.1
Incentives	10	3.6	6	5.5	7	4.1
Environmental protection	–	–	3	9.4	–	–
Market regulation	–	–	9	4.2	9	3.1
Agriculture	–	–	–	–	10	2.9

Source: Judith Bara, 'The 2005 manifestos: a sense of déjà vu?', paper presented at the Elections, Public Opinion and Political Parties Conference, September 2005

manifesto to Labour's effectiveness in office. (Labour's manifesto extolling, and the opposition parties attacking, Labour's record.) Labour placed more emphasis on health, welfare and culture than the Conservatives, while the Conservatives placed more emphasis on incentives, market regulation and agriculture. The Liberal Democrats' focus on 'demographic' groups in 2005 stood in marked contrast to their manifesto in 2001 (when this ranked seventh). This change may reflect the centre party's attempt to appeal to certain groups (such as the young and public sector workers) and exploit disillusion with the Labour government.

More revealing than analysis of specific issues is Figure 17.2, which traces the ideological progression of the British parties over the post-war period. We can see how this affects their ideological positions in relation to each other. To do this one can look at left–right differences more directly. All one needs do is group 'left-wing' issues together and add up the percentage of references to them. Then one groups 'right-wing' issues together and adds up their percentage score. Finally one can take the combined percentage for left-wing issues and subtract this from the combined

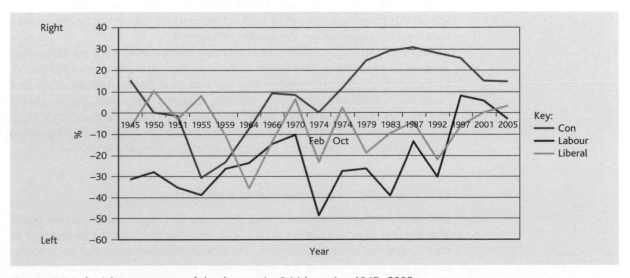

Figure 17.2 Left–right movements of the three major British parties, 1945–2005

Table 17.3 Creating a left–right scale from party manifestos

Negative items (left wing)	Positive items (right wing)
Nationalisation	Free enterprise
Controlled economy	Economic orthodoxy
Welfare: positive	Social services expansion: negative
Regulation of capitalism	Incentives
Economic planning	Freedom
Protectionism: positive	Protectionism: negative
Military: negative	Military: positive
Peace	Effective authority
Education expansion: positive	Constitutionalism: positive
Internationalism: positive	National way of life: positive
Decolonisation	Traditional morality: positive
Labour groups: positive	Law and order
Democracy	Social harmony

Source: Budge *et al.*, Mapping Policy Preferences, Oxford: OUP, 2001, p. 2

percentage for right-wing issues. That gives us a 'scale' running from +100 per cent (all references in a manifesto are to right-wing issues) to −100 per cent (all references in a manifesto are to left-wing issues). In practice, of course, each manifesto will contain references both to left- and right-wing issues, so they will never be totally right wing or totally left wing. Neither will all topics mentioned by parties fit into this particular ideological distinction. This means that on average the main British parties fall near the middle of the left–right space, as we have already seen in Figure 17.1. The positions they take in specific elections vary more, of course, but only within a narrow range of +30 towards the right and −50 towards the left.

Table 17.3 lists left- and right-wing issues. As the essence of the left-wing position is support for government regulation and intervention domestically and the creation of governmental bodies to do the same internationally, the topics picked out as leftist are all the statements that have a bearing on these questions. They include nationalisation (takeover of businesses by government), regulation and control of the economy, provision of welfare and education (again by government) and peace and international cooperation. The right opposes these emphases and puts a stress on freedom from government. The free market needs some government support to keep it going, which is provided by law and order at home and military alliances abroad. All these elements can be seen in Conservative policies up to 1997, which have been characterised as 'free market, strong State'.

Measuring left–right differences in this way enables us to trace the ideological progression of the three main British parties over the whole of the post-war period. In Figure 17.2 left–right positionings are measured on the upright dimension (from +35 – relatively right wing – to −50, relatively left wing). The horizontal dimension is time. Each election can be identified by its particular date: 1945, 1950, 1951 and so on until 2005. This evidence can be used to examine the proposition that there has been 'ideological convergence' among British parties.

Left and right – convergence or divergence?

Differences between the parties were very large in 1945, the post-Second World War election in which Labour won a large majority and started a programme of intervention and reform in all areas. The Conservatives realised that the reforms, particularly the creation of the Welfare State, were popular and that to win elections they had to accept them. By emphasising such left-wing positions they came very close to Labour from 1955 to 1964, the heyday of the social democratic con-

Plate 17.5 'Old Labour' trade unionists, like Arthur Scargill, and left-wingers, like Tony Benn, accused Tony Blair of betraying 'socialism'

Source: Peter Brooks/The Times, 17th September 1996, Centre for the Study of Cartoons & Caricature, University of Kent

sensus. Both parties accepted the Welfare State and a mixed economy, in which the government owned large sectors of industry. However, the convergence was due partly to Labour's own move to the right as it toned down its (increasingly unpopular) emphasis on nationalisation. Meanwhile, the Liberals wandered about between the other two parties with no fixed position.

All this changed after the 1966 election as the Conservatives generally moved to the right; up to 1997, in fact, they remained relatively far to the right. The gap between the two main parties widened as Labour moved dramatically left in 1974 and again in 1983. Only in 1997, as 'New Labour', did it make a dramatic shift to the right, largely by playing down economic intervention while continuing to support welfare and education. This move to the right paralleled that of the Conservatives leftwards in the 1950s: 'If you can't beat 'em, join 'em!' Unlike the earlier Conservative change, the move did not bring Labour close to its main rival as the Conservatives still remained much further to the right. In both 1997 and 2001, the Liberal Democrats were further than Labour. So the 1997 election saw ideological convergence only up to a point. In 2005 Labour moved back to the left and 'passed' the Liberal Democrats as the centre party moved a little to the right. The Conservatives have remained virtually unchanged since 2001. Thus, for the first time since 1992, the parties are in their 'proper' order with Labour on the left, the Liberal Democrats in the centre and the Conservatives on the right. It appears that the 1997 and 2001 elections represented a mild – and temporary – departure from the 'normal' positions of the parties.

The end of ideology?

Ideology is a term with highly negative connotations for many people. It has associations with Marxism and thus with sterile debates among fanatics and extremists about abstract principles. It is also associated with totalitarian regimes that murdered millions in the name of 'racial purity' or 'the victory of the proletariat'. Even when manifested in democratic politics ideology is seen as preventing agreement and maintaining artificial party differences, which get in the way of national unity and successful problem solving.

No wonder, then, that many commentators have predicted an 'end of ideology' at various times in Britain's post-war history. 'Ideology' has been particularly associated with the left. Thus the electoral defeat of Labour in the 1980s and its modification of socialist principles have been seen by many as necessary to creating a more rational and balanced society in Britain.

The positions taken up by the parties, even in 1997 and 2001, were still quite sharply differentiated. It is difficult, moreover, to maintain that there would be no significant differences in Britain today if John Major had won in 1997, if William Hague had won in 2001 or even if Michael Howard had won in 2005. Ideology provides parties with a general course to steer the nation by should they get into power; though progress towards that goal may be as steady as a drunkard's walk.

Past experience suggests that convergence is usually a temporary phenomenon. Convergence in the 1950s was followed by divergence in the early 1970s and early 1980s. Convergence in 2001, for example, was followed by divergence in 2005. There is no 'inevitable' trend towards general agreement. If this did come to pass the parties would lose their identity and with it their separate existence, and would cease to offer alternative choices to electors. A drawing together is always likely to be followed by a drawing apart to traditional policy positions. No 'end of ideology' seems in view, no matter how much party squabbles irritate the public.

The positive contribution of party ideology to electoral choice

Is this necessarily a bad thing? Although 'ideology' has bad connotations it can be regarded as the same thing as holding to firm political principles. Having principled politicians rather than self-servers and office seekers is generally regarded

BRIEFINGS

17.9 Conditions for electoral control over public policy

To summarise the relationship between party representation and electoral choice one can specify four conditions for electoral control over future government policy:

1. Parties must offer voters a choice.

2. Voters need to be aware of the choice.

3. People must vote on the basis of the choice.

4. The party in control of the government follows policies consistent with the options it placed before the electorate (party accountability).

All these conditions require that the parties subscribe to different ideologies to generate policy choices for voters and to give them an incentive to carry through their programme in government.

as good. If the 'end of ideology' amounts to the 'death of principle' this cannot be a good thing.

As the discussion at the beginning of the chapter also indicates, it is impossible to operate in politics without an ideology. People need to have a set of beliefs and assumptions about the way the world works in order to understand it at all. Socialism could only be abandoned by replacing it with another ideology. Neo-liberalism and free market beliefs are in this general sense just as much ideologies as Marxism. Indeed, far and away the most ideological politician in recent British politics has been Margaret Thatcher, the right-wing Conservative Prime Minister from 1979 to 1990.

We cannot escape having ideological parties, so the only question is whether parties should have different ideologies or all share the same one. The general conclusion we can draw from our examinations of party programmes is that they are likely to remain different.

This has positive advantages for the role parties play in representing the views of the British electorate. Consider what would happen if parties did all share the same ideology and offered electors the same policies in their programmes. This would mean that whichever party electors voted into government the same policy would be pursued. Voters would then have no opportunity to choose between policies. Differences in ideology guarantee that different solutions will be offered by different parties and that electors can weigh them up and decide between them with some probability of determining which will actually be pursued.

The doctrine of the party mandate rests on the idea that electors are able to choose between programmes in this way. The core of the argument is that a majority or plurality vote for a party in the general election can also be interpreted as an endorsement of that party's policy programme. This gives the party the authority to put its policies into effect when in government. If all parties offered the same programme governments would lack the authority of a mandate, because no one would know whether electors had really endorsed their programme or had simply been deprived of the opportunity to express an opinion.

BRIEFINGS

17.10 The party mandate

The idea of a party mandate assumes that the party winning most votes in an election will form a government that will carry through its electoral programme, because this has been supported by a majority or plurality of electors. The details of the argument are as follows:

- Electors choose between parties at least in part on the basis of their programme.

- Such programmes are distinguishable from each other, so they offer electors a basis for choice.

- The party that gains most votes forms the government.

- The party or parties that form the next government have a responsibility to carry out their programme in government, because this is a major basis on which they were elected.

- They also have the authority to carry out their programme in government, because it has been selected by the largest number of electors as the best.

- Parties do carry through their programmatic priorities in government.

Ideology has another positive contribution to make in a party democracy such as Britain. It gives parties an incentive to carry through their programme when they get into government. Many voters are cynical about whether governments will actually carry out election promises or will simply ignore their commitments as soon as they take

▶

office. The Wilson governments (1964–70, 1974–6) were particularly criticised, having gained office with the promise of economic expansion through state planning and ending by restricting economic activity and creating high unemployment. Their failures prompted a swing to the left discussed in Chapter 16.

In contrast, no one could say that the highly ideological Margaret Thatcher did not vigorously carry through her programme of restricting government and promoting the free market. Thatcher did this because, as well as promising such measures to the electorate, she actually believed in them very strongly.

In theory, governments could be punished retrospectively for breaking earlier election pledges. Some analysts argue that electors would not vote for such a government because they could not trust it to carry through policies they otherwise find attractive. In practice, however, this seems a rather weak sanction because of the lapse of time involved and the many circumstances that will have intervened to make earlier pledges irrelevant or incapable of fulfilment.

While external sanctions or election penalties may be weak, ideological imperatives to carry through the programme may be quite strong, as the case of Thatcher shows. Ideology can thus play a very important role in promoting party accountability. It might be preferable to have 'conviction politicians' saying and then doing what they believe rather than opportunists following the changing whims of public opinion or doing the minimum they think they can get away with.

Alternatives to party democracy

Party democracy

Either (1) the widespread distribution of power within a political party and/or (2) a system of national democracy resting on competitive parties.

At the start of the twenty-first century, parties seem to be exerting a more pervasive influence on general debate than ever. Our evidence shows that they are still divided in ideological terms, and that this situation is likely to continue. It clearly has many advantages in presenting electors with sharp policy choices and guaranteeing that most governments will carry them through.

Many, however, find the constant squabbling between parties deeply dispiriting. It is epitomised by televised debates from Parliament, where Labour and Conservatives appear to shout each other down, with no attempt to debate the merits of the case or to find agreement. Surely things would be better if the good people on all sides came to a problem without party prejudices and found the best solution that genuinely served the national interest? David Cameron, the new Conservative leader, said as much when he accepted the leadership of his party.

The problem lies in discovering what is in the national interest and how best to achieve it. Does it exist at all or is it simply a projection of the interests of one group, for example the City of London or the south-east 'Establishment', at the expense of others? The national interest is perhaps most easily identified in foreign affairs – keeping Britain strong and influential in the world. Even here, however, there has been much criticism of Britain's subservience to the United States and of the costs an overextended world role has imposed on society.

The 'best people' coming together outside their parties would still, therefore, face policy dilemmas, and divide and argue over them. There are no easy or obviously 'best' solutions to political problems. That is why parties and their ideologies have evolved, to ensure that no major interest or grouping in society lacks an advocate to promote its views on any problem about which it is concerned. As Winston Churchill remarked of democracy in general, 'Democracy is the worst form of Government except for all the other forms that have been tried from time to time'. The same can be said of parties and their ideologies. If they did not exist today they would rapidly re-emerge, as they are so essential to democratic debate and choice and to the control of electors over government. In that sense, British democracy cannot do without them, whatever their incidental defects.

Summary

This chapter has examined the different party ideologies that exist in Britain today and how they help maintain party identity and distinctiveness. In particular it has looked at:

- the different 'families' to which British parties belong and how they have evolved over time;

- the way in which party families can be 'placed' in terms of an underlying left–right ideology, centred on differences about the nature and extent of government intervention in society;

- how the left–right positions of the main parties can actually be measured from their election manifestos and used to track changes in their ideological positions over time (Figure 17.2);

- how ideology assists voters as they make choices between alternative programmes for society and to electoral control over government actions, and hence to the general functioning of representative democracy in Britain.

Essays

1. What is ideology? Why is it useful for parties to have one? Or: What are 'political principles'? Why is it useful for parties to have these?

2. What does it mean to say that a party is to the 'left' or to the 'right' in politics?

3. Why is it important that British electors should be presented with different party programmes in an election?

Projects

1. Read three party manifestos without their identifying labels, analyse them and try to guess: (a) which party they belong to; (b) whether they were published at the same election. Give reasons for your judgement.

2. Analyse the reasons for ideological change on the part of the British parties with reference to Figure 17.2.

Further reading

The nature of political ideologies in general is discussed in Andrew Heywood, *Political Ideologies: An Introduction* (Basingstoke: Palgrave Macmillan, 2003); Robert Leach, *British Political Ideologies* (Basingstoke: Palgrave Macmillan 2002). Applications to British election manifestos are made in Ian Budge *et al.*, *Mapping Policy Preferences: Estimates for Parties, Electors and Governments 1945–1998* (Oxford: OUP, 2001) and in Judith Bara and Ian Budge, 'Party policy and ideology: still New Labour?' in Pippa Norris (ed.), *Britain Votes 2001* (Oxford: OUP, 2001) pp. 26–42, reproduced in *Parliamentary Affairs*, **3**, 2001, pp. 590–606. A review of party families and ideologies, as well as of other aspects of British parties, can be found in Paul Webb, *The Modern British Party System* (London: Sage, 2000). Two useful articles on the ideology of New Labour are Michael Freeden, 'The ideology of New Labour', *Political Quarterly*, **70** (1), 1999, pp. 42–51 and J. Buckler and B. Voldwitz, 'New Labour's ideology', *Political*

Quarterly, **71** (2), 2000, pp. 101–4, which criticises Freeden. On the Conservatives, see J. Garnett and P. D. Lynch, 'Bandwagon blues: the Tory fightback fails', *Political Quarterly*, **73** (1), 2002, pp. 29–37. For a comparison of the British party system with other European parties, see Ian Budge *et al.*, *The Politics of the New Europe* (Harlow: Addison Wesley Longman, 1997).

Useful web sites on party ideologies

Hot links to these sites can be found on the CWS at www.pearsoned.co.uk/budge.

In Chapter 16 we provided an extremely comprehensive list containing links to the main political parties as well as the more important party factions.

There are a number of political ideology sites that cover Britain and the world. The Keele Guide to Political Thought and Ideology on the Internet (www.keele.ac.uk/depts/por/ptbase.htm) is an A–Z guide to political thought, theory and ideologies. In addition to this you can also visit the Social Science Information Gateway (www.sosig.ac.uk/roads/subject-listing/World-cat/polideol.html) for a general introduction to the leading currents in political thought.

In more specific terms, the LockeSmith Institute offers an excellent account of the formative years and historic development of classical Liberalism (www.belmont.edu/lockesmith/); on the same topic, very interesting insights can be found in the Stanford Encyclopaedia of Philosophy (http://plato.stanford.edu/entries/liberalism/). With regard to neo-liberal theory, a brief historical account of its evolution can be found at www.globalissues.org/TradeRelated/FreeTrade/Neoliberalism.asp and a more academic approach is available at www.globalpolicy.org/globaliz/econ/histneol.htm. The main trends within Conservatism and its potential evolution are described and critically assessed in www.ukconservatism.freeuk.com. A very insightful analysis of the main currents within Marxism is available from the above-mentioned web site of Keele University.

Concerning the specific ideological features of the main British parties, a good deal of information can be obtained from a careful reading of the political speeches given by their respective leaders.

A complete list of party manifestos since 1945 is available at www.psa.ac.uk/WWW/elections_uk.htm.

Data collected by the party manifestos project (Budge *et al.*) that codes and counts party policy commitments is available from the book *Mapping Policy Preferences* (Oxford: Oxford University Press, 2001) and its associated CD-Rom.

chapter 18

Parliament: the House of Lords and the House of Commons

The previous two chapters have emphasised the fact that Britain is a party democracy rather than a parliamentary democracy. That is, elections decide which party is to form the government rather than what individual is going to represent a constituency in Parliament. MPs get elected because of their commitment to a particular party (and its manifesto) rather than on their own merits. Once elected they are expected to vote either with the government or opposition, except on the rare occasions when their party does not take a position on an issue, or they are given leave to dissent on what the party managers define as an issue of conscience.

In constitutional theory MPs are required to hold the government to account, to ensure that legislation and the actions of ministers are adequately scrutinised and that proposals are tested to ensure they are workable. In political reality, however, most MPs for most of the time have little inclination and scope to act independently of parties. They have spent many years as a party member, activist and candidate and want to maintain good relations with friends, colleagues and party members. Many have ambitions to get as far up the 'greasy ladder' as they can and inevitably hope to impress (or ingratiate themselves with) their leaders. It is important to remember that 'parliamentary government' means 'government *through* Parliament', rather than 'government *by* Parliament'.

The chapter covers:

- the structure of Parliament and the relationship between the House of Lords and the Commons
- parliamentary scrutiny of administration (as distinct from legislation) and the work of select committees
- MPs' interests and business links
- party discipline in Parliament and backbench rebellions
- the role of third parties.

Government and Parliament

To administer the country, Her Majesty's Government must have the support of the majority of elected members of the House of Commons and be confident of retaining that support for the duration of the five years of a Parliament. Usually, but not invariably, a single party wins an absolute majority of seats at the general election and thus forms the government on its own. The growth of third parties (Liberal Democrats, Welsh and Scottish Nationalists and so on) means that a 'hung' Parliament, where no clear Conservative or Labour majority exists, is a very real possibility. However, since 1945 the government of the day has lacked an absolute majority on only three occasions: between the February and October 1974 general elections (when Labour governed as a minority), between 1977 and 1979 (when Labour lost its slender majority as a result of by-election defeats) and between November 1994 and April 1995 (when the whip was withdrawn from eight Conservative Euro-rebels). To be sure, the 1950–1 and 1964–6 Labour governments both had very small majorities, as had the 1951–5 Conservative government, but both were still able to govern quite effectively even so.

The first past the post electoral system more often produces governments with a clear majority (see Chapter 15). Since the principle of collective responsibility

Plate 18.1 In theory Parliament is sovereign, but many feel that it is routinely ignored by the executive

Source: Empics

applies to all government ministers, they must vote with the government or resign. In order to prevent the government from packing its benches with people bound to vote for it, the number of ministers who can sit in the Commons is limited by statute to 95 (though there were only 85 in March 2006). However, parliamentary private secretaries (PPS), who act as unpaid assistants to ministers, are also bound by collective responsibility and there are no statutory limitations on their number. The number of PPS appointments has increased in recent years under Labour (from 32 in 1997 to 57 in March 2006). The effective 'payroll vote' who must vote for the government in the Commons in March 2006 was 142. Thus, fully 40 per cent of Labour MPs must vote with the government or lose their jobs. As long as the government can persuade 85 per cent of its backbenchers to vote with them, they can get their legislation through.

We have already seen that governments claim a mandate for the proposals set out in their manifesto, which is itself the product of lengthy discussions within political parties (see Chapter 16). By the time that most proposals have been put into a bill before Parliament the party leadership will have been familiar with the issues for very long periods of time and regard it as their task simply to make sure that legislation is enacted. Ministers use appeals for party unity to claim the loyal support of their own MPs who, as we have seen, are usually in a substantial majority. Yet in addition to providing support for the government, Parliament also has the important roles of scrutinising and debating. It is on this aspect that this chapter concentrates. As we shall see, the obsessive secrecy of British governments, and their desire to control the flow of information to their own advantage, undermines Parliament's role as a forum for informed criticism and constructive debate. Together with the government's firm control over procedures and legislation, governments deprive ordinary MPs of significant political influence, except at times of crisis. To understand how governments exert such control we turn first to the structure of Parliament and the nature of its business.

Structure of Parliament: the House of Lords

'Parliament' is frequently equated with the House of Commons but also includes the House of Lords. The membership and powers of the Lords have been the subject of sporadic, and occasionally intense, debate since the early twentieth century. Despite promises in the 1997 Labour manifesto to work towards a more 'democratic and representative' chamber, the present House of Lords contains no one that most ordinary people would think of as democratically selected.

Membership of the House of Lords

The unreformed Lords

The House of Lords as it existed before the House of Lords Act 1999.

Before 1999 the following were members of the **unreformed House of Lords**:

- those appointed under the Life Peerages Act, 1958, who serve for life
- the 26 most senior bishops in the Church of England, who serve while they hold office
- hereditary peers who inherited their titles as a result of 'accidents of birth'
- the 12 Lords of Appeal in Ordinary (senior members of the judiciary).

Until 1999 the vast majority of members were hereditary peers who sat with the Conservatives. The inappropriateness of the hereditary principle and the

Plate 18.2 The pageantry of the state opening of Parliament contrasts with efforts to 'modernise' the institution

Source: Empics

The partially reformed Lords

The House of Lords after the House of Lords Act 1999 but before any further reforms to its composition and powers.

Conservative bias was already clear in 1911, when the Preamble to the Parliament Act stipulated: 'It is intended to substitute for the House of Lords as it at present exists a Second Chamber constituted on a popular instead of a hereditary basis, but such substitution cannot be immediately brought into operation.' This turned out to be the constitutional understatement of the twentieth century. It was not until 1999 that most hereditary peers finally lost the right to sit and vote in the House. The word 'most' is significant here. In an effort to avoid a prolonged parliamentary battle about Lords reform the remaining hereditary peers were allowed to elect 92 of their number to continue to sit in the **partially reformed Lords**. From 2008 onwards the Lords of Appeal in Ordinary will also cease to sit in the upper house when a new Supreme Court is established (see Chapter 19).

Most members of the House of Lords (around 600 out of 721) are now life peers, appointed by the monarch on the advice of the Prime Minister (who by convention consults with other party leaders). A small number of these are 'People's Peers' appointed on the recommendation of an Appointments Commission, established in 2000. This body also vets party appointments for propriety. The Prime Minister, however, determines how many party nominees and People's Peers are appointed. A Prime Minister who finds himself frustrated by the Lords could, in theory, appoint a large number of sympathetic peers in order to get legislation through; however this would be at some political cost and Tony Blair gave assurances that he would not resort to this tactic.

The powers of the House of Lords

The democratically elected House of Commons is the most important chamber for the simple reason that the government must secure Commons' support for all legislation. Furthermore, a government must, by convention, resign if it is defeated on a 'vote of confidence' in the Commons. Strong party discipline and the political ambition of MPs mean that the Commons usually defers to the government. The practical significance of these Commons powers is, therefore, doubtful. The House of Lords, by contrast, has limited powers in relation to legislation and does not hold a vote of confidence. However, as we shall also see, its greater independence from the executive makes it arguably a more significant check on the power of the government.

The formal powers of the Lords are set out in the Parliament Acts 1911 and 1949 as follows:

- It can delay any bill, other than those that are certified as a 'money bill' (financial measure), for up to one year. This power is more extensive than it might first appear:

  - Many bills relating to local taxation and spending are not certified as 'money bills', so the powers of the Lords are significant. (The bills to introduce the 'poll tax' and 'council tax' were not money bills.)

  - The Lords have great potential power in the final year of a Parliament, since a government knows that a defeat in the Lords will block legislation unless it wins another election.

- It has an absolute power to veto bills that try to extend the life of a Parliament beyond five years (an important constitutional long-stop to prevent a government keeping itself in power).

- It has the power to reject secondary legislation (those rules and regulations made by ministers in the form of statutory instruments or orders in council by authority delegated to them by acts of Parliament). It treats such legislation no differently from primary legislation.

The House of Lords also has a role in relation to the judiciary. Senior judges can only be removed by the monarch on an address presented by both Houses of Parliament. Taken as a whole, however, the Lords' powers are quite modest in comparison with second chambers elsewhere in the world. The US Senate can veto any legislation, is required to ratify treaties and can block key presidential appointments (including those to the Supreme Court). The Lords' powers are further limited by the fact that they abide by the 'Salisbury convention' that they will not oppose measures that were included in the government's election programme. A defeated government can, moreover, always reintroduce legislation, unless it is in the final year of Parliament (which explains in part why governments, especially Labour governments, are reluctant to go into a fifth year and risk having their programme blocked by the Lords). Ultimately, the elected Commons can get around the Lords by using the Parliament Acts of 1911 and 1949, which allow a bill to become law without the Lords' consent if certain conditions are satisfied. This power is not used very often. Recent examples include:

- *War Crimes Bill 1991*, which allowed the courts to prosecute war criminals.

- *European Parliamentary Elections Bill in 1999*, after the Lords had rejected the proposal for a 'closed regional list' system of proportional representation for elections to the European Parliament on no fewer than six consecutive votes.

- *Sexual Offences (Amendment Act), 2000*, which lowered the age of consent for homosexual sex to 16.

- *Hunting Act 2004*, which outlawed hunting with hounds.

The Lords have the power to make the government think and/or restate their case but can ultimately be overridden by a government early in a Parliament or with a fresh electoral mandate. This is perhaps as it should be in a democratic nation, though some think that it provides too few safeguards for fundamental liberties.

The role of the partly reformed House of Lords

The unreformed Lords lacked democratic legitimacy and, as a result, viewed itself as primarily a 'revising' chamber to improve legislation by amendment. The hereditary peers who dominated the House thus tended to defer to the Commons. Labour governments were usually able to get their legislation through the Lords even when it was not outlined in their manifesto and not, therefore, subject to the Salisbury convention. Some government measures were watered down or occasionally blocked by the Lords, but this was surprisingly rare.

The fact that the partially reformed House of Lords is almost entirely appointed led to concerns that it would soon be stuffed with 'Tony's cronies' and that a Labour majority would replace the Conservative majority. To most people's surprise this is not what has happened. To be sure, there has been a slight rebalancing of party membership but Labour has a bare plurality, not a majority, in the partially reformed House of Lords. In November 2005 Labour had just 210 out of 721 (29.1 per cent) members. The Conservatives had 208 (28.9 per cent), the Liberal Democrats 74 (10.3 per cent) and the crossbenchers (independents) 192 (26.6 per cent) (see Figure 18.1). Many of the crossbench peers tend to vote with the Conservatives, so the government's task is even more difficult than it might first appear.

The existence of a permanently 'hung' second chamber means that ministers must think very carefully about how to deal with the Lords. They must rely on the strength of their arguments rather than appeals to party unity. It is arguable, therefore, that the members of the unelected chamber are more likely to behave as effective 'watchdogs' than the people's elected representatives!

The fact that members of the House of Lords were appointed by the Prime Minister also led to fears that the House would turn out to be compliant. Experience has again demonstrated such fears to be largely groundless. The fact that they are not subject to re-election by voters or even reselection by the parties provides them with real independence. Since many peers are coming to the end of their

Figure 18.1 Party composition of the House of Lords, November 2005

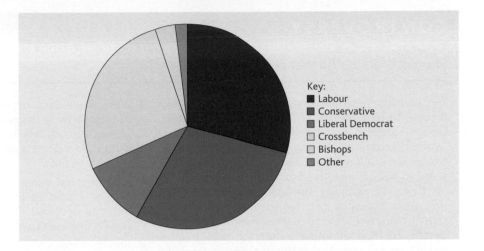

Key:
- ■ Labour
- ■ Conservative
- ■ Liberal Democrat
- □ Crossbench
- □ Bishops
- ■ Other

political careers they have more experience and less ambition than their fellow parliamentarians in the Commons. They are, accordingly, less likely to defer to the executive and Prime Mminister.

The current members of the Lords have come to regard themselves as having greater legitimacy and they have become correspondingly more likely to challenge the executive. The growing assertiveness of the partially reformed Lords is illustrated by the fact that in the 1997–2001 Parliament the government was defeated 108 times in the House of Lords. In the 2001–5 parliament it was defeated 245 times. In recent years, therefore, government bills have regularly passed back and forth between the two Houses of Parliament (a process called 'parliamentary ping-pong').

A major source of conflict has been the government's 'anti-terror' policies. The Lords, like members of the senior judiciary, have become increasingly alarmed by the way in which ministers have responded to perceived terrorist threats by introducing draconian legislation that restricts civil liberties. Many Lords have come to see themselves as one of the few checks and balances in an unbalanced constitution and as providing the government with an opportunity for 'sober second thought'.

> Parliament should take the long view, and resist the temptation to grant powers to governments which compromise the rights and liberties of individuals. The situation which may appear to justify the granting of such powers are temporary – the loss of freedom is often permanent . . . Too many ill-conceived measures litter the statute book as a result of such rushed legislation in the past.
>
> (Second Report of the Joint Committee on Human Rights, HC 372, HL 37, 2001–2, para. 76)

Recent Home Secretaries have become wearily familiar with the need to offer concessions to their Lordships on such matters. In 2004 the Lords resisted government proposals to restrict trial by jury in the case of complex fraud trials and blocked attempts to abolish the office of Lord Chancellor (see Chapter 19). In March 2005 they scored another notable victory when they got the government to promise that provisions in the Prevention of Terrorism Act 2005 would be reviewed early in the next Parliament. In early 2006 they voted against proposals in the terrorism bill to make it illegal to 'glorify' terrorism. While ministers frequently claimed the support of public opinion, the Lords clearly found such arguments less than convincing, particularly when they were based on opinion polls or focus groups rather than support for a manifesto as expressed by an election victory.

CONTROVERSY

Should there be further reforms of the Lords?

The partially reformed House of Lords was widely thought to be a prelude to further reform. The 2001 Labour manifesto was wonderfully ambiguous, saying, 'We are committed to completing House of Lords reform, including removal of the remaining hereditary peers, to make it more representative and democratic' (as if simply removing the remaining Lords would succeed in making it more representative and democratic!). Many would like to see the reforms 'completed' by the creation of either a fully or substantially elected second chamber and/or the alteration of its powers.

Governments on the whole oppose elected second chambers, since this would increase the legitimacy of that body and make it more difficult for the government to drive its legislative programme through Parliament and/or to act quickly and decisively when it needs to do so. The partially reformed House is an irritant to the government and has made it think again when it would have liked to act quickly. Their Lordships have clearly not been a major irritant, however, since otherwise the Prime Minister would have tried to reduce its powers and/or flooded it with his appointees.

It is possible to argue that Labour's 'half-baked' reforms have produced a compromise that works. It may well be that, just like the 1911 Parliament Act, the House of Lords Act 1999 turns out to be rather more long-lived than anyone would have expected. Opposition politicians, commentators and lawyers, however, tend to prefer a wholly elected second chamber on simple democratic grounds. Others would like to see a substantially elected second chamber, in order to leave room for appointments of individuals – especially those without party affiliations – on merit.

The proposition that the Lords should be elected raises a number of questions:

■ *When should elections take place?* If they are held at the same time as the general election and under the present system, they would replicate these results. If they are held at a different time turnout would probably be low.

■ *What electoral system should be used?* If the same system is used as for the Commons the results might be replicated. If they use a more proportional system the results would be very different.

■ *How can competing mandates be reconciled?* An elected second chamber would have its own claim to legitimacy and there may be battles between the two houses, resulting either in 'gridlock' or calls for abolition of the second chamber. This is the main reason why the Wakeham Committee, which reported in 2002, decided against recommending any changes in the powers of the Lords.

Most of those who advocate reform appear to believe that the present powers of the Lords to block rather than veto legislation should be retained. Others, however, would like to see the Lords be given greater powers in order to protect the constitution or human rights. Indeed, if the **fully reformed Lords** were elected by a more proportional system it could be argued to have more legitimacy than a House of Commons elected by first past the post. Not surprisingly, many politicians think that reform of the House of Lords raises more questions than are worth asking.

The real question, as with electoral reform (see Briefing 15.1), is whether it is better to have a constitution that concentrates power in the hands of the 'winner' or whether it is better to diffuse power. The question again boils down to this: is it better for governments to be able to act quickly and decisively or slowly and consensually? Since the future is uncertain, no answer is obviously correct.

Structure of Parliament: the Commons

A fully reformed Lords

Various proposals to 'complete' House of Lords reform, including either an elected element and/or modified powers.

The House of Commons currently has 646 members elected by first past the post (see Chapter 15) and meets for 200–250 days of the year, on a reasonably continuous basis from late September through to July or August. General debates, questions to and statements from ministers and legislative activity take up full meetings of the House (see Table 18.1 for times). Much work is done in specialised committees, which meet both in the mornings and later in the day, in tandem with meetings of the whole House.

Table 18.1 Sitting hours of the House of Commons

House of Commons	
Monday–Tuesday	14.30–22.30
Wednesday	11.30–19.30
Thursday	10.30–18.30
Friday	09.30–15.00
Westminster Hall debates	
Tuesday and Wednesday	09.30–11.30 and 14.00–16.30
Thursday	14.30–17.30

In theory MPs are watchdogs looking out for the interests of their constituents and ensuring good government. In practice they are largely partisans out to support their own team and do down their opponents. Roughly three-quarters of the days in which Parliament sits are reserved for government business (legislation, ministerial statements and so on). There is little time for either the opposition or backbench MPs to raise issues.

BRIEFINGS

18.1 Parliamentary stages of a government bill

First reading	The bill is introduced in the Commons. The first reading precedes the House's order to print the bill. There is no debate or vote at this stage. The bill automatically goes through.
Second reading	Minister introduces bill and the House considers its principles. Debate printed in *Hansard*, the official report of debates. This is the first stage at which the government can be defeated. Money resolutions authorising any part of a bill that involves a significant charge on central government funds are dealt with after this stage.
Committee stage	A **standing committee** of about 18 MPs deals with the details of the bill, going through it clause by clause. A new committee is appointed for each bill. Membership reflects the composition of the House and it is therefore dominated by government MPs. Occasionally the whole House may consider a bill, especially if it is of constitutional importance (e.g. the House of Lords Bill, 1998/9), but also those requiring rapid passage and certain financial measures (e.g. the Finance Bill).
Report stage	The House may make further amendments. This stage enables those who were not members of the standing committee to move amendments. The delay between the committee and report stages allows governments to consider amendments. The House may amend or reverse changes at report stage.
Third reading	This is the final Commons stage and is usually taken directly after the report stage. No amendments are taken at this stage and debates tend to be short.
House of Lords	The legislative procedure in the Lords is broadly similar to that in the Commons.
Royal assent	The Crown must give assent for a bill to pass into law (such assent has not been withheld since 1707).

Notes: (1) A few draft bills have been subject to pre-legislative scrutiny by Select Committees. (2) Before second reading, programme motions may be moved to set out a timetable for the conclusion of proceedings. This ensures the government gets its legislation through on time. (3) A bill must normally complete all its stages in one session of Parliament. There are new provisions, however, for bills to be carried over into the next session.

Standing committees

Committees of the House of Commons that examine bills after their second reading in order to improve them before their third reading.

Private members' bills

These are introduced in Parliament by backbench MPs or peers on their own initiative (or occasionally at the instigation of the government).

The House of Commons is presided over by the Speaker of the House of Commons who is elected by fellow MPs. Together with various deputies, the Speaker is responsible for ensuring that procedures follow the rules set out in Erskine May (the 'bible' for procedure). It is the government, however, that has the largest impact on the Commons. The extent to which governments dominate the Commons is illustrated by the fact that the 'Leader of the House of Commons' is actually a Cabinet minister rather than a senior backbencher, whose prime responsibility is for ensuring that the government gets its business through the Commons. The extent to which parties dominate Parliament, furthermore, is illustrated by the fact that the Leader of the House negotiates with a shadow House Leader in the main opposition party about the conduct of business. Much parliamentary business is also agreed between the respective party whips (referred to as 'the usual channels').

Private members' bills, which are introduced by backbench MPs, sometimes with government backing, and private bills, which are sponsored by an outside body (normally a local authority) also go through these general stages. Without government support, however, such bills are unlikely to reach the statute book.

Scrutiny of legislation

At general elections voters judge governments, at least in part, by their ability to carry out their manifesto promises. Even if voters are not particularly enthusiastic about specific proposals, party members often expect their ministers to enact the legislation hammered out in party deliberations. As we have seen in Chapter 17, governments take their manifestos very seriously. There are also incessant demands for government to 'do something' about social or economic problems; especially in the media. Since ministers do not like to look 'out of touch' with the public mood, these factors produce a constant pressure for government to legislate.

Since the government party normally commands an overall majority of the House of Commons and can usually count on party discipline, government bills are almost always approved, although amendments are often made in the course of the bill's passage through Parliament. Individual ministers are judged by their ability to get bills through Parliament with as little fuss, and as few amendments, as possible. Opposition MPs are equally judged by their ability to embarrass ministers. Partisanship is embedded in the scrutiny of legislation. At least one minister will be on the standing committee considering a bill, together with a front bench opposition spokesperson. The participation of the front bench spokespersons ensures that most debate about the bills takes the form of partisan point scoring rather than any serious attempt to improve legislation. The committees are usually given little time to scrutinise the most detailed and complex legislation. By and large most bills pass as originally drafted by the government. The vast majority of those amendments that are accepted, moreover, are initiated by the government itself, sometimes in response to strong pressure from its own backbenchers, and less often in response to the House of Lords.

The result is predictable. Every year the government produces a large volume of bills and delegated legislation. Every year a large number of poorly thought-out and poorly drafted bills and regulations have become law. Many require later amendment by Parliament or judicial creativity in order to identify what the law actually is or to iron out contradictions with other legislation.

Delegated legislation

Many Acts of Parliament give ministers the power to make laws, rules and regulations in relation to highly technical issues that could not easily be contained within the 'parent' legislation. This 'delegated legislation' can have far-reaching consequences for those individuals who are affected by it, so it would seem to be vital that Parliament has the opportunity to scrutinise it.

Despite the volume and significance of such legislation, parliamentary scrutiny is limited. Most 'statutory instruments' become law 40 days after they are laid on the table of the House unless they are annulled (the so-called 'negative procedure'). Some instruments are laid for information only. A very few are made subject to a positive vote before they come into effect (the 'affirmative procedure'). The Joint Committee on Statutory Instruments is responsible for scrutinising legislation and drawing the House's attention to issues, but is often overwhelmed by the volume of legislation that takes this form.

Scrutiny of the executive

Parliamentary scrutiny of government actions means a critical review of what ministers have done, or intend to do, and is important for two reasons. First, the wider discussion accompanying the review, sometimes conducted by experts, may improve the quality of the policies being pursued. Second, in constitutional theory Parliament is the main national institution that represents the views of the population. Potentially, at least, it can express these views more freely than press and television, not being constrained by censorship and libel laws. In other words, the government is accountable to the people through Parliament.

Select committees

Select committees

Committees of the House of Commons and the House of Lords that consider general political issues which are wider than a particular piece of legislation. The Public Accounts Committee of the House of Commons, which considers all accounts of money appropriated by Parliament, is a major example.

The major way in which the legislature scrutinises the executive is the select committee (see Table 18.2). These include those that monitor specific departments and those that are allocated specific issues. Members of these committees are selected to serve for the length of a Parliament and have the opportunity to gain considerable expertise on complex issues. The party whips put forward nominations for membership to the Committee of Selection, but the final appointment is a matter for the House as a whole.

There have been constant complaints that the government whips (and their masters in the executive) have had too much influence on the selection process. In 2001 the Labour whips tried to remove Gwyneth Dunwoody (Transport) and Donald Anderson (Foreign Affairs). Both had proved thorns in the sides of ministers. In a remarkable display of 'parliamentary independence' Labour MPs voted against the wishes of the whips and secured both Dunwoody's and Anderson's re-election. Ms Dunwoody, in particular, proceeded to criticise the government on aspects of transport policy. In general, however, the House rarely puts partisan considerations aside.

Membership of select committees again reflects the composition of the Commons and so they are dominated by government MPs. Ministers, shadow ministers, party whips and parliamentary private secretaries do not normally serve on them. The committee structure, therefore, provides ordinary backbench MPs with an opportunity to gain expertise on policy areas and in holding the executive to account. One of the few aspects of parliamentary 'modernisation' that may have increased the effectiveness of the Commons in holding ministers to account has been the decision to award committee chairmen an additional salary. This may encourage some MPs to focus on scrutiny of the executive as an alternative career path. At the very least it may provide them with greater independence and with some of the backbone demonstrated by their colleagues in the Lords. Party loyalties, however, will reduce the impact of such reforms.

Table 18.2 The select committee system

Departmental committees
- Constitutional Affairs
- Culture, Media and Sport
- Defence
- Education and Skills
- Environment
- Food and Rural Affairs
- Foreign Affairs
- Health
- Home Affairs
- International Development
- Northern Ireland Affairs
- Office of the Deputy Prime Minister
- Science and Technology
- Scottish Affairs
- Trade and Industry
- Transport
- Treasury
- Welsh Affairs
- Work and Pensions

General concerns
- Broadcasting
- Environmental Audit
- Food Standards
- European Scrutiny
- Public Accounts
- Public Administration
- Regulatory Reform

Committees dealing with matters internal to Parliament
- Modernisation
- Standards and Privileges
- Speaker's Committee (responsible for oversight of the Electoral Commission)

Joint Committees of the Lords and Commons
- Human Rights, Statutory Instruments
- Financial Services and Markets
- House of Lords Reform

Others
- Liaison Committee
- Security and Intelligence Committee[1]

Note: [1] Made up of MPs appointed by the Prime Minister (see Chapter 21).

The departmental select committees have a remit to examine 'the expenditure, administration and policy of the principal government departments . . . and associated public bodies' of a department; they themselves decide on issues of interest to them and they are expected to investigate aspects of government administration. Each committee has a small staff and evidence is gathered by inviting submissions from outside bodies, holding oral hearings and conducting fact-finding visits. (The Public Accounts Committee is especially well supported since it is assisted by the National Audit Office and Auditor and Comptroller-General.) The committees have powers to call witnesses and documents, but this does not always mean that

Plate 18.3 The US equivalents of the Foreign Affairs Select Committee are important players in the US political system. In the United Kingdom they are minor political figures. Do you know who these people are?
Source: Empics

they can obtain evidence. In the early 1990s Ian and Kevin Maxwell successfully deflected an inquiry into a pensions scandal by pleading that answers would damage their defence in an impending trial. The committees have no power to compel Members of Parliament (and therefore ministers) to attend. Most will do so in order to deflect charges of a 'cover up'. Two Conservative government ministers, however, successfully refused to answer select committee questions: Lord Young over the privatisation of Rover cars and Sir Leon Brittan over the 1986 Westland Helicopters affair. In general, ministers and officials can expect tougher questioning from opposition members.

When a committee has completed its evidence gathering it tries to produce a consensual report. These reports can go through several drafts and the committee may vote on parts of it. When this happens the votes are noted in the final document. The published report sometimes attracts newspaper and television coverage ('An influential committee has today condemned . . .'), but – in truth – most represent compromises and are bland. When the committees cannot agree they may produce both a majority support (usually written by government MPs) and a more critical minority (written by opposition MPs). This inevitably reduces their impact.

Some committees, such as the Public Accounts Committee, have developed formidable expertise and reputations. Their reports generally have some impact in the media and highlight concerns. Most reports, however, tend to gather dust on the shelves. There is little opportunity to debate these reports on the floor of the House itself, though the opening of Westminster Hall as a parallel debating venue has allowed around 24 reports a year to be debated in that venue. Governments are required to respond to reports but often produce bland, non-committal memorandums. Although some committees have produced well-regarded reports on important issues and act as a magnet for pressure groups that wish to communicate their concerns or demands, they have little direct impact on policy. The sheer existence of these committees, however, must act as a deterrent to those ministers or civil servants who might be called to appear before it. The threat of being 'named and shamed' may subtly alter behaviour.

The Liaison Committee

The chairmen of all the select committees form a Liaison Committee, which has tried to create a 'Commons view' of policy, as distinct from a partisan view. This meets to decide which reports should be debated in the House and approves expenditure by committees. From 2002, moreover, the Prime Minister offered to appear before the committee twice a year, in order to increase his accountability to Parliament. He is given advance notice of the general topics to be covered. The sessions have generally been held to be a success, though Blair's generally confident performance has attracted little media coverage. It is unlikely that future prime ministers will cancel such appearances and so prime ministerial accountability has increased a little as a result.

Parliamentary questions

The role of committees in scrutinising administration is supplemented by oral or written questions that individual MPs can put to ministers, including the Prime Minister, in meetings of the full House. Written questions in particular, to which answers are published in Hansard, can be useful for extracting factual information from the government. Oral questions, by contrast, tend to be framed to make – or extract – a partisan point, and often involve point scoring. Question Time is therefore an opportunity for ministers to demonstrate their ability (or inability) to think on their feet. Parliamentary whips note the performance of both ministers and backbenchers and include these in their reports to the party leadership. It is not unknown for the party managers on both sides to supply questions to their own backbenchers in order to bolster or embarrass a minister.

Ministers can prove evasive and occasionally downright misleading. In autumn 2001 Stephen Byers, the Secretary of Transport, denied he was taking over Railtrack while he was actually doing so. Such behaviour, however, is not advisable. The truth came out in a court case and Byers later apologised to the House.

BRIEFINGS

18.2 Partisan questions

How do exchanges such as this promote accountability?

Mr O'Brien (Eddibsury) (Con): Does the outgoing Prime Minister – *[Interruption.]* Does he agree with the chairman of the Cheshire Police Authority, Labour Councillor Peter Nurse, when he says in his recent letter to the Home Secretary: 'Restructuring policing with such haste and without considering the long-term implications is dangerous and not in the interests of the people of Cheshire'?

The Prime Minister: That is precisely why we must consult fully on it, which we will, and ensure that we get the right proposals for policing in the Hon. Gentleman's area and others. However, I point out that he has record numbers of police in Cheshire, just as he has record numbers of people across the entirety of the public services. On every score – health, education and crime – things are better today than they were in 1997.

Jeff Ennis (Barnsley, East and Mexborough) (Lab): Can my Right Hon. Friend tell me how he will deal with a young, handsome, intelligent, charismatic politician, such as myself – *[Laughter.]* – and how Parliament can better engage ordinary people in the political process?

The Prime Minister: I have always thought that my Hon. Friend was a model to follow, although I have never quite managed it myself. The best way to make progress is to continue with the strong economic growth and the investment in our public services that we have seen across the whole of the public services. Every single indicator has improved since 1997.

Source: Hansard, 7 December 2005

Opposition days

The opposition parties can initiate debate on aspects of government policy on the 'supply' days allotted to them in the parliamentary timetable. These are used to criticise selected aspects of policy, and to promote the opposition party's alternatives, although at a very broad level. Given the secretiveness of both the government and the Civil Service and the influence of party rivalries, it is unusual for these set debates to influence policy. There is also some provision for emergency debates at the discretion of the Speaker.

Government and party

The presence of both the actual government and of the alternative government (the official opposition) in the House of Commons has both advantages and disadvantages. It means that the chief policy makers directly face elected representatives for most of the year, which makes for close and intimate communication. It also means that proceedings are dominated by ritual quarrels between the government and the opposition, which make it difficult for the Commons to organise itself as an entity distinct from party and to express an independent point of view.

Almost all members of a British government must be members of one or other House of Parliament (the exceptions are certain law officers) and in practice the large majority are MPs. The government continues for as long as it commands the confidence of a majority of MPs, in effect the support of the majority party. Party cohesion is therefore central to the functioning of parliamentary democracy as it currently operates in Britain. It is the responsibility of the party managers (**whips**) to secure party cohesion; they apply a variety of sticks and, more frequently, carrots to maintain discipline.

Whips

Officials appointed by parliamentary parties in the Lords and the Commons to promote party discipline and manage party business in Parliament.

Party unity in the Commons

Even when a minority of MPs disagree with their party leadership they normally vote loyally for them against the other party or parties for the sake of party unity and

BRIEFINGS

18.3 Organisation and management of parliamentary parties

There are two aspects to the way MPs are organised in Parliament. One is the methods by which the party leadership keeps control over its followers. This is particularly important for the party in government: with a disciplined party majority the government can do almost anything. Dissent gives an impression of disunity and weakness and at worst leads to humiliating defeat for the government. The same consideration holds, less forcibly, for the opposition parties.

The second aspect is the question of how backbench MPs (those who do not hold office in the government or the 'shadow Cabinet') organise themselves to take action independently of the leadership, so making the House of Commons more of an autonomous body and less of a mechanical register of the strengths of the parties. The most significant of such backbench bodies is the '1922 Committee'. The committee is open to all Conservative MPs, who elect their own executive committee and chair, but is in effect a sounding board for Conservative backbenchers. Meetings are an obvious focus for party discontent, as in 1992–7 over the issue of Europe.

Both major parties also have many policy committees, and 8–10 regional groupings, all for backbench MPs. All-party backbench committees on numerous (usually non-contentious) subjects also provide a 'Commons voice' on policy issues, though party considerations always loom large.

The leadership controls its party in two ways:

1. The meeting of the full parliamentary party agrees policy. Members of the leadership and government attend. As the latter generally consists of the 'payroll vote', all of whom are bound to support official policy, the leadership typically needs to secure the support of an additional 100 MPs to decide party policy, which all members of the parliamentary party are then bound by party rules to support. With the support of no more than 200–250 of all MPs, therefore, the government can dominate the Commons.

2. The whips (the name comes from whippers-in of foxhounds at a hunt, hardly flattering for backbench MPs!). There is a whips' office in each of the major parties, with a chief whip, deputy and four or five others, who are each assigned to a regional grouping of backbench MPs.

   The whips' job is complex. They have to ensure that all MPs turn up for important votes (their summonses are also confusingly called 'whips': a 'three-line whip' is underlined thrice to indicate its importance). Primarily, however, they have to maintain party loyalty and discipline. They do this in three ways:

   (a) By passing information about party morale and opinion up to the leadership and by passing reassuring messages from the leadership down to backbenchers.

   (b) By rewarding loyalty, nominating favoured MPs for desirable committee assignments, trips abroad and other 'treats'. Most importantly, they advise leaders on promotion to junior ministerial office when in government.

   (c) By punishing disloyalty. Whips prefer rewards to sanctions but can punish dissenters by withholding patronage and, in serious cases, by 'withdrawing' the whip; that is, suspending or expelling dissenting MPs from the party. If suspension becomes permanent MPs will lose their party's endorsement at the following election and thus, in all probability, fail to be re-elected. But this sanction damages the party as much as the MP. It is rarely deployed.

Labour has supplemented these parliamentary arrangements by creating a general Party Disciplinary Committee, which can suspend MPs – as it did in the case of George Galloway, the former Labour MP who attacked government policy on Iraq in 2003. Sanctions and rewards only work, of course, because MPs stand or fall together as a party and are strongly motivated to support 'their' opposition or 'their' government. Discipline is much less effective, however, when deep ideological divisions occur.

in order to keep 'their' government in office. The presence of a large **payroll vote** gives the government the advantage. Conversely, it acts against the House developing views independent of the government in office. Although the position of the leaders of the other main party (recognised as Her Majesty's Official Opposition) is more akin to that of an ordinary MP, their enforcement of a united front against the government also inhibits the House from developing a 'Commons' view of most matters. Most issues are viewed through the distorting lens of partisanship.

The principle of collective responsibility means that those on the payroll vote must publicly defend any government policy as if it were their own, even if they privately disagree with it; their only alternative is to resign office. Internal party disputes, with occasional exceptions, are fought out in inter-departmental memoranda and in Cabinet committees, rather than in public debates in Parliament. The last thing parties want is the political embarrassment and electoral damage of internal clashes aired in a general debate. Collective responsibility and party cohesion operate to maintain at least the semblance of a united, effective government and opposition and, in doing so, they reduce the possibility of MPs expressing independent points of view in Parliament.

Payroll vote

Those members who must vote with the government or lose their positions. It includes ministers and parliamentary private secretaries.

Electoral mandate versus continuing parliamentary scrutiny

Electoral mandate

The idea that a party whose policies are approved by a majority of voters has the duty and authority to carry them through as a government.

There are major obstacles to informed parliamentary debate about policy alternatives. The first is the way in which parliamentary procedures are designed to facilitate set-piece Conservative–Labour battles. The domination of business first by the government, and second by the leadership of the next largest party, constitutes the major obstacle to independent initiatives by the House of Commons as such.

This institutional monopoly is buttressed both by constitutional doctrine and the entrenched attitudes of many MPs. A common parliamentary view is that the government's ultimate responsibility to serve popular wishes is guaranteed by exposure to a general election at the end of its term. The task of the majority parliamentary party is therefore to support the government and of the opposition parties to maintain opposition morale, and sap the government's, by ceaselessly criticising ministers. As the House of Commons is simply an arena for partisan encounters it can have no collective and independent role vis-à-vis the government. Neither should it, since that would blur the responsibility of the majority party for government policy, on which it will be judged at the next election.

This belief is in turn linked to a broader idea that the government is in the best position to understand the public interest, and should be left to get on with the task of governing unhindered between elections. This outlook colours opinions on a wide range of constitutional issues that extend beyond the character and procedures for parliamentary debate. For example:

- *Reform of the current electoral system is undesirable* because it generally allows one major party to take responsibility for the record of the government (see Chapter 15).

- *Accountability of the leadership to party members is undesirable* because it makes leaders less able to act decisively on their own initiative (see Chapter 16).

- *Government secrecy is desirable* because it discourages too much outside intrusion into government business (see Chapter 21).

Support for strong, unfettered government thus reduces effective day-to-day scrutiny in Parliament. The justification is that 'the public interest' can only be served in this way. Governments should not be put under pressure to meet immediate demands, for to do so might result in an inability to govern in the longer-term interest and to plan for the future. In turn the opposition should set out an alternative government programme for the next election, supported by its MPs. Nobody in the major parties should engage in independent action outside the party line.

The case for MPs adopting a more independent and critical attitude towards the government is that most of what gets done during its term of office is only tenuously related to the broad lines of policy presented at the preceding election. The implementation of the main commitments in the government's party manifesto requires many intermediate decisions, some of which may be debatable. Moreover, much of the business of government is unrelated to electorally endorsed party policies and is carried out by unelected civil servants. Wider and more informed discussion might improve rather than hamper the business of the government. A growing belief that this is so has spurred MPs to develop procedures for discussing the justification, and likely outcomes, of government policy, on a broadly non-party basis.

The government and journalists

The obstacles to even establishing simple facts about what the government is doing are hard to exaggerate. The selective management of information by the government is best illustrated in the parliamentary context by the '**lobby system**' of specialist journalists attached to Parliament.

The parliamentary 'lobby' is a name given to specially privileged parliamentary correspondents of the main newspapers and television and radio channels who spend most of their time in the 'lobbies' of Parliament. They are given confidential information and have ready access to ministers, but rarely to civil servants. It is understood that in return they will reveal only what they are expressly authorised to publish. Failure to observe the understanding leads to exclusion from the lobby's privileges. Thus much of the political information that is published is divulged at the initiative of the government, and consists of what the government wants to reveal rather than what journalists think it ought to reveal.

Two recent developments have undermined this traditional way of managing the news. The first is the increasing practice by ministers and civil servants of privately 'briefing' selected journalists, usually in order to resist or promote policy proposals within the government. This is a common tactic by departments wishing to resist budget cuts, and is pursued even by figures such as the joint chiefs of staff, the military commanders. Such briefings can shade into the unauthorised 'leak' of news by nominally subordinate officials or junior ministers opposed to policies backed by their superiors. They always represent selective management of information in the interest of those doing the briefing.

The other process undermining the lobby system is the development of a more independent stance on the part of a minority of political journalists. This is linked to the spread of 'investigative journalism' where stories are pursued at the initiative of the newspapers or, more rarely, television editors (see Chapter 14). Journalists and newspapers have been prepared to risk prosecution either under the Official Secrets Act, under the D-notices circulated by governments to prevent discussion of topics relating to national security, or under the severe British libel laws, for refusing to reveal the sources of their information. The editors of some newspapers have withdrawn from the lobby (notably the *Independent* and the *Guardian*) and now explicitly quote their official sources.

In spite of this, the ethos of the lobby system still predominates in British government. Information is for insiders rather than outsiders and the government (or at least its constituent ministers and administrators) determines who shall be insiders. MPs depend heavily on published material for their own information, to supplement erratic personal contacts and the selective confidences of party leaders. The government's management of news deprives MPs of a major source of information just as much as it deprives the general public.

Live radio and television coverage of parliamentary proceedings has not changed this situation. What is broadcast tends to be the set debates (on the Queen's Speech, or the budget, for example) and the weekly Prime Minister's Questions, which

Lobby system

The name given to specially selected correspondents of the main newspapers, TV and radio stations who are given confidential information by the government on a non-attributable basis. Not to be confused with 'the lobby', or pressure group system in Parliament.

have become ritual gladiatorial contests between the government and opposition leaderships. Only if Parliament itself develops procedures for uncovering and evaluating important information will broadcasts be more illuminating.

This accepted, the set-piece exchanges typical of the big debates or of Prime Minister's Questions do perform a democratic function. They oblige prime ministers and ministers to state their positions clearly and to defend them. They have to convince their own supporters, and the wider public to whom they are exposed through the mass media, as well as put up a defence against the attacks and taunts of the opposition parties. For most of the time these exchanges are simply theatre; but it reflects the importance attached to such occasions that Tony Blair (and his predecessors as Prime Minister) typically spend the morning before Prime Minister's Questions closeted with their officials second-guessing the questions that will be asked and rehearsing answers. Occasionally, a single speech can make a difference, as Sir Geoffrey Howe's thinly veiled attack on Margaret Thatcher following his resignation as Foreign Secretary did in 1990. Ann Widdecombe's criticism of Michael Howard ('there is something of the night about him') damaged his chances of leadership in 1997.

Interests: proper and improper representation

The representation of interests lies at the heart both of constitutional theory and of the actual practice of parliamentary and party politics. As Chapter 13 pointed out, an immense variety of groups and organisations are affected by government policy and therefore seek to influence it in their favour. Their most common and effective means of lobbying is by direct contact with government ministers and officials rather than with MPs, which underlines the general predominance of the executive over Parliament in Britain.

However, sometimes a specific piece of legislation can have very important consequences for particular groups. For example, even such a seemingly boring and technical matter as regulation of hygiene on caravan sites could gain or lose site

BRIEFINGS

18.4 The Modernisation Committee

As we have already noted a Modernisation Committee was established in order to review parliamentary procedures. It is chaired by the Leader of the House of Commons, a cabinet minister. There have been six Leaders of the House between 1997 and March 2006, resulting in little continuity. There have, however, been a large number of published reports and some innovations in parliamentary procedure.

The basic problem with the committee is that the term 'modernisation' means different things to different people:

1. To government it means simply improving their ability to drive legislation through Parliament. 'Modernisation' in this sense has included:

   ■ the increased use of 'timetabling', which produces a strict timetable that reduces the time available for debate

   ■ the introduction of 'carry over bills', which allows the government to reintroduce bills that did not get through in the previous session.

   The government has also generally opposed efforts to increase the effectiveness of select committees.

2. To back bench MPs, constitutional commentators and others modernisation means improving the ability of the Commons to hold the executive to account. Modernisation in this sense has included:

   ■ starting Prime Minister's Questions at 12 noon on Wednesday in order to attract more media attention

   ■ ensuring the Prime Minister appears twice yearly before the Liaison Committee

   ■ increasing the resources available for select committees

   ■ the introduction of additional salary for select committee chairmen

   ■ opening a parallel debating chamber in Westminster Hall

   ■ the publication of draft bills in order to enable select committees to engage in pre-legislative scrutiny (assisted by a Scrutiny Unit within the Committee Office).

3. To just about everyone 'modernisation' also means doing away with some of the more archaic and sillier aspects of Parliament. Modernisation in this sense has included:

   ■ reforming its anti-social working hours (some of these reforms have now been reversed; see Table 18.1 for current times)

   ■ improving office space available for MPs

   ■ stopping the wearing of top hats to make a point of order during a division

   ■ referring to members of the public as 'strangers'

   ■ making Parliament more accessible by opening it to visitors on Saturdays.

Parliament operates the way it does because it is largely in the interest of the government (and of the opposition, the potential government) to continue. The 'winner takes all' aspect of the electoral system means that loyalties to party invariably trump loyalty to Parliament. Revealingly, when MPs were given the opportunity to remove the whips from the selection process altogether it showed just how partisan most MPs are! Dennis Skinner, the left-wing Labour MP, declared, 'The newfangled select committees would have handed over power to the political enemy – the Tories – who were going to sit on a joint committee to select Labour members of Parliament!'

Scrutiny of the executive will only be addressed once the 'winner takes all' approach has gone. Certainly the Scottish Parliament, in which no party has an absolute majority, has introduced strong committees in a deliberate attempt to tone down party hostility and create a less partisan culture. Major changes at Westminster would follow if the Liberal Democrats held the balance between the two major competitors. With the growth in third-party support, and certainly after any change in the method of electing MPs, this is a possibility. The confrontation between Conservatives and Labour has certainly frustrated any attempt to change the procedures that facilitate it. The expectation by both that they will eventually form a strong majority government militates against any change that might make Parliament more effective in scrutinising them.

owners millions of pounds: it all depends on whether they or the water companies are legally obliged to provide the requisite water facilities. Water companies will therefore also be drawn into this debate.

It was traditionally taken for granted that MPs should not only represent outside interests but be personally linked to them, particularly land, commerce, industry, the City of London and the professions. It was far better, it was assumed, that MPs have personal experience of the 'real world' than be full-time parliamentarians, and that they depend on inherited wealth or paid employment for their livelihood rather than on the taxpayer.

This relaxed attitude towards MPs' links with outside interests was largely abandoned by the end of the twentieth century. One reason is that most MPs have become full-time political professionals: they have no outside employment; devote all their time to committee work and (increasingly) to constituents' problems; and depend on a fairly modest parliamentary salary and permitted expenses for their livelihood. This is particularly true of Labour MPs, who are drawn mainly from the 'talking professions' of teaching, law and journalism. But it is increasingly true of Conservative MPs too, who are less likely than a generation ago to have inherited or accumulated significant private wealth. The advantage of MPs having private means or significant outside earnings (as a barrister, for example) is that it confers a degree of personal political independence; the danger of relying on a parliamentary salary alone is that it exposes MPs to the temptation of accepting an often generous fee for lobbying on behalf of a particular interest.

A second reason is that the scope of governmental and parliamentary action broadened immensely in the course of the twentieth century. When governments regulated only a few aspects of the economy, and firms could act much more freely and independently, the business interests involved in Parliament were few in number and clearly defined. Now almost everything the government does has financial implications for some companies and interests. Even when it decides to disengage from part of the economy, by privatising a state-run industry, for example, the way it chooses to do so (the nature of the share offer or the new regulatory regime) can have enormous financial implications for City interests and private companies. In these circumstances it can be very beneficial for the affected interests to have MPs quietly interceding on their behalf.

Third, as the culture of political deference has gradually declined, so the mass media have become less reticent and trusting about the connections between MPs, especially ministers, and outside interests. Clear evidence of corruption is rare; the details of any situation are usually fuzzy and the motives of the people involved ambivalent and complex. It is difficult to know whether a wealthy businessperson makes a substantial gift to the Labour Party in the hope of a legislative favour, a knighthood, an invitation to Number 10 or out of genuine ideological sympathy – it may be all of these. It is equally difficult to tell whether a government decision that happens to benefit the donor was taken in gratitude for or anticipation of a donation or entirely irrespective of it in the public interest. What has changed is the media's assumptions. They no longer automatically give politicians the benefit of the doubt but presume selfish motives unless the contrary can be proved. For example, during the Conservative governments of the 1980s and 1990s a number of ex-ministers and senior officials joined the boards of major companies. Even though the ministers and officials abided by the Cabinet Office rules regulating such practice, the media would ask whether the prospect of such appointments affected the decisions of the minister when they were still in office. Similarly the media, encouraged by the Conservative opposition, sought to imply that the businessmen appointed to the New Labour government by Tony Blair in 1997, such as Lord Simon and Lord Sainsbury, were subject to conflicts of interest even though they had dispensed with the shares they held in their companies.

In order to deal with the problem, Parliament in 1975 required MPs (and Lords) to register their interests and financial links in writing (the Parliamentary Register of Interests) and to declare their interest before participating in a debate or committee. However, by the 1990s this provision appeared to be ineffective. Some MPs failed to declare all their interests in the Register, whether through genuine inadvertence or deliberate concealment, and the Register did not stop MPs from declaring a connection with a public relations company specialising in parliamentary lobbying and accepting a 'consultancy fee' or favours for lobbying on behalf of an undisclosed particular interest. It also transpired that in the 1992–7 Parliament some MPs were being paid (at £1,000 per question!) by outside organisations to ask parliamentary questions on their behalf. Neil Hamilton's failure to declare his connection with Mohamed Al Fayed, the owner of Harrods, and other paid activities on behalf of Ian Greer Associates (a parliamentary lobbying company) is but one notorious example.

Individual links with special interests are to some extent legitimised by the fact that the parties to which they belong have institutionalised links with the same or similar interests. The Conservative Party has historically received substantial donations from major companies such as Hanson, Dixons and Marks & Spencer and from business associations such as Aims for Industry seeking to promote free enterprise. It has also accepted more dubious donations from wealthy overseas businessmen. A substantial proportion of Labour MPs were sponsored by trade unions, which have contributed to their election expenses, although the practice has declined. Successive Labour leaders, including Harold Wilson, James Callaghan and Tony Blair, have relied on donations from wealthy but initially anonymous sympathisers to pay for their private office, general election campaign headquarters and for policy research.

A run of minor parliamentary scandals and dubious practices during the 1992–7 Major administration led to the impression that Parliament and politicians were becoming '**sleazy**'. This hit the Conservatives harder than Labour, because of their more extensive business links and their ability while in government to do more for their sponsors. In response to widespread disquiet, John Major took the unprecedented step of setting up an extra-parliamentary permanent committee (the Committee for Standards in Public Life) under an Appeal Court Judge, Lord Nolan, to investigate these matters. In 1996 the Conservative government, despite fury among some of its backbenchers, reluctantly accepted most of its recommendations for much wider disclosure of interests and for a prohibition against MPs accepting payment for lobbying. There is now a Code of Conduct for MPs and a Parliamentary Commissioner for Standards, who is empowered to investigate complaints about MPs. The Commissioner reports to the Standards and Privileges Committee of the House of Commons, which then makes recommendations to the House. The Commissioner cannot, however, investigate complaints against ministers acting as ministers. These are dealt with separately via informal inquiries, such as that produced by Sir Gus O'Donnell into the financial activities of Tessa Jowell, in early 2006.

In their Fifth Report, under the chairmanship of Lord Neill, the Committee for Standards in Public Life reported on party finance. Its recommendations for greater transparency were accepted by the Labour government. The Political Parties, Elections and Referendums Act 2000 required the parties to declare the names of donors for all donations above £5,000. The register of donations held by the Electoral Commission can now be examined by members of the public via the internet.

Although plausible allegations of 'sleaze' have somewhat abated since 1997 the Labour government has not avoided them altogether. The most notorious example was the so-called 'Ecclestone Affair'. The Labour government came to power promising to ban tobacco sponsorship of sport. Bernie Ecclestone, the owner of Formula One Racing, successfully lobbied to have the ban postponed in the case of his sport. It later emerged that Ecclestone had donated £1 million to Labour and

Sleaze

A popular term referring to the corrupt and improper behaviour of public officials.

Plate 18.6 Elizabeth Filkin was removed as Parliamentary Commissioner for Standards, it is said, because she was too assiduous in her role

Source: Empics

was contemplating a further substantial donation. All this happened before the new rules relating to publication of donations so Blair referred this second donation to the Committee for Standards in Public Life. Lord Neill proceeded to astonish the Prime Minister by saying that not only should the additional donation be declined but the original £1 million donation should be returned! The government has also been criticised by the Commissioner for Public Appointments for favouring its political sympathisers in appointments to quangos, in particular to NHS trusts.

Some MPs have criticised the new system of regulation as being unfair and there were particular criticisms of Elizabeth Filkin, the second Commissioner. The tenuousness of the arrangements for checking improper links between MPs and special interests was illustrated by the effective sacking of Filkin (some thought because she had been too active in investigating MPs' interests). The Committee for Standards in Public Life recommended in 2002 that the Commissioner's post be made non-renewable for five to seven years in order to prevent the House exerting undue influence on the office holder and in order to increase public confidence in the system. The Commissioner now has little incentive to 'take it easy' on MPs.

Party discipline in Parliament and its relaxation

The major reason for parliamentary weakness in the face of the executive is the loyalty given by MPs to their party, particularly when their party is in power. This raises two crucial and related questions. What mechanisms are available to secure MPs' loyalty? And under what circumstances does loyalty break down? The rights and wrongs of party loyalty are bound up with issues of democratic theory. On the one hand, party discipline is a prerequisite for effective government and for communicating the principles and policies of the parties to the electorate. It enables the electorate to know where the parties stand and on that basis to make a rational choice between them. On the other hand, the individual MP was elected by the voters of his or her constituency and has obligations to represent their interests and views. The eighteenth-century MP Edmund Burke even suggested that sometimes an individual MP may owe it to his constituents to go against their wishes if he believed it was for their own good! MPs sometimes defy party discipline, therefore, in order to vote with their conscience or with the wishes of their local constituents. This tension between the electoral mandate for the party and the individual MP's duty to conscience and constituency has increased in recent years.

Maintaining party cohesion

Parties maintain cohesion by a variety of strategies and mechanisms. The leader of the majority party is also Prime Minister and can appoint MPs to ministerial office – or, just as important, offer the prospect of office in the future – as a reward for loyalty. The Prime Minister can also award honours and make appointments or nominations to outside bodies (for example, to the European Commission) as to a lesser extent can the leader of the opposition. The Prime Minister has the power to dissolve Parliament and call a general election through a formal request to the Queen. The uncertainty of the result prevents this threat being made very often – after all, it could lead to electoral defeat and the Prime Minister relinquishing office – but it can promote cohesion on a particular issue. In July 1993, for example, one day after the Conservative government's defeat by 324 to 316 on the Social Policy Protocol of the Maastricht Treaty, John Major declared the issue a 'vote of confidence' and secured a reversal of the decision by 339 to 301.

The party leadership is supported by party officials known as whips, selected from MPs not in the government (or in the shadow Cabinet, in the case of the opposition party). One of the whips' powers is withdrawal of the 'whip' from a dissident, with resulting loss of access to parliamentary order papers and back-bench party committees. The ultimate sanction is expulsion from the parliamentary party, involving loss of the party's endorsement at the next election and near-certain electoral defeat.

The whips allocate backbench MPs to standing committees on government bills, recommend them for select committee appointments and choose MPs for parliamentary and party delegations abroad. They can provide a host of small favours for MPs with health, family or financial problems. Such incentives improve the atmosphere on the backbenches and encourage loyalty. Prime Ministers rely on whips for advice about appointments to junior government posts, which are the stepping stones to more senior positions.

Ironically 'ideology' (adherence to a particular doctrine or programme) is more likely to lead to party division than unity. 'True believers' are more likely than pragmatists to put doctrine before party and to reject the compromises that all governments have to make. From the 1950s to the mid-1980s this posed more problems for Labour than the Conservatives because the Labour Party was divided between the doctrinaire 'socialist left' and pragmatic 'social democrats' over a wide range of issues (see Chapter 16). However, Conservative MPs became noticeably more ideological under Mrs Thatcher's premiership and by the 1992–7 government dissent became endemic within the Parliamentary Conservative Party. This coincided with the influx of new-style Tories in the 1980s who, like Mrs Thatcher herself, did not come from the traditional male, public school, armed forces and colonial service stereotype, in which acceptance of authority and loyalty to the institution was paramount. The new-style Conservative MPs were more likely to be upwardly mobile meritocratic individualists for whom loyalty to party was less important, and they were encouraged in this view by Margaret Thatcher's sporadic disloyalty to John Major after she ceased to be Prime Minister. They chose the issue of 'British sovereignty' against 'Europe', which symbolised 'Thatcherism' versus 'Majorism', as the cause for rebellion. Meanwhile Labour, desperate to avoid a fifth election defeat in 1997, preserved an uncharacteristic unity despite the reservations of many on the left about Tony Blair's abandonment of traditional positions. The Labour leadership tightened the standing orders that regulate backbenchers' freedom to dissent and the electronic pager issued by the whips to each Labour MP became a symbol of the leadership's 'control freakery'.

Dissent within parliamentary parties

All governments are vulnerable to rebellions if they persistently ignore the views of their MPs and appear to be heading for defeat at the next election. Local constituency parties will be less inclined to disown rebels if they themselves are critical of the party leadership for deviating from party principles or for governmental incompetence. Ideologues with an 'all or nothing' approach ignore the danger that public dissent might weaken the government in the eyes of voters and increase the prospect of defeat.

Party discipline was strong under both Labour and Conservative governments during the 1950s and 1960s. It began to crumble during the 1970–February 1974 Conservative government led by Edward Heath. Internal tensions grew after the government's economic U-turns on its manifesto and as a result of its commitment to joining the European Economic Community (now the EU) – consistently the most divisive issue in post-war British politics. An identifiable body of Conservative MPs emerged with a hard line on monetary policy and social issues. They gradually took over the leadership of the party with the election of Margaret Thatcher as party leader in 1975 and Prime Minister in 1979. Semi-public dissent by the 'wets' from the prevailing monetarist orthodoxy increased after 1980.

Backbench rebellion became endemic during the 1974–9 Labour governments of Wilson and Callaghan. It reflected growing disillusion with the economic performance of the government and rooted objections to devolution to Scotland and Wales. No less than 45 per cent of all whipped divisions in the 1978–9 session saw some Labour MPs voting against the government. What is more, only 62 backbench Labour MPs (19 per cent of the total) cast no dissenting votes, while 40 cast more than 50, and 9 more than 100. The secession of the Social Democrats in 1981–2 can be traced to these increasing factional tensions among Labour MPs in the late 1970s (see Chapter 16).

The watering down of Thatcher's policies under John Major (1990–7) made diehard members of the party disgruntled. They found a cause to rally round in opposition to 'Europe'. The Major government's progressive loss of its modest majority through by-election losses (1992–7) meant that even small groups of determined opponents within the party could force its hand. The limit to the leadership's power to impose party discipline was demonstrated when it withdrew the whip from eight Eurosceptic rebels in November 1994 (another resigned the whip in sympathy). The withdrawal gave the rebels publicity, underlined the party's divisions, and left the government even more vulnerable to defeat in the House of Commons. Within a year the party was forced to readmit them without guarantees of their future compliance.

The Labour government elected in 1997 was far more united than its Conservative predecessor. In its first two full parliamentary sessions there was less rebelliousness than in any full-length Parliament since the 1950s. In the 703 divisions one or more Labour backbenchers rebelled in a mere 35. The large cohort of newly elected women Labour MPs were particularly loyal, contrary to the assumption that they might shake up both Parliament and the Labour Party and promote a new agenda. This exceptional parliamentary cohesion was assisted by tougher party management but also by an acute awareness of Labour backbenchers of the role played by disunity in keeping the party in opposition for 18 years after 1979. An even more important factor was the government's successful record of economic management and its high standing in the opinion polls. However it was not entirely immune, particularly on various aspects of welfare reform, especially proposals to reduce welfare benefits to the disabled.

In the second term, Labour backbench MPs became increasingly rebellious. They voted against the party whips on a total of 259 occasions (or 20.8 per cent of all divisions). Some of these rebellions, moreover, were very large. As many as 65 Labour MPs voted against the whip over foundation hospitals in 2003 and 72 voted against the government on the second reading of the Higher Education Bill introducing 'top-up fees' in the same year. Yet even these were dwarfed by the rebellions over Iraq. In the final vote before the war in March 2003 fully 139 Labour MPs voted against the war and the government, making it the largest rebellion since the repeal of the Corn Laws in the nineteenth century. This new found rebelliousness spilled over into revolts on aspects of the government's 'anti-terrorist' legislation and the last months of the 2001–5 Parliament were dominated by battles about the civil liberties implications of the government's proposals.

The fact that the government's majority was cut from the dizzying level of 162 in 2001 to 66 in 2005 has shifted the balance of power in Parliament in favour of the backbenches. In these circumstances any Prime Minister has to worry about his ability to take his or her backbenchers with them. While some expected this smaller majority to produce greater discipline, the initial behaviour of backbench MPs suggested that this might not be the case. In November 2005 the government suffered its first defeat in the Commons since 1997 on proposals to detain terrorist suspects for up to 90 days. The sheer novelty of the defeat caused speculation about the Prime Minister's immediate future.

BRIEFINGS

18.5 Why did Labour MPs became so rebellious in the second term?

Labour MPs did not appear to become any more rebellious because of turnover of MPs. Fully 85 per cent of all MPs in the 2001–5 Parliament had served in the 1997–2001 Parliament. There appear to be essentially four reasons for this increased rebelliousness.

The issues

The government introduced a series of reforms that trampled on traditional Old Labour sensitivities about the nature of the NHS (foundation hospitals), education (top-up fees) and the welfare state (further reforms of welfare payments). In addition, government policy towards Iraq, support for Bush's 'war on terror' and the introduction of anti-terrorist legislation also sparked fears among members of Labour's liberal wing.

The decline of self-discipline

By the middle to the 2001–5 Parliament memories of Labour's 18 years in opposition were fading. Moreover, the Conservative Party under Iain Duncan-Smith did not appear to be a great threat to Labour's re-election chances. This made it appear less costly to follow the party line.

Rebellion got easier with practice

Voting with the other side is not easy. Not only do most MPs want to 'back their side', they do not want to be thought of as helping 'the other side'. MPs have to walk through the division lobbies with the 'other side'. Once this has been done each successive rebellion became a little bit easier.

The presence of a backbench leadership

By the second term the Labour backbenches included many former ministers (such as Frank Dobson, Robin Cook and Clare Short) who could not hope for a return to office and who could lead opposition.

Source: See Philip Cowley and Mark Stuart, 'Parliament', in Anthony Seldon and Dennis Kavanagh (eds), *The Blair Effect 2* (Cambridge: Cambridge University Press, 2005), pp. 20–42.

The role of third parties

The House of Commons is so dominated by the battle between Her Majesty's Government and Her Majesty's Loyal Opposition that so far we have given little attention to third parties. Yet if Parliament is to develop a function beyond sustaining the government and official opposition, the role played by the smaller parties may prove crucial. Because they are placed outside the main struggle between government and opposition they can make criticisms that are not simply directed at doing the government down.

Third-party representation in Parliament has grown, if somewhat erratically, since the 1950s, as Figure 18.2 shows. Fully 75 MPs were elected in 1997, the largest number since 1931. In 2001 this figure increased to 80 and in the 2005 election to 93 (in a House of Commons made up of 646 rather than 659 MPs). Of these, 27 were regionalist MPs, particularly concerned with issues affecting their own part of Britain they are not strongly interested in general British issues, or at any rate will be willing to trade support on these for regional concessions if the government is in a tight corner (as the dying Major administration found to its cost when dependent on the votes of a few Ulster Unionists in 1995–6). The Liberal Democrats are the party most likely to act as a genuine third voice on questions of general British concern. It is for this reason that their parliamentary growth is shown separately in Figure 18.2.

Liberal Democrat strength in Parliament has grown in fits and starts since their initial recovery in the early 1960s. The electoral system, however, prevents them from translating their substantial share of votes into parliamentary seats. This creates a vicious circle. The number of Liberal Democrat MPs has been too limited to break the hold of Conservatives and Labour over parliamentary procedures and the adversarial style of debate it engenders. This culture also extends to select committee proceedings and appointments. For example, only one Liberal Democrat chaired a select committee in the 1997 Parliament although in many ways Liberals would be ideal in forging a 'Commons view' outside the main party battle. The parliamentary weakness of the Liberals means that they cannot force through the electoral reforms that would end it. Thus the 'third force' that might help to

Figure 18.2 Percentage of third party and Liberal MPs, 1945–2005

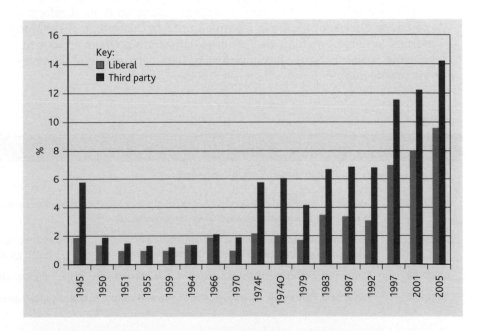

develop a genuinely autonomous role for Parliament is normally disadvantaged by the latter's institutional bias towards the two main parties.

As we point out in Chapter 15 it is quite possible that there will be a hung Parliament either at the next election or shortly afterwards. The Liberal Democrats may well hold the balance of power and demand electoral reform as a precondition of their cooperation in a coalition. If either of the major parties accepts this condition it is likely to produce a permanently hung Parliament which will shift the culture of the House of Commons and produce a legislature that is less dominated by the major parties and by contestation and confrontation.

Summary

This chapter shows that:

- Parliament at the present time is dominated by the two major political parties. Most MPs owe their election to party support and thus tend to support their party and shield it from criticism, whatever their private doubts.

- This means that Parliament's main role is to sustain the government and provide a forum for the opposition to criticise it.

- However, some weakening of major party cohesion and increased third-party representation have allowed backbench MPs to assume a slightly more independent role in questioning aspects of government policy.

- This has been expressed by voting against some government legislation, and by more vigorous questioning and investigation by select committees.

- Scrutiny and questioning of the administration are probably more important and justifiable activities for Parliament than querying the principles underpinning legislation. Important legislation has been given a 'mandate' through the government party's electoral success. The details of implementation, however, have not, neither have the many major administrative decisions made by the Civil Service. A useful role of committees is simply to provide more information about the workings of British government.

- Parliament plays only a peripheral part in government. It could play a modestly useful role in scrutinising the administration, if it were better organised to do it. Most reform will have to wait until third parties or dissident MPs are in a position to force change out of the leadership of one of the major parties. In spite of rhetoric, the Labour government is no more anxious to diminish its present or prospective power than any other government. Thus major reform of the House of Commons is not on the immediate horizon.

MILESTONES

Milestones in parliamentary development

1295–1306	Edward I summons representatives of boroughs and counties, as well as Lords, to consent to taxation. In return he redresses grievances they complain about
1306–1532	This practice continues and the Parliament clearly divides into two Houses (Lords and Commons). The Commons establishes itself as the more active House, with power to grant taxation
1532–59	Parliament confirms the Royal Succession and sanctions the major religious changes
1640–51	Parliament fights civil war against the Crown and wins. It establishes its supremacy over the law courts

Milestones in parliamentary development continued

1688–9	The Glorious Revolution. Parliament transfers Crown from James II to William and Mary and establishes exclusive power to raise money and sanction military forces. Members given personal immunities
1701	Parliament settles Protestant succession
1715–1832	The 'eighteenth-century constitution'. Government has to be acceptable both to the King and the Commons majority. From time to time party caucuses ('Whigs', 'Tories') form to manage the majority
1832	Great Reform Act. Election becomes the clear and exclusive basis of membership of the House of Commons. Government is now totally dependent on a Commons majority. Monarch withdraws from active politics
1867–8	Second Reform Act institutes mass male franchise. Mass-membership parties impose discipline on MPs in return for sponsoring their election. 'Elective dictatorship' of government commences
1874–86	Imposition of procedural devices to ensure government legislation passes in spite of filibustering by Irish nationalists ('guillotine' to curtail debate on clauses etc.)
1911	Lords cannot oppose financial legislation and can only delay legislation for three years
1922	Government of Ireland Act sets up Northern Irish government and Parliament
1949	Parliament Act limits delaying power of House of Lords to one year
1970	Growth of dissent from the party line among backbench MPs
1972	European Communities Act significantly limits parliamentary sovereignty
1973	Abolition of Northern Irish government and Parliament
1979	Creation of system of departmental select committees to scrutinise administrative actions
1994–6	Scott Committee reveals extent to which governments may mislead the Commons
1994	Government sets up Committee of Inquiry into Standards in Public Life, under Lord Nolan
1995	Nolan Report recommends public disclosure of MPs' interests and party donors
1996	MPs obliged to register all details of outside contracts with a new parliamentary commission
1997	Creation of the Modernisation Committee
1998	Devolution to Wales, Scotland and Northern Ireland
1999	House of Lords Act: hereditary peers lose their voting rights, except for 92 who retain them during a 'transitional period'.
2001–3	Debate over how Lords' members should be selected: Liberals and Conservatives come out for largely elected House with same general power
2003	Largest revolt since the repeal of the Corn Laws over Iraq War
2005	Labour government's first defeat in the Commons since 1997 over proposals to detain terrorist suspects

Essays

1. Could we still have a democracy in Britain without Parliament? If so, how would it function? If not, what is the irreplaceable contribution that Parliament makes?

2. 'The second chamber is a vital protection against an over-mighty executive.' Discuss.

3. Why do MPs nearly always vote as the whips instruct them, even when they have doubts about their party's line?

4. What can a parliamentary select committee do that an investigative journalist cannot?

Projects

1. On the basis of the 2005 Labour Party manifesto and the Queen's speeches made in the present Parliament, estimate the extent to which the government has fulfilled its election pledges up to this point.

2. On the basis of newspaper accounts and Hansard calculate the amount of dissent within the Parliamentary Labour Party and the Parliamentary Conservative Party during the present Parliament.

3. 'Shadow' two select committees in this Parliament on the basis of newspaper reports. Do you feel that one is more effective than the other? Why?

4. Outline the reforms that you think are necessary for the Commons to operate better.

Further reading

General works on Parliament are Philip Norton, *Parliament in British Politics* (Basingstoke: Palgrave Macmillan, 2005); Peter Riddell, *Parliament under Blair* (London: Politicos, 2002). Also useful is John Alder, *Constitutional and Administrative Law* (Basingstoke: Palgrave Macmillan, 2005), Chapters 9–11. For a longer study of parties in Parliament, see Jack Brand, *British Parliamentary Parties* (Oxford: Oxford University Press, 1992), and for the work of party whips see Keith Alderman, 'The government whips', *Politics Review*, **4** (4), 1995, pp. 23–4. Committees are discussed in T. Morgan, 'Teeth for the Commons watchdog', *Politics Review*, **8** (4), 1999, pp. 6–10. See also Anthony King, *Does the United Kingdom Still Have a Constitution?* (London: Sweet & Maxwell, 2001) and Dawn Oliver, *Constitutional Reform in the UK* (Oxford: Oxford University Press, 2002) who both provide overviews of the larger constitutional issues.

On the House of Lords see Meg Russell, 'What are second chambers for?', *Parliamentary Affairs*, **54** (3), 2001, pp. 442–58; Donald Shell, 'The future of the second chamber', *Parliamentary Affairs*, **57** (4), 2004, pp. 852–66 and also 'Labour and the House of Lords: a case study in constitutional reform', *Parliamentary Affairs* **53** (2), 2000, pp. 290–310; Thomas Bird, 'The House of Lords: national treasure or confounded nuisance?', *Talking Politics*, **18** (1), 2005, 20–2. See also the House of Commons Research Paper, *House of Lords Developments since January 2002* (http://www.parliament.uk/commons/lib/research/rp2003/rp03-085.pdf).

For recent discussions on the reform of the House of Commons, see Riddell, *Parliament under Blair* esp. Chapter 9; the Hansard Society Commission Report, *The Challenge for Parliament: Making Government Accountable* (London: Hansard Society, 2001); 'What's new? Parliamentary reform and political parties', *Politics Review*, **11** (1), 2002, pp. 6–7; Moyra Grant, 'The theory and practice of parliamentary reform', **16** (2), pp. 78–81; Philip Cowley and Mark Stuart, 'Parliament', in Anthony Seldon and Dennis Kavanagh (eds), *The Blair Effect 2* (Cambridge: Cambridge University Press, 2005); Tony Wright, 'Prospects for parliamentary reform', *Parliamentary Affairs*, **57** (4), pp. 867–76. See also the House of Commons Research Paper, *Modernising the House of Commons 1997–2005* (http://www.parliament.uk/commons/lib/research/rp2005/rp05-046.pdf).

On the question of backbench revolts see Philip Cowley's various publications including: *Revolts and Rebellions: Parliamentary Voting under Blair* (London, Politicos, 2002), *The Rebels: How Blair Mislaid his Majority* (London: Politicos, 2005).

Hot links to these sites can be found on the CWS at www.pearsoned.co.uk/budge.

For a complete list of political parties' web sites see Chapter 16 of this book. The Westminster parliamentary structure is described thoroughly in www.parliament.uk, which also provides general information on representative democracy in the United Kingdom as well as in-depth information on both chambers and their members. Acts of the UK Parliament are available at Her Majesty's Stationery Office (www.hmso.gov.uk/acts.htm). POLIS is the Parliamentary Online Indexing Service (www.polis.parliament.uk); it provides an excellent database on all sorts of issues related to parliamentary activities in the United Kingdom. Other useful information about Parliament may be obtained from the Committee on Standards in Public Life (www.public-standards.gov.uk) and the Royal Commission for the Reform of the House of Lords (www.lords-reform.org.uk).

For information on the Scottish Parliament, visit www.scottish.parliament.uk. Information on the Welsh Assembly is available at www.wales.gov.uk; for data on the Northern Ireland Assembly, visit www.ni-assembly.gov.uk. The institutional structure and the list of members of the European Parliament are available at www.europarl.eu.int; for a more specific search, visit the UK Office of the European Parliament at www.europarl.org.uk/uk_meps/MembersMain.htm.

The best (and certainly the most fun) source of information about what is happening in Parliament is www.revolts.co.uk (which is run by Philip Cowley of the University of Nottingham). The web pages contain discussion papers, updates and even competitions.

In addition to the parties themselves, there are many institutions devoted to the design of the parties' political agendas and their implementation through Parliament. In this respect, it might be worth looking at some of the issues raised by some of the most prestigious think tanks in the United Kingdom. The Centre for Policy Studies is closely related to the Conservative Party. On its web site you will be able to find a wide range of academic articles combining policy making and conservatism; visit it at www.cps.org.uk/start.htm. For the case of the Liberal Democratic Party, we suggest you visit the Centre for Reform at www.cfr.org.uk; finally, the Fabian Society (www.fabian-society.org.uk/int.asp) and the Institute for Public Policy Research (www.ippr.org) are quite representative of New Labour thinking.

PART 6

Order

chapter 19

The courts and the judiciary

As we have seen in Chapter 4, Parliament is sovereign in the British constitution and this formally remains the case despite Britain's membership of the European Union, devolution to Scotland, Wales and London and its various treaty obligations. Unlike the US Supreme Court, the British courts have no power to declare Acts of Parliament 'unconstitutional'. British judges have, furthermore, traditionally deferred to the executive on a whole range of issues, not least those relating to national security (see Chapter 21). Britain has also hitherto had a 'political' constitution in which many important decisions were governed by conventions that were 'policed' by politicians rather than the courts (see Chapter 4). Thus, while Justices of the Supreme Court in the United States have become major political figures, British judges have – with a few notable exceptions – remained above the political fray. Few politicians felt it necessary to address the judiciary or to factor their reactions into their calculations, let alone warn of the dangers of 'judicial supremacism'.

Yet judges have always had an important role in British politics. Many of the laws that regulate behaviour are the product of the 'common law', which is entirely judge-made. Judicial decisions have had profound implications for individuals' ability to obtain justice, remedy for a breach of contract, compensation for damages caused by negligence and redress for their grievances. While Acts of Parliament override earlier common law, Parliament has not always expressed its wishes clearly and judges have always had to adjudicate where the law is either ambiguous or contradictory. In recent years the volume of legislation produced by Westminster has increased enormously and – as we saw in Chapter 18 – much of it has not been subject to proper scrutiny. Unsurprisingly, some legislation has proved to be contradictory or unworkable. The judges have, therefore, been forced to step in to clear up the mess that Parliament and the executive have caused.

As the final interpreters of the law the judges have always had considerable potential power and have exercised influence intermittently throughout British history. However, as the modern British state became more powerful and it became increasingly clear that Parliament did not hold those who wield power to account, the judiciary became more assertive. Local authorities, tribunals and ministers of the Crown have all increasingly been made to account for their actions to the courts via 'judicial review'. Constitutional changes have added further to the power of the courts. Both the European Communities Act 1972 and the Human Rights Act 1998, for example, have required the judges to adjudicate in cases where laws or high political principles conflict.

The steady encroachment of the courts on issues traditionally reserved for politicians has provoked conflict. Not only have ministers criticised judges with increasing regularity and increasing force, the judiciary itself has felt the need to bite back and criticise politicians for failing to respect them. The resulting greater visibility of judges in the political landscape has led some authors to speculate as to whether the United Kingdom is in the course of developing a 'legal constitution' in which the judges become an autonomous power that is able to resist the will of the executive.

Judges have ceased to be anonymous figures on the margins of the political process. They have made an increasing number of interventions on a range of issues relating to public policy and this too has brought them into conflict with the executive.

This chapter accordingly:

- reviews the proper 'constitutional' role of the courts, the 'separation of powers' and the 'rule of law'
- describes the court systems and recent reforms
- examines the political role of the judges, the growth in 'judicial review' and their 'extra-judicial' activities
- describes the appointment, background and outlook of the judges.

The separation of powers, the rule of law and judicial independence

Law

A body of rules enforced by the power of the State.

It is widely believed that most societies have a natural tendency to concentrate the power of government in the hands of a single individual and that this must be resisted or it will produce autocratic (and bad) government. There are many ways of thinking about the structure of 'government'. Most constitutional thinkers, however, divide it into three branches: the legislature (which makes the laws), the executive (which enforces the **law** and makes government policy) and the judiciary (which interprets and applies the laws to specific cases). It is generally argued that these functions should be separated so that no individual has complete power (a proposition known as the 'separation of powers'). It is also argued that there should be 'checks and balances' to ensure that no individual part of government becomes over-mighty. These constitutional principles predate the principle of parliamentary sovereignty and exist in an uneasy tension with it.

The British constitution reflects the threefold division between the three parts of government: the legislature (in the form of Parliament), the executive (in the form of the Prime Minister, Cabinet and Civil Service) and the judiciary (in the form of the hierarchy of courts discussed below). As we have seen in Chapter 4, however, in the British constitution one branch of government is sovereign. The doctrine of parliamentary supremacy means that Parliament can override any other part of government. It can make any law, act retrospectively and rewrite the constitution. As we have seen in Chapter 18 the electoral system produces a government with a significant majority and party loyalty ensures that the government can usually, if not inevitably, get its way. Writing in the nineteenth century Walter Bagehot referred to this fusion between the executive and legislature as the 'efficient secret' of the British constitution; but it is a secret that also threatens to produce something approaching autocratic government. If the separation of powers is to have any meaning, therefore, it is vitally important that the courts are able to act as a check on the executive. It is here that the 'rule of law' is of such importance.

The rule of law

The proposition that public officials should act under the law and are not above the law. It is contrasted with autocratic or arbitrary government.

The **rule of law** simply means that all power in a community should be subject to general rules. This means that public officials should act under – and not above – the law. Any attempt to 'do justice' simply by setting aside formal rules or departing from established precedents is held to smack dangerously of arbitrary government. Not surprisingly, therefore, some critics equate the rule of law with a rigid formalism, a pedantic adherence to the letter of the law or as a game by which those who know the rules exploit others. Nevertheless, there is a widespread consensus that any public body should establish that it does have the power to act. This naturally implies officials should not determine the limits of their own powers and that the limits of their powers must be determined by a properly independent and impartial judiciary.

Many constitutional thinkers (and, in particular, many lawyers) regard judicial independence as a fundamental part of the constitution. Although senior judges are

Plate 19.1 The British courts used to be a marginal institution in the United Kingdom. With developments in judicial review and human rights law they are now one of the more important institutions
Source: Alamy/Peter Horee

appointed on the recommendation of the Lord Chancellor and Prime Minister, they are subsequently protected from political pressure in the following ways:

■ Their salaries are charged on the Consolidated Fund and are not subject to annual review by the House of Commons.

■ MPs cannot comment on cases currently before the courts (the so-called *sub-judice* rule).

■ They also enjoy judicial immunity for all acts said and done in court and are, therefore, not subject to improper outside pressure (including public opinion).

■ Ministers are required to uphold the continued independence of the judiciary.

■ Ministers are required not to use their 'special access' in order to influence the court's judgments (s.3 Constitutional Reform Act (CRA), 2005).

■ Senior judges cannot be sacked by ministers. Judges in the High Court and above remain in office during good behaviour until they reach the normal retirement age of 70 (though this can be extended to 75 in the case of senior judges). In law they can be removed on an address to the Crown brought by *both* Houses of Parliament. This power has not been used since 1830.

■ The Lord Chancellor is subject to a special requirement to uphold the independence of the judiciary (s.1 CRA 2005). He is also required to swear the following oath: 'I do swear that in the office of Lord High Chancellor of Great Britain I will respect the rule of law, defend the independence of the judiciary and discharge my duty to ensure the provision of resources for the efficient and effective support of the courts for which I am responsible. So help me God.'

The effective independence of the judiciary provides them with enough autonomous power to leave them free to decide cases according to their understanding of the law: the words used in statute, well-known rules of construction and judicial **precedent**. They are free to provide impartial judgments that favour no particular group. If they feel that they are unable to be partial (or, just as important, to be seen to be impartial), they must decline to hear the case ('recuse themselves'). Failure to do so may lead to an appeal. This is very rare, but happened in a high-profile case in 1998. Lord Hoffman, one of the most senior and experienced judges in the land, heard a case relating to the application to extradite General Pinochet, the former dictator of Chile, to Spain. Hoffmann was also a director and chairperson of Amnesty International Charity Limited. Amnesty International itself intervened and made representations in the case. Although the General's lawyers did not allege that Hoffman was biased, the appearance of bias was enough for the Lords to set aside their own judgment. A different panel of judges heard the case a second time. They came to the same conclusion: that Pinochet did not enjoy diplomatic immunity and could be extradited. In March 2000 Jack Straw declined to extradite the General to face charges in Spain on the grounds of his ill-health.

In principle judicial independence and professional norms should ensure that there is great confidence in the judiciary. In the past, however, judges were said to be reactionary, conservative (with a small 'c'), anti-Labour or anti-trade union. More recently, they have been accused of being unduly liberal or driven by a 'human rights' agenda that ignores the rights of society to protect itself from threats (criminals, terrorists and asylum seekers). In every generation critics have argued

Precedent

A decision or practice of the past that is accepted as a guide for the present. In the law, precedents are past decisions of the courts that are thought to apply to similar legal problems or situations in the present.

Plate 19.2 Lord Hoffmann's short judgment in the Pinochet case caused embarrassment when it was revealed that he had links with Amnesty International, a party to the case. The House of Lords had to hear the case again

Source: Empics

that since judges are unelected they should defer to Parliament (and, in effect, the executive). This is an issue that we will return to at the end of this chapter.

Having covered these basic considerations, it is now time to examine the structure of the court systems in the United Kingdom.

Court systems in the United Kingdom

The court structure of England and Wales (it differs in Scotland and Northern Ireland) is summarised in Figure 19.1. In the localities are the magistrates' courts, which outside the main conurbations are staffed by part-time, unpaid laypeople.

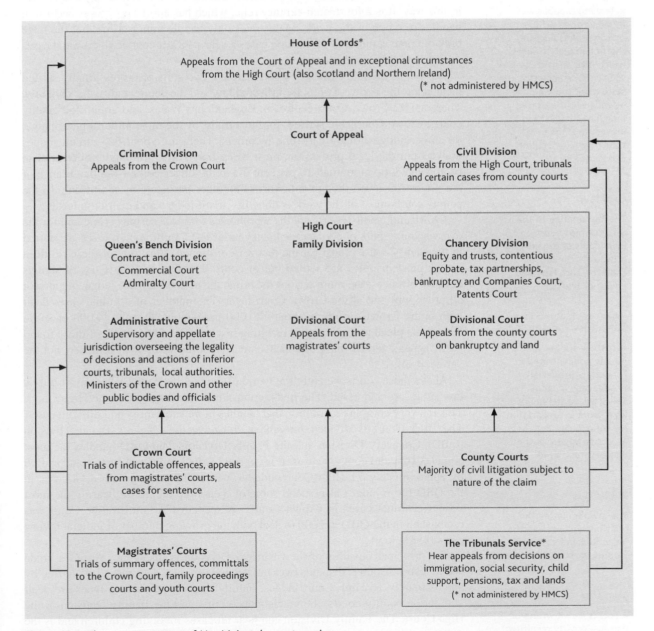

Figure 19.1 The court structure of Her Majesty's court service

Source: http://www.hmcourts-service.gov.uk/aboutus/structure/index.htm. Reproduced under the terms of the Click-Use Licence

These are local notables, appointed by secret committees nominated by the Lord Chancellor. There are over 30,000 magistrates, known as justices of the peace (JPs) roughly half of whom are male and half female. Although magistrates' courts are sometimes described as 'the people's courts', JPs are in no sense representative of the populations in their areas. There is no direct public participation in their selection. JPs do, however, have more contact with local communities than professional, full-time judges. They deal with most minor crime and also decide whether more serious cases should be sent for trial by judge and jury in the Crown Court. The crimes they deal with are minor but they have, and very often use, the power to imprison for up to six months. Although they are aided by legally trained clerks the biggest problem about the magistrates' courts is the significant variation from area to area in sentencing practices.

England and Wales is the only jurisdiction in the world to rely on lay magistrates in this way. It is a fourteenth-century relic, which has enormous power because it handles so much of the work. Magistrates only handle minor crime, but the huge bulk of crime is minor. Two million cases a year – 98 per cent of all criminal cases – start and end with magistrates.

As well as the magistrates' courts, there are two sorts of professionally staffed local court: the Crown Courts for **criminal law** and the county courts for **civil law**. There are 92 Crown Court centres in England and Wales, and about 260 county courts. Crown Courts are staffed, for most trials, by the most junior type of judge, the circuit judges, or by part-time recorders. There are about 624 circuit judges drawn from the legal profession, most being **barristers**. Although **solicitors** can be appointed, no more than 10 per cent of circuit judges come from that branch of the profession, even though solicitors outnumber barristers by ten to one. In the county courts most of the work is done by circuit judges and district judges.

Crown and county courts are the workhorses for more serious crime and for the overwhelming bulk of civil cases. Each year over 2.5 million civil cases are started in the county courts, most for the recovery of money. Very few of these result in a trial; most disputes are settled out of court. The Crown Courts try all serious criminal offences; the more serious the crime the more senior the judge, but almost all crime will end at the Crown Court level. The number of criminal cases dealt with in the Crown Courts is about 120,000 per annum. In only 34,000 or so do defendants plead not guilty, thus resulting in a full trial. Only 8,000 of those found guilty appeal, and the bulk of appeals are against the severity of sentence, not the verdict itself.

Above these courts we enter the world of the real legal elite where most **public law** issues are addressed. The first step up in the legal system is the High Court. This is a very complex institution that handles more substantial and difficult cases. The High Court is divided into three divisions, the Queen's Bench Division (QBD), Chancery Division and the Family Division. The QBD handles the most complex **tort** and contract cases. It is headed by the Lord Chief Justice and staffed by approximately 71 High Court judges. As well as dealing with civil cases in the QBD these judges also spend some of their time on circuit hearing the most serious criminal cases in Crown Courts. A specialist Administrative Court was established in the QBD in 2000 to deal with the growing number of judicial review cases (see below).

The principal business of the Chancery Division is insolvency disputes, trade and industry disputes, disputes over intellectual property and trusts. It is staffed by approximately 16 High Court judges. Family disputes of various types are dealt with in the county courts, the magistrates' courts and the Family Division of the High Court. The Family Division can hear all cases involving children and is the only court that has jurisdiction in wardship matters. It is staffed by approximately 19 High Court judges.

Criminal law

Relates to a public and moral wrong (such as murder, manslaughter, theft or sexual offences) which is of such great social importance that the state itself must punish the offender. In the United Kingdom the decision to prosecute is taken by the Crown Prosecution Service (CPS).

Civil law

The law relating to the relationships between individuals or organisations. It includes the law of contract, tort, land and equity or trusts.

Barristers and solicitors

Barristers are lawyers, mostly concentrated in London, who specialise in advocacy in court. Solicitors do the bulk of legal work in preparation for court judgments but access to appear in the courts is restricted.

Public law

The law regulating the relationship between the individual and state or various parts of the state.

Tort law

A tort is a civil wrong or damage mostly resulting from negligence.

The Court of Appeal is divided into the Criminal Division and the Civil Division. It is staffed by the Lord Chief Justice who heads its Criminal Division, the Master of the Rolls who heads its Civil Division, and by 33 Lord Justices of Appeal. (Lord Justices are not Law Lords. Law Lords sit in the Appellate Committee of the House of Lords (see later).) The Criminal Division hears appeals from the Crown Courts and handles in the region of 7,000 appeals a year, most of which are appeals against the sentence imposed rather than the verdict itself. The Civil Division hears approximately 1,000 appeals a year from decisions of the High Court, county courts and certain tribunals.

Most jurisdictions have only one court of appeal, but Britain has two. Above the Court of Appeal is the Appellate Committee of the House of Lords, which is technically a committee of the House of Lords. (It is also commonly known as the 'Judicial Committee of the House of Lords' or simply 'the House of Lords'). This consists of 12 specially created life peers known as the Lords of Appeal in Ordinary (more commonly '**the Law Lords**'). These are lawyers who have reached the very summit of the legal profession. By convention, two will be Scots lawyers. This court is also the ultimate Court of Appeal from Scotland but only on civil matters. On criminal cases the High Court of Justiciary in Edinburgh gives the final rulings.

The House of Lords handles fewer than 200 cases a year and there is no automatic right of appeal to it. 'Leave' (permission) to appeal is granted either by the Lords themselves or by the Court of Appeal. It only handles those cases that have far-reaching implications. Unlike all other courts, the House of Lords has the power to overrule itself (a power acquired in 1966). This has enabled the law to adapt new conditions when there is an urgent need to do so. The Constitutional Reform Act 2005 will create a Supreme Court, which will move out of the House or Lords and to its new site by 2009.

There are two other legal structures that have a potential impact on politics. At a level lower than the High Court are innumerable tribunals and appeal tribunals, which handle a massive and diverse range of disputes between individuals and public bodies. There is also the Judicial Committee of the Privy Council, which is essentially the Law Lords under another name. This Committee acts as a final court of appeal from certain Commonwealth and colonial countries. It also deals with disputes between Westminster and Holyrood in relation to Scottish devolution.

Courts in Northern Ireland, although separate, closely resemble the English, with less emphasis on lay magistrates and juries. The law administered there derives largely from English common law, modified for Irish conditions and shaped to some extent by acts of the former Northern Irish Parliament between 1922 and 1972. There is an Appeal Court in Belfast, but the House of Lords has ultimate jurisdiction.

The Scottish system is more distinctive. While there are district courts with lay magistrates, the major court is the Sheriff Court, with jurisdiction over a considerable population and area, and powers to try all but major criminal and civil cases. The sheriff is a professional lawyer. At the centre of the system are the 18 senators of the College of Justice in Edinburgh, who staff both the chief civil court, the Court of Session, and the chief criminal court, the High Court of Justiciary. Other judges than those who tried the original case sit as a Court of Criminal Appeal, which is the final authority. There are also appeals in civil cases from the Outer to the Inner House of the Session, but the final authority is the Appellate Committee of the House of Lords, sitting with two Scottish Lords of Appeal.

These institutional differences are reflected in the different nature of the law administered in Scottish courts. This diverges from the English system in two major ways. The actual law, in the sense of the legal rules applied by courts, often

The Law Lords

The highest court in the United Kingdom. Also known as the Lords of Appeal in Ordinary, the Appellate Committee of the House of Lords and (from 2009) Justices of the Supreme Court.

BRIEFINGS

19.1 The Supreme Court and Lord Chancellor

The House of Lords is the highest court in the United Kingdom. Unusually among such courts it is physically located within the upper (or second) chamber of Parliament. Also unusually the Law Lords are allowed to take part and, what is more, to vote in the House of Lords (though, by convention, they do not take part in partisan debates).

These features of the House of Lords are striking exceptions to the 'separation of powers' doctrine. They were defended on the usual grounds that the system worked well, that the upper chamber benefited from having access to the best legal advice available and that the Law Lords also found it useful to keep themselves informed about political developments. Nevertheless, it did produce some problems:

- The Law Lords could often find itself hearing a case relating to legislation that they had previously voted on (though they could preclude themselves from doing so).

- The Law Lords could appear to have conflicts of interest and look less than impartial. In January 1997, they heard an appeal in the morning over the decision by the Home Secretary relating to the length of time that the killers of Jamie Bulger should spend in detention and then moved downstairs in the building to vote against the same Home Secretary's proposals to impose mandatory life sentences for repeat offenders. Imagine how this might have seemed to the Home Secretary!

The position of the Lord Chancellor was even more anomalous since he had three roles: head of the judiciary (and often active member of the Appellate Committee), senior member of the executive (Cabinet) and member of the legislature (he chaired the House of Lords). He has also traditionally acted, in effect, as the voice of the judiciary within government. In short, the Lord Chancellor was required to wear a large number of hats all at once and there was always the possibility of a conflict between these various roles.

The Constitutional Reform Act (2005) (CRA) effectively removes both these anomalies. The Law Lords will no longer sit as a committee of the House of Lords and will no longer vote in the legislature. They will have their own budget, staff, and ultimately their own building. Their powers are fundamentally unaltered.

Lord Irvine's tenure as Lord Chancellor (1997–2003) was sometimes controversial. He personally decided which cases he would sit on and chose to sit on cases where the government had a decided interest in the outcome. Shortly before the 2001 election he wrote to barristers who were known to be supporters of Labour, inviting them to make donations. Critics wondered aloud whether these decisions might not influence his decision as to who would be elevated to become a Queen's Counsel and muttered darkly about conflicts of interest.

Lord Falconer was appointed as the Secretary of State for Constitutional Affairs and Lord Chancellor in 2003. Although a practising barrister, he was not thought to be sufficiently qualified to be a senior judge (and he was vulnerable to accusations that he had not got the post on merit because he was Tony Blair's former flatmate). It was accordingly announced that he would not act in a judicial capacity. It was later announced that the office of Lord Chancellor be abolished, but this caused an outcry in the House of Lords, the senior judiciary and the legal profession as a whole. Some feared that the courts would no longer have the ability to communicate their concerns discretely via the Lord Chancellor (as they had done in the past). The Lord Chancellor and Lord Chief Justice produced a 'concordat' on future reforms and many of these proposals were included in the resulting CRA.

The CRA states that the Lord Chancellor will no longer sit as a judge, will no longer exercise judicial functions and must have certain qualifications (exactly what these are is decided by the Prime Minister). Many of the Lord Chancellor's remaining functions will be transferred to the Lord Chief Justice or other senior judges. The CRA imposes a duty on ministers to uphold the independence of the judiciary by not seeking to influence their decisions via their 'special access' and places a special duty on the Lord Chancellor to support the judges. It also gives the Lord Chief Justice the ability to make representations to Parliament on any matter relating to administration of justice.

In July 2006, Baroness Hayman became the newly elected chair of the Lords. With these reforms in place the UK will have a clearer separation of powers. Physical distance from Parliament may also subtly alter the relationship between the judiciary and the executive and make the former more assertive.

differs from equivalent rules in England. Property law, for example, retains much more of the feudal inheritance than does the English law of real estate. These differences are becoming greater now that separate legislation for Scotland is produced by the new Scottish Parliament. It seems likely, for example, that there will be greater freedom of information than in England under new Scottish legislation. Second, the sources of Scots law, and the general theory of law are different. Although this difference can be exaggerated, Scots lawyers operate under a system heavily influenced by Roman law, as in Continental Europe. There is no room here to discuss Scotland separately. Much of what is said here will still be true of Scottish courts and judges, but not all. It will certainly be the case, however, that any conclusions about the autonomy and political importance of English judges will apply equally to Scottish judges (and for that matter to Northern Irish judges).

The political role of the courts

The growing recourse to legal action to resolve political disputes means that the higher courts have an important role mediating between:

- individuals and all branches of government

- central and local government

- British central and local government and the European Union.

Conservative legislation of the 1980s, particularly the laws regulating industrial relations and trade union activities, extended the supervisory and decision-making powers of the courts into new areas, where they often find themselves in conflict with powerful political interests.

All this has happened in a system where the courts lack what has often been taken as the distinguishing mark of a 'political' jurisdiction, that is, the power of **'constitutional review'**. Constitutional review in its layperson's sense means a system in which laws and other acts of the legislature can be overruled by a court if they are held to conflict with constitutional rules, basic human rights or any other laws treated as superior to ordinary legislation. In *Marbury* v *Madison* (1803), for example, the Supreme Court decided that it could invalidate those Acts of Congress or the state legislatures that contradicted the constitution. Courts with similar powers exist in Canada, Australia and Germany among other countries and, as we have seen in the *Factortame* case (1993) in Chapter 4, the European Court of Justice has similar powers (regarding EU law) in relation to member states such as Britain. A little-mentioned fact about such national courts, however, is that many seldom use it! Only a handful of congressional acts have been overruled in the United States since the 1930s. In Canada, Australia and Germany the use of a court to veto legislation is even rarer. Nevertheless, no one will try to argue that these supreme courts are not politically important. In each of these countries the courts are real political 'players' and their likely attitude towards legislation must be taken into account by legislatures.

When this sort of power belongs to a court its judges are clearly of political importance. Until recently most experts would have agreed that no such power belonged to English courts: no Act of Parliament could be brought before a court and challenged as to its basic lawfulness. (Scottish courts have asserted vague claims to do this on occasion, but have never actually done so). This is part of the general doctrine that Parliament is supreme (Chapter 4).

Constitutional review

The process by which laws and other acts of the legislature can be overruled by a court if the court holds them to conflict with constitutional rules, human rights or other laws treated as superior to legislation.

In recent years there has been a significant growth in the political importance of the courts. The judges have developed the principles of judicial review to a point where they are now prepared to scrutinise the actions of all public bodies to ensure that their decisions are *legal*, *fair* and *reasonable*. This has increased the risk of dispute between the judiciary and the legislature or (more accurately given the executive's domination of Parliament) between the judiciary and the executive. This is illustrated by the (well-chosen) title of one recent book on the subject *Trial of Strength: The Battle Between Ministers and Judges over Who Makes the Law*. The author rightly omits any mention of Parliament, though both the judiciary and ministers claim the authority of Parliament in their battles with one another.

Judicial review

Judicial review is simply the High Court's power to ensure that public bodies (ministers, local authorities, tribunals and so on), do not act unlawfully. This method of seeking a redress of grievance is *only* appropriate where there is no alternative remedy available and where the application is brought promptly (and in any event within three months) of the events complained of. Thus, many applications are brought out of time and never reach a formal hearing.

This supervisory role is justified by two approaches: the **ultra vires** approach and the *common law* approach. These have radically different implications for both the scope of judicial review and for the relationship between the judges and the executive.

> **Ultra vires**
>
> Where a public body (minister, local authority or tribunal) acts 'beyond the powers' granted to them by Parliament.

The *ultra vires* doctrine

The first approach treats judicial review as simply a means of ensuring that public bodies (ministers, local authorities, tribunals and even private companies carrying out public duties) do not exceed the powers that are granted to them. Where such a body acts outside the scope of the powers that are given to it by Parliament it is said to have acted 'unlawfully' or (in Latin) '*ultra vires*' (meaning 'beyond powers'). The courts have regularly declared that they are not interested in the 'merits' (i.e. the 'rightness' or 'wrongness' of the act), merely in its legality. Where a court finds that a public body has acted unlawfully it can quash the original decision, require the decision maker to decide again or prohibit them from acting in an unlawful manner. It cannot substitute the decision with its own.

While judicial review is entirely 'judge-made' law its justification is, according to this view, essentially democratic. The courts are merely ensuring that public bodies comply with the will of Parliament. Thus, if a local authority is given a subjectively worded (and inherently vague) power to do X, the courts assume that the scope of that power is limited by the objects of the legislation and that the authority does not have the power to do Y. Determining the meaning of words is, of course, exactly what most lawyers (and most judges) spend all their careers training to do!

In the past 50 years the *ultra vires* doctrine has been developed to cover cases where the public body has:

- *Made errors of law* or (in certain cases) *errors of fact*.

- *Acted out of ulterior motives* (e.g. used their powers to produce partisan advantages).

- *Fettered their discretion* (e.g. by applying a rigid rule and failing to consider the specific facts of a case).

- *Acted so unreasonably that no reasonable authority could ever have come to it.* This final ground for review, discussed first in the *Wednesbury* case of 1948, has caused particular problems since it comes close to allowing the court to arrive at a view about the 'merits' of a decision and risks replacing the decision of a public body with that of a judge.

We have seen in Chapters 2 and 3 that the scope of government activity has expanded throughout the twentieth century and that various public bodies have been given extensive discretionary powers (in order to resolve disputes or make decisions about eligibility for benefits). In particular, there has been a massive growth in the number of administrative tribunals:

- asylum and immigration

- finance and tax tribunals

- lands tribunal

- pensions appeal tribunal

- social security and child support commissioners

- Gender Recognition Panel (created in 2004 to ensure transsexual people acquire the rights of their acquired gender).

We have also seen in Chapter 18 that Parliament is often unable (or simply unwilling) to hold ministers to account (let alone other public bodies such as the various quangos, councils and tribunals). In many cases, therefore, judicial review offers individuals their *only* chance of seeking a redress of their grievances.

Many of the judicial review cases relate to decisions taken by the executive. Powerful public figures rarely like their powers to be checked by others. It was no surprise, therefore, that ministers tried to rein in the judges by putting 'ouster clauses' into Acts, which declared that their 'decisions' could not be challenged in the courts. These attempts failed. The *Anisminic* case (1969) established that the courts would always assume that Parliament granted powers on the assumption that the body concerned would not exceed their powers. This was a matter for the courts – and for the courts alone – to determine. It is not easy, therefore, to exclude judicial review.

The *ultra vires* doctrine treats judges as the watchdogs of Parliament who ensure that ministers, officials and public bodies operate within the powers granted to them. For that reason they are unlikely to review non-statutory powers, such as the 'prerogative powers' exercised by the monarch on the advice of ministers of the Crown. Even where the powers were granted under statute, however, judges sometimes deferred to ministers, especially in relation to matters of national security.

This is illustrated by an old case from 1942. Defence regulations issued in 1939, for example, gave the Secretary of State the power to detain individuals where there was 'reasonable cause to believe' that they had hostile associations. In *Liversidge* v *Anderson*, however, the House of Lords declined to make the minister show that his beliefs were reasonable and, in effect, added the words 'if the Minister believes (he has reasonable cause to believe)'. The effect in this case (which long predates the Human Rights Act) was to deny an individual their liberty despite the express wording of the statute!

In this case Lord Atkin criticised his brother judges. He declared: 'I view with apprehension the attitude of judges who on a *mere question of construction* when face to face with claims involving the liberty of the subject show themselves *more executive minded than the executive* . . . In this country, amid the clash of arms, the laws are not silent. They may be changed, but they speak the same language in war as in peace. It has always been one of the pillars of freedom, one of the principles of liberty for which on recent authority we are now fighting, that the judges are no respecters of persons and stand between the subject and any attempted encroachments on his liberty by the executive, alert to see that any coercive action is justified in law' (emphasis added).

Lord Atkin was in a minority in 1942 but his words have a modern ring to them. As we shall later see, Lord Hoffman said much the same thing in a case about powers to detain terrorist suspects without trial in 2005 (see Briefing 19.3).

In addition to the *ultra vires* doctrine the courts have also developed tests of '**natural justice**' or 'procedural impropriety'. The process began in earnest with the case of *Ridge* v. *Baldwin* (1964), which related to the sacking of the Chief Constable of Brighton. The courts have set aside various decisions where:

- *There has been a violation of statutory procedures.*

- *The decision maker is biased* (or might be thought to be biased).

- *There has not been a fair hearing* (e.g. has not been given a chance to put their case).

- *There is a failure to give reasons for decisions* (e.g. dismissal from office without being told why).

The net effect of various court judgments is that decisions within government are increasingly made in the way that they are made in court: according to publicly stated procedures.

The principles of *ultra vires* and *natural justice* have been used to justify substantial judicial activism in the post-war period. In 1980 there were a mere 533 applications for judicial review, but by 2000 this had risen to 4,247 (see Figure 19.2). Not all these applications were accepted and resulted in a full hearing. Many of these applications and hearings related to immigration matters and the decisions reached by various tribunals. The decisions often had implications for government

Natural justice

Procedural rules designed to ensure fairness, including the right to a hearing, lack of bias on the part of the decision-maker and so on.

Figure 19.2 Applications for permission to seek judicial review, 1980–2000

Source: HMSO. Reproduced under the terms of the Click-Use Licence

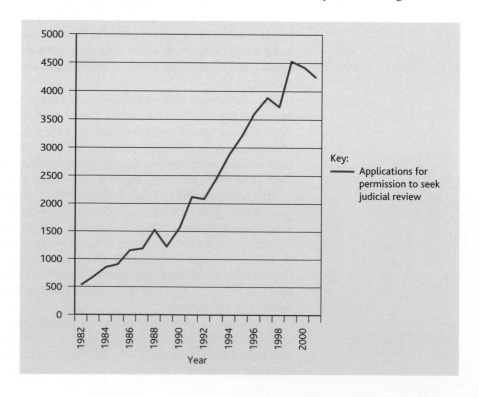

Key:
—— Applications for permission to seek judicial review

departments and ministers, who have responded angrily. In February 2003 David Blunkett expressed fury with a judge for ruling new rules relating to the payment of welfare benefits to asylum seekers illegal. He said: 'I'm fed up with having to deal with a situation where Parliament debates issues and the judges overturn them'. Both ministers and the courts, of course, claimed to be upholding the will of Parliament, but this has barely concealed the naked struggle for power, especially in relation to those 'grey areas' that are not clearly the responsibility of any part of government.

This conflict between the judges and ministers has intensified in recent years as a result of continued developments in the common law and the Human Rights Act 1998.

Developments in the common law

The second (and newer) approach to judicial review extends it considerably by suggesting that the courts have an inherent power to protect individual (or community) rights and interests. According to this view, judicial review is not simply about serving the intention of Parliament but is rather rooted in the common law and constitutional principles such as the separation of powers. This justification has been used to:

- *Extend the scope of review to prerogative powers and non-statutory bodies*. In 1985 the court allowed workers to challenge the government's actions, based on a prerogative power, to ban trade unions at GCHQ (though they ultimately did not overturn the ban).

- *Shift the emphasis from reasonableness to proportionality*. In late 2004, for example, the House of Lords held that the indefinite detention of terrorist suspects without trial in Belmarsh prison was disproportionate (since the same goals could have been achieved with less draconian legislation) (Briefing 19.3).

This new approach has increased the danger of conflict between the executive and judiciary. The proposition that the courts can judge whether the actions are 'proportionate' seems close to suggesting that the courts can consider the 'merits' of a decision and, in effect, replace the decision made by ministers with their own.

There are, however, limits to judicial review. Some judges (speaking generally or writing extra-judicially) have questioned the concept of the supremacy of Parliament, the courts have made it clear that any Act of Parliament which interfered with basic democratic rights, such as the right to free speech, would require express and very clear provisions; otherwise the courts would assume that Parliament meant not to interfere with such rights. If the Act did use such words the courts would have little choice but to apply it. Similarly, there are clear limits on the court's willingness to review decisions made under prerogative powers. Some powers, such as the granting of passports and the management of the Civil Service can be reviewed by the courts, since they relate to issues of procedure that the courts feel able to pass judgment on. Others, relating to the appointment of ministers or the dissolution of Parliament, will not be reviewed since the courts have no especial claim to expertise about such issues.

The Human Rights Act 1998

The Human Rights Act (HRA) gave further effect to the European Convention on Human Rights (ECHR) in British law. Not all of the 18 articles of the ECHR were included in the HRA. Those that were given further effect include:

2. Right to life

3. Prohibition on torture

4. Prohibition on slavery and forced labour

5. Right to liberty and security

6. Right to a fair trial

7. No punishment without trial

8. Right to respect for private and family life

9. Freedom of thought, conscience and religion

10. Freedom of expression

11. Freedom of assembly and association

12. Right to marry

14. Prohibition on discrimination

16. Restrictions on political activity of aliens

17. Prohibition on abuse of rights

18. Limitation of use on restrictions of rights.

Although many British politicians were sympathetic to the general approach enshrined in the ECHR they were concerned that a foreign court should not be seen to override Parliament. Thus, although the British government ratified the convention in 1951 (and it came into force in 1953) Britons did not obtain the right to directly petition the European Court of Human Rights in Strasbourg until 1966. Until the HRA the courts took into account the ECHR where a parliamentary statute was ambiguous or where the common law was unclear.

The HRA was enacted in such a way as to preserve the supremacy of Parliament. It requires ministers to include a statement on legislation that they believe its provisions to be compatible with the ECHR or a statement that they do not. If this were to happen, of course, the courts will be made aware of Parliament's intention to legislate in these terms. The main provisions of the HRA are as follows:

- s.3 requires courts to interpret all legislation (statutes and delegated legislation both past and present) in such a way as to be compatible with the ECHR 'so far as it is possible to do so';

- s.4 declares that when it is not possible to interpret legislation in a way that is compatible with convention rights the court may issue a 'declaration of incompatibility';

- s.6 makes it unlawful for any public authority to act in a way that is incompatible with convention rights.

The courts do not have the power to strike down an Act of Parliament. They do have the power to strike down delegated legislation if it cannot be interpreted as being compatible with convention rights. If a declaration of incompatibility is made there are 'fast-track' procedures that allow a minister to bring a statutory instrument before Parliament in order to remove the conflict.

A great deal of comment has focused on those dramatic instances when the courts have issued a declaration of incompatibility under s.4. Yet while this appears to represent a dramatic exercise of judicial power it is s.3 that provides the courts with a 'quasi-legislative' power and may lead to concerns about the law been altered by unelected judges. After all, if the courts make a declaration under s.4 of the Act, the ball is firmly back in Parliament's (for which read 'the executive's') court. They can choose to revise legislation to make it compatible with convention rights or not. S.3 can be regarded as authorising the courts to make whatever changes are possible to ensure that all past and future law is compatible with convention rights.

This is illustrated by the case of *Ghaidan* v. *Mendoza* (2004). This related to the 1977 Rent Act, which allowed the 'spouse' of a protected tenant to succeed to the tenancy on the tenant's death. A further amendment allowed 'couples living together as man and wife' to enjoy the same rights. In this case, however, the couple were homosexuals. The tenant had died and his partner tried to claim his rights to succeed under the 1977 Act as the surviving partner. (If he had not won his case he would still have been allowed to make a claim for tenancy as a member of the 'family', but under less favourable terms.) The House of Lords held that while the wording of the Act was unambiguous, it was possible to interpret it as referring to homosexual couples, since to do otherwise would violate article 8 of the ECHR (respect for private life) and article 14 (relating to discrimination). The court argued that it was clear that the thrust of the legislation was to protect couples.

This case illustrates the way in which s.3 provides the court with authority to 'rewrite' legislation. It also illustrates how the HRA has increased the rights of individuals, since a similar case heard before the HRA had come into effect decided that a surviving homosexual partner had no right to succeed as tenant. It also shows how different judges can come to different decisions. One of the five Law Lords who heard the case, Lord Millett, agreed that the effect of the Act was discriminatory and thought that this discrimination should be removed. However, he felt it was not 'possible' to interpret the Act in such a way as to be compatible with the ECHR. He maintained that arguments that the homosexual couple had formed a loving and stable relationship were irrelevant because the Act focused on the status of the couple ('man and wife' or 'living as man and wife') not whether

BRIEFINGS

19.2 The courts, asylum and welfare payments

The Labour government became increasingly concerned about the number of people claiming asylum in the late 1990s. Ministers, the national press and public opinion were convinced that there were many 'bogus' asylum seekers, using the asylum system in order to move to Britain and claim welfare payments.

David Blunkett, a 'no-nonsense' (some would say 'populist') Home Secretary, introduced a series of reforms to combat the problem. One of these was a regulation that those who claimed asylum must do so at the first possible opportunity (which would usually be when they first entered the country), otherwise they would lose their entitlement to welfare payments. When the case was heard by Mr Justice Collins in February 2003, he found in favour of several asylum seekers who claimed that this new system was unfair (especially since the immigration officials who interviewed asylum seekers did not try to establish why the individual had not claimed asylum on entry to the United Kingdom, and many asylum seekers fleeing persecution were often confused or ignorant about the rules). This judgment provoked a great deal of criticism from the Home Office. Mr Justice Collins was vilified in the popular press. Richard Littlejohn, the *Sun* columnist, complained 'Judges take no account of the will of Parliament or the will of the British people.' ('Men in wigs and the magic words', the *Sun*, 21 February 2003).

The Home Office appealed. In *R* v *Secretary of State for the Home Department* ex. parte *Q and others* (2003) the Court of Appeal agreed with Mr Justice Collins and recommended that a new (and fairer) system be introduced. They regarded the case as a simple application of principles of natural justice and the HRA.

The Court of Appeal was evidently unmoved by the opinions of the press.

BRIEFINGS

19.3 The courts and anti-terrorist legislation

International developments and the increasing threat of home-grown terrorism have increased the importance of issues such as asylum, immigration and crime. In 2001 David Blunkett, the Home Secretary, speculated about the need to suspend the HRA in order to provide the police with enough powers to tackle the threat. The government responded to increasing public concerns by introducing new powers to detain those suspected of links to terrorism under s.23 of the Anti-terrorism, Crime and Security Act 2001. Blunkett himself issued a series of speeches in which he proclaimed his determination to overcome judicial opposition.

Those who were detained under the Act could leave the country if they could find a state willing to accept them, but some could not and some faced the real threat of torture or execution. They could not, therefore, simply be deported. A wholly new category of person had been created who was too dangerous to release but too rights laden to deport. Nine of the individuals held at Belmarsh prison in South London appealed to the courts.

The case of *A and others* v *Secretary of State for the Home Department; X and another* v *Secretary of State for the Home Department* was heard by the House of Lords in 2004. In a mark of the importance of the case nine (rather than the usual five) Law Lords gave judgment. Eight of the nine decided that these actions were incompatible with convention rights under the HRA because (1) they discriminated against non-British nationals and (2) the detentions were 'disproportionate'. They issued a declaration of incompatibility under s.4 of the HRA.

Most of the judges who heard this case expressed themselves in the cautious language of judges. Lord Hoffmann, however, echoed Lord Atkin's comments from 60 years earlier in *Liversidge* v *Anderson* in declaring that '. . . The real threat to the life of the nation, in the sense of a people living in accordance with its traditional laws and political values, comes not from terrorism but from laws such as these. That is the true measure of what terrorism may achieve. It is for Parliament to decide whether to give the terrorists such a victory.'

The ruling was widely viewed as a disaster for the government's policy. The detainees, however, remained in prison until Parliament introduced a new system of 'control orders', which restricted those individuals' freedoms in prescribed ways (e.g. by requiring them to remain at certain addresses, not communicate with certain individuals and so on). This new system was compatible with convention rights.

In the aftermath of the July 2005 bombings in London, the demand to 'do something' increased again (see Chapter 21) and there was much muttering about the weakness of the courts. In October 2005 Lord Phillips, the new Lord Chief Justice, declared, 'It is never right for a minister to tell a judge how to interpret legislation. Occasionally one feels that a politician is trying to browbeat the judiciary, and that is wholly inappropriate'. Several judgments subsequently reinforced judicial independence.

In *A and others* v *Secretary of State for the Home Department (No 2)*, (2005) the Law Lords overruled the Court of Appeal and declared that evidence obtained through torture of third parties was not admissible in court. The court also held that there was an obligation to inquire how the evidence was obtained (though they did not go as far as some judges wanted by making the prosecution demonstrate beyond all reasonable doubt that the evidence had not been obtained by torture). Lord Bingham declared, 'The principles of the common law, standing alone, in my opinion compel the exclusion of third-party torture evidence as unreliable, unfair, offensive to ordinary standards of humanity and decency and incompatible with the principles which should animate a tribunal seeking to administer justice'. The court also held reliance on such evidence inadmissible as a result of the HRA.

In contrast with the aggressive approach taken by David Blunkett, the then Home Secretary Charles Clarke welcomed the ruling as clarifying the law. This was widely taken as suggesting that the new Home Secretary would seek to work with the courts in producing workable legislation, rather than engage in a war of words via the media.

they had a loving and stable relationship. He preferred, therefore, to make a declaration of incompatibility under s.4 and leave it for Parliament to sort out the issue. The majority of the court disagreed, but the case demonstrates that there may be clear differences of opinion as to whether it is 'possible' to interpret legislation so that it is compatible with the ECHR.

BRIEFINGS

19.4 Judicial autonomy: sentencing

Another area of conflict between ministers and judges has related to penal policy. In general most politicians have responded to public (and media) concern by promising to 'crack down' on criminals and 'get tough' on trouble-makers. Judges have often expressed grave doubts as to whether increased penalties and custodial sentences will work (and can cite report after report in support of that view). Nevertheless, 'populist' politicians have tried to reduce the judiciary's room for discretion in various ways:

- Michael Howard (1994–7) was a Home Secretary with strong 'law and order' credentials. He introduced mandatory minimum sentences. The prison population rose from around 40,000 to 60,000.

- Jack Straw (1997–2001). In opposition Straw matched Howard's 'tough' policies almost point for point. In office he introduced a number of reforms, such as increased use of tagging. Nevertheless the prison population rose from around 60,000 to 66,000 during his tenure at the Home Office.

- David Blunkett (2001–4) was a Home Secretary with authoritarian instincts. He introduced new guidelines designed to ensure that some (particularly repugnant) murderers would get long sentences. The judiciary and many judges objected to the removal of their discretion. In May 2003 Blunkett told the Police Federation: 'There has been a rumour that I am not at all pleased with the judges. This is completely untrue. I just like judges to live in the same real world as the rest of us.' Sir Oliver Popplewell, a former judge, responded, 'The job of a judge is to interpret the law,' he said. 'Politicians hate people being independent. They want to control it. It is control freakery.'

The senior judges were appalled by efforts to curb their discretion and by the growing size of the prison population. They pointed out that the practice of allowing a politician to fix the terms of prisoners violated article 6 of the ECHR. In 2002 Lord Woolf (speaking extra-judicially) argued that the Home Secretary should no longer play a part in fixing the sentence for those imprisoned for 'life'. The Home Office declared, 'The government believes it is necessary for the maintenance of public confidence in the criminal justice system that decisions relating to the length of time a murderer spends in custody and release are taken by the Home Secretary, who is directly accountable to Parliament'. Many of the tabloid newspapers agreed, arguing that it would be wrong if murderers such as Myra Hindley (the 'Moors Murderer') were ever released in the face of public opposition.

In the case of *R (Anderson)* v *Secretary State for the Home Department* (2002), however, the Law Lords sided with Lord Woolf. They held that the Home Secretary's role was incompatible with article 6 of the ECHR and they issued a declaration of incompatibility under s.4 of the HRA. He does still have a role in those cases of prisoners serving fixed sentences of 15 years or more.

None of this helped Myra Hindle. She died in 2002 aged 60.

Some view the new common law and human rights approaches positively. Lawyers, such as Dawn Oliver, argue that the court's approach will prevent public bodies from arbitrary interference by decision makers and thus promote accountability and trust. Ministers and members of the governing party have not been so happy. Judges view themselves as doing nothing more than consistently applying the rule of law and protecting the rights of unpopular minorities. Unlike elected politicians they were unlikely to be moved by public opinion or the arguably mob-like tendencies of the popular press.

Given the political importance of all these issues, it is likely that there will be continued 'turf wars' between the courts and the executive about who is best suited to make decisions on certain issues. Ironically, having given the courts the power to check its legislation for its human rights implications, some members of the Labour government almost immediately began to complain about the implications of the HRA: it was as if they had not thought through the implications of their decision.

Extra-judicial activities

The relationship between politicians and judges has soured for other reasons that have little to do with their decisions in court. In the past 20 years or so, judges have made an increasing number of interventions in politics more broadly defined.

Until the mid-1980s judges' public statements were covered by the so-called 'Kilmuir rules' issued in the mid-1950s, which discouraged judges from participating in public debates about policy in order to preserve their impartiality. These were relaxed in the late 1980s by Lord McKay, the Conservative Lord Chancellor, who permitted judges to put across their views in media interviews, public lectures and 'think pieces' for academic journals, subject to general safeguards. Many senior judges have taken the opportunity to air their views on matters of vital importance to their profession (and of broader society). Some have seen it as vitally important to explain their position or reasoning to a wider public in order to ensure that their judgments gain wider acceptance. Each time they have intervened, however, they have risked becoming involved in matters of public controversy and – worse – risking their reputation for impartiality, which might undermine confidence in the legal system. As we have already seen, some have been unable to conceal their exasperation with those 'populist' ministers who desire to lock as many people up as possible (or necessary to generate a favourable headline!) On occasion their statements have caused ministers difficulty. In November 2003, for example, Lord Steyn condemned the United States for its detention of terrorist suspects at Guantanamo Bay in Cuba: a statement that could hardly be calculated to improve relations with the United States.

Another source of contention has resulted from the way in which judges have been used by the government to chair various inquiries. Governments have invariably turned to the senior judiciary when they want to produce an authoritative report on major issues of public controversy. Examples include:

- Lord Scarman's report on the inner city riots (1981)

- Lord Nolan's report on Standards (First Report of the Committee for Standards in Public Life), 1995

Plate 19.3 Lord Woolf, the Lord Chief Justice, clashed with ministers during his period of office
Source: Empics

BRIEFINGS

19.5 Ministerial criticism and the courts

Hansard 27 April 2004

Lord Lester of Herne Hill asked Her Majesty's Government:

Whether, following comments by the Home Secretary on the release of an Algerian man suspected of having terrorist links, criticism by Ministers of the Crown of decisions of the courts in cases to which they are party is an attack on the rule of law.

The Secretary of State for Constitutional Affairs and Lord Chancellor (Lord Falconer of Thoroton): My Lords, the rule of law is fundamental to our constitutional democracy and must be safeguarded accordingly. This Government have always strongly defended the rule of law and will continue to do so. Given this responsibility, the Government are not in the same position as other litigants who are entirely free to express views about decisions against them. But the Government are entitled to disagree with particular decisions, both in Parliament and as part of our wider executive responsibilities, without undermining in any way judicial independence and the rule of law. I have discussed the approach that I have set out with my right honourable friend the Home Secretary and the noble and learned Lord the Lord Chief Justice. We all agree that this is the right approach.

Lord Lester of Herne Hill: My Lords, I thank the noble and learned Lord the Lord Chancellor and Secretary of State for that careful, considered and helpful reply. This is not the first occasion on which the present Home Secretary has made an instant and angry attack on a judicial decision without, of course, the judge having any opportunity to reply. He did so in an asylum case early last year. If the noble and learned Lord has further discussions with the Home Secretary, will he bring home to him, in addition to the helpful formula about which he told us, how harmful it is to the rule of law to make such attacks? . . .

Lord Falconer of Thoroton: My Lords, I think that the line that must be drawn is between legitimate disagreement, which is plainly permissible even for the Government, as long as it is measured, and something that is intemperate and undermines the rule of law. In the light of remarks that have been made, I have closely considered the detail and am quite satisfied that my right honourable friend was measured in what he said. One must be careful to distinguish what he said from what else was said about the issue by other people . . .

- Lord Scott's report on the sale of arms to Iraq (1996)
- Lord Philip's report into BSE (or 'mad cow disease') (2000)
- Lord Saville's inquiry into 'Bloody Sunday' (which was established in 1998 but which had still to report in March 2006)
- Lord Hutton's report on the death of Dr David Kelly (2004).

In principle, judges seem the people best suited to establishing the facts and coming to conclusions on the basis of the evidence. However, the idea that judges should work to the terms of reference imposed by ministers does appear to violate the separation of powers. Judicial involvement has often backfired and judges have been accused of various biases. The most recent example was the Hutton Report, which exonerated the government in the wake of the death of Dr David Kelly. The report was painstaking, authoritative and regarded by opponents of the Iraq War, some Conservatives and conspiracy theorists, as a 'whitewash' (see Chapter 15).

The Inquiries Act (2004) introduced a requirement that ministers obtain the agreement of senior judges before engaging the services of a judge. This will ensure that the courts always have sufficient judges to fulfil their judicial functions.

Plate 19.4 Lord Hutton became one of a long line of judges who has produced a report at the request of the executive (into the death of Dr Kelly)

Source: Empics

Appointment of judges

Writing in 1997 Professor John Griffith said: 'The most remarkable fact about the appointment of judges is that it is wholly in the hands of politicians' (*The Politics of the Judiciary*). High Court, circuit judges and magistrates are appointed by the Lord Chancellor, who is a member of the government; the most senior judges are appointed by the Prime Minister after consultation with the Lord Chancellor (who takes 'soundings' to ensure that the nominee has the required skills and character). Almost all High Court judges are appointed from the ranks of QCs (Queen's Counsel), who are senior barristers. (The Lord Chancellor also decides who are to become QCs.)

It is unlikely that senior judges will be appointed because of their political allegiance to the Prime Minister of the day. Today 'being a known supporter of a political party seems to be neither a qualification nor a disqualification for appointment' (Griffith, op. cit., p. 16). Senior appointments may still be controversial. For example, it is known that in 1996 the right wing of the Conservative Party 'strongly resisted' the appointment of Lord Bingham as Lord Chief Justice and Lord Woolf as Master of the Rolls.

Because senior judicial appointments tend to be made from the most experienced barristers, the choice of candidate at any one time is extremely limited, possibly

Table 19.1 Characteristics of the senior judiciary

	Total	Former barrister	Former solicitor	Men	Women	Ethnic minority
Law Lords	11	11	0	10	1	0
Heads of Division	4	4	0	4	0	0
Court of Appeal	33	33	0	31	2	0
High Court judge	106	104	2	94	10	1
Circuit judge	624	537	87	537	67	6
Recorder	1,417	1,289	128	1,117	199	60

Source: www.dca/gov.uk/judicial

not extending beyond five or six suitable people. Officially no regard is had to gender, race, religion, secular orientation or political affiliation. As Table 19.1 shows, very few women, ethnic minorities or solicitors had reached the highest levels of the judiciary by late 2005. Less than 4 per cent of recorders (the lowest level of judge in Table 19.1) are drawn from ethnic minorities and just 14 per cent are women. Above this level both groups are even less well represented. (Dame Brenda Hale became the first ever woman Law Lord in January 2004.)

Women and ethnic minorities are well represented at the bar among the younger cohorts. It may simply be, therefore, that the tendency to appoint judges in their 40s may explain the current unrepresentative nature of the senior judiciary. Only time will tell whether this is the case.

Since they have spent their professional lives working as barristers they are overwhelmingly likely to have come from privileged backgrounds. There have been many studies of the social background of senior judges over the years. Overall these show that about 80 per cent of the senior judiciary are the products of public schools and of Oxford or Cambridge; that they have an average age of about 60; that 95 per cent are men; and 100 per cent are white. Clearly, such a socially restricted group is likely to share some particular attitudes and social and political orientations.

From April 2006 a Judicial Appointments Commission, comprising a majority of lay people, will have responsibility for making selections for most appointments.

BRIEFINGS

19.6 How has the EU affected English judges?

On the face of it the increased power of the European Court of Justice might seem to threaten the powers of English courts and judges, by limiting their independence of action and autonomy of judgment. In fact the opposite seems to be true. The activity of the ECJ has impinged on the higher English courts in three ways:

1. It has encouraged them to take a stronger stand on judicial review of legislation in general, not just on EU matters.

2. It has given English courts the power to disapply parliamentary legislation if they think it runs counter to the EU treaties. While they have to refer the final decision to the ECJ, delaying the effects of legislation (often until after the next general election) could be tantamount to nullifying it.

3. On specific interpretations of law the ECJ's often 'progressive' attitudes have nudged the English courts into a more supportive attitude towards, for example, gender equality.

It should be noted, however, that in most matters the ECJ simply enunciates general principles, in keeping with the practice of Continental supreme courts. It leaves to national courts the responsibility of deciding, for example, whether discrimination has actually taken place. This leaves ample scope for construction and interpretation, which give the courts their power.

It will have the power to advertise vacancies, scrutinise candidates and recommend appointments. The Commission can submit a single name to the minister (Lord Chancellor). He can reject the name, but must give reasons. He cannot reject the next nominee. As before, it must select candidates according to merit and no additional criteria (such as diversity) are likely to be applied. The new procedure is unlikely, therefore, to result in a more representative bench.

Politics and the judges

Judges have traditionally regarded themselves as impartial interpreters of the law. They regard their interpretations of the law as being largely based on established rules of statutory construction, precedent and case law, so that the correct legal answer is usually 'obvious' to anyone with the required skills. This does not mean, of course, that judges are 'neutral', they cannot but help make 'political' decisions: society requires them to do so! Nor does it mean that judges do not ever disagree with each other. The law is rarely unambiguous. Many of the words in statute and many of the powers granted to public bodies, for example, are inherently subjective and it is possible for reasonable people to come to very different – but equally reasonable – conclusions. When they disagree it is often a result of genuine differences about the meaning of words, the interaction of various statutes and their understanding of the intent of Parliament.

It is perhaps worth reminding ourselves that judges are, in a sense, the least powerful branch of government. They cannot legislate in any conventional sense and, provided that Parliament has used clear words, must give effect to legislation. If the executive cannot live with a court decision it can always go back to Parliament, redraft its proposals and override any objections. There might be some delay, but there is little doubt that the executive will get their way in the end. Moreover, the courts can only decide the cases brought before them. They cannot roam around the law looking for conflict and picking fights: they must passively wait for individuals to bring their grievances before them. This makes it difficult to argue, as some have tried to do, that Britain is in danger of lapsing into judicial supremacism.

A common argument is that since judges share a common social background they also share common attitudes or predispositions that lead them to certain conclusions. This argument seems plausible in the sense that the senior judiciary consist of a very small group of individuals (no more than 160) who share similar backgrounds, similar training and interact with each other on a regular basis. In particular, it is often argued that judges are either 'Conservative' with a large 'c' or 'conservative' with a small 'c'. In *The Politics of the Judiciary*, for example, Professor John Griffiths pointed out that the judges appear to be predisposed in favour of 'Conservative' causes:

■ allowing employers to sue trade unions for losses resulting from industrial action (*Taff Vale* (1906));

■ permitting ministers to detain suspects without trial (*Liversidge* v *Anderson* (1942));

■ supporters of grammar schools against attempts to enforce comprehensive school policies (*Secretary of State for Education and Science* v *Metropolitan Borough of Tameside* (1976));

■ domestic ratepayers who objected to a subsidised public transport policy (*Bromley London BC* v *GLC* (1983));

- supporting the right of chief constables and the Home Office to supply rubber bullets against a local police authority's wishes (*R* v *Home Secretary, ex parte Northumbria Police Authority* (1988));

- ministers who imposed a ban on broadcasting the voices of terrorists (*R* v *Secretary of State for the Home Department, ex parte Brind* (1991)).

These cases are occasionally reinforced by unfortunate extra-judicial statements, such as Lord Denning's suggestion that the 'Birmingham Six' could not be released because to do so would suggest that the police had perjured themselves. The conservative traditions of the courts (their penchant for formal language, pageantry, gowns and wigs) may also accentuate their reputation for conservative political views.

The idea that judges shared political predispositions as a result of their background seems plausible until we remember that, as we saw in Chapter 15, there is no one-to-one correspondence between social characteristics and political beliefs. Several judges have acquired reputations for advancing distinctly 'liberal' views. In the 1980s Lord Scarman became a hero to the Afro-Caribbean community after publication of his report about the inner city riots, which supported 'community policing'. In the 1990s Lords Woolf, Steyn and Hoffman all developed similarly 'liberal' reputations. Writing in the *Spectator* in 1995 Boris Johnson, the future Conservative MP, clearly regarded many judges as being closet supporters of the Labour Party. This was perhaps understandable. The Conservative Party had been in power for 16 years at the time and their ministers had got very used to being rebuked by the courts. After Labour had been in power for some years they had much the same experience.

Griffith's main argument, however, was not that judges are conservative because of their upbringing and training. Judges are conservative because they are judges. The judiciary in every society, whatever the background of its individual members, is bound to be conservative (with a small 'c'), since its task is to maintain order and the stability of the state. He argues, 'To some, the judicial view of the public interest appears merely as reactionary conservatism. It is not the politics of the extreme right. Its insensitivity is clearly rooted more in unconscious assumptions than in a wish to oppress. But it is demonstrable that on every major social issue which has come before the courts during the last thirty years . . . the judges have supported the conventional, established and settled interests. And they have reacted strongly against challenges to those interests. This conservatism does not necessarily follow the day-to-day political policies associated with the party of that name. But it is a political philosophy nevertheless' (Griffiths, op. cit., pp. 340–1).

Griffiths is correct in part. Judges have given 'conservative' judgments and have been especially assiduous in the protection of property rights. It could be argued, however, that in doing so they did little more than express relatively orthodox views about the 'public interest'. It could also be argued that historically the courts deferred to Parliament and – since the Conservative Party has been dominant in Parliament – this has made the courts appear conservative too.

Despite their association with conservative traditions, the courts have sometimes changed with the times to reflect social change. Until the late 1980s, for example, it was impossible for a husband to be found guilty of raping his wife. As social views changed, so did the courts. (Parliament – revealingly – never introduced this change.) From 1991 the courts accepted that a wife could retract consent to intercourse during marriage. In recent years the British courts have handed down a large number of judgments that have overturned the established way of doing things and have by no means always deferred to those in authority. This is not, moreover, simply the product of the HRA. Many of the most important developments in the law, such as the case relating to the banning of trade unions at GCHQ in 1985, predate the HRA and were based on the common law. To be sure, the courts did not overturn the government's decision in this instance, but they did establish the important principle that the exercise of some powers could be reviewed. Those relating to the management of the civil service, the granting of compensation to the victims of crime or the issuing of passports could be reviewed while others (relating to diplomatic relations, treaties and defence) could not. At the time many thought that the Lords' judgment in the GCHQ case was conservative. It later became clear to everyone (not just lawyers) that the Lords had opened a tiny crack which enabled them to examine a whole range of government decisions and subject decision making to public scrutiny.

Deference to the executive appears to be on the wane. In 1994 the House of Lords found the Home Secretary guilty of contempt of court, rejecting his argument that he enjoyed Crown immunity (*M* v *Home Office* (1994)). In the recent cases relating to terrorism the courts have insisted that the executive must behave legally, procedurally fairly and proportionately. It must be doubted whether the courts would now produce a finding so supportive of executive power as they did in *Liversidge* v *Anderson* in 1942; though the courts cannot be entirely insensitive to public demands to control criminals and terrorists.

Many have objected to the HRA on the grounds that it has given power to unelected judges. Some advocates of a 'political constitution' have argued that many of the decisions that are made by judges should be made by politicians, since they are accountable to voters. Others have welcomed the increased role given to the judges and the movement towards a 'constitutionalism' in which political activity is regulated by the courts. It is perhaps important to remind ourselves that Parliament demanded that the judges take a role (s.3 of the HRA says that the courts 'must' interpret legislation so as to be compatible with convention rights as far as it is possible to do so). It is also necessary to remember that the 'judicialisation' of politics has curbed the power of the executive, never Parliament. While some judges clearly have doubts as to whether parliamentary sovereignty provides sufficient protections for minorities and human rights, they have not directly challenged the authority of parliament in their judgments. Whether Britain should give the courts such a power in a written constitution is, however, another story (see Chapter 4).

Plate 19.5 MAC (Stan McMurty) cartoon in the *Daily Mail*, 10 September 1996. A 12-year-old boy, beaten by his stepfather with a cane after he tried to stab another child with a kitchen knife, takes his case to the European Court of Human Rights

Source: MAC (Stan McMurty) Daily Mail

'Before you decide what action to take over my smashing up your car, father, I'd like you to meet my lawyer, my social worker and a bloke from the European Commission of Human Rights . . .'

CONTROVERSY

Should judges be elected?

Some people feel that judges now have such power that they should be made directly accountable to the electorate as in some parts of the United States. This would mean that judges would have to factor in what the public think about an issue when arriving at a judgment. They could not simply listen to the so-called 'experts' such as psychologists, social workers and the like. If they did not 'listen to the voters' they would run the risk of being voted out of office, like all 'other' politicians.

This proposal is viewed with horror by many lawyers and judges. They consider the fact that judges are appointed according to 'merit' rather than 'political belief' to be a great virtue. If judges knew that they would be subject to such pressures they may set aside precedents and distort their judgments to fit prejudices. The only organisations that are likely to be able to mobilise voters, furthermore, are the parties. If litigants and defendants knew that judges were subject to selection by party and election by voters this would undermine faith in the legal system.

'Blunkett should stop these judges rampaging about! With on-the-spot fines!'

Plate 19.6 Some ministers came to regret giving the judges increased powers under the Human Rights Act. The courts often declared ministers' actions incompatible with convention rights and were bitterly criticised by some, such as David Blunkett, the former Home Secretary

Source: Michael Heath/The Mail on Sunday, 18th May 2003, Centre for the Study of Cartoons & Caricature, University of Kent

Summary

This chapter has discussed the workings of courts and the thinking of judges. It has reached these conclusions:

- The courts play a vital role in establishing a rough separation of powers and provide a check on a strong executive.

- Judicial independence is vital to ensure the rule of law.

- The court system is highly complex. Most conflicts between the executive and judiciary occur at the High Court and above.

- The political role of the courts has been growing. This is not simply due to the impact of EU law, devolution and the HRA. It also stems from the volume of politically related legislation (for example, the trade union laws) passed in the last 30 years and changes in the senior judiciary.

- In interpreting this and other legislation judges are often thrown back on their own reasoning because laws are unclear. They have to use their own personal opinions as a guide.

- The judges must be influenced at the margin by their own values, but these are not necessarily 'conservative' or 'Conservative'.

- Recruitment patterns are not likely to be changed much in the foreseeable future so we may expect judgments also to continue along the same lines.

- The judges used to be relatively unimportant actors on the political stage. They are now among the most important.

MILESTONES

Milestones in legal development 1846–2009

1846	County courts established for small civil disputes
1873–5	High Court established for major civil disputes. Court of Appeal established
1876	House of Lords becomes highest court of appeal
1942	House of Lords decision in *Liversidge* v *Anderson*
1948	Court of Appeal establishes 'reasonableness test' in the *Wednesbury* case
1949	Civil legal aid established
1953	UK becomes party to European Convention on Human Rights but the treaty is not incorporated into UK domestic law
1964	Major developments in field of 'natural justice' and right to a fair hearing *Ridge* v *Baldwin*
1966	Law Lords decide that the House of Lords is no longer strictly bound by previous decisions
1969	House of Lords rejects attempts to prevent judicial review in *Anisminic* case
1972	Crown Courts replace assizes and quarter sessions
1972	European Communities Act incorporates EU law into UK law
1974	Juries Act abolishes property qualifications for jurors, who are to be drawn from the electoral register
1977	Reforms to system of administrative law
1981	Supreme Court Act lays down current jurisdiction of the High Court and its three divisions
1985	*GCHQ* case establishes that some prerogative powers can be subject to judicial review

Milestones in legal development 1846–2009 continued

1986	House of Lords holds that courts have the power to examine actions taken under prerogative powers in the *GCHQ* case
1985	Solicitors lose their monopoly over conveyancing
1990	Courts and Legal Services Act: barristers lose their monopoly of arguing cases in court; cases involving less than £25,000 to go to county courts; cases involving more than £50,000 to the High Court. *Factortame* case – European Court of Justice rules that UK courts can suspend the provisions of Acts of Parliament which appear to contravene European law until a definitive ruling can be made
1994	Barristers' monopoly to appear in High Court abolished. Woolf Report, Access to Justice, recommends radical streamlining of civil litigation
1997–9	Substantial reforms of civil legal aid scheme imposed by government, cutting financial support to claimants and litigants
1998	The Human Rights Act to give fuller effect to the ECHR (into force from October 2000)
2002	Establishment of the Administrative Court, Home Secretary loses role in determining sentences of most life prisoners
2004	House of Lords declares indefinite imprisonment without trial of terrorist suspects held in Belmarsh prison to be incompatible with convention rights *(A and others* v *Secretary of State for the Home Department; X and another* v *Secretary of State for the Home Department)*
2005	House of Lords declare third-party evidence obtained under torture inadmissible in British courts and require government to inquire how evidence obtained
2009	Current proposed start date for new Supreme Court

Essays

1. To what extent do judges want to make political judgements and to what extent are they forced into making them?

2. How would judges' decisions be different if they came from different social backgrounds?

3. What is meant by the 'political role of the judiciary'? Why is it increasing?

4. 'Ministers are more in touch with public opinion than judges. Judges don't understand what people want. That is *exactly* why ministers should not decide on *either* specific immigration cases *or* the sentences handed down to criminals.' Discuss.

Projects

1. Find law reports for Scotland and for England and Wales that deal with a similar kind of case. On the basis of the law reports, determine the extent
to which the different legal systems of Scotland and of England and Wales produce different results.

2. Find out all that you can about three current members of the Appellate Committee of the House of Lords. What do they share in common? Do they have any significant differences?

Further reading

The classic work on English courts and judges is John A. G. Griffith, *The Politics of the Judiciary* (London: Fontana, 5th edn, 1997). Other useful books are Dawn Oliver, *Constitutional Reform in the UK* (Oxford: Oxford University Press, 2002), esp. Chapters 5, 6 and 18; David Judge, *Political Institutions in the United Kingdom* (Oxford: Oxford University Press, 2005); Hilaire Barnett, *Britain Unwrapped: Government and Constitution Explained* (London: Penguin, 2002). Also useful are R. Stevens, *The Independence of the Judiciary* (Oxford: Oxford University Press, 1993), and P. Madgwick and P. Woodhouse, *The Law and Politics of the Constitution* (Hemel Hempstead: Harvester Wheatsheaf, 1995). David Robertson in *Judicial Discretion in the House of Lords* (Oxford: Clarendon Press, 1998) deals in depth with the highest court in the system. Joshua Rosenberg *Trial of Strength: The Battle Between Ministers and Judges over Who Makes the Law* (London: Richard Cohen Books, 1997) is a particularly readable account of the struggle between ministers and judges. Also useful is Louis Blom-Cooper's 'Government and the judiciary', in Anthony Seldon and Dennis Kavanagh (eds), *The Blair Effect 2* (Cambridge: Cambridge University Press, 2005).

On relationships between English (and Scots) law and Continental systems see, for a specific review, Chapter 14 of Ian Budge *et al.*, *The Politics of the New Europe* (London: Addison Wesley Longman, 1997).

Useful articles on the changing relationship between politics and law, and politicians and judges in Britain are L. Foster, 'The encroachment of the law on politics', *Parliamentary Affairs*, **53** (2), 2000, pp. 328–46; D. Woodhouse, 'The law and politics: in the shadow of the Human Rights Act', *Parliamentary Affairs*, **55** (2), 2002, pp. 254–70; Philip Norton, 'Judges in British politics', *Talking Politics*, **16** (2), 2004, pp. 60–2; Hannah Roberts, 'The Last Lord Chancellor', *Politics Review*, **14** (3), pp. 14–16.

Useful web sites on politics and law

Hot links to these sites can be found on the CWS at www.pearsoned.co.uk/budge.

As a first step we suggest that you visit the web site for the Department for Constitutional Affairs (www.dca.gov.uk). This contains a large amount of information about the structure of the courts, the case load and judicial appointments. For more specific information on legal issues visit www.judiciary.gov.uk or the Government Legal Service at www.gls.gov.uk. It might also be worth looking at the web site of the Law Commission for England and Wales (www.lawcom.gov.uk). In addition, the Government's Court Service (www.hmcourts-service.gov.uk) is an executive agency of the Lord Chancellor's Department. It covers policy, legislation and the magistrates' courts' activities. The Crown Prosecution Service is responsible for prosecuting people in England and Wales charged by the police with a criminal offence; visit them at www.cps.gov.uk.

The process of European integration has strengthened the influence of the European Union in the functioning of the legal systems of all its country members. Visit the European Court of Justice at www.curia.eu.int. On the web site of the Council of Europe (www.coe.int) you have access to the full text of the European Convention for the Protection of Human Rights; the Human Rights Act is available at www.hmso.gov.uk/acts/acts1998/19980042.htm. The International Court of Justice represents a crucial step towards juridical globalisation; their web site is available at www.icj-cij.org.

A great deal of information and critical analysis is available from the Judicial Studies Board (www.jsboard.co.uk) and the Law Society (www.lawsociety.org.uk). Justice is one of the UK's leading legal and human rights organisations. You can visit it at www.justice.org.uk. You can also visit Liberty's web page (www.liberty-human-rights.org.uk).

chapter 20

The police and policing

The central dilemma of the police service is that they do not have enough resources to enforce all the laws all the time and must, to some extent, develop their own priorities independently of democratically elected politicians. The police in Britain link with both local and central government and the courts. Officially they are under the supervision of police authorities, composed in part of local councillors and in part of other local people and magistrates. Britain is almost unique in Europe in not having a national police force directly under the Ministry of the Interior (Home Office). Instead it has many different, mainly local, police forces. The question of who actually controls them is ambiguous, as we shall see. But there is no doubt that political control of the police is more dispersed than it is on the Continent.

The relationship of the police to courts and judges is more straightforward. The police uphold the law and work with the Crown Prosecution Service to bring criminals to trial. However, since there are many laws and only limited power to enforce them, the police are forced to set priorities about which they will enforce, just as judges are forced to fall back on their own opinions. The police are not therefore just executors of policy made by local or central government or judges. They also make day-to-day policy decisions themselves, partly in order to pursue their own priorities but also because they lack guidance from elsewhere.

This chapter focuses on police in England and Wales and considers:

- the principles, pressures and politics underlying and shaping modern policing
- the history of the British police and how this influences the way they operate today
- police accountability: for what are they responsible and to whom?
- police procedures and the individual citizen
- the politicising of policing
- law and order legislation
- recent developments in policing.

The principles underlying policing

Police

The civilian organisation established to enforce the criminal law and maintain order.

'The **police**' have been variously regarded as a key social and political institution, a law enforcement agency, a social service and a symbolic site of power. They can be regarded as homogeneous and treated as a complex organisation of hierarchical command, or as pluralist and as harbouring many conflicting goals and interests.

This chapter focuses on the organisational aspects and their relationships with other organisations. It largely focuses on policing in England and Wales because the legal system in Scotland is rather different.

Policing

The processes and arrangements, usually but not always involving the police, established to maintain social order. All societies have to maintain order and so all engage in policing, although not all do so through a civilian police force. (The UK, for example, uses social workers and other professions to 'police' parts of society).

Legitimation

The process of making something morally acceptable in the view of the population.

There are three major influences shaping modern '**policing**' in Britain:

1. *Function*. The police have to maintain order and both prevent and detect crime. This makes them highly visible through their activities of patrol and surveillance. Their duties here also include control of crowds, gatherings (such as the recent Countryside Alliance and Anti-Iraq War demonstrations in London) and other potential sources of disruption.

2. *Legitimation*. The police need to ensure that what they do is acceptable to the public. Prevention of crime is difficult and the detection of offenders even more so. Both rely on the goodwill and assistance of the public. Detection relies on witnesses, confessions, informants, the general gathering of intelligence and, increasingly, the use of technology (e.g. matching databases, DNA testing and evidence from CCTV cameras). These activities have to be seen to be legitimate and agreed to reflect the exercise of power on behalf of an elected body. The legitimated use of force by the police must be seen to be used on behalf of the community. It must also be seen to be impartial (not seen to favour particular social or political interests above others).

3. *Autonomy*. The police seek to influence their own development. As a key institution of the state and as a large-scale organisation, the police seek to maximise their resources, power and status. This is not to say that 'the police' act as one: there are conflicts within the police service, between the 43 different forces, between ranks, between officers and so on.

These three underlying influences can be seen at work in all aspects of police activity that we shall examine in this chapter.

A brief history of British policing

Historically, policing was regarded as a communal responsibility and every adult male had an obligation to play his part. During the eighteenth century a wide variety of forms of policing flourished and there were piecemeal initiatives to establish a formally administered system. By the mid-eighteenth century, the system of watchmen was being criticised by many as inadequate, and in 1750 two magistrates, Henry Fielding (author of *Tom Jones*) and his brother John, created the Bow Street Runners, a small police force. In 1798 another magistrate, Patrick Colquhoun, established a police force for the Port of London and in 1800 this became a statutory force, recognised and part-funded by government.

Parliament was not enthusiastic, indeed it was downright hostile, towards proposals for a police force. Parliamentary committees considered and rejected the idea of a police for London in 1770, 1793, 1812, 1818 and 1822. Opposition to the proposal reflected a mix of concerns. The landed and merchant classes were wary about what a police force might do and the need for higher taxes to pay for it. There was also a general mistrust of the Continental model of state-controlled police and their association with spies and informers. Nonetheless, Sir Robert Peel's Policing Bill for the creation of a Metropolitan Police Force finally did succeed in 1829. This laid the foundations of modern policing.

The guiding principles behind the bill remain pertinent today. These emphasised the independence of the police from direct political control or interference and strict internal disciplinary systems to prevent the abuse of authority. The police were also encouraged to develop good relations with the public, to be 'civil and obliging to all people of every rank and class', while taking care never to

Plate 20.1 The police are called to perform a range of social functions, including controlling demonstrators as in this Countryside Alliance protest

Source: Empics

compromise their authority. The important legacy of this mix of the 'helping hand' and 'figure of authority' was the image of the 'benign British bobby'. A further consequence of earlier mistrust was the local nature of the forces set up outside London. These were created by local authorities to police their own area and were under the supervision of a local 'watch committee'. Despite amalgamations, the tradition of local forces with supervision by local representatives still survives and accounts for the patchwork of local forces that we have in Britain today (though this is changing: see Briefing 20.6).

From 1945 to the 1970s: consensus and controversy

It has been observed that:

> The 1950s were the heyday of cross-party consensus on law and order, as on other social issues. The police were generally regarded as national mascots, totems of patriotic pride, routinely referred to as role models for the world. The pedestal on which the police stood is illustrated by the popularity of the TV series *Dixon of Dock Green*, in which the central character was a kindly, avuncular PC who captured the cosy stereotype of the British bobby which then prevailed in the public imagination.
>
> Robert Reiner, *The Politics of the Police*, p. 710

The cosy *Dixon of Dock Green* image was challenged by a series of scandals that damaged public confidence in the police. The Home Secretary established a

BRIEFINGS

20.1 Police powers

The legal status of police powers has developed in a peculiar way. It derived less from Parliament than from two 'landmark' legal judgments:

1. *Fisher* v *Oldham Corporation* (1930). It was held that a police officer is not the servant of any local authority and acts on their own 'original' authority. They are answerable only to the law.

2. *R* v *Metropolitan Police Commissioner, ex parte Blackburn* (1969). The court held that the police commissioner's principal duty was to 'enforce the law of the land'. Lord Denning declared that the Metropolitan Commissioner 'is not the servant of anyone, save of the law itself. No Minister of the Crown can tell him that he must, or must not, keep observation on this place or that; or that he must, or must not, prosecute this man or that one. Nor can any police authority tell him so. The responsibility for law enforcement lies on him. He is answerable to the law and the law alone.'

Royal Commission and its report in 1962 provided a review of the role, organisation and accountability of the police. This resulted in the 1964 Police Act. The most enduring contribution of the 1964 Act proved to be the tripartite mechanism for supervision of the police, involving local authority police committees (in London the Home Secretary performed the role), chief constables and the Home Office.

For some time this seemed a reasonably effective structure. It was only as society and policing changed that its weaknesses became apparent. Calling the police to account is not a straightforward matter. As we have seen, police powers that have been defined by the courts as inherent to the police themselves and not subject to scrutiny by outside bodies (Briefing 20.1).

More stringent requirements concerning accountability and appropriate conduct were perhaps seen as unnecessary while consensus reigned and the 'British bobby' was still a folk hero in the national consciousness. We now know from autobiographies and archive research that – even in the 'golden age' of the 1950s – some police officers were flawed heroes. However, it was the exposure of corruption within the Metropolitan Police in the late 1960s and 1970s that truly tarnished the image, with members of specialist squads being charged with receiving bribes and corrupting the course of justice.

New structures

The first moves at post-war reform were not procedural but organisational in nature, and were more related to the concurrent restructuring of local government than to burgeoning scandals. They stemmed from the report in 1962 of the Royal Commission mentioned earlier. Its recommendations were effected in the 1964 Police Act, which combined many smaller forces.

Before the amalgamation consequent on the 1964 Act, Britain had a very large number of local police forces – over 170. Apart from the Metropolitan Police covering London, and a few forces in the other larger cities, most forces were small by today's standards. Their average size was around 600, and some were as small as 150. The small size and small area they policed made these forces very local, and local politicians had, in one way or another, a good deal of influence over them.

By the early 1960s the sheer inefficiency of having many small forces, combined with a growing concern about lack of uniformity, led to the appointment of the Royal Commission. This prompted an often impassioned debate about whether the entire structure should be replaced with one national police force, accountable to Parliament, as is the model throughout the rest of Europe. The debate was often confusing because the key issue, accountability to political control, could be argued in several ways. Opponents of a national police force feared political intervention and a highly partisan police under government control. At the same time, many of the proponents of a single national force argued that there was far too little democratic control in the current system, and a single force would be more democratic because of its accountability to Parliament. The Metropolitan Police, it was argued, had never been politicised, even though the Home Secretary acted as the police authority.

The number of forces was to be cut enormously by amalgamations that merged county (largely rural) and borough (largely urban) forces. This happened in several stages, and there are now only 43 police forces in England and Wales. The smallest forces have at least 1,500 officers, and the average is around 3,000. A few, like the West Midlands Police, are much bigger than anything that existed before; one of its chief constables is on public record as saying he could not control it. Similarly, the Thames Valley Police, with nearly 5,000 officers, covers three entire counties.

Police accountability and control

Accountability

To have to answer for one's conduct, or be subject to review or evaluation by a higher body.

The question of control of these forces immediately became a serious problem, and has remained so. The 1964 Act envisaged a three-cornered control system, with political authority (and budgetary obligations) shared between the Home Office, chief constables and new bodies, called 'police authorities', consisting of both local magistrates and local councillors. The basic doctrine is that no one can give chief constables any orders about how to carry out their job. They can be sacked for incompetence, but not directed. (Incidentally, the sacking of the Chief Constable in Brighton resulted in *Ridge* v *Baldwin* (1964), one of the leading cases on 'natural justice' noted in Chapter 19.) As noted, the courts have held in subsequent case law that police authorities cannot intervene to order a police force to do anything particular in the carrying out of its functions.

In fact, the police authorities have almost no powers. They need Home Office approval to appoint a chief constable; they can be ordered by the Home Office to dismiss their chief constable; and, because so much of the finance comes from the government, directly or otherwise, they have little financial power over the police. The Home Office sets minimum and maximum staff levels, equipment tables and so on, so their influence is limited. This became clear in 1988 in a major case where the Northumbria Police Authority tried to get the courts to forbid the Home Office from interfering with its own preferred policy. The case in question (*R* v *Home Secretary, ex parte Northumbria Police Authority* (1988)) is probably the most significant legal ruling on police and politics in the twentieth century.

The Home Office decided that it would authorise the acquisition of plastic bullets for use by police forces, and hold these centrally for distribution to any force that convinced Her Majesty's Inspector of Constabularies (HMIC) that it might need them. The Chief Constable of Northumbria decided that he might have a need for such weapons, but his police authority took the policy decision that he should not have them, and refused to approve his purchase of plastic bullets out of funds he was granted. The Home Office authorised him to have them. The police authority went to court, asking for an order to quash the Home Office decision. The court held that the Home Office did have the power to provide weapons to a police force against the wish of that force's own police authority. Even more, it held that the Home Office had this power, not because of the 1964 Police Act, but under the 'royal prerogative' (see Chapter 4). One judge declared,

> a prerogative of keeping the peace within the realm existed in mediaeval times, probably since the Conquest and . . . it has not been surrendered by the Crown in the process of giving its express or implied assent to the modern system of keeping the peace through the agency of independent police forces. I therefore conclude that, if the necessary power had not been available under section 41 of the [Police] Act of 1964, [it] would have been within the prerogative powers of the Crown.

What this means is that the central government has an automatic right to fix local police policy, whether or not Parliament has specifically given it this right! The only control on weaponry, and probably on any policy question where a chief constable wants something is, therefore, the central government. The powers of the police authority are simple: it is entitled to one yearly report by the chief constable on the activities of the force. It is also entitled to ask for other reports on specific matters. But chief constables can refuse to make these reports if they feel they should not give them! In contrast, the Home Office can demand any report or investigation it likes, and the chief constable must then report.

Police forces are, therefore, entirely under the control of the chief constables, subject to the regulation of the Home Office. There are only 41 chief constables of English and Welsh forces. There are about a dozen inspectors of constabulary, and perhaps 50 policy-level civil servants controlling the use of police throughout the UK. This is a significant level of concentrated power.

The question arises whether this situation constitutes a move towards a national police force (see also Briefing 20.6). The debate on a national force has never been properly resolved. Most chief constables do not wish for one, and no government has ever suggested its creation. But it is often suggested that a de facto national force already exists. Some critics have argued that the government prefers to have a system that operates effectively as one force but with the formal trappings of a series of separate forces. This avoids parliamentary control, making the police even more independent of democratic control than they would otherwise be.

The basic argument behind the thesis that Britain already has a de facto national force rests on the proposition that there is a small national police elite from whom all senior police officers are recruited. Apart from chief constables themselves, there are two other ranks – deputy chief constable and assistant chief constable – that make up the membership of an extremely powerful pressure group, the Association of Chief Police Officers (ACPO). These senior officers, and junior colleagues aspiring to membership, share similar experiences. They have all been on senior officers' courses at the police college in Bramshill; they all have some sort of national experience, such as being a staff officer to an inspector of constabulary or being seconded to the Home Office; and they have all served in several forces, almost certainly including a stint in 'the Met'. Their career patterns are interesting. Although they have all started as constables, and will usually have taken seven or eight years to become sergeants, they will have gone through the next five ranks, to assistant chief constable, at the rate of about two years per rank. They are high-flyers, and the need to move from force to force in order to fly so fast leads to a much more national outlook. As with any small elite, these officers know each other well, have attended endless courses and seminars together, and have formed their ideas and attitudes in concert. Most important of all, they are members of ACPO.

ACPO is not an official governmental organisation, and technically is simply the professional organisation of senior police officers, part-trade union, part-club, part-official representative for professional views, something like, say, the British Medical Association. However, it is funded by the Home Office and sends delegates to Home Office conferences and committees. The importance of ACPO became particularly apparent during the 1984–5 miners' strike. The problems of policing the nationwide dispute were beyond the capacity of any one force, so ACPO invoked the use of an established agreement providing for a National Reporting Centre (NRC) to coordinate demand and supply of support to forces policing the dispute. Although technically chief constables could refuse to cooperate with other forces, the Home Office made it quite clear that it would use legal powers to enforce cooperation if the NRC did not work. It felt that the need to cooperate was intense, and at least in terms of staff supply the British police became effectively a national force, under ACPO control, for over a year.

The arrangement produced a nationally coordinated policy of providing police support to colleagues under pressure and putting up roadblocks to prevent convoys of pickets rushing to particular collieries from all over the country. Effectively, this meant that operational decisions in some areas far from the crisis points were being made in the light of operational needs hundreds of miles away. (The policy was, incidentally, of dubious legality.)

Chief constables deny that ACPO and the NRC constituted a national force. But significantly, they have also argued that if they had not organised themselves unofficially, the government would have created a national force. It is unclear that saying there is no de jure national force because there is a de facto one means very much. This combination of independence from local control, dependence on the Home Office, a small national elite of common-minded professionals, and ACPO's coordinating role, adds up effectively to a national force. Other factors, such as the increasing importance of specialised units, nearly all run by the Metropolitan Police based in the capital, and a serious concern for a uniform position to be taken in Europe as the frontiers go down, encourage this move to centralisation.

Police procedures and the individual citizen

There have been two crucial changes enforced by recent legislation that have materially affected police work. The most important was the passing of the 1984 Police and Criminal Evidence Act, known universally as 'PACE', which was partially based on the report of the Royal Commission on Criminal Procedure published in 1981. This Act managed to offend both civil libertarians and the police! Civil libertarians object, for example, to the general power the Act gave to stop and search people or vehicles where an officer has reasonable grounds for suspecting possession of stolen or prohibited objects. In fact, to a large extent, this part of the Act just formalised a mass of separate stop and search powers and probably did not change police procedure very much, Indeed, it probably increased the degree of

Civil liberties

The freedoms that should not normally be constrained by others, whether private individuals or the state.

caution in use of stop and search. **Civil liberties** groups remain critical of the Act because ACPO's evidence to the Royal Commission stressed the need for new legal powers for the police and in many ways PACE provided these. However, PACE also introduced measures that the police did not welcome.

PACE enormously changed procedures for questioning suspects and for taking down what they say and any statements they make. Police critics of the Act argue that they are seriously hampered by the need to tape record all interviews, and to have a complete and contemporaneous account of the entire interview process. Secondly, a suspect's rights to have a solicitor present, and to say absolutely nothing to the police, mean that police cannot risk detaining and interrogating anyone until they already have enough evidence to win a committal in a magistrates' court.

Plate 20.2 Peter Schrank cartoon in the *Independent on Sunday*, 23 February 1997. Three men, jailed 18 years previously for the murder of Carl Bridgewater, were freed amid allegations of 'serious, substantial and widespread police malpractice' after new methods proved that the confession used to condemn the three had been obtained under false pretences

Source: Peter Schrank/The Independent, 23rd February 1997

In other words, they have had to abandon the practice of relying on confession evidence. There is still pressure to make a conviction impossible merely on the basis of a confession, which is already the law in Scotland.

In fact, PACE has simply put into statute rights that already existed in judges' rules, making them very much more effective. In the words of one expert: 'The old informal procedures for crime control, based on fabricating evidence, have had to go.'

PACE had an interesting side-effect on statistical measures of police effectiveness. The 'clear-up rate' for crime declined substantially. In part this is because, before PACE, detectives could often persuade offenders to confess to a series of other crimes that they would ask to be 'taken into consideration' (TIC) in court. Criminals are very much less willing to cooperate with police in this way now, and 'TIC' clear-up has dropped considerably. The fact that police were so dependent on these admissions suggests that PACE was very much needed.

The second statutory restriction on the police to come out of the 1981 Royal Commission was the creation of the Crown Prosecution Service by the Prosecution of Offences Act 1986. This is, constitutionally, a more radical change than PACE, which (at least in theory) simply gave statutory recognition to received practice. In the past, the police used to take the decision to prosecute, but this responsibility passed to the CPS solicitors, who are full-time salaried officers. The CPS is organised regionally but under the ultimate control of the Director of Public Prosecutions, a central government officer who had always had this power for certain very serious crimes.

The previous fusion of responsibilities mattered principally because there is always a considerable element of discretion involved in the decision to prosecute, and in what evidence will be used by the prosecution. Discretion covered both which crimes to prosecute and when to prosecute any particular offender. There may be some value in discretion in the first sense, because community standards on, say, pornography do vary. In fact, the police can still exercise some discretion in this area by simply refusing to investigate crimes they do not want prosecuted. The police also used their discretion not to prosecute cases that were simply not worth taking to court.

This use of discretion was effectively using court appearances as a method of social control, as a policing activity, rather than as a legal consequence of clear guilt. For example, the police often merely cautioned, or simply talked to, young offenders guilty of minor affrays or disturbances of the peace. But if there were complaints about behaviour on a certain housing estate, they would suddenly start to prosecute instead. This constituted an inappropriate use of the discretion to prosecute. The CPS uses objective, nationally determined guidelines in this sort of case.

Discretion on whether to prosecute really depends on how high a probability of conviction there should be before a prosecution is launched. The rate of conviction in a jury trial where there is no plea of guilty often surprises people because it is only around 70 per cent. As the cost and suffering of going to trial can be devastating, even for those acquitted, no prosecution should be launched lightly, however certain the police may be in their own minds that they have the right person. There is no doubt that the CPS demands a significantly higher probability of conviction before it will prosecute than the police used to expect. The CPS is also keener to check that evidence is reliable and all police procedures are water-tight, thus further enforcing civil rights against police enthusiasm.

The CPS was subject to controversy in 1998 when Dame Barbara Mills, the Director of Public Prosecutions, resigned over the failure to prosecute police corruption cases amid perceptions of delay in bringing cases to court. The CPS was restructured into 42 offices matching police forces, and was given additional funds to help it keep up with caseloads.

The politicisation of policing

During the 1970s, the police and their role became increasingly politicised, reflecting a broader social context of tension and conflict. Political and industrial protest, and the anxieties provoked by rising crime rates, led to a new strategy put forward in the Conservative 1979 election campaign. As Mrs Thatcher declared on 28 March 1979: 'The demand in the country will be for two things: less tax and more law and order.' The support of the 'rank and file' Police Federation was immensely valuable in making 'law and order' a vote-winning issue for the Conservatives. Deeply hostile towards Labour after a pay dispute in 1977, the Federation provided a well-publicised, openly political endorsement of Tory policy.

Once elected to government, the Conservatives delivered what they had promised to the police: greatly enhanced pay awards and increased budgets for recruitment and resources. In turn, the police were supposed to deliver their part of this bargain. They had been given the rewards in advance; now there could be no excuses for losing the 'fight against crime'. Of course, once mutual admiration and rhetoric were put aside, it became apparent that the practical problem of crime control could not be reduced to a simple formula of 'more police equals less crime'. Crime rose and, with fluctuations here and there, it continued to do so throughout the 1980s, although the statistics improved somewhat in the 1990s.

While this suggested that 'more policing' was not working, two key and symbolic episodes of the first half of the 1980s kept the police high on the Thatcher government's list of 'favourites'. These were, first, the inner city riots of 1981 and, secondly, the miners' strike of 1984–5.

In urban riots then and since, the police have first contained disorder and then moved in to enforce order. Their efforts at 'community policing' after rioting, in line with the Scarman Report of 1981, helped prevent further outbreaks of protest, although 20 years later controversy again rose around police and community

BRIEFINGS

20.2 Political aspects of policing

Discrimination, minorities and the police

Prejudicial treatment of minority groups has long been a key issue for critics of the police. Considerable evidence suggests that, while police policy has belatedly but increasingly sought to stamp out sexual and racial discrimination and increase recruitment of ethnic minority officers, prejudice nonetheless remains part of what is known as the 'canteen culture'. In everyday policing, the disproportionate 'stop and search' of black youths has been one expression of this.

Tensions between black youths and the police were the volatile background against which the inner city riots of 1980–1 flared, first in Brixton, south London, and then in Toxteth, Merseyside; Moss Side, Manchester; and Handsworth, Birmingham. The first event was investigated by a senior judge, Lord Scarman, whose Report on the Brixton Disorder (1981) made recommendations concerning the need for police and community consultation.

The Prevention of Terrorism Act 2005: the police as policy advocates

In late 2005, the Labour government tried to introduce detention without trial for up to 90 days for terrorist suspects in a new Prevention of Terrorism Act. These proposals were supported by chief constables such as Sir Ian Blair, the Commissioner of the Metropolitan Police. Tony Blair told the BBC that 'The security services and the police are advising us that we need these powers to defeat those who are planning and plotting terrorist activity in our country.' In the debate in the House of Commons, the Home Secretary reported that every chief constable he had contacted had supported the proposals.

Despite the support of the police, the proposals were rejected. Opposition parties and civil liberties groups such as Liberty criticised senior police officers for getting involved in politics. Sir Ian responded that it was their duty to give politicians 'professional advice'. Others felt that this was entirely a matter for Parliament and that the police had allowed themselves to be seen as taking sides.

relations leading up to and following riots in Asian communities in Bradford and elsewhere.

Financial scrutiny and the push for reorganisation

The police, like other public services, have come under increased financial scrutiny in recent years. As crime rose, despite high investment in police pay and resources, the yardstick of 'value for money' was introduced. The first step in this direction was the 1983 Financial Management Initiative requiring the setting of objectives and priorities, efficient allocation of resources, and the planning of policing. After a period of relative immunity from public expenditure cuts, the police experienced the push towards centralisation and privatisation already applied to most other public services. The language of accountancy became paramount, with HM Inspectorate of Constabulary being given a more substantial and critical remit to monitor efficiency (as measured by a 'matrix of performance indicators'), and the Audit Commission and National Audit Office also evaluating aspects of policing. The police responded with hesitant and small-scale reforms but not to the satisfaction of the government. By the 1990s more far-reaching changes were envisaged, first through the 1993 Sheehy Report on pay, conditions and rank structure, and then through a 1996 Home Office Review of Police Core and Ancillary Tasks.

Both initiatives were embarrassing failures for the government. The Sheehy Report attracted derision in the press, criticism from a significant alliance of

BRIEFINGS

20.3 Police effectiveness and 'value for money'

Just how effective are the police? In recent years the adequacy of government policy concerning law and order has become more and more politically sensitive. The increase in the importance of the issue has come about largely because, until the 1997 general election, the Conservative Party had always been able to present itself as much more concerned about law and order than Labour, and Conservative governments since 1979 considerably increased resources for crime control.

It is necessary first to get some sense of scale on the problem. Talking to the Police Superintendents Conference in 2002, the Home Secretary, David Blunkett, announced that police numbers in England and Wales were the highest on record and now totalled 129,603. This included 20,000 in the Metropolitan Police, but not around 40,000 civilian employees. By 2005 this had increased to 141,230. This makes the English police roughly half the size of the French police, and not much more than one-third the size of the Italian forces: that is, Britain has roughly one police officer for every 450 inhabitants, France one for every 250.

Second, unlike their European counterparts, the British police are a general duty and entirely civilian force, handling every aspect of policing. Elsewhere in Europe, the police are more functionally specialised, usually with a paramilitary organisation like the French gendarmerie or the Italian carabinieri, who are primarily responsible for public order. It is a predominantly (although decreasingly) unarmed force, and one that has always tried to police consensually.

In this last respect the British police have probably improved since the severe criticisms of heavy-handed tactics in the 1981 Scarman Report. Usually senior officers will avoid using serious force to contain ethnic rioting in case it exacerbates the situation, although this has not been the policy in industrial disputes. On the whole this has paid off, and public order policing is fairly effective without being too oppressive. In the other sense of use of force, the use of deadly force with firearms, there has been a clear rise in the number of criminals, or disturbed people, shot to death by the police in recent years. But the total numbers are too small to constitute a significant rise.

Assessing how effective the police are in detecting and 'clearing up' crime other than public order offences is a methodological nightmare. Crime statistics are unreliable. Taking an uncritical view, property offences continue to dominate recorded crime, accounting for 91 per cent of all notifiable offences recorded by the police in England and Wales in 1997. Over half of theft offences and one-quarter of all recorded crimes are vehicle-related theft; 23 per cent of recorded crimes are burglaries; 1 per cent are drug offences (including trafficking and possession) and public order offences. Violent crime (including violence against the person, robbery and sexual offences) account for around 8 per cent. The detection rate, however, remains very low: roughly one-third of crimes are cleared up, with the rate dropping marginally every year.

It should immediately be noted that, even were these figures reliable, they do not justify the use that some politicians make of them. Nine-tenths of all crime is crime against property, and the overwhelming bulk of that is very minor, where the cost of the stolen or damaged property is less than £200, and often very much lower.

Labour and police, and well-organised and high-profile opposition from the united police ranks. The result was serious dilution of Sheehy's recommendations. The second initiative, the 1996 Review of Core and Ancillary Tasks, was supposed to fit in with the government's drive to push services into the market sector wherever possible. However, the promise of a 'big bang' actually resulted in little more than the 'whimper' of transferring various minor tasks to local authorities and private companies.

As relations between the police and the Conservatives deteriorated, so they warmed with Labour. The culturally conservative character of the police might have reacted strongly and adversely against the 'loony left' of the old metropolitan administrations, but the sound bites of emerging 'new realism' in the Labour Party were rather more palatable.

New Labour: tough on crime, tough on the causes of crime

Views of the police within the Labour Party have varied over time. In the 1960s some on the left argued that changes in the strategy of policing, with moves to patrol cars and 'firebrigade policing' (i.e. responding to calls rather than being on the beat), meant that the police were increasingly remote from the communities they served. The corruption cases of the 1970s, followed by revelations about the number of deaths in police custody (274 between 1970 and 1979), sparked further distrust (even though most – but not all – deaths arose from natural causes). Police confrontations with demonstrators (protesting about unemployment, nuclear weapons and so on) and strikers (the long-running dispute at Grunwick, the steel strike in 1980 and the miners' strike of 1984–5) created tensions with many left-wing groups. The local elections of May 1981 were particularly significant, with the councils of all of the metropolitan areas now being dominated by a more middle-class, assertive and radical Labour politician. These provided opportunities for the questioning of police policy, generating acrimonious but important debates about the actual nature of police accountability and leading to several high-profile clashes between police authorities and chief constables. James Anderton, the Chief Constable of Greater Manchester, for example, had a long-running feud with his police authority. Given this history of Labour antipathy towards the police, post-1979 Conservative administrations had good reason to think that their stance on the police and 'law and order' was far more appealing to voters.

There were some in the Labour Party who took note of Mrs Thatcher's success (see Chapter 17). Indeed, the issues of crime and policing provided an early indication of New Labour thinking on social policy. In early 1993 Tony Blair declared, 'We need to be tough on crime and tough on the causes of crime'; a 'sound bite' that immediately passed into common usage and summarised a new approach to crime. From that moment on New Labour combined its traditional emphasis on dealing with the social and economic conditions that promote crime with a new-found 'toughness'. Critics on the left branded this approach authoritarian, reactionary, illiberal or populist. They feared that however 'tough' Labour promised to be, the Conservatives would be tougher. While there are reasons for doubting the wisdom of such policies, there is little doubting their electoral success. Between 1992 and 2001, the Conservative lead over Labour as the party best able to deal with the problem of crime evaporated.

As Home Secretary, both Jack Straw and David Blunkett, among the closest associates of the Prime Minister, have been responsible for the 'being tough on the crime' (and terrorism) parts of the package. Both have been much criticised by human rights groups for their restructuring of immigration policy and in particular for proposals to streamline court procedures, limit jury trial and restrict the rights of defendants. At the same time, the government's particular stress since 2001 on efficient service delivery has also led to confrontations with the police, as with other public sector workers, about the introduction of unpopular changes in working practices in return for pay increases.

Police, public and the law

In reviewing the law relating to the police since the 1980s, the first point to make is that there has been a great deal of it! This is partly related to the stamp that successive Home Secretaries wished to make on policy, but it was also driven by electoral strategy, the need to be constantly producing 'new ideas'. The key piece of legislation is undoubtedly the Police and Criminal Evidence Act 1984, already

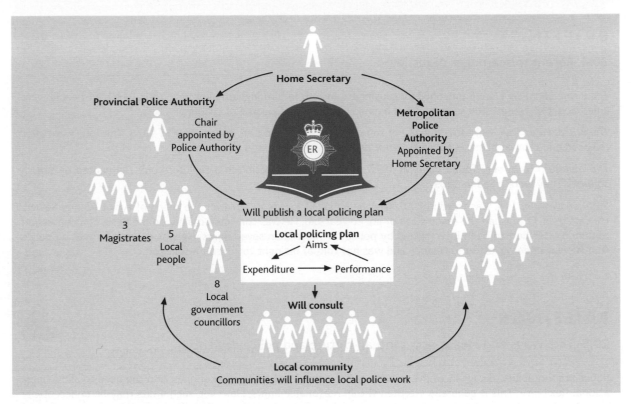

Figure 20.1 The new police authorities of April 1995

discussed. Subsequently, legislation on police powers was produced at a furious pace, from the Public Order Act 1986 to the Police and Magistrates' Courts Act 1994 and then the Crime and Disorder Act 1998, which placed a responsibility on the police to work with the local political authority and other services with the aim of reducing crime.

The 1994 Act, in particular, reshaped the tripartite structure of police account-ability noted earlier, reducing membership of the police authorities, giving them wider powers within a 'business-oriented' brief, and making them accountable to the Home Secretary. Critics say that these committees are now little more than mini-quangos and are far from being democratically representative of local people. Figure 20.1 shows the structure of the new police authorities.

Clearly the strengthening of police powers was one of the dominant motifs of 'law and order' legislation since the 1980s. Some obviously felt that the wisdom of this trend was highly questionable as another and darker theme emerged in par-allel. This concerned the misuse of police powers and the miscarriage of justice. A dramatic sequence of appeal cases revealed serious police malpractice (e.g. suppression or falsification of evidence and wrongful arrest), resulting in appalling miscarriages of justice. Earlier disclosures of corruption had, it seemed, produced few enduring lessons for the police. As David Rose remarks: 'If police detectives could steal or take bribes, it did not take a vast leap of the imagination to consider that they might also present evidence produced by fabrication or duress' (*In the Name of the Law*, London: Jonathan Cape, 1996, p. 43). The cases exposed a dis-maying picture of dishonesty, impropriety and callousness on the part of some police officers (see Briefing 20.4).

Unsurprisingly, a recurrent concern for reformers and critics of the police is the question of how to detect and prevent police deviance, corruption and prejudicial mishandling of cases. It was hoped that the calling of an inquiry into the criminal

BRIEFINGS

20.4 Recent miscarriages of justice

The Birmingham Six were imprisoned for causing explosions in Birmingham pubs in 1974 in which 21 people were killed and 162 injured. The six were freed from jail in 1991 and cleared of charges.

The Bridgewater Four were found guilty of murdering 13-year-old Carl Bridgewater in 1978. The four were later released and cleared because police evidence against them was found to be wrong.

The Guildford Four were found guilty in 1975 of causing an explosion in a Guildford pub frequented by British soldiers. They were freed in 1989.

Stephen Downing, 44, was freed in 2001 after being jailed for life in 1974 for the killing of typist Wendy Sewell. He was then 17 but had the reading age of an 11-year-old. He was convicted mainly on the basis of a confession obtained after he had been interrogated by police for more than seven hours. He was never informed by police that he was under arrest or in custody and was not told of his right to consult a solicitor.

BRIEFINGS

20.5 The 'Ways and Means Act': canteen culture and police deviance

Police accountability always faces the problem of balancing strict application of rules with the need to allow operational flexibility. This is generally accepted within reasonable limits. However, such limits may be unacceptably stretched by the informal police culture ('canteen culture'), and invocation of the fictitious 'Ways and Means Act' as a form of justification. An important investigation of police culture and police perceptions of the public was a study commissioned by the Metropolitan Police and undertaken by the Policy Studies Institute (PSI) in the early 1980s (Smith and Gray, 1983). The research found evidence of disturbing levels of racism and sexual discrimination. The PSI report also distinguished between three types of 'rule' within police culture: the 'working', the 'inhibitory' and the 'presentational' (ibid., pp. 169–72). The first type represents the 'accepted' way of working but is by no means always in line with formal regulations. Inhibitory rules are formal rules that carry organisational weight and must therefore be followed, even if seen as unnecessary by officers. Presentational rules highlight the disparity between how the police are supposed to act and how they actually act.

This analysis implies that if regulation of the police is to be effective, it must involve a high degree of self-regulation and require a commitment by police officers at all levels to high standards of conduct. Imposing new systems and new institutions may not be enough. It is just as important to develop a culture of compliance.

D. J. Smith and J. Gray, *The Police in Action*, London: Policy Studies Institute/Gower, 1983

justice system under Lord Runciman would offer a programme for sweeping reforms. In the event, the Report of the Royal Commission on Criminal Justice (1993) suggested very few. New Labour proposals for relaxation of controls on the police (e.g. suspension of rights in cases of suspected terrorism) may exacerbate the problem.

Issues in policing

The police attract a great deal of attention and criticism either because they have been placed on a pedestal or because of the importance of their powers. It should, of course, also be emphasised that the police perform an unenviable and difficult task and receive a great deal of deserved praise, and public and political support. However, there are areas for future development and reform.

Police forces have faced recurrent criticism for being predominantly male and white. Forces have sought to improve recruitment of women and ethnic minority officers. According to figures from Her Majesty's Chief Inspector of Constabulary (HMCIC), in 1997/8 less than 16 per cent of officers were women and only 2 per cent were from ethnic minorities. The police – like the judiciary – are not representative of British society. This fact undoubtedly hinders their efforts to engage the support of some ethnic minority communities.

This observation illustrates that the police make only a particular kind of contribution to 'policing'. The general public do a great deal of 'police work', regulating young people, providing surveillance and intelligence (Neighbourhood Watch, Crimestoppers). Various public and private bodies employ inspectors, investigators, wardens and guards. The 'boundaries of policing' are increasingly blurred, most significantly because of the unrelenting growth of the private security sector. A mixed market now flourishes and readers might note some interesting echoes of eighteenth- and nineteenth-century arrangements for policing society. In no small measure, policing has been 'privatised' and is now a matter for many bodies other than the police themselves.

The National Criminal Intelligence Service (NCIS), created in 1992, incorporates several formerly distinct databases and under the 1997 Police Act is now supported by a new National Crime Squad (NCS). In the post-Cold War era, the involvement of the security services, first in operations against domestic terrorism, and now in relation to the 'war on terrorism and on drugs' (authorised under the Security Services Act 1996), has also been a development to note. This represents the involvement in criminal investigation of a highly centralised yet largely invisible and unaccountable agency. In the future, cooperation between NCIS, the NCS and the security services (MI5 and MI6) will create a very powerful, centrally directed police establishment. Does all this represent an Orwellian vision of Big Brother police agencies, or is it simply a practical response to the increasing diversity and incidence of serious organised crime?

BRIEFINGS

20.6 Police authority mergers

In late 2005 the Home Secretary announced that he would invite the existing police forces and authorities to produce their own proposals for merging with neighbouring forces. The main reasons for this merger were said to be the need to produce organisations of sufficient size to deal with terrorism and the growth of serious organised crime. Despite protests from many local authorities, opposition MPs and some police forces about the policy, the authorities consulted at a local level and produced their own plans. The Home Office provided feedback on the proposals. Lancashire and Cheshire, for example, will merge to form a new North West police force, while Staffordshire, West Mercia, Warwickshire and West Midlands will amalgamate to become a new West Midlands police force.

The Home Office's strategy of asking local authorities and forces to come up with their own proposals was clearly designed to reduce concerns about lack of consultation and joining together areas with long rivalries. It retained considerable influence over the process. The Home Office was so determined to push ahead with the mergers that it even rejected the conclusions of a Number 10 report, which warned that mergers 'could be a costly, protracted exercise which does not always deliver expected benefits and inevitably causes distraction for management and staff'.

If these mergers were to go ahead there would be around 24 police forces in total. Some regard the mergers as another small step towards the creation of a genuinely national police force on the continental model, raising questions of excessive powers and accountability. Others regard it as a long-delayed recognition of the need to increase the size and efficiency of police forces.

BRIEFINGS

20.7 Jury trials: the jewel in the crown of British justice?

It is widely believed that juries constitute the 'jewel in the crown' in the British legal system and that any attempt either to reform the system or to restrict access to jury trials must, as a result, make the legal system less just, less reliable and less democratic. In the late 1990s Jack Straw, the Labour Home Secretary, tried to restrict the right to a jury trial in around 18,000 cases, by allowing magistrates to determine exactly where the case would be heard. This would have had the effect of speeding up the legal process, thus helping the government to demonstrate that it believed in 'tough' summary justice. It was suggested that this proposal would have saved around £100 million per year. A coalition of lawyers and civil liberties groups mobilised to defeat the proposal in the House of Commons and Lords.

In 2003 David Blunkett, the new Home Secretary, again tried to limit access to jury trials by introducing a new Criminal Justice Bill. There was again a great deal of opposition to these plans and, in the event, access to jury trials was limited only in the case of complex fraud cases or where there were fears of jury tampering. Further restrictions on the right to trial by jury are not possible without the support of both Houses of Parliament. (The same Act, incidentally, also removed the 'double jeopardy' rule, whereby an individual could not be tried for the same offence twice.)

In June 2005 Lord Goldsmith, the Attorney General, said the government had 'absolutely no plans' to restrict further the right to jury trial. The opposition parties remained unconvinced.

Is trial by jury such a precious thing that it should be preserved? The following points should be noted:

- All civil law cases (with the exception of those relating to defamation or libel) are tried by a judge sitting alone.
- A small fraction of the criminal cases (about 1 per cent) that come before a court are tried by jury. The vast majority are tried in a magistrates' court by three magistrates.
- 'Trial by jury' is really 'trial by judge and jury'. Judges decide on the admissibility of evidence and the procedures followed. They also advise the juries on issues of law. Juries decide on matters of fact (whose version of events are to be believed).
- Some crimes are 'triable either way' (either by magistrates or by a jury). The decision is left to the accused, but this gives them an incentive to pretend that they wish to go to Crown Court. This inevitably delays things.
- In Northern Ireland a system of judge-only trials (the 'Diplock courts') was introduced in the 1970s in relation to terrorist actions. This was done both to prevent potential intimidation of jurors and to avoid the difficulties of finding a fair jury in a deeply polarised community.

Little is actually known about how effective the system of jury trials actually is (and there is legislation that actually prevents research on this subject). There is deep scepticism among some lawyers about the ability of ordinary people to understand the complex issues in some cases. As one judge famously put it,

> Gentlemen of the jury, the facts of this distressing and important case have already been put before you some four or five times, twice by prosecuting counsel, twice by counsel for the defence, and once at least by each of the various witnesses who have been heard; but so low is my opinion of your understanding that I think it necessary, in the simplest language, to tell you the facts again.

There is also a risk that jurors evaluate the performance of the prosecution and defence advocates, rather than the guilt or innocence of the defendant. Restricting access to jury trials would save money that could be used elsewhere in the legal system. It is arguable that lawyers like jury trials simply because they can feather their own nests!

On the other side, trial in front of a judge might stack the odds in favour of the prosecution. Judges, like magistrates, could become 'case hardened' and inclined to believe the police or other authority figures rather than ordinary witnesses. 'Ordinary people' are best able to judge the honesty of witnesses (an issue that is of crucial importance even in complex fraud trials). The democratic principle of counting heads and spreading the task of thinking among twelve people rather than one person suggests that juries are more likely to get the answer right than a judge sitting alone.

Perhaps the strongest argument in favour of jury trial, however, is that there is widespread support for it. A MORI poll in early 2002 suggested that fully 81 per cent of those polled thought that juries were fairer than a judge sitting alone. If people lose confidence in the legal system, they may become less active citizens and less likely to assist the police, and the quality of policing may decline to the cost of us all.

Source: See Helena Kennedy, *Just Law: The Changing Face of Justice and Why It Matters to Us All*
(London: Vintage, 2005), chapter 4

Recent developments

Shortly after the 1997 general election, Labour's new Home Secretary, Jack Straw, enjoyed a warm reception on his first visit to a Police Federation annual conference and in October that year he told delegates at his party conference: 'We said we would make Labour the party of law and order. And we did.' So what policies have been pursued since Labour came to power – are they new or do they largely represent continuity with the 'old' party of 'law and order', the Conservatives?

Some on the left of the party (or its still significant liberal wing) complain that they see little difference between the crime control policies of the new government and those of its predecessors. Prior to the 1997 election there did indeed emerge a new consensus between the parties on several relevant matters and clearly there is some continuity today. The 1998 Crime and Disorder Act, however, illustrates significant differences between the new and previous governments. The Act placed particular emphasis upon the prevention and reduction of crime, linked to a requirement that the police develop closer working partnerships with local authorities to implement community safety strategies. In these new arrangements for inter-agency cooperation, the police become just one among several agencies that must work together and, importantly, local government has a key role. While the Conservatives had refused to acknowledge links between social conditions and crime, Labour readily adopted the connection as a target for policy, creating a Social Exclusion Unit, introducing proposals to prevent and tackle juvenile crime and announcing a new strategy to reduce the misuse of drugs. All three initiatives reflected both compromise and tension between old-style Labour welfarism and New Labour's strategy of being tough but showing compassion where appropriate. Action against social exclusion includes creating opportunities for employment and education but also commitments to regenerating social and community life in deprived areas. Policing and community safety play significant roles here, and the 1998 Act also created a framework for intervention that coupled prevention with deterrence. Relevant measures include: anti-social behaviour orders (ASBOs) that restricted certain freedoms; parenting orders, requiring parents to take responsibility for the behaviour of their children; and curfew orders, which are temporary, apply to children under the age of 10 and are designed to prevent young children being on the streets after a certain time. All these community measures require the involvement and support of the police if they are to be effective. A preventive agenda is evident here and central to it is a concern to help young people and families. However, we can also hear quite clear echoes of the tough 'zero tolerance' approach that has been borrowed from the politics of US policing. At the 1998 Labour conference, Tony Blair proposed the introduction of 'order maintenance' into 25 crime 'hot spot' areas throughout Britain. This included a more targeted use of police patrols, based on the belief that random patrols were largely ineffective in deterring crime or catching criminals. Such measures blended the reactive aspects of zero tolerance with crime prevention.

This proposal became part of a promise to increase the number of police officers on the street, delivered to the party conference of the following year, 1999, but the pledge quickly became the subject of a political dispute. In 1995 John Major had made a similar promise to his party conference, but chief constables used their discretion over budgets to spend money on new technology. Labour's idea was for a fund to which specific bids must be made, in order to constrain chief officers and ensure the money was used for recruitment. In itself this seemed an imaginative way to compel police chiefs to spend funds as government intended. However, the question then arose of just how many extra police officers would actually be recruited. Mr Straw insisted the plan was to recruit 5,000 officers 'over and above' the recruitment plans of the police service. A leaked memo and questions from the shadow Home Secretary, Ann Widdecombe, cast doubt on this, suggesting the effect would merely be to stabilise current total numbers by replacing officers leaving and retiring. Three years later the Police Federation was still complaining about shortages of regular officers forcing 'rookies' on to the beat. It accused government of a 'boom and bust' policy. By the end of its second term, police numbers had increased significantly under Labour. There was continued muttering, however, about the amount of bureaucracy that the police had to deal with, among other things as a result of ensuring that their activities were compliant with the Human Rights Act 1998.

In 2003 the government introduced Police Community Support Officers, full-time employees whose job was to support the police by dealing with truants, controlling crowds, patrolling, gathering intelligence and generally increasing the visibility of the police force on the street. By March 2006 there were about 6,200 of these and the Chancellor of the Exchequer announced plans to double their numbers in his budget that month.

Human rights

The rights each human has to personal freedoms, respect and dignity. There have been various attempts to define these, such as the United Nations Declaration of Human Rights (1948) and the European Convention on Human Rights (1951).

Policing, civil liberties and human rights

The government intended the Human Rights Act 1998 to signal a commitment to equal treatment, justice, and freedom from unwarranted interference. Clearly sensitive to such trends, the report of HMCIC (1998) noted that equal opportunities training for police officers was in need of improvement and suggested that impressive-sounding policy and strategies still have a long way to go before they make a real impact on the predominantly white police organisation.

Despite the introduction of the HRA, critics continue to see some developments in policing as endangering civil liberties and human rights. The record of deaths in police custody continues to give rise to concern, attracting the attention in 1998 of the United Nations Committee Against Torture; the use of CS gas spray by the police is increasingly controversial following reports of deaths said to be connected to improper use of the weapon; and further cases of police misconduct and corruption have come to light. One commissioner of the Metropolitan Police acknowledged that there may be up to 250 corrupt officers serving in this force, suggesting that the pursuit of an unknown number of criminal investigations may be compromised.

The extension of police powers caused some people worries. For example, the capacity for police surveillance was increased under the 1997 Police Act, which gave police similar powers to the security services to employ hidden cameras and microphones ('bug and burgle' powers) during the investigation of serious crimes. A new national database holding over 3 million DNA samples from active criminals has been promised by Tony Blair, and both he and the Home Secretary have stated that they wish to see the extension of drug testing of people arrested and charged by the police. Such developments are strongly criticised by civil liberties commentators.

Critics also point to the difficulty of making the police accountable for their actions or, in some important cases, their inaction. There have so far been fewer revelations of miscarriages of justice than in the 1980s and early 1990s. However, some have surfaced, particularly relating to police mishandling of cases involving ethnic minorities.

The electorate appear to feel less safe today than when New Labour came to power, despite the fact that crime has fallen substantially in recent years. Indeed, people are actually 40 per cent less likely to be a victim of crime in 2004 than in 1995. Figure 20.2 shows that crime has been falling in recent years. The growing mismatch between perception and reality represents one of the central conundrums in British public policy. Some inevitably blame the media for focusing on violent

Figure 20.2 Crime trends in England and Wales, 1995–2004/5 (indexed: 1995 = 100)

Notes: 1995–9 – calendar years; 2001–5 – financial years. The data are from the British Crime Survey (this data differs from crime figures recorded by the police).

Sources: *Home Office Statistical Bulletin 11/05, July 2005; Crime in England and Wales 2004/2005*, Table 2.01, p. 25 (for 1995–7 and 2001–5); *Home Office Statistical Bulletin 10/04, July 2004: Crime in England and Wales 2003/2004*, Table 2.01, p. 21 (for 1999). Reproduced under the terms of the Click-Use Licence

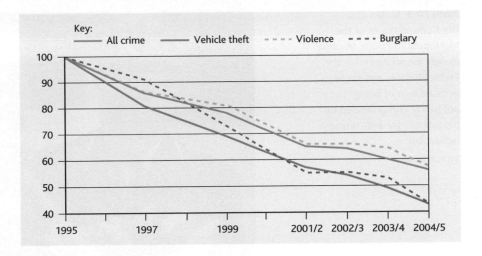

crime (which, unlike most other crimes, has increased). Some blame the government's for 'spinning' the figures and distorting reality (though the data were compelling: crime *had* fallen). Others have pointed to the government's hyperactivity in the field of crime and terrorism as a source of insecurity. It may be that 'talking tough' about crime and terrorism and increasing the visibility of the police stimulates rather than removes fears. Whatever the case, there is little doubting the potency of crime as an electoral issue (see Chapter 15).

The growing sense of insecurity undoubtedly increased following the 9/11 attacks in New York, the 2004 Madrid bombings and the 7/7 attacks in London, which caused increased pressure on the forces of 'law and order'. The Labour government acted by providing the police, security services and immigration authorities with sweeping new powers in the Anti-Terrorism Crime and Security Act 2001 and the Prevention of Terrorism Act 2005 (see Chapter 21). Some of these were found to be incompatible with human rights by the courts and had to be hastily revised (see Chapter 19). Many critics thought that the tendency of government to introduce new legislation did little to improve security and may have actually reduced it by lulling people into a false sense of security. Indeed, some regarded the 'war on terrorism' as little more than an excuse to gather more police powers.

Some senior officers expressed awareness of these concerns. In his Reith lectures in late 2005, Sir Ian Blair, the Commissioner of the Metropolitan Police, distinguished between a 6 July and 7 July police force. He called for a more vigorous debate on the nature of the modern police force via:

■ creation of a select committee on the Police

■ citizens' panels to discuss issues

■ openness on operational issues

■ more informed debate in the media.

Such reforms may help to establish more broad-based consent for policing, but they also require the police to become less defensive and more willing to engage in debate. Better policing may depend on changing the culture of the profession: something that is very difficult to do.

Plate 20.3 Sir Ian Blair, the Commissioner of the Metropolitan Police, became closely associated with the Prime Minister and some accused him of being politically compromised by his support for anti-terrorist legislation

Source: Empics

BRIEFINGS

20.8 Anti-social behaviour orders

All crime, apart from violent crime, has fallen in recent years but many people still feel less safe. Attention has shifted from property crime towards behaviour which – while in itself not criminal – makes life difficult or inconvenient for the community. This includes the harassing of pensioners in shopping centres, noisy neighbours keeping people awake all night with their loud and raucous parties or even the wearing of paramilitary uniforms designed to intimidate others. In the wake of the 2005 general election campaign, Tony Blair emphasised a new 'Respect' agenda.

One of the most controversial policies introduced to deal with these problems was the anti-social behaviour order, created by the Crime and Disorder Act 1998. ASBOs are civil orders issued by magistrates at the request of the police or local authorities, which place restrictions on the activities of individuals (described by the media variously as 'yobs', 'tearaways' or 'neighbours from hell'). Some ASBOs were served on children as young as 10 and on pensioners ('OAPs on ASBOs', the media declared!). Some young people were put in jail for breaching the conditions of their ASBO. Civil liberties groups such as Liberty protested against the policy, claiming that it amounted to imprisonment without having been convicted of a crime. They claimed that ASBOs had been used to victimise some vulnerable groups. One councillor in Manchester responded, 'I'm tired of being lectured on civil liberties by people who live in Surrey.' Between 1999 and December 2004 a total of 4,649 ASBOs were served in England and Wales.

Source: See Polly Toynbee and David Walker, *Better or Worse: Has Labour Delivered?* (London: Bloomsbury, 2005), pp. 224–5

Plate 20.4 Stephen Lawrence inquiry suspects leaving the court and gesturing at Lawrence family supporters

Source: Empics

The Stephen Lawrence murder and the Macpherson inquiry

On 22 April 1993 Stephen Lawrence, a young black teenager, was murdered in an unprovoked attack carried out by white assailants. The police investigation into his death was grossly inadequate and the racist nature of the attack given little attention. A campaign by Stephen's family called for an official inquiry into the police handling of the case, failure to follow up information available at the start of the investigation, and lack of success in providing evidence that could lead to prosecutions. This call was resisted by the Metropolitan Police and rejected by Conservative Home Secretaries. In 1998 Jack Straw, the Labour Home Secretary, asked Sir William Macpherson, a former High Court judge, to chair an official inquiry into the case. Sir William examined three specific allegations against the police – that they were incompetent, racist and corrupt. Reporting in 1999, Macpherson did not find evidence of corruption but concluded that the police investigation had been 'marred by a combination of professional incompetence, institutional racism, and a failure of leadership by senior officers'. He was clearly frustrated by senior officers who were unable to agree their accounts of conversations about the investigation, concluding that some officers must have lied. His highly critical report could not be lightly dismissed by the police.

Naturally, comparison was made with the report prepared by Lord Scarman in 1981, which found evidence of racism within the police and made recommendations concerning police–community relations and the need for racism-awareness training for the police. Macpherson's reminder of the intervening lack of progress in improving police recruitment of minorities and changing police culture was disturbing. HMCIC had acknowledged these particular problems in its 1998 report and noted the 'continued and disturbing evidence of racist, sexist and discriminatory behaviour within forces'. However, Macpherson went further than either Scarman or HMCIC and argued that racism was a problem that could be viewed as pervasive throughout the Metropolitan Police (and, by implication, throughout the police service nationally). The report referred to the idea of '**institutional racism**' to describe this state of affairs, defining it as:

Institutional racism

The collective failure of an organisation to provide an appropriate and professional service to people because of their colour, culture or ethnic origin.

Plate 20.5 The Metropolitan
Police sheds crocodile tears
over the failure to convict
the murderers of Stephen
Lawrence

Source: New Statesman,
26 February 1999

> The collective failure of an organisation to provide an appropriate and
> professional service to people because of their colour, culture or ethnic origin.
> It can be seen or detected in processes, attitudes and behaviour which amount
> to discrimination through unwitting prejudice, ignorance, thoughtlessness and
> racist stereotyping which disadvantage minority ethnic people.
>
> Sir William Macpherson of Cluny, *The Stephen Lawrence Inquiry: Report
> of an Enquiry* (London: The Stationery Office, 1999), para. 6.34

The Macpherson Report made 70 recommendations and the Home Secretary
accepted most of these. Clearly, the agenda for the government and, more than
ever, for the police, now includes serious initiatives for a change in institutional
culture. Such change needs to be more sensitive to the problem of racism, to civil
liberties and to human rights issues. This is, of course, an 'ideal' agenda and
readers will by now be fully aware that the police service is a rather conservative
organisation. In coming years the politics of policing will partly revolve around
tackling police resistance to fundamental change. At the same time it must be
emphasised that, since the 1980s, it has not been only domestic issues that have
shaped the police agenda but also international pressures such as the 'war on drugs'
and now the 'war against terrorism'. Critics argue that the latter has given rise to
a new era of policing of 'suspect' groups as 'risk populations', such as immigrants
and Islamic minorities who have come under scrutiny for possible terrorist connections. Labour has adopted a tougher anti-immigration stance and supported the
extension of police and security service powers in the face of a terrorist threat.
In such a climate, fundamental change, in the sense of increasing police sensitivity
to racism and human rights issues, may be harder to accomplish than previously
hoped.

BRIEFINGS

20.9 Police complaints and Jean Charles de Menezes

The Police and Criminal Evidence Act 1984 established the Police Complaints Authority in order to investigate complaints against the police. In April 2004 this became the Independent Police Complaints Authority (IPCA), partly as a result of flaws revealed by the Stephen Lawrence Inquiry. It is run by 17 commissioners who act independently of the police and government, and none of whom has ever worked for the police. The IPCA is staffed by lawyers and health and education specialists.

On 22 July 2005, shortly after the London tube suicide bombings and a subsequent series of failed bombings, armed police officers shot and killed a Brazilian, Jean Charles de Menezes, at Stockwell tube station in London. The officers apparently believed that he was either a terrorist or another suicide bomber. His family lodged a formal complaint and the case was referred to Mike Grant, an IPCC senior investigator. He was asked to report in due course to three commissioners: Mehmuda Mian Pritchard, Naseem Malik and David Petch.

The case brought into sharp focus the police's policy of 'shoot to kill', which allowed police officers to shoot suspects where they believed that they represented an immediate threat to themselves or to the public. Critics argued that the policy was bound to result in accidents and that particular parts of the community (ethnic minorities) were more likely to suffer than others. Defenders of the policy pointed out that, in certain dangerous situations, the police could hardly wait for a suspect to make the first move. If an ordinary citizen honestly and genuinely believes that they are about to be attacked and kills someone, they are not guilty of murder, and the same should apply to police officers.

The IPCA had not reported as at March 2006.

Plate 20.6 The parents of Jean Charles de Menezes visit the scene of the Stockwell shooting. The shooting of Jean Charles de Menezes raised issues about police use of firearms, the 'shoot to kill' policy and accountability in 2005

Source: Empics

BRIEFING

20.10 National identity cards

The Labour Party manifesto of 2005 contained a promise to introduce a voluntary system of national identity cards should it be re-elected. Charles Clarke, the new Home Secretary, introduced a bill early in the new parliament to do just this, but encountered a great deal of criticism of his proposals. Some of these criticisms related to general principles; others to the specific proposals.

Advocates of national identity cards argue that a system of identity cards is essential. They point out that:

- Britain is one of few countries in the EU that does not currently have a system of national identity cards.

- Everyone carries identity documents. Having an authoritative form of identity would help people open bank accounts, take out loans and so on.

- False identities have often used by those involved in terrorism.

- The inclusion of biometric data makes it difficult to fake the cards and the data have a variety of uses.

- The cards will make it easier to ensure the integrity of the UK's borders and monitor the movements of asylum seekers.

- The cards will make it more difficult for people to claim welfare benefits that they are not entitled to.

- There will be safeguards designed to ensure that the information is not abused by those government officials with access to it.

Civil liberties groups, such as Liberty, on the other hand, argue that:

- International comparisons are irrelevant. Some European countries still have an identity scheme as a legacy of their Fascist government!

- Other forms of identity are entirely voluntary. Even if the national identity card is voluntary, organisations will insist on producing it for all sorts of purposes. It will soon become de facto compulsory.

- National identity cards will not deter crime.

- National identity cards will do nothing to prevent terrorism. The Madrid bombers in 2004 all used their own passports. They wanted the world to know who they were.

- Most welfare fraud consists of claiming benefits to which one is not entitled: mistaken identity accounts for a small fraction of cases.

- The system will be expensive and the burden will fall most heavily on the poor (costing around £75–100).

- The police and other authorities may use the information to identify certain groups and discriminate between them. This may undermine their ability to 'police' certain areas effectively.

- The cards will not be safe. Even biometric data can be copied and there will soon be a black market in these cards. Terrorists and criminals will soon make copies.

- The introduction of cards represents another unacceptable expansion of state power and another step towards a 'Big Brother' state. The risks outweigh the benefits.

Others argue that, since current proposals suggest that the cards will be 'voluntary', they will not work.

Clearly, the case for and against national identity cards is complex. Those who are instinctively suspicious of government are likely to oppose it. Those who are not likely to welcome it. (Mr Clarke accused critics of 'liberal woolly thinking and spreading false fears'!) There is also a partisan element to the debate. Many Conservatives, particularly traditional Conservatives, would doubtless be able to accept these proposals if they came from a Conservative government!

The issue of identity cards prompts strong opinions. Both 'sides' have a tendency to overstate the strength of their case. In the end the issue boils down to this: are the benefits likely to exceed the costs? Since the future is uncertain, the answer is not obvious.

Summary

The police are not 'apolitical' and the politics of policing are a complex business. This has been amply demonstrated by the questions and problems raised in this chapter, chief among them:

- police organisation and accountability: who is really in control?

- moves from a local to a national organisation

- procedural reforms and individual rights in relation to the police

- the politicisation of policing

- recent reforms

- the issue of institutional racism

- national identity cards

- recent developments in the law relating to crime and terrorism, which have significantly shifted some of the most deep-seated presumptions in the British legal system.

MILESTONES

Milestones in the development of British policing

1829	Sir Robert Peel's Metropolitan Police Act
1830–60	Establishment of county and borough forces under local control
1856	County and Borough Police Act establishes Home Office inspection of, and grants for, local police authorities
1960	Establishment of the Royal Commission on the Police
1962	Report of the above
1964	Police Act amalgamates 117 police forces into 43. Tripartite control by chief constables, police authorities and Home Secretary
1972	Bains Committee recommendation that chief constables should be as accountable as local authority chief executives is rejected
1976	Police Complaints Board (PCB) established
1979	Central government controls over local government expenditures also mean central control over police expenditure
1981	The Brixton disorders (10–12 April) and the Scarman Report, which criticised aggressive tactics used by the Metropolitan Police
1984	Police and Criminal Evidence Act consolidates police powers but introduces better safeguards for suspects
1984	Police Complaints Board replaced by Police Complaints Authority
1984–5	Miners' strike; employment of national coordination and control
1986	Creation of Crown Prosecution Service
1988	Court of Appeal gives Home Secretary powers to override police authorities on matters of equipment and expenditure
1993	Royal Commission on Criminal Justice (Runciman Report)
1994	Police and Magistrates' Courts Act reduces police authorities to agents of Home Secretary
1995	First woman chief constable appointed. Metropolitan Police Commissioner states that some police routinely carry firearms

▶

Milestones in the development of British policing continued

1997	Police Act creates a new National Crime Squad and gives the police enhanced powers to mount surveillance operations
1998	Crime and Disorder Act places emphasis on cooperation between police, local authorities and other agencies; introduces ASBOs to curb anti-social behaviour
1999	The Macpherson Report
2001–3	International terrorist attacks spark US-led 'war on terrorism' and suspension of human rights in cases of suspected British terrorists
2002	Police Reform Act replaces Police Complaints Authority with Independent Police Complaints Authority
2005	London bombings (7/7)

Essays

1. Are 'the police' a police 'force' or a police 'service'? What are the implications of these different terms?

2. One conclusion of the Scarman Report was that 'public tranquillity should have a greater priority than law enforcement if the two conflicted' (Reiner, 1994, p. 725). Discuss in relation to the policing of minority communities, making reference to the Macpherson Report.

3. 'The fact that the British police are answerable to the law, that we act on behalf of the community and not under the mantle of government, makes us the least powerful, the most accountable and therefore the most acceptable police in the world' (Sir Robert Mark, Metropolitan Commissioner, *Policing a Perplexed Society* (London: Allen & Unwin, 1977, p. 56). Discuss.

Projects

1. Using newspaper reports, contrast the priorities of any two local police forces in enforcing specific laws.

2. Using press and television reports, discuss whether recent decisions of the IPCA will increase or decrease confidence in the regulation of the police.

Further reading

P. Joyce, *Law, Order and the Judiciary* (London: Hodder & Stoughton, 1999) is a good overview of this general area, well written and comprehensive; Robert Reiner, *The Politics of the Police* (Oxford: OUP, 3rd edn, 2001) is generally regarded as the best introduction to the study of the police and policing; see also C. Elmsley, *The English Police: A Political and Social History* (Hemel Hempstead: Harvester Wheatsheaf, 1991) on the history of the police; L. Lustgarten, *The Governance of the Police* (London: Sweet & Maxwell, 1986) is the classic study of the police and the constitution. See Thomas Quinn, 'Tony Blair's second term' in John Bartle and Anthony King (eds), *Britain at the Polls, 2005* (Washington: CQ Press, 2006); Polly Toynbee and David Walker, *Better or Worse: Has Labour Delivered?* (London: Bloomsbury, 2005), chapter 6; D. Woodhouse, 'Politicians and the judges: a conflict of interest', *Parliamentary Affairs*, **49** (3), 1996, pp. 423–40, for recent specialised discussions.

On the proposed mergers of constabularies, see Her Majesty's Inspector of Constabularies, *Closing the Gap* (London: Home Office, 2005; http://inspectorates. homeoffice.gov.uk/hmic/inspect_reports1/thematic-inspections/closinggap05.pdf).

For a police perspective on recent developments affecting their profession, see Sir Ian Blair's Dimbleby Lectures for the BBC (http://www.reform.co.uk/filestore/ pdf/The%20Richard%20Dimbleby%20Lecture%202005.pdf).

Useful web sites on the police and policing

Hot links to these sites can be found on the CWS at www.pearsoned.co.uk/budge.

There are a number of very good web sites that cover key aspects of police, policing and crime in the United Kingdom. The first stop for students is the web site for the police services of the UK (www.police.uk). The Metropolitan Police web site is available at www.met.police.uk.

The Home Office offers a comprehensive account of the guiding principles of criminal law and police reform at www.homeoffice.gov.uk/new_indexs/ crim_jus.htm. In addition, the government maintains an individual web site on police reform (www.policereform.gov.uk). The government's Criminal Policy Group (http://www.homeoffice.gov.uk/cpg/cpg.htm) works in conjunction with the Home Office, aiming to ensure the effective delivery of justice, through efficient investigation, detection, prosecution and court procedures. Police Law (www.policelaw.co.uk) is an independent organisation that provides insightful information and analysis of all aspects of British criminal law.

Rethinking Crime and Punishment (www.rethinking.org.uk) is an independent organisation that aims to raise the level of public debate about the use of prison and alternative forms of punishment in the UK. You can also obtain useful information on crime and the strategies oriented to prevent it at www.crimeconcern. org.uk. The Police Complaints Authority web site is available at www.pca.gov.uk.

chapter 21

Security and secrecy

Police efforts to maintain order have been increasingly supplemented over the post-war period, most spectacularly by private security firms. Related groups such as Customs and Excise also operate to detect crime in their specialised areas. Ordinary citizens have been drafted in, notably through Neighbourhood Watch schemes, and have been encouraged to use 'hotlines' to name those suspected of social security frauds. Many public spaces are now covered by 24-hour camera surveillance.

Wherever we go and whatever we do in Britain, therefore, we may be under surveillance and scrutiny by someone, even our neighbours. Much of this activity is initiated by the security and intelligence services, whose functions have been expanded in recent years to combat serious crime, such as international terrorism and drugs trafficking.

All modern states have security services to protect themselves against terrorism, subversion and violence, but they present democracies with dilemmas nonetheless. First, one of the most important principles of democratic government is that no person or organisation is above the law. As we shall see, however, the courts have traditionally given ministers and the security services considerable leeway when interpreting the legality of their actions. If the 'rule of law' means that the security services should comply with the European Convention on Human Rights, it is difficult to argue that the British security services operate fully within these parameters. Second, all branches of a democratic state should be publicly accountable, but the security services are under a blanket of secrecy, for obvious reasons. Third, to be effective the security services must have powers necessary to operate secretly and effectively against the enemies of the state, but they must not be used by the government against its own citizens. In other words, governments must use the security services for the public interest, not for their own political purposes. Nor must the security services be able to take the law into their own hands and act against either the government or its citizens.

Every modern state faces these dilemmas and none has an easy solution. Yet the British state appears to gives its security and intelligence organisations wide discretionary powers that remain resistant to accountability, and to conceal their actions behind an unusual cloak of secrecy. How and why this is the case is discussed in this chapter. It covers:

■ the rise of security and secrecy as a political issue

■ the security and intelligence services

■ laws and conventions about secrecy

■ accountability

■ freedom of information and open government

Throughout the chapter it must be kept in mind that the security and intelligence services are secret and it is not, therefore, possible to say much about them with certainty.

Plate 21.1 The government argued that the police and security services needed new powers in the wake of the London bombings of July 2005. Were they crying wolf or seeking to protect their citizens?

Source: Empics

The rise of security and secrecy as a political issue

As we have already indicated, there is always a tension in a liberal democratic society between the need for society to defend itself from those who wish to undermine it and the preservation of basic civil liberties and freedoms. There is considerable agreement across the political divide on the need to strike a balance between the conflicting demands of security and liberty, but different groups draw the lines in different places. Liberals have traditionally been sceptical about the need for giving the state greater powers over individuals. They insist that those who are responsible for enforcing such laws are subject to the rule of law. Many socialists have been similarly suspicious of the security services, particularly when their operations were directed against 'socialist' states, such as the former Soviet Union.

Conservatives, on the other hand, have emphasised the need of the state to protect itself from those who would threaten to undermine it from either within or without. Although they are committed to the 'rule of law', they have traditionally been willing to give the security services many discretionary powers. To some extent, however, the disagreements are based on power rather than ideology. Governments of all ideological inclinations tend to see the advantages of increasing the powers of the security services and protecting their activities under a shield of secrecy.

In the 1950s and 1960s **national security** was not a major political (or partisan) issue. The success of wartime intelligence operations against Germany and the fear of communism during the Cold War helped to sustain support for the security services and the secrecy that surrounded their operation. The issue grew, however, as a result of a sequence of events in the 1970s and 1980s, including:

National security

Policies designed to maintain the established political order. In Britain's case this means defence of its parliamentary democracy.

- The 'troubles' in Northern Ireland (see Chapter 10).

- *The spread of Northern Irish terrorism to the mainland*: the bombings in Birmingham and Guildford in 1974, Harrods (1983), Brighton (1984) (which nearly killed Margaret Thatcher and severely injured Norman Tebbit, a senior Cabinet Minister), the Stock Exchange (1990), Warrington (1993), Manchester (1996) and Canary Wharf (1996).

- *Rising levels of serious crime*: including large-scale international drugs and crime rings.

- *Failures of the security system*: several intelligence and security personnel were revealed to have acted as Soviet spies – among others, the double agents Guy Burgess, Donald MacLean and Kim Philby, as well as (Sir) Anthony Blunt, Sir Maurice Oldfield (former head of MI6), George Blake (an officer of the Secret Intelligence Service), the Portland Spy Ring, John Vassall and Michael Bettaney. There were also allegations that Sir Roger Hollis (a former director-general of the Security Services) and John Cairncross of MI6 were Soviet agents, although Hollis was cleared by an official inquiry in 1974 and later by evidence of a Soviet defector.

- *International terrorism*: the 9/11 attacks in New York (2001), the Bali bombings of 2002, the bombing in the Egyptian resort of Sharm el-Sheikh in 2005, and the 7 July 2005 bombings in London, together with recurrent rumours about plots to use the poison ricin on the London underground or poison water supplies, have raised anxiety to an altogether new level.

- *The proliferation of weapons of mass destruction*: there have been growing fears that terrorist groups would acquire weapons of mass destruction from 'rogue states' such as Iraq, North Korea or the former Soviet states.

These events contributed to a growing concern about security. At the same time, however, there was also mounting concern about growing government power, and threats to individual rights and civil liberties. These fears were fuelled by:

- The growing power and centralisation of the police and their apparent lack of accountability (Chapter 20).

- The growing power of central government, especially the Prime Minister and Cabinet, and the apparent weakening of the legislature and local government (Chapters 5 and 12).

- The growing amount of information held about people by private companies (e.g. the databases held by banks, supermarkets and so on).

- The growing power of the security services as a result of legislation increasing their responsibilities.

- The growth of technology for surveillance and the centralisation of computer records (fears increased by proposals to introduce national identity cards: see Chapter 20).

- An increasing awareness of the secretive nature of the British state, and of the ways in which the Official Secrets Act was used. In the 29 years between 1945 and 1974, a mere 34 people were prosecuted under the Official Secrets Act. In the 8 years between 1978 and 1986, the number prosecuted was 29.

- A series of events involving the security forces and government secrecy with allegations about either government misuse of secrecy, or security services abuse of power. In the United States there was a sharp decline in trust in government after the 'Watergate' scandal, which revealed that President Nixon had tried to cover up attempts to bug political opponents by his supporters. In the UK the failure to find weapons of mass destruction (WMD) after the Iraq War led some to conclude either that the government had exaggerated the threat posed by Saddam Hussein's regime or that it had simply 'lied' about it in order to justify a decision made for other reasons.

- Television programmes (such as the popular BBC programme *Spooks*) and films (such as the film *Enemy of the State*) have raised awareness of security and secrecy.

Heightened concern about security has, therefore, coincided with heightened concern about the growth of unaccountable (and unchecked) power of the state. The resulting clash between national security and liberty has produced political conflicts:

- between the House of Lords and Commons (over the government's efforts to introduce national identity cards)

- between the parties (with the opposition parties, and particularly the Liberal Democrats, taking a consistently sceptical approach to increased powers for the police and security services)

- within the Labour Party (over national identity cards and detention of terrorist suspects without trial)

- between the courts and ministers (over detentions without trial and the use of third-party torture evidence)

- among the public as a whole (who broadly support efforts to increase police powers) and minorities (such as Muslims) who fear being victimised under the new legislation.

While the traditional left–right issues of the economy, taxation, welfare and the role of the trade unions have become less important as a result of New Labour's repositioning in the centre, security and secrecy have become increasingly significant issues.

The security services have been drawn into the political limelight and the problems they pose for democracy have become a political issue. While the need for effective security seems more urgent than ever, there is a strong suspicion that security services and the police have sometimes acquired powers that they don't really need (or which will not make a difference to security) and that the government has enforced secrecy, not in the public interest, but in order to protect

BRIEFINGS

21.1 Operations of the secret state

Tisdall and Cruise missiles, 1984 Sarah Tisdall, a clerk at the Foreign Office, believed her minister, Michael Heseltine, was deceiving the public about the arrival of Cruise missiles at Greenham Common in order to minimise public opposition. She released information to the *Guardian*, was prosecuted and received a six-month prison sentence.

Ponting and the *Belgrano* affair, 1985 Clive Ponting was a high-flying civil servant who released information suggesting that the government had concealed the true circumstances of the sinking of the Argentine battleship *General Belgrano* in the Falklands War of 1982. Ponting defended himself in court on the grounds that he was acting in the public interest. He was acquitted by the jury despite the summing up of the judge, who equated the interests of the nation with that of the government of the day!

Political vetting in the BBC, 1985 It was revealed that MI5 had an office in the BBC in order to vet job applicants. It was promised that the practice would stop.

Phone tapping, 1985 A former member of MI5, Cathy Massiter, claimed in a TV documentary that MI5 routinely tapped the phones of trade union officials and CND leaders. (The security services claimed that they did not do so as a matter of routine, but did act where specific individuals were thought to be subversive.)

***Spycatcher*, 1987–8** The government tried to ban the book by Peter Wright, formerly of MI5, even though it was easily available abroad. The government sent the Cabinet Secretary, Sir Robert Armstrong, to an Australian court to try to ban publication there. This was itself a controversial political use of a civil servant, and Sir Robert caused more criticism by admitting that the government had been 'economical with the truth'. Among other things, Wright claimed that some members of MI5 had tried to destabilise the Wilson Labour government, and that MI5 'bugged and burgled its way across London'.

Zircon, 1987 A film about the British spy satellite, Zircon, made by the journalist Duncan Campbell, was seized by the Special Branch from the Edinburgh offices of the BBC, together with five other programmes in the same series. The government claimed that the film was a danger to state security, but critics argued that the government wanted to conceal the fact that the Zircon project was behind schedule.

Defending the Realm, 1991 Evidence from an ex-security services official, Robin Robison, was presented in a *Guardian*/ITN *World in Action* inquiry, claiming that the security services regularly engage in unauthorised spying on, among others, Britain's EU partners, to discover their negotiating positions, on commercial companies and on trade union leaders. He claimed that the security services concealed some of this activity from ministers.

Surveillance of MPs and ministers The memoirs of ex-minister Alan Clark suggested that MPs and ministers are under MI5 surveillance. This has been consistently denied by the security services.

The Scott Inquiry, 1996 The official inquiry into arms to Iraq revealed how secretive the British government is at the highest levels, and how little is known even by MPs.

The Shayler Affair, 2002 David Shayler, a former MI5 officer, published allegations that the service had – among other things – tried to arrange the assassination of Colonel Gadaffi, the Libyan leader. Shayler was prosecuted under the Official Secrets Act and sentenced to six months in prison. This led to demands that 'whistleblowers' within the security services should be given protection.

The failure to find weapons of mass destruction Intelligence reports published before the Iraq War (together, it is fair to say, with various United Nations reports) suggested that Iraq had an active programme to create weapons of mass destruction and that it might have links with groups such as al-Qaeda. In the event no weapons of mass destruction were found and no links with terrorist groups were ever established. These failures added to the belief that the intelligence services were willing to lie or, at the very least, distort information in order to provide the government with the excuse it wanted to invade Iraq.

State censorship Examples of government censorship of TV include among others, *Yesterday's Men* (1971), *Real Lives* (1985, about politicians in Northern Ireland), *The War Game* (1965), *A Question of Ulster* (1972) and the Zircon affair (see earlier in this briefing). The government also strongly criticised the BBC for its reporting of the Suez War, the Falklands War and the US bombing of Libya, and the Independent Broadcasting Authority for showing *Death of a Princess* (1980) and *Death on the Rock* (1988).

its own reputation. There are also fears that the powers of the security services have been used by governments to spy on citizens, and claims that the security services themselves have engaged in covert operations against citizens and even the government. To understand how this might be so it is necessary to understand the nature of the security services and the laws and conventions under which they operate.

Security and intelligence agencies

Little is known for certain about the British security services, and it is difficult to sort out fact from fiction. From 1993 some official information has been released, and web sites have opened. The UK has three main intelligence and security agencies – the Secret Intelligence Service (SIS – better known as MI6), the Security Service (better known as MI5), and the Government Communications Headquarters (GCHQ). They were placed on a legal basis by the Intelligence Services Act 1994, and two Security Service Acts of 1989 and 1996.

Spending on these agencies has increased rapidly in recent years as a result of perceptions of increased risk. Their combined budget for 2002/3 was £893 million. This was planned to increase to £1,553 million by 2007/8 (see Figure 21.1). Some have cynically argued that the security and intelligence services have deliberately exaggerated the threat to the UK posed by terrorists in order to acquire additional powers and increase the size of their budgets. Most people do, however, appear to feel that the threat is significantly greater than before.

To the three agencies we should add three more with a different status and paid for from different funds, namely the Defence Intelligence Staff, the Special Branch, and the National Criminal Intelligence Service. All six are concerned

Figure 21.1 Spending on national security, 2002–8
Source: UK Security Service

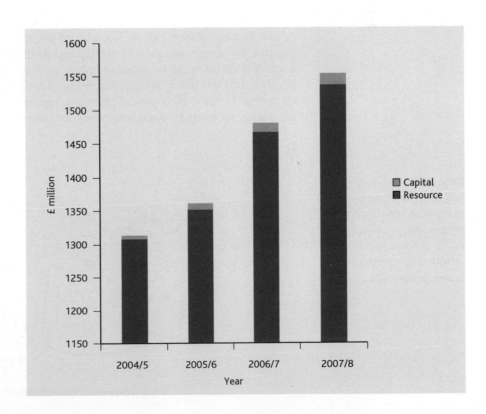

BRIEFINGS

21.2 The Butler Report

The invasion of Iraq was justified partly on the basis that Saddam Hussein's regime had an active programme designed to produce weapons of mass destruction. Several allegations, including the claim that Iraq could deploy WMD within 45 minutes, were emphasised in a dossier published shortly before the war, which was designed to influence public and parliamentary opinion. When the Coalition forces failed to find WMD after the war, the Prime Minister decided to establish a committee to review the intelligence on which the conclusions had been based.

The committee comprised five privy counsellors: Lord Butler (the former Secretary to the Cabinet), Sir John Chilcot (former Permanent Secretary at the Northern Ireland Office), Field Marshal The Lord Inge, Michael Mates MP (former Minister for Defence) and Ann Taylor MP (former Leader of the House of Commons). It was given access to relevant papers, visited Washington and interviewed many of those responsible for drawing up the intelligence reports. The resulting report was 196 pages long and published in July 2004.

In a crucial part of the report (paragraph 465) it was stated, 'the language in the dossier may have left with readers the impression that there was fuller and firmer intelligence behind the judgements than was the case: our view, having reviewed all of the material, is that judgements in the dossier went to (although not beyond) the outer limits of the intelligence available'.

This carefully worded statement was widely interpreted as implying that, although the government had not lied about WMD it had either seen what it wanted to see or had been reckless about the truth when it drew up its dossier. Others interpreted it as suggesting that the Prime Minister had been in the words of *The Economist* magazine a 'sincere deceiver'.

The Butler Report provided some reassurance about the performance of the intelligence services but little for the Prime Minister or Cabinet.

Source: See *Review of Intelligence on Weapons of Mass Destruction* (London: HMSO, 2004); www.archive2.official-documents.co.uk/document/deps/hc/hc898/898.htm

in one way or another with the security of the nation, and the intelligence this requires. To some extent there is overlap and duplication between these agencies. Some feel that it might be better to reduce the number of agencies. Others fear, however, that this would produce larger and more powerful organisations that are more able to abuse their powers. Possible replication and competition between these agencies might be thought to be a small price for liberty.

Plate 21.2 The failure to find weapons of mass destruction after the end of the Iraq War increased public cynicism about security and intelligence
Source: Cartoon Stock

"I see weapons of mass destruction!"

BRIEFINGS

21.3 The security services

There are six major organisations charged with responsibility for national security. They are as follows:

The Security Service (MI5)

The domestic intelligence service is charged with 'protecting the UK against threats to national security from espionage, terrorism and sabotage, from the activities of foreign powers, and from actions intended to overthrow or undermine parliamentary democracy by political, industrial or violent means'. Since the Security Service Act 1996, its role has been expanded to cover work against serious crime. It employs about 1,900 full-time staff and is headed by a director, currently Dame Eliza Manningham-Buller. In 1992 it took over from the police the responsibility for gathering intelligence about the IRA on the British mainland. MI5 is also engaged in political vetting, and with 'the preventing and detection of serious crime, and for connected purposes'. It cooperates closely with SIS and GCHQ (see below), and with foreign police and intelligence agencies. Its headquarters are in Thames House, Millbank, London SW1.

The Secret Intelligence Service (SIS, better known as MI6)

A government report on the national intelligence machinery states that the main job of the SIS is to produce secret intelligence on Britain's interests in the fields of security, defence, and foreign and economic policies. Less is known about it than the Security Service. Its headquarters are at Vauxhall Cross, London, and it employs about 2,300 staff. Its role has also been expanded to cover the war against drugs. The chief of the Secret Intelligence Service, John Scarlett, is known simply as 'C'. His appointment was controversial because he had previously been chair of the Joint Intelligence Committee and was thought to have too close connections with Tony Blair. He worked closely on the production of the dossier setting out the government's case for the Iraq War and was one of the key witnesses in the Hutton Inquiry into the death of Dr David Kelly (see Chapter 14).

Government Communications Headquarters (GCHQ)

The existence of GCHQ was officially acknowledged in 1983 as the result of a spy scandal. It is famous for its wartime work on decoding German messages enciphered by the 'Enigma' machine. It is mainly concerned with government coding and decoding, and with the use of satellites and listening posts to monitor communications. It works closely with its equivalents in the United States, Canada, Australia and New Zealand. Its headquarters in Cheltenham employs about 7,000 people. It was the subject of political controversy in 1984 when the government banned its workers from trade union membership (allegedly under pressure from the Americans after a spy scandal) (see Chapter 19). Trade union rights were restored by the Labour government in 1997.

Defence Intelligence Staff (DIS)

Part of the Ministry of Defence and funded from the defence budget, the DIS is mainly concerned with foreign military threat assessment and intelligence, but also with the internal security of the armed forces. The DIS is estimated to have a total staff of about 4,600 civilians and military people.

Special Branch

As Branch 12 of the Special Operations of the Metropolitan Police, Special Branch is especially concerned with gathering and analysing intelligence on extremist political and terrorist activity. It works under the direction of a senior officer of the Metropolitan Police and is, therefore, accountable to the Home Secretary. The Special Branch works closely with MI5. Its responsibilities include intelligence work, enforcing official secrets laws, the security of VIPs, watching ports and airports, and making arrests for MI5. It employs about 2,000 people in its central and local offices.

The National Criminal Intelligence Service (NCIS)

The youngest of the intelligence agencies, the NCIS was established in 1992 in order to collect and analyse intelligence about serious and organised crime. It is mainly concerned with economic crime, drugs, illegal immigration, vehicle crime, West African organised crime, serious sex offenders, counterfeits, football hooliganism, kidnap and extortion, and wildlife crime. It works closely with foreign intelligence agencies and contains the UK division of Interpol. Outside its headquarters in London it has offices in Birmingham, Bristol, Glasgow, London, Manchester, Wakefield and Belfast. It has a staff of 900 and falls under the authority of the Home Secretary.

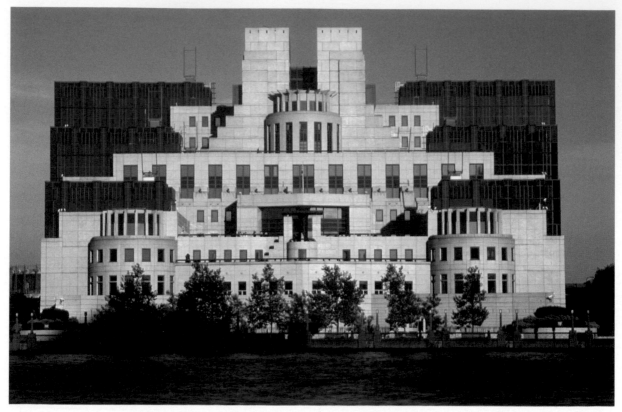

Plate 21.3 MI5's impressive Thames headquarters can be seen by visitors to London
Source: Alamy/Steve Atkins

Recent anti-terrorist legislation

Terrorism Act 2000

Before 9/11 the principal legislation relating to terrorists was the Terrorism Act 2000, which outlawed certain terrorist groups such as al-Qaeda and allowed the Home Secretary to add new groups to the list of 'proscribed organisations'. The Act gave powers to investigate terrorism, wide stop and search powers and the power to detain suspects after arrest for up to 14 days. It also created new criminal offences of inciting terrorist acts, seeking or providing training for terrorist purposes at home or abroad, and providing instruction or training in the use of firearms, explosives or WMD. It further provided additional powers for Northern Ireland, which must be reviewed annually.

Anti-Terrorism, Crime and Security Act 2001

This Act was introduced shortly after the 9/11 attacks to cut off the supply of funding to terrorists, to initiate new 'streamlined' immigration procedures and new provisions enabling government agencies to share information, and to improve the security of the nuclear and aviation industries. Parts of the Act were repealed after the House of Lords judgment in the 'Belmarsh' case (see Chapter 19).

Plate 21.4 The futuristic headquarters of GCHQ at Cheltenham, which monitors communications all over the world
Source: Empics

Prevention of Terrorism Act 2005

The Home Office introduced a system of 'control orders' that permitted the imposition of obligations on individuals designed to stop their participation in terrorist activity. Control orders can limit the use of certain types of communication and/or restrict movement. The Home Secretary applies to the court for such orders on the basis of intelligence information, but may also impose a provisional order providing that this is reviewed by a court within 7 days. The applications may be heard in open court or, where the intelligence information is sensitive, in closed session. If the court allows the order, it will automatically be sent for judicial review. These orders are limited to 12 months at a time, although a fresh application can be made after it has expired. The Home Secretary is required to report to Parliament about how many such orders are made.

Regulation of Investigatory Powers Act 2005

The Regulation of Investigatory Powers Act 2000 (RIPA) gave the security and intelligence agencies the authority to engage in covert surveillance, providing that the activity is necessary for national security and proportionate. The 2005 Act updates the law in relation to the interception of communications on the web and by other means. It includes new powers to tackle the problem of 'strong encryption', which makes it virtually impossible for the authorities to decode messages (a decision that has prompted vigorous debate about censorship among users of the web).

Concerns about recent anti-terrorist legislation

Although the UK has never had a Bill of Rights that protects individual liberties (the 'Bill of Rights' from 1689 relates to Parliament), there has been a long tradition of civil liberties. It is often said (with some justification) that Britons can do anything they like, as long as there is not a specific law against it. Many hoped that the Human Rights Act 1998 would usher in a new era of liberty. Unfortunately for its advocates, the HRA coincided with the emergence of new threats and these have prompted the Labour government to legislate in order to protect national security.

The growth of the 'security state' has raised a number of concerns:

- The rushed way in which the legislation was introduced was indicative of a panic. Critics believe that increased police powers are not the answer to the threats posed by terrorism. These can only be solved by traditional policing within established rules, improved cooperation with other countries and so on. Some argue that most of the legislation is either counterproductive (will help recruit people to terrorist causes) or more concerned with reassuring rather than protecting voters (and that it will promote a false sense of security).

- Much of the legislation was rushed through with little serious parliamentary scrutiny and it did not receive the intense discussion that it merited. Potentially 'bad laws' may have perverse or unintended consequences.

- Many laws provide the agencies with discretionary powers that might be abused. The Terrorism Act 2000, for example, gives the police the power to arrest a person (without a warrant) if they suspect them of being a terrorist. This does not tie the power of arrest to a specific offence and does not require the officer to give reasons for the arrest. The same Act gives officers the power to search within a defined area. In *R (Gillam)* v *Metropolitan Police Commissioner* (2004), police used their powers to search a student who was protesting against arms sales! The courts held that this was unlawful because the powers were related only to terrorism.

- There was a fear that the security services and government were, in effect, gathering a wide range of powers that will stay permanently on the books.

- Continuing concerns have been expressed about the lack of accountability (see below).

Some people feel that some of the presumptions that have, hitherto, laid at the heart of the British legal system have been displaced in recent years. The Criminal Justice and Public Order Act 1994 already removed the 'right to silence', allowing juries or magistrates to make such inferences from the defendant's silence as 'appear proper'. The Terrorism Act 2000 reversed the presumption of innocence, with suspects having to show 'beyond a reasonable doubt' that they did not possess items for terrorist purposes. The Anti-Terrorism, Crime and Security Act 2001 permitted detention without trial (until declared illegal by the House of Lords) and the Prevention of Terrorism Act 2005 permitted the imposition of restrictions on liberty without formal trial. The new immigration system excludes suspects and their lawyers from the hearings when intelligence evidence is being discussed. Moreover, this 'intelligence' often falls well short of the normal standards demanded by the British courts. (It was partly on the basis of faulty intelligence that the UK went to war in Iraq.) Some lawyers and civil liberties groups fear that in trying to combat terrorism the UK may have become a terrorist in itself. Others feel that these claims are grossly exaggerated and that the pedantic emphasis on the 'legal niceties' risks letting terrorists go free and/or that national security warrants the granting of such powers to the police and security agencies.

Who is right? As in so many cases, the answer is far from clear. How should the uncertain risk that an individual might perpetrate a crime be traded off against the certain fact that they will be denied their liberty? Since the future is uncertain, there is no clear answer. Those who give priority to liberty will be suspicious of all restrictions. Those who give priority to security will welcome such powers (subject to proper safeguards).

Accountability

One of the principal concerns of those who are alarmed by what they see as the growth of the 'security state' is the fact that the security and intelligence agencies are, to a large extent, unaccountable for their actions. The Prime Minister has overall responsibility for intelligence and security matters. The services are under the day-to-day control of their respective directors, who in turn, are personally responsible to a minister (see Figure 21.2). Two main committees of central government are responsible for the work and coordination of the various branches of the security services: the Ministerial Committee on the Intelligence Services and the Joint Intelligence Committee.

The Ministerial (Cabinet) Committee on the Intelligence Services (CSI)

The terms of reference of the committee are to 'keep under review policy on the security and intelligence services'. It is chaired by the Prime Minister and its members are the Deputy Prime Minister, the Home, Defence, and Foreign Secretaries, and the Chancellor of the Exchequer. This committee is assisted by the Permanent

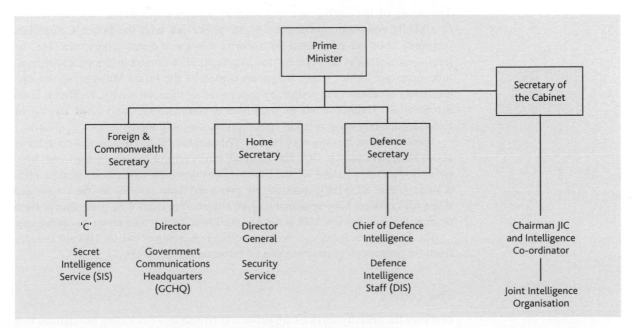

Figure 21.2 Ministerial and Cabinet responsibility for the intelligence services

Source: HMSO. Reproduced under the terms of the Click-Use Licence

Secretaries' Committee on the Intelligence Services (PSIS), chaired by the Cabinet Secretary.

Joint Intelligence Committee (JIC)

This is part of the Cabinet Office and under the authority of the Cabinet Secretary. It is chaired by a senior member of the Cabinet Office and is the main body for advising on intelligence priorities, and for gathering and assessing results that are provided to ministers and other senior officials. A key individual is the intelligence coordinator.

The Intelligence and Security Committee

Intelligence and security agencies are not directly accountable to Parliament, and ministers can refuse to answer any parliamentary question related to national security. The House of Commons has a nine-member Parliamentary Intelligence and Security Committee, which – uniquely among parliamentary committees – is appointed by the Prime Minister. Members are 'notified persons' under the Official Secrets Act (see below). The chair of the committee in March 2006 was Paul Murphy, the former Secretary of State for Northern Ireland, who replaced Ann Taylor, former Leader of the House of Commons, after the 2005 general election.

The committee examines the spending, administration and policy of the intelligence services. It issues a brief annual report, and other reports on specific matters. The reports are not very informative or controversial. They are, however, first presented to the Prime Minister and censored to remove sensitive material. Other select committees have not been successful in recent attempts to interview security officials, or in attempts to scrutinise the security agencies. The National Audit Office does, however, scrutinise the accounts of the agencies.

Commissioners and tribunals

The heads of the intelligence and security agencies themselves are not subject to a public complaints procedure, as the police are with the Police Complaints Authority, but are monitored by security service commissioners: one for the intelligence services and one for the interception of communications. Both commissioners are former senior judges appointed by the Prime Minister, so the system really amounts to oversight by judges rather than the courts. In March 2006 Sir Swinton Thomas acted as intelligence commissioner and Lord Brown of Eaton-Under-Heywood acted as interception commissioner.

There is also an Investigatory Powers Tribunal established to examine complaints about MI5, MI6 and GCHQ. The tribunal works entirely in secret. Between 1989 (when it was set up) and 1996 the tribunal considered 187 complaints against MI5, rejecting them all. MI5 documents are protected from scrutiny by the courts and when MI5 officers have appeared to give evidence in court they have always been unidentified and hidden. MI5 is not required to tell the police about its operations.

The Security Service, the Secret Intelligence Service and GCHQ are exempt from the provisions of the Freedom of Information Act 2000.

The courts

In theory the security services are subject to British law (including the statutes that created them and the Human Rights Act). However, the courts have traditionally been reluctant to intervene in relation to national security.

Plate 21.5 John Scarlett, the former chair of the Joint Intelligence Committee, was a controversial appointment as director of MI6. He had worked closely with Alastair Campbell, the Prime Minister's press secretary, on the preparation of the government's case for the invasion of Iraq

Source: Empics

As we saw in Chapter 19, the House of Lords was willing to read words into legislation in order to provide the Home Secretary with enough power to justify his decision to intern an individual in the case of *Liversidge* v *Anderson* (1942). In the GCHQ case relating to the banning of trade unions in 1985, the courts held that the workers would have had a legitimate expectation to be consulted about the ban 'but for national security'. In that case Lord Diplock stated:

National security is the responsibility of the executive government; what action is needed to protect its interests is, as the cases cited by my learned friend, Lord Roskill, establish and common sense itself dictates, a matter upon which those upon whom the responsibility rests, and not the courts of justice, must have the last word. It is par excellence a non-justiciable question. The judicial process is totally inept to deal with this sort of problem.

Lord Hutton (the author of the Hutton Report on the death of Dr David Kelly) went further in *R* v *Shayler* (2002), arguing that the courts would assume good faith on the part of security officials. No wonder, one might think, that he was asked to conduct the inquiry into the death of Dr David Kelly (see Chapter 19)!

More recently, of course, the Lords has intervened to protect individuals detained under the Terrorism Act 2001 and to prevent reliance on third-party evidence procured by torture. In the Belmarsh case, however, the House of Lords reiterated that 'Great weight should be given to the judgment of the Secretary of State, his colleagues, and Parliament on that question because they had been called upon to exercise a pre-eminently political judgment.' The judges accepted the minister's view that there was a public emergency which justified acting other than in accordance with the European Convention on Human Rights. They found against the minister because the relevant Act *discriminated* between British and non-British nationals and because the detentions were not *proportionate*.

Standards of conduct

In effect, no more than the dozen people who are members of the Cabinet Committee on Intelligence Services and of the Joint Intelligence Committee have first-hand information about the security services. Half of these are unelected and the other half are among the busiest politicians in the land. In short, the security services seem to be largely 'self-tasking': they set their own goals, choose their own means and monitor their own activity. They are beyond the scrutiny of all but a few overworked politicians, and perhaps even beyond that. According to Peter Wright in *Spycatcher* and Robin Robison in the TV programme *Defending the Realm*, the Prime Minister and the Cabinet do not know half of what goes on.

In the absence of stronger forms of accountability, the real safeguards are the professional standards that are inculcated within the various organisations. The directors of MI5 and MI6, therefore, are both responsible for ensuring that the agencies carry out their statutory duties and that they remain politically impartial. Both agencies maintain Codes of Practice designed (they claim) to ensure that the rule of law is paramount and that the methods of investigation are proportionate to the particular threat. They report annually to the Prime Minister and Home Secretary (in the case of MI5) and Prime Minister and Foreign Secretary (in the case of MI6). Suspicions inevitably remain that the agencies bend the rules (either when they feel a desperate need to, according to their supporters, or routinely, according to their critics).

Some hoped that the role and size of the security services would be reduced after the collapse of the Soviet Union, but instead its activities were expanded to include 'the prevention and detection of serious crime, and for connected purposes'. It is no longer only concerned with national security but also with duties that were previously reserved for the police. At the same time MI5 is charged with vague duties – serious crime and connected purposes – but unlike the police it is not subject to democratic accountability.

The secret state

The British state as a whole, not just its security and intelligence agencies, works within a framework of laws and conventions that give it substantial powers to protect itself from public scrutiny. The centrepiece of the system is the Official

BRIEFINGS

21.4 Instruments of the secret state

Privy counsellor's oath

Since the year 1250, members of the Privy Council have been required to swear, in the presence of the monarch, an oath dealing with secrecy, among other things. Only senior government and opposition members are privy counsellors, but membership is for life.

Royal prerogative

Crown powers that are in the hands of ministers are held not to be subject to parliamentary approval or scrutiny. They are, as is the rest of the 'unwritten constitution', vague and undefined and give governments great scope to do what they want (see Chapter 4).

D-notices

The job of the D-notice system ('D' is for defence) is to prevent the publication of information that is not in the public interest. The old D-notice Committee, made up of representatives from the Ministry of Defence and the media, has been reconstituted as the Defence, Press and Broadcasting Advisory Committee. It no longer issues D-notices but what are called Press and Broadcasting Advisory Notices.

Government Directive, 1952

This directive stated the convention that ministers 'do not concern themselves with the detailed information which may be obtained by the Security Service in particular cases but are furnished with such information as may be necessary for the determination of any issue on which guidance is sought'.

Public Records Act 1958 (the 30-year rule)

Under the Public Records Act, certain government papers are not publicly available until they are 30 years old, or longer in some cases. The Act covers about 40 categories of document, including those about living people, confidential government information, state security and Ireland.

The Official Secrets Act, 1989

The Act covers the following subjects: security, defence and international relations; crime and its investigation; warrants issued under the Interception of Communications Act (1985) and the Security Services Act (1989) and information that these warrants produce; and secret information provided by foreign governments and international agencies.

- Release of information that is deemed 'harmful' to the public interest is a criminal offence. It is no defence to argue that public disclosure of the information is in the public interest, or that the information is publicly available abroad.
- Disclosure of information covered by the Act is harmful in itself; the prosecution is not required to prove that disclosure has probable or actual harmful effects.
- The Act covers Crown servants, members of the security services, government contractors and journalists. Editors who encourage journalists to disclose such information are liable to prosecution.

Security Services Act, 1989

The 1989 Act gave MI5 (not MI6) a statutory basis, and a broad range of rather vaguely defined functions. These were expanded in 1997 to include the prevention and detection of serious crime and connected purposes. The Act also provided for a security services commissioner to review phone-tapping warrants, and a tribunal to revoke improper warrants. Critics argue that the commissioner and the tribunal are weak and ineffective.

Regulation of Investigatory Powers Act, 2000

This updates the Interception of Communications Act of 1985 to cover electronic communications. The Act gives law enforcement organisations (that is, police forces, intelligence services, Customs and Excise and the Inland Revenue) blanket powers to intercept, monitor and track all electronic communications (email and internet). It can do this secretly (it cannot be revealed in court) in the interests of national security, preventing or detecting crime, preventing disorder, public safety, protecting public health and 'in the interests of the economic well-being of the United Kingdom'.

Secrets Act of 1989, which replaced the hugely controversial Official Secrets Act 1911. Section 1 of the 1911 Act made it an offence to engage in conduct contrary to the safety or interests of the state, including the disclosure of information of use to enemies. In most cases this section has been uncontroversial. It was Section 2 that caused trouble. This made it a crime for anyone employed by the state to pass on official information to those not authorised to have it. The section was so broadly and vaguely worded that it included almost any information: the number of paper clips used by a government department or the number of cups of tea consumed in the canteen.

It is widely held that Section 2 suppressed legitimate discussion about British government, a belief supported by a series of incidents. The judge who tried the journalists who revealed that the government was supplying large quantities of arms to Nigeria (1971) said that the section should be pensioned off. The 1972 Franks Committee on Official Secrecy recommended repeal. A string of events in the 1970s and 1980s brought the issue to the surface again, but nothing was done until 1988 when a private member's bill to reform the Act was defeated by the government, which then passed its own Official Secrets Act in 1989.

Section 1 of the 1911 Act remained unchanged in the 1989 Act, which concentrated on Section 2. The government claimed to have liberalised the law by dropping many of the items covered by the 1911 Act. Critics claim that the new Act simply excludes harmless information that has not been a problem in the past, while at the same time increasing secrecy in other areas, including those raised by the *Spycatcher*, Tisdall and Ponting cases, all involving officials who leaked information about government activities that they thought harmed the public interest. Critics also argue that the definitions of what is 'harmful' are both broad and vague: it is estimated that the Act creates about 2,300 offences. In short, it is said that the 1989 Act increased rather than decreased state secrecy by tightening the government's grip on a range of broadly and vaguely defined matters, by expanding the range of people to whom they applied ('notified persons'), and by eliminating the most important grounds that might be used in defence by those prosecuted under the Act.

Freedom of information and open government

Freedom of information

Free public access to government information and records as required by citizens.

Critics of the Official Secrets Act and of the broader apparatus of state secrecy in Britain do not deny the need for some secrecy. What they argue is that Britain is unnecessarily secretive compared with most other western states, and that it needs legislation that positively requires the government to release certain sorts of information to citizens, if they require it. This is not a matter of military information, espionage or the 'war against terrorism', but information that the state holds about its citizens and organisations relating, for example, to individual health records or tax payments, or to issues such as mad cow disease or the arms to Iraq affair. In recent years the matter of freedom of information has become one of the most controversial in the UK.

Many western democracies have freedom of information acts that guarantee citizens the right to see a wide variety of documents, both state and personal. State secrets in these countries are exempt, of course, but they are more narrowly and precisely defined than in Britain. Although there are many practical difficulties with freedom of information acts (documents can be 'lost', destroyed or suppressed), countries such as the United States and Sweden have operated them successfully for many years. The UK, however, did not get its Freedom of Information Act until 2000, and even then, critics claim, it got an inadequate one.

Open government

The relatively unconstrained flow of information about government to the public, the media and representative bodies. In open government it is the government, not the citizen, who decides what information to release, but under freedom of information it is citizens, not the government, who decide what information they want.

Freedom of information

Pressures for freedom of information provisions have increased over the past decade, prompted by the tightening of official secrets legislation in the 1989 Official Secrets Act, although Major's Conservative government did promote open government in 1992 by making public some government documents, such as the rulebook on procedures for ministers, the list of Cabinet committees, some records not previously released under the 30-year rule, and even information about MI5. The Citizen's Charter of 1991 also promised more open government and information. A code of practice was introduced in 1994 that promised: (a) secrecy only where there is good reason for it; and (b) increasing amounts of information.

Major's initiative did not satisfy the freedom of information lobby, especially since the government rejected two private member freedom of information bills in 1992 and 1993, and then expanded the powers of MI5 with the Security Service Act of 1996. The Scott Report on the arms to Iraq affair, published in 1995, and the government's handling of the BSE (mad cow) scare revealed a deep-seated culture of secrecy at the highest levels.

Two pressure groups took the lead in campaigning for freedom of information:

- *Charter 88* – a broad alliance of people and organisations to press for a range of constitutional changes, including freedom of information and open government.

- *Campaign for Freedom of Information (CFOI)* – created in 1984 with the backing of some leading, all-party politicians and senior ex-civil servants. It now has 90 supporting and observer organisations.

Some progress was made with the Data Protection Act (1984), and the CFOI was able to promote private members' bills that resulted in the Local Government (Access to Information) Act 1986, the Access to Personal Files Act 1987, the Environment and Safety Information Act 1998, and the Access to Health Records Act 1990.

Labour came to power in 1997 with freedom of information as a manifesto commitment. Blair promised an end to obsessive and unnecessary government secrecy, and to work on the presumption that information should be released. In the event, the Freedom of Information Bill was delayed, and when it was presented to Parliament, it turned out to be a watered-down version of what had been promised. After controversial and hurried progress through Parliament the Act was passed in 2000, but it did not come into force until 2005.

Freedom of Information (FOI) Act, 2000

The main provisions of the Act are as follows:

- Individuals already had the right of access to their own personal information held on computers and some paper files, under the Data Protection Act 1998. The FOI Act extends these rights to all types of information, whether personal or not.

- Approximately 70,000 'public authorities' and 'publicly owned companies' are covered by the Act.

- The Act is enforced by an Information Commissioner, who combines responsibility for freedom of information and data protection, and a new Information Tribunal.

- There is a duty laid on authorities that do not disclose information to show that this is in the public interest.
- There are many exemptions to the Act. It does not cover any of the intelligence and security agencies, and information will not be released that will cause harm to:
  - national security
  - internal discussion of government policy
  - law enforcement
  - personal privacy
  - business activities or information that could unfairly damage a company's commercial standing
  - the safety of individuals, the public and the environment
  - references, testimonials, or other matters given in confidence.

The delay in implementing the Act gave those in all branches of government time to prepare for the change and (some cynics suggested) time to lose (or destroy) particularly embarrassing documents. Criticism of the Act concentrated on the Act's 23 exemptions that ministers can use to preserve secrecy, including one 'catch-all' clause that enables ministers to withhold information that is not in the public interest or that prejudices the conduct of public affairs. Under a 'right-to-silence' provision, ministers can even refuse to acknowledge whether information exists at all. The Ministry of Defence, for example, denied that it had any documents that assessed the implications of replacing its Trident nuclear submarines, even though the decision *must* shortly have to be taken by government! There have also been criticisms of the speed with which departments have responded to requests. Some, such as the Treasury, have proved to be remarkably slow, while others, including the Ministry of Defence, have gained reputations for answering requests speedily. It appears that most of the information to date has been released without charge, though there are suggestions that fees may have to increase if the demand for information becomes too heavy. This would have the effect of reducing the flow of information.

It is too early to say what effect, if any, the increased availability of information will have on the decisions taken by either consumers or voters. It does seem likely, however, that the FOI will help voters intrude into the policy-making process. The UK does seem to have taken a small step towards a slightly more open – and more accountable – form of government.

Summary

- All democracies struggle to reconcile the requirements of national security with the protection of civil liberties.
- Political developments have heightened the importance of national security issues.
- The Labour government's response to these new threats has been to expand the powers given to the security and intelligence agencies, prompting intense debate as to whether fundamental liberties have been eroded.

- Many of the agencies charged with protecting national security are only weakly accountable to Parliament or the courts and are surrounded by secrecy.

- The British government remains one of the most secretive in the western world.

- The Freedom of Information Act 2000 has had limited success in producing open government.

MILESTONES

Milestones in British security and secrecy

1911	Official Secrets Act
1958	Public Records Act. Designated documents not available for 30 years after the event, or longer if the Lord Chancellor decides
1968	The Fulton Committee on the Civil Service argues that it is too secret and recommends more openness
1972	The Franks Report on Section 2 of the Official Secrets Act recommends its repeal and replacement with a new, and narrower, official information act
1977	ABC trial: journalists tried and sentenced for disclosing defence information
1984	MI5 officer Michael Bettaney sentenced to 23 years' imprisonment for spying
1984	The Tisdall case about disclosing arrival of US Cruise missiles. Data Protection Act
1985	The Ponting case about the sinking of the *General Belgrano* – Ponting claimed the government lied
1985	The Prime Minister states that security service members will not appear before select committees of the House of Commons. The European Court of Human Rights states that British law about phone tapping is insufficiently clear. This results in the Interception of Communications Act
1986	Local Government (Access to Information) Act
1986–7	The *Spycatcher* affair: government tries to suppress a book about security service lapses
1987	The Zircon affair: TV film impounded by security services
1989	Security Services Act; Official Secrets Act
1990	Access to Health Records Act. MPs Jonathan Aitken and Sir Richard Body claim that MPs are under MI5 surveillance
1991	A TV programme, *Defending the Realm*, claims that MI5 routinely spies on EU partners, commercial organisations and trade union leaders, and keeps much of this secret from ministers
1991	Citizen's Charter promises more open government
1993	Home Secretary states that the head of MI5 will not appear before the Home Affairs Select Committee of the Commons. Ex-minister Alan Clark claims that ministers are under MI5 surveillance. Limited official information released about MI5
1996	Scott Inquiry shows how secretive British government is at the top levels, and how little Parliament knows. Security Services Act
1999	Proposals for new freedom of information and anti-terrorist acts
2000	Regulation of Investigatory Powers Act. Freedom of Information Act. Terrorism Act
2001	Anti-Terrorism Crime and Security Act extends powers to seize terrorist funds, and introduces new immigration procedures and detention without trial
2002	Freedom of Information (Scotland) Act passed by the Scottish Parliament
2002	Publication of the case for the Iraq War
2003	Iraq War
2004	Publication of the Butler Report, House of Lords declares that detentions under the Anti-Terrorism Crime and Security Act 2000 are incompatible with convention rights under the HRA
2005	Prevention of Terrorism Act 2005

Essays

1. 'It is essential that any democracy has powerful security and intelligence services and it is vital that they are not overly constrained by purely theoretical concerns about either the rule of law or the abuse of human rights'. Discuss.

2. Is the Freedom of Information Act 2000 fundamentally flawed, as some claim?

3. The public interest is the basis of government powers to monitor private communications and the basis for it withholding information. What is the public interest and who should define it?

Projects

1. Using official and private web sites, find out what is known for certain and what is only rumour and hearsay about the security and intelligence services.

2. Debate the merits and deficiencies of the Regulation of Investigatory Powers Act 2000 and the Freedom of Information Act 2000.

Further reading

Little is known and not much has been written about the security services in Britain. Most textbooks barely even mention them. Books that do deal with the subject include Jon Alder, *Constitutional and Administrative Law* (Basingstoke: Palgrave, Macmillan, 2005), chapter 19; Helena Kennedy, *Just Law: The Changing Face of Justice and Why it Matters to Us All* (London: Vintage, 2005), especially chapters 2 and 15; P. Birkinshaw, *Reforming the Secret State* (Milton Keynes: Open University Press, 1991); S. Dorril, *The Silent Conspiracy: Inside the Intelligence Services in the 1990s* (London: Heinemann, 1992); Seamus Milne, *The Enemy Within: The Secret War Against the Miners* (London: Verso, 2004); R. Norton-Taylor, *In Defence of the Realm? The Case for Accountable Security Services* (London: Civil Liberties Trust, 1990); and Philip Davies, *MI6 and the Machinery of Spying* (London: Frank Cass, 2004).

See also David Beetham, Pauline Ngan and Stuart Weir, 'Democratic audit: an inauspicious year for democracy', *Parliamentary Affairs*, **55** (2), 2002, pp. 400–15, and Iain Byrne and Stuart Weir, 'Democratic audit: executive democracy in war and peace', *Parliamentary Affairs*, **57** (2), 2004, pp. 453–68 for critical assessments of recent developments.

You can now read the memoirs of a former director of MI5. See Stella Rimington, *Open Secret: The Autobiography of the Former Director of MI5* (London: Hutchison, 2001). The book tells us little that we did not know already but is worth noting.

You can read the Butler Report (Review of *Intelligence on Weapons of Mass Destruction*). (London: HMSO, 2004); www.archive2.official-documents.co.uk/document/deps/hc/hc898/898.pdf.

On the growth of terrorism see the special edition of *Political Quarterly* published in August 2002 (volume **73** (3)). This contains articles by leading scholars in the field of security, terrorism and counter-terrorism. See also John Gray, *Al Qaeda and What It Means to be Modern* (London: Faber, 2003).

On freedom of information, see M. Rathbone, 'The Freedom of Information Act', *Talking Politics*, **13** (3), 2001, pp. 165–70, and M. Flinders, 'The politics of accountability: a case study of the freedom of information legislation in the United Kingdom', *Political Quarterly*, **71** (4), 2001, pp. 422–35.

Useful web sites on security and secrecy

Hot links to these sites can be found on the CWS at www.pearsoned.co.uk/budge.

In the wake of the terrorist attacks of 9/11, issues related to intelligence and security have become more important than ever before. Global security provides an excellent introduction to the organisation and the different institutions of Britain's intelligence agencies at www.globalsecurity.org. The official web site of MI5 can be found at www.mi5.gov.uk, and of GCHQ at www.gchq.gov.uk. A great deal of information about the National Criminal Intelligence Service is available from www.ncis.co.uk. It is worth consulting the United Kingdom mission to the UN at www.ukun.org. Official documentation on the national intelligence machinery can be obtained from www.archive.official-documents.co.uk/document/caboff/nim/natint.htm. The full text of the Anti-terrorism, Crime and Security Act 2001 can be obtained from www.hmso.gov.uk/acts/acts2001/20010024.htm, the Official Secrets Act 1989 is on www.hmso.gov.uk/acts/acts1989/Ukpga_19890006_en_1.htm and for the Security Services Act 1996 visit www.hmso.gov.uk/acts/acts1996/1996035.htm.

A visit to the Lord Chancellor's Department web site on freedom of information at www.lcd.gov.uk/foi/foidpunit.htm would also be useful. The Freedom of Information Act 2000 is available at www.legislation.hmso.gov.uk/acts/acts2000/20000036.htm. The Information Commissioner (www.dataprotection.gov.uk) enforces and oversees the Data Protection Act 1998 and the Freedom of Information Act 2000. The Campaign for Freedom of Information monitors existing access rights and provides practical guides to help people use them; visit it at www.cfoi.org.uk. Liberty is an independent organisation devoted to the protection of civil liberties and human rights; its web site is available at www.liberty-human-rights.org.uk.

SISG is the Security and Intelligence Studies Group (www.rdg.ac.uk/SecInt/), a specialised group of the UK Political Studies Association. We suggest you also visit the International Centre for Security Analysis (Department of War – King's College London) at www.icsa.ac.uk.

PART 7

Policy

chapter 22

Foreign and defence policy

A major justification for keeping the extensive, and expensive, security apparatus described in the previous chapter is Britain's position in world affairs. Its role as a major power means that it is vital for hostile states and interests to know about government intentions and policies. By the same token, it is important for Britain to know about theirs. This justifies large investments in decoding and intelligence gathering (spying) abroad, and placing some restrictions on freedoms at home to prevent foreign spies doing the same things here.

This rather chilling picture of Britain being unable to trust its allies and of countries constantly surveilling and undermining each other rests on a particular view of states. This defines them by their possession of a particular territory that they have to control and defend against aggressive neighbouring states. States are thus always in potential conflict with each other, no matter how united and friendly they seem. But it is not only states that present a threat to Britain. As the events in Ireland over many decades, on 11 September 2001 in the United States and 7 July 2005 in the United Kingdom showed, terrorist groups can operate almost anywhere in the world and do not necessarily depend on any one state for support. This dimension to British and world politics adds further complexity to the business of making defence and foreign policy.

This chapter will:

■ describe the main actors and institutions in British foreign policy making

■ outline the 'realist' and 'idealist' views of foreign policy

■ briefly review the major events and developments in British foreign policy since the 1950s and examine the way in which these have been influenced by Britain's structural and geographical position halfway between Europe and overseas

■ trace the changes in the world that have influenced Britain's post-war foreign policy

■ analyse the motivations and assumptions governing Britain's foreign policy under the Labour government since 1997 and the consequences of these for its anti-terrorist capacity and military role and capabilities

■ ask how successful Britain has been in achieving a world order to its government's liking and assess whether Britain really does remain a 'big player' in international affairs.

Foreign and defence policy making in Britain: actors and institutions

Even more than with other areas of public policy, foreign policy making in Britain is dominated by the executive. The two key Whitehall departments – the Ministry of Defence (MoD) and the Foreign and Commonwealth Office (FCO) – implement policy. The responsible Cabinet secretaries make policy, although the Prime

Minister is always closely involved both with foreign policy and with strategic defence decisions. Within the Cabinet, the Overseas and Defence Policy Committee is the main forum for foreign policy discussions. Parliament plays virtually no role in the actual formulation of policy, although via select committees and debates it can act as a focus for criticism and advice.

The FCO is unusual among Whitehall departments in having few direct constituents. Instead, it oversees the Diplomatic Service, which in turn protects and advances British commercial and diplomatic interests in embassies and consulates throughout the world. As with most other diplomatic services, it operates (at least in part) according to a set of externally agreed international rules governing the behaviour of foreign governments and international organisations such as the North Atlantic Treaty Organisation and the United Nations. In most international political contexts there is, therefore, a foreign policy 'line' that puts negotiation, tact and compromise first, and confrontation second. Nonetheless, the FCO can be subject to pressures both from within government and from societal interests. Relief organisations may work to change the government line in Afghanistan, for example, or human rights groups may call for an embargo on arms sales to autocratic regimes.

The MoD is a very different political animal. It directly serves the very important constituency of the armed services and, indirectly, arms manufacturers and suppliers. Often there is potential or actual conflict of interest between the two departments. At the time of the Falklands War, for example, it was the obligation of the FCO to seek a political solution, while the MoD was obliged to continue its preparations for armed conflict should diplomatic initiatives fail. The Falklands episode also demonstrates just how intimately involved are prime ministers when Britain engages in armed conflict overseas. At some stages of the crisis Prime Minister Thatcher was taking decisions almost on her own.

Other departments, including the Department for the Environment, Food and Rural Affairs, the Department of Trade and Industry, and the Treasury, can also be closely involved in foreign policy, and liaison committees, interdepartmental groups and exchanges of personnel help facilitate policy coordination.

As we saw in Chapter 8, the EU increasingly impinges on foreign and defence policy. Joint projects such as the 'Eurofighter' Typhoon combat aircraft have a clear EU dimension. And, generally, the moves towards a common defence and foreign policy have crucial implications for the future of the whole policy area.

Realism and idealism

The view that states need to be on perpetual guard against each other is the so-called realist view of international relations. It is termed 'realist' because its proponents claim to be able to see beyond governments' protestations of good intent and desire for the common good to their 'real' motives, which on this view are always selfish and aimed at material and territorial gain at the expense of their neighbours.

As most other states are too small and weak to hurt Britain, historically this analysis has mostly concerned the 'big players' – that is, France, Germany, Russia, the United States, Japan and China, although most recently it has also included 'rogue' states such as Serbia (until 2000) and Iraq (until 2003). 'Realist' assessments of the world are most influential in regard to military affairs, where decision makers are usually obliged to adopt a 'worst case' view in order to know what their capabilities should be to ward off the worst threats. Of course, it also dominated assessments during the Cold War (1948–88) when the US-led NATO alliance (of

BRIEFINGS

22.1 The Soviet Union and the Warsaw Pact

The collapse of the Russian Empire in the First World War (1917) led to a political takeover by the Communist Party after a civil war (1918–22). The empire was reconstituted within a reduced territory as the Union of Soviet Socialist Republics (USSR). The republics were created as political units to satisfy the aspirations of the minority peoples of the old empire, who had been conquered by the Russians. However, the Russian Federal Socialist Republic (RFSR) remained the largest and predominant republic. In any case, all the republics and the USSR as a whole were effectively ruled by the Communist Party, which was the real centre of power.

The USSR was attacked by Nazi Germany in 1941 and bore the brunt of fighting over the next four years. Soviet troops gradually pushed the Germans back and occupied eastern Germany and east–central Europe. Communist regimes modelled on the Soviet one were forcibly installed in all these countries, while the Soviet frontier was extended to take in all the territory of the old empire.

These actions led to a break with the USA and Britain. Hostility and frontier incidents prompted the formation of a western military alliance in 1949, the North Atlantic Treaty Organization, covering the USA, Canada, Britain and most countries of western Europe. NATO left troops and bases in Europe, notably in Germany and Britain, which were confronted by the forces of the Warsaw Pact, dominated by the USSR.

The confrontation between those opposing sides was known as the Cold War and lasted from 1948 to 1989. The inefficiency of the Soviet system brought it to an end, as the USSR was unable to sustain either a functioning economy or a high-technology arms capacity that could compete with the USA. The countries of east–central Europe instituted democracy, while the minority republics of the USSR broke away to become independent, leaving Russia itself as the successor state.

BRIEFINGS

22.2 The United Nations

The First World War (1914–18) killed around 20 million people through fighting, famine and disease, mostly in Europe. To help avoid conflict in the future, the victors hoped to create a world body that would bring nation states together and help them resolve disputes peacefully. This was the League of Nations. The League held regular assemblies but became increasingly ineffective as national conflicts intensified in the 1930s. It was also weakened by the fact that the USA and USSR were never members. It did, however, do useful work through its specialised organisations, particularly for refugees in the 1920s, and was associated with bodies such as the International Labour Organization (ILO), which tried to get world agreement on working conditions.

Such bodies were inherited by the League's successor organisation, the United Nations, set up in 1946 after the Second World War (1939–45). This tried to avoid the weaknesses of the League by having, besides a General Assembly in which all states had a vote, a Security Council of major powers: the United States, the Soviet Union (now Russia), China, Britain and France. Each of these can veto UN action, but if they agree, they can apply considerable pressure on states that have broken international agreements. The UN has proved a useful umbrella both for intervention where order has broken down and for policing disputed borders. The intervention in Bosnia (1992–5) was a mixture of both. The UN has been relatively ineffective in stopping fighting, however, because member states often disagree on objectives and are reluctant to pay for costs.

Like the League, the UN does much useful work through specialised agencies for refugees, education, children and health, and also works for international agreements on the environment. The secretary-general appointed by the Assembly has become a world figure, but as a result is often controversial and opposed by one or other of the superpowers. The activity of the UN marks another breakdown in the traditional view of the state as a sovereign entity controlling everything that happens within its own borders.

which Britain was a leading member) confronted the Soviet Union and its allies, sometimes violently but never in full-scale war.

With the end of the Cold War and the growth of inter-governmental cooperation channelled through organisations such as the United Nations and the European Union, another analysis of international relations has gained support. Termed 'idealism', this sees countries as having many common interests that they can maximise only through full cooperation. Often such cooperation involves setting up international regimes and organisations that may even take over sovereign power from states in certain areas. To a considerable extent these 'idealist' assumptions are the ones that led to the formation of the EU. They also have a considerable affinity to the nineteenth-century idea that countries could attain peace and prosperity by opening themselves to each other through free trade, as described in Chapter 2. Indeed, an alternative label for the idealist position is (international) liberalism.

As we shall see, both 'realism' and 'idealism' have influenced British foreign and military policy. Like most general ideas, however, they do not give complete answers to the practical decisions faced by governments. For example, the concepts have but limited application in the fight against international terrorism. Terrorism is often inspired not by state-based nationalism, but by broader religious or ideological causes that cut across nations and continents. Thus, increasing terrorist threats require different military and diplomatic tactics from those appropriate to fighting the Cold War and other 'traditional' conflicts involving nation states.

Post-war developments in British foreign policy

A summary of major events and developments is given in the milestones section at the end of the chapter. For convenience they are grouped under three headings: general international developments involving Britain; decolonisation – the process of disengagement from the colonial empire that in 1945 covered almost a quarter of the globe; and the European Union, already discussed in Chapters 8 and 9.

The problem of **decolonisation** was a major preoccupation of the first half of the post-war period, as it carried potential threats to British investment and trade and might involve the army in unwinnable colonial wars. As the colonies became independent, however, Britain's direct involvement diminished and government attention shifted to the accelerating moves towards economic and political union in Europe, culminating in the 'deepening and widening' of the European Union in the 1990s.

Some have seen this shift of attention from overseas to Europe as evidence of the decline of Britain from a world power to a regional, European power. But this is to ignore the major preoccupation of British governments throughout the post-war period, which was neither the empire nor the European Union but the Cold War, the standoff between NATO (led by the United States and backed heavily by Britain) and the Soviet Union. This involved a state of constant military readiness on both sides, the stockpiling of huge nuclear and other military weapons, and the maintenance of large armies. As part of their commitment to NATO, the Americans maintained important air and army bases in Britain and Germany, to confront the Soviet forces stationed in central and eastern Europe.

The **Cold War** sometimes erupted into local conflicts, although the Americans and Russians never confronted each other directly. Thus in Korea (1950–3) US troops, supported by Britain and other NATO allies, fought North Korean and Chinese troops backed by the Soviet Union. In Vietnam (1964–75) US troops with local support fought local communist troops backed by the Soviet Union. In

Decolonisation

Colonies are foreign territories dominated by stronger states by means of military and economic power. Decolonisation, therefore, is the process of withdrawing from colonial relations with foreign countries so that they gain the autonomy of an independent sovereign state.

Cold War

The state of international relations between the West and the Communist bloc, which stopped short of outright war but involved intense hostility, the stockpiling of arms and the maintenance of large armies in case war should break out.

Afghanistan (1979–89) Soviet troops fought local guerrillas armed and financed in part by the United States.

With the collapse of the Soviet Union and communism in eastern and central Europe between 1989 and 1991, British foreign policy has been redirected towards maintaining stability and peace in a multi-polar world. Hence, the major foreign engagements of the last ten years have involved Bosnia, Kosovo, East Timor and Afghanistan, invading and occupying Iraq in the Middle East and fighting international terrorism.

Changing world context

Clearly, the developments we have traced have not taken place in a vacuum. British politics and interests have changed in response to other events taking place around them. For example, the British would hardly have abandoned their empire of their own volition. They got out because they sensed their presence would no longer be tolerated by the colonised populations, or even perhaps by the two superpowers, the United States and Soviet Union. In this section, we outline the major changes in the world context that influenced British responses in the post-war period. These policy changes are reflected in a changing climate of ideas as to how foreign policy should be conducted.

Changing climate of ideas

Ideas are often discounted as a source of influence in politics, in part because of the realist view that what matters are resources and power. No matter what governments say, they will always try to do each other down because all they 'really' care about is maximising their own state interests.

Such a 'hard-boiled' view of international relations often attracts people because it cuts through the pretence and hypocrisy with which governments often mask their own self-interest. It is true up to a point and in many situations. But, by the same token, ideas and ideals often exert an independent influence on events. For example, in order to understand how subsistence farmers were mobilised throughout the Third World against well-equipped colonial armies, one needs to appreciate the force of nationalism and calls for social justice.

Not surprisingly, therefore, material changes in global economics and politics have been accompanied in the post-war period by changes in the overall climate of ideas. Four of these are worth highlighting. One was that the 'white man's burden' view of empire – in which the colonising powers claimed to be on a civilising mission that would grant independence to colonial peoples 'when they were ready for it' – became increasingly unacceptable. It was replaced by embarrassment about the domination and exploitation of the Third World that colonialism implied. Unfortunately for the newly liberated colonial populations, however, this change in attitude was not accompanied by much of a willingness on the part of the ex-colonial powers to make up for earlier exploitation.

A second change in the climate of opinion after 1945 was the apparently increasing appeal of communism as a mobilising ideology of the dispossessed. Anti-imperialists throughout the Third World frequently saw the economic and political difficulties that their countries faced, even after decolonisation, as deriving from the global capitalist system of production, distribution and exchange. Between 1945 and 1975 over 30 countries 'succumbed' to the attractions of Marxist–Leninist ideology (and, as we saw, the British were often combating it in the colonies). After 1980, however, this seemingly inexorable tide of socialism

BRIEFINGS

22.3 The international human rights movement

The United Nations launched a Universal Declaration of the Rights of Man [sic] when it was founded. Although another of its principles was mutual non-interference in the internal affairs of states, in practice gross breaches of rights have led to UN or NATO intervention (for example, in Bosnia from 1992 onwards).

Mutual policing of rights was, in fact, institutionalised by the Helsinki Accords of 1975, signed between the NATO and Warsaw Pact countries. Britain and the United States have also made protests about violation of human rights in China. Under the auspices of the Council of Europe, Britain and other members have submitted themselves to the jurisdiction of the European Court of Human Rights, to which individuals and groups in Britain can appeal against the British government. The European Court of Justice, in practice, applies the European Convention on Human Rights in its own jurisdiction, and Britain has incorporated it into its domestic legislation (see Chapter 19).

Supplementing these governmental initiatives, voluntary organisations such as Amnesty International, with headquarters in London, have policed each country's own observance of basic rights and procedures, publicised abuses and sent observers to trials to monitor what is going on. Britain has been reasonably supportive of their efforts, though sometimes subject to criticism itself.

went into rapid reverse. With the success of the Islamic revolution in Iran after 1978, with Moscow's conflict with Islamic forces in Afghanistan after 1979, and with the collapse of socialism in eastern Europe and in the Soviet Union (1989–90), communism's appeal as a vehicle for mobilising deeply felt grievances declined significantly.

A third major change in the post-war climate of international opinion was an increased interest in, and commitment to, the promotion of individual human rights. In part this emphasis reflected a conscious rejection of the 'collective rights' stressed by communism. But it also reflected a genuine humanitarian effort on the part of western governments and non-governmental organisations (such as Charter 88 and Amnesty International) which sought to extend internationally the protective cover of human rights legislation.

A fourth set of ideas emerged in the 1990s around the goal of establishing a New World Order based on spreading freedom and democracy to all nation states. Although agreement among the leading democratic powers on exactly *how* this was to be achieved was never established, international forces did fight wars in Bosnia, Kosovo, Afghanistan and Iraq that resulted in the overthrow of aggressive regimes. In the case of Afghanistan, of course, the intention was to eliminate a regime that directly succoured international terrorism. In all these cases, Britain played a crucial role either directly through military action or as a key ally of the United States. By 2003, the toppling of regimes that harbour terrorists became the main goal of the New World Order led by the United States with strong support from Britain.

Globalisation

Nationalist movements in the old empires were not, of course, fuelled wholly by ideas. European rule produced economic development, which in turn brought social and political tensions. The process of urbanisation, together with the expansion of education and mass communications, fragmented old social networks, rendering the indigenous populations of the colonies much more susceptible to the new, radical ideas. By developing the colonies, the imperial powers created the very conditions in which anti-colonial oppositions could thrive.

The British were astute enough to realise this early on, putting the more congenial members of the opposition in power and integrating them and their newly independent countries into the western political and trading system. In doing so, they contributed to the process of 'globalisation' that has transformed the world over the last 50 years. Globalisation relates primarily to the process whereby all parts of the world, even the most remote and isolated, have been linked up by western trade and communications. Therefore, the way people live and work, the way they dress, the food they consume, the things they do – even the way they think – has become more similar. There are very few subsistence economies left that produce only for themselves. Even the largest western economies are not self-sufficient any more, but depend on networks of traders and producers in other parts of the world.

Before 1945 countries with relatively powerful economies tended to use their economic and military muscle to extend their direct political influence beyond their current national boundaries. European **imperialism** in the nineteenth century, and German and Japanese expansionism in the 1930s involved precisely this sort of extension. Since 1945, however, nation states have increasingly recognised that economic security and global influence can be achieved without direct or indirect political control, as the cases of post-war Germany and Japan have demonstrated.

A related change in the international system has been the massive increase in world trade and financial exchanges. These increases have both reflected and reinforced the revolutions in transport technology and global communications that have occurred since 1945. Although direct comparison is difficult, the available figures suggest that the volume of world trade in goods and services in 2006 was more than 30 times greater than it had been in 1950. The volume of currency exchanges and capital transfers, spurred on by **trade liberalisation** and deregulation, was so great by the turn of the millennium that it was beyond the capability of national governments even to monitor them effectively. This expansion of the financial sector, in particular, has served to increase the significance of international markets and market forces. Economists sometimes speak about the permeability of national economies, meaning the extent to which capital, labour, goods and services can be either introduced into or extracted from a given country. There can be little doubt that, over the last 50 years, the average level of permeability has increased considerably. The consequence of this has been a corresponding decrease in the decision-making autonomy of national governments, which have found their economic policy strategies increasingly vulnerable to international market pressures.

Reflecting economic globalisation and integration, one can observe a parallel growth of '**international regimes**'. Regimes are sets of international 'rules of the game' accepted by states because of the importance of joint rather than independent decision making in many areas. States are prepared to accept regime-imposed restrictions on their decision-making autonomy on two conditions: first, that the benefits of any cooperation sponsored by the regime more than outweigh the costs entailed by any loss of autonomy; and second, that the regime is able to ensure that states which fail to cooperate (or which 'free ride' on the concessions made by others) are suitably penalised.

In the post-war period, international regimes have proliferated to such an extent that we cannot even attempt to describe them all here. Three examples, however, indicate the wide range of contexts in which international regimes have developed. In the economic sphere, the World Trade Organization (previously the General Agreement on Tariffs and Trade) has been remarkably successful, through a series of negotiating rounds that have brought down trade barriers and expanded world trade. In the security sphere, the Conference on (now the Organisation for) Security and Co-operation in Europe made an important contribution to the

Imperialism

The practice of one nation controlling or dominating another state or territory, usually by military and economic means, and to the advantage of the imperial power.

Trade liberalisation

The process whereby international trade is increasingly opened up to market forces (free trade) by reducing trading tariffs, import and export controls, and other forms of protection.

International regimes

Sets of international institutions and 'rules of the game' that are created and accepted by states in order to promote international cooperation and integration, as opposed to independent decision making and national competition.

softening of East–West relations in the years immediately before the end of the Cold War. Finally, in the ecological sphere, the Vienna Convention (1985) and the Montreal Protocol (1987) established and extended guidelines for reducing chlorofluorocarbon (CFC) production in order to protect the earth's ozone layer and the Kyoto Protocol on Climate Change (1997) proposed a reduction in the emission of 'greenhouse' gases.

Ensuring compliance with a regime's rules is always a difficult matter in practice, and in some instances a major country has withdrawn in its support, as the United States did with the Kyoto Protocol with the new Bush Presidency in 2001. Nonetheless, the enormous growth of regime-like organisations and practices since 1945 represents an important change in the international environment in which Britain now operates. To a lesser extent it also reflects the commitment of successive UK governments to the construction of regimes that would themselves facilitate further international cooperation (a practical application of 'idealist' principles).

Motivations and assumptions of British foreign policy

Foreign policy is largely constrained by developments in the surrounding world. No country can simply devise a policy and carry it through, unaffected by external events. Any attempt to ignore these would be self-defeating.

British foreign policy is no exception and has clearly had to respond to the developments traced earlier. The real question is whether it has been a good or bad response. Has it succeeded in advancing British interests as well as could be expected within the inevitable constraints, or has it squandered resources while not achieving its objectives? We will be able to judge this better after analysing policy in this section and considering British capabilities, both general and military, in the following one.

The key question with regard to foreign policy, as with any other policy, is: whose interests are being served? It is a mistake to assume that there is any readily identifiable general British 'national interest' to be served by its foreign policy. Usually there are competing interests, one of which successfully asserts a claim to be the 'national interest' while the others lose out.

It is only fair to say, however, that the major motivation behind post-war policy, to defend liberal democracy and the capitalist system against communist attempts to subvert it, enjoyed widespread support among all sections of the population. Thus, on the major lines of British policy – managed de-colonisation, staunch membership of NATO, support for international organisations and regimes operating on broadly democratic liberal lines (the UN, WTO) – there was broad agreement.

On some of the more detailed implementation of policy, there might naturally be dissent. Three major areas are the European Union, nuclear deterrence and the relationship with the USA.

European Union

The decision to join the European Union, taken by a Conservative government in 1972, was attacked by the trade unions and Labour Party as a sell-out to European capitalist interests that would thwart left-wing plans for a radical overhaul of British society. Paradoxically, by the 1990s the EU was seen by the Conservative right in exactly parallel terms, as a leftist constraint on radical free market reform in Britain! Both reactions demonstrated the structural and cultural difficulties the British had in coping with the capitalist–protectionist traditions of France and Germany, so alien to support for a totally free market in Britain.

Nuclear deterrence and unilateral disarmament

Nuclear deterrent

The threatened use of nuclear weapons to prevent aggression on the part of foreign states, on the grounds that the aggressor nation will suffer too much damage to make the venture worthwhile.

Few groups in Britain advocated leaving NATO. There was considerably more support for giving up the independent British **nuclear deterrent**, which was seen as expensive and unreliable in light of US capabilities. Protests against British nuclear and, to a lesser extent, chemical weapons reached a head in the 1960s, when the Campaign for Nuclear Disarmament could muster up to half a million people in its protest marches. In the 1980s there were other protests against the stationing of US nuclear missiles on British soil.

The 'special relationship' with the United States

British leaders (including Tony Blair and Gordon Brown) have long argued that Britain has a special relationship with the United States, based on a common language and traditions and a history of opposing common foes (Germany, Japan, the Soviet Union). The relationship took its most concrete form inside NATO, where Britain actively backed up the US leadership. Most other NATO members were content to let the United States carry a disproportionate share of common defence costs. Britain, in contrast, allocated a significantly higher proportion of its GDP to defence. In 1979, for example, the United Kingdom spent 4.7 per cent of GDP on defence compared with Germany's 3.9 per cent. In the 1990s the purchase from the United States of Trident submarines to carry nuclear missiles still went on, even under Labour, while the new government reaffirmed its commitment to development of a Eurofighter, estimated to cost £15 billion.

Plate 22.1 Both Bush and Blair were seriously damaged politically over the reasons for going to war in Iraq

Source: Cartoon Stock

In the post-Cold War era, Britain has consistently supported American policy in the Gulf War (1991), Bosnia (1995–7), Kosovo (1999), Afghanistan (2002–) and Iraq (2003–), even when American actions have been given at best a lukewarm reception from other EU states such as Germany and France. In 2002–3, the British gave the strongest support to the Bush administration to topple the Saddam Hussein regime in Iraq. This almost unquestioning loyalty to the Americans has led many to argue that the United Kingdom is America's 'poodle', or is still trying to emulate its imperial past by slavishly supporting the exercise of American power. This critique raises the question of British defence and foreign policy capability. Why should a mid-sized power with a mid-sized economy play such a prominent role in global affairs?

British capabilities in the post-Cold War era

Britain has always had a large 'defence establishment' made up of arms producers, the armed forces and supportive officials in Whitehall. For many years it was argued that an overemphasis on defence industries was 'distorting' the economy by starving 'civilian' industries such as car manufacturing of capital and technological help. Whether or not this is true, the high priority given to defence industries has resulted in the development of arms manufacturing into one of the most successful and largest areas of the British economy. Britain is one of the three leading arms exporters in the world (along with the USA and France). British armaments firms such as British Aerospace depend heavily on British taxes to provide a protected market where they can recoup costs on weapon development and subsidise overseas sales. Their close relationships with the civil servants of the Ministry of Defence have meant that massive cost overruns and delays on weapons development have not only been tolerated, but paid for, by British taxpayers. Often these have escalated to five or six times the original cost of a project. Until recently, the Ministry of Defence has been astonishingly tolerant of this and was not held closely to account for its expenditures, even in the most cost-conscious and cost-cutting days of Conservative government. The argument that national security is involved seemed to silence critics, who may also be under pressure from the security services as mentioned in the previous chapter.

The argument that military investments have distorted economic ones does seem to have some validity, but these effects are not unique to Britain. Exactly similar subsidies to arms firms and the blurring of civil and military expenditures have occurred in France and the USA. It seems that any country with a sizeable military force is liable to run into these problems.

The armaments industry is powerful partly because it has protectors and supporters right up to the highest levels of government. High-ranking ministers have had past links with arms firms or have taken up positions with them after leaving office. So also have retired civil servants, particularly from the Ministry of Defence. Their technical expertise may have some market use, but they are more likely valued for their political and administrative contacts.

There is also an institutionalised pressure group right at the heart of government that will always speak up for defence contracts. This is the Joint Chiefs of Staff Committee, representing the high commands of the army, navy and air force. Naturally the generals, air marshals and admirals are anxious to see their forces well equipped. They have two reasons for this: first, they have a genuine concern that the military should have the capability for what is demanded of them; and second, the more that is spent on the armed forces, the more important they and their commanders become in the governmental structure. Influence correlates with budgets, so budget cutting constitutes a major threat.

BRIEFINGS

22.4 The career of Jonathan Aitken, journalist, arms dealer, politician, criminal, prison reformer

Jonathan Aitken is a nephew of one of the pre-war media moguls, Lord Beaverbrook (Max Aitken). He was prosecuted under the Official Secrets Act in 1971, when he reported in the *Sunday Telegraph* that arms sales to Nigeria were much larger than the government claimed. After he was acquitted, he went on to engage in the arms trade himself, becoming particularly involved in the huge arms deals of the 1980s with Saudi Arabia.

At the same time he became a Conservative MP and rose rapidly, becoming Chief Secretary to the Treasury – second in command of finances – in the 1990s. He continued to accept hospitality from Saudi Arabians engaged in the arms trade. Mohamed Al Fayed, who was pursuing a personal vendetta against the British Establishment, leaked receipts to the *Guardian* from a stay of Aitken's at the Ritz Hotel in Paris that had been paid for in this way. Government ministers are not supposed to accept such hospitality in case they are influenced improperly.

The case contributed to the accusations of sleaze facing the Major government and Aitken resigned from his post in a reshuffle, in order to wield 'the sword of truth' in a libel charge against the *Guardian*. This had to be abandoned in 1997, amid accusations of perjury against him. Aitken's final disgrace came in 1999 when he was jailed for this perjury offence. Following his prison sentence Aitken became a devout Christian and champion of prison reform. However, his attempt to return to politics in 2004 was vetoed by the then Conservative leader Michael Howard.

Aitken's career illustrates the close connection between the arms trade, politics and journalism in Britain, and the role of the Official Secrets Act and severe libel laws in suppressing relevant political information. It is still unclear what the influence of arms dealers over government policy really is, but their ability to gain high-level political representation and to influence aid-for-trade deals, such as the Pergau Dam in Malaysia, indicates that it is great. What facts we have come mostly from investigative journalism, to which, paradoxically, Aitken contributed at the beginning of his career.

Plate 22.2 Michael Cummings' cartoon in *The Times*, 26 July 1997: the government grants export licences for more Hawk jets to Indonesia and sponsors an international arms fair – after Labour pledges that it 'would not permit the sales of arms to regimes that might use them for internal repression or internal aggression'. More than 200,000 innocent people have died in East Timor and internal dissent has been ruthlessly suppressed in parts of Indonesia

Source: Michael Cummings/ The Times, 26th July 1997

By the same token, decisions about what weapons to buy generally sets off a struggle within the armed forces. Is money to be invested on ships for the navy, new fighters for the air force or tanks for the army? Each service desperately tries to ensure that it is not downgraded relative to the others. Withdrawal 'east of Suez' in the late 1960s meant that the navy was no longer so important for guarding extended communication routes to India and south-east Asia. It was compensated to some extent, however, by the shift in delivery systems for the nuclear bomb from aircraft to submarines. The expeditions to the Falklands and the Gulf again demonstrated the importance of the navy in carrying troops to where they were needed. However, airlifts were also very important, and air offensives were a crucial element in both these cases, as also in Bosnia, Kosovo, Afghanistan and Iraq. That is one reason why the Royal Air Force (RAF) has managed to retain political support for an expanded rapid deployment capability for moving troops and equipment around the world.

The need for an effective army is unchallenged, whether to fight off a large-scale invasion of Europe or, more recently, to undertake limited war or peace-keeping operations (which often, in fact, develop into low-intensity conflicts). The question, as always, is: what kind of army with what kind of equipment? Should it be equipped to fight at all levels, even if some possibilities are less likely than others are? The concern of governments in the twenty-first century is to get as much value for money as possible – especially given the pressure to increase spending in such areas as health and education. In one sense, the demise of the Cold War and the emergence of a war on terror and on small but aggressive states such as Iraq has made these choices easier, for what is needed today is a highly trained, well-equipped and highly mobile defence capability. This need not involve a large army (Britain has one of the smaller armies in relation to its size in Europe). Neither does it have to be very expensive. As can be seen from Table 22.1, defence spending in the United Kingdom has in fact been slowly declining in recent years – especially if expressed as a percentage of GDP. Note also that British defence spending is not particularly out of line with that of its larger NATO allies. None of this is to argue that the defence establishment is happy with the contraction of the armed forces. But recent events do show that even with relatively small forces, Britain can still play a major international role.

Following the terrorist attacks of September 2001, the Americans became much more willing to use troops abroad in order to establish domestic and international peace. Given the vast size of their armed forces, it is therefore likely that, as in Afghanistan and Iraq, they will provide the main force supported by smaller British (and other) forces. Britain may in fact be establishing a 'niche' role in the New World Order as a seasoned peacekeeper and loyal ally of the Americans. This was confirmed by a 2004 government White Paper, 'Delivering Security in a Changing World', which confirmed a shift away from conventional warfare to limited rapid deployment actions, namely:

- We should be able to mount three small-scale operations (such as in Kosovo in March 2004) or medium-scale operations (such as in Afghanistan in 2001) at the same time.

- The United Kingdom should be able to lead a medium-sized European operation where the United States is not involved.

- Larger-scale operations (such as recent operations in Iraq) are only likely to take place as part of a US-led coalition.

- Potential threats from hostile submarines or from the air have reduced significantly.

Table 22.1 Trends in defence spending, NATO states, 2000–4, defence standing as a percentage of GDP

	2000	2001	2002	2003	Estimated 2004
NATO total	2.6	2.6	2.7	2.7	..
NATO – Europe	2.1	2.0	2.0	2.0	..
Belgium	1.4	1.3	1.3	1.3	1.2
Bulgaria	*	*	*	*	2.4
Czech Republic	2.1	2.0	2.0	2.1	1.9
Denmark	1.5	1.6	1.6	1.5	1.5
Estonia	*	*	*	*	1.6
France	2.6	2.5	2.5	2.6	2.6
Germany	1.5	1.5	1.5	1.5	1.4
Greece	4.9	4.6	3.4	2.8	2.9
Hungary	1.7	1.8	1.7	1.7	1.5
Italy	2.1	2.0	2.1	2.1	1.8
Latvia	*	*	*	*	1.3
Lithuania	*	*	*	*	1.4
Luxembourg	0.7	0.8	0.7	0.7	0.8
Netherlands	1.6	1.6	1.6	1.6	1.7
Norway	1.8	1.7	2.1	2.0	1.8
Poland	1.9	1.9	1.9	1.9	1.9
Portugal	2.1	2.1	1.6	1.6	1.7
Romania	*	*	*	*	2.2
Slovakia	*	*	*	*	1.8
Slovenia	*	*	*	*	1.6
Spain	1.2	1.2	1.4	1.3	1.3
Turkey	5.0	5.0	4.4	3.8	3.5
United Kingdom	2.5	2.5	2.4	2.4	2.3
North America	2.9	3.0	3.3	3.4	..
Canada	1.1	1.2	1.2	1.2	1.2
United States	3.1	3.1	3.4	3.8	3.9

* Not a member.
Source: NATO

■ The more favourable security situation in Northern Ireland should allow further reductions to forces committed there in support of the civil authorities.

In July 2004 a Defence White Paper called 'Future Capabilities' explained how these objectives would be achieved by addressing three new themes:

■ **Effectiveness** – focusing on improving the effect that our systems and forces can deliver rather than the number involved.

■ **Technology** – using the latest advances to improve everything from communications to strike ability.

■ **Efficiency** – the need to spend our money wisely and to make savings that can be diverted to enhance front-line capabilities.

To this end the armed forces are being reorganised with a reduction in traditional naval capacity (destroyers and frigates), but the commissioning of two new super carriers, each capable of carrying up to 50 combat aircraft. Similarly, the army's tank force would be reduced but rapid deployment forces would be increased, as would the RAF's heavy airlift and helicopter capacity.

Plate 22.3 Members of the British Army bring humanitarian relief to the people of Imam Anas, Iraq
Source: Topfoto

Already by 2007 disputes over procurement of weaponry for these new programmes had emerged, and particularly over whether the new carrier-based aircraft that was to be jointly developed with the United States would have aircraft engines sourced in the United Kingdom or the United States, and which contractors would be responsible for the carriers.

British foreign and defence policy: the party political dimension

One of the most interesting aspects of the foreign and defence policy area is that Labour and Conservative governments have broadly adopted the same strategic stances. It was the 1945–50 Labour government that first took up a realist confrontational stance towards the Soviet Union – a stance that, in spite of opposition from the Labour left, was adhered to by all governments right until the collapse of the Soviet Union in 1991. Indeed, apart from contrasting attitudes on the EU, it is very difficult to discern major differences between Labour and Conservative governments in any area of foreign policy in the last 50 years. They may criticise each other in opposition, and Labour, in particular, may promise to deliver a foreign policy that pays more attention to considerations of human rights than do the Conservatives, but once in office these differences usually diminish or even disappear.

This certainly applies to the Labour government elected in 1997. On coming to office Robin Cook declared that foreign policy would have a strong 'ethical dimension' and not one where 'political values can be left behind when we check in our passports to travel on diplomatic business' (cited in Hamill, 1997, p. 29). Indeed, both Robin Cook and Prime Minister Blair promised to change the values of the 'foreign and defence policy establishment' by ensuring that, among other things, Britain would not sell arms to undemocratic states that then proceeded to use them against their own people. On 21 May 1997 the government signed up to the 'Ottawa Process' – a Canadian-led initiative to ban the production and stockpiling of anti-personnel mines. In addition, the government did not stand formally in the way of the extradition of the former dictator General Pinochet to Spain to face prosecution for war crimes.

In spite of these initiatives, however, the fundamentals of foreign policy, including the pattern of arms sales, remained the same as under the Conservative government. By the late 1990s, Britain had become the second largest defence exporter in the world after the USA. In no instance did it reverse a past pattern of major arms sales, including the sale of Hawk jets to Indonesia – a country known to have used force of arms against dissident citizens. In effect, the commercial imperatives of the arms industry have taken precedence over humanitarian concerns. To be fair, however, Britain does not sell arms to a number of countries on strategic and political grounds. And these states (including North Korea, Cuba, Iran and many African countries) usually have very poor records on human rights.

The absence of fundamental differences between the parties also applied to the events following the terrorist attacks on the United States in September 2001. Tony Blair together with his Foreign Secretary, Jack Straw (who replaced Robin Cook in the second Labour term), gave total support to the American actions in Afghanistan and Iraq, thus strengthening further the special relationship with America. Tory leaders fully supported the government's position. Indeed, most of the opposition to British engagement initially came from within the Labour Party and the trade union movement, although as events in Iraq came to a head after 2003, the anti-war coalition broadened to include a large cross-section of society.

Support for the USA fits well with Tony Blair and Gordon Brown's belief in a world order underpinned by democracy and the rule of law. The policies that result from this, including support for American leadership, often carry with them considerable risks. These include not only the loss of life and suffering that goes with military action, but also the loss of intra-party support and of prestige and influence that can result from military and diplomatic failure. So, in spite of the relative decline in Britain's forces and in the domestic economy, Britain continues to play for very high stakes on the world stage. No other European country has taken on such a role. In this regard, Britain's international influence remains far greater than could be expected from a medium-sized European power.

Summary

Following a brief outline of the major actors and institutions in foreign and defence policy, this chapter has reviewed British foreign and military policy over the post-war period. This has been dominated by three developments:

1. decolonisation (1945–64)
2. increasing involvement with the European Union, culminating in the possibility of economic and monetary union at the start of the millennium
3. European and world security, seen by British governments as best secured by a close alliance with the USA inside NATO.

▶

In the light of these:

- British governments have been criticised for trying to do too much abroad in support of the USA (the 'special relationship').
- Although money could have been saved on costly defence projects, it is difficult to see what else, broadly, Britain could have done. Major mistakes have been avoided and the NATO alliance 'won' the Cold War.
- Overlaying this strategic need is the question of the protection of human rights and the pressures to pursue an ethical foreign policy. However, such objectives often conflict with commercial imperatives, as the experience of the Blair government shows.
- As the major US ally, Britain under Tony Blair has taken a highly interventionist stance in world affairs since the terrorist attacks in September 2001. The Conservatives supported him in this stance. Such a strategy carries with it a risk not only of domestic opposition to the use of military force, but also of opposition from abroad and especially the European Union.

MILESTONES

Milestones in post-war foreign policy

World		Decolonisation		European Union	
1945	Defeat of Nazi Germany and Japan				
1946	Foundation of UN				
1946–8	Growing tensions between United States and Soviet Union initiate Cold War. US Marshall aid stabilises economic situation in the United Kingdom and western Europe	1948	Independence of India, Pakistan, Burma, Ceylon and Palestine		
1949	Communist takeover of China	1950–4	Mau-Mau war in Kenya		
1949	Foundation of NATO, the US-dominated military alliance against the Soviet Union. UK leading initiator and member	1951–60	Guerrilla war in Malaya	1951	Treaty of Paris: the six – Belgium, the Netherlands, Luxembourg, France, Italy and West Germany – form European Coal and Steel Community (ECSC)
1950–3	Korean War: NATO confronts China				
1948–55	Britain develops nuclear bomb	1956	Abortive invasion of Suez by UK with France and Israel	1957	Treaty of Rome: European Economic Community aims at free market of six countries
1950–73	World economic growth and liberalisation of trade under GATT	1956–62	Guerrilla war in Cyprus		
		1960	Ghana becomes first African colony to gain independence		

Milestones in post-war foreign policy continued

World		Decolonisation		European Union	
1962	Attempt by Soviet Union to place missiles in Cuba brings the United States and Soviet Union to brink of nuclear war	1960–2	Peaceful independence of most African, Caribbean and Pacific colonies	1962–3	British application to join EEC rejected
1964–75	US defeat in Vietnam War, tensions within NATO. United Kingdom stays aloof	1960–3	Breakdown of British rule in South Arabia	1966	De Gaulle establishes right of national veto within the EC (Luxembourg compromise)
1962–79	US–Soviet relaxation of Cold War, mutual arms limitation	1962–4	Successful confrontation with Indonesia in Borneo		
1967	Devaluation of sterling	1964–94	White regimes in Rhodesia and South Africa first consolidate power, then negotiate handover to African majority	1968	British application rejected
1972	Discovery of oil in British North Sea	1968–72	British military withdrawal from east of Suez		
1973–7	Steep rise in world oil prices initiates inflation and periodic economic recessions	1970–96	Northern Irish terrorism	1973	United Kingdom, Ireland and Denmark join EEC
1979–88	Renewed arms race provokes economic crisis in Soviet Union and ends Cold War on US terms	1982	Falklands War: sea-borne British expedition reconquers islands from Argentina	1979	Direct elections to European Parliament
1989	Central and eastern European regimes democratise and create free markets			1985–6	Single European Act undermines national veto by introducing qualified majority voting on measures to achieve a single market
1989–93	World economic recession			1986	Spain and Portugal join EC
1991	Soviet Union splits between Russia, Ukraine and other successor states				
1991	Gulf War: NATO against Iraq			1992	Treaty of Maastricht plans for economic and political union. United Kingdom 'opts out' of Social Chapter
				1992	Black Wednesday: United Kingdom forced out of European Monetary System
1992–5	Bosnia crisis ended by NATO intervention			1993	EMS reorganised with broader exchange rate bands
1993	Further liberalisations of world trade under GATT			1994–7	Plans for single currency and closer union increasingly attacked by UK Conservative government

▶

Milestones in post-war foreign policy continued

World		Decolonisation		European Union	
1993–8	Gradual world recovery from recession			1995	Finland, Sweden and Austria join EU
		1997	UK returns Hong Kong to China	1997	Amsterdam Summit fails to move to closer union. New Labour government accepts Social Chapter and welcomes EMU
1999	War in Kosovo provokes a NATO military response			2000	EU moves haltingly towards a common defence and foreign policy
2001–2	Terrorist attacks on the United States provoke strong British backing for American action in Afghanistan. Taliban regime toppled			2002	EU supports action in Afghanistan but is more cautious than United Kingdom and United States
2002–3	US and UK military intervention in Iraq			2002–3	Germany and other EU states oppose intervention in Iraq
2003–7	Continuing insurrection in Iraq accounts for death of more than 100 British service personnel			2003–7	United States accused of human rights abuses in Iraq and at Guantanamo Bay
2005	7 July bombings in London kill 56 and injure over 700			2005–7	Iran accused by United Nations and all leading states of building nuclear weapons facilities North Korea performs a nuclear device test

Essays

1. How do you account for British support for the United States in the war in Iraq? Is British participation in the 'national interest'?

2. What effect, if any, has the European Union had on British foreign policy?

3. Why does the UK have an independent nuclear deterrent? Is it a good thing?

4. What were the main differences between Labour and Conservative positions on foreign policy in the period since 1990? How significant were they?

Projects

1. Catalogue the ways in which recent Labour governments have fought the 'war on terrorism'. Have these efforts compromised civil liberties in Britain?

2. In what ways are defence contractors privileged in British politics? Answer with respect to *one* major weapons system developed since the 1980s.

3. Provide a systematic account of British decolonisation since 1945. How successful was it in establishing stable, democratic regimes?

For a critical overview of British foreign policy, see David Sanders, *Losing an Empire, Finding a Role: British Foreign Policy since 1945* (London: Macmillan, 1990). Bernard Porter, *The Lion's Share: A Short History of British Imperialism* (Harlow: Longman, 1988) gives the background to decolonisation. On arms sales, see Mark Phythian, *The Politics of British Arms Sales since 1964* (Manchester: Manchester University Press, 2000). On the special relationship, see John Dumbrell, *A Special Relationship: Anglo-American Relations since 1960* (Basingstoke: Macmillan, 2000). On ethics and New Labour, see James Hamill, 'New Labour, ethics, foreign policy', *Politics Review*, November 1997, pp. 29–33. On Blair's foreign policy, see Anthony Seldon and Dennis Kavanagh (eds), *The Blair Effect, 2001–5* (Cambridge: Cambridge University Press, 2005), Chapters 17 and 18. On the Labour government and Iraq, see John Kampfner, *Blair's Wars* (London and New York: Free Press, 2003) and Con Coughlin, *American Ally: Tony Blair and the War on Terror* (London: Politicos, 2006).

Accessible articles on foreign policy in general with an emphasis on the British role can be found in *International Affairs*, the quarterly journal of the Royal Institute of International Affairs.

Hot links to these sites can be found on the CWS at www.pearsoned.co.uk/budge.

A general introduction to some of the landmarks in British foreign relations is available from http://britishhistory.about.com/cs/foreignpolicy/. For a more specific site, we suggest you start by looking at the Ministry of Defence site at www.mod.uk; in its 'about us' section you can find a full list of links to all the main defence institutions in the UK. In addition the Foreign and Commonwealth Office (www.fco.gov.uk) provides insightful information on global and regional foreign relations. The Department for International Development (DFID) is the UK's government department working to promote sustainable development and eliminate world poverty; visit it at www.dfid.gov.uk. The British Foreign Policy Resource Centre at King's College London (http://foreign-policy.dsd.kcl.ac.uk/index.htm) offers an extraordinary range of useful material, with sections covering issues from academic essays on British foreign policy to the war against terrorism. The 2001–2 publications of the Foreign Affairs Select Committee can be obtained from www.publications.parliament.uk/pa/cm/cmfaff.htm. The Department of Trade and Industry has a useful section on world trade (www.dti.gov.uk/worldtrade/).

Britain has always been substantially involved in a series of international organisations. Currently the process of European integration occupies a privileged place on the agenda; the Foreign and Commonwealth Office has an excellent section on the relations between Britain and the EU, you can find it at www.fco.gov.uk/servlet/Front?pagename=OpenMarket/Xcelerate/ShowPage&c=Page&cid=1007029391674. The Organisation for Security and Cooperation in Europe (OSCE) is the largest regional security organisation in the world. It is active in early warning, conflict prevention, crisis management and post-conflict rehabilitation. Visit its web site at www.osce.org.

It is also worth visiting the web sites of the major international organisations in which Britain participates. The European Union (www.europa.eu.int), NATO (www.nato.int), the Council of Europe (www.coe.int) and the United Nations (www.un.org). We suggest you also visit the Royal Institute of International Affairs (www.riia.org).

chapter 23

Environmental policy

Environmental problems raise important questions about the capacity of modern governments to solve difficult dilemmas. This chapter begins with an example of how environmental policies can lead to major domestic and international disputes. It then goes on to look at:

- changes in the character of environmental problems
- the leading policy actors and institutions in the United Kingdom
- the long-standing British philosophy of pollution control
- new pressures, especially from developments within the EU
- the difficulties that confront the New Labour government in any attempt to implement its ambitious environmental goals.

During the spring and summer of 1999 what had, up to that point, been a relatively quiet backwater of public policy erupted into intense and prolonged front-page headlines. The subject was genetically modified foods. In February the *Daily Mirror* ran THE PRIME MONSTER as a headline, when Tony Blair said that he would be prepared to eat genetically modified food. Other newspapers, previously noted more for their Conservative Party sympathies than anything else, started to refer to 'Frankenstein foods' and published lists of common supermarket items that were genetically modified. The Prince of Wales, long known for his support of organic farming, publicly challenged supporters of genetic modification to defend their stance. With memories of the food scare surrounding BSE and the eating of beef fresh in their minds, retailers began withdrawing stocks that had previously sold well. By July, Greenpeace was organising raids on farm trials of genetically modified crops, pulling them up and claiming to be acting according to the popular will. The European Union began to reform its own policies on the control of genetically modified organisms.

Although the eruption of intense public debate took place between May and August 1999, the issues had surfaced the year before when in August Dr Arpad Pusztai, a scientist working at the Rowett Institute in Aberdeen, had made a public statement saying that the growth of rats experimentally fed on GM potatoes had been stunted. This claim immediately sparked enormous scientific controversy, with august bodies such as the Royal Society establishing a committee to investigate – and ultimately reject – its scientific validity. But whatever its scientific merits the incident sparked enough concern to lead the government to review the arrangements for controlling the development of biotechnology and to ask its chief medical officer and chief scientist to review the evidence on the safety of genetically modified foods.

The events of 1999 could not have been more badly timed from the government's point of view. In May the joint report from the chief medical officer and chief scientist argued that there was no evidence that eating GM food was unsafe but proposed new public bodies to regulate biotechnology developments. That report coincided with one from the British Medical Association, which argued that there should be a moratorium on the planting of GM crops following the publication of a paper in the scientific journal *Nature* which claimed to show that in the United States monarch butterflies were killed by eating pollen from GM maize. The leaking of a government paper to the *Independent on Sunday*, advocating the establishment of a 'central co-ordinated rebuttals strategy' did not help the government's cause. Suggesting the need to enlist eminent scientists to explain the government's point of view, it could be read as the government being partial towards the biotechnology industry.

The problems lay deeper than these coincidences, however. On coming to office, New Labour needed tangible ways in which it could demonstrate that it was the party of production rather than redistribution. Just as Harold Wilson had referred to 'the white heat of the technological revolution' to show that Labour was the modernising party in 1964, so New Labour after its election victory in 1997 began explicitly to support the development of biotechnology as the engine of economic growth for the twenty-first century. When it found itself out of step with public opinion on biotechnology issues, it did not know whether to persist in its original strategy or to retreat to a point where it could portray itself as a guardian of public safety, impartially regulating a technology that might be useful but which could be discontinued if it were shown not to be safe.

However, even if the government had consistently presented itself as the neutral regulator of public safety, it would still have had difficulties, since the safety and environmental hazards associated with modern technology pose risks that are inherently difficult to control in ways that make sense to members of the public. The problems involved in handling the issues associated with GM crops are simply examples of the central problems of environmental policy. In particular, there is a whole range of issues, spanning food safety, the control of chemicals and the control of climate-changing gases, that pose significant but unquantifiable risks to human health and the environment in ways that are bound to cause political controversy. In a situation in which uncertainty is high and public concern intense, how can a British government strike the right balance between environmental protection to the high standards expected of it, and a commitment to prosperity and economic competitiveness?

Behind this problem lay others. How should the United Kingdom deal with the pollution legacy of past industrial activity, which left hazardous chemicals in the environment? How best can the complex and difficult choices be made between policy options, all of which, in the light of that legacy, involve environmental damage? How far can these policy choices be made in ways that pay attention to the technical/scientific aspects of the issues without also engaging with broader issues of public opinion and sentiment? What role is there for European institutions in providing a forum within which international differences can be discussed and resolved? How well adapted, in short, are British political institutions in dealing with the politics of the environment?

Environmental problems

Environmental problems arise in many different ways and from many different sources (see Table 23.1). Sometimes the problem is local, as when a person's bonfire pollutes the neighbouring environment. Sometimes it occurs on a regional

Table 23.1 Environmental problems, characteristics and causes

Environmental problem	Main sources	Related human activities	Expected effects
Protecting wildlife	Pesticides, land-use development	Agriculture, transport, house building	Loss of species
Global climate change	Carbon dioxide, methane, CFCs	Power generation, transport	Temperature rise, unpredictable and dangerous weather
Ozone depletion	CFCs	Aerosol use, refrigerators	Loss of protection against sun's radiation
Increase of acid in environment	Sulphur dioxide, nitrogen oxides, ammonia	Fossil fuels	Crop and building damage, ill health
Over-enrichment of waterways	Phosphates, nitrates	Fertiliser, sewage	River pollution
Dispersed dangerous substances	Chemicals	Most modern production processes	Damage to human health, e.g. lower fertility

scale, as when a river basin is polluted. And sometimes it is worldwide, as is the case with global climate change. Human activity has had effects on the environment for centuries. At one time northern Europe was covered in forests before they were cut down for agriculture, a process of deforestation that is mirrored in developing countries today. Moreover, environmental issues inevitably arise from a large number of social activities and government policies. Industrial development causes problems of land use and pollution. Boosting agricultural crop production through incentive payments leads farmers to an increased use of pesticides and fertilisers that, in turn, cause the pollution of rivers and chemical residues in the food chain. Transport provision takes land for road building, and causes air pollution through the burning of fossil fuels. The specification of building regulations has implications for energy consumption, and tax law can affect how people consume resources. Environmental policy is both a separate sphere of government activity and a dimension of many government activities.

The term 'environmental policy' in the United Kingdom covers a wide field of government activity, including pollution control for discharges to air, water or land; the control of nuclear power; the release of genetically modified organisms into the environment; land-use planning; building conservation; the protection of the countryside, including plants and wildlife; and urban regeneration. Within the United Kingdom there is a long history of public policy measures directed at some of the most serious environmental problems. Industrial air pollution in the nineteenth century led to pressure from landowners for controls, and in 1865 the Alkali Inspectorate was formed to regulate major industrial sources of pollution. In the late nineteenth and early twentieth centuries, legislation led to slum clearance and the rebuilding of housing to higher environmental standards. In 1947 the post-war Labour government passed the Town and Country Planning legislation, which imposed restrictions on developments and created green belts around British towns. In 1956 clean air zones were established to prevent the recurrence of the urban smog that had caused 4,000 deaths in London in 1952. In 1969, in the wake of a worldwide upsurge of public concern and interest in environmental matters, a permanent Royal Commission on Environmental Pollution was established to help formulate policy. And in 1974 the Control of Pollution Act was passed, which brought together previous pieces of legislation. In the 1980s the UK began to move towards the establishment of a separate Environment Agency, a move that was completed in 1995, and in the 2000s major policy initiatives began to develop in a context in which European and global concerns were becoming prominent.

In terms of the control of pollution, modern environmental policies typically involve regulation: that is to say, the specification by government or a government agency of the standards of pollution control that a product or a process has to meet. For example, there are regulations governing car exhaust fumes that manufacturers have to conform to, and on the volume of gases that can be emitted from a major electricity-generating plant. Bathing and drinking waters are subject to quality standards, and factories are not allowed to discharge unauthorised pollution into rivers. There are controls on where waste can be dumped, as well as bans on the use of certain chemicals. Building and other forms of development are subject to planning controls, and certain areas may be designated as national parks or sites of special scientific interest because of the plants or animals they contain. The regulations may not always be enforced stringently, and there are many disputes about the standards. But the point remains that the most important policy instrument of environmental policy is regulation, and much of the substance of environmental policy concerns the content and strength of those regulations.

However, in recent years influential voices have been urging that effective environmental policies require a wider set of instruments. In particular, many policy analysts have argued for a greater use of economic instruments to tax environmental 'bads' and encourage environmental 'goods'. The same analysts have often pointed out that in practice political systems already have economic incentives in place that have implications for the environment, but they may not always be beneficial. For example, agricultural subsidy programmes may encourage intensive farming with consequent use of fertilisers and pesticides that may be environmentally harmful. So the need is not only to devise new economic instruments but also to scrutinise the effect of those already in place. In comparative terms the UK has not been a leader in the adoption of economic instruments or the scrutiny of potentially harmful economic incentives to wasteful use of the environment. During the 1990s, as we shall see, this pattern began to change – with political consequences.

Policy actors and institutions

Around the politics of environmental regulation has grown up a varied policy community of those who take an interest in the way that standards are set and enforced (see Briefing 23.1). Until 1997 the Department of the Environment was the principal ministry in England and Wales, with its counterparts located in the Scottish and Northern Ireland Offices. The New Labour government of 1997 merged the environment department with transport and regional planning, to create a new superministry, the Department of the Environment, Transport and the Regions (DETR). After the 2001 election, there was a further reorganisation, with the creation of the Department for Environment, Food and Rural Affairs (Defra), which combined the environment section of the DETR with the old Ministry of Agriculture, Fisheries and Food (MAFF). Transport, which in 1997 had been identified as a major environmental issue, was hived off from the Department of Transport, Local Government and the Regions. It was re-designated as the Department for Transport.

Environmental policy in the UK is embedded in a network of specialist advisory groups and committees, of which the most important is the Royal Commission on Environmental Pollution. Within Parliament there is a great deal of environmental interest and expertise in the House of Lords. Two Lords committees in particular, that on science and technology and an environment subcommittee of the European

Union Committee, have been especially active. Successive environment committees in the House of Commons have also played an important role on various issues. The Labour government established a new House of Commons committee, the Environmental Audit Committee, in December 1999.

Environmental policy is an area in which there are well-established pressure groups, many with a high degree of skill and extensive resources, making them well able to take political action. Some have a long history, with large and influential memberships. For example, the Royal Society for the Protection of Birds is the largest wildlife protection group in Europe with an active, vocal and persuasive membership. As well as managing its own reserves it also has a campaigning arm. It became increasingly active from the late 1970s on issues to do with pesticide use, farming practices such as the rooting out of hedgerows encouraged by the Common Agricultural Policy, and the need to provide international protection for migrating species. Other organisations, such as Friends of the Earth and Greenpeace, campaign on issues of air pollution, water pollution and waste disposal. Friends of the Earth, which started as a radical outsider group in the 1970s, has since been incorporated into the world of routinised government consultation

> **Environmentalism**
>
> A concern with the natural environment (including many things from the physical environment affecting 'the quality of life') and the belief that its protection should be given more importance and economic growth less.

BRIEFINGS

23.1 Main actors in British environmental policy institutions

Department for Environment, Food and Rural Affairs Incorporating an environment component and an agriculture component. The Department is the main policy-making department, although the Department for Transport, and the Department of Local Government and the Regions have some environment responsibilities, as do the territorial ministries. The Secretary of State is assisted by ministers responsible for specific aspects of environmental policy.

Environment Agency Created in 1995 by a merger of the National Rivers Authority and Her Majesty's Inspectorate of Pollution. Responsible for detailed standard setting and implementation of pollution control measures and river basin management.

Parliamentary committees The Environment, Food and Rural Affairs Committee of the House of Commons shadows the department. There is also an Environmental Audit Committee, which examines how far general government policy is consistent with environmental concerns. The Commons Committee on Science and Technology has taken an interest in environmental questions, as has its counterpart in the House of Lords. A subcommittee of the House of Lords European Union Committee is also concerned with scrutinising EU environmental legislation. All these committees have produced important reports on issues of environmental policy.

Royal Commission on Environmental Pollution The major advisory body on matters of pollution control policy. Responsible for introduction of major concepts of environmental policy, most notably integrated pollution control, and for some influential reports on lead in petrol and transport policy.

Other advisory bodies The Sustainable Development Commission; Advisory Council on Business and Environment; Genetic Manipulation Advisory Committee. Two new advisory bodies created at the end of 1999 include the Human Genetics Commission and the Agriculture and Environment Biotechnology Commission.

Local authorities Important responsibilities for solid waste regulation (county and unitary authorities) and for local environmental controls (district authorities).

European Union Important source of pressure to raise standards (see Briefing 23.4).

Environmental groups Friends of the Earth, Greenpeace, the Council for the Protection of Rural England, the Royal Society for the Protection of Birds, the World Wide Fund for Nature, Surfers against Sewage, the National Society for Clean Air, Transport 2000, GeneWatch.

Affected interests Electricity supply industry, water industry, road hauliers, farmers and the general public as consumers and drivers of private cars.

and discussion. In addition to these formal organisations, there are now many local and informal groups, some of which are mobilised by what they see as threats to the environment. Protesters building tree houses and tunnels to stop the Newbury bypass or the new runway for Manchester airport fall into this category.

Other actors who should also be included as members of the environmental policy network include **think tanks**, journalists and other opinion formers, including various scientific researchers whose work bears on policy questions. Some of the general think tanks, such as the Centre for Policy Research on the right and the Fabian Society or the Institute for Public Policy Research on the left, have published work on environmental policy from their own perspectives. In addition, there are specialist think tanks and research organisations (for example, the Institute for European Environmental Policy or the International Institute for Environment and Development) that have played an important role in diffusing knowledge and understanding of policy problems. During the 1980s and 1990s there also grew up a significant body of specialist journalists in the media, many of whom were extremely knowledgeable about environmental issues, and who kept in touch with both the developing scientific research and the work of the pressure groups.

Environmental policy is something no one likes to be seen to be against. Consequently, opposition to measures to protect the environment usually takes the form, not of questioning the goal of environmental protection, but of questioning the costs, and in particular questioning whether the improvement in the environment justifies the costs that are incurred. During the 1980s the Central Electricity Generating Board, the nationalised industry responsible for electricity production, led the resistance to tighter international controls on air pollution (see next section). And in the 1990s doubts about the costs of water pollution regulation were raised by Ofwat, the government body responsible for regulating water industry prices. In addition, at various times the Confederation of British Industry has expressed doubts about the imposition of environmental costs. Perhaps more important, however, has been the structural power of those groups, such as farmers or the road construction industry, whose political clout makes it difficult to devise suitable policies to control pollution or modify existing land-use practices.

> **Think tank**
>
> An organisation set up to develop public policy proposals and to press for their adoption by government.

Issues in environmental policy

Scientific uncertainty

Policies to protect the environment go back many centuries. The main lines of the British approach were laid down in the late nineteenth century with a series of measures to control air and water pollution (see the milestones section at the end of the chapter). During the last 20 years, the modern politics of environmental policy has revolved around the question of how far the UK government can accept the new philosophy of environmental protection known as 'sustainable development'.

The traditional British way of thinking about pollution and environmental policy became firmly established among key policy makers from 1900 until the mid-1970s (see Briefing 23.2). Briefly put, this tradition placed a great deal of emphasis on the scientific understanding of environmental problems and on the need to ensure flexibility and informality in the imposition of environmental regulation. The key idea was that pollution and environmental risk were inseparable from human activity, so the task of the environmental regulator was to understand the risks and to control those that were most damaging to the environment. As Lord Ashby, the distinguished biologist who first chaired the Royal Commission on Environmental Pollution, argued in the 1970s, the task of environmental policy is

BRIEFINGS

23.2 Phases of UK environmental policy

Nineteenth century to mid-1970s: the 'traditional philosophy' phase   Environmental control standards were entrusted to specialist inspectors, negotiating on a cooperative basis with industry.

Mid-1970s to 1988   Attempt by policy makers to hold on to the traditional philosophy in the face of domestic and international criticism. Domestically, groups such as Friends of the Earth questioned the closed nature of the traditional regulatory system. Internationally, there was criticism of the slow and hesitant response of the UK government to problems of pollution, and the United Kingdom was dubbed 'the dirty man of Europe'.

1988–97: the period of transition   In September 1988 Margaret Thatcher made a speech to the Royal Society emphasising the seriousness of the problem of global warming. In 1989 the European elections showed strong support for the Green Party. UK policy began to shift, accepting the need for a precautionary approach and stressing the importance of integrating environmental concerns with all aspects of public policy.

1997 onwards: implementation of sustainable development?   The New Labour government has committed itself to action on global climate change and action to control the harmful environmental effects of car use. There have also been developments in environmental taxation. New bodies have been established to help control biotechnology and new forms of public consultation have been experimented with.

not to eliminate pollution, but to optimise it. In other words, the traditional approach was to regulate effectively, but in such a way as to recognise the capacity of the environment itself to assimilate a certain amount of pollution. The traditional British philosophy of pollution control was therefore built on the principle of 'dilute and disperse'.

The record of pollution control that was built on this philosophy was impressive for its time. However, by the late 1970s, it was increasingly recognised that there were new problems that were not easy to deal with using the principle. The problem that came to symbolise these new challenges was that of 'acid rain'. When coal and other fossil fuels are burnt they give out a series of gases, most notably sulphur dioxide, which reacts in the atmosphere to form sulphuric acid. This sulphuric acid is then deposited in the form of rain, snow or mist, causing damage to crops, buildings, soils and fresh waters. As part of its policy to disperse pollutants from urban centres, the UK government had favoured a policy of building tall chimney stacks. These stacks dispersed their plumes over long distances, crossing national boundaries and contributing to a generally worsening problem in Europe.

The difficulty with acid rain as an issue was that, unlike many of the traditional problems of pollution, the scientific understanding of the effects of acidifying pollution was uncertain and contested. For example, although sulphur dioxide is given off in the burning of fossil fuels, it is also given off naturally by volcanoes and some sea species. Determining how much was due to human sources and how much to these naturally occurring ones is a complex problem. It is equally complex to trace the effects of emissions. It was often thought, for example, that given its prevailing south-westerly winds the UK exported most of its acid pollution to northern Europe. But research in the late 1980s showed that, with complex air currents, some acid rain was carried from northern England to the Highlands of Scotland.

This story was repeated in a large number of cases throughout the 1980s and 1990s. It was clear that rivers were suffering damage from excessive nitrates, but was this due to fertilisers, plough patterns or sewage sludge? How far was it possible to say that sewage pollution caused health problems for swimmers, when those who did not go into the water when they went to the beach reported as many symptoms of gastric illness as those who did? Were very small quantities of pesticide residues in drinking water really a health hazard? How far was it correct to say that a significant rise in global temperatures could be predicted from observed trends? It was, of course, precisely this issue of scientific uncertainty that was at issue in the controversy over GM foods.

These scientific uncertainties and the contestable hypotheses to which they gave rise began to undermine the traditional UK philosophy of pollution control. Where cause and effect relationships are contested or uncertain, it is difficult to base environmental regulation purely on scientific evidence. In the face of this difficulty, a number of other countries, including Germany, the Netherlands, Denmark, Sweden and Norway, began to push for precautionary action to control pollutants even when the evidence of their damage was difficult to establish. The UK came under considerable political pressure, especially in the EU (see later), to adopt the precautionary principle, which requires policy makers to take action against environmental risks, even when the causes of those risks are poorly understood.

Cross-cutting nature of environmental issues

Another important feature of the changing politics of the environment has been the recognition that environmental considerations cut across all aspects of public policy. One area this affected was the privatisation policies of the Thatcher governments. Both the water industry and the electricity industry were major sources of pollution. When they were nationalised they had the protection of their 'sponsoring ministries', which spoke up for them in government during the making of policy. They were also prevented from making investments in pollution control by Treasury spending limits that restricted capital spending by the nationalised industries. With privatisation, however, this constraint has been lifted. In the case of water in particular, large investments have been necessary to meet various international obligations. This has led Ofwat to question how far these pollution control measures are necessary. In other words, a new institutional tension has been built into the British policy system between those who favour environmental protection and those who stress the cost of stringent measures.

Another feature of this cross-cutting character of environmental issues has been the need to deal as much with problems of consumption as with problems of production. Since environmental damage arises often as the by-product of everyday activities, environmental policy also needs to deal with issues of lifestyle and the control of consumption. This is most obvious in the case of transport and the significantly increased use of cars in recent years. Margaret Thatcher favoured what she called 'the great car economy' and in the late 1980s significant increases in road building took place or were planned. Moreover, the deregulation of bus services and the withdrawal of subsidies to the railways made the car an economically more attractive option for many households. Public expenditure cuts, and a new thinking about the extent to which roads generate increased traffic, led to a serious reduction in the road-building programme under the Major government. A legacy has been laid down, however, that will make it difficult to develop alternative forms of transport to the car.

There have been important measures to control emissions from car exhausts and to limit the noise of vehicles, but the benefits of these measures are often offset by the increase in the number of cars being driven on the road. The Royal Commission on Environmental Pollution, in an authoritative report, summarised the situation as follows:

> At present pollutants from vehicles are the prime cause of poor air quality that damages human health, plants, and the fabric of buildings. Noise from

Plate 23.1 Sizewell B nuclear power reactor on the Suffolk coast, north of Aldeburgh

Source: Topfoto

> vehicles and aircraft is a major source of stress and dissatisfaction, notably in towns but now intruding into many formerly tranquil areas. Construction of new roads and airports to accommodate traffic is destroying irreplaceable landscapes and features of our cultural heritage. The present generation's cavalier and constantly increasing use of non-renewable resources like oil may well foreclose the options for future generations. This is doubly irresponsible in view of the risks from global warming.
>
> Royal Commission on Environmental Pollution, 18th Report, 1994, p. 233

However, the chief problem for any government in response to this sort of issue is how to implement any feasible changes in priorities and organisation.

The principal way in which the pressures to secure greater policy integration have been played out in practice is in terms of the machinery of government. The creation of the DETR in 1997 can itself be seen as an example of this tendency. Bringing environment and transport together (not for the first time: something similar was done in the early 1970s) reflected a policy perception that the solution to environmental problems lay in the better planning of transport provision. The splitting of environment and transport in the reorganisation of 2001 suggested to some observers a lowering of this priority. But it could also be seen as evidence that environmental issues cut across many fields of public policy, including the newly salient agricultural policy.

In addition, however, the Labour government had inherited from the Conservatives a commitment for all ministries to report on their environmental performance, together with a commitment that key Cabinet ministers would meet regularly to discuss the environmental implications of their work. Early in its period of office, in November 1997, the government set up a new House of Commons committee, the Environmental Audit Committee, to scrutinise the extent to which environmental concerns were being integrated into government policy. At the time, John Prescott described it as a 'terrier to bite our ankles'. With John Horam, a former Labour MP turned Conservative via the Social Democrat Party, the new committee quickly started biting. Having ascertained the information in one of its inquiries that the Cabinet Committee on the Environment had only met twice in its first year, it extracted the thought from Michael Meacher, the relevant minister, that this was a good sign because it indicated consensus on the major issues! It has subsequently gone on to highlight the extent to which there is a shortage of established procedure and environmental management information in the running of Whitehall.

Another topic to which the Environmental Audit Committee has turned its attention is the development of policy on the use of economic instruments for environmental goals. From its earliest days the committee started to press the Treasury on the extent to which taxes could be used to discourage the consumption of environmental 'bads' or encourage the consumption of environmental 'goods'. Although the Treasury refused to appear before the committee in the run-up to the 1998 budget, subsequent policy developments were to mark one of the most important developments in environmental policy of the Labour government.

Development of eco-taxation

The turning point in using taxes for environmental purposes came with the budget of March 1999. Trumpeted by Patricia Hewitt, the economic secretary, as 'the largest and most radical package of environmental tax reforms ever announced in this country', the budget did indeed contain some significant proposals. The policy of increasing fuel taxation higher than the rate of inflation each year, which the Labour government had inherited from the days of Kenneth Clarke as chancellor, was confirmed, as were higher tax rates for solid waste going to disposal in landfills. There was also mention of the possibility of introducing environmental taxes on pesticides and a planned tax on aggregates. However, the most important development was the introduction of a climate change levy that would introduce taxation on companies emitting greenhouse gases in their production processes. In March 1998 the government had asked Lord Marshall, the former president of the CBI and the chairman of British Airways, to chair a task force on the use of economic instruments to control greenhouse gas emissions. The task force reported positively in November of that year, and the scheme was put into effect in 2001.

At this point we encounter a familiar pattern of environmental policy not only in the UK but throughout the developed world. The budget announcement set in train a predictable set of reactions from those adversely affected by the proposals. The proposals on the climate change levy allowed for a reduction in the rate of tax to be paid, provided the industry in question undertook voluntary energy-saving measures. Industrial representatives therefore started to lobby to increase the scope of voluntary agreements, while energy-intensive industries also began to lobby for exemptions, on the grounds that the costs of the tax would be disproportionately heavy in their case. Coincidentally, a global rise in oil prices was taking place at that time, leading to increased complaints from commercial vehicle operators about the increased cost of fuel from the policy of increasing taxes faster than inflation, culminating in their taking direct action in September 2001, blocking the movement of fuel from depots. In other words, a political dynamic took over in which relatively small groups in society that bear concentrated costs from a measure have an incentive to lobby hard against its introduction and they meet little opposition because the potentially large number of beneficiaries are only affected to a small degree.

As a result of this lobbying activity, the next major budget announcement of the Chancellor, Gordon Brown, conceded ground on the matter, and the policy was adopted that there would be greater flexibility in the application of the climate levy, while the fuel escalator policy was ended. Despite these concessions the introduction of environmental taxes on the scale proposed can still be seen as a major turning point in policy, even though other possible environmental taxes, including water pollution charges that have proved successful in the Netherlands and Germany, have also been quietly shelved. To have accepted a role for environmental taxes of the sort contained in the climate change levy is important and it is reasonable to expect that influential members of the environmental policy community will push for even more such measures to be adopted.

Sustainable development

> **Sustainable development**
>
> Development that meets the needs of the present without compromising the ability of future generations to meet their needs.

Another important element in the dynamic of policy is the rise of the principle of '**sustainable development**' in international policy discourse. This is an idea that originated with a UN Commission on Environment and Development in 1987 chaired by Mrs Gro Harlem Brundtland, the Norwegian Prime Minister. The Brundtland Report defined sustainable development as development that meets the needs of the present without compromising the ability of future generations to meet their needs (see Briefing 23.3). The importance of this concept is that it challenged an assumption that was strongly built into much conventional environmental policy, namely that environmental improvements had to be bought at the expense of economic growth. The Brundtland Report pointed out that economic growth not only did environmental damage but also prevented economic development in the future: for example, through overfishing or the depletion of natural resources.

The politics of sustainable development are intrinsically international. The most important manifestation of this was the Earth Summit in 1992 in Rio de Janeiro, at which governments signed up to a number of international agreements, including ones on biodiversity and climate change. In 2002 there was a high-level follow-up to Rio in Johannesburg, which was intended to produce implementation plans in several key areas of sustainable development, including energy use, corporate accountability, chemicals and the marine environment. The UK government's participation at first had an element of farce, when it was announced that the environment minister, Michael Meacher, would not attend on the grounds that

---

BRIEFINGS

23.3 The idea of sustainable development

'Humanity has the ability to make development sustainable – to ensure that it meets the needs of the present without compromising the ability of future generations to meet their own needs.

'Sustainable global development requires that those who are more affluent adopt lifestyles within the planet's ecological means – in their use of energy, for example.

'The objective of sustainable development and the integrated nature of the global environment/development challenges pose problems for institutions, national and international, that were established on the basis of narrow preoccupations and compartmentalised concerns. Governments' general response to the speed and scale of global challenges has been a reluctance to recognise sufficiently the need to change themselves. The challenges are both interdependent and integrated, requiring comprehensive approaches and popular participation.'

Source: World Commission on Environment and Development, *Our Common Future* (the Brundtland Report), Oxford: Oxford University Press, 1987, pp. 8–9

members of the government did not wish to seem to be indulging in expensive overseas trips, only for this decision to change when Friends of the Earth offered to pay for Mr Meacher's expenses.

When at the summit the UK government, together with other European Union governments, pushed rather unsuccessfully for agreements in their key areas of concern. In particular, the EU states pushed for a commitment to increase to 10 per cent the use of renewable energy sources in the overall global mix by 2010. They were opposed by both a coalition of developed countries, including the United States, Australia, Canada and Japan, and a group of developing countries, including China, which objected to the proposal. Eventually, in the face of this opposition, the EU states had to back down, settling for a mere declaration of intent to promote renewable technologies. This particular instance represented a pattern across other areas of discussion, in which declaratory commitments replaced targeted action plans. Despite these setbacks, Margaret Beckett, as Secretary of State in Defra, hailed the summit as a new path.

Sustainable development is also an important topic of debate within UK environmental policy. The idea was first endorsed in the Conservative government's White Paper, 'This Common Inheritance' (Cm 1200, London: HMSO, 1990), which sought to examine how far the principle of sustainable development could form the basis for public policy measures. The problem of how to achieve sustainability in fields as diverse as agriculture, transport and energy consumption as well as the search for cleaner technologies that are compatible with the requirements for sustainability dominated much thinking and policy argument over the subsequent decade within environmental policy networks.

One important consequence of these debates is that many now argue there is no simple conflict between proponents of environmental protection and the business community. Business and industry are still responsible for a great deal of pollution. But there are segments of business – for example, within the pollution control industries or in the field of mass transport – that have an interest in pushing the case for more stringent environmental protection. There is a lot of questioning as to whether proponents of more sustainable alternatives – for example, the organic farming industry – are competing on equal terms, in respect of the public subsidies available, with their more established counterparts.

These issues – the need for precaution as well as scientific certainty, the integration of environmental policy with general public policies, the growing interest in economic instruments and the implications of sustainable development – have transformed the politics of the environment in the last 20 years. The traditional assumption that environmental regulation was largely a specialist affair, limited to engineers and civil servants negotiating about technical standards of control, has given way to the idea that environmental standards are part of social and economic life. The policy networks around environmental policy are therefore more crowded, with new actors emerging on the scene, and with issues in sharper dispute. The way in which the disposal of GM foods hit the national and international headlines is just one small illustration of the new politics of the environment. Moreover, these politics, as with others areas of public policy, are being increasingly carried out not only within the framework of the European Union, but also in a global international context.

Role of the European Union

From the beginning of the 1980s, the EU has been one of the principal forces operating on the British system of environmental protection, reshaping many of its main characteristics. Indeed, there is no other area apart from agriculture where the

EU has been so influential in changing the assumptions and standard operating procedures of UK policy.

Environmental policy was not originally part of the Treaty of Rome and so was not one of the original functions of the European Economic Community (as it then was). There are two reasons why environmental policy came to occupy a central place in EU policies. First, there is often a connection between the creation of a single market and environmental regulation. For example, if one country imposes high standards on vehicle exhaust emissions, requiring that cars sold within its borders meet those high standards, this policy in effect erects barriers to trade in vehicles manufactured in other countries where standards are not so high. Indeed, some of the earliest EU legislation on the environment was concerned with harmonising standards on the permissible level of noise from vehicles.

The second reason for the EU's interest in environmental policy was that it could be seen as a way of securing greater legitimacy for the processes of European integration. EU leaders responded to the upsurge of public interest in the environment in the late 1960s and early 1970s, adopting a declaration on the importance of environmental protection in 1972. The declaration led to some policy developments during the 1970s and early 1980s, although environmental regulation was not formally included in the competences of the EU until the Single European Act of 1987.

There are a number of different actors within the EU (see Briefing 23.4). However, decisions on environmental policy have been crucially shaped by the policy stances of the member states and in particular, given its size and centrality, by the position of Germany. Until the early 1980s Germany had a similar environmental policy to the UK: for example, being sceptical of the international action to control acid rain that the Scandinavian countries had been proposing. For domestic political reasons this position began to change in 1982 and was consolidated by the conversion of the Christian/Liberal coalition government in 1983 on the acid rain issue. From then on, Germany began to use the EU as a major forum within which to press for the imposition of higher environmental standards on products and manufacturing processes. First, it pushed for measures to reduce acid rain by more stringent controls on sulphur dioxide emissions from electricity power stations and other large furnaces. This initial pressure was followed by support for a wide-ranging series of measures including higher standards on vehicle emissions, tighter control of water pollution and reductions in the volume of packaging waste and measures to control the disposal of wastes in landfill sites. On these points the other 'green' member states, Denmark and the Netherlands, often supported Germany in the Council of Ministers. This dynamic was particularly important in the 1980s, but was modified by the weakening of the German government's environmental commitment for much of the 1990s, a weakening that has recently been joined by Denmark.

In the middle of the 1980s, the UK found itself in the position of opposing higher environmental standards in the EU, thus earning for itself the unenviable title of the 'dirty man of Europe'. From one point of view this was justified. The UK was always going to find it difficult to meet the high environmental standards demanded by countries that had a higher per capita income (and which therefore could afford to spend more) and that had, especially in the case of Germany, world-class engineering and pollution control industries. Moreover, the UK government did not enhance its reputation by its poor implementation of measures to which it had agreed. For example, when it came to implementing the bathing waters directive, the UK designated only 27 beaches in the whole of the UK as places of traditional bathing. Not only did the list exclude Blackpool and Brighton; it also meant that officially the UK claimed to have fewer bathing beaches than land-locked Luxembourg!

BRIEFINGS

23.4 Main actors in EU environmental policy

The Commission   The Commission has a Directorate with responsibility for environmental policy. Its principal concern is to draft directives that govern the use of resources and control permissible levels of polluting discharges into the environment. There are now some 300 pieces of environmental legislation.

The Council of Ministers   All environmental measures have to be agreed by the Council of Ministers, representing the member states. Since 1992 most measures can be agreed by qualified majority voting. Over the last 20 years those member states with the most positive environmental reputation have been Austria, Denmark, Finland, Germany, the Netherlands and Sweden. During the 1990s German interest weakened, as has Danish interest more recently. Those with concerns for economic growth and development include Greece, Ireland, Portugal and (especially) Spain. In between are France and Italy. The UK has often found itself in opposition to measures proposed by the environmental 'leader' states.

European Parliament   The main actor here is the Environment Committee. It has the reputation of taking a strong 'pro-environment' line: for example, on the control of car exhaust emissions or controls on landfill sites.

European Court of Justice   The court plays a role in enforcing compliance with environmental measures, and a number of its judgments – for example, on the legality of measures taken by member states to impose environmental regulations on products – have had a significant effect on policy.

European Environment Agency   This was established in 1995 in Copenhagen. Its brief is to collect data and information, rather than implement environmental measures. However, some see it as the forerunner of a European environment inspectorate.

Environmental impact assessment

A requirement of the European Union, which came into effect in 1988, requiring all public and private projects above a given cost to be subject to environmental appraisal in which the advantages and disadvantages from the environmental point of view are laid out.

Yet in some ways the reputation of the UK as an environmental laggard in the EU is one-sided. On some issues of EU environmental policy the UK has been a pioneer: for example, it was the UK that pressed for important legislation on wildlife protection, most notably the protection of migrating birds. The UK also pioneered the policy of agricultural set-aside, by which farmers are paid to protect their land rather than farming it intensively. Similarly, the UK introduced the principle of integrated pollution control into EU environmental policy, by which emissions to air, water and soil are controlled as a whole. Moreover, on some questions, the UK was not alone in opposing proposed measures. Spain was hostile to the control of sulphur dioxide from power stations, neither France nor Italy wanted catalytic converters on small cars and France was also opposed to the proposal for a carbon/energy tax.

Despite the conflicts over environmental policy in which Britain has been engaged, there is no doubt that the effects of EU policy on UK law and practice have been considerable. For example, some of the main measures of the 1990 Environmental Protection Act conformed to the requirements of the 1984 EU directive on air pollution control. Much of the capital cost of water pollution control measures of the 1990s has been incurred through accepting EU standards on bathing and drinking waters. Over the next few years, significant sums of money will be spent on replacing lead water piping in order to meet tighter standards on lead in drinking water.

Britain's future position in the environmental politics of the EU is more difficult to identify. The sharp antagonisms of the 1980s softened in the 1990s, not least because the EU itself lost momentum in the field of environmental policy after the difficulties of ratifying the Maastricht Treaty. With its own economic problems after reunification, Germany's environmental initiatives became less pressing, particularly after its committed environment minister Klaus Töpfer was replaced.

By way of contrast, the UK failed to regain environmental powers in a number of fields under the doctrine of 'subsidiarity', which it tried for in the wake of the 1992 Edinburgh Summit. Moreover, the accession of Sweden, Finland and Austria has augmented the pro-environment group of countries in the Council of Ministers, and led to changes in the Treaty of Amsterdam (1998), which strengthen environmental provisions. In large part, the position the UK takes in the EU and other international forums will depend on how it is able to deal with precautionary measures, integration of environmental with social and economic policy, and sustainable development.

By the beginning of the 1990s, the issue of global climate change had come to dominate discussions of European environmental policy. Global climate change involves the prediction that over the next 50 years or so the earth's atmosphere would warm up with unpredictable effects. Ironically, the issue had been thrust into prominence by Mrs Thatcher's speech to the Royal Society in September 1988, when she appeared to accept the seriousness of the problem. Under the Conservative government the difficulty as far as the UK was concerned was that the solution seemed to involve a tax on carbon fuels or on energy more generally, in order to cut consumption. The UK was not prepared to cede more tax-raising powers to the EU, thus undermining the possibility of joint action by member states.

The Labour government made the issue a priority, in part helped by the fact that the substitution of gas-fired energy production in place of coal-fired production promised to reduce greenhouse gas emissions anyway. The issue is an interesting one since it shows how the UK's relationship to global environmental issues is mediated through its membership of the EU. The most significant meeting took place in Kyoto in December 1997, when there was agreement among the nations present to cut emissions of greenhouse gases by 2008–12 to 5 per cent below their level in 1990 and 30 per cent below their projected levels. However, it was the EU that entered into this agreement on the part of its member states, and subsequent bargaining was necessary in the Council of Ministers to share out the burdens of meeting this target.

In fact, reductions in the emission of greenhouse gases into the environment in the UK were achieved between 1996 and 2002, although they began to creep upwards thereafter (Figure 23.1).

As can be seen, this performance was broadly in line with the targets sets by the **Kyoto Protocol**, although only part of the credit for this can be taken by the government, given that some reductions have been achieved by a general trend towards reduced emissions in such areas as vehicular exhaust.

The Kyoto Protocol on Climate Change

This was negotiated in 1997 to set targets to stabilise and reduce the emission of greenhouse gases in order to arrest climate change. By 2006, 162 countries had signed the accord, although the United States has refused to ratify it.

Figure 23.1 Emission of greenhouse gases in the United Kingdom, 1990–2004

Source: Social Trends, **36**, 2006, Figure 11.2, Office for National Statistics. Reproduced under the terms of the Click-Use Licence

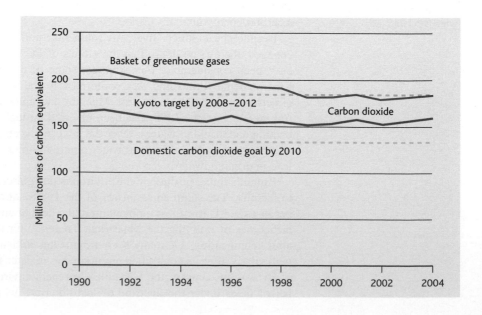

New Labour: new environmental policy?

In its 1997 election manifesto the Labour Party offered the oft-quoted assertion that environmental policy 'is not an add-on extra, but informs the whole of government, from housing and energy policy through to global warming and international agreements'. This assertion suggests that those drafting the manifesto had some understanding that environmental issues could not be contained within one segment of public policy. The politics of the environment and of sustainable development challenge assumptions about the workings of the economy, the organisation of transport and communications, as well as the responsibilities that government owes to present citizens and future generations and the responsibilities that citizens owe to one another. After more than two terms in office, how is the challenge of sustainable development likely to work itself out?

The most obvious and politically salient area of challenge is transport policy. The original merging of the ministries of transport and the environment in 1997 was intended to signal the priority to be given to dealing with congestion and transport pollution. The demerger in 2001 marks the failure of that strategy, as does the slowness of the Labour government in delivering on its aim of producing a workable integrated transport strategy. The failure of Railtrack and the difficulties of establishing its successor quickly on a sound basis have also contributed to the challenge. Without a feasible alternative, many people are forced into daily reliance on the car, in ways that are not ultimately sustainable. And while the Conservatives under David Cameron have also made sympathetic noises about the need to assign emissions controls to the top of the political agenda, it remains to be seen whether their policies would, in practice, be any different in substance from those of successive Labour governments. Less urgent, but in some ways more difficult to handle, are the environmental problems arising from the growth of low-cost air travel, which offer a growing market in cheap travel, using a fuel that remains untaxed. Whether the Labour government will be able to confront this new form of consumerism remains to be seen.

The brigading of environment and agriculture in the same ministry also points to areas of continuing challenge. So far the government has not been successful in its attempts within the European Union to secure fundamental reform of the Common Agricultural Policy, a policy that is both wasteful of resources and environmentally damaging. The growth of a political movement around the Countryside Alliance means that the issues of rural policy have in general become more difficult to handle. Also, there remains the issue of genetically modified crops and the decisions that will have to be taken once the current round of field-scale trials is complete. Such crops are inherently controversial with some arguing that they have the potential for environmental benefit because they require a lower use of pesticides, and others arguing that their development is hindering the emergence of sustainable organic agriculture. Behind this particular issue there lies a more general question about the extent to which the government can manage the process of innovating in biotechnology.

The third area of political controversy may well concern land-use developments. Although the road-building programme is not extensive, the government launched a discussion document in 2002 on the expansion of airport facilities, containing suggestions of the need for a massive growth in runway capacity. And by 2006 plans were firmly in place to build a second runway at Stansted, with the possibility of a third runway at Heathrow. Already these suggestions have prompted the mobilisation of opponents around some of the main airports targeted for expansion. Land-use planning issues are also raised by the reform of planning legislation and in particular by the passage of the Planning and Compulsory Purchase Act 2004, which restructured the planning system in England and Wales. Although the new law emphasised the importance of sustainable development and increased public participation in planning at the local level, it reduced it at the regional level and in some ways centralised decision making in the hands of the Office of the Deputy Prime Minister. Land-use planning remains, along with the National Health Service, one of the most lasting legacies of the post-war Labour government. In theory the government is committed to 'sustainable development', but this is difficult to reconcile with the pressure on land from commercial developments, especially in the south-east of England. Opposition to the massive house-building plans and airport expansions in this region could provoke considerable opposition, perhaps in the form of direct action.

In short, environmental policy is not one item of policy but raises issues that challenge assumptions in many areas of policy. At present this is more recognised in the rhetoric of policy than in the reality. How far the British political system can adapt to the challenges is an open question.

Summary

- Environmental policy raises important questions about the international dimension of public policy and the ability of the British political system to cope with the challenges of environmental management.

- Environmental policy covers a wide range of issues, but the usual way in which governments deal with environmental problems is by regulation. The politics of the environment is thus primarily concerned with the stringency of this regulation, but new instruments – such as the use of environmental taxation – are also coming into play.

- The UK's system of environmental regulation has a long history. But in some ways the perception of Britain's 'proud record' of environmental policy has inhibited adaptation to new issues and approaches, especially problems of scientific uncertainty, overall policy integration and sustainable development.

- The EU has been a major force in reshaping Britain's environmental policy. At one stage the United Kingdom stood out against EU policy making, but the picture is more subtle than a simple tale of British intransigence would suggest.

- The present government faces the challenges posed by the idea of sustainable development, especially in the areas of transport, agriculture and land-use planning.

MILESTONES

Milestones in the development of UK environmental policy

1865   Alkali Inspectorate created. The world's first national pollution inspectorate, it was responsible until the 1980s for regulating air pollution from industry

1947   Town and Country Planning Act creates the framework within which local authorities can control building and other development with the aim of protecting the countryside and enhancing town life

1952   London smog, caused by the burning of domestic coal fires, responsible for 4,000 deaths, the event that triggered the 1956 Clean Air Act, by which local authorities could create smokeless zones

1969   Harold Wilson as Prime Minister establishes the Royal Commission on Environmental Pollution, a standing Royal Commission to report on matters of environmental policy

1974   Control of Pollution Act, the first attempt to begin to codify national pollution control standards

1983   German government 'conversion' on the issue of acid rain. Germany begins to push for tougher pollution control standards in the EU, and the United Kingdom often seeks to resist the pressure

Milestones in the development of UK environmental policy continued

1986 The Alkali Inspectorate is merged with other pollution inspectorates to create Her Majesty's Inspectorate of Pollution, the beginnings of a separate environment agency

1987 Single European Act makes environmental policy a normal EU responsibility for the first time. Except when related to the single market, voting in the Council of Ministers is by the principle of unanimity

1988 Mrs Thatcher makes speech to the Royal Society in September referring to the problems of global warming

1990 Environmental Protection Act, the first major piece of legislation since 1974; aimed to introduce a modern regime of pollution control, particularly in respect of air pollution and waste management. Conservative government publishes *This Common Inheritance* in September, a statement of its policies towards sustainable development. Stronger on machinery of government issues than on substantive policy

1992 Government pursues the policy of regaining some EU environmental powers to the member states under the principle of subsidiarity

1995 Environment Act establishes the Environment Agency, bringing together the National Rivers Authority and Her Majesty's Inspectorate of Pollution

1997 Government creates new super department (Environment, Transport and the Regions), which should aid the coordination of environmental policy

1997 Kyoto Protocol sets international and national targets for emission of greenhouse gases

2001 Newly re-elected Labour government abolishes Department of Environment, Transport and the Regions and creates Department of Environment, Food and Rural Affairs

2004 Government announces that it has met the emission targets of the Kyoto Protocol

2004 Government passes the Planning and Compulsory Purchase Act

2006 UK emissions increasingly exceed the Kyoto targets

Essays

1. What are the main institutional difficulties in the way of producing a coherent environmental policy in the UK? How might they be overcome?

2. What is the Kyoto Protocol? What has been the position of British governments on the protocol?

3. What are the obstacles to a UK government pursuing policies promoting the goals of sustainable development? Can those obstacles be overcome?

Projects

1. Compare and contrast the positions of the major party manifestos on the subject of environmental policy in the 1997 and 2005 elections.

2. Identify all the major interests affected by a policy of stressing public transport rather than the car, and say whether each interest would be for or against the policy.

3. Assess the impact of the Kyoto Protocol on Climate Change. Why have some countries signed the protocol but others not?

Further reading

A useful general book on environmental politics in Britain is Robert Garner, *Environmental Politics: Britain, Europe and the Global Environment* (Basingstoke: Macmillan, 2000). On the difference between UK and Japanese policy on global warming, see Shizuka Oshitanti, *Global Warming Policy in Japan and Britain: Interactions Between Institutions and Issue Characteristics* (Manchester: MUP, 2006).

On green political thought, see A. Dobson, *Green Political Thought* (London: Routledge, 2000) and the short article by B. Jones, 'Green thinking', *Talking Politics*, **2** (2), 1989/90, pp. 50–4, September 1995. M. Robinson, *The Greening of British Party Politics* (Manchester: Manchester University Press, 1992) discusses the issue from the point of view of pressure groups and parties. R. Garner, 'How green is Labour?', *Politics Review*, **8** (4), 1999, pp. 26–8, assesses the Labour government's green credentials in its first term, and J. Callaghan, 'Environmental politics, the New Left and the new social democracy', *Political Quarterly*, **71** (3), 2000, pp. 300–8, compares the position of Labour on the environment with other European social democratic parties.

A good book on comparative environmental policy is Andrew Jordan, Rudiger K. W. Wurzel and Andrew R. Zito (eds), *'New' Instruments of Environmental Governance? National Experiences and Prospects* (London: Frank Cass, 2003), which can be usefully complemented by the essays in A. Jordan (ed.), *Environmental Policy in the European Union* (London: Earthscan, 2005). A. Weale *et al.*, *Environmental Governance in Europe: An Ever Closer Ecological Union?* (Oxford: Oxford University Press, 2003) provides coverage of the politics of environmental policy at both the EU and the member state level. T. O'Riordan and J. Jager (eds), *Politics of Climate Change* (London: Routledge, 1996) is a collection of essays on climate change, including a chapter on the UK.

Useful web sites on environmental policy

Hot links to these sites can be found on the CWS at www.pearsoned.co.uk/budge.

The protection of the environment has acquired a central role in the government's agenda in the last decade. There are many web sites of institutions dealing with environmental policies. The first stop is the government's Environment Agency (www.environment-agency.gov.uk) and the Department for Environment, Food and Rural Affairs at www.defra.gov.uk. The Institute for European Environmental Policy (www.ieep.org.uk) is an independent organisation dedicated to the analysis and development of European environmental policy. Environmental Data Services (www.ends.co.uk) is an independent publisher; on its web site you have access to daily information on a wide variety of topics related to environmental policies and strategies; it also provides excellent links to sites devoted to the analysis of issues such as air pollution, waste and recycling, and environmental law. You can access it from www.ends.co.uk/links/index.htm.

The Policy Library (www.policylibrary.com/environment/index.htm) offers a very comprehensive section on environmental policies. The Chartered Institute of Environmental Health (www.cieh.org.uk) is a professional and educational body, dedicated to the promotion of environmental health.

The Centre for Social and Economic Research on the Global Environment is based at the University of East Anglia. It works with the aim of mitigating environmental problems in both developed and developing economies; visit the centre at www.uea.ac.uk/env/cserge/. You can also visit the Environmental Change Institute at Oxford University (www.eci.ox.ac.uk). For information on legal aspects of environmental protection, visit the US-based Environmental Law Institute (www.eli.org).

In Chapter 13 of this edition you can find a comprehensive list of web sites belonging to pressure groups in the UK, which includes a wide variety of non-governmental organisations, interest groups and social movements devoted to the protection of the environment. Some of the most important ones are Friends of the Earth (www.foe.org) and Greenpeace International (www.greenpeace.org).

chapter 24

Economic policy

Previous chapters showed how many aspects of security and foreign policy are insulated from democratic scrutiny and debate. This and the two following chapters will examine contrasting styles of decision making on the economy, social affairs and equal opportunities. Of all these, management of the economy is the 'master' policy area. Put simply, the level and quality of almost all government-provided services depend on public spending, and spending in turn is a product of the ways in which governments manage the economy. The chapter will first attempt to place spending in Britain in a comparative and historical context. It will then distinguish between macro and microeconomic policy and move on to discuss the institutional context and the style and substance of decision making in this area. The chapter will conclude by pointing up the extent to which international events are now a major influence and how this will affect the likely direction of policy making over the next few years. It therefore covers:

- the historical and comparative context of economic policy

- the basics of economic policy

- the institutional context, characterised above all by centralisation

- the style and substance of policy making: a new orthodoxy?

- the internationalisation of economic policy making.

Economic policy in historical and comparative context

As was shown in Chapters 2 and 3, Britain has had an unusual and fascinating economic history. It was the first country to move from a feudal agricultural economy to one based on cash crops and modern farming methods. It was then, in turn, the first economy to industrialise. By the first third of the nineteenth century, Britain had established itself as the leading industrial nation and by the second third of the century the British economy was easily the largest in the world. It is important to know how Britain came to assume this position. Even today, the making of economic policy is influenced by this distinctive past.

Three key facts relating to Britain's economic history have affected the nature of policy making in this area:

1. Britain was – and, many would argue, remains – a world leader in the extension of free market principles. In marked contrast to such countries as France, Germany, Japan and Russia, Britain's industrialisation occurred with little direct intervention from the central government. Private capital was the driving force

behind both the construction of infrastructure (canals, railways, roads, utilities) and the development of manufacturing and extractive (mining) industries. As a result, governments proved reluctant to intervene directly in economic affairs until the traumatic events of the great depression and the Second World War forced their hand (see Chapter 3). At the same time Britain was a champion of free international trade, so has long pursued policies that opened up export and import markets among all trading nations.

2. Britain's political system is highly centralised. From the very beginning, therefore, economic policy making has been directed from the centre. It has also been executive led. Unlike political systems with federal arrangements or the separation of powers, in Britain lower-level governments, the courts and even Parliament have played a minimal role in economic policy. Until 1997 the central bank (the Bank of England), which in comparable systems played a major role in economic management, was also subservient to the executive.

3. Since the First World War, economic policy in Britain has been in almost continuous crisis. This has resulted in the elevation of economic policy to the top of the political agenda. Only very rarely have other policy issues overtaken economic affairs in importance. Hence it was economic questions rather than foreign policy or social issues that tended to make or break governments for most of the twentieth century.

When discussing public policy it is usual to distinguish between the institutional context and the style and substance of how policy is made. Before we examine these points, however, we need to provide some basic information on the nature of economic policy itself.

Economic policy: the basics

Macroeconomic policy

The branch of economic policy that deals with total or aggregate performance of the national economy, including monetary policy (money in circulation and interest rates), savings and investment levels, inflation and exchange rates.

Microeconomic policy

The branch of economic policy that deals not with the total performance of the economy, but with the performance and behaviour of individual economic actors, including firms, trade unions, consumers, and regional and local governments.

The most fundamental distinction in economic policy is between **macro** and **microeconomic policy**. Macroeconomics is concerned with the total or aggregate performance of the economy, including savings and investment totals, monetary policy (how much money is circulating in the economy, interest rate levels or the cost of borrowing) and the exchange rate of the pound in relation to other currencies. Monetary policy is in turn one of the determinants of the general level of activity in the economy and, in particular, of the level of inflation. Microeconomics is concerned not with aggregates but with the behaviour of individual economic actors such as firms, trade unions, consumers, and regional and local governments. Clearly the two are related. How firms and consumers behave greatly influences the amount of money circulating in the economy (the money supply) as well as the overall level of demand for goods and services and the savings rate. These in turn will inform macroeconomic management.

As far as policy is concerned, many free market economists believe that most of economic policy should be confined to macroeconomic management, and that governments should do as little as possible to interfere with individual firms and consumers. Such an approach implies minimal levels of taxation and of government spending, and therefore a minimal level of government debt. Put another way, it implies that governments should be concerned with macroeconomic policy but not with the microeconomics of the economy. As we all know, however, governments in Britain have legislated to affect the behaviour of all economic actors and they are intimately involved in microeconomics. Manufacturing firms, for example, are taxed in several ways, their labour markets are regulated (employee safety, job

Plate 24.1 Lloyd's, home of the famous insurance exchange – a symbol of the City's continuing importance in international finance

Source: Alamy/Robert Harding Picture Library

security, equal opportunity), the safety and quality of their products are regulated by law, and government plays a major role in providing for or regulating their production environment (environmental controls, the provision of roads and utilities, planning law and so on). The EU and local governments as well as central government play some part in this process.

The policy universe covering this microeconomic environment is highly complex and the product of numerous pieces of legislation enacted at a number of levels over a period of time. Often these laws are contradictory or incompatible. High 'on costs' (employer social security contributions) may conflict with job security. Competition or anti-monopoly policy and planning policy may result in reduced profits and therefore reduced government revenues. Much of the time governments are concerned to find a balance between these conflicting objectives, or to find the optimal tradeoffs between them. Because microeconomic policies affect the behaviour of individuals, they tend to be highly politicised. Consumers, firms,

BRIEFINGS

24.1 Characterising economic policy: institutions and actors in approximate order of importance

Monetary policy (interest rates, money supply, exchange rates)

Institutions	Actors
Bank of England	Monetary Policy Committee chaired by the
(European Union, if Britain joins EMU)	Governor of the Bank of England
Treasury	(European Central Bank, if Britain joins EMU)
International financial markets	Chancellor of the Exchequer
	Prime Minister
	Treasury
	Market investors and speculators
	Organised interests

Fiscal and spending policy (taxation, government spending)

Institutions	Actors
Treasury	Prime Minister
Cabinet and Cabinet departments	Chancellor and First Secretary to the Treasury
Public Accounts Committee and Parliament	Treasury officials
European Union	Cabinet ministers
International financial markets	Spending department officials
	Members of Parliament
	Organised interests
	Local governments
	EU officials
	Market investors and speculators

Other microeconomic policies (labour market, industrial, regional, environmental, health and safety, and competition policy)

Institutions	Actors
Cabinet	Prime Minister and Cabinet
Cabinet departments	Ministers
European Union	Departmental officials
Organised interests	EU officials
Parliament	Interest group spokespersons and officials
Local authorities	Members of Parliament
	Local government councillors and officials

Economic management

The process whereby governments assume, to varying degrees, the task of managing the national economy by means of macro and/or microeconomic policies.

taxpayers and workers are acutely aware of changes in taxation, competition policy or trade union law and are therefore likely to mobilise to protect their interests.

Macroeconomic policy is, by definition, an easier area both to characterise and to manage. Only central authorities can direct broad changes in the economy and in practice this means the executive branch of the central government. In addition, central banks are always closely involved in monetary policy, and the more independent they are of central control, the less party political monetary policy becomes. This is a point we will return to later. This said, all aspects of **macroeconomic management** ultimately affect individuals, so they can be highly controversial. If, for example, the government decides that the economy is overheating then it is likely to raise taxes and and/or reduce government spending. Both decisions are likely to be resisted by a range of political and economic actors.

Institutional context

As with so many other aspects of British politics, the most notable institutional characteristic of economic policy making is its highly centralised character. Part of this derives from the British parliamentary system, with its dominant executive, and part from the inherent weakness of regional and local government in Britain (Scotland and Wales excepted). In many other countries, lower-level governments – for example, the *Länder* (federal states) in Germany – play an important role in microeconomic policy. In others, such as the United States, national legislatures are intimately involved in the budgetary process.

Centralisation within the executive is also high in the United Kingdom, so the lead actors are the Prime Minister, the Chancellor and the Treasury. It is significant that the Prime Minister is also the First Lord of the Treasury, so emphasising the important historical role of the Treasury in British politics.

The pre-eminence of the Treasury stems from the fact that it is the institution responsible not only for providing the government with advice on general questions of economic policy, but also for enforcing government spending priorities and rules on all other departments. Hence, the 'spending departments' negotiate over the detail of their budgets with the Treasury. Its civil servants have the highest status in Whitehall, and the Chancellor of the Exchequer is widely regarded as the most senior minister in the Cabinet bar the Prime Minister.

Of course, 'the Treasury' is a building staffed with civil servants. Formally, it is not a decision-making body at all. Its job is to implement the policies of the government of the day. In this sense, the key institutional actors are the Prime Minister, the Chancellor, the First Secretary to the Treasury and the Cabinet. In reality, the Cabinet as a collective entity plays a relatively minor role in economic management. Even the key Cabinet committees in the area are not central players. In the Blair governments, the Ministerial Committee on Economic Affairs, Productivity and Competitiveness was more an advisory than a decision-making body. Of course, individual Cabinet ministers will lobby hard for their departments in the appropriate Cabinet forum, and of course, general questions of economic management are discussed in Cabinet. But the core decision making is done by the Prime Minister, Chancellor and First Secretary. They may work in ad hoc groups, or they may be influenced by outside advisers – much as Margaret Thatcher was by Sir Alan Walters – but they are unlikely to depend on the collective will of the Cabinet.

The Treasury will have a 'view' on economic management and its influence is very hard to measure. Treasury officials have almost always been fiscal conservatives or averse to increasing government debt. Since the Thatcher era they have also become significantly more hostile to government intervention in industry and in the economy generally. What role Margaret Thatcher and her ministers played in this, compared with a changing intellectual mood on the role of government, is very difficult to say. But we do know that the Prime Minister made a number of key appointments to the Treasury that greatly helped her cause. She appointed an outsider, Terry Burns, as Chief Economic Adviser (he was a professor at the London School of Economics rather than a career civil servant), and worked hard to get Peter Middleton appointed as Permanent Secretary. Burns and Middleton were both committed to fiscal orthodoxy and a reduction in the role of government, and they dominated the Treasury for most of the 1980s.

Controversy on the policy role of the Treasury has waned significantly since the Thatcher era. The reasons for this relate to the rise of a new orthodoxy in economic policy that pervades not only much of British government but also governments elsewhere.

Plate 24.2 Tony Blair and Gordon Brown launch a Labour Party poster in London during the final week of campaigning for the May 5 election in 2005

Source: Corbis/Stephen Hird

Central banks are key players in economic policy in almost all political systems, including the British. As the institutions responsible for setting interest rates, controlling the money supply and defending the national currency on the foreign exchanges, they are of obvious importance. Unusually among democracies, the Bank of England has traditionally shared with the government the responsibility for setting interest rates. Until the 1990s this was primarily the government's prerogative, although the Bank always gave advice. Under John Major the balance shifted towards the Bank. The Chancellor and the Governor of the Bank would meet monthly, the Chancellor would take the decision, but the minutes of the meeting were published later, so revelation of any rifts between the Bank and the government was delayed. Many previous governments used interest rate policy to manipulate the economy for political advantage (Chapter 3) and this innovation was designed to depoliticise the whole process.

On coming to power in 1997, the new Chancellor, Gordon Brown, announced that in future the Bank would be given the freedom to set interest rates, subject only to the advice of a group of experts appointed by the government (a group of eight economists and bankers known as the Monetary Policy Committee (MPC), most of whom are appointed by the Chancellor). This unexpected change – there was no reference to it in the Labour manifesto – effectively gave to the Bank the same freedom enjoyed by many other EU central banks. Only under emergency conditions can the government give instructions to the Bank on interest rates and then only for a short period. Most commentators agree that this move proved successful. The MPC is mandated (by the government) to target inflation at 2.5 per cent and during its first two years of operation it acted swiftly to raise interest rates when the economy was seen to be overheating and to reduce them when the economy

Plate 24.3 The Bank of England. Chancellor of the Exchequer Gordon Brown gave the Bank freedom to set interest rates on New Labour coming to power in 1997 and set up a separate regulatory body for financial institutions
Source: Alamy/Elmtree Images

was slowing down. With inflation firmly under control after 2000, the MPC reduced rates to their lowest levels in 40 years during 2001 and 2002 and then gradually increased them between 2003 and 2006. Interestingly, the Chancellor, Gordon Brown, has broadly supported these decisions.

While the Treasury and the Bank of England are undoubtedly the core economic policy-making institutions, there are numerous other institutional actors with some influence. All the major spending departments, and in particular those directly concerned with economic matters such as the Department of Trade and Industry, play some role. The DTI is concerned with micro rather than macroeconomic policy, although in its liaison with numerous private sector firms over such matters as competition policy and aid for small business it is, by definition, immersed in the concerns of individual economic actors. The same is true of the role played by local authorities. Although their spending powers have been greatly reduced over recent years (Chapter 12), they continue to plan land use, which can greatly affect the investment decisions of companies.

Until the privatisations of the 1980s and 1990s, the nationalised corporations were important economic actors. Often their pricing and investment decisions were used by central government as instruments of government policy. For example, if government wanted to rein in spending, it would cut new investment in British Rail or British Steel. Similarly, the corporations were used as examples in incomes policy: pay rises for rail workers or miners might be held down to encourage restraint in the private sector.

The role that Parliament plays in economic policy is, in effect, a very small one. The Public Accounts Committee (PAC), which is the most important of Parliament's

BRIEFINGS

24.2 Organised interests and government in economic policy making

In some countries, peak associations (the equivalent of the British Trades Union Congress or Confederation of British Industry) are directly incorporated into the economic decision-making process. Such systems are usually labelled 'corporatist'. Austria is usually identified as a corporatist system, and there are elements of corporatism in other countries such as Germany and Japan. Scholars agree that Britain has never had corporatist political arrangements. Major corporations or unions are rarely consulted before important decisions are taken. More often they will lobby to protect their interests, but there is no guarantee that their wishes will be heeded. For example, during the 1980s, Conservative governments systematically reduced the powers of trade unions. More revealing was the government's rejection of pleas by manufacturing industry during the early 1980s that its policies were leading to rapid deindustrialisation. The determination to continue with monetarist policies showed just how far removed industry was from central decision making.

The US political scientist Charles Lindblom has pointed out, however, that businesses – but not trade unions – are uniquely privileged in economic policy because they can always threaten that anti-business policies will lead to recession and unemployment. In other words, they do not need to be directly involved in decision making; instead they have a hidden veto on the policy agenda. Today this seems almost a truism, and it is certainly the case that all governments now talk in terms of maintaining a good environment for business investment and profits. Given Britain's status as a major trading nation over many generations, UK governments have been particularly keen to serve the interests of the City of London (see Chapters 2 and 3), which may however encourage short-termism so far as industry and manufacturing are concerned.

Source: C. Lindblom, *Politics and Markets*, New Haven, CT: Yale University Press, 1977

select committees, meets twice a week and is charged with scrutinising the government's accounts and ensuring that government spending provides value for money. Although important, this function does not relate directly to the formulation of economic policy. Generally there are clear limits to the ability of Parliament to keep the government accountable in any detailed way (Chapter 18).

Apart from the PAC, Parliament's role is limited – as it is with most aspects of public policy – to the collective power of backbench MPs. When they can muster a majority against the government they can be very effective, but this rarely happens. Indeed, the only example in the last 20 years of a government's being defeated on a major economic question was when an alliance of opposition and dissenting Conservative MPs rejected the rise in VAT on fuel from 8 to 17.5 per cent in the November 1994 budget.

Finally, what role do organised interests play in economic policy? It is clear from earlier discussions that groups are rarely involved directly. Firms and unions may make comments on (say) a rise in taxation or interest rates, and they may lobby hard in favour of or against one policy or another. Sometimes their demands are heeded, as with the transitional relief from the uniform business rates granted to business during the early and mid-1990s.

Business, in particular, is privileged in relation to other organised interests as it has an indirect veto on a range of economic policies. Governments are very aware that policies that challenge the free market environment can lead to recession and unemployment. It is rarely necessary for business leaders to threaten such consequences should particular policies be adopted. All of the actors in the policy process are aware of it and this in turn helps mould a pro-business policy agenda. Because of Britain's history as a trading nation, governments have been particularly deferential to the financial markets of the City of London. As will be discussed later, maintaining the value of the pound on the foreign exchanges was for long a major priority of successive governments.

Style and substance of policy making

Monetarism

A revised version of neo-classical economics that, contrary to Keynesianism, argues that government should minimise its involvement in economic matters, except for controlling the money supply as a way of holding down inflation.

Economic policy making in Britain in the twentieth century took the form of almost continuous crisis management (Chapter 3). British efforts to sustain the free convertibility of sterling into gold, followed by the Great Depression, the Second World War and the near bankruptcy of the post-war years, were quickly followed by decades of 'stop–go' policies. Successive governments, intent on maintaining the value of the pound on the foreign exchanges, were forced into periodic bouts of deflation only to be followed by electorally inspired reflation.

By the late 1970s controlling inflation became the top priority and, with the election of Margaret Thatcher in 1979, the fight against inflation was seen as inexorably linked to the supply of money circulating in the economy. **Monetarism**, as it came to be known, dominated British politics during the early and mid-1980s. It was highly controversial, not only because of its uncertain intellectual pedigree, but also because, if implemented fully, it could be highly deflationary. At a time when unemployment was in any case rising, monetarism was viewed by many as involving increased unemployment as a deliberate tool of economic policy.

The monetarist experiment was abandoned once it became clear that the relationship between the money supply (which in any case was notoriously difficult to measure) and inflation was tenuous at best. What the episode demonstrates, however, is the extraordinarily centralised and closed nature of economic policy making in Britain. The Prime Minister, Chancellor (Sir Geoffrey Howe) and personal Downing Street and Treasury advisers (Alan Walters and Terry Burns) decided on the policy and it was implemented. Many in Margaret Thatcher's Cabinet objected, as did many Conservative backbenchers. Many Treasury officials were sceptical, as were most economists.

Since the mid-1980s there have been two more major crises. One of them is a typically insulated instance of economic policy making and the other – British

BRIEFINGS

24.3 Monetarism and British politics

On coming to power in 1979, the Conservatives were already converted to the belief that the control of the money supply (the amount of cash and credit circulating in the economy) was the key to controlling inflation. Margaret Thatcher and her intellectual guru, Sir Keith Joseph, accepted the analysis of the Nobel Laureate economist Milton Friedman, who had long argued that rising inflation was linked to governments' neglect of monetary targets. Accordingly, the government adopted a medium-term financial strategy that set specific targets for one of the Treasury's broader money supply indicators (M3, which denoted cash and accounts at UK banks). In order to curb the money supply, interest rates were raised and public expenditure cut. In addition, the standard rate of value added tax (VAT) was almost doubled. The immediate effects of these changes were to fuel inflation and to depress the economy. Economists assured the government that this was a short-term phenomenon, or a necessary dose of medicine to guarantee long-term economic health. In the event, the recession bottomed out in 1982 and a slow but steady recovery set in thereafter. By 1983 it was becoming obvious that the objective performance of the economy, including the inflation rate, was only loosely linked to the money supply. The Treasury set ever-higher monetary targets, but these were almost always overshot. Meanwhile, inflation was falling steadily. By 1985 monetary targets, although set, were no longer the main guiding principle of government policy.

Monetarism was important because it demonstrated how a determined Prime Minister could almost unilaterally change the direction of economic policy. Monetarism also became a catch-all phrase to describe 'Thatcherite' policies. In fact, by the end of the 1980s Thatcherite policies bore very little relationship to the strictly economic definition of monetarism.

Exchange Rate Mechanism

The ERM was the first stage of a European Union plan for financial integration. As part of the European Monetary System introduced in 1979, the ERM was designed to minimise currency exchange fluctuation among members of the EU belonging to the system.

European Monetary System

The third and final stage of European financial integration, EMS provides for a single European currency (the euro), to replace existing national currencies, and a European central bank.

membership of the **Exchange Rate Mechanism** and of the European currency – is highly atypical. The first crisis occurred after the stock market 'crash' in October 1987. The Chancellor of the Exchequer, Nigel Lawson, feared that the consequences would be deflationary and therefore stimulated the economy with interest rate cuts. The crash did not have the expected effect, however, and the fall in the cost of money further stimulated an already overheated economy. Credit became extremely easy to obtain and consumer debt soared. By mid-1988 the boom was widely recognised as inflationary; property prices were soaring and the government was obliged to take draconian corrective measures in 1989 and 1990. These events contributed to the deepest recession of the post-war era.

The second crisis grew in part out of a major rift between the lead policy makers in the economic policy arena: Prime Minister Margaret Thatcher and her Chancellor, Nigel Lawson. The issue was British membership of the ERM and of the **European Monetary System**. Lawson supported membership, while the Prime Minister was vehemently opposed. Lawson's resignation in 1989 was partly inspired by this disagreement. But the ERM supporters finally won the day and Britain joined in October 1990. Only the threat of a Cabinet revolt caused Thatcher to change her mind. This was, therefore, one of the rare instances when economic policy making moved beyond a small coterie of Downing Street and Treasury officials.

British membership of the ERM was a failure. In September 1992, the UK was forced out of the currency agreement. The issue continued to dominate economic debate for the next dozen years and more, but now in the form of Britain's position on the single European currency. The unusual nature of this policy issue is well demonstrated by the fact that the Conservative governments of John Major could not make a clear commitment one way or another on the question. So deep were the divisions in the Conservative Party that the government's hands were effectively tied. No other economic issue in recent British political history has been diffused into the rank and file of a party in this way. The typical mode, as with monetarism and the Lawson boom, is for decisions to be taken by a few lead actors and then implemented irrespective of the opposition.

Plate 24.4 By Labour's third term, many in the business community were accusing Chancellor Gordon Brown of stifling enterprise with regulations and high taxes
Source: Cartoon Stock

While Britain's membership of European Monetary Union remains a vitally important issue, it has not divided the Blair government as it did Major's. Blair's 'wait and join EMU only when the conditions are right' policy is broadly supported by the Cabinet and Parliamentary Labour Party. In addition, Blair was Prime Minister at a time when an unusual degree of consensus applied to the fundamentals of economic policy. There are a number of reasons for this, including the almost universal perception that the primary aim of economic policy should be the control of inflation. As a result, the controversial issues that dominated most of the post-war period – the proper economic role of the state, the extent of public ownership, the timing of stop–go policies, monetarism and the relationship between the trade unions and the government – have, at least for the time being, largely passed from the political agenda.

This almost certainly made Tony Blair's job easier. He was, of course, still obliged to operate in the same institutional environment as his predecessors. And

BRIEFINGS

24.4 The new orthodoxy in economic policy

When, in October 1997, the Deputy Prime Minister John Prescott announced to the Labour Party conference that he would not renationalise the railways, he was conforming to what is an almost universally supported orthodoxy in economic policy. This consists of the following assumptions:

■ **The primacy of keeping rates of inflation low** over all other objectives. It used to be the case that low rates of unemployment and high rates of growth were governments' top priority, with low inflation a poor third. Now, with the internationalisation of capital, governments almost everywhere see low inflation as the prerequisite for economic well-being.

■ **Fiscal responsibility** During the 1960s and 1970s some British governments believed that it was possible to 'spend their way out of trouble' or stimulate the economy through borrowing and spending to speed recovery. Today governments are convinced that the only way to spend responsibly is to finance expenditure with taxation. Government borrowing is permissible but should not rise to more than 3 per cent of gross domestic product. Moreover, any borrowing should be used for investment by the government rather than consumption. This came to be known as Gordon Brown's 'Golden Rule'. During periods of sustained growth, as in the late 1990s, the deficit should be reduced well below 3 per cent.

■ **Low, preferably indirect, taxation** is a good thing; high direct taxation is a bad thing. At one time Labour governments supported the idea of high progressive personal income taxes and low indirect taxes (taxes on expenditure such as VAT). Today economists argue that high income taxes distort consumer preferences and undermine efficiency. Indirect taxes leave the consumer the choice to save rather than spend, or to spend on low-tax rather than high-tax items. The Blair government has broadly accepted this view, as did the Major government. The main difference between them is Labour's preference for a much lower starting rate of income tax for the low paid, which was set at 10 per cent in 1999.

■ If possible, **the market rather than the state should provide goods and services**. Until recently, Labour governments believed in nationalisation and the Conservatives in privatisation. Today all parties accept the advantages of privatisation. Labour accepts the need for more regulation of companies previously in public ownership, but does not propose any major renationalisation. Even the failure of Railtrack in 2002 was followed not by outright nationalisation, but by a state-supported investment company, Network Rail. It is unlikely that the Conservatives would have acted differently.

■ A major debate in the Labour Party used to be between supporters of an economy protected from outside competition and those who believed in **free trade**. Today this debate is all but over. All leading Labour politicians support open international markets, with only a very minimal state role in protecting British industry. Put another way, Labour governments are enthusiastic supporters of free and open competition at home and abroad.

on occasion 'traditional' economic crises, such as the public sector labour disputes of the winter of 2002–3, erupt to disturb the relatively benign policy environment. Let us look at the nuts and bolts of the most important part of this environment – the budgetary process – in more detail.

Budgetary process

Until the late 1960s, the budgetary process was conducted in much the same way as it was 100 years earlier. It consisted of an annual round of expenditure approved by the government on an ad hoc basis. No systematic survey of spending, or planning of future spending, was involved. On the recommendation of the Plowden Report in 1961, the government accepted the need for annual expenditure surveys, which were finally adopted in 1969. The system was known as the Public Expenditure Survey Committee (PESC). Over the years, and especially since the economic traumas of the 1970s, this process has become more thorough and more systematic.

Until the election of a Labour government in 1997, the system worked like this:

1. The process started with the estimates procedure whereby officials from the spending departments report to the Treasury on their spending needs over the next three years.

2. These estimates were then summarised in the PESC, which reported to the Chief Secretary to the Treasury. The Chief Secretary in turn reported to the Cabinet, which made an estimate on spending needs over a five-year period.

3. This was followed by a series of bilaterals or face-to-face negotiations between spending department ministers and Treasury ministers. This was the first phase of the spending round. It was characterised by horse trading, confrontation and intense negotiation. A great premium was placed on the quality of argument. Intellectually gifted and aggressive ministers were more likely to squeeze something out of the Treasury than their less gifted colleagues.

4. The results of these negotiations were passed on to Cabinet committees and thence to the full Cabinet for approval. If a minister failed to agree with the Treasury, the request was sent to the 'Star Chamber'. This was a Cabinet committee made up of senior Cabinet members who heard the arguments and adjudicated disputes between the disagreeing parties. The Star Chamber's decisions were usually final. Ministers might have tried to appeal against their decision to the full Cabinet, but were unlikely to gain much satisfaction.

5. Predictably, most disputes involved the large spending departments – Health, Social Security, Defence and Education – that serve large and politically powerful constituencies. As can be seen from Table 24.1, spending has remained at a high level since 1971, accounting (today) for about 40 per cent of GDP. In comparative perspective over time, note that government spending is high in most countries, although there has been some levelling off and decreases in recent years. All governments are now committed to holding spending and government debt down. Given that the public continue to assign a high priority to health, education, housing and social security (see Table 25.1), the pressures for increases can be appreciated. Indeed, spending on social security, health and education now dominate the national budget (Figure 24.1). Note also the relatively low proportion of spending devoted to defence. Just £24 billion was spent on defence in 2002 – less than 6 per cent of total government spending. For most of the post-war period, defence was one of the largest items in the government budget.

Table 24.1 General government total outlays as a percentage of GDP, 1985–2004

	1985	1990	1995	1999	2000	2004
Australia	37.3	33.0	35.7	32.4	33.0	36.6
Austria	50.3	48.8	52.5	49.9	48.8	49.3
Belgium	57.1	50.5	50.2	47.4	46.7	49.3
Canada	45.2	45.7	45.0	38.7	37.7	41.7
Czech Republic	–	–	43.9	43.8	46.1	41.5
Denmark	–	53.6	56.6	52.5	50.6	58.9
Finland	42.6	44.4	54.3	47.1	43.6	52.5
France	49.8	47.5	51.4	49.6	48.7	49.8
Germany	45.6	43.8	46.3	46.2	43.3	43.2
Greece	43.8	47.5	46.7	43.3	43.3	46.0
Hungary	–	–	56.2	50.0	47.5	44.6
Iceland	35.3	39.0	39.2	39.1	38.8	48.1
Ireland	50.7	39.9	38.0	31.9	29.2	35.6
Italy	49.5	52.9	51.1	46.7	44.8	45.4
Japan	29.4	30.5	34.4	36.1	36.8	30.3
Korea	17.6	18.3	19.3	23.3	22.9	31.3
Luxembourg	–	41.3	42.8	39.8	38.5	44.8
Netherlands	51.9	49.4	47.7	43.8	41.6	46.2
New Zealand	–	48.1	38.6	38.8	38.2	41.2
Norway	41.5	49.7	47.6	45.8	40.8	47.9
Poland	–	–	47.0	43.4	43.7	40.2
Portugal	39.3	39.3	41.0	40.6	40.3	45.4
Slovak Republic	–	–	41.0	54.2	52.2	45.7
Spain	39.7	41.6	44.0	39.6	38.8	38.4
Sweden	60.4	55.9	61.9	55.0	52.2	58.3
United Kingdom	–	39.1	42.2	37.1	37.3	40.8
United States	33.8	33.6	32.9	30.2	29.9	31.9

Source: *OECD in Figures*, 2005 edn, Paris. © OECD, 2005

Figure 24.1 Central government spending by function, 2005–6

Source: HM Treasury, www.hm-treasury.gov.uk. Reproduced under the terms of the Click-Use Licence

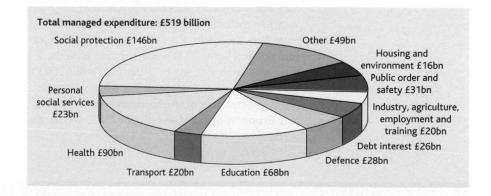

6. The budget was then consolidated in a finance bill that was presented to the House of Commons in November. Since 1993 both the expenditure side and the income (taxation) side have been combined in the November budget (previously, the taxation measures were announced in the spring). The finance bill is then referred to House committees, and individual measures are debated before votes are taken. While this process takes some time, major amendments are very rare. Indeed, we earlier noted that the government's defeat on the increase in VAT on fuel in 1994 was a very unusual event and one that can partly be attributed to the government's very small Commons majority at that time.

Figure 24.2 Central government receipts, 2005–6

Source: HM Treasury, www.hm-treasury.gov.uk. Reproduced under the terms of the Click-Use Licence

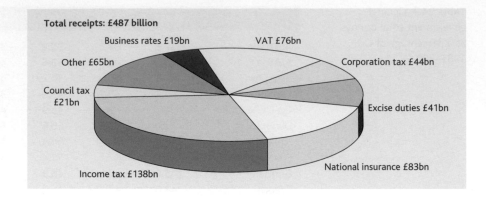

Total receipts: £487 billion

Business rates £19bn — VAT £76bn — Corporation tax £44bn — Excise duties £41bn — National insurance £83bn — Income tax £138bn — Council tax £21bn — Other £65bn

The fundamentals of this system remain in place. But when elected in 1997 New Labour tried to make the system more amenable to longer-term planning by guaranteeing the three-year departmental expenditure limits (DEL), thus eliminating the annual expenditure round which was used under the old system to secure ad hoc increases. Other changes included a shift to 'resource accounting budgeting' or an emphasis on counting expenditure when commitments are made rather when invoices are paid. As a result, it was hoped that value for money would be achieved. Finally, the government announced 'cross-sector coordination' or 'joined-up government' when allocating resources. As of 2005 the government continues to experiment with novel means of rationalising the public expenditure control system.

Within the machinery of Whitehall, negotiations over spending are intensely political. But the same is rarely true of decisions affecting revenue. In the November budget the Chancellor announces, in a highly ritualised manner, forthcoming changes in taxation. These are deemed to be strictly confidential, with only the Prime Minister and the Treasury team privy to their contents. Indeed, it is rare for even senior Cabinet ministers to be party to these decisions. Of course, much speculation surrounds the process and leaks are not uncommon. Once announced, the decisions may prove highly controversial (as with the case of VAT on fuel) but they are very rarely successfully challenged. Almost all the major changes in UK taxation, including the shift from direct to indirect taxation over the last 20 years, have been the result of a relatively closed decision-making process involving very few political actors. Such was the case with the 2002 decision to increase national insurance contributions by 1 per cent from 2003 to fund large increases in health spending. In effect, this added 1 per cent to the marginal rate of income tax for those in employment. Almost certainly this decision was taken by the Chancellor and Prime Minister alone. Figure 24.2 shows the percentage distribution of tax revenues in 2005/6.

Internationalisation of economic policy

Economic policy in Britain has been affected by external events for many decades. Recently, however, the constraints imposed by the international environment have grown in importance. Let us summarise these briefly.

European Union

The EU impinges on British economic policy in a number of ways. Most of these affect micro rather than macroeconomic policy. EU regulatory, environmental and

Stability and Growth Pact

The Stability and Growth Pact was adopted at the Amsterdam meeting of the European Council, 1997, to ensure smooth progress towards fiscal convergence (single monetary policy) and price stability within the EU.

competition policy have precedence over British law. In addition, should Britain join the single currency (or European Monetary Union) then the crucial aspects of macroeconomic policy – interest rates and exchange rate policy – would be set by a European central bank rather than by a government or the Bank of England. Only fiscal (taxation and expenditure) policy would be left in the central government's hands, although even here it would be subject to the rules of the **Stability and Growth Pact**.

International capital markets

Since exchange rate and other controls on the movement of capital were abolished in Britain and the other leading trading nations during the 1970s and 1980s, the pressure on all economic authorities to follow certain policies has been intense. These policies include low levels of inflation and public (government) debt. If the markets sense that inflation or debt is out of control, investors will move out of what is considered a vulnerable currency. In order to maintain the value of currencies, governments will be forced into taking drastic corrective measures, including cuts in spending and raising interest rates and taxation. The alternative would be to let the currency fall, which in an import-dependent economy would result in more inflation. As can be seen from Figure 3.1, the inflation picture is complex. Figure 24.3 shows the size of the public sector debt/surplus over the period 1996 to 2011 projected. Generally, debt during periods of recession and falls during booms. As of 2006, debt was on the rise but to relatively modest levels compared with the early and mid-1990s. The projections to 2011 are based on certain economic assumptions, such as continued economic growth that may not, of course, be fulfilled. Most commentators agree that public debt is being held at a reasonable level in Britain. Expressed as a percentage of GDP, it was increasing

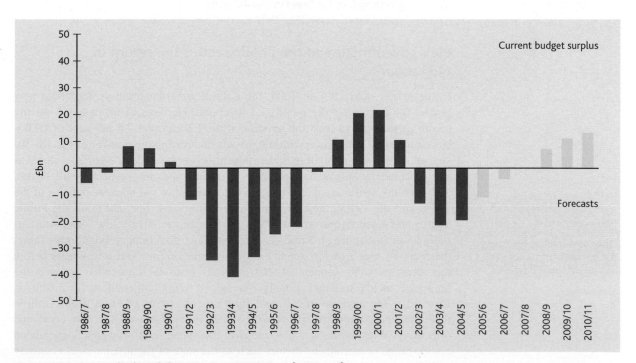

Figure 24.3 Current budget deficit/surplus, 1996–2011 (projected)

Source: House of Commons Library Research Paper 06/12, *Economic Indicators*, March 2006. Reproduced under the terms of the Click-Use Licence

Figure 24.4 Net debt as a percentage of GDP, 1997–2005

Source: Office of National Statistics at http://www.statistics.gov.uk/cci/nugget.asp?id=206. Reproduced under the Click-Use Licence

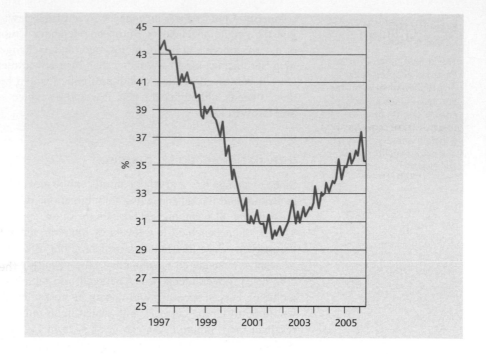

in 2006 (Figure 24.4), but at 37 per cent it is low compared with comparable countries such as the United States and Germany. Generally, the centralised and unitary nature of economic policy making in Britain gives to incumbent governments all the tools necessary to control the level of government expenditure and income, and therefore the level of public debt.

Blair government and the public sector: the return of old Labour?

In the period from 2001 to 2005, the Labour government announced bold new targets for improving the quality of the public services. This included raising health spending to at least the average in the EU (around 7/8 per cent of GDP), easing transport congestion within ten years and raising the number of the 18–30-year-old age group going into higher education to 50 per cent. Naturally, this was accompanied by substantial increases in public spending especially in health. Although this looks like a return to the old 'spend, tax and borrow' policies of the 1960s and the 1970s, there are important differences. For one thing the **Public Sector Net Cash Requirement** (**PSNCR**) remained relatively low – and substantially lower than during the mid years of the Major government. For another thing, the economy was growing steadily with low inflation for a full seven years before the increases were announced. No previous post-war chancellor enjoyed the luxury of such a situation. Finally, the largest single expenditure (in health) is financed by an increase in National Insurance. In terms of fiscal responsibility, therefore, the government plans were quite compatible with the new economic orthodoxy. Whether this remains true over the longer term, of course, depends on a wide range of extraneous factors such as the state of the international economy and the economic competence of the government. Most economists agree that, should the economy falter, Gordon Brown's spending plans may not be sustainable over the next economic cycle.

Public Sector Net Cash Requirement

The total amount borrowed by government to finance its annual expenditure.

Summary

This chapter has shown how highly centralised economic policy making in Britain is:

- Even within the executive, very few political actors are involved in the key decisions. This applies to both monetary and fiscal policy.

- Until recently, monetary policy was the shared prerogative of the Chancellor of the Exchequer and the Bank of England. Since 1997, however, the Bank has been the dominant influence in setting interest rates. The Prime Minister, Chancellor and the Treasury remain the key players in setting levels of government spending and taxation.

- Other Cabinet ministers play a reactive rather than proactive part in this process. Parliament's role is usually confined to approving decisions and to a limited form of supervision. Other interests such as business and the unions play an indirect role, although they may be closely involved in the detailed implementation of aspects of microeconomic policy.

- Government options in this area are, however, greatly circumscribed by the need to maintain the confidence of business. This applies both domestically and, as far as the money markets are concerned, internationally.

- In addition the European Union plays an increasingly important role in microeconomic policy. Should Britain join the single currency then the EU's role in macroeconomic policy will become dominant.

- Labour governments have adhered to a new orthodoxy in economic policy, although there are dangers that increased social spending in the 2004–7 period will conflict with agreed borrowing targets should the economy falter.

MILESTONES

Milestones in recent economic policy making

1961	Publication of the Plowden Report on the need for more systematic control of public spending
1969	Public Expenditure Survey Committee system introduced to plan expenditure in advance
1976	Introduction of the 'Star Chamber' to arbitrate disputes over departmental spending
1979–80	Margaret Thatcher's monetarist experiment begins
1983–5	Monetarism quietly dropped as a guiding principle in economic policy
1987	Stock market crash followed by overstimulation of the economy
1989–93	Deepest recession of the post-1945 period
1990	Britain joins the Exchange Rate Mechanism of the European Monetary System
1992	Britain is forced out of the ERM ('Black Wednesday')
1993	Spending and taxing side of the budget consolidated into one November budget
1994	Government defeated over further increases in VAT on domestic fuel
1997	New Labour Chancellor, Gordon Brown, announces that the Bank of England is immediately to be given the freedom to set interest rates
1999	Budget establishes a new 10 per cent income tax starting rate for the poorest working families
2002	Budget includes large increases in health spending, financed by a 1 per cent increase in National Insurance (in effect a 1 per cent increase in income tax for all those in employment). Budget surplus becomes a (small) deficit
2005–7	Government borrowing increases in order to finance increased social spending. Gordon Brown's financial prudence is tested in the context of a slowing economy

Essays

1. Who are the main actors in economic policy making in the UK? How has membership of this group changed since the 1980s?

2. Critically assess the Labour government's handling of the economy between 1997 and 2007.

3. What effect has membership of the European Union had on economic policy in the UK? Answer with reference to the period since 1986.

4. 'One of the most significant developments of recent years has been the convergence of Conservative and Labour parties on the fundamentals of economic policy.' Discuss.

Projects

1. Write a departmental brief from one of the major spending departments (Defence, Social Security, Health, Education, Transport, Home Office) justifying expenditure to the Cabinet Star Chamber. Write a Treasury reply, arguing for reduced expenditure.

2. How does the European Union affect British economic policy? Answer with respect to *one* of the following:

   (a) trade policy

   (b) interest rate and currency policy

   (c) labour market policy.

3. Explain the differences between Labour's first nine budgets (1997–2006) and the subsequent expenditures. Answer by providing statistics on changes between departments and on the overall level of spending.

Further reading

For an account of recent changes in economic policy, see Anthony Seldon and Dennis Kavanagh (eds), *The Blair Effect, 2001–5* (Cambridge: Cambridge University Press, 2005), Chapters 8 and 9. Wyn Grant's *Economic Policy in Britain* (London: Palgrave, 2002) provides a good up-to-date introduction to economic policy making. On Gordon Brown's tenure as Chancellor, see Robert Peston, *Brown's Britain* (London: Short Books, 2006). A good summary of New Labour economic and social policies is provided by Gerald R. Taylor (ed.), *The Impact of New Labour* (London: Macmillan, 1999). See also Wyn Grant, 'The changing nature of economic policy', *Politics Review*, **10** (4), 2001, pp. 14–17. On the Thatcher years, see Andrew Gamble, *The Free Economy and the Strong State* (London: Macmillan, 2nd edn, 1994). For an account of changes in expenditure control, see Simon James, *British Cabinet Government* (London: Routledge, 2nd edn, 1999).

Useful web sites on economic policy

Hot links to these sites can be found on the CWS at www.pearsoned.co.uk/budge.

In Britain, economic and fiscal policy is dominated by the Chancellor of the Exchequer; the main policy goals and achievements can be found at www.number-10.gov.uk. There are other relevant sites related to economic and fiscal policies, including the Treasury site (www.hm-treasury.gov.uk), the Bank of

England (www.bankofengland.co.uk) and the Department of Trade and Industry www.dti.gov.uk. Some useful information is available at the government's Centre for Management and Policy Studies (www.cmps.gov.uk). It might also be worth looking at the British Chambers of Commerce (www.chamberonline.co.uk/index.jsp). The Confederation of British Industries is at www.cbi.org.uk. You can find the Trade Union Congress at www.tuc.org.uk.

There are a number of think tanks and research groups where economic theories receive critical assessment. Some of them are: the Institute of Fiscal Studies (www.ifs.org.uk), the National Institute for Economic and Social Research (www.niesr.ac.uk), the Centre for Economic Policy Research (www.cepr.org), the Adam Smith Institute (www.adamsmith.org.uk) and the Institute for Economic Affairs (www.ie.org.uk) The *Financial Times* (www.ft.com) and *The Economist* (www.economist.com) offer regular market, financial and economic analysis.

In the Policy Library web site, under the entry on economic policy, you can find an excellent set of resources on topics such as agriculture, employment, business and taxation. We strongly suggest you visit the site at www.policylibrary.com.

chapter 25

Social policy

Few issues in Britain arouse as much controversy as social policy. The vast majority of the population support free health care provided by the National Health Service, free high-quality primary and secondary education, adequate old age pensions and unemployment benefits. Yet to a greater or lesser extent, all of these benefits are perceived to have been reduced in value or quality by successive governments. Many of the problems associated with state social provision in Britain are related to the sometimes painful transition from the **universal benefits** promised at the inception of the Welfare State in the 1940s to the much more **selective** system that economic and political realities have imposed since the 1980s. Much of this chapter will be devoted to explaining why this transition has occurred and why the pressures for more selectivity continue to increase even when the public expect higher standards of social provision. The chapter will cover:

- problems in defining 'social policy'

- the Welfare State in Britain: its foundations and principles

- the four main areas of social provision – income maintenance, housing, health and education – over the last 25 years

- policy areas examined in their institutional context. A special emphasis is placed on the efforts by New Labour to improve the quality of the public services.

Defining social policy

Universal and selective benefits

Universal benefits are welfare benefits distributed to all groups and individuals who are eligible, irrespective of their particular circumstances, compared with selective benefits for which eligibility is determined according to individual circumstances such as income, age or disability.

What constitutes social policy depends on both historical and geographic circumstances. In some countries what we regard as social support is provided by families or the market. If social policy is defined as *state* support for people in need (a definition adopted by this chapter), it is clear that within countries, the definition changes over time as it does between countries. In Britain, for example, state support for housing has moved from a limited form of municipal provision before the Second World War, to near universal provision for 'general needs' housing after the war, back to a minimal level of support today. In many poorer countries, state-provided benefits are limited to education. Even in rich industrialised nations such as the United States and Japan, social policy means something very different from what it means in the United Kingdom. In the United States, for example, housing is rarely considered a part of social policy and there is no system of universal health care. Instead, the market is the major provider in these areas. In Britain today, the definition is changing as the political and public support for state provision of housing has fallen.

BRIEFINGS

25.1 Universalism, selectivism and the Welfare State

In many developed modern economies, such as the United States, most state welfare benefits are provided on a selective basis: that is, eligibility is determined by individual circumstances. Income, disability and age are the usual criteria employed when potential recipients' eligibility is tested. Benefits may be selective both in terms of the social group eligibility and in terms of the level of support. State pensions, for example, are obviously only available to the old and survivors (those widowed), and the amount of the pension may vary according to circumstance and past employment record.

In other systems, benefits are provided on a universal basis. All social groups may be eligible and the benefits may be distributed on a flat-rate basis, which means that the same benefit is given to everybody, irrespective of circumstances. Elements of both systems prevail in most countries. Even in the self-reliant United States, elementary and secondary education is organised on a universal basis.

The British Welfare State as implemented by the Labour government after 1945 was based more on universal than selectivist principles. Everybody was entitled to health care, including dental care. Public housing was for 'general need' and rents were unrelated to income. Family allowances were flat rate as were elements of the old age pension.

The founders of the system were not so naive as to believe that it could be introduced without considerable cost. How then would it be funded? Three devices would be employed to ensure the system was viable. First, Keynesian demand management would be the dominant tool of macroeconomic policy. As a result the country would enjoy full employment; the poverty, illness and dislocation associated with mass unemployment would be avoided. Second, much of the system would be self-financing through contributory national insurance stamps. Eligibility for unemployment benefit, for example, would be directly linked to this system. Third, although never explicitly stated, a system of rationing would reconcile the demand for, and the supply of, certain services. Waiting lists would prevail for some hospital treatments and for public housing.

In spite of numerous problems, the Welfare State worked well for most of the post-war period. Even in the early twenty-first century, elements of universalism – for example, in the NHS – persist.

Welfare State

A system in which the state takes responsibility for at least the minimum conditions of social and economic security by providing public services such as housing, health care, sickness and unemployment benefits, and pensions.

Very generally, social policy covers those areas where the government (or the state), rather than the market, plays a major role in providing for the physical well-being of families and individuals. Governments came to play this role because of the failure of markets to provide acceptable standards of provision. Usually, although not always, it was electorally powerful socialist or Labour parties that legislated for social provision. Often they came to power following periods of serious economic dislocation.

In Britain, for example, the Labour government elected in 1945 legislated to create what became known as the Welfare State, or a system of social support designed to protect every citizen from the physical insecurities of life.

The British Welfare State

The British welfare system was largely a product of the Great Depression of the 1930s and of the Second World War. Although the rudiments of a pension and unemployment insurance system were introduced by the Liberals soon after the turn of the century, it was not until the election of a Labour government in 1945 that the construction of the **Welfare State** began. The mass unemployment of the 1930s had demonstrated how inadequate social protection was in the absence of comprehensive state aid. Low levels of unemployment assistance (known as 'the dole') were means tested or available only to families close to destitution. Families

BRIEFINGS

25.2 Foundations of the British Welfare State

Income maintenance

1942   Beveridge Report on social security

1945   Family Allowance Act: family allowances

1946   National Insurance Act: unemployment benefit, disability, old age and survivors' pensions

1948   National Assistance Act: income support for those not covered by national insurance

Housing

1946   Housing Act: central government subsidies for local authority housing

1949   Housing Act: council housing designated as 'general needs' and not just for the working class

Health

1948   National Health Service Act: creation of the National Health Service

Education

1944   Education Act: secondary education available to all, free of charge; 11-plus exam would select the academically gifted for grammar schools

Employment

1944   'Employment Policy' White Paper: official recognition of Keynesian full employment policy; also recognised the need for regional policy to reduce economic disparities between the regions

whose means were above these low levels of income had to make do as best they could. Other services, including health, housing and secondary education, had to be paid for or were freely available only on a very limited basis.

By the end of the 1940s, an intellectual and political consensus was emerging in favour of a greatly enhanced role for government in economy and society. The Second World War had demonstrated how massive government spending could quickly remove the blight of mass unemployment, and politicians became convinced that Keynesian economics, or demand management, could be used to keep unemployment at acceptably low levels for the foreseeable future. During the late 1930s and early 1940s, the government commissioned a number of reports into almost all aspects of social and economic life from land-use planning to education and employment. The most famous of these, the Beveridge Report, concerned social welfare.

Beveridge argued that, with the new tools of economic management that would ensure that mass unemployment would never occur again, the government could afford to provide a complete system of social protection for those who, through misfortune, inadequacy or dependency, could not provide for themselves. The new system would be built on the principles of universal care: the state would provide flat-rate benefits irrespective of the ability to pay. Hence, public (or council) housing would be provided on a 'general needs' basis. Rents would be the same for all tenants irrespective of income. Health services and a flat-rate family allowance would be provided on the same basis. This comprehensive system of welfare would ensure that everybody was secure 'from the cradle to the grave'. The Labour government legislated to produce just such a system, which was fully in place by 1950.

BRIEFINGS

25.3 Aneurin Bevan on housing and health

The following extracts reflect the views of the Labour politician Aneurin Bevan who was health minister between 1945 and 1951, and introduced the National Health Service in 1948:

> I said that in my view it was entirely undesirable that on modern housing estates only one type of citizen should live. I referred to them then as 'twilight towns', and said it was a reproach to our modern social planning that from one sort of township should come one income group. I said that, if we are to enable citizens to lead a full life, if they are each to be aware of the problems of their neighbours, then they should be all drawn from the very different sections of the community and we should try to introduce in our modern villages what has always been the lovely feature of English and Welsh villages, where the doctor, the grocer, the butcher and farm labourer all lived in the same street . . . I believe it is a necessary biological background for modern life, and I believe it leads to the enrichment of every member of the community to live in communities of that sort. We believe that it is essential that local authorities should also provide accommodation for single persons, for persons who are following a professional life, and that they should provide for old people.
>
> *Source*: Bevan in 1949, recalling his intentions in 1945, quoted in D. McKay and A. Cox, *The Politics of Urban Change*, London: Croom Helm, 1979, p. 118

> Allowing for all sensible administrative measures to prevent waste, the plain fact is that the cost of the health service not only will, but ought to, increase. Most of the hospitals fall far short of any proper standard; accommodation needs to be increased, particularly for tuberculosis and mental health – indeed some of the mental hospitals are very near to a public scandal and we are lucky they have not so far attracted more limelight and publicity. Throughout the service there are piling up arrears of essential capital work. Also it is in this field, particularly, that constant new development will always be needed to keep pace with research progress (as, recently, in penicillin, streptomycin, cortisone, etc.) and to expand essential specialist services, such as hearing aids or ophthalmic services. The position cannot be evaded that a nationally owned and administered hospital service will always involve a very considerable and expanding exchequer outlay. If that position cannot, for financial reasons, be faced, then the only alternatives (to my mind thoroughly undesirable), are either to give up – in whole or in part – the idea of national responsibility for the hospitals or else to import into the scheme some regular source of revenue such as the recovery of charges from those who use it. I am afraid that it is clear that we cannot have it both ways.
>
> *Source*: Bevan in 1950, quoted in R. Klein, *The New Politics of the NHS*, Harlow: Addison Wesley Longman, 3rd edn, 1995, p. 32

Utopianism

A form of ideology that claims that it is possible to create a perfect or near-perfect society. Some utopias are constructed by their creators not as feasible societies but as models against which to compare the real world.

Given its scope – some would say its **utopianism** – the Welfare State worked remarkably well and was widely copied in other countries. There are a number of reasons for its initial success. First, full employment was indeed established quickly after the war, so Keynesian demand management appeared to work. Not until the 1970s did mass unemployment re-emerge. Full employment kept the cost of the Welfare State down and government revenues up.

Second, benefits were established at modest levels. Unemployment benefits and old age, survivors' and disability pensions were to be self-financing. Employees would pay national insurance stamps out of their wages; these stamps were to be stuck on to a national insurance card that would act as proof of eligibility for benefits. And, initially at least, welfare benefits were low. In addition, the school leaving age was 15 and only a minority of pupils stayed on after 16, with a tiny minority going on to higher education. Health care standards were, by today's norms, low and inexpensive. Limited supplies of housing and health facilities ensured that the system worked. In effect, a system of rationing prevailed that involved long waiting lists.

Table 25.1 Priorities for public spending by class, 2000

	Salariat*	Self-employed	Working class
First priority for extra public spending	%	%	%
Health	46	43	48
Education	37	33	30
Public transport	6	4	3
Roads	2	6	4
Housing	1	2	5

* Salaried employees.

Source: *British Social Attitudes*, 17th Report, 2000, Table 3.2

Third, a remarkable degree of consensus on the status of the Welfare State emerged. People from all regions, ages and social classes were agreed that it was a good thing. Almost everybody used the health service, the vast majority of children went to state schools, private pensions were available only to a minority of the middle classes. Even council housing attracted a wide social mix, at least during the serious housing shortages prevalent during the 1940s and 1950s.

The system worked adequately until well into the 1960s, and indeed Labour governments legislated to extend and improve benefits during this decade. By the 1970s welfare spending had become easily the largest item on the national budget. Politicians on the right were arguing that unless spending was curbed the system would become untenable. During the 1980s Conservative governments began to roll back the Welfare State, a process that continues in some areas, such as income maintenance, to this day. At the same time, public support in the United Kingdom for welfare spending remained high, with health and education the top priorities for extra spending. Even by 2000 this support prevailed across all social classes (Table 25.1). A good way to understand how and why this transition has occurred is to examine each of the main components of social policy in turn. In addition, we will examine the main actors and institutions involved in these policy areas.

Income maintenance

Almost certainly the greatest actuarial problems in the income maintenance area apply to old age pensions. The flat system created by Beveridge (all would receive the same pension having paid enough national insurance contributions) was expected to become more expensive over time, but by the 1960s it was, in real terms, twice as expensive as envisaged. More people were living longer and the political pressures for maintaining or increasing the level of benefit proved considerable. By the 1970s, governments were convinced that the system was in need of long-term reform. Poverty among the old remained a serious problem, which the flat-rate system could not solve except at huge expense. In 1975 the government compromised by introducing a State Earnings Related Pensions Scheme (SERPS), which added an earnings-related element to the system. However, this too was projected to become very expensive and in 1986 the Conservatives legislated to restrict the scope of the SERPS system.

By the 1990s governments were under even more pressure to reduce the real value of the old age pension. In 1980, the Conservatives linked pension increases to prices rather than to earnings, so the relative value of the pension declined over time, but even so the cost of state pensions could become prohibitive in the longer

Table 25.2 Projected
dependency ratios
1994–2061

	Child dependency	Elderly dependency	Overall dependency
1994	34	30	64
2001	33	29	62
2011	30	31	60
2021	28	30	58
2031	29	39	68
2041	28	43	72
2051	28	43	71
2061	29	44	73

Note: This table shows 1994-based projections, for number of children and people over retirement age to every 100 people of working age. The ratios take account of the change in state pension age for women from 60 years to 65 years between 2010 and 2020.
Source: *Social Trends*, **27**, 1997, Table A.2, HMSO. Reproduced under the terms of the Click-Use Licence

term. As can be seen from Table 25.2, the number of people in the UK likely to be dependent on the working population will increase substantially in the decades after 2020, and it is the old whose dependency will increase the most. As a result, politicians from all political parties are now committed to making the provision of state pensions selective by replacing them for most of the working population with private pension schemes. Given the special status that the flat-rate state pension has assumed in the minds of most voters, this proposal is bound to be politically controversial.

Family poverty was originally tackled through the provision of National Assistance or welfare payments, available to all those past school leaving age not in receipt of unemployment benefit and who were in need. In addition, a flat-rate family allowance was payable to second and subsequent children (it was assumed that the first child could be cared for if one parent was working). While National Assistance was selective (i.e. it was means tested), everybody from the Queen down was eligible for family allowances. Over the years, this system has been modified, although, remarkably, the flat-rate element in Family Allowance (now called Child Benefit) remains. The main changes have been:

- In 1968 family allowances became taxable, but the 1975 Child Benefit Act actually strengthened the flat-rate principle by making the allowance payable to all children. One-parent families received a higher level of benefit.

- In 1966 National Assistance was replaced with Supplementary Benefits. These means-tested payments were available to all in need, including pensioners and the unemployed who could not manage on the flat-rate pension or unemployment benefit.

- By the early 1970s it was clear that many families were in a '**poverty** or income support **trap**'. If an adult took a job, the family income could fall, given that the earned income (net of tax) could be less than the state benefits forfeited once employment began. Legislation to reduce this disincentive to work was passed in 1971 (Family Income Supplement) and 1988 (Family Credit). These laws allow benefit recipients to work without losing all their benefits. While this is helpful for some families, a general consensus had emerged by the late 1990s that the disincentive effect of the benefit system remained considerable for many families. Given the array of benefits (including Housing Benefit), individuals and families have to make complex calculations when taking employment. The

Poverty trap

The idea that the Welfare State creates a vicious cycle of poverty for some social groups by imposing welfare systems that discourage people from taking responsibility for their own life or finding work. The cycle tends to continue, some claim, into the next generation of children who grow up in such a system.

system also provides an incentive for benefit recipients to work while receiving benefits without declaring their income.

■ In 1982 the government removed earnings-related supplements to unemployment benefit and made such benefits taxable. Gradually during the remainder of the Conservative period in office, the relative value of benefits was reduced and eligibility criteria were tightened.

■ In a 1998 Green Paper, 'A New Contract for Welfare', the Labour government stressed the need to 'empower' the poor and thus remove dependency. This and subsequent government publications have emphasised the mutual responsibility of the needy, the government and the business community to tackle low incomes together. Labelled a 'New Deal' for younger people, lone parents and the disabled, this policy has been directed towards increasing opportunities to exploit the untapped resources of the under-employed. To this end businesses have been encouraged to provide work for this largely unused labour force. The 1999 budget introduced a new minimum income guarantee of £200 per week per working family with children, with tax credits and income tax reductions so that families at and slightly above this level would pay no income tax at all. Non-working adults in families would be required to seek work.

■ The new system, labelled the Working Families Tax Credit (WFTC), together with similar tax credits for children and the disabled, removed most of the disincentive for the less well paid to work. In April 2003, the system was overhauled again and the scope of the benefits was widened. The new credits were known as Child Tax Credit (CTC) and the Working Tax Credit (WTC). All political parties agree that these schemes are a good thing, although by 2005 the CTC was not working as smoothly as intended – mainly because HM Revenue and Customs was unable to monitor closely people who moved from eligibility to non-eligibility as their incomes rose. As a result they came to depend on credit payments that they were not entitled to.

■ In the early 1980s, the Thatcher government removed the link between earnings and the old age pension (Basic State Pension or BSP), thus heralding an era where the real value of pensions gradually eroded. In addition, in 1988 the private sector was given incentives to supplement the BSP with private schemes. Many of these schemes provided poor value for money and by 2005 the whole question of how to fund the pension system returned to the centre of the political stage. The Blair government introduced a Minimum Income Guarantee (MIG) or a system of welfare benefits to supplement the BSP. In 2003 this was renamed the Pension Credit, which remained a welfare payment for those with inadequate income in old age. The government also promised to restore the link between earnings and the Basic State Pension in 2012.

Actors and institutions

Unlike economic policy, where key decisions can often be made by a few senior politicians and officials, income support policy tends to change incrementally and is often infused with interest group activity. This is particularly true of pensions policy. Given that almost all the population will eventually become pensioners, the issue is politically highly salient. In the past, politicians from all parties have expressed sympathy for poverty among the old. Groups such as Age Concern are active in keeping the issue in the public eye, and the vulnerability of the old ensures that any policy changes that occur have to be implemented over the longer term. Family support policy has a slightly different status. Public support for poor families is lower, and the Conservative legislation of the 1980s shows that relatively major changes can be wrought without serious political repercussions. This said, pressure groups (such as the Child Poverty Action Group) and individual members of Parliament are likely to be active in support of or against particular proposals.

Given the premium on expertise in this policy area, individual Cabinet ministers and their officials are usually closely involved in income support policy making. Indeed, by the early part of the twenty-first century, the more than 20 different benefits available to the needy, administered by several departments, required a high level of expert input to inform any future reforms.

New Labour policy

As noted, New Labour's stance on income maintenance is quite similar to that of the previous Conservative government. Labour accepts the need to supplement (or eventually replace) the flat-rate pension with a system of private pensions. More surprising is the Labour Party's conversion to 'workfare' or a system of family support designed to oblige parents, and particularly single parents, to work rather than depend on state help. Coupled to this objective is a commitment to expand both nursery education (which will enable working mothers to take employment), institute training for the unemployed, encourage business to play a major part in providing employment and provide a minimum income guarantee for working families and the old. During its first two terms Labour faithfully worked towards meeting these objectives, which it called a 'New Deal' or welfare to work strategy. These policies do, of course, represent a sea change from the universalist welfare policies of the 1970s.

Related was the new emphasis on coordinating different aspects of social policy in what was called 'joined-up' government. Hence the creation of the Social Exclusion Unit in the Cabinet Office in 1997 represented an attempt to coordinate all those government departments, including Social Security and Education, whose brief covered helping those such as the poor, homeless, truants and others excluded from the mainstream of British society.

As a result of these changes and a healthy economic environment, government spending on social security (all income maintenance including pensions) levelled off during the late 1990s and early 2000s, although note how it started to increase again when the economy slowed after 2002 (Figure 25.1).

Figure 25.1 Real growth in social security benefit expenditure, United Kingdom, 1977–2005

Note: From 1990/1 data are for financial years.
Source: *Social Trends*, **36**, 2006, Figure 8.1, Office for National Statistics. Reproduced under the terms of the Click-Use Licence

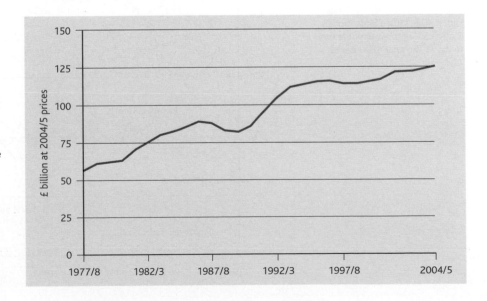

Housing

In 1946 the Labour government legislated to provide a new system of housing subsidies channelled through local authorities. This and later legislation identified council (public) housing as 'general needs' accommodation. In other words, the private sector was to be relegated to secondary status and most housing would be provided by local councils. Although the Conservatives later assigned a much more prominent role to the private sector, both parties accepted that council housing would be the source of new housing for the working-class population. Serious housing shortages meant that during the 1950s and early 1960s Conservative and Labour politicians vied with each other over who could build the most houses.

Unlike income support, the housing policy system closely involved local authorities. They were the recipients of government housing grants but were left much on their own when making decisions about the location and management of housing estates. As housing was in short supply, a 'waiting list' system was created whereby local government housing departments decided on eligibility for housing. Family size, income and job status were the main criteria employed. Only in 1972 did (a Conservative) government apply a systematic means test, whereby rent rebates were given to needy tenants both in the public and private sectors. Until that time everybody in council housing paid the same rent, irrespective of income.

As can be seen from Figure 25.2, public sector housing construction remained at a high level through to the mid-1970s. Generally, Conservative governments and local authorities favoured the private sector while Labour favoured the public sector. At the same time, public housing was increasingly viewed as housing for the disadvantaged, a perception that was strengthened by the construction of large, anonymous housing estates during the 1950s and 1960s that were increasingly occupied by disadvantaged families. Figure 25.2 shows how council housing construction fell from the mid-1970s on. This was initially a result of fiscal emergency, but after 1979 it was the direct result of Conservative government policy.

Figure 25.2 Housebuilding completions by sector, United Kingdom, 1951–2004/5

Source: *Social Trends*, **36**, 2006, Figure 10.3, Office for National Statistics. Reproduced under the terms of the Click-Use Licence

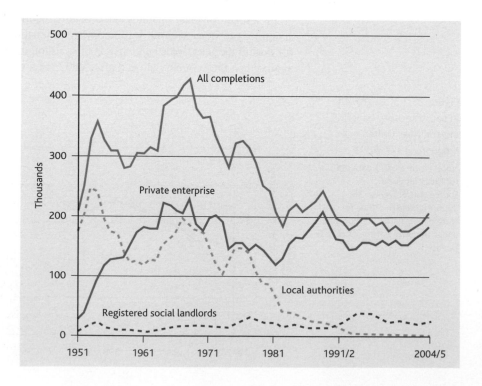

Margaret Thatcher's administrations (1979–90) disliked publicly provided housing. They believed that it undermined self-reliance, encouraged local authority overspending and aggravated class divisions. As a result they progressively cut government housing grants and launched the largest single change in housing policy since the Second World War: the sale of council houses to tenants. The major changes in this and other areas were:

- In 1980 tenants were given the right to buy their houses. A system of discounts on the price was available depending on length of tenure.

- In 1982 Housing Benefits were introduced. Council rents had increased steadily, although individual authorities retained some freedom to subsidise them. For those who could not pay these rents because of poverty or disability, a system of rebates was available.

- In 1986 and 1988 the government provided further incentives for council house sales. Councils could sell to housing associations and private landlords. The discounts available to sitting tenants and council flat tenants, where the property was particularly hard to sell, were increased.

- In 1989 the government effectively ended local authority rent subsidies. In future, local authorities would have to charge an 'economic rent' with rebates available to the disadvantaged in the form of Housing Benefits.

- Throughout their tenure in office, the Conservatives attempted to increase the role of private landlords. This was the smallest and least efficient part of the housing market and they believed that labour mobility would improve with a larger and more flexible private rental sector. A new form of 'regulated tenancies' was created with reduced security of tenure for tenants. Conservative efforts here were less than successful, however. Ultimately, the failure to stimulate this part of the market relates to underlying factors, including restrictive planning laws on land use and public disquiet with private landlords, which even radical Conservative governments were not prepared to challenge.

In the late 1990s and early part of the twenty-first century, social housing (as it is now called) is provided mainly by housing associations and through Housing Benefits. Indeed, housing associations have become the major providers of social housing in the system. Local authority housing remains important, but it is declining rapidly and consists mainly of large estates occupied by disadvantaged families. Meanwhile, owner occupation has soared and now accounts for some 67 per cent of the total housing stock (Figure 25.3).

Actors and institutions

Unlike income maintenance, the key actors in social housing in Britain have been local governments. They remain important as administrators of the remaining council housing stock and of Housing Benefits, although their discretion over these policy areas is now quite limited. Central government decisions during the 1980s and the 1990s were taken with little reference to local government preferences. Organised interests in this area, including pressure groups representing the poor and homeless, have usually played a reactive rather than proactive part. In some ways it is easier to cut capital spending on social housing rather than current expenditure on such things as pensions or Housing Benefits. The latter groups have numerous recipients who are highly sensitive to marginal changes in their incomes. Capital spending cuts are felt in the longer term, involve few immediate victims and are therefore politically easier to impose.

Figure 25.3 Stock of dwellings by tenure, Great Britain, 1981–2001

Source: Social Trends, **36**, 2006, Figure 10.6, Office for National Statistics. Reproduced under the terms of the Click-Use Licence

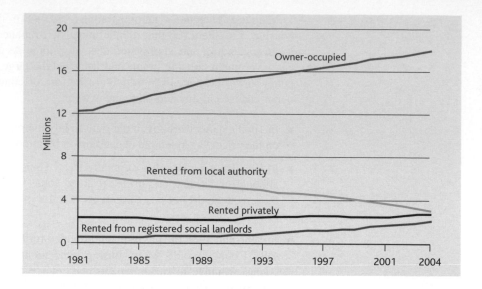

New Labour policy

Although housing shortages remain and many people live in poor housing conditions, the issue has slipped in political importance compared with health, education and pensions. Politicians from all parties believe the private sector should play the dominant role in housing provision. Housing Benefits are now the main means by which the state helps house the disadvantaged, and in this sense housing policy has become inseparable from income support policy. New Labour recognises this fact and has not proposed a reversal of council house sales and a return to traditional public housing. Instead, it supports an extension of owner occupation to the less advantaged through tax and interest-deferred mortgages together with the provision of social housing for those who are ineligible for mortgages.

Health

State-provided health care has assumed a very special status in British society. As noted earlier, the utopian vision of the founders of the National Health Service was that health care would be provided on a universal basis. Unlike housing and many aspects of income maintenance, much of the health care system in the early part of the twenty-first century, and in particular primary doctor and hospital care, remained free and universally available. However, the increasing cost has brought constant pressure for reform, and some services, including dental care, are now provided on a selective basis. In addition, market-like mechanisms have been introduced into the system, changing what might be called the culture of health care in the United Kingdom.

The 1948 system

When the NHS was created in 1948 its administrative structure was a compromise between existing and new institutions. (The following description applies to England and Wales; Scotland had a separate system.) General practitioners (GPs) worked much as they had before the reforms, except that their revenue came from government rather than patients; many health services remained in the hands of local authorities. The major innovation was the creation of 14 new regional hospital boards. Within each region, most hospitals were run by locally appointed hospital management committees, but an elite of teaching hospitals were run by boards of governors with direct links to the Ministry of Health.

The 1974 reforms

During the 1950s and 1960s a number of serious problems emerged with this structure. Regions varied enormously in size, resources tended to move towards an elite of teaching hospitals, little in the way of planning for the whole system was possible. When, during the 1960s, a major hospital-building programme was launched, every regional board required major new capital expenditure, but there was no means whereby priorities could be set. Therefore, both Labour and Conservative governments agreed that reform was needed. What transpired was a new structure that was eventually implemented in 1974. The regional boards (now regional authorities) were given the job of overall strategic planning, and a new tier of 90 area health authorities was created to manage direct care. The rationale was to facilitate better management and control of the service from the centre. At the same time, democratic accountability was enhanced through the creation of a system of advisory committees and community health councils. These were made up of laypeople and interest group spokespersons nominated by local governments, voluntary organisations and regional authorities.

The 1982 reforms

Among the problems with the 1974 structure was a perception that the system was run in the interests of the producers (the health care professionals) rather than the consumers (patients). At the same time, local government involvement seemed unnecessary. In 1979, the Conservative government published a consultative document, *Patients First*, which recommended a number of changes. These culminated in the 1982 reforms that abolished area authorities and created 192 district health authorities (DHAs). Local government participation in DHAs was reduced and that of local experts and notables increased. In addition, the government devolved greater management responsibility to the DHA level. In the ensuing decade, government spending on health was reduced, at least in relation to the rest of the post-1955 period (Figure 25.4), and much of the pressure on spending was felt by the DHAs.

Figure 25.4 Total NHS spending, percentage increase per annum, 1951–89

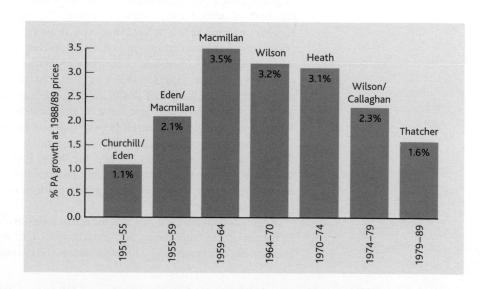

Plate 25.1 Ambulances at the Accident and Emergency department of St Thomas' Hospital in London
Source: Getty Images/Graeme Robertson

Further reforms, 1991–2006

Organisational change during the 1970s and the 1980s was informed by what might be called 'managerialism', or the belief that improved managerial structures and lines of accountability would improve efficiency and therefore the quality of service provided to the public. However, during the 1980s a new administrative philosophy assumed that bringing in market forces rather than improving management structure would enhance efficiency. A White Paper, 'Working for Patients' (Cm 555, London: HMSO, 1989), argued that NHS institutions acted as both providers and purchasers of health care. In other words, they might provide hospital care but they would also have to purchase hospital supplies and services. Moreover, a conflict had arisen between these two functions because the health service was more producer than it was consumer oriented. Much as with the Civil Service before the Next Steps reforms, the White Paper argued that the institutional structure of the service gave health care professionals (doctors, nurses and so on) an incentive to improve their status and conditions of service rather than to make patient care the top priority.

Again, as with the Civil Service, the answer was to change the incentive structure of the service by introducing market principles into the system. Accordingly, the government designated a system of providers (NHS trusts and general practitioners)

BRIEFINGS

25.4 The economics of health care

The search for increased efficiency in some social policy areas, and especially in health care, is beset by a structural economic problem that, unless checked, means that the cost of health care will spiral ever upwards. With most items we buy as consumers, the more that is invested in the productive process, the lower the unit costs of production become. Investment in a car factory, for example, reduces the labour input, increases productivity and ultimately reduces the real cost of the product. Capital investment in health, however, can have perverse results. New equipment bought by a hospital usually results in an increased demand for labour to operate it. Worse, the complexity of such things as dialysis machines and CAT (computerised axial or computer-assisted tomography) scanners requires highly trained operative staff. (In the car factory, required skill levels typically fall as capital investment increases.) Given that labour is the most expensive item in most organisations, this means that increased investment in health results in increased costs.

This problem is compounded by the fact that, in the economist's parlance, the demand for health care is highly inelastic: that is, it responds only imprecisely to variations in price. If you have the money to pay for a life-saving operation, you are likely to pay for it irrespective of the cost. In addition, the health professionals (doctors, nurses and so on) are in a good position to organise and negotiate higher wages. This is what has happened in the USA, where health care accounts for 17 per cent of GDP.

In Britain the government is, in effect, a monopoly supplier and employer of health services and labour, so it has been able to hold costs down through rationing and central financial controls. An ageing and more demanding public has, however, greatly increased the pressure for more spending on health, which will almost certainly rise steadily in the future. Given the constraints on the NHS, increasing numbers of the more affluent have turned to private health care.

These problems have shifted the emphasis in health care from curing illness to preventing illness.

who would bid for business (or draw up a contract) with a purchaser (district and family health authorities, GP fundholders).

Most commentators agree that the reforms of the 1990s had both desirable and unwanted consequences. By some measures (waiting lists, outpatient services) some improvement occurred, although measuring performance is notoriously difficult. The district health authorities, which were the key purchasers on behalf of consumers in the system, seemed to be more attuned to GPs than to patients. Critics also pointed to the rapid increase in the number of managers in the system. But the main problem was that the reforms did not significantly increase the quality and the quantity of health care delivery that the public expected. The economics of health care are such that some degree of rationing by price or availability is necessary in any system. The reforms of the 1990s recognised this. In effect, the rationing element that has always been present in the NHS was made more explicit. Not surprisingly, the public were quick to notice this and to demand more and better provision.

Actors and institutions

As can be inferred from what we have said already, health care professionals have always been intimately involved in the politics of health care. Expertise is so crucial in this policy area that their involvement – and cooperation – is crucial. The Department of Health and its predecessors have also been key actors because of their intimate links with the institutional structure of the NHS. Until the 1990s change came only slowly to the system, in part because of the entrenched power of professionals, and in particular hospital doctors.

The public's role has also been crucial, not in terms of the day-to-day management of the system, but in terms of what has always been a strong public commitment to free universal health care. Conservative reforms were condemned by the opposition as 'backdoor privatisation'. This was the worst possible criticism in the British context. In fact, only dental care has effectively been privatised. Moves towards market-like transactions have changed the culture of the NHS but not who pays for NHS services (the taxpayer). The Labour critique was enough to disturb the electorate, however, and almost certainly contributed to the Conservative government's defeat in 1997.

As in so many other areas, the role of local governments in health care has all but vanished, while central financial controls have strengthened.

New Labour policy

In December 1997 the New Labour government published a White Paper, 'The New NHS: Modern, Dependable', which identified three themes for reform: partial abolition of the internal market, mandating GPs to join primary care groups (now called primary care trusts) and improving clinical care. Although, in opposition, Labour promised to abolish the NHS internal market, it proved reluctant to implement a wholesale abolition. Instead, it concentrated on trying to reduce the transaction costs associated with the internal market by streamlining the relationship between the purchasers of health care (primary care trusts) and the main providers (the NHS hospital trusts). In some respects the Labour reforms went further than the Conservatives – and in the same direction – for now GPs are required to form conglomerates covering 100,000 people. They are governed by a board, a chief executive and an executive board. By 2005, 305 such primary care trusts had been established. These in turn had set up long-term service agreements with the NHS trusts. Overseeing these relationships are the 28 strategic health authorities, which monitor performance and standards. This structure is shown in Figure 25.5. Most commentators agree that the new system works adequately. In effect, the Labour reforms endorsed the changed management and operating culture of the service and accepted the main change instituted by the Tories: placing GPs at the centre of a system based on 'buying' services from NHS trusts.

There can be no doubt that Labour was committed to maintaining free universal care for the vast majority of the population. The political salience of the issue is very high and Labour has made promises in the area that are truly impressive – if they can be met. These include raising expenditure on health up to and beyond the EU average of around 8–9 per cent of GDP. But by 2003, the NHS seemed still to be in crisis. Hospital consultants – the group that has traditionally held most power in the system – refused to go along with new conditions of service that

Figure 25.5 The NHS in England

Note: Slightly different although broadly equivalent arrangements apply in Wales, Scotland and Northern Ireland.

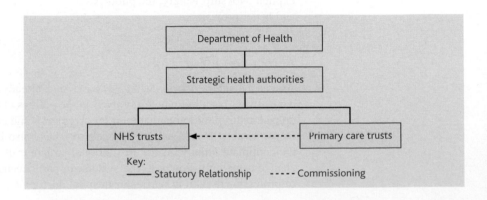

would require them to spend more of their time on NHS patients. Without their full cooperation, the government's plans for better hospital care were threatened. It is also interesting to note that the Conservatives have also changed their stance to one of supporting increased spending – although they continue to differ from Labour on the way the service should be managed.

By 2003 the Labour government's commitment to an improved health service was shown in the allocation of a further £2.5 billion in the 2003/4 budget. In 2004 the government published another document, *The NHS Improvement Plan: Putting People at the Heart of Public Service*. Among other things, this proposed to reduce the maximum waiting time for hospital treatment to 18 weeks by 2008. Finally, in 2005 yet another plan, *Creating a Patient Led NHS: Delivering the NHS Improvement Plan*, announced a 'patient led' system providing patients with a choice of services and treatments, including by 2008 a choice between four or five hospitals.

Education

While, historically, Britain has long been regarded as a world leader in the public provision of health care, it has never been regarded as a great innovator in the provision of state education. Unlike many countries, including France and the United States, elite secondary education has traditionally been provided by the private rather than public sector (through the perversely named 'public school' system). Not until the passage of the 1944 Education Act did the central government assume full responsibility for universal free primary and secondary education up to the age of 15 (16 from 1971). Since 1944, education policy has revolved around two related themes: comprehensive versus selective education, and the relationship between educational standards and the management and funding of schools. We will add a note on higher education following a discussion of these two points.

To select or not to select?

The 1944 Act formally recognised three different sorts of secondary school: grammar for the academically gifted, modern for the mass of the population and, in some areas, technical for those with vocational skills. Very soon, secondary modern schools assumed a low status and grammar schools high status. Critics pointed to the fact that entry to grammar schools, decided by an examination at the age of 11, was closely correlated with social class. Liberal-minded Conservative ministers and local politicians were among such critics. When elected in 1964, the Labour government pledged to reform the system by introducing one sort of school, the neighbourhood or community comprehensive, which would cater for all abilities. In October 1965, local authorities were instructed to draw up plans for the reorganisation of education by introducing comprehensive schools and, once re-elected in 1974, Labour made the change mandatory. The resulting change in school type is shown in Table 25.3.

While comprehensive schools made sense in rural areas where the provision of two sorts of school was not viable, the reforms proved highly controversial in many urban and suburban communities. Many Conservative-controlled authorities refused to comply, although the vast majority adopted the new system. In 1979, the new Conservative government removed the directive and later actively encouraged authorities to maintain grammar schools.

The crucial issues in this debate were parent choice and educational standards. On the right, commentators argued that comprehensive schools drawing on poorer

Table 25.3 Number of school pupils: by type of school

	1970/1	1980/1	1990/1	2000/1	2003/4	2004/5
Public sector schools						
Nursery	50	89	105	152	150	142
Primary	5,902	5,171	4,955	5,298	5,107	5,045
Secondary						
Comprehensive	1,313	3,730	2,925	3,340	3,456	3,457
Grammar	673	149	156	205	216	217
Modern	1,164	233	94	112	107	107
Other	403	434	298	260	235	220
All public sector schools	9,507	9,806	8,533	9,367	9,271	9,189
Non-maintained schools	621	619	613	626	654	652
Special schools	103	148	114	113	109	107
Pupil referral units	–	–	–	10	13	15
All schools	10,230	10,572	9,260	10,116	10,048	9,963

Source: *Social Trends*, **36**, 2006, Table 3.3

communities tended to develop a culture of underachievement. Gifted children from such areas were not given the chance to develop their potential, as they had no choice but to attend 'dump' schools. Worse, according to the right, a new cohort of teachers infused with egalitarian educational notions were aggravating this culture of underachievement by emphasising children's development as personalities rather than as individuals trained in essential skills. Right-wing think tanks such as the Institute for Economic Affairs and the Adam Smith Institute became increasingly vocal during the 1970s and were beginning to influence expert and political (Conservative) opinion.

The Conservatives were also keen to encourage private education and in 1980 introduced an Assisted Places Scheme that gave a small number of lower-income parents a subsidised place for their child at an elite private school. Although highly controversial at the time, the scheme remained small in cost and scope until its abolition by New Labour in 1997.

Standards and management

As with health care, debate moved forward rapidly during the 1980s to revolve around the question of the individual incentives of teachers and managers in the educational system. Local authorities were the traditional managers of education, but the Conservatives became increasingly critical of their management standards. In two Education Acts, one passed in 1986 and the other in 1988, the government devolved the day-to-day management of schools to school governing bodies. It also allowed schools to opt out of local authority control altogether and be maintained directly by central government.

In combination, these laws increased the power of 'managers' over educational 'professionals'. Boards of governors, which include elected parent governors, hire and fire, and manage school finances. Increasingly, they have to conform to central financial directives and to central performance indicators. A National Curriculum is now in place requiring pupils to study English, maths and science and seven foundation subjects. League tables on examination performance are widely published and classroom teachers are formally assessed and graded. Parents can now make comparisons between schools and, in theory at least, can choose which is best for their child. As with health care, these reforms have had good and bad consequences. By most criteria, educational attainment is improving.

However, the pressures on teachers have been considerable – many have taken early retirement – and the new school-level management structure has been used as an instrument of national policy rather than local discretion.

Higher education

Higher education escaped major reform until the 1990s. After the Second World War, free higher education was available to all those able to get a place at university, with maintenance grants available on a means-tested basis. Until the 1960s, when higher education was greatly expanded, this meant that a tiny minority (under 5 per cent) of 18-year-olds enjoyed university education. Expansion in the 1960s was not accompanied by any reform, so the system became increasingly expensive. Cuts in the real value of the maintenance grant helped, but were insufficient to prevent the system from experiencing a serious fiscal crisis when further expansion occurred from the late 1980s onwards. The government instituted much tighter central controls through a newly created quango, the University Funding Council (now the Higher Education Funding Council). By the mid-1990s it was clear that, for the system to survive in the absence of greatly increased funding, students would have to make some contribution towards the cost of their education. The Conservatives were already drawing up plans to this effect before their defeat in 1997. Once elected, Labour promptly announced the introduction of tuition fees for all students with rebates for those on a low income. It also abolished what remained of the student grant system.

The government soon accepted that this new regime disadvantaged students from poorer backgrounds and promised a complete overhaul of the system of student finances. At the same time, in 2001 the government set a target of 50 per cent of the 18-year-old age group to be in higher education. In 2003 the government finally produced a long-awaited White Paper on higher education that proposed the reintroduction of a (very limited) form of maintenance grant for those on low incomes. More importantly, universities were to be given the freedom to charge fees up to a maximum of £3,000. Most commentators agreed that this, together with a more targeted system of research resources, was likely to result in a two-tier system: an elite headed by Oxford and Cambridge, and a large number of universities whose primary function would be teaching rather than research. Interestingly, the Scottish Parliament voted to reject tuition fees, so a three-tier system may come to prevail: elite English and Welsh universities, 'other' universities and Scottish universities.

Actors and institutions

Education is not unlike health in that it is an area where expertise is at a premium. Therefore, educational professionals have always been important actors in the system. Local governments, too, were important players until the Conservative reforms of the 1980s. Today school boards of governors have assumed a new importance, but they are subject to increasingly close central control. Teachers too are now more circumscribed both in the ways in which they teach and in their role in day-to-day management. Parents, in spite of the rhetoric of 'empowerment' contained in various educational reforms, remain more passive than active actors in the system. Unlike parents in the US system, for example, they have no direct say in the financing of schools.

Again as with health, the most important decision-making institutions operate in central government, for it is the Department for Education and Skills that sets the financial priorities and monitors school and teacher performance.

New Labour policy

It would be misleading to talk of a consensus between the major parties on educational matters, but much more agreement exists than might be expected. Labour has abolished the Assisted Places Scheme, but the scheme was a minor part of the system. The 1998 School Standards and Framework Act led to the creation of up to 25 education action zones, consisting of two or three secondary schools together with their feeder primary schools. Action forums made up of parents, representatives from businesses and local education authorities were given the job of raising standards. Elsewhere in the system, selective schools remain but parental ballots determine whether grammar schools should continue on an exclusively selective basis. The new emphasis on standards reflects Labour's desire to persuade many middle-class parents to shift from private to state education, which can only be done by improving some state schools. In 2005 the government published the Education and Inspections Bill. This proved highly controversial because it proposed devolving more power to individual schools by giving them the choice to become educational trusts. Fearing that this would herald a return to selection (i.e. schools choosing the most able students), Labour backbenchers sought assurance that the new system would be strictly non-selective. A second version of the bill specifically prohibited selection and was duly passed by the House of Commons in March 2005. However, many Labour MPs continued to fear that the increased autonomy given to schools would lead to more rather than less divergence in educational standards.

Given these developments, what distinguishes Labour from Conservative in this policy area? Most of the differences are in emphasis rather than substance. Substantively, Labour is more committed to nursery education than were the Conservatives and has promised nursery places for all 4-year-olds and subsidies for nursery attendance for 3-year-olds. But in most areas, Labour governments have simply modified Tory policies. If anything, they have been tougher on 'failing' schools and have given considerable support to the idea of specialist schools. But the main dilemma for Labour is the same one that faced the Tories: do you try to improve *all* schools or simply *most* schools? Labour governments have often been muddled in their thinking on this subject. Specialist 'beacon' schools seeking excellence in science, art or music, and the continuation of grammar education suggest a more elitist approach. At the same time, ministers insist that they want to create a good educational environment for everyone. This dilemma extends to other areas of social policy, of course. In many ways, New Labour is meritocratic and market oriented. Yet it remains committed to helping the 'socially excluded' and working towards a society where everyone is educated and participating fully in social and community life.

Summary

This chapter has summarised the major changes in social policy that have occurred since the inception of the Welfare State:

- In all the areas under discussion, a move from universalism to selectivism has occurred. More recently, the main values underpinning reform attempts have shifted from those associated with managerial efficiency to those associated with consumer choice and the discipline of the market.

- More and more, policy takes heed of the personal incentives of individual actors and how reforms can harness individual incentives to particular ends, such as reduced costs and improved quality in health care or education. Even in income maintenance this transformation is under way, with the prospect that private pensions and workfare will replace universal flat-rate benefits in the longer term.

■ While differences between Labour and the Conservatives remain, there are few fundamental differences between the parties in most social policy areas. New Labour is committed to the state employing market-like solutions to a range of problems. In housing, the private sector is now accepted as the main provider. Income maintenance benefits have become increasingly selective. Education and health remain predominantly state-provided services for the foreseeable future, but in both areas market-like transactions have partly replaced hierarchical bureaucratic relationships.

■ In terms of the institutions and actors involved in policy, central government ministers and bureaucracies continue to dominate. The independent influence of professionals (doctors, teachers and so on) may, in turn, decline in relation to the 'users', 'customers' and 'clients' in the system – parents, patients and benefit recipients.

■ The unanswered question, however, relates to the power of the consumer: that is, the patient, client or parent. Reforms have promised consumer 'empowerment'. It remains to be seen whether reforms will empower the public or merely result in increased central control over the quality and price of services.

MILESTONES

Milestones in post-war social policy

1944–9	Foundation of the Welfare State
1952	Conservatives introduce charges for prescriptions and optical and dental treatment
1965	Directive calls for local authorities to draw up plans for comprehensive education
1966	Supplementary benefits replace National Assistance
1971	School leaving age increased to 16
1972	Means-tested rent rebate scheme provides assistance to tenants in public and private sectors
1974	National insurance contributions are earnings related. Pension increases are linked to prices or earnings, whichever is the greater
1974	Health service reorganised. Regional and area health authorities created to coordinate family, hospital and community care
1975	Local education authorities directed to implement comprehensive school plans
1977	Child Allowances replaced with Child Benefit. Benefit is available to all children, with increased rate for single parents
1978	State Earnings Related Pension Scheme links pensions to earnings
1980	Pensions linked to prices only, thus reducing their relative value
1980	Assisted Places Scheme introduced. Local authorities given the right to keep selective schools
1981	Local authority tenants given the right to buy their homes. Incentive to buy is further strengthened in 1986 and 1988
1981	Housing Benefit available to provide subsidies for rent and rates
1982	Earnings-related supplements to unemployment benefit abolished. Unemployment benefits taxable
1983	NHS reforms create district health authorities as main management units in the system
1986 and 1988	Education Acts devolve day-to-day management of schools to school governors. Schools given the choice to opt out of local authority control. National Curriculum introduced
1988	Family Credit introduced to encourage families on income support to work
1989	Government ends subsidies for council housing. Local authorities required to set economic rents, with Housing Assistance for the needy

▶

Milestones in post-war social policy continued

1991 and 1993	Major NHS reforms. Service divided into providers and purchasers. Regional authorities abolished. Central financial controls strengthened
1997	Labour government announces introduction of tuition fees in higher education. Social Exclusion Unit created in the Cabinet Office
1998	School Standards and Framework Act sets up education action zones and gives parents the right to change the admissions policies of grammar schools
1999	Budget announces a minimum £200 weekly income guarantee for all families with working parents and children. Major NHS reforms reorganise the service around primary health care groups
2001–2	Chancellor announces huge increases in NHS spending
2004	Ten-year plan to improve provision by the NHS is announced
2006	Education and Inspection Bill is passed, promising more school autonomy and higher standards for all

Essays

1. Why historically has Britain spent less on health care than most comparable countries? How is the government attempting to redress this?

2. What is the distinction between 'welfare' and 'workfare'? Answer with specific reference to the changes introduced by Labour since 1997.

3. Why did the government introduce tuition fees for university students? What have been the consequences of this move?

4. In 1970 most people rented their housing. Today more than two-thirds are owner-occupiers. To what extent has public policy been responsible for this change?

Projects

1. How much choice of schools do parents and pupils have in your immediate area? What are the differences between the various schools and how do these differences present a challenge for government policy?

2. Interview senior and junior medical and administrative staff at your local NHS trust hospital. From the responses, how would you characterise the main problems facing the NHS today?

3. Break down social spending (health, housing, education, income maintenance) in the UK and *two* other major EU countries. What accounts for the differences?

Further reading

A good introduction to the subject is provided by Kenneth Blakemore and Edwin Griggs, *Social Policy: An Introduction* (Milton Keynes: Open University Press, 2006). On New Labour and social policy, see Anthony Seldon and Dennis Kavanagh (eds), *The Blair Effect, 2001–5* (Cambridge: Cambridge University Press, 2005), Chapters 12–14. On the relationship between government and social policy, see Nicholas Deakin (ed.), *Welfare and the State* (London: Routledge, 2003). On health, see Michael Moran, 'Health policy, choice and rationing', *Politics Review*,

14, April 2005. For a sense of the government's goal on health, see *Creating a Patient Led NHS: Delivering the NHS Improvement Plan*, Department of Health, 2005. The various publications of the King's Fund, a charity devoted to health policy research, should also be consulted. A good account of housing policy is provided by Brian Lund, *Understanding Housing Policy* (London: Policy Press, 2006). On changes in education after 1997, see Michael Fielding (ed.), *Taking Education Really Seriously: Three Years Hard Labour* (London: Routledge Falmer, 2001).

Useful web sites on social policy

Hot links to these sites can be found on the CWS at www.pearsoned.co.uk/budge.

In general, social policy concerns the health, education and welfare of British citizens. As an introduction you can visit the British Council, particularly its account of the transformation of the British Welfare State in the recent past at www.britishcouncil.de/e/governance/pubs/gerpp303.htm. The most important governmental institutions related to social policy are the Department of Health (www.doh.gov.uk), the Department for Education and Skills (www.dfes.gov.uk), the Department for Work and Pensions (www.dwp.gov.uk), the Social Exclusion Unit (www.socialexclusionunit.gov.uk), and the Office of the Deputy Prime Minister's Housing and Housing Policy section (www.housing.odpm.gov.uk). New Deal is a key part of the government's welfare to work strategy; its web site is available at www.newdeal.gov.uk. Information on social policies for children is available from the Child Support Agency (www.csa.gov.uk).

The Joseph Rowntree Foundation (www.jrf.org.uk) is one of the largest social policy research and development charities in the UK; its web site provides excellent information on housing, education, child support and other important areas. The New Policy Institute maintains a web site devoted to the monitoring of poverty in the UK; among other valuable sources it offers a good deal of statistical information on income distribution. Visit it at www.poverty.org.uk. There are a variety of other sites that can prove useful for a proper understanding of how social policy works in Britain, including the National Health Service (www.nhs.uk), the Social Security and Child Support Commissioners (www.osscsc.gov.uk) and the Pension Service (www.thepensionservice.gov.uk).

In addition, you can consult the National Health Service Confederation (www.nhsconfed.net), the Association of University Teachers (www.aut.org.uk) and the National Institute for Social Work (www.nisw.org.uk).

chapter 26

Citizenship and equal opportunities

In contrast to the original objectives of the Welfare State, which emphasised equality of condition in the provision of a wide range of benefits, policies designed to provide equal opportunity for women, ethnic minorities and other disadvantaged groups must by definition be selective in scope. When legislation was first enacted in this area during the 1940s, it was concerned with discrimination against disabled people. Since then it has been widened to embrace discrimination based on race, gender and sexual preference. The political salience of the issue has varied over time, and since the first legislation was passed the values underpinning public policy have changed very substantially. This chapter outlines the main legislative changes and evaluates the effectiveness of the law in this important area. The actors and institutions involved are also discussed and some basic data on inequality in Britain today are presented. The chapter examines:

■ some problems of definition associated with equal opportunity

■ inequality and discrimination in Britain

■ equal rights for women

■ legislation to help the disabled

■ race relations

■ immigration and citizenship

■ sexual preference

■ the future of equal opportunity legislation.

Equal opportunity: a political and semantic minefield?

Discrimination

The practice of distinguishing (usually in order to disadvantage) between individuals or social groups on grounds or criteria (such as race, religion, gender or colour) that are not relevant to circumstances.

Equal opportunity laws are designed to reduce entrenched inequalities in society. They have come about because the income, employment, housing and educational conditions pertaining to certain social groups are persistently inferior to those of the general population. Such inequalities may result directly from **discrimination**, which in turn may be overt, covert or structural. Typically, overt discrimination is easy to identify and to eradicate. Advertisements for rental housing stating 'no coloureds' – not unusual in the UK during the 1950s and early 1960s – can be identified quickly and proscribed by law. Covert discrimination is more difficult to deal with. Estate agents may have a stated policy of non-discrimination, but a tacit understanding between renter and agent might exclude minority applicants.

Structural discrimination is the most problematical of all. To continue with the housing analogy, during the 1960s and 1970s many local authorities used 'house-keeping standards' as one of the criteria for eligibility for council housing. Some ethnic minorities failed to meet the prescribed standard, which was culturally biased in favour of white families.

Some feminists argue that a typical example of structural discrimination today applies in science education. Very few women enrol on engineering and science undergraduate courses and even fewer on postgraduate courses. As a result, there are very few female engineers and scientists in the job market. The problem stems not from discrimination at entry but from the fact that few women choose school or university courses in these areas. This may be the exercise of free choice or it may be that biases in the system discourage women from pursuing 'male' subjects and instead direct them into the more 'female' arts and humanities.

Problems with gender discrimination are sometimes rooted in biological differences. Until quite recently (and very recently indeed as far as the armed forces are concerned), pregnancy was an adequate basis for dismissal from a job. Thus few women were able to build continuous and successful careers unless they remained childless. In order to deal with such problems, governments have legislated to ban discrimination and provide for equal opportunity – although legislation does not always work as intended. For example, pregnancy continues to affect women's career chances in spite of what looks like appropriate legislation.

Few subjects arouse so much passion. There are a number of reasons for this. First, policies designed to redress discrimination against the disadvantaged must focus on the circumstances of social groups as well as individuals. Because a group (e.g. women) as a whole is disadvantaged, this does not, of course, mean that all members of that group are disadvantaged. As a result, group-based anti-discrimination policies are often criticised for 'favouring' women or minorities over males or whites. This problem is particularly acute in a society where liberal, rather than collectivist, values are well established. Many of the values that make up our society are based on the value of the individual, whose merit or worth, not membership of a particular group, should, we believe, determine rewards. Equal opportunities policies, however well intentioned, are often difficult to reconcile with such beliefs (see Briefing 26.1).

A second and related problem concerns the nature and level of government response to inequality and discrimination. Laws may be designed to combat overt discrimination and they may also tackle structural discrimination. They may go even further and attempt to reverse the effects of a long-established pattern of discrimination. In the United States such laws are called *affirmative action measures*. Their objective is to allow women and minorities to 'catch up' with whites and males. Typically, they apply in employment and education and involve the use of quotas and 'balancing' to ensure that workplaces, schools and universities hire or enrol women and minorities in proportion to their numbers in the local or national population. British governments have eschewed affirmative action measures as unfair to equally qualified individuals who are not members of disadvantaged groups.

The Labour Party has, however, employed affirmative action through its use of 'Emily's List' or the idea that women-only shortlists for the selection of candidates should be adopted in some constituencies. In 2001 Iain Duncan Smith instigated reforms in the Conservative Party requiring measures to increase the numbers of women and ethnic minority candidates among those selected as Conservative candidates. This trend continued with his successor, Michael Howard, and in particular his successor in turn, David Cameron, who is assiduously trying to change the old-fashioned image of the Conservative Party.

Affirmative action (positive discrimination)

Policies designed to provide groups with redress for a past pattern of discrimination. Such policies often take the form of legal requirements that organisations should take positive steps to increase their numbers of minority groups.

BRIEFINGS

26.1 Liberalism and equal opportunity

One of the most difficult problems associated with equal opportunities policy is reconciling rules and regulations designed to assist social groups with the fact that in liberal societies each citizen's worth is measured in terms of individual merit. When we apply for a job or a place at university, we assume that what determines success is our qualifications or A-level scores, not membership of a particular social group. Liberal values are offended by those collective notions of worth that prevail (or have prevailed) in some Muslim states, where gender or religion determines access to employment and education, or in South Africa under apartheid, where race determined access.

When there has been a long-established pattern of discrimination, some argue that society has a duty to seek redress for past transgressions through the use of affirmative action. Affirmative action can, however, mean a number of things. It can mean the use of race or gender quotas where a minimum number of places is reserved for, say, entry to a university. In such a situation it is possible that the best qualified of the minority group will have qualifications inferior to those of the majority group. In the United States, the courts have effectively banned quotas of this sort, arguing that they constitute a violation of the equal protection of the law guaranteed by the constitution. As problematical are affirmative action measures that adopt a general policy of favouring particular social groups without specifying numbers. These too have been under attack from the courts, although their exact legal status remains unclear.

The term 'affirmative action' is often used interchangeably with 'positive discrimination', or the application of policies that discriminate in favour of some social groups. Generally, positive discrimination is used to create a 'level playing field' for the disadvantaged. It could apply, for example, to the provision of special English-language classes for non-native speakers, or special educational help for children from poor areas. In other words, it involves policies that allow certain groups to 'catch up' with the general population through special training and education.

In Britain the use of affirmative action is rare. British anti-discrimination laws take the individual, not the group, as the basic unit, and the law's objective is to provide redress for demonstrable grievances against individuals, rather than reverse a pattern of discrimination against groups. However, there is a limited form of affirmative action for the employment of the disabled, and in one form or another positive discrimination has been a part of British social policy for many years.

These intra-party reforms apart, British equal opportunities policy has developed incrementally. Even today it is incomplete, as the evidence on income and jobs shows. We examine this before proceeding to a discussion of the politics of equal opportunity legislation.

Inequality and discrimination in Britain

Equality of condition

The ideal objective of providing all citizens with equal access to income, wealth, education, employment and other aspects of social life.

All societies display a degree of wealth and income inequality. **Equality of condition**, or the same income and wealth for all, is clearly impossible to achieve. Most societies strive for **equality of treatment**, meaning that the same rules and standards apply to all social groups. Equality of treatment is similar to **equality of opportunity**, the main difference being the emphasis on rules guaranteeing equality of treatment rather than individuals' circumstances, which is implicit in equality of opportunity.

In fact, there can never be complete equality of opportunity given individuals' widely varying inherited, home and educational backgrounds. Equality of opportunity should, therefore, be seen as an ideal goal rather than an absolute. Equality of treatment is more achievable. Rules and regulations can be standardised so that, in theory at least, all citizens are treated equally. This distinction helps us separate out all those economic differences and inequalities that derive from employment,

Equality of treatment

The application of the same rules and standards to all individuals and social groups.

Equality of opportunity

The practice of ensuring that individuals compete on equal terms for goods, benefits and life chances, such as education, employment or housing, even though the outcome may be unequal.

Disposable income

More often known as 'take-home pay', disposable income refers to income after taxes have been paid.

educational and geographic factors, from those that derive from overt, covert or structural discrimination.

Of course, in reality, discrimination may be practised against almost anyone, including poor whites and the old. But our natural sense of justice is most offended by systematic and institutionalised discrimination against ethnic minorities, women, the disabled and sexual minorities. Hence, the liberal conscience was outraged at apartheid in South Africa and segregation in the American South. Similar feelings are aroused by the treatment of women and homosexuals in some Muslim states.

Measuring discrimination is difficult, to say the least. By definition, covert discrimination is not measurable and, while we may be able to identify the rules and procedures that make up structural discrimination, we can rarely measure the effects of such rules accurately.

What we can do is identify income inequalities by social group. Britain has a sizeable ethnic minority community. As can be seen from Table 26.1, in 2001 8.4 per cent of the population of Great Britain (which excludes Northern Ireland) consisted of ethnic minorities. While the definition of 'ethnic minority' is highly contentious, the categories itemised in Table 26.1 are those recognised by the government as constituting minority groups. Note that, the Chinese population apart, ethnic minorities in Britain are much younger than the general population. As a result their numbers are likely to increase proportionately over time, irrespective of future immigration patterns.

Table 26.2 shows the extent of male unemployment by ethnic minority in Great Britain. Note the very dramatic concentration of unemployment (which is correlated with low incomes) among the minority populations. In fact, these figures are worse than they appear when geographic location is taken into account. Most of the British minority population is concentrated in London and the Midlands, where employment and **disposable incomes** are relatively high. Relatively few live in some of the lowest-income areas: Northern Ireland, the north-east, Merseyside and the Glasgow area. Only in what used to be the textile towns of Lancashire and Yorkshire is there a congruence of high minority population and generally low local incomes.

Table 26.1 Population of Great Britain by ethnic group and age, 2000–1

	Under 16	16–34	35–64	65+	Total (millions)	Ethnic groups as a percentage of total population
White	20	25	39	16	53	92.9
Black Caribbean	23	27	40	10	0.5	0.9
Black African	33	35	30	2	0.4	0.7
Other black	52	29	17	–	0.3	0.5
Indian	23	31	38	7	1.0	1.8
Pakistani	36	36	24	4	0.7	1.2
Bangladeshi	39	36	21	4	0.3	0.5
Chinese	19	38	38	4	0.1	0.2
None of the above	32	33	32	3	0.7	1.2
Other ethnic minorities[1]	30	34	33	3	0.8	1.4
All ethnic minorities	–	–	–	–	4.8	8.4
All ethnic groups[2]	20	26	39	15	57.1	100%

Notes: [1]Includes those of mixed origin. [2]Population living in private households.
Source: *Social Trends*, **32**, 2002, Table 1.4, Office for National Statistics. Reproduced under the terms of the Click-Use Licence

Table 26.2 Employment rates[1] by ethnic group, age and highest qualification, 2000–1[2]

	Males				Females			
	Higher qualification	Other qualification	No qualification	All aged 16–64[5]	Higher qualification	Other qualification	No qualification	All aged 16–59[5]
White	89.9	81.7	58.4	80.4	85.1	72.5	47.7	70.9
Black	83.5	62.3	48.6	64.8	77.4	56.3	32.6	57.6
Indian	92.1	72.1	52.7	75.5	80.4	59.9	36.4	60.1
Pakistani/ Bangladeshi	82.9	57.7	49.5	59.7	68.6	30.2	7.2	24.7
Other ethnic groups[3]	85.4	56.9	50.9	64.4	68.2	42.5	28.1	47.7
All ethnic groups[4]	89.7	80.5	57.7	79.5	84.3	71.0	45.5	69.3

Note: [1] Percentage of the working age population in employment. [2] Combined quarters: spring 2000 to winter 2000–1. [3] Includes those of mixed origin. [4] Includes those who did not state their ethnic group. [5] Includes those who did not state their qualifications.
Source: *Labour Force Survey*, Office for National Statistics. Reproduced under the terms of the Click-Use Licence

As far as economic activity rates are concerned (the percentage of each social group that is in the workforce), women are generally less active than men, and whites are generally more employed than ethnic minorities (Table 26.2). Note the particularly low participation rates among Asian and particularly Pakistani/ Bangladeshi women. Note also the high rate of workforce participation for the more educated from all ethnic groups. These figures are, of course, different from unemployment rates, which measure the numbers of people actively seeking work.

Data on income, employment, educational or housing inequality in no way prove the existence of discrimination. What they do show, however, is a pattern of inequality that persists over time and which almost certainly is related to discrimination in one form or another. This perception has led successive governments

New Commonwealth

A coded term used to refer to non-white Commonwealth countries.

BRIEFINGS

26.2 Defining ethnic minorities in Britain

Over the years both the official and unofficial labels attached to Britain's ethnic minority population have changed considerably. During the 1950s and 1960s, 'immigrant' and 'coloured' were used almost interchangeably. Both are condescending. 'Coloured' has passed from the official vocabulary and 'immigrant' is obviously inappropriate for the majority of the ethnic population born in Britain. Later, the census used the coded term BPBNC or 'both parents born **New Commonwealth**' to distinguish 'black' from 'white' immigrants and their descendants. The official labels in use today are reproduced in Table 26.1. While these are more accurate and sensitive, they remain very broad categories. The use of the term 'black' is gradually being replaced by the hyphenated 'Afro-'. Using 'black' as a shorthand for all ethnic minorities is also passing from the political vocabulary. Of course, no one is literally black, any more than anyone is literally, white; in reality, the minority population is extraordinarily heterogeneous in its origins. West Indian or Afro-Caribbean includes people from very different island cultures. Indian applies to all those from a vast and complex medley of cultures, religions and languages. Only the Chinese population is relatively homogeneous, the vast majority having originally come from Hong Kong.

Even these distinctions can be offensive, for most of Britain's ethnic minorities have been born in Britain and are as British as the royal family or anyone else. By many measures the Welsh, Irish and Scots are also 'minorities' but, Catholics in Northern Ireland apart, their treatment is not a political issue because they suffer from little discernible discrimination.

Labels are, however, a necessary evil. If discrimination and inequality are to be identified and dealt with, it is necessary to collect the relevant statistics.

Figure 26.1 Unemployment rates of men by ethnic group, Great Britain, 2004

Source: *Social Trends*, **36**, 2006, Figure A4, Office for National Statistics. Reproduced under the terms of the Click-Use Licence

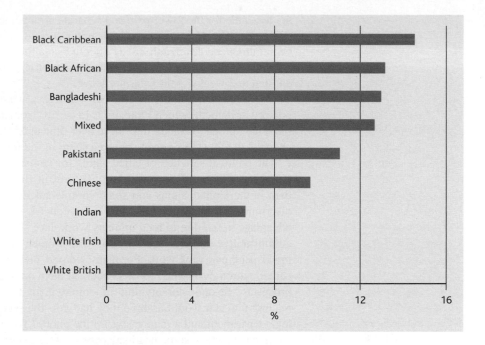

to legislate to reduce or remove discrimination, and to provide redress for aggrieved parties. The following sections will provide an account of this legislation and the politics surrounding it as it has affected gender, disability and race.

Gender

Unlike race, gender has been on the political agenda for many generations. Equal pay for men and women working in the same job has been a trade union demand since the end of the nineteenth century, but it was not until 1970 that legislation was enacted to achieve this end. The Equal Pay Act of 1970 allowed women to claim equal pay if their work was of 'equal value' to that of men. This law was amended in 1983 to comply with an EC directive on equal pay that required equality of remuneration without a formal job evaluation of the work concerned and without regard to physical differences between the sexes.

In 1976, the government acted to outlaw discrimination based on sex or marital status in employment, education, housing and public facilities. The law set up an Equal Opportunities Commission (EOC) to process complaints and refer them to industrial tribunals. As with the Commission for Racial Equality, the EOC has limited enforcement powers, although its provisions have gradually been strengthened by European Union directives, particularly in the areas of social security and welfare.

Two major omissions in the law have been partly addressed in recent years. The first concerns maternity, paternity and pregnancy. European directives on maternity leave and pay were issued during the 1970s and 1980s, but it was not until 1996 that these were formalised in law. Under the 1996 Employment Rights Act, women have the right to paid time off both for antenatal care and after the birth of their child, with the right to return to work. As of April 2006 pregnant employees were entitled to a minimum of 26 weeks' leave with pay, provided 21 days' notice is given. Benefit is paid at a rate of 90 per cent of full pay, provided the employee has worked for a minimum period and earns at least £80 a week. Lower benefits are available for the lower paid and separate arrangements are in place for the self-employed. These provisions are an improvement on previous benefits and have been introduced as a result of EU directives – although benefits are not as good in the United Kingdom as in some other EU countries. From April 2003 fathers were entitled to 2 weeks' paid paternity leave.

The second omission concerns pension rights, which relate to the date of compulsory retirement, which typically is lower for women than for men. The government has agreed to standardise these over time at 65. In addition, the law has been changed to allow a divorced spouse a share of the former partner's pension.

The political salience of equal rights for women has gradually increased over the years, although the women's movement in Britain has often been less vocal than in the United States and some continental European countries. While overt discrimination in employment has been reduced, women continue to be at a disadvantage in relation to men in many workplace situations. Men hold most senior administrative and managerial posts, and women are greatly over-represented in lower-paid, part-time work. For many women, pregnancy results in an interrupted career pattern even when those concerned have no wish to undermine their career prospects. Sexual stereotyping in employment remains. How many students reading this text would assume they had got 'the secretary' if they phoned a college department and a man answered the phone? As can be seen from Table 26.3, women have made some headway over the longer term, but in such professions as accountancy, the law and medicine they still have a long way to go.

The 'pay gap' between men and women remains at around 20 per cent (see Figure 26.2) and tends to grow during the middle years of life when earnings are typically at their highest. Moreover, in spite of the fact that Britain has had a Sex Discrimination Act for almost 30 years, employers continue to find ways of passing over women for appointment and/or promotion, find cause to sack them if they are pregnant, and generally treat them unfavourably. Part of the reason for this is that there is no statutory body charged with the job of providing redress. As mentioned, the EOC, which was created in 1976, provides only a referral service to employment (formerly industrial) tribunals. Moreover, incomplete information on

Table 26.3 Women's employment over 100 years

Profession	End of nineteenth century		End of twentieth century	
	Men	Women	Men	Women
National government	88,894	11,666	143,370	206,120
Police	44,734	0	130,030	16,580
Armed forces	134,061	0	176,800	13,090
Barrister, solicitor, advocates	23,089	0	57,660	22,150
Medical practitioners	21,519	113	65,890	29,550
Veterinarians	3,725	3	5,090	2,080
Nurses, midwives and related	650	56,829	81,350	899,140
Teaching professional	57,772	157,358	325,230	530,890
Domestic housekeepers, cleaners, etc.	123,098	1,601,656	121,310	688,110
Chartered and certified accountants	9,129	50	83,220	22,670
Farming	1,043,780	74,695	356,170	91,530
Milliners, dressmakers, tailors, etc.	145,755	566,943	12,060	17,570
Coalmine labourers	587,542	3,833	20,770	160
General labourers	659,124	3,022	91,660	7,740
Authors, writers, journalists	5,539	689	4,517	3,418

Source: *The Times*, 11 May 2000, p. 8

Figure 26.2 Gross hourly earnings by sex and whether working full or part time, Great Britain, 1986–2004

Source: *Social Trends*, **36**, 2006, Fig. 1.3, Office for National Statistics. Reproduced under the terms of the Click-Use Licence

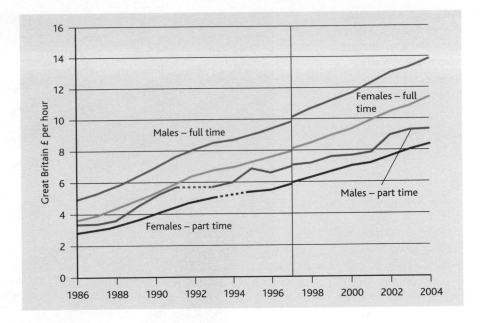

women's pay means that much discrimination goes undetected. Therefore, the EOC has repeatedly called for the creation of 'pay audits' or systematic audits by industrial and commercial sectors to find out how, exactly, different social groups are treated.

With the election of a Labour administration with the largest government and parliamentary representation of women ever, it is likely that women's issues will be given greater prominence over the next few years. Certainly, both in its response to EU directives and its stance on relevant British legislation, Labour has been more supportive of sex equality than were the Conservatives. Of all women's issues, childcare and the position of working mothers are likely to head the political agenda. Labour has made changes to the welfare system to encourage single mothers to work (see Chapter 25). However, the effects of these reforms will be limited in the absence of universal state provision for childcare and training programmes for single parents. Although extra resources for nursery education have been allocated by Labour governments, most commentators agree that it will be many years before the incentive structure for single parents is changed in ways that will remove their disadvantaged status.

Disability

The 1944 Disabled Persons (Employment) Act defined a disabled individual as a 'person who, on account of injury, disease or congenital deformity, is substantially handicapped in obtaining or keeping employment'. Disabled people could, voluntarily, register under the Act. As amended in 1958, the Act required employers of more than 20 people to employ a 3 per cent quota of registered disabled people. This law was widely flouted – employers could apply for exemption – and it was poorly enforced. Worse, the legislation did nothing to change the environment in which disabled people worked. Instead it assumed that disability was a permanent handicap and employers should patronise disabled people's condition by giving them 'suitable' work. Car park and passenger lift attendants were officially identified as the most appropriate jobs for the disabled!

By 1970 attitudes towards disability were changing and the Chronically Sick and Disabled Persons Act of that year placed on local authorities a duty to see to the general needs of the disabled. Under the Act authorities are obliged to identify the local disabled population and to provide them with help. The Act was well intentioned, but the actual provision of such things as suitable housing, home helps and the adaptation of facilities to the needs of the disabled was to be financed by limited local authority budgets. Local authority finances were increasingly hard pressed from the mid-1970s onwards and, as a result, provision was patchy and incomplete.

By the 1990s the pressure for more effective legislation was mounting. Disability was increasingly seen in terms of equal opportunity. In other words, people with disabilities should, as far as possible, be given access equal to that of the general population to jobs, housing, education and public facilities. In other countries, and notably in the United States and Australia, legislation had been passed requiring schools, universities, employers, and providers of transport and other public facilities to make special provisions for the disabled. In Britain, however, the Conservative governments of the 1990s were reluctant to pass equivalent legislation. They argued that it would prove an expensive burden on employers and (perversely) would be resented by the disabled themselves. Instead they opted for legislation that, although it strengthened the rights of the disabled, fell far short of the mandatory provisions of the US and Australian legislation. Hence the 1995 Disability Discrimination Act makes it unlawful to discriminate on grounds of disability in employment; requires employers of more than 20 people to accommodate the needs of the disabled; and establishes a right of access for the disabled in transport, higher education and some other areas.

The law also created a National Disability Council to provide advice on freeing the disabled from discrimination. Crucially, however, a number of loopholes in the law made most of its provisions advisory rather than compulsory. For example, there is no requirement that newly built restaurants, pubs or cinemas provide access and toilet facilities for the disabled. Many do, but equally many do not.

This issue is likely to increase in importance during the next few years, partly because the number of disabled is increasing and partly because economic activity rates among the disabled remain low (particularly for women) (Table 26.4). In addition, advocates for the disabled have become more effective and vocal. In the parliamentary debates on legislation for the disabled, the Labour opposition was always more supportive of compulsion in the law than were the Conservatives. Once in government New Labour did legislate to provide for better access for the disabled to public buildings, and benefit levels were increased above the rate of inflation. In 2000 the government created the Disability Rights Commission (DRC) whose job was to eliminate all discrimination against the disabled and to investigate complaints of discrimination. But the DRC lacks enforcement teeth and when it came down to hard choices between more state aid for the disabled and fiscal prudence, the government often chose the latter. For example, it was accused of discriminating against the disabled when it tried to make benefits more selective by reducing the amount available to those with other sources of income. This issue illustrates nicely one of the central dilemmas of Labour's social policy: how do you target benefits to the most needy without giving the impression that many existing recipients of benefits are scroungers and a burden on the state? For many disabled people, being denied benefits because they have other sources of income seems insulting because they believe that their benefits are a *right* that should be available irrespective of income. Interestingly, the European Union has been much less active in issuing directives in this area than it has over discrimination based on

Table 26.4 Economic activity status of disabled people by gender, 2001

	Males	Females	All
In employment[1]			
Working full time (%)	43.5	22.9	33.8
Working part time (%)	5.6	21.6	13.1
All in employment (%)	49.1	44.6	46.9
Unemployed[2] (%)	5.1	3.2	4.2
Less than one year (%)	3.1	2.3	2.7
One year or more (%)	2.0	0.9	1.5
Economically inactive (%)	45.8	52.2	48.8
All disabled (= 100%)(millions)	3.6	3.2	6.8

Notes: [1] Males aged 16 to 64 and females 16 to 59 with current long-term or work-limiting disability. [2] Based on the ILO definition.
Source: *Social Trends*, **32**, 2002, Table 4.8, Office for National Statistics. Reproduced under the terms of the Click-Use Licence

gender, although the 1997 Treaty of Amsterdam declared that it was EU policy to improve workplace and transport access for the disabled throughout the EU.

Race

Race has been an important issue in British politics at least since the 1950s. For much of the nineteenth and early twentieth centuries, Britain had the reputation as a haven for those subject to religious and political persecution in other European countries. Until the First World War, immigration controls were minimal and successive waves of Jews, socialists and Marxists settled in Britain during these years. Their numbers were, however, relatively small. Overt discrimination against Jews, which had become commonplace in many continental countries during the 1930s, was relatively rare in Britain. After the Second World War, a further wave of refugees arrived in Britain from the continent. Again, numbers were limited (by official policy) and again these groups of Jews, Poles and other eastern Europeans were assimilated with relative ease.

In 1948 the Labour government passed the British Nationality Act, which allowed Commonwealth citizens to settle in the UK. The assumption was that, with decolonisation, a new Commonwealth of Nations sharing a language and common traditions could move freely from one state to the other. At the time, it was not expected to result in mass immigration. The citizens of the 'White Commonwealth' – Australia, New Zealand, Canada – enjoyed high living standards and had little incentive to migrate to Britain. Citizens of the 'Black Commonwealth', including newly independent India, rarely had the economic resources to migrate to what was a very distant land. During the 1950s, however, the British economy suffered from shortages of labour and some employers such as London Transport actively recruited cheap, unskilled workers from the West Indies and elsewhere. By the late 1950s the numbers of immigrants from the West Indies and the Indian subcontinent had increased substantially. Racist attitudes were widespread, as was discrimination. In 1958 a race riot in the Notting Hill area of London raised the political salience of the issue.

Unrestricted entry of Commonwealth citizens ceased in 1962 with the passage of the Commonwealth Immigrants Act. Thereafter, all Commonwealth citizens were subject to immigration control except those holding British passports issued in Britain. A system of work vouchers was created that had to be issued by employers before entry was permitted.

Overt discrimination against ethnic minorities (at the time generally called 'coloureds') was commonplace and was not proscribed until the passage of the 1965 Race Relations Act. As amended in 1968, this law banned 'whites only' advertising, prohibited discrimination in housing and employment, and set up a Race Relations Board to mediate disputes concerning discrimination. Most commentators agree that the 1960s legislation was minimalist in scope. Conciliation rarely worked and large areas such as education were excluded from the law.

The much more effective Race Relations Act of 1976 banned direct and indirect discrimination in employment, education, public facilities and housing. The definition of discrimination was expanded to include nationality, citizenship and ethnic origin, and a Commission for Racial Equality (CRE) was established to receive and process complaints. The CRE was instructed to tackle both direct and indirect discrimination and to refer unresolved complaints to an industrial tribunal for settlement.

Although the 1976 law was a great improvement on earlier legislation, the CRE's powers are quite limited. It cannot take on 'class' actions or complaints about discrimination against whole groups of complainants as opposed to individuals, its sanctions under the law are limited and difficult to enforce, and its operations have been consistently underfunded. Part of its brief was to advise governments on how best the law might be improved. This it has done, but none of the Conservative governments in the 1979 to 1997 period acted on its advice.

Against this background of anti-discrimination law, the politics of race changed dramatically from 1968 to 1997. During the 1960s race became an important electoral issue, especially following the Conservative Enoch Powell's 'rivers of blood' speech in 1968. Powell likened the effects of immigration in Britain to the excesses of ancient Rome: 'As I look ahead I am filled with foreboding. Like the Roman, I seem to see the River Tiber foaming with much blood.' Although he was immediately sacked from the shadow Cabinet, Powell's views were not unpopular in many parts of the country. He persisted with his demagoguery and later called for a stop to all immigration, accompanied by compulsory repatriation.

During the 1970s and the 1980s, a racial element emerged in electoral politics. In a number of West Midlands seats race was a factor in determining electoral outcomes. As leader of the opposition, Margaret Thatcher said in 1978 that she understood that the 'British character' might be 'swamped' by immigrants from different cultures. And although overt cultural nationalism – some might say **racism** – of this kind was rare in public life, it was apparent to most in the minority communities that Conservative governments were at best lukewarm supporters of an enhanced state role in fighting discrimination.

A further incident in 1992 confirmed in the minds of many minority voters that some local Conservative parties held unacceptable racial views. In Cheltenham, a highly qualified black candidate, John Taylor, was nominated to fight the parliamentary seat. However, he was confirmed only after an unseemly row in the local party where overt racist views were expressed. Only national publicity and pressure from Central Office facilitated Taylor's nomination. He was subsequently defeated in the general election but was later appointed a Conservative life peer.

Although the Conservative Party has always been identified as anti-immigrant, it has never come remotely close to endorsing discrimination and has usually been quick to condemn overtly racist attitudes and actions. Far-right parties, such as the National Front, which have racist platforms, have had very limited success in British politics. In the post-war period they have never won a parliamentary seat and have won only a few local elections. Indeed, in comparison with the major continental states including France, Germany, Spain and Italy, Britain has no tradition of far-right political parties or far-right racist politics.

Most ethnic minorities in Britain vote Labour. There is a class and a race element to this pattern, in that minorities tend to have lower incomes. But more vote Labour than would be expected from this fact alone. In many inner city constituencies the ethnic vote has been crucial in swinging the result to Labour. So it is not surprising that as a party it has been more supportive of minority interests than have the Conservatives.

One major problem for the minority communities has been racially inspired harassment and violence by whites and a widespread perception that the police have been less than vigilant in stamping out racial incidents. Such incidents are common, especially in the London area, and should be considered a serious public order problem. As can be seen from Table 26.5, racial incidents are at a high and rapidly increasing level – although it is very difficult to find reliable statistics in this area. Many incidents go unreported and an apparent increase in attacks may be the result of an *improved* race relations environment when victims are more likely to trust the police to act and thus more likely to report incidents. During the late 1990s and early 2000s, the government made special efforts to raise police consciousness of the issue. In London the reaction to the failure by the police to catch the killers of Stephen Lawrence, who was stabbed to death in a racial attack

Racism

The practice of discriminating between individuals or groups on racial grounds.

Table 26.5 Racial incidents reported to the police in England and Wales, 1994–2000

	1994/5	1995/6	1996/7	1997/8	1998/9	1999/2000	% change 1994–2000
England and Wales	11,878	12,222	13,151	13,878	23,049	47,814	330
Metropolitan police area	5,480	5,011	5,621	5,862	11,050	23,346	307

Source: *Statistics on Race and the Criminal Justice System*, 2000, computed from Table 8.1, Home Office 2000, available at www.homeoffice.gov.uk

in 1995, led to accusations that the police force was infused with a culture of racism. This was precisely the finding of the Macpherson Report, which was set up to investigate police handling of the killing. Since then, efforts have been made to reform police attitudes and practice.

Antipathy towards police forces that have taken a less than firm hand in this area may help explain periodic outbreaks of rioting in British cities. These assumed serious proportions in the early 1980s and again in the early 1990s and in 2001. In almost all cases, the rioting has centred around conflict between the police and ethnic minorities. These problems persist in spite of the fact that many forces have instituted racial awareness programmes and have made special efforts to recruit minorities.

The condition of minorities in Britain is certainly not one of unrelieved gloom. Educational standards among many Asian and Afro-Caribbean British are generally high. Intermarriage and cohabiting – often an indicator of good race relations – are also high as regards the Afro-Caribbean and the white population. Indeed, around one-third of all Afro-Caribbean males have white partners. The 2005 intake of MPs included 15 (out of 659) from ethnic minorities among their number – a low figure, but significantly up on the historic average.

Immigration and citizenship

Throughout the long history of immigration into Britain, governments have never created a separate category of immigrant labour with a status inferior to that of the 'native' population. Once admitted, immigrants and their children have similar rights and privileges to other citizens. This is in contrast to countries such as Germany and Switzerland that have made extensive use of temporary migrant labour, many of whom enjoy limited civil rights. This is not to deny the existence of serious flaws in British immigration laws (see Briefing 26.3). All sorts of anomalies and restrictions exist and over the years governments of all political complexions have made migration to Britain more complicated. It is merely to state that the citizenship status of legal immigrants is better than in many European countries.

The immigration debate took on a new relevance after 1999 when the number of people seeking political asylum increased substantially following the war in Kosovo and continuing economic and political dislocation in such countries as Afghanistan and Iraq. By 2000 the government was receiving nearly 98,000 asylum applications, in 2001 over 76,000, and in 2002 around 100,000. Since then the figure has declined but the number of applicants being accepted for settlement has actually increased (see Figure 26.3). This was more than in any other EU country – although not, in the case of some countries, in relation to population. Of these a relatively small number were successfully processed – most remained dispersed in the community in specially provided housing or, in the case of those awaiting deportation, in detention centres. All asylum seekers receive state

Plate 26.2 French police find allegedly illegal immigrants in a lorry at Calais bound for Dover

Source: Corbis/David Pollack

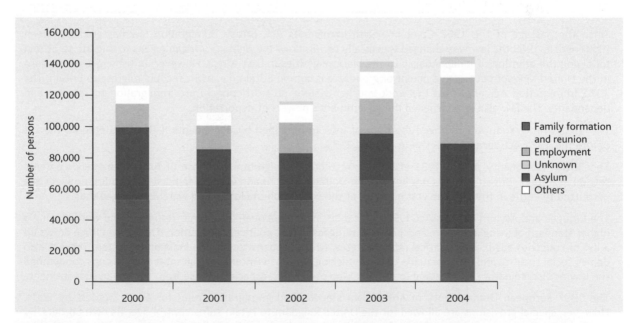

Figure 26.3 Grants of settlement by broad category of grant, excluding European Economic Area nationals, 2000–4

Note: Includes nationals of Czech Republic, Cyprus, Estonia, Hungary, Latvia, Lithuania, Malta, Poland, Slovakia and Slovenia before 1 May 2004, but excludes them after this date.

Source: *Social Trends*, **36**, 2006, Fig. 5.6, Office for National Statistics. Reproduced under the terms of the Click-Use Licence

benefits – although only because of a judicial ruling in 2003 that overturned a government ruling limiting some benefits.

Generally speaking, the British system of processing asylum seekers is one of the most legalistic in Europe. In some cases, the process can drag out for years. The popularity of Britain as a destination is not easy to explain but is almost certainly related to the fact that communities of Kosovans, Bosnians, Iraqis, Afghanis and others already exist in the United Kingdom, especially in London. Britain also has a relatively relaxed 'official regime'. As yet there is no system of national identity cards (although all asylum seekers are issued with identity cards) and restrictions on freedom of movement and employment are minimal. However, in 2005 the government introduced an identity cards bill to make the use of identity cards for all citizens mandatory. This measure is highly controversial and some doubt remains as to whether it will eventually be passed into law.

In 2006 the government introduced a new points system for would-be migrants that set priorities based on the skills of the applicant. Therefore highly skilled computer or health professionals would be given a high priority for admission compared with semi- or unskilled workers.

The whole question of citizenship received increased attention during the early 2000s, in part because of the asylum controversy, but also because of the large number of people given the right to reside in the UK (called a grant of settlement). By 2004 this figure was approaching 150,000 a year. Concern that these newcomers would not be properly assimilated into British society caused the government to introduce a citizenship 'test' called *Life in the UK* before citizenship was granted. Immigrants can apply for citizenship after five years in the country or three years if married to a British spouse. Although mainly of symbolic significance, the test

BRIEFINGS

26.3 Immigration law in Britain

Since the passage of the 1962 Commonwealth Immigrants Act, British immigration law has gradually been tightened. In 1968 the law was changed specifically to withdraw the rights of African Asians to migrate to Britain following the granting of independence to the black majorities in East Africa. However, British citizens not born in the United Kingdom but with a parent or grandparent born in Britain (i.e. whites) could migrate to Britain. The 1971 Immigration Act abolished the work voucher system, so restricting future immigration to spouses and dependants. The law also strengthened the government's powers of deportation.

The 1988 Immigration Act removed the right of men to be joined by dependants if they had entered the UK before the 1971 Act became effective in January 1973.

The British Nationality Act of 1981 effectively restricted immigration to those of British parents or parents settled in Britain. 'British' citizens not born in the United Kingdom and with no familial links to Britain were not permitted to settle in the UK. The vast majority of the population of Hong Kong were categorised thus.

The Refugee and Asylum Seekers Act 1996 made a distinction between 'economic' refugees, who were seeking a higher standard of living in Britain, and 'political' refugees fleeing political persecution. The Home Office draws up a list of countries eligible for political refugee status, which happens to exclude India and Pakistan. The Act also denies social security and other benefits to those seeking asylum in Britain. Immigrant welfare groups condemned the law as discriminatory and leading to the break-up of families, especially those from the Indian subcontinent.

The 1997 European Union Treaty of Amsterdam standardised immigration rules for all EU borders by 2004. However, special provisions are allowed for the United Kingdom to retain some control over its own borders. By 2003 the government was prepared to relax immigration controls further in order to encourage immigration by skilled workers in such areas as health and education, and this system was formalised in 2006 with the introduction of a points system based on applicants' skills.

did show how much more seriously the government was taking the question of British identity. This was also reflected in the increased emphasis on civic education in schools and in the debate on the meaning of 'Britishness'.

Sexual preference

It was not until 1967 that a Labour government voted to remove the ban on homosexual relations between consenting adults in England and Wales. (The ban remained in force in Scotland until 1980 and in Northern Ireland until 1982.) Until then, homosexuality was a criminal offence punishable by imprisonment. However, the new law applied only to consenting adults over the age of 21, although heterosexual relations were permitted at the age of 16. At the same time, homosexuals received no protection against discrimination in employment or housing.

With changing attitudes towards sexuality in general, homosexuality became generally more acceptable during the 1980s and 1990s, although in some areas and notably in the armed forces and the police service, the subject remained taboo.

In 1994 the Conservative government reduced the legal age of consent for homosexuals to 18, and the pressure to standardise the law for all at the age of 16 was increasing. When elected in 1997, the Labour government pledged to do just that and after a long parliamentary battle the law was changed in November 2000. Thus the age of consent for all is now 16 in England, Scotland and Wales, and 17 in Northern Ireland. The government succeeded only after invoking the Parliament Act to overcome resistance in the House of Lords where a determined Tory peer, Baroness Young, led the opposition.

Another area of great controversy concerns Section 28 of the 1988 Local Government Act. This reads: 'A local authority shall not a) intentionally promote homosexuality or publish material with the intention of promoting homosexuality; b) promote the teaching in any maintained school of the acceptability of homosexuality as a pretended family relationship.'

Gay rights activists including such groups as Stonewall and Outrage quickly condemned Section 28 as a mandate to discriminate against homosexuals, and when elected in 1997 the Labour government promised to repeal it. However, as with the age of consent, the government at first faced considerable opposition from the House of Lords, and more recently has not found parliamentary time to change the law. It has been established that the law does not apply to schools and most local authorities have not explicitly invoked Section 28. Paradoxically, in Scotland, where support for Section 28 has been high, the law was repealed by the new Scottish Parliament in June 2001. Given that the government remains pledged to repeal – and action under the European Convention on Human Rights may yet force repeal – a change in the law is almost certain.

By 2003 even the Conservatives were broadly supportive of an extension of gay rights and the first Tory MP to come out as gay (Alan Duncan) did so without losing his shadow ministerial post.

The European Court of Human Rights has already forced the government to act in the area of gays in the armed forces. In spite of a 1997 electoral pledge to lift the ban on homosexuals in the forces, the government refused to do so but was forced to reverse its decision by a unanimous European Court of Human Rights decision in September 1999. European law has been vital in producing the first ever ban on discrimination against homosexuals in Britain. The government acted in this area in 2003 in order to comply with an EU directive deriving from the 1997 Treaty of Amsterdam.

Finally on 5 December 2005 the law was changed to enable homosexual people to enter into civil partnerships that gave to couples the same legal rights (for example, in terms of inheritance) as heterosexual couples. This proved very popular and in the first six weeks of the new system over 3,600 couples entered into civil partnerships.

Politics of equal opportunity: what does the future hold?

Political correctness

A controversial term to describe the use of language about socially sensitive matters, such as race or gender, in a way that is designed not to give offence. Often the implication is that politically correct language is silly or absurd.

Our discussion demonstrates how attitudes have changed over time. Political discourse as it affects disability, race, gender, immigration and sexual preference is very different today from that prevailing in the 1970s, let alone the 1940s or 1950s. This is reflected in semantics – in that we use a different language to describe the issues – and in behaviour, in that discrimination is now relatively rare. Some argue that there has been a 'backlash' against tougher anti-discrimination laws. Certainly disquiet has been expressed at what are often viewed as the strident demands of the '**politically correct**'. A number of leftist local authorities were much derided during the 1970s and 1980s for what were considered their extreme policies in support of the disabled and sexual and other minorities.

The reality of inequality and discrimination in Britain is, however, that a framework of law was laid down in the 1970s that, although updated and amended since, in no way compares with the reach of the law in a number of other countries including the Netherlands and Australia. Many loopholes exist in British laws and some forms of discrimination on grounds of age and sexual orientation remain lawful. Given the changes that have occurred in the disability, gender and race areas, it seems probable that these issues will assume a similar status in due course. As noted, governments have already been obliged to act in order to conform with EU directives.

Labour governments have extended opportunities and removed discrimination, but not if this has meant spending more money on social benefits available to large, undifferentiated categories of disadvantaged citizens. This was nicely demonstrated in late 1999 when, faced with a backbenchers' revolt, the government was forced to modify some of its reforms designed to make benefits for the disabled more selective. As part of the New Deal for the disadvantaged (see Chapter 25), the government announced that incapacity benefits would be increased for those most in need. The term 'need' was broadened to include not only the extent of disability but also potential recipients' financial circumstances. Although the government did accede to some of the backbenchers' demands, the principle that physical need alone would determine eligibility was effectively abandoned.

Summary

- The provision of equal opportunities for women and disadvantaged minorities has become an important issue in British politics over the last 30 years. All the political parties support equal opportunities, but the Conservatives have trodden more cautiously in this area than have Labour. Indeed, the framework of law that was laid down by Labour governments in the 1970s has remained largely unchanged.

- Generally, the British have eschewed affirmative action as a form of redress for past discrimination and have instead opted for redress based on proven individual grievances. Both the Commission for Racial Equality and the Equal Opportunities Commission operate on this basis.

- The framework of protective laws provided for ethnic minorities and the disabled in Britain, although flawed in many respects, compares favourably with that of many European countries. Britain has tended to lag behind other EU states in the provision of equal opportunities for women, however.

- With the increasing political salience of immigration, recent governments have emphasised the importance of citizenship and identity.

- As far as sexual preference is concerned, Labour governments, although more liberal than the Conservatives, have been very cautious in instituting change. On such issues as gays in the armed forces, the European Court of Human Rights has forced their hand.

- The political salience of the issue is likely to increase in the years ahead, in part because the Labour government is likely to play a more proactive, if fiscally cautious role, and in part because inequality and discrimination remain a serious disadvantage for many social groups.

MILESTONES

Milestones in equal opportunities policy

1944 and 1958	Disabled Persons Acts establish quotas for the employment of the disabled
1948	British Nationality Act allows access to the UK for Commonwealth citizens
1958	Notting Hill riots in London
1962 and 1968	Commonwealth Immigrants Acts restrict immigration, introduce work vouchers and deny access for African Asians
1968	Enoch Powell's 'rivers of blood' speech
1965 and 1968	Race Relations Acts provide limited redress for discrimination
1970 and 1983	Equal Pay Acts
1970 and 1976	Chronically Sick and Disabled Acts charge local authorities to see to the needs of the disabled
1975	Sex Discrimination Act outlaws sex discrimination and sets up Equal Opportunities Commission
1976	Race Relations Act outlaws race discrimination in employment, education and other areas, and sets up Commission for Racial Equality
1981, 1985, 1991, 2000	Widespread race riots in British cities. British Nationality Act confines entry to United Kingdom to those with British ancestry
1986	Disabled Persons Act requires educational and other facilities to provide for the disabled
1996	Refugee and Asylum Seekers Act restricts asylum and denies social benefits to asylum seekers
1996	Employment Rights Act gives women the right to maternity pay and leave
1997	Record intake of women into the new Parliament
1998	Government announces a New Deal for the disadvantaged and those in need, involving more training and the targeting of benefits
1999	European Court of Human Rights outlaws British ban on gays serving in the military
2000	Legal age of consent for homosexual and heterosexual relations standardised at 16 (17 in Northern Ireland)
2001–3	Asylum seeker numbers increase greatly. Government encounters serious difficulties in processing applications and toughens its rhetoric
2003	EU directive requires governments to act to end discrimination against homosexuals
2004	Government announces intention to introduce a 'citizenship test' for immigrants
2005	Civil partnerships or same-sex unions are given full legal status

Essays

1. Outline the law protecting ethnic minorities from discrimination in Britain. How effective is it? What changes would you make to protect minorities from discrimination?

2. Describe the laws outlawing discrimination based on gender. How, if at all, might they be improved?

3. Why has legislation banning discrimination against homosexuals been delayed for so long? Should homosexuals be given the same rights as other minority groups?

4. Why is the 'asylum seeker' issue so controversial in British politics? How does British policy differ from that in other EU countries?

Projects

1. Research the pattern of immigration into the UK compared with other EU states. What explains this pattern? Answer with respect to the role of public policy as well as cultural and economic factors.

2. Write a report on the state of gender equality in the UK today. Answer with respect to either employment or education.

3. Taking your own school or college as an example, write a critical report on the facilities and educational opportunities available to the disabled. Write a report on how policy might be changed to provide the disabled with a more equal opportunity to use these facilities.

Further reading

A good account of racism in Britain is John Solomons, *Race and Racism in Britain* (London: Palgrave, 2003). See also Andrew Pilkington, *Racial Disadvantage and Ethnic Diversity in Britain* (London: Palgrave, 2003). On asylum and immigration, see Matt Hall, 'The race card: asylum and immigration in contemporary politics', Parts 1 and 2, *Talking Politics*, **14**, 2 and 3, 2005. On access of minorities and women to the British Parliament, see Pippa Norris and Joni Lovenduski, *Political Recruitment: Gender, Race and Class in the British Parliament* (Cambridge: Cambridge University Press, 1994). On the politics of gender equality, see Esther Breitenbach, *The Changing Politics of Gender Equality in Britain* (London: Palgrave, 2001). On citizenship and women's rights, see Ruth Lister, *Citizenship: Feminist Perspectives* (London: Palgrave, 2003). An excellent account of equal opportunity and social policy is provided by Barbara Bagilhole, *Equal Opportunities and Social Policy* (London: Longman, 1997). On asylum and immigration, see Jef Huysmans, *The Politics of Insecurity: Security, Migration and Asylum in the EU* (London: Taylor and Francis, 2006). The Commission for Racial Equality, the Equal Opportunities Commission and the Disability Rights Commission all provide good up-to-date reports on inequality and discrimination.

Useful web sites on equal opportunities

Hot links to these sites can be found on the CWS at www.pearsoned.co.uk/budge.

Equal opportunities for women, ethnic minorities, disabled people and those with alternative sexual orientations have become important issues for government and politics in Britain. A good starting point is the government's Commission for Racial Equality (www.cre.gov.uk) and the Equal Opportunities Commission (www.eoc.org.uk); it is also recommendable to check the Women and Equality

Unit (www.womenandequalityunit.gov.uk), and the Women's National Commission (www.cabinet-office.gov.uk/wnc). Her Majesty's Stationery Office (www.hmso.gov.uk) has official statistics on labour force trends with respect to race, gender and disability. Funded through the European Social Fund, Equal is an initiative which tests and promotes new means of combating all forms of discrimination and inequalities in the labour market; visit it at www.equal.ecotec.co.uk. The TUC campaigns against discrimination at work and in wider society. It has a special section devoted to equality at www.tuc.org.uk/equality.

Citizenship21 (www.c21project.org.uk) is an independent organisation devoted to the protection of civil rights and the promotion of equal treatment for every British citizen; a similar line of campaigning is supported by Liberty (www.liberty-human-rights.org.uk). For the protection of people with disabilities, visit the Disability Net at www.disabilitynet.co.uk. A variety of organisations aim to promote equal treatment for gays, lesbians and transgendered people; some of them are Lesbian and Gays Employment Rights (www.lager.dircon.co.uk), Stonewall (www.stonewall.org.uk) and Outrage (www.outrage.org.uk).

PART 8

Assessment

chapter 27

Problems, policies, processes and democracy, 1997–2006

The Blair governments, from their initiation in 1997, set themselves an ambitious agenda of domestic reform and democratic renewal. Ironically, however, they will probably be remembered for their Iraq intervention in support of the US Bush administration.

This chapter cuts across the detail of earlier discussions to ask what has driven government policy in the last ten years and whether it has been successful in tackling the problems left over by previous administrations. Has there been significant institutional change? Or have the basically nineteenth-century conventions and processes of the British constitution proved resilient enough to continue into the third millennium, just as they underpinned twentieth-century politics? What are the implications of all this for the quality of British democracy? That is the question posed at the beginning of the book, which we consider explicitly at the end.

Our discussion covers the following points:

- world crises and the 'war on terror': effects on foreign and domestic policy
- Europe versus the United States: Britain's place within the EU
- globalisation: the final collapse of British manufacturing?
- economic management: free markets, strong state?
- redressing inequality? New Labour's social policies
- institutional reforms: will they go further?
- democratic deficits: how far has constitutional reform gone?
- party policies for the future.

Free market, humane society: New Labour's programme

On winning the 1997 election, the New Labour government took over most of the problems that confronted its predecessors and adopted many of their solutions. It had to, in order to convince the middle classes of London and south-east England that it would not endanger the economic boom which Britain experienced in the closing years of Conservative government (1994 onwards). At the same time, it also promised a more humane and responsive government, which would address the growing inequalities that the boom had produced and at the same time govern more efficiently.

This New Labour programme had four main elements.

Neo-liberal economics

It accepted the massive privatisation of government enterprises carried through under the Conservatives: the sale of steel, coal, railways, buses, telecommunications, etc. to private owners. It went even further and accepted 'contracting out' and 'hiving off' in the public services – that is, wherever possible having functions like cleaning or computer and clinical services provided by private firms. This in turn implied a recognition that the free market could on the whole provide goods and services more efficiently and cheaply than public suppliers, under the right conditions. These conditions included low taxes and low inflation – key elements in traditional economics. To foster business confidence, the government immediately gave the Monetary Policy Committee of the Bank of England powers to set national interest rates independently. From 1997 to 1999 New Labour actually stuck to Conservative expenditure targets rather than setting its own, in order to convince the public of its own economic soundness. And it never raised the level of income tax. In terms of the economy, therefore, Labour almost totally accepted Thatcherism (i.e. getting the state out of the economy) and created a '**neo-liberal consensus**' on economics.

Neo-liberal consensus

Agreement among different political groups and parties about neo-liberal policies: that is, the political belief that individual rights should be protected by maximising freedom of choice, limiting the powers of government and promoting market economics.

Public services

What kept Labour distinctive, however, was its insistence on strengthening the public services – particularly the National Health Service. Although the Conservative governments of 1979–97 had been critical of the NHS, they had left it largely as it was because of overwhelming public support for it, consistently running at about 80 per cent. Labour supported the idea of public social provision with much more conviction than the Conservatives. Its argument was that the strong economy produced by its conversion to orthodoxy would generate the finance necessary to fund better and more extended general services.

This support extended beyond health into the broader social sphere – where indeed many of the health problems faced by the NHS originated. Blair's pre-election slogan 'Tough on crime, tough on the causes of crime' indicated that anti-social behaviour, drug and alcohol abuse, poverty, poor living conditions, unemployment and ignorance would be prevented before they arose. Thus the police but also social workers would be strengthened. Many problems arose from the sharply unequal distribution of wealth among different classes and social groups, which were accentuated by the operation of the strictly profit-oriented private economy. Some of the wealth generated by this should be used to help the disadvantaged and create equality of opportunity for all. One way to do this was to make up very low levels of income through personal allowances, while at the same time getting everyone to work who could. 'Education, education, education', another Blairite slogan, saw the schools as the main avenue of social advancement and of participation in society and economy.

Constitutional reform

A third element of the 1997 and subsequent manifestos was 'bringing government closer to the people' in terms of constitutional reform. We have already seen how this resulted in Welsh and Scottish as well as attempted Northern Irish devolution, and in the restoration of Greater London as a political entity. Full acceptance of the European Convention on Human Rights and the passage of a Freedom of Information Act both quickly followed. Attempts to change the House of Lords from a nominated to an elected body stalled, however, as did reform of national voting rules. Although two systems of proportional voting were introduced for devolved and European elections, 'first past the post' and the resulting 'elective dictatorship' of New Labour remained at Westminster.

In part this was because Labour's reform programme for more efficient public services increasingly ran into political opposition from elements within the party itself, as well as affected professionals and local governments. The unchallenged power of the Cabinet and Prime Minister to force measures through Parliament was seen as a necessary basis for efficient administration and could not be weakened.

Europe

A final feature of Labour's overall programme was the promise to 'put Britain at the heart of Europe'. As the Conservative Party became increasingly sceptical about European Union – even of the powers previously ceded to the Union – Europe seemed likely to emerge as a clear dividing line between the main parties (Liberals and most of the minority parties also supported it). Closer integration seemed a natural line to take, as it fitted into Labour's constitutional project. Most EU members put a high emphasis on social services and social support for their population, so it was easy for Labour in 1997 to accept the European Social Charter and a minimum wage. Accepting the Human Rights convention and thus extending the jurisdiction of the EU's European Court of Justice was also a natural feature of constitutional reform.

The great unresolved question was, however, whether Britain would join the European Monetary Union (EMU) and thus accept a common currency with the rest of the EU. This was never done. Without acceptance it was difficult to be 'at the heart of Europe'. As we shall see, events after the millennium quickly moved Britain away from Europe anyway.

New Labour has often been criticised for coming too close to the Conservatives and making its policies practically indistinguishable from Thatcherism. This certainly is true of its economics, but in the other areas it is clearly unfair. With its concerns about social inequality and public services, and 'New Starts' for Europe and the regions, the 'Third Way' between Thatcherism and old-style socialism had real substance, which received a ringing endorsement in 1997 and a less enthusiastic one at the elections of 2001 and 2005.

Iraq and the 'war on terror'

What happened to New Labour after 2003 forms an interesting example of how programmes and policies – even those endorsed in elections – frequently get derailed by events over which governments have little or no control. In the case of New Labour, this was al-Qaeda's attacks on the US on 11 September 2001.

Final casualty figures put the dead at 3000. This was bad enough. Far greater was the shock to US self-esteem and self-security. The attack gave the right-wing Bush administration a project – even a crusade – to make the world safe for the United States by asserting its power, particularly in the Middle East, which was vital for oil supplies.

Britain joined a UN-approved invasion of Afghanistan where al-Qaeda was based: Bush then prepared an invasion of Iraq on much more dubious grounds. Under a particularly brutal dictator, Saddam Hussein, Iraq had indeed been a force for instability in the region and had invaded its small neighbour, Kuwait, in 1990–1. In the first Gulf War 1990–1, the first President Bush had pushed Iraq back with UN approval and British backing. UN sanctions had then been imposed on Iraq in the 1990s, while international arms inspectors monitored its destruction of long-range and chemical weapons, in spite of Iraqi obstruction and aggressive rhetoric.

Saddam's regime, like that of many other Third World dictators, was oppressive and corrupt. However, it was also militantly secularist with nothing in common with Islamic terrorists linked to al-Qaeda. In order to make a case for war wider than just finishing his father's work, the second Bush claimed that Saddam had links with the international Islamist conspiracy and was preparing weapons of mass destruction. None was ever found, so retrospectively the invasion had to be justified in terms of the oppressive regime and restoring democracy in Iraq. That was all very well, but the question remained: why Saddam – rather than Gaddafi (Libya), Musharraf of Pakistan and many other dictators who lined themselves up with the Anglo-US invasion?

Blair not only sent troops into Iraq alongside the Americans but played the major part in justifying the war with suspect and sometimes doctored intelligence information. In part this was deployed to defuse the opposition to war of the major EU partners, France and Germany. In siding with the United States, Blair sacrificed any chances he otherwise had of bringing them along on reforms of agricultural and competition policy inside Europe.

Support for the Bush project was very much in line with British nurturing of the 'special relationship' with the United States during the post-war period (although Blair's Labour predecessor Harold Wilson had resolutely refused to get involved in the United States' disastrous intervention in Vietnam, 1964–72). Traditionally, the 'special relationship' had been justified in terms of the influence it gave Britain over the superpower's foreign policy. Once assured of British support, however, the Bush administration seems to have decided no concessions were necessary either on the war or on other matters to which the Blair governments were committed, such as writing off debt for the Third World and – most significantly – combating global warming and climate change. Indeed, until 2005 the Bush administration consistently denied there was any evidence for the latter and tried to undermine any international agreements to combat it.

In light of their opposition to British initiatives in these other spheres, all of more long-run importance than international terrorism, it is hard to understand the UK government's total subservience to American foreign and military policy. This had costs not only in Europe but also at home, increasing social tensions with the British Muslim community (over a million people) and within the Labour Party itself. Support can only be explained in terms of the Prime Minister's personal commitment, as other members of the government would have been at the least more circumspect in their dealings with the United States.

Blair's support extended beyond Iraq, to an endorsement of a 'long war' against terrorism to be fought by the West under US leadership throughout the Muslim world, from Morocco through the Middle East to Indonesia. This may involve overt and covert military operations, surveillance, economic and political pressure on governments – or their outright subversion – along with kidnappings, suspension of human rights, secret prisons and torture.

The price of active British involvement in the 'war on terror' can be briefly summarised as the undermining of many of New Labour's policy ambitions, as follows.

Democratic renewal and government responsiveness

In fact the Iraq intervention has been continued regardless of majority opposition. Internally, rights to open trial and appeals against detention at administrative discretion have been suspended on the UK mainland in a way that never happened with the more extensive Irish terrorism of 1972–96. The government has been widely seen as lying about matters like WMD and as actively involved in manipulation of media news and public opinion.

Social harmony

Intervention in Muslim countries and legislation against 'incitement to terrorism' aimed at radical clerics has alarmed and disorientated the British Muslim minority

Table 27.1 Public support and opposition to military intervention in Iraq, 2003–5

	Right %	Wrong %	Don't know %	
2003: 18 March	50	42	9	Commons debate
20 March	53	39	8	Start of war
23 March	56	37	7	
25 March	56	35	9	
27 March	59	35	6	
30 March	54	38	7	
1 April	54	40	6	
3 April	55	38	7	
6 April	60	35	5	
8 April	63	32	6	
10 April	66	29	5	US troops enter central Baghdad
13 April	60	35	6	
3–4 May	57	34	9	Bush declares war over (1 May)
30 May–1 June	58	35	7	
22–4 July	50	41	9	Kelly death (18 July)
September	49	41	10	Mid-point of Hutton Inquiry
25–6 September	43	42	15	End of evidence to Hutton Inquiry
2–3 October	46	47	8	After Labour Party conference
23–4 October	46	41	13	
13–14 November	43	45	11	Prior to Bush visit to UK (from 18 November)
18–19 December	53	33	14	After capture of Saddam Hussein (13 December)
2004: 12–14 January	48	42	10	
30–1 January	50	39	11	After Hutton Report (28 January)
26–7 February	49	42	9	Clare Short UN bugging row (26 February)
6–8 May	43	49	8	After US, UK torture pictures (from 27 April)
8–10 July	42	50	8	Immediately before Butler Report
10–11 September	39	49	12	
17–18 September	38	52	10	
1–2 October	42	48	10	After Labour Party conference
8–9 October	40	47	14	Following death of Kenneth Bigley and report of Iraq survey group
22–3 October	42	47	11	Following decision to send UK troops to central Iraq
26–8 October	36	54	10	
2005: 20–2 January	35	56	9	

Source: www.yougov.co.uk

and supplied indigenous suicide bombers for the London attacks of July 2005. As Muslims feel more under threat, they may express their disquiet through civil disobedience.

Political disunity and discontent

Iraq has also got in the way of another New Labour project – maintaining party unity and winning elections. The Labour Party has traditionally been committed to peaceful internationalism and support for the UN. An invasion undertaken without UN backing and indeed against the wishes of the majority of its members has thus split MPs and activists. An opposition group among the former have extended their opposition to the Blairite choice agenda, particularly those parts involving private selection and competition in the public services.

Many activists have dropped out of the party, while formerly loyalist voters have abstained. This contributed to the fall in turn-out in the General Elections of 2001 and 2005 – from above 70 per cent in the 1990s to around 60 per cent today. Minority groups, previously nearly unanimous in support of Labour, are now split. These factors are estimated to have cost Labour around 3 per cent of its vote at the last election, causing it to be elected to government on the smallest percentage of votes for 80 years – 36 per cent.

However, Labour *did* win in 2005. The main reason was that the Conservatives offered no alternative over Iraq or terrorism. The Liberals, who did, continued their slow increase in seats. But under the single-member simple plurality voting system, they had no chance of gaining power. Despite leading Labour in the polls after his election as Conservative leader in late 2005, David Cameron is unlikely to better his long-term position unless he changes these policies. It is, however, dangerous for New Labour to rely on the weakness of its opponents, while pursuing policies that weaken its traditional political base.

Alienation from 'Europe'

We have already commented on the fact that Britain's major partners in the EU, France and Germany, strongly opposed the Iraq invasion. Although Poland, Italy and Spain initially joined Bush's 'coalition of the willing', the bitter split with the traditional supporters of closer union hardly put New Labour at the 'heart of Europe'. This was such an important consequence of the war that it deserves longer examination in the next section.

Europe versus the United States: Britain's place in the European Union

In choosing to support the United States so wholeheartedly from 2001 on, the Blair governments were certainly following a path marked out by their predecessors, particularly in the early part of the post-war period. Then Britain had been the closest supporter of US leadership of the military alliance against the Soviet Union, NATO. Much was made then of the 'special relationship' between the two powers, in which (from the British point of view, at least) the United States supplied the muscle and the UK the wisdom and experience. Doubts have been raised, however, about whether the United States saw Britain as much more than a loyal spear-carrier and possibly as a less important ally than Germany.

The strength of the relationship weakened when Blair's Labour predecessor, Harold Wilson, refused support for the United States' unsuccessful Vietnam War

(1965–72). This helped convince the French that the UK would not necessarily be a US stooge inside Europe, and they lifted their veto on British membership of the EU (then the EEC) in 1972. Till the end of the century, US and EU interests ran along broadly parallel lines. So Margaret Thatcher's strong support for President Reagan in the 1980s was not too contentious, particularly with the end of the Cold War. Her extreme defence of British interests within the EU, which earned the UK the soubriquet of a 'bad European', was counterbalanced by acceptance of the Single European Act (1986), the most important step towards integrating the Union as a market. The Major governments from 1990 to 1997 accepted most EU initiatives towards closer union, against increasing opposition from their own Conservative Party and in spite of 'opting out' on social issues and currency union.

By immediately 'opting in' on the Social Charter and the Convention on Human Rights, the first Blair government moved closer to the 'heart of Europe'. It was not, however, going to imperil its economic boom by joining the euro, and having missed the most favourable time politically to do so, never did. After 2001 it had so clearly opted for the United States over its major European partners that it lost some of the leverage it previously had for advancing its preferred policies within the EU. Certainly so far as enlargement went, it supported the incorporation of ten new members (mainly in central and eastern Europe) which took place in 2004.

Plate 27.1 British troops in action in Iraq

Source: Getty Images/AFP

It also promoted negotiations with Turkey on its application to join, which were initiated in 2005.

The problem with both policies was that they were also strongly urged on the EU by the United States. So were the British preferences for trade liberalisation by the EU and an emphasis on its role as part of the world free market rather than as a political union to counterbalance the United States. The British role within the EU, in other words, was increasingly perceived by its partners in some policy areas as surrogate spokesman for the United States, earning it a position on the fringes of European debate rather than at its centre. Hopes that the new eastern European members would share the British viewpoint and counterbalance the Franco-German axis that dominates EU decision making have been partly undermined by the rapid integration of their economies with the German.

It seems from the perspective of the mid-2000s, therefore, that the Blair governments have almost made the choice between Europe and the United States that has hung over British governments since their loss of empire. Few things are ever final in politics. But neither a New Labour Prime Minister in succession to Blair nor a Conservative one seems likely to reverse it. What remains puzzling is what return Britain gets from participation in the 'war on terror' given US reluctance to make policy concessions anywhere else.

Globalisation – the continuing decline of British manufacturing?

Globalisation is shorthand for the increasing trade links and communication between all countries in the world. It is, of course, a process that has been developing ever since the first European voyages of exploration. The technological advances of the twentieth century – instant communication, air travel, rapid development and transmission of new technologies – have now, however, come to a head to the extent that changes which previously took centuries or decades now occur within a few years.

The practical consequence for Britain has been the collapse of first old and then some new industry in the face of Japanese and now Chinese competition. Shipbuilding and textiles are only the two most dramatic of these. Manufacturing has now shrunk to less than 20 per cent of British GDP and is certain to decline further.

Such decline would have taken place anyway as Japan and China entered the marketplace. It has been accelerated by the elimination of national barriers to trade, which has allowed low-cost countries to undercut high-cost ones. British governments, with their inherited enthusiasm for free trade ideas (see Chapter 2) have, however, strongly supported trade liberalisation – never hesitating to put the interests of investors and consumers in cheap goods and greater choice ahead of the interest of producers in steady jobs and better working conditions.

The sustained economic boom since the 1990s was based on a massive expansion of service industries, particularly centred on finance. As the Far East developed manufacturing, Britain provided investment, technology and expertise in handling transactions. One question mark over the future is how far the new industrial giants may not provide their own services later on and how Britain will develop then. The other European countries face the same problems but from a substantial industrial base, owing to the protectionist practices still strong in the EU. Germany, in particular, is well placed to integrate its advanced technology with the underexploited resources of the new EU members in the East, so to that extent is less dependent on developments overseas.

As pointed out in Chapter 2, the Industrial Revolution in Britain developed in the peripheries owing to the availability of water and coal there. Services and administration were always concentrated on London and the south-east. The decline of manufacturing has therefore had different effects in different areas of Britain, increasing differences and political tensions between peripheries and centre.

During the economic boom these have to some extent been glossed over by the growth of subsidiary financial centres like Leeds and Edinburgh. The London conurbation, served by a relatively cheap and efficient transport network, has for some purposes extended out to Birmingham and Cardiff. On the political side, the fact that Labour dominates the Welsh and Scottish executives as well as Westminster means that they have little interest in directly challenging central policies even if they have diverged marginally on some points. Fiscal autonomy for Scotland might, however, become a real possibility under the twin impacts of economic downturn and change in political control. One could well see nationalist parties gaining strength again under such conditions.

Economic management: free markets, strong state

Some downturn seems increasingly likely as China, serviced by Japan, dominates world markets and catches up on technology and services. Even given its success in providing services, Britain has been running a deficit in terms of importing more than it sells abroad. Combined with the major US deficit now running at more than 6 per cent of GDP a year, this creates a structural imbalance in world trade which is only sustained by Chinese willingness to accept US debt. It is not in China's interest to pull the plug, of course, as it would then lose its major export market. But if it did, the whole fragile structure of world relationships would collapse, bringing the British economy down with it.

A second looming problem is the extent to which climate change may impose increasing economic costs and so undermine the premises of steady growth and unlimited expansion on which the free market operates. Certainly New Labour's economic model, personified in the 'Iron Chancellor' Gordon Brown, has been to pursue growth and non-interference at least as far as a Conservative government would have done: for example, loosening local planning regulations that businesses claimed were restricting their growth.

To do so the government has kept local government in England under a tight grip, curtailing its powers by legislation and keeping its expenditure within rigid limits dictated by the Public Sector Net Cash Requirement (i.e. the total amount that the government wants to borrow to finance itself), set by the Treasury. Grants to councils have been tied to specific purposes approved by government. Many powers in areas like education have been taken over by central government, with, for example, the imposition of a National Curriculum and transfer of individual schools outside council control.

All this smacks of the Thatcherite emphasis on a strong state as a guarantee of a free market and the supply of skills it needs – or that business thinks appropriate for it to have. The 'elective dictatorship' at Westminster has helped the government beat down elements in the Labour Party who might oppose these developments, which the Conservatives can criticise only marginally and largely ineffectively.

New Labour argues that an enterprise-driven economy is the most efficient means of ensuring employment and jobs. Thus it justifies its adoption of Thatcherite tenets in terms of old social democratic values. It adds, as we have seen, that only a strong economy can provide the revenues necessary for strong public services that will, among other things, support its victims.

It is, of course, difficult to keep these two areas apart. Public spending inevitably impacts on economic activity, which may then create additional problems for the public sector. A practical example of this is the pensions crisis from 2003 onwards. Changes in the taxation of investments to generate more government revenue, combined with a downturn in the value of stock market investments from 2000 to 2006, caused many company pension schemes for employees to devalue their assets, leaving them substantially short of their liabilities. Rather than making these up, or waiting till the price of shares recovered, most companies closed the schemes down, or restricted payouts.

This then left millions short of the income they expected in retirement, creating new problems for a government worried about pensioner poverty on a very minimal state pension. New Labour has also been accused of imposing stealth taxes through, for example, increasing compulsory national insurance payments for both employees and employers.

Redressing inequality? New Labour's social policies

New Labour's main inheritance from its old Labour past has always been based on a recognition that a profit-orientated economy will not automatically take care of the problems it creates, particularly of poverty or inequality. The state must step in to redress them by providing certain minimal standards for all – and better than that, an opportunity particularly for the young to get a footing in the free market.

From acceptance of the European minimum wage to credits for poor families, the Blair governments have consistently tried to direct money to those in need. This has been perhaps the most consistent feature of all their social policies, for which the major credit goes to the persistence of Gordon Brown as Chancellor of the Exchequer and second man in the controlling dyarchy. Combined with making the health service more efficient and better funded, and championing lower-class and ethnic education in schools, these measures have improved the quality of life for those at the social bottom.

Coupled with more generous provision has been an attempt to get all these groups into work – regarded by Blair and Brown as the best social benefit of all – and to improve the efficiency of provision for them. Police, social and medical workers have been better paid under New Labour. But all public service professionals have been reorganised, usually several times, and subjected to relentless targets and inspection on whatever criteria were uppermost in the government's priorities at the time, usually to deflect media campaigns. As one exasperated professor commented, politicians are reluctant to allow professionals to do what they are trained to do.

Of course, one can carry criticism of the 'nanny state' too far. In the NHS, for example, government interventions have tipped the balance between professionals, empowering general practitioners in relation to hospital consultants and weakening the stranglehold the latter had over hospital administration. In part this has been achieved by employing more professional managers and administrators, and opening up services to private contractors, particularly where there are long waiting lists.

In education too, New Labour's solution to inequality of provision has often been to take schools out of local government control, setting them up as independent trusts with more or less selective entry. This has been justified as necessary to ensure that bright children from underprivileged groups get their chance to rise. To old Labour this has seemed like a return to the old system of grammar schools with selective entry biased in favour of the middle class, and has provoked significant parliamentary revolts by Labour MPs. It is significant that Wales and Scotland have stuck to the established comprehensive system.

Plate 27.2 Blair and Brown, the two dynamic personalities behind New Labour
Source: Getty Images

Tight central control, 'hiving off' to the private sector, competition, reorganisation and inspection – all by central government – are features of the market-led approach to efficiency inherited by New Labour from its Conservative predecessors. However, its distinguishing feature remains a concern with the quality of the public services – partly to induce the middle classes to stick with them and thus provide a supportive political base, and partly with the laudable aim of ensuring that the disadvantaged also get the best service possible.

This may compensate for demoralised public service professionals with high rates of drop-out and retirement, where there is still a sharp divide between private and public provision. Opportunities and attainments seem to have expanded for the middling levels of the social structure but not for the lowest 20 per cent. Nearly half of the relevant population went into higher education in 2005. But this left universities in a state of perpetual crisis from under-funding and increasingly subservient to changing government priorities and initiatives.

The political management of national reform: have institutions changed and can they cope?

New Labour has been criticised for its nanny state. But in truth much of the impetus for detailed regulation and continued inspection and checking came from the Conservatives' 'strong state', determined to enforce compliance of the public services with its 'Citizen's Charters', and from EU directives designed to cover all eventualities in safety, hygiene, health standards and political correctness. However, Labour's 'continuing revolution' implied continual state intervention and supervision, and the limitation of local autonomy in many areas. All this implied that the central institutions were to do more policy-wise, which in turn increased problems of coordination between them.

How far, therefore, have they been streamlined or adapted to cope with their constantly increasing workload? The short answer is: very little. Problems of actually implementing policy goals on the ground seem to be increasing and coordination between one part of the government and another often seems non-existent. Given the Prime Minister's earlier emphasis on 'joined-up solutions', this seems surprising.

Implementation and coordination have, however, been problems not only for New Labour but also for its predecessors. The problem may well rest with the ability of the 'elective dictatorship' in Britain to take whatever action it wants where it wants, coupled with its inability to keep its attention fixed on any one policy for long, given the continuing flow of new problems. Iraq is again a case in point. The Prime Minister in the midst of his second government diverted his attention from home affairs for a full year under the pressure of international events.

On the face of it, devolving powers to Scotland and Wales, and perhaps Northern Ireland, divested central government of domestic concerns for one-sixth of the UK population. However, these areas were often dealt with at the tag-end of general British legislation, and implementation handled by a devolved administration anyway. So the reduction in central workload was more apparent than real.

Devolution was the only major change in the machinery of government carried through by New Labour. How then have coordination and oversight of major policies been carried through? Various counts have identified anything from 70 to 80 autonomous spending units in the government, each responsible for particular (major and minor) areas of policy. The most important are the 25–30 ministries, such as Education. Each has a political head – sometimes a whole political team – supervising its work. While a ministry can always carry on with administering policy in its own area under existing legislation and regulations, what it does has implications for other areas. And it may not be achieving what the government wants anyway. How to manage programmes over a range of departments is a problem constantly facing central decision makers.

Constitutional textbooks usually see the Cabinet, grouping the political heads of all the main ministries, as the essential coordinating committee. Under the Blair governments, however, the Cabinet has met less than ever and has figured in the news more as a block on some proposals – for example, on a total smoking ban in 2005 – than an originator of policy. Cabinet committees grouping relevant ministers clearly do perform a certain amount of coordination, and there was a War Cabinet to conduct the Iraq invasion. The general problem, however, is the tremendous work pressure on ministers, now with an extra European and world

BRIEFINGS

27.1 The 'elective dictatorship' in British government

'Elective dictatorship' is a shorthand term (coined by Lord Hailsham) used to describe the situation whereby the leadership of the majority party in the House of Commons forms a government that can do more or less what it wants, with only weak constitutional and legislative checks. This is possible because of (a) tight internal discipline which ensures that the MPs of the majority parliamentary party will always vote to uphold the government (Chapter 18); and (b) the unwritten constitution, whose conventions are more or less what the government says they are (Chapter 4).

Although some limitations have been placed on governments through EU legislation, devolution, judicial review and investigative journalism, these are relatively limited and weak.

dimension added to meetings. This means that they often miss Cabinet and its committees even where their agreement is essential.

In an age of instantaneous communication, much can be done by email and telephone between ministers and civil servants. Probably this accounts for much of the discussion and decision making that was previously done in face-to-face meetings. It is hard to escape the impression, however, that ministers often learn about each other's doings as much from media reports as from exclusively government sources, except in their own specialised areas.

In the absence of more formal means, joined-up government seems under the first Blair government to have been carried on between the three most powerful figures in the government – Blair, Brown and, until 2006, Prescott. Having agreed a course of action, they then informed other ministers in a series of bilateral contacts. Prescott as Deputy Prime Minister ceased to be an independent participant and became more of the Prime Minister's enforcer in the later governments.

It is hard to avoid the impression, however, that right from the start, and increasingly from 2001, government policy has been made mainly on the basis of prime ministerial initiatives, communicated through bilateral meetings with affected ministers, and sometimes barely that. Blair's preferred method for enforcing such initiatives has been to set up special task forces of civil servants, sometimes with nominated outsiders, to carry through the remit he gives them. A good example is the Social Exclusion Unit, which operated around 2000. In support, the Prime Minister's personal office has expanded and he has had his 'kitchen cabinet' of political intimates and advisers.

This personal rather than institutional style of governing is shared with many of Blair's predecessors, from Thatcher and Heath back to Lloyd George from 1916 to 1922. Lloyd George even had his 'garden suburb' of advisers and civil servants located in the grounds of Downing Street. The undefined British constitution, with its vague but potent attribution of powers to a Prime Minister, allows him or her to do this. The power is personal, however, and the mechanisms keep shifting between incumbent and incumbent.

This is likely to be true if Gordon Brown, Chancellor of the Exchequer in all the Blair governments, succeeds as Prime Minister. In the Treasury (i.e. the Ministry of Finance and Economic Affairs), Brown has been the sole minister to operate autonomously of Blair within his own sphere, which he has defined very broadly. It has not only covered economics, taxation and expenditure, but has also extended to tax credits and social subsidies for the poorest families and individuals. The ministry nominally in charge of these is the Department of Social Security, but Brown has forged special links with that ministry in order to see through the implementation of the anti-poverty programmes.

The Treasury is the ministry that traditionally has been the coordinator for other departments, in so far as they are coordinated. This is through so-called 'Treasury control', whereby Treasury teams audit other departments' yearly expenditure and review their future plans. Formalised under the 'Comprehensive Spending Review', all departments had to justify their spending and keep within Treasury targets. Indeed, the Treasury under Brown has taken a proactive role, binding ministers to his approved policies through 'public service agreements' with the Treasury.

Insofar as there has been systematic, institutionalised coordination and close monitoring of policy implementation over the last 10 years, this has come paradoxically from the Treasury not from Downing Street. It has been directed primarily at the two central areas of New Labour policy, the economy and public services. Relative successes in these areas can probably be attributed to Brown rather than Blair. When and if Brown succeeds as Prime Minister, it is unlikely that he will relinquish this power base. By putting his own nominee into the Treasury, he can keep control of it as Prime Minister.

There could hardly be a sharper contrast of administrative style than that within the New Labour governments between Brown and Blair – the one systematic and institutionally based in persistent pursuit of clearly defined, limited, objectives; the other inspirational, sporadically interested in a wide range of areas, and using ad hoc 'task forces' which cut across institutional boundaries. The Brown approach, broadening out from established departments and processes, is likely to survive longer and to extend itself over the government if the latter becomes Prime Minister.

Brown's methods are a logical development of the 'elective dictatorship', where the leader of the majority party assumes total control of government, even though New Labour has so far seen a dyarchy rather than a purely 'presidential' leadership. If, however, a power-sharing or coalitional arrangement emerges as a result of no party having an absolute majority after the election of 2009/10, we may expect the emergence of a detailed coalition agreement on policy, with a two-party cabinet adjudicating disagreements and coordinating ministries shared between the parties. With a hung parliament and consequent power sharing, presumably with the Liberal Democrats, much more would change than forms of government coordination. A first victim would be the elective dictatorship itself. We consider this possibility in the next section.

Democratic deficits: how far has constitutional reform gone?

An important part of New Labour's appeal in 1997 was the promise of democratic renewal and reform. The elective dictatorship was never felt more keenly than under Margaret Thatcher (1979–90) when a right-wing minority gained power owing to splits among the opposed majority and proceeded to impose its vision on the rest of the country. In the process, of course, majority opinion shifted: it is never a one-way dialogue between governors and governed, and New Labour had to adapt to the new economic realities created on the ground by the Conservative administrations. Nevertheless there was a general desire for greater governmental responsiveness and accountability in 1997. How far has New Labour met this?

In general, one might again say that the reforms initiated by New Labour were victims of the 'war on terror', although they might have run out of steam anyway. The first Blair government carried through the easy bits. The more difficult ones, involving reductions in central government power, were first postponed and then never carried through, partly because giving up central power is always very difficult.

Nevertheless, giving devolution to Scotland and Wales after popular referendums in the affected areas was a radical step that no British government had undertaken before. It was a step towards bringing government closer to the people in those regions, particularly in light of the more proportional election system adopted there. In comparison, accepting a more proportional European voting system and expelling hereditary peers from the House of Lords were small steps. The Freedom of Information Act was severely limited and incorporation of the European Convention on Human Rights simply confirmed tendencies to judicial review of government decisions which were already developing, under the promptings of the European Court of Justice.

Constitutional reform stopped in 1999 and has never effectively resumed, for one simple reason. The unreformed constitution gives central government great powers to effect changes if it wants to do so. The New Labour programme involved substantial and often market-oriented reforms of the public services which Blair and Brown were convinced were right. The traditional Westminster system gave them a basis to force reforms on an unwilling party and an unconvinced, sometimes hostile public, and in the face of negative media comment. Like all governments, they were reluctant to devolve such powers and in the end did not do so.

Blair in particular reinforced his position by using government secrecy and selective leaks to 'spin' the media. Public opinion forms in relation to the choices put before it and Blair's press adviser, Alastair Campbell, was determined that choices were presented in a way that favoured government. The flow of government information was ruthlessly manipulated to ensure positive popular reactions. Nowhere was this more evident than in the softening up of opinion before the Iraq invasion, with government exaggerating the threat posed by Saddam in order to get public opinion on its side. When public opinion shifted under the impact of successive revelations of government 'spin', the Prime Minister kept the country at war regardless.

This flouting of general preferences is part of the explanation for the political apathy and electoral abstention that have shown themselves in the new millennium. Despite more elections with more responsive voting systems, the fact remains that British general elections offer voters little opportunity to shape policy on central issues such as the Iraq War where both major parties agree. Only with a change in election rules towards more proportional voting will popular choices become more determining. And such a change is only likely to happen when Liberal Democrats hold the balance of power in a 'hung' parliament. This may happen in the general election of 2009/10 but only time will tell.

CONTROVERSY

Coalition government versus single-party government

Arguments for single party government based on first past the post

1. The two major parties offer electors a clear-cut choice between alternative government programmes.

2. A cohesive parliamentary majority ensures that the government programme gets through and the electoral mandate is fulfilled.

3. The largest single number of electors is represented by the party that gets into power.

4. The disadvantages of basing government on a popular minority are outweighed by the advantages of strong effective government.

5. Single-party government encourages adversarial politics, particularly between the two largest parties, as they are very much in a win or lose situation, and this clarifies the debate on the key political issues.

Arguments for coalition government based on proportional representation

1. Some coalition governments are formed by parties that have fought the election with a common programme of government, as an electoral alliance (Germany, Scandinavia). If they get a majority, they have a mandate just as much as a single-party government.

2. Many coalitions are strong and cohesive and have a clear programme of government (Sweden, Germany, the Netherlands).

3. Coalitions are usually based on a popular majority that includes the 'middle' voter. Even though the supporting majority has not all voted for the same party, policy has a greater chance of representing majority rather than minority wishes.

4. Coalitions can be strong and effective too, as Germany and the Netherlands demonstrate. The Scottish Executive, formed by a coalition of Labour and Liberals, has clearly been effective.

5. Coalitions generally encourage compromise and negotiation between the partner parties, and sometimes with the opposition too. No party and its supporters will lose out entirely under coalition government because all parties have to bear in mind that they might be partners with the others in a future coalition.

Party policy for the future

A great deal therefore depends on what policies the political parties endorse for the next general election, and whether they offer a real choice on the policies that electors think are most important. At the moment, the prospects are not encouraging. After three successive election defeats the Conservatives have concluded that the only way to beat New Labour is to join it in policy terms. They have therefore elected as leader a look-alike of the younger Blair, David Cameron, and abandoned hardline policies of lower taxation and cuts to public services. Both main parties are committed to support for the United States and the 'war on terror'. 'Europe' seems dormant as a British issue for the next five years. Cameron's task therefore is to convince the public that the Conservatives really have changed in terms of support for public services and that they will manage the free enterprise economy more competently than Labour. Until the economy really experiences a downturn, this programme is likely to bring the Conservatives only level with Labour at best, and thus will usher in a hung parliament where Liberal Democrats hold the balance of power.

The Liberal Democrats are the most radical of the three main British parties, and have a vested interest in pressing for a reform of the Westminster election system that will bring in proportional representation. They also oppose Iraq and are sceptical of over-close involvement with the Americans in the long 'war on terror'. In terms of socioeconomic policy, they have moved substantially towards acceptance of the free market and support for strong public services, as urged by New Labour. Nevertheless their empowerment represents the best chance for the extension of constitutional reform in Britain. Their steady build-up of parliamentary seats and the probable stand-off between the main parties makes the election of 2009/10 the most likely to bring about radical political change since the failed hopes of 1997.

Summary

This chapter has reviewed the record of New Labour in government from 1997 to 2006 and concluded that:

- New Labour has significantly strengthened the public services in Britain in comparison to preceding governments.

- However, political and institutional reform stalled after 1999. Government has been brought closer to the people in Wales and Scotland, but the 'elective dictatorship' of Westminster has been strengthened elsewhere.

- Iraq and the 'war on terror' have decisively shifted the United Kingdom from engagement in Europe to support for the United States. They have also had adverse internal effects on social harmony and democratic rights inside Britain.

- These policies will only be reversed and real democratic reform take place if a hung parliament in 2009/10 gives the Liberal Democrats a pivotal role in a parliament otherwise balanced between the two major parties.

MILESTONES

Milestones for democracy under New Labour 1997–2006

Note: Positive developments for democracy are marked with '+' and negative ones with '−'

1997+	General election. Victory of Labour seen as a reaction against 'sleaze' under Conservative governments
1997+	Scottish and Welsh referendums allow affected minorities to have their own say on devolution of powers to a Parliament/Assembly

Milestones for democracy under New Labour 1997–2006 continued

1998+	Northern Irish referendum on devolution
1999+	Devolved Parliament/Assemblies elected and start to function: elected London Mayor and Assembly set up. Local referendums and consultations to decide on form of government within each local authority
1999+	Incorporation of European Convention on Human Rights into British legal systems safeguards rights more and extends judicial scrutiny of legislation
1999+	Abolition of hereditary membership of House of Lords
1999+	Freedom of Information Act passed, although access to information is more limited than expected
2000–	'Cabinet' system imposed on local government with secret executive meetings in place of previous open committees
2001–4–	'Spin': systematic 'handling' and manipulation of media by government in order to influence public opinion
2001–	General election sees turnout fall from 70 to under 60 per cent
2003–	Invasion of Iraq by Britain in support of Bush administration with substantial opposition ignored by government
2003–4–	Failure to agree on elected House of Lords
2003–	Hutton and Butler inquiries publish unprecedented information about government actions but produce crisis at BBC for 'misreporting'
2003–2006–	Prevention of Terrorism Acts and use of emergency executive powers lead to police raids, detention without trial and restrictions on freedom of speech
2005–	General election with low turnout sees Labour elected to government with only 36 per cent of vote and 20 per cent of electorate supporting them
2005–6+	Courts and House of Lords challenge some of government's more restrictive anti-terrorist legislation
2005–6–	Iraq intervention continues despite majority opposition

Essays

1. To what extent have New Labour governments been successful in achieving their objectives of 1997?

2. What is the 'Third Way'? Why did it drop out of political discussion after 2000?

3. Why did Britain participate so enthusiastically in the 'war on terror' under New Labour?

Projects

1. Prepare an audit of the constitutional reforms undertaken by Labour since 1997. Assess how these reforms have been affected by the Iraq War.

2. Prepare an audit of the relative advantages and disadvantages of plurality versus proportional voting systems. Answer by comparing Britain with at least two other European countries.

3. Assess the democratic benefits of having a written rather than unwritten British constitution.

Further reading

For a sympathetic assessment of New Labour's achievements in power, see Polly Toynbee and David Waller, *Better or Worse? Has Labour Delivered?* (London: Bloomsbury Publishing, 2005); see also Anthony Seldon and Dennis Kavanagh (eds.), *The Blair Effect, 2001–5* (Cambridge: Cambridge University Press, 2005). For institutional change, see David Richards and Martin J. Smith *Governance and Public Policy in the UK* (Oxford: Oxford University Press, 2002). New Labour's record on democracy up to the Iraq War is assessed in Stuart Weir *et al.*, *Democracy under Blair: A Democratic Audit of the United Kingdom* (London: Politicos, 2002). A succinct guide to 'Europe' is Duncan Watts and Colin Pilkington, *Britain in the European Union Today* (Manchester: Manchester University Press, 2005).

Useful web sites on new politics, new democracy

Hot links to these sites can be found on the CWS at www.pearsoned.co.uk/budge.

British democracy and politics are changing at a pace hardly ever seen before. A wide variety of issues that were regarded as secondary in the past have come to occupy the very centre of the political scene. Students of politics in Britain and around the world have privileged access through the internet to the ideological debates, decision-making processes and legislative bodies where these changes occur. One of the leading arguments for changes in the UK system relates to the widening of political participation. Most of the decisions taken in this respect are available from www.number-10.gov.uk. However, the government is not the only institution putting forward strategies for change; every political party has its own way of conceiving a 'wider democracy'. A full list of the main political parties in Britain is available from www.bubl.ac.uk/uk/parties.htm.

The main advocate of constitutional reform in the UK is Charter88, whose web site is available at www.charter88.org.uk. The Lord Chancellor's Department site (www.lcd.gov.uk) covers constitutional issues in England. The question of devolution is one of the epicentres of the debate on widening democracy; a recommendable starting point is the government's site at www.cabinet-office.gov.uk/constitution/devolution/devoluton.htm.

Current issues and debates in British politics are the main concern of www.ukpolitics.org.uk and www.britpolitics.com. For the most relevant academic centres devoted to the analysis of politics in the UK, see the useful web sites section in Chapter 1 of this book. Finally, the role of the media in democratic change and the main web sites on this aspect of politics are analysed in Chapter 14.

Glossary

Accountability To have to answer for one's conduct, or to be subject to review or evaluation by a higher body. The doctrine of ministerial accountability, for example, holds that government ministers are answerable to Parliament for their actions.

Administration Either (1) the process of coordinating and implementing public policy through the machinery of public administration; or (2) another word for government – as in 'the Blair administration'.

Affirmative action Policies designed to provide groups with redress for a past pattern of discrimination. Such policies often take the form of legal requirements that organisations, such as universities, businesses or state bureaucracies, should take positive steps to increase their numbers of minority groups that have suffered discrimination in the past. Known as affirmative action or reverse discrimination in the United States, the term 'positive discrimination' is often used in the United Kingdom.

Agenda-setting theory Argues that the media cannot determine what people think, but can have a strong influence over what people think about. By focusing on some issues but not others, the media can highlight the importance of some issues in the public mind.

Balance of payments (balance of trade) A method of analysing the record of economic relations between a given country and the rest of the world, the balance of payments measures the surplus or deficit of exports over imports over a period of time. In practice, measuring the balance of payments is a complicated matter, but it is useful as a shorthand indicator of whether a country is 'paying its way' or spending more than it earns abroad.

Barristers and solicitors Barristers are lawyers, mostly concentrated in London, who specialise in advocacy in court. They have more prestige than solicitors, who do the bulk of the legal work in preparation for court judgments but whose access to appear in the courts is restricted.

Benchmarking The practice of measuring public sector cost efficiency against the standards of the private sector.

Beveridge Report Resulted in the Welfare State, in which the government ensures the basic social and economic necessities of its citizens by financing and providing goods and services such as education, health care, housing and social security.

Bill of Rights A formal statement of the rights and privileges that may be actually or theoretically claimed by citizens. Unlike a modern Bill of Rights, however, the one passed by Parliament in 1689 was more concerned to restrict the royal prerogative and assert the powers of Parliament. Britain's modern Bill of Rights dates not from 1689 but from the Human Rights Act of 1998.

Bloc vote The practice whereby the trade unions used to cast their votes in a single bloc at the Labour conference in order to maximise their impact. Thus, even if a union executive voted 51 per cent for A and 49 per cent for B, all its votes would be cast for A.

Boundary reviews The process of redrawing constituency boundaries in order to ensure constituencies are approximately the same size.

Broadsheets Serious national daily and Sunday papers, so called because of their former size (most are now in smaller formats). Daily broadsheets are *The Times*, the *Daily Telegraph*, the *Guardian*, the *Independent* and the *Financial Times*.

Cabinet The committee of the leading members of the government who are empowered to make decisions on behalf of the government. The Cabinet is mainly, but not entirely, formed by heads of important departments of state and others who perform important functions of state.

Cabinet collegiality The feeling among Cabinet members that they must act closely and cooperatively together, even when they conflict over policy issues and departmental interests.

Cabinet government The theory that the Cabinet, not the Prime Minister, forms a collective political executive that, therefore, constrains the power of the Prime Minister. In Cabinet government, the principle of collective responsibility ensures that the Cabinet either makes or is consulted about all important political decisions.

Cadre parties Parties of like-minded and wealthy 'notables' who used their own money to fight political campaigns and relied upon their own personal supporters. Good examples are the Conservative and Liberal parties in Britain between about 1830 and the Reform Act of 1867.

Cartel An arrangement between economic interests to limit competition by controlling their market in some way.

Cause groups (promotional groups) Promote a general cause or idea. Unlike interest groups their members are not drawn from particular occupations but may come from a wide variety of social backgrounds.

Celtic fringe Coined around 1900 to describe the northern and western peripheries of the British Isles (Scotland, Wales and Ireland) that voted Liberal, Labour or Nationalist rather than Conservative. The term is now used to refer to the Celtic periphery of the UK (Scotland, Ireland and Wales) whatever their voting patterns.

Civil liberties The freedoms that should not normally be constrained by others, whether private individuals or the state. Civil liberties are often used as an argument against the extension of state power into areas of life regarded as private – for example, the enforced use of seat belts in cars or crash helmets for motorbike riders. Civil libertarians are those who use these arguments, or who are particularly conscious of the importance of civil liberties.

Civil law The law relating to the relationship between individuals or organisations. It includes the law of contract, tort, land and equity or trusts.

Civil servant A servant of the Crown (i.e. the government) who is employed in a civilian capacity (not a member of the armed forces) and who is paid wholly and directly from central government funds (not local government, nationalised industries or quangos).

Civil Service anonymity Civil servants are the confidential advisers of ministers and must not be asked questions about politically controversial matters or the policy advice they give.

Civil Service impartiality The principle that civil servants should be politically neutral and serve their Cabinet ministers regardless of which party is in power and of what they may personally feel about their minister's policies.

Civil society The aspects of social and economic life (primarily voluntary associations and private organisations) that are outside the immediate control of the state. A strong civil society based on a large number and wide variety of private associations and organisations is thought to be the basis for democracy.

Class Among the many and varied definitions of class, the most useful ranks the social and economic status of people according to their occupation, most notably into manual (working-class) and non-manual (middle- and upper-class) groups, and then into subgroups or strata of these categories.

Coalition government Where two or more parties combine to form the government, in contrast to single-party government where all the offices of government are held by members of the same party. Britain had single-party government for most (but not all) of the twentieth century.

Codification of the constitution Producing a written constitution that makes it clearer, and more precise, explicit and systematic.

Cold War The state of international relations between the West and the Communist bloc that stopped short of outright war, but involved intense hostility and the stockpiling of arms and maintenance of large armies in case war should break out. The Cold War started in a serious manner in 1947, at the time of the Berlin blockade and airlift, but gradually died away in the 1970s as a result of international agreements and arms limitations.

Collective responsibility The principle that decisions and policies of the Cabinet are binding on all members of the government, who must support them in public, to maintain a united front, or resign their government post.

Committee of Inquiry A committee appointed by the government, but mainly composed of members outside Parliament, and charged with the job of inquiring into and reporting on a particular matter. Recent examples are the Nolan Committee on Standards in Public Life, the Scott Committee into 'arms to Iraq', and the (Lord Roy) Jenkins Committee on electoral systems.

Common law Law that is overtly made by judges and which has become part of custom and precedent.

Community charge or 'poll tax' The local tax that replaced the rates (or property tax), in which every adult resident of a local authority paid the same amount. It came into operation in 1990 and was replaced by the council tax in 1993.

Community law The treaties, legislation and case law of the European Court of Justice, which are the legal basis of the European Union.

Constitution A set of fundamental laws that determine what the central institutions and offices of the state are to be, their powers and duties, and how they relate to one another and to their citizens. Most constitutions are written and codified in a single document, but in Britain it is partly written but uncodified. Constitutional documents set the limits and powers of government and often state the rights and freedoms of citizens.

Constitutional conventions Unwritten understandings based on custom and practice that are held to be binding and are commonly observed even though they are not enforced by law or sanctions. An example in the British constitution is that of the Crown assenting to bills passed by Parliament.

Constitutional review The process by which laws and other acts of the legislature can be overruled by a court if the court holds them to conflict with constitutional rules, human rights, or other laws treated as superior to legislation. Prior to joining the European Economic Community, no British court had this power.

Constructionism The practice by which the courts define and interpret the meaning of Acts of Parliament, especially where they are vague or general.

Content regulation Regulation of the content of the media by public bodies. Regulation of political content applies mainly to the electronic media (because of spectrum scarcity), and requires that news and current affairs programmes are accurate, balanced and impartial, but it also applies to the print media so far as pornography, violence and public decency are concerned.

Core executive The network of institutions, people and practices that collect at the apex of power around the Prime Minister and the Cabinet, including the most powerful civil servants of Whitehall, the Cabinet Office and the Prime Minister's Office. The core executive integrates policy in an otherwise rather fragmented decision-making structure.

Core party support The minimum voting support it is estimated a party can gain in a given election. The idea behind the concept is that core supporters are the diehard voters for a party in a given election.

Core voters Those voters who are strongly predisposed to support a party election after election. Parties do not need to persuade their core voters that they are the best party, merely to turn out and vote.

Corporatism A system of policy making in which major economic interests work closely together within formal structures of government to formulate and implement public policies. Corporatism requires a formal government apparatus capable of concerting the main economic groups so that they can jointly formulate and implement binding policies. In this sense, Britain has never been a corporatist state, but had in the 1960s and 1970s a looser form of tripartite system.

Council tax The local tax that replaced the community charge in 1993, in which, like the rates, payment is related to property values and levied on all occupants of property. Business rates are set by central government and levied on non-domestic property.

Criminal law Relates to a public and moral wrong (such as murder, manslaughter, theft or sexual offences) that is of such great social importance that the state itself must punish the offender. In the United Kingdom the decision to prosecute is taken by the Crown Prosecution Service.

Crossbench (non-aligned) groups Pressure groups that are not aligned with a party and try to maintain party political neutrality (such as crossbench groups in Parliament).

Cross-media ownership When the same person or company has financial interests in different forms of mass media – radio, TV and newspapers.

Cross-pressures Cross-pressures occur where political forces or influences push in different directions – for example, where someone with Labour sympathies reads a Conservative paper. Cross-pressures are likely to encourage moderate, centre-of-the-road political attitudes and behaviour, or political inactivity in response to the difficulties they cause.

Decolonisation Colonies are foreign territories dominated by stronger states by means of military and economic power. Decolonisation, therefore, is the process of withdrawing from colonial relations with foreign countries so that they gain the autonomy of a sovereign state. In the case of the British Empire, colonial countries often became members of the Commonwealth.

Democratic Audit A private body that monitors and publishes regular reports on democracy and political freedom in Britain – see http://www.democraticaudit.com

Democratic deficit A phrase usually applied to the EU to describe a lack of democratic accountability in its decision making. It is usually argued that the European Parliament is too weak in relation to the Commission, and especially the Council of Ministers.

Deregulation The opposite of regulation, this involves the weakening or removal of state regulations in the interests of market competition. Deregulation was accompanied by privatisation in Britain in the 1980s and early 1990s.

Devolution The delegation of specific powers by a higher level of government to a lower one. Unlike a federal system where the powers of the lower level are constitutionally guaranteed, devolved powers can always be taken back by the higher authority.

Discrimination The practice of distinguishing (usually in order to disadvantage) between individuals or social groups on grounds or criteria (such as race, religion, gender or colour) that are not relevant to the circumstances under consideration.

Disposable income More often known as 'take-home pay', disposable income refers to income after taxes have been paid.

Disproportionality (the opposite of proportionality) Occurs when the seats in a representative body are not distributed in relationship to votes. Proportionality (proportional representation) occurs, therefore, when there is a closer relationship between the distribution of seats and votes. The British 'simple plurality' (first past the post) electoral system is often criticised for its disproportionality insofar as it advantages large parties and discriminates against small ones.

Economic management The process by which governments assume, to varying degrees, the task of managing the national economy by means of macro and/or microeconomic policies. Government economic intervention may become so broad and pervasive that management turns into planning. Monetarism is associated with the idea that the government's role should be limited largely to management of the money supply, but Keynesian theory advocates more interventionist economic planning.

Egalitarian Political views or policies based on a wish to achieve equality, or less inequality.

Elective dictatorship The term used to describe the British political system as one in which, once elected, the leadership of the majority party in the House of Commons can do more or less what it wants without constitutional checks and balances, until it faces the electorate at the next general election.

Electoral mandate The idea that a party whose policies are approved by a majority of voters has the duty and authority to carry them through as a government.

Electoral system A set of procedures for translating votes received by party candidates into shares of parliamentary seats.

Electoral volatility Large changes in voting behaviour from one election to another.

Environmental impact assessment A requirement of the European Union, which came into force in 1988, requiring all public and private projects above a given cost to be subject to environmental appraisal in which the advantages and disadvantages from the environmental point of view are laid out.

Environmentalism A concern with the natural environment (including many things from the physical environment affecting 'the quality of life') and the belief that its protection should be given more importance, and economic growth less. Environmentalists are sometimes referred to as 'ecologists' or 'conservationists'. In the 1970s and 1980s environmentalists began to form themselves into social movements and green parties.

Episodic groups Groups that are not normally political, but become so when circumstances require. For example, football clubs are politically involved only when issues such as football ground safety or hooliganism become a political issue.

Equality of condition The ideal objective of providing all citizens with equal access to income, wealth, education, employment and other aspects of social life.

Equality of opportunity The practice of ensuring that individuals compete on equal terms for goods, benefits and life chances, such as education, employment or housing, even though the outcome may be unequal. Equality of opportunity does not involve treating all individuals as equals. For example, the mentally or physically handicapped should not be treated in the same way as those who are not so handicapped.

Equality of treatment The application of the same rules and standards to all individuals and social groups.

Essex Model A method of explaining past election results and predicting future ones based on a statistical analysis of the changing economic basis of previous election results.

Establishment A vague term referring to the elite of public and private life who, some claim, run Britain irrespective of which party is in government. The Establishment consists of the small number of 'the great and the good' in the Civil Service, military, church, universities, political parties and business. Usually with public school and Oxford and Cambridge backgrounds, they are said to follow a consensus, middle-of-the-road and conservative approach to government and politics.

Ethnicity A mixture or combination of different social characteristics (which may include race, culture, religion or some other basis of common origin and social identity) that give different social groups a common consciousness, and which are thought to divide or separate them in some way from other social groups.

EU law The treaties, legislation and case law of the European Court of Justice, which are the legal basis of the European Union.

Euro The name of the official common currency adopted by 11 members of the EU (Austria, Belgium, Finland, France, Germany, Ireland, Italy, Luxembourg, the Netherlands, Portugal and Spain), with fixed conversion rates in their own currencies. Euro notes and coins were issued on 1 January 2002.

European Monetary System The third and final stage of European financial integration, EMS provides for a single European currency (the euro) to replace existing national currencies, and a European central bank.

Europhiles Those who are generally well disposed to the further integration of Europe within the framework of the European Union.

Eurosceptics Those who are not generally well disposed to the further integration of Europe, at least within the framework of the European Union.

Exchange Rate Mechanism The ERM is the first stage of a European Union plan for financial integration. As part of the European Monetary System introduced in 1979, the ERM was designed to minimise currency exchange fluctuation among members of the EU that belonged to the system. Each currency had an exchange rate against the European Currency Unit, and was supposed to fluctuate within a band either side of this exchange rate. Britain joined the ERM in October 1990, but international currency speculation against the pound drove it out again in September 1992 (Black Wednesday).

Executive One of the three branches of government (with the legislative and judiciary). The executive is concerned with making government decisions and policies rather than with passing laws. In Britain the political executive is the Prime Minister and the Cabinet; in the EU the main executive is the Council of Ministers.

Executive agencies Also known as 'Next Step agencies', these are the semi-autonomous agencies set up to carry out some of the administrative functions of government that were previously the responsibility of Civil Service departments.

Factions Enduring (and often organised) groups within parties that share common attitudes or place particular emphasis on certain parts of a party's core beliefs.

False consciousness The state of mind induced in the working class by the ruling class in order to conceal the real nature of capitalism.

Federal A political structure that combines a central authority with a degree of constitutionally defined autonomy for sub-central units of government – usually territorial units of government such as states, regions or provinces. In discussions about the European Union in Britain, however, the term 'federal' is sometimes used as a code word by those critical of the idea of a 'European superstate', and sometimes as a word to describe a political structure, national or supranational, which is decentralised.

Federal party A party in which power is located in different bodies that affiliate to the party organisation.

Federation A political organisation in which power is divided between a central authority and other units, usually geographical, that retain some independent authority in the system. The term is a controversial one in Britain because it can either mean a fairly centralised form of government (e.g. a United States of Europe) or a loosely organised one, in which the member states retain much autonomy.

Fire brigade groups Pressure groups formed to fight a specific issue and dissolved when it is over (e.g. the Anti-Poll Tax Federation).

First past the post Also known as the single-member simple plurality system (SMSP), this translates votes into seats by awarding each seat to the candidate who gets most votes (a plurality) inside a small constituency.

Fiscal policy A type of macroeconomic policy that uses taxation and public expenditure to manage the economy. Fiscal theories are particularly associated with the work of J. M. Keynes (*General Theory of Employment,*

Interest and Money, 1936) who argued that fiscal tools should be used to promote economic development while avoiding the economic cycles of 'boom and bust'.

Framing effects (of the media) The argument that the media can exercise a subtle but strong effect on how public opinion thinks about politics in a general way, and how it reacts to particular events. For example, by focusing on bad news, the media can produce 'videomalaise'.

Franchise In its political sense, the right to vote. In Britain the male franchise was extended in 1832, 1867, 1884 and 1918. The female franchise was partly introduced in 1918 and completed in 1928, by which time Britain had a universal franchise.

Free trade The idea that international trade should not be restricted by protection in the form of tariffs, customs duties or import quotas that are designed to protect the domestic economy from foreign competition. Free trade policies are sometimes called 'laissez-faire' (allow to do) policies.

Freedom of information Free public access to government information and records. Freedom of information is a necessary condition of open government. Under the public record acts of Britain, some government records are open after 30 years.

Fully reformed Lords Various proposals to 'complete' House of Lords reform, including an elected element and/or modified powers.

Functional integration A form of international integration based on pragmatic cooperation between states in specific areas of (usually) economic activity. The European Coal and Steel Community is an example. Functional integration is often contrasted with political integration that involves more ambitious blueprints for supranational government.

GATT General Agreement on Tariffs and Trade – the series of agreements heavily promoted by the USA since the Second World War and designed to promote free trade in all products throughout the world.

Globalisation The growing linkage of all countries of the world with each other through travel, tourism, trade and electronic communication. As anything done in one area now affects all the others, this means that countries such as Britain can act less and less on their own and so creates a need for international political institutions such as the UN and the EU.

Glorious Revolution of 1688 Established the King's dependence on the support of Parliament and was thus a first step towards parliamentary and constitutional government.

Golden voters Swing voters in marginal constituencies. Shifts in their behaviour are amplified by the first past the post system, producing dramatic shifts in the parliamentary strength of the parties.

Government A general term that refers either to the body that forms the political executive (as in 'the Labour government'), or the institutions that form the constitutional system (as in 'the British system of government'). In the second sense the government consists of those institutions that make the binding rules and decisions in a given territory.

Gross domestic product The total value of all the goods and services bought and sold in the domestic economy.

Harmonisation The attempt of the EU to create common product standards and specifications among its member states in the interests of a free and genuinely common market.

Hegemonic In popular language, the term refers to an idea or practice that is widely accepted as correct, but the term originally meant a social class (the capitalists) or nation state that is so powerful that its view of the world is accepted even by those whose interests are not served by such a world view.

Human rights Western ideas about 'rights' are traceable through the English Magna Carta, the US Declaration of Independence and the French Declaration of the Rights of Man. The 1948 UN Universal Declaration of Human Rights proposed a number of fundamental rights, including those of 'life, liberty and security of the person', 'freedom of movement' and 'of thought, conscience and religion'.

Hung parliament A situation in which no single party has a majority over all other parties in the House of Commons. In the current 646-member Parliament a party needs 324 seats to gain an overall majority. If no party gains 324 seats, there is said to be a 'hung' parliament.

Idealism The view of politics, especially international relations, that emphasises the role of ideals and morality as a determinant of state policies, and hence the possibility of peaceful cooperation.

Ideology A system of ideas, assumptions, values and beliefs that help us to explain the political world – what it is and why, and what it should be. Conservatism, liberalism, socialism, fascism and anarchism are the main examples. Sometimes the word is used to describe a set of political ideas that are false or misleading. Marxists use the word in this way to describe the political ideas used by the ruling class to conceal the real nature of capitalism from the workers.

Imperialism The practice of one nation controlling or dominating another state or territory, usually by military and economic means, and usually to the advantage of the imperial power. Imperialism (as in the British Empire) is often distinguished from colonialism in that it implies a greater degree of political integration of territories and their citizens, and in so far as imperialism is sometimes claimed to be a feature of advanced capitalism. The term 'imperialism' is now sometimes loosely applied to a strong international financial or cultural influence, as in 'US imperialism', which involves US films, clothes and speech.

Incomes policy Government policy designed to secure economic growth and stability by regulating incomes and wages on the grounds that excess demand may be inflationary. Incomes policy was sometimes accompanied by a matching prices policy – hence prices and incomes policy.

Indicative planning The practice of the state indicating targets or goals for such things as employment, inflation and output, without necessarily taking action of its own to achieve them.

Insider groups (established groups) Pressure groups that are able to work closely with elected and appointed officials in central or local government.

Institutional racism The collective failure of an organisation to provide an appropriate and professional service to people because of their colour, culture or ethnic origin. It can be seen or detected in processes, attitudes and behaviours that amount to discrimination through unwitting prejudice, ignorance, thoughtlessness and racist stereotyping, which disadvantage minority ethnic people.

Interest groups (sectional groups) Pressure groups that represent the interests of particular economic or occupational groups, especially business organisations, professional associations and trade unions.

Inter-governmental consultative organisations Allow national states to cooperate on specific matters while maintaining their national sovereignty. They contrast with supranational or federal organisations that wield some power over nation states.

International regimes Sets of international institutions and 'rules of the game' that are created and accepted by states in order to promote international cooperation and integration, as opposed to independent decision making and national competition. Major examples include the General Agreement on Tariffs and Trade, the Organisation for Security and Cooperation in Europe, and the Organization for Economic Cooperation and Development.

International reserve currency A currency that many Third World countries not directly linked with the sponsor country choose to make payments in, because it has a stable value.

Investigative journalism In-depth and often critical journalism involving research that is usually time consuming and expensive. Examples include the *Washington Post*'s digging into the Watergate Affair in the United States and the *Guardian*'s persistent inquiry into the cash for questions affair in Britain, 1995–7.